ROUTLEDGE HANDB CONTEMPORARY MY

After decades of mismanagement and direct military rule, Myanmar's contested transition to a more democratic government has rapidly shifted the outlook in this significant Southeast Asian nation. Since 2011, the removal of Western sanctions and new foreign investments have resulted in high rates of economic growth and an expanding middle class, albeit from a very low base. In a result unthinkable a few years earlier, former political prisoner and Nobel laureate Aung San Suu Kyi and her party, the National League for Democracy (NLD), formed a national government in early 2016. However, despite significant political and economic reforms since the liberalisation process commenced, the transition to civilian rule remains constrained by the military's 2008 Constitution, which guarantees that it operates unfettered by civilian oversight. As a result, although some ethnic conflicts have abated, others continue to fester and new conflicts have erupted. With a daunting task ahead the NLD government has made some progress in removing the vestiges of repressive military-era laws but many remain untouched and some of the practices of the new government provide unwelcome reminders of the country's authoritarian history.

This timely Handbook describes the political, economic, and cultural dimensions of this crucial period of transition in Myanmar. It presents explanations for contradictory trends, including those that defy some of the early narratives about the comprehensive transformation of Myanmar. The Handbook also considers the impact of major environmental, strategic, and demographic trends which help underscore that Myanmar's development will be an ongoing task. In addition to introductory and concluding chapters by the editors, the body of the Handbook is divided into seven core sections:

- Fundamentals
- Spaces
- Cultures
- Living
- Governance
- International
- Challenges

Written by an international team of scholars, with a mix of world-leading established academics and talented emerging researchers, the Handbook provides a rigorous scholarly overview of

Myanmar's politics, economics, and society. As Myanmar opens to Western businesses and government agencies, this is an invaluable reference book that will provide a foundation for further research and offer the first port of call for scholars, students, and policy makers working on Myanmar and Asia.

Adam Simpson is Director of the Centre for Peace and Security at the Hawke Research Institute and Senior Lecturer in International Studies at the University of South Australia. He is also Adjunct Research Fellow at the Centre for Governance and Public Policy at Griffith University, Australia.

Nicholas Farrelly is an Associate Dean of the College of Asia and the Pacific at the Australian National University and Director of the ANU Myanmar Research Centre.

Ian Holliday is Vice-President and Pro-Vice-Chancellor (Teaching and Learning) at the University of Hong Kong.

ROUTLEDGE HANDBOOK OF CONTEMPORARY MYANMAR

Edited by Adam Simpson, Nicholas Farrelly and Ian Holliday

Routledge
Taylor & Francis Group
LONDON AND NEW YORK

First published 2018
by Routledge
2 Park Square, Milton Park, Abingdon, Oxon OX14 4RN

and by Routledge
52 Vanderbilt Avenue, New York, NY 10017

First issued in paperback 2020

Routledge is an imprint of the Taylor & Francis Group, an informa business

British Library Cataloguing-in-Publication Data
A catalogue record for this book is available from the British Library

Library of Congress Cataloging-in-Publication Data
Names: Simpson, Adam (Adam John), editor. | Farrelly, Nicholas, 1982- editor. | Holliday, Ian, editor.
Title: Routledge handbook of contemporary Myanmar/edited by Adam Simpson, Nicholas Farrelly and Ian Holliday.
Description: New York: Routledge, 2018. | Includes bibliographical references and index.
Identifiers: LCCN 2017028742| ISBN 9781138820777 (hardback) | ISBN 9781315743677 (ebook)
Subjects: LCSH: Burma–Politics and government–21st century. | Burma–Social conditions–21st century. | Burma–Economic conditions–21st century.
Classification: LCC DS530.65 .R68 2018 | DDC 959.105–dc23
LC record available at https://lccn.loc.gov/2017028742

ISBN 13: 978-0-367-58096-4 (pbk)
ISBN 13: 978-1-138-82077-7 (hbk)

Typeset in Bembo
by Sunrise Setting Ltd, Brixham, UK

For Lisa and Kyela

CONTENTS

FIGURES

TABLES

CONTRIBUTORS

Ardeth Maung Thawnghmung is Professor and Chair of the Political Science Department at University of Massachusetts, Lowell. Her areas of specialisation are Myanmar/Southeast Asian politics, ethnic politics and political economy. She is the author of *The 'Other' Karen in Myanmar* (2012), *Beyond Armed Resistance* (2011), *Karen Revolution in Burma* (2008), and *Behind the Teak Curtain: Authoritarianism, Agricultural Policies and Political Legitimacy in Rural Burma/Myanmar* (2004).

John H. Badgley published his first article on Burmese politics in 1959 and returned frequently to the topic in subsequent decades. *Red Peacocks* (2009) is his most recent book, co-edited with Aye Kyaw. Since 2008 he has co-directed Myanmar Library Aid Foundation with Dr Thant Thaw Kaung.

Jared Bissinger is a development economist who has been working in and on Myanmar since 2009. He is currently working with the International Labor Organization in Yangon, and has previously consulted with a wide range of organisations including the World Bank, The Asia Foundation, Overseas Development Institute, AusAID and others.

David Bradley is Professor of Linguistics at La Trobe University in Australia; President, UNESCO Comité International Permanent des Linguistes; Fellow, Academy of Social Sciences in Australia; and Fellow, Australian Academy of Humanities. His research focus is the Tibeto-Burman languages of Myanmar and surrounding areas, particularly Lisu, Lahu and Myanmar language.

Matthew Bugher is a Lecturer at the School of Global Studies at Thammasat University in Thailand. He is an American lawyer admitted to the New York State Bar and specialising in human rights documentation and advocacy. He has worked on human rights issues relating to Myanmar since 2009, contributing to projects by Amnesty International, Aegis Trust, the Harvard Law School International Human Rights Clinic, and the International Commission of Jurists.

Charles Carstens is a PhD candidate in the study of religion at Harvard University. He holds a Masters of Theological Studies from Harvard Divinity School and a BA in Economics from Carleton College. His dissertation investigates theories and practices of power expressed through historical, poetic, administrative and ritual texts of pre-colonial Burma. His research interests include historiography, secularism, aesthetics, identity and ethics.

Li Chenyang is Professor and Director of the Center for Myanmar Studies, Yunnan University.

Violet Cho is a PhD candidate in anthropology at the Australian National University. Originally from Hpa'an, she grew up in the Thai-Myanmar borderlands and worked as a journalist with Karen and Burmese media in exile. She is currently conducting research on pwa k'nyaw (Karen) everyday life across the India-Myanmar maritime borderlands.

Céline Coderey received her MA and PhD in Anthropology from the University of Provence in France. She has studied the different conceptions of health, disease and therapeutic practices in Myanmar's Rakhine State. She has particular interests in Theravada Buddhism, astrology, traditional medicine, alchemy and local spirits cults. She is a Research Fellow in the Asia Research Institute at the National University of Singapore.

Melissa Crouch is a Senior Lecturer in the Law Faculty, at the University of New South Wales, Sydney. Her publications include *Law and Religion in Indonesia* (2014), *Law, Society and Transition in Myanmar* (2014), *Islam and the State in Myanmar* (2016) and *The Business of Transition: Law Reform, Development and Economics in Myanmar* (2017).

John Dale is Associate Professor of Sociology at George Mason University, specialising in transnational social movements and the political sociology of globalisation. His current research explores emerging transnational networks of social entrepreneurs and social enterprises using 'smart' technologies to solve social problems in the pursuit of sustainable and democratic social change, and examines their influence on urban and community governance, the development of 'knowledge economies', and practices of human rights and humanitarian action. He is author of *Free Burma: Transnational Legal Action and Corporate Accountability* (2011) and co-author (with Anthony Orum) of *Political Sociology: Power and Participation in Modern World* (2009).

Renaud Egreteau is a 2015–16 Fellow at the Wilson Center, Washington, DC, where he researches the parliamentary affairs in post-junta Myanmar. He taught comparative politics at Sciences Po Paris (2008–9) and the University of Hong Kong (2009–13) and held a visiting fellowship from the Institute of Southeast Asian Studies (ISEAS) of Singapore (2015). He recently authored *Caretaking Democratization: The Military and Political Change in Myanmar* (2016).

Nicholas Farrelly is Associate Dean in the College of Asia and the Pacific at the Australian National University, where he also serves as Director of the ANU Myanmar Research Centre. In 2006, Nicholas co-founded *New Mandala*, which is now a prominent website on Southeast Asian affairs. He recently completed an Australian Research Council fellowship focused on political change in Myanmar, for which he spent 6 months in Naypyitaw.

Christina Fink is a Professor of practice of international affairs at the George Washington University's Elliott School of International Affairs. She is a cultural anthropologist and the author of *Living Silence in Burma: Surviving under Military Rule* (2001). Over the past 20 years, she has engaged extensively with civil society organisations in Myanmar and Thailand.

Thomas Förch is a financial market professional and is currently heading the Deutsche Gesellschaft für Internationale Zusammenarbeit GmbH (GIZ) project on Financial Sector Development in Myanmar. Previously he held positions with GIZ as advisor to the Indonesian Central Bank and as financial sector expert at GIZ headquarters. Before joining GIZ, he worked in the financial services industry in Switzerland.

Charlotte Galloway is a Senior Lecturer in the School of Art and Design, Australian National University. A frequent visitor to Myanmar, Charlotte regularly lectures at the Department of Archaeology University of Yangon, and the Field School of Archaeology at Pyay. She has worked on museum collection projects at Sri Ksetra and Bagan, and is a UNESCO expert contributing to Bagan's nomination for world heritage listing.

Tyler Giannini is a Clinical Professor of Law at Harvard Law School (HLS), where he also co-directs its Human Rights Program and International Human Rights Clinic. Prior to coming to HLS in 2004, he founded and directed EarthRights International and spent a decade working on rights violations in Myanmar while living in Thailand. His Myanmar-related work has included investigating international crimes in the country as well as serving as co-counsel in the Doe v. Unocal case, a corporate accountability suit against a US corporation for its complicity in abuses surrounding the Yadana gas pipeline.

Inga Gruβ is a cultural anthropologist. Her doctoral research among Myanmar migrants in Phang Nga province explored the ways in which perceptions of time and place intersect and shape everyday goals. Recently, she has become increasingly interested in the intersection of migration and health. She works as a researcher at the Center for Health Research in Portland, USA.

Jürgen Haacke is Associate Professor in International Relations at the London School of Economics.

Ian Holliday is Vice-President and Pro-Vice-Chancellor (Teaching and Learning) at the University of Hong Kong. He has published widely on Myanmar politics, and is the author of *Burma Redux: Global Justice and the Quest for Political Reform in Myanmar* (2011).

Cindy Joelene is a Research Associate at the Myanmar Development and Resource Institute – Center for Economic and Social Development (MDRI-CESD).

Kim Jolliffe is an independent researcher, writer, analyst and trainer, specialising in security, aid policy and ethnic politics in Myanmar/Burma. He has worked in the region since 2007, particularly in state- and non-state-controlled regions in Myanmar and with refugee and exile communities on its borders. Kim has written policy guidance, provided training and assisted programmes for local civil society and community-based groups, UN and other inter-governmental bodies, INGOs, research institutions, security think tanks and analysis firms. He has an MA from the King's College London, War Studies Department.

Lee Jones is Reader in the School of Politics and International Relations at Queen Mary, University of London. His work focuses on political economy, social conflict and domestic and international politics in Southeast and East Asia. His publications include *ASEAN, Sovereignty and Intervention in Southeast Asia* (2012), *Societies under Siege: Exploring How International Economic Sanctions (Do Not) Work* (2015) and, with Shahar Hameiri, *Governing Borderless Threats: Non-Traditional Security and the Politics of State Transformation* (2015).

Thomas Kean is editor-in-chief of *Frontier Myanmar*, a weekly English-language magazine based in Yangon that was launched in July 2015. He has been working as a journalist in Myanmar for nine years and edited the English edition of *The Myanmar Times* from January 2010 to April 2016.

Marie Lall is a South Asia expert (India, Pakistan and Burma/Myanmar) specialising in political issues and education. She has written widely on these topics and is the author/editor of six books and a monograph. Her book *Understanding Reform in Myanmar, People and Society in the Wake of Military Rule* was published in 2016. She is a Professor in Education and South Asian Studies at the UCL Institute of Education and currently serves as UVL's Pro-Vice-Provost for the region including Myanmar. She has held a number of fellowships and visiting posts at world-renowned universities in Japan, Australia, Germany, India and Pakistan. She received her MPhil from Cambridge in 1993 and her PhD from the London School of Economics in 1999.

Ma Khin Mar Mar Kyi is the 'Excellence in Gender Research' award-winning anthropologist and the Daw Aung San Suu Kyi Senior Gender Research Fellow. She is also the inaugural Burmese and female Senior Research Fellow, at the University of Oxford. She has written articles and book chapters. Her latest article, based on her extensive research in Rakhine state, is 'Women and Myanmar's Religious Protection Laws: why are women supporting Myanmar's Religious Protection Laws' and she is also co-editor of *The Oxford-Myanmar Policy Brief Series*, Oxford University. She is currently co-investigating an ESRC-funded project entitled 'Gender, Buddhist Nationalism, and Violence in a Political Transition in Myanmar'. The project builds on Dr Mar's series of previous researches on gender related religion, gender politics, human security, child protection, education, peace studies, political economy, masculinities, adolescent and men's health deploying transformative methodologies for social change.

Dr Mar is also a Senior Advisor to many organisations including the UN, DFID, EU and Australian Government, a co-founder of the Oxford-Myanmar Academic Initiatives and a winner of many prestigious awards including, the 'Unsung Hero Award' and the 'UN 100 Years 100 Women Award'. She serves as a Trustee and Board Member of many organisations including Oxford-Myanmar Academic Initiatives, E-Tekkatho, the Australian Myanmar Institute. She is a Regional Lead of Oxford Analytica.

Gerard McCarthy is a doctoral fellow in the Department of Political and Social Change at the Australian National University and a visiting fellow at the University of Yangon. From 2015 until mid-2016 he conducted fieldwork in provincial Myanmar exploring welfare, patronage and ethnic politics, informal taxation and Buddhist nationalism. His research has been published by the Institute of Southeast Asian Studies, Chiang Mai University Press and the *Journal of Contemporary Asia*. He also works as a consultant and contributes to popular and policy outlets including ABC News, *The Guardian*, the International Growth Centre, *The Myanmar Times*, *New Mandala* and the United States Institute of Peace.

Maitrii Aung-Thwin is Associate Professor of Myanmar/Southeast Asian History at the National University of Singapore, and editor of the *Journal of Southeast Asian Studies*. His research is concerned primarily with nation-building, identity politics and resistance in Myanmar. He is the author/co-author of *A History of Myanmar since Ancient Times: Traditions and Transformations* (2013), *The Return of the Galon King: History, Law, and Rebellion in Colonial Burma* (2011) and *A New History of Southeast Asia* (2010).

Patrick Meehan completed his PhD in Development Studies at the School of Oriental and African Studies, University of London, in 2016. His research focuses on the political economy of drugs, conflict and state formation in Myanmar's borderlands. He has been conducting field research in Myanmar since 2011. He has previously published in the *Journal of Southeast Asian Studies* and *Critical Asian Studies*.

Jacqueline Menager is a PhD candidate at the Coral Bell School of Asia Pacific Affairs at the Australian National University. Her PhD dissertation focuses on the role of elite young people in contemporary Myanmar. She has lived and travelled in Myanmar and the wider Southeast Asian region since 2009. She has published on the topics of youth entitlement, viral rumours and political identity in contemporary Myanmar.

Ikuko Okamoto is Professor, Faculty of Global and Regional Studies, Toyo University, Tokyo, Japan. Currently her major research interests include agricultural and rural development, rural finance and natural resource management, particularly in Myanmar. Her major publication is *Economic Disparity in Rural Myanmar* (2008).

Morten B. Pedersen is Senior Lecturer in International and Political Studies at the University of New South Wales Canberra (Australian Defence Force Academy) and a former senior analyst for the International Crisis Group in Myanmar. He has spent more than six years on the ground in Myanmar and has worked as a policy advisor for, among others, the European Commission, the Australian government, the United Nations, the World Bank and Nobel Peace Prize laureate Martti Ahtisaari.

Phyo Win Latt is a PhD candidate in History at National University Singapore.

Elliott Prasse-Freeman is a PhD candidate in Anthropology at Yale.

Jayde Lin Roberts is an interdisciplinary scholar of the built environment and Myanmar Studies specialist. Her book, *Mapping Chinese Rangoon: Place and Nation among the Sino-Burmese*, was published by the University of Washington Press in June 2016. She is a tenured faculty member at the University of Tasmania and a 2016–18 Fulbright US Scholar in Myanmar. Her Fulbright-funded research examines discourses of development in Yangon during a period of rapid urbanisation.

Mandy Sadan is Reader in the History of South East Asia at the School of Oriental and African Studies, University of London. She has been researching the social and cultural history of the Kachin region since the mid-1990s. She has written a number of articles and *Being and Becoming Kachin: Histories Beyond the State in the Borderworlds of Burma* (2013). Her most recent publication is the edited volume *War and Peace in the Borderlands of Myanmar: The Kachin Ceasefire, 1994–2011* (2016).

Samantha Samuel-Nakka is a PhD student in Sociology at George Mason University, USA. She earned her MSc at the London School of Economics in International Development and Gender and her BA from Kings College London in Development Geography. Her research focuses on the politics of social inclusion, processes of marginalisation, indigenous peoples' rights and gender-based violence.

Andrew Selth is Adjunct Associate Professor at the Griffith Asia Institute, Griffith University, and the Coral Bell School of Asia Pacific Affairs, Australian National University. He has been studying international security issues and Asian affairs for over 40 years, as a professional diplomat, strategic intelligence analyst and research scholar. He has published six books and more than 60 peer-reviewed works, most of them about Myanmar. His latest major work is *Burma, Kipling and Western Music: The Riff From Mandalay* (2017).

Adam Simpson is Director of the Centre for Peace and Security within the Hawke Research Institute and Senior Lecturer in International Studies, University of South Australia. He is Adjunct Research Fellow at the Centre for Governance and Public Policy, Griffith University. He previously taught at the University of Adelaide where he remains an Associate in the Indo-Pacific Governance Research Centre. He completed some of the work for this volume during time as a Visiting Research Scholar at the Centre for Southeast Asian Studies, Kyoto University. He has also held visiting positions at SOAS University of London, Queen Mary University of London and Keele University. He has published in journals such as *Society and Natural Resources, Pacific Review, Third World Quarterly* and *Environmental Politics*. He is the author of *Energy, Governance and Security in Thailand and Myanmar (Burma): A Critical Approach to Environmental Politics in the South* (2014; updated edition, 2017).

David Steinberg is Distinguished Professor Emeritus of Asian Studies at Georgetown University, and was for ten years director of Asia Studies there. Previously he was a Representative of the Asia Foundation in Korea, Hong Kong, Burma and Washington, DC; Distinguished Professor of Korea Studies, Georgetown University; and President of the Mansfield Center for Pacific Affairs. Earlier, as a member of the Senior Foreign Service, US Agency for International Development (USAID), Department of State, he was Director for Technical Assistance in Asia and the Middle East, and Director for Philippines, Thailand and Burma Affairs. He is the author of 14 books and monographs, including: *Modern China–Myanmar Relations: Dilemmas of Mutual Dependence* (2012, with Fan Hongwei); *Burma/Myanmar: What Everyone Needs to Know* (2010); *Turmoil in Burma: Contested Legitimacies in Myanmar* (2006); and *Burma: The State of Myanmar* (2001). Professor Steinberg was educated at Dartmouth College, Lingnan University (Canton, China), Harvard University, and the School of Oriental and African Studies, University of London.

Su Mon Thazin Aung completed her PhD in Politics and Governance Studies at the Department of Politics and Public Administration, University of Hong Kong. Her research focuses on elite politics and executive government in Myanmar. She has also contributed to research-training projects in Myanmar.

Matthew J. Walton is the Aung San Suu Kyi Senior Research Fellow in Modern Burmese Studies at St Antony's College, University of Oxford. His research focuses on religion and politics in Southeast Asia, with a special emphasis on Buddhism in Myanmar. His first book, entitled *Buddhism, Politics, and Political Thought in Myanmar*, was published in 2016. He has published articles on Buddhism, ethnicity and politics in Myanmar in the *Journal of Burma Studies, Journal of Contemporary Asia, Asian Survey* and *Social Research*. He is one of the co-founders of the Myanmar Media and Society project and of the Oxford-based Burma/Myanmar blog *Tea Circle*.

Zaw Htet is a doctoral candidate in the Department of Politics and Public Administration, University of Hong Kong. For several years he has worked for non-profit organisations and UN agencies in Myanmar and Thailand.

ACRONYMS

3DF	Three Diseases Fund
AAPP	Assistance Association of Political Prisoners
ADB	Asian Development Bank
AFPFL	Anti-Fascist People's Freedom League
AIPMC	Association of Southeast Asian Nations Inter-Parliamentary Myanmar Caucus
ALTSEAN-Burma	Alternative ASEAN Network on Burma
AMFA	Association Médicale France-Asie
AMRDP	All Mon Regions Democracy Party
AN	Austronesian
ANP	Arakan National Party
ASEAN	Association of Southeast Asian Nations
AusAID	Australian Agency for International Development (now Australian Aid)
BCP	Burmese Communist Party
BGF	Border Guard Force
BSPP	Burma Socialist Programme Party
CBM	Central Bank of Myanmar
CBO	community-based organisation
CEDAW	Convention on the Elimination of All Forms of Discrimination Against Women
CESR	Comprehensive Education Sector Review Programme
CinC	Commander-in-Chief
CRC	Convention on the Rights of the Child
CSO	civil society organisation
CTUM	Confederation of Trade Unions of Myanmar
DDR	disarmament demobilisation and reintegration
DfID	Department for International Development
DKBA	Democratic Karen Buddhist Army
EAG	ethnic armed group
EAO	ethnic armed organisation
EIA	environmental impact assessment

EITI	Extractive Industries Transparency Initiative
EU	European Union
FAO	Food and Agriculture Organization
FATF	Financial Action Task Force
FDA	Food and Drug Administration
FDI	foreign direct investment
FIL	Foreign Investment Law
FSWG	Food Security Working Group
GAD	General Administration Department
GEN	Gender Equality Network
HSBC	Hong Kong & Shanghai Banking Corporation Holdings
IA	Indo-Aryan
IBRD	International Bank for Reconstruction and Development
ICC	International Criminal Court
ICCPR	International Covenant on Civil and Political Rights
ICESCR	International Covenant on Economic, Social and Cultural Rights
ICG	International Crisis Group
ICJ	International Court of Justice
IDA	International Development Association
IDP	internally displaced person
IFI	international financial institution
IGO	inter-governmental organisation
ILO	International Labour Organization
IMF	International Monetary Fund
INDC	Intended Nationally Determined Contribution
INGO	international non-governmental organisation
ISI	import-substituting industrialisation
IT	information technology
JICA	Japan International Cooperation Agency
KDA	Kachin Defense Army
KIO	Kachin Independence Organization
KNPLF	Karenni State Nationalities People's Liberation Front
KNPP	Karenni National Progressive Party
KNU	Karen National Union
LRC	Local Resource Centre
LUC	Land Use Certificate
MCDC	Mandalay City Development Committee
MDEF	Multi Donor Education Fund
MDG	Millennium Development Goal
MIMU	Myanmar Information Management Unit
MK	Mon-Khmer
MNDAA	Myanmar National Democratic Alliance Army
MoE	Ministry of Education
MOECAF	Ministry of Environmental Conservation and Forestry
MoF	Ministry of Finance
MONREC	Ministry of Natural Resources and the Environmental Conservation
MPC	Myanmar Peace Centre
MPF	Myanmar Police Force

MPSI	Myanmar Peace Support Initiative
MPT	Myanmar Posts and Telecommunications
MSF	Médecins Sans Frontières
MSG	Multi-Stakeholder Group
MY	Miao-Yao
NCA	National Ceasefire Agreement
NCEA	National Commission for Environmental Affairs
ND Burma	Network for Human Rights Documentation – Burma
NDA-K	National Democratic Army-Kachin
NDSC	National Defence and Security Council
NGO	non-governmental organisation
NHRC	National Human Rights Commission
NLD	National League for Democracy
NLUP	National Land Use Policy
NMSP	New Mon State Party
NNER	National Network for Education Reform
NSC	National Security Council
NV	National Verification
ODA	official development assistance
OECD	Organization for Economic Cooperation and Development
OHCHR	Office of the High Commissioner for Human Rights
OIC	Organisation of Islamic Cooperation
OSF	Open Society Foundations
PNO	Pa-O National Organisation
PSLO	Palaung State Liberation Organisation
RC	Revolutionary Council
RNDP	Rakhine Nationalities Development Party
SEZ	Special Economic Zone
SLORC	State Law and Order Restoration Council
SNDP	Shan Nationalities Democratic Party
SOE	state-owned enterprise
SPDC	State Peace and Development Council
SSNA	Shan State National Army
SSPP	Shan State Progress Party
TAN	transnational advocacy network
TB	Tibeto-Burman
tCO2eq	tonnes of carbon dioxide equivalent
TK	Thai-Kadai
UEC	Union Election Commission
UN	United Nations
UNDP	United Nations Development Programme
UNEP	United Nations Environment Programme
UNESCO	United Nations Educational, Scientific and Cultural Organization
UNFC	United Nationalities Federal Council
UNFCCC	United Nations Framework Convention on Climate Change
UNICEF	United Nations Children's Fund
UPR	Universal Periodic Review
URDI	Urban Research and Development Institute

US	United States
USAID	United States Agency for International Development
USDA	Union Solidarity and Development Association
USDP	Union Solidarity and Development Party
UWSP	United Wa State Party
WHO	World Health Organization
WLB	Women's League of Burma
YCDC	Yangon City Development Committee
YMBA	Young Men's Buddhist Association

NOTES ON LANGUAGE

Throughout the book we have endeavoured to use the most practical version of Myanmar/Burmese words and names. In the translation from Myanmar to English there is inevitably variation in the Romanisation of some words and we have tried to be consistent. We have generally used the Myanmar government's terminology for most names and places. While the authority and legitimacy of the government in Myanmar has improved since the NLD government came to power in 2016, the ongoing structural power of the military over the government's affairs ensures that its legitimacy remains contested in some parts of the country, particularly those where civil conflict endures. We have therefore allowed authors some flexibility in the use of names and terminology.

Ethnic Bamar (Burmans) and most ethnic minorities in Myanmar (except the Chins, Kachins and Nagas) have no family name. We have therefore followed the custom adopted by other academics specialising in this region by citing Myanmar authors in the text and reference list by their first, rather than last, names.

ACKNOWLEDGEMENTS

With 40 chapters and 43 authors, this volume has been a challenging undertaking from the beginning and has only been possible with the ongoing cooperation of the contributing authors in keeping to the various deadlines. Myanmar experienced momentous political changes during the preparation of the manuscript, and since many of the authors were intimately involved in these developments we are extremely appreciative of their efforts in focusing on this project.

Many thanks go to Research Associate Mish Khan at the Australian National University who did an excellent job on the final formatting of the manuscript. Thanks are also due to Dorothea Schaefter, Jillian Morrison and Lily Brown at Routledge who patiently waited for delivery of the manuscript.

Adam would also like to thank the Centre for Southeast Asian Studies at Kyoto University where he prepared part of the manuscript during a six-month fellowship from February to July 2016. In particular, he would like to thank colleagues, Associate Professors Yoshihiro Nakanishi and Pavin Chachavalpongpun, and Centre Director, Professor Yasuyuki Kono, for their generosity and collegiality during his time there.

Adam Simpson, Nicholas Farrelly and
Ian Holliday

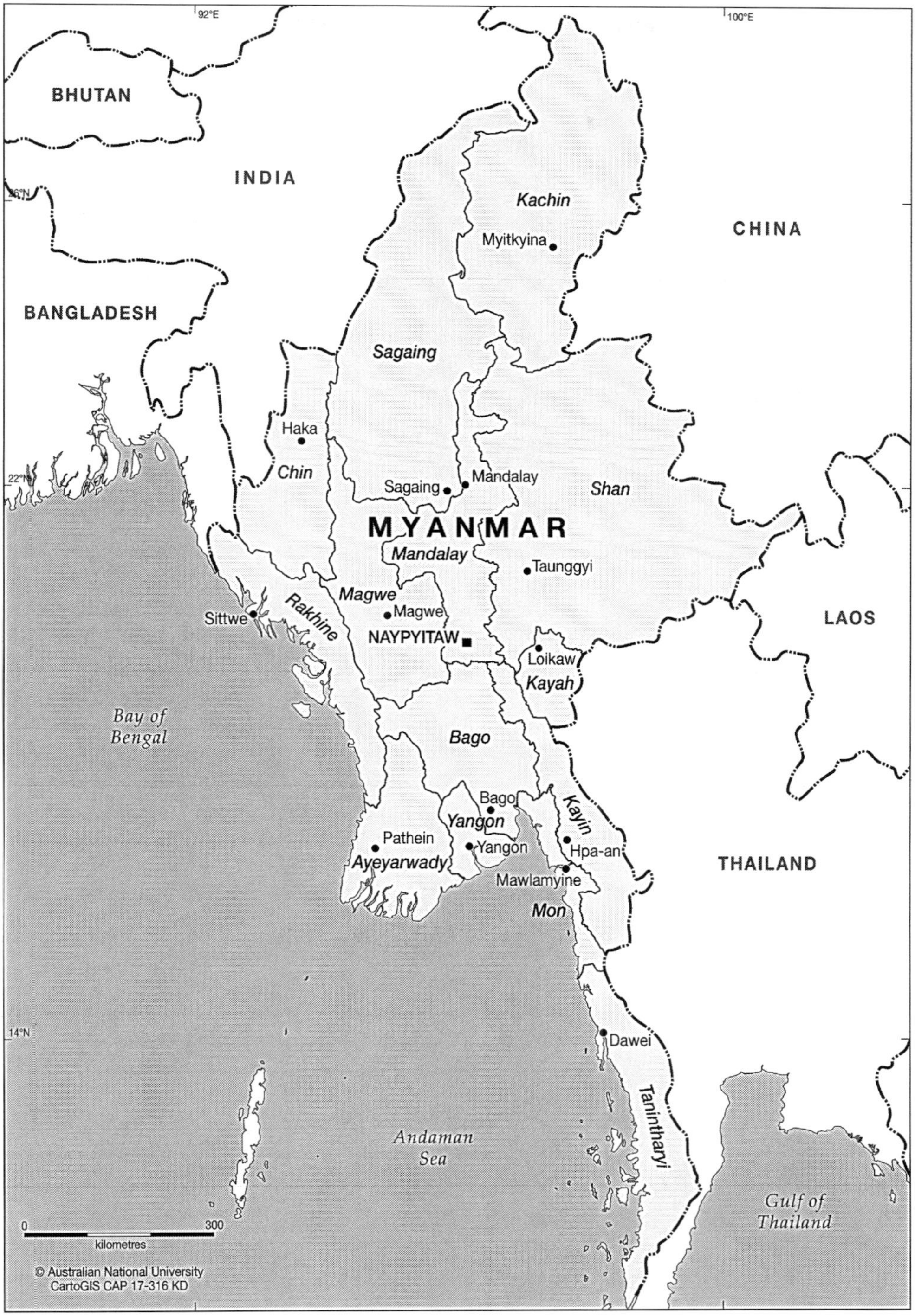
92°E
100°E
BHUTAN
INDIA
26°N
CHINA
Kachin
Myitkyina
BANGLADESH
Sagaing
Haka
Chin
22°N
Sagaing
Mandalay
Shan
MYANMAR
Mandalay
Taunggyi
Magwe
Magwe
Rakhine
Sittwe
NAYPYITAW
LAOS
Loikaw
Kayah
Bay of
Bengal
Bago
Bago
Kayin
Yangon
Pathein
Yangon
Hpa-an
Ayeyarwady
THAILAND
Mawlamyine
Mon
14°N
Dawei
Tanintharyi
Andaman
Sea
Gulf of
Thailand
0
300
kilometres
© Australian National University
CartoGIS CAP 17-316 KD

Introduction

1

EXPLAINING MYANMAR IN FLUX AND TRANSITION

Nicholas Farrelly, Ian Holliday and Adam Simpson

Flux and change

After decades of direct military rule, Myanmar's contested transition to more democratic government has rapidly shifted the outlook in this significant Southeast Asian nation. Changes at the political level have astounded many observers. The National League for Democracy (NLD) government that took office in 2016 now shares power with its old enemies in the armed forces. Ethnic minorities who fought for greater autonomy anticipate fresh rounds of negotiations with the central authorities. The economy has boomed, recently growing at a rate of around 8 per cent. In some urban neighbourhoods, the rate of economic growth is surely much higher. People are on the move, taking advantage of new employment prospects and business opportunities to improve conditions for themselves and their families. Many who were locked out of the political process are emboldened to have their say, including across a vast spectrum of largely unregulated social media. Even traditional broadcasters and publishers have the freedom to test the limits of open debate. It is a time of immense flux and change, defined by the partial resolution of a complicated history that saw long-running conflict between democrats and militarists, conservatives and ethno-nationalists. Their battles are now fused to a society rapidly shifting its priorities and, with them, the expectations of the rest of the world.

Under these conditions, there is a need to take stock of recent changes and place them in Myanmar's historical context while considering the uncertainties that will continue to define day-to-day experiences. This volume sets out to explain the political, economic, cultural and strategic dimensions of this vibrant period of transition in Myanmar. The primary challenge is to get to grips with contradictory trends, including those that defy some of the early narratives about the comprehensive transformation of Myanmar life. The reality for tens of millions of people is uneven and inconsistent, and often unpredictable. Much is still unfinished and tentative. For instance, the principles for decision-making and allocating power have changed with the priorities of the new political institutions and those who seek to manage them. People have higher expectations and yet inequality and disenfranchisement, in both political and economic realms, will take a long time to be addressed; the necessary compromises with the military and associated structural powers within society exacerbate the difficulties for making effective policy. Depending on how they deal with the range of countervailing forces, the country's decision-makers, including the democratic ones, risk alienating large sections of society. A careful balance is prudent but that does not imply that it is easy to maintain.

The search for stability is apparent in Myanmar's 2008 constitution, which established a national framework for consolidating the long-term influence of the armed forces. When it was endorsed at a manipulated referendum in the wake of the devastation of Cyclone Nargis, hopes were very low that any significant changes to Myanmar society would follow. The fear at the time was that the armed forces, long entrenched in supreme political positions, would maintain their habitual dominance, even if cosmetic changes occurred. It did not help that at the general election held in November 2010 the Union Solidarity and Development Party (USDP), the successor to the military regime, won a big majority of the contested seats (Turnell 2011). Combined with the military's constitutionally mandated allocation of 25 per cent of legislative seats, at both the national and regional levels, this ensured there was no serious competition for power (for an explanation see Holliday 2012). Ethnic minority legislators were accommodated by a system that, by design, worked to ensure the continuity of establishment rule, with the interests of the armed forces at its core (Jones 2014). This system received a significant jolt in April 2012 when the NLD polled strongly at by-elections. With NLD leader Aung San Suu Kyi and her party members elected to the legislature, the international reception of Myanmar's changes shifted quickly. The NLD presence added legitimacy to a system that was, under the USDP, only fractionally democratic (Than 2013). By the time of the November 2015 general election, the armed forces were clearly comfortable with the idea of an NLD-led government taking a greater share of legislative and executive power. The elected politicians now share power with unelected military officers. It is currently an uneasy coalition. The story of contemporary Myanmar needs to account for these momentous shifts.

Beyond the realm of elite politicking and negotiation, life in Myanmar has mutated in many other important respects. While gradual changes across society are apparent, there is also radical disjuncture when it comes to the economy, technology and culture. Under the former military government, information was very closely controlled and a nationwide propaganda machine dictated the content of public discussion. There was no room for debate in a system regulated to defend the narrow perspectives of the ruling military clique. With the abolition of prepublication censorship procedures in August 2012, Myanmar's newspaper, magazine and book publishers welcomed a fresh chance to test the limits of free expression (Wiles 2015). This liberalisation was matched by the rapid expansion of Internet-enabled mobile phone technologies (see Ling *et al.* 2015). Two foreign companies, Telenor from Norway and Ooredoo from Qatar, won licences to unfurl new national networks that quickly created millions of new users. People who had never before read an uncensored newspaper were flooded with information through the anarchy of Facebook connections. Before long, any semblance of official control over the flow of information melted into the digital haze.

Other connections have also blossomed during recent years, especially through international players keen to get more involved in Myanmar's transition. Under the military government a range of links were curtailed through sanctions imposed by the Western democracies (see Pedersen 2008). For decades, Myanmar's most important foreign ties included sympathetic neighbours like China, Singapore and Thailand. Many other countries avoided doing business or making friends while the country's leadership had such a poor reputation. This isolation from global investment flows, cultural outputs and political sentiments has shifted with incredible speed, and there is now an impressive range of worthwhile links being forged. A local middle class, albeit a small one, is assertively embracing its connections to international markets and the opportunities that come with such rapid economic growth (see Farrelly 2015). They are joined by mushrooming numbers of foreign professionals, businesspeople, teachers and humanitarians, all eager to be involved in one of this century's major national transformations. Investment and innovation, which were both impeded under the military government, are now embraced by Myanmar people looking to catch-up on the benefits of living in the 21st century.

Such benefits—in heath, wealth, education and security—do not flow evenly across society. People who prospered under the military government have generally secured their financial and social status, and are well placed to continue extracting maximum returns from the improved national economy. The so-called 'crony' class, which enjoyed patronage from the top military generals, retains its unmatched economic muscle even though it now contends with newly aggressive and well-resourced competitors. At the other end of the spectrum, there is continued destitution and hardship. With 70 per cent of the population still living in rural areas, and a growing urban underclass attracted to the cities by the prospect of better wages, there is an immense distance between rich and poor, especially when gender and age inequalities are taken into account (Faxon *et al.* 2015; Teerawichitchainan and Knodel 2015). Such inequity is amplified in ethnic minority areas that often still suffer the effects of long-running civil wars. Many of those wars remain unfinished, as ethnic leaders wait to negotiate with the new democratic government. Religious contention is also a major issue, especially in northern Rakhine State where the Rohingya minority struggles with persistent mistreatment (see Kipgen 2013; Simpson 2017). While the conclusions are often disheartening, the great disparities of contemporary Myanmar life are essential components of this book's analysis.

Our book also considers the impact of major environmental, strategic, demographic and cultural trends. These forces, often at a regional or global scale, will test Myanmar's ability to juggle its domestic concerns with the great risks of our era (Simpson and Park 2013). The country is vulnerable, in many unseen respects, to potential disruptions and even disasters. Sitting astride the 'crossroads' of Asia, bumping against the giants of China and India, Myanmar enjoys a very small buffer when it comes to changes beyond its own borders (see Thant Myint-U 2011). Future upheavals—whether man-made or natural—will often come unexpectedly, just as Cyclone Nargis did in 2008. We cannot forget how that storm may have killed as many as 140,000 people, left to fend for themselves against rising waters and howling winds. In the future, the ultimate challenge for the leaders of Myanmar will be to offer adequate insulation against a world and a region in almost constant flux. Until now, it has been reasonably straightforward for Myanmar's people to accept such uncertainty while their lives have, in general, seen substantial improvement. The problem for the government and for society is that such a positive trajectory should not be taken for granted.

In response to this complex story, our book is structured thematically to showcase the great diversity of life in Myanmar today. It benefits from a wave of new research that is being conducted right now, often under conditions of refreshingly open access and scholarly freedom (see Farrelly 2016). Most of the tiresome restrictions on academic and analytical work have dissipated as the government and other key institutions become more comfortable with the relatively free flow of ideas. New debates are emerging that go well beyond the stale binary of dictatorship and democracy. A rising generation of Myanmar thinkers, artists, writers and policy-makers actually has little experience, at least as adults, of military rule. For them, the shifting sands of transitional politics and economics are the only standard they truly know. In this erratic context, our book takes a comprehensive look at contemporary Myanmar from a variety of disciplinary perspectives, including history, sociology, anthropology, linguistics, political science, economics and international relations. The chapters also highlight the emergence of a new cohort of scholars who have already devoted many years to the study of Myanmar life, and for whom the conditions of military dictatorship are quickly fading from view. Their contributions to our collective understanding are helping to modify existing perspectives and rejuvenate the conceptual basis for explaining contemporary Myanmar.

Part 1—Fundamentals

The book begins by considering the fundamentals of Myanmar life that provide the context for the analysis of contemporary Myanmar: the state, the defence services, democracy, and ethnicity and identity. The modern Myanmar state draws on influences from the old Myanmar dynasties and the difficult period of British colonial rule. These legacies were then moulded by the devastating experience of long-running internal political conflict along ethnic and ideological fault lines. To account for this history, Maitrii Aung-Thwin explains the origins and ideology of the Myanmar state. Since before independence from Britain in 1948, the country has absorbed political, economic, administrative and cultural influences from the armed forces. Usually referred to as the Tatmadaw, they first seized direct control of the government machinery in 1962 and held on to their supreme position until handing power to a civilianised regime in 2011. Across those decades the armed forces first endorsed an idiosyncratic interpretation of socialist economic principles before, at the end of the Cold War, switching to a system that evolved in crony-capitalist directions. As we learn from Andrew Selth, nationalism remained the core value and organising principle for the military and helped to sustain its mission as the primary custodian of national unity and internal security.

In seeking to consolidate power, the armed forces have faced resistance from a broad range of democratic forces. During the decades of authoritarian rule, there was limited space for democratic activism, with great efforts made to eliminate dissent. Those who called for greater democracy tended to do so at risk to their livelihoods and freedom. Many were locked up in trying conditions, bludgeoned by a political regime that accepted no deviation from its dictatorial model. It is no wonder that many escaped across the borders, seeking any chance at a happier life. John Badgley and Ian Holliday explore attempts to implement some form of democracy in Myanmar, and offer an appraisal of factors that have often impeded those efforts. Such local variation is also apparent in the country's ethnic landscape, where official categorisations interact, often uneasily, with the jumbled experiences of everyday life. Ethnic identity remains a fundamental element of Myanmar society, helping to structure the full range of day-to-day interactions. There are cultural, linguistic and religious dimensions to such identities, which also often have profound implications for political, economic and conflict dynamics. Violet Cho's chapter offers a thorough overview of these fundamental issues, providing a useful corrective to undue emphasis on Myanmar's majority Bamar Buddhist culture. Friction between minorities and majorities has proved enduringly complex and resistant to the most even-tempered attempts at resolution.

Part 2—Spaces

After decades of official delineation, it is now common to explain Myanmar's spaces in terms of the majority Bamar population and the many ethnic minorities. On the map, there are seven Bamar majority Regions and seven ethnic majority States. This bifurcation is supposed to balance their divergent interests and ensure a level of integration for the minorities, usually summarised as the Mon, Kayin (Karen), Kayah (Karenni), Shan, Kachin, Chin and Rakhine (Arakan). Instead of focusing attention on this official impression of geography, this book looks closely at the ways that other spatial groupings end up shaping Myanmar life. This starts with an analysis by Nicholas Farrelly of Myanmar's capital, Naypyitaw, a city built for the explicit purpose of re-positioning power. It is in Naypyitaw, a creation of the former military government, that a system of watchful bureaucratic management has been amended to give space for the creation of new political institutions, including the legislature, executive and judiciary. In Naypyitaw the armed forces also retain significant physical and symbolic presence, ever mindful of the potential for dissent and rebellion.

While Naypyitaw is a recent addition to urban Myanmar, Jayde Lin Roberts takes a close look at some of the country's other cities and the people who live in them. Her analysis of urban development contrasts with what we learn from Ardeth Maung Thawnghmung about conditions in rural Myanmar, where around 70 per cent of the population live. It is also in rural Myanmar that hardship is greatest for those who struggle on the margins of the modern economy. While living conditions in the cities have improved greatly, many farmers and fisherfolk subsist at the very margins of society. Patrick Meehan and Mandy Sadan further explore such marginal spaces with an analysis of Myanmar's borderlands. The country shares borders with five neighbours—Bangladesh, India, China, Laos and Thailand—all of which present important challenges to the rush for centralisation and cohesion. In many cases, these borderlands have weathered generations of conflict and lawlessness, with no guarantee that old grievances will not re-emerge.

Nowadays Myanmar's spaces need to be assessed in other, more abstract, realms. Gerard McCarthy writes about the proliferation of cyber-spaces that have changed expectations of political, cultural and economic interaction across the country and in the rest of the world. These spaces were heavily controlled by the former military dictatorship, but with the swift expansion of access to mobile Internet-enabled technologies the people of Myanmar have rushed to colonise their new-found, online world. To consider some of the other anomalous spaces in Myanmar today, Nicholas Farrelly analyses the places where the government has struggled to exert full control. His chapter looks at the variety of autonomous areas, special regions, special economic zones and other exceptions to the ordinary patterns of spatial governance. These places tend to generate new economies and cultures that thrive in areas of deniability and exchange.

Part 3—Cultures

With so much movement and interaction, Myanmar's cultural diversity is one of its most striking attributes. Culture, across time and space, is a deeply political concern, closely tied to experiences of antagonism and inequality. It is also in culture that much of the joy and value of life can be found. To begin the cultural assessment, David Bradley introduces the country's rich linguistic heritage with a wide-ranging survey of the different languages spoken around the country. What emerges is a detailed account of one of the world's great polyglot societies, where a mastery of different languages is commonplace. The question of religious diversity also requires considered attention, especially in a context where elements among the Buddhist majority have mobilised around a group of newly emboldened, chauvinistic political leaders. In his chapter on religion, Charles Carstens examines the social tensions intrinsic to the categorisation of religious faith and national belonging. Charlotte Galloway then considers Myanmar's artistic outputs in all their varied colours and attributes. The political dimensions of art during Myanmar's transition from the military deserve our specific attention.

The chapter by Tom Kean appraises public discourse and the media. Based on a decade working for newspapers in Myanmar, his analysis clarifies the extent to which greater free expression has become possible during the years of political transition. The expansion of the public sphere and the proliferation of new voices challenge us all to consider the role of debate and contention in Myanmar life. Such contention is also a primary concern for Inga Gruß, who writes about the role of diaspora cultures. Millions of people from Myanmar have left the country over recent decades, with huge numbers, perhaps around two million, settling in Thailand, with smaller diasporic populations in China, India, Malaysia and Singapore, and also in some of the Western democracies. These groups—each with their considerable internal diversity—clarify the extent to which Myanmar society is integrating foreign influences and developing strong connections to the rest of the world. These discussions of cultures conclude with a chapter by Jacqueline Menager. She looks intently at the ways that young people have challenged old cultural priorities and helped to create their identities in a rapidly changing social landscape.

Part 4—Living

For all of these changes, life in Myanmar is still framed, to a very significant extent, by the decisions and policies of the former military government. The consequences of their mismanagement of the economy and exclusion from the global commercial mainstream will matter for many years to come. This legacy complicates all sorts of decisions, especially those that concern the allocation of political and economic power. Lee Jones explains the structure of the national political economy, delving into the relationships and interests that drive decision-making. His analysis offers appropriate consideration of the mechanisms that keep the military and its allies in positions of ongoing importance. Ikuko Okamoto follows, by contrast, with an analysis of agriculture, which remains the primary sector for employment and a significant driver of national economic output. Vast areas of the country, especially in the most fertile regions of central and lower Myanmar, are set aside for rice production. Increasingly sophisticated cropping techniques and access to appropriate agricultural technologies are changing opportunities for millions of people who live in Myanmar's rural hinterlands. Delivering a higher standard of living for rural people is judged a singular priority for the ruling NLD.

The expansion of banking and financial services is another major factor reshaping contemporary Myanmar life. In the past, it was almost impossible to use modern banking facilities in Myanmar, and foreign visitors were expected to carry their own supplies of cash in pristine US dollars. It was an endlessly frustrating and antiquated system. Thomas Förch explains the challenges for implementing a more transparent, efficient and effective finance system, which better meets the needs of the people, business and government. Foreign Direct Investment and trade are other issues receiving increased attention under transitional conditions. During the years of direct military rule, Myanmar was barred from participating in the ordinary business of global commerce even though it managed to develop significant economic links with its neighbours, most notably China, Thailand and Singapore. Myanmar is also benefiting from the transformative potential of the telecommunications revolution, including in areas like online banking. Nowadays, as Jared Bissinger explains, Myanmar is better connected to the global economic system, with some major new investors seeking to understand the country's prospects as one of Asia's last so-called 'frontier' markets.

Part 5—Governance

Since the military surrendered its direct control in 2011, a new set of political institutions has emerged to help manage the range of governance challenges. In general, these new institutions have been surprisingly adaptive, making the most of the extra space for creative responses to old problems. Ian Holliday and Su Mon Thazin Aung begin this section with an explanation of the role of the executive, headed by a President, two Vice-Presidents and the the innovative new position of State Counsellor, designed specifically for Aung San Suu Kyi. The President appoints the cabinet and a number of other important positions, and holds considerable sway over the tone of national leadership. That executive is forced, under the 2008 Constitution, into regular conversation with the legislature, at both the Union and State/Region levels. Across Myanmar, there are more than 1,000 elected legislators who are expected to manage the law-making process. Given the number of new laws drafted and debated, the legislatures have proved busy since they first took office in 2011. With the NLD's 2015 general election victory, there has also been a significant change in the legislative line-up. Renaud Egreteau and Cindy Joelene offer a careful assessment of the legislative role during this transformative period. The NLD legislative team certainly faces significant challenges to secure and enhance the country's nascent democratic reputation. This analysis of legislative practice is followed by Melissa Crouch's treatment of the judiciary, another institution that has been forced to adjust its performance to the more democratic outlook of recent years. Shifting to arrangements where 'rule of law' is consistently implemented will take more time and effort.

It is to the benefit of Myanmar's transition that, under current conditions, the executive, legislature and judiciary are subjected to greater scrutiny than ever before. While certain kinds of information about government activities are still carefully guarded, there is a fresh spirit of relative openness alongside an appetite for improved civic engagement. Civil society actors, as explained by Christina Fink and Adam Simpson, make a range of other contributions to national governance. Under the military dictatorship such groups, both at home and abroad, struggled for adequate resources to support activities across humanitarian, advocacy and development fields. Marie Lall discusses changes to Myanmar's education system in the next chapter. Major injections of international development assistance have been crucial to the progress in this area. Health is another major concern with respect to the well-being and prosperity of the people. Céline Coderey explores the current character of the health system and the challenges faced by this sector in the years ahead.

Part 6—International

All of Myanmar's domestic political, cultural and economic changes are occurring in the context of continuously shifting international expectations. This section begins with a big picture chapter about global engagement with Myanmar by David Steinberg. It makes sense that such engagement has played a constructive role in the transition from long-term military rule, while there are still reasons to worry about the extent to which foreign players will help to consolidate Myanmar's tentatively democratic situation. As Jürgen Haacke explains, there is also a complex regional dimension to Myanmar's international entanglements, including its status within the Association of Southeast Asian Nations. Renaud Egreteau and Li Chenyang then look at the immediate neighbourhood and the ways that Myanmar seeks to cooperate with its closest economic and political partners. At all three levels, there is increased competition among international actors, almost all of whom see new potential in Myanmar's changed political landscape. With China, the United States and India all now making more assertive moves, the foreign policy equation will only become more complex in the years ahead.

There are further layers of international engagement and contention that require concerted attention. John Dale and Samantha Samuel-Nakka look at the role of international non-government organisations as they advocate on behalf of policy reform in Myanmar. They are joined in some of these tasks by the international organisations that have become very active in creating space for creative interventions. These entities tend to be focused, as argued by Tyler Giannini and Matthew Bugher, on their commitments to international law. There are also those groups working in Myanmar that bring an explicitly developmental agenda. Ian Holliday and Zaw Htet examine how this works in practice. They also clarify the extent to which international assistance is benefiting the people of Myanmar at this crucial stage of national development.

Part 7—Challenges

After so much recent flux, some significant challenges confront the people and government of Myanmar. At the top of the list are the peace process and the push for national reconciliation. Kim Jolliffe discusses the frustrations of getting final agreement, at the national level, from the country's different ethnic, military and political interests. Any consideration of a nationwide peace agreement needs to grapple with the country's incomplete democratisation and the continued human rights abuses in some areas. Morten Pedersen goes on to explain the hard realities for those seeking to make further progress towards a more peaceful and inclusive society. There are gender aspects to these topics that rarely receive sufficient attention. In her chapter, Khin Mar Mar Kyi presents a feminist perspective on the reform required of Myanmar society if its people are ever going to achieve their collective goals.

Other challenges for Myanmar in the years ahead will require new resources for nation building. Previously, this was managed through the narrow guidance of the military, with its preference for cohesion and deference. Matthew Walton considers whether different approaches to nation building may be possible in the years ahead. Such proposals will need to grapple with the major problems of class and inequality. Myanmar society is now heavily stratified, with a preponderance of opportunities flowing towards those who already claim higher socio-economic status. Elliott Prasse-Freeman and Phyo Win Latt look at the types of policies that could help to adjust this situation. Finally, Adam Simpson draws our attention to Myanmar's environmental and natural resource management challenges. These will ultimately determine the extent to which the country can provide a sustainable standard of living to its people.

Over the horizon

In the final chapter we examine possible futures for Myanmar. This chapter suggests that while the recent trajectory of economic, political, social and cultural development is promising, the blunt fact is that Myanmar continues to face some potentially grim scenarios. The management of political and ethnic contention will remain a concern for many years to come. Other internal security issues and matters of social cohesion will require constant government supervision and the goodwill of the people-at-large. At the same time, Myanmar will need to deal with rapidly shifting regional and global circumstances across the full gamut of environmental, geostrategic and economic circumstances. And the NLD government will be forced to make continued accommodations with the armed forces if it hopes to avoid a showdown that could unravel all of the recent moves towards partial reconciliation and democratisation. If Myanmar's leaders struggle for a long-term consensus about the distribution of power then their ability to respond to other challenges will be greatly diminished.

Looking at Myanmar's immediate neighbours—especially Thailand and Bangladesh—the difficulties of securing a new democracy are readily apparent. In recent years, Myanmar has enjoyed a great deal of positive international attention which, when combined with new levels of local exuberance and energy, have helped to quickly shift the direction of local politics. With an economy that is growing strongly, and with hopes for many future positive developments, it is easy to get caught up in the excitement of Myanmar's moment in the sun. Already, however, darker moods and harsher trends are becoming apparent. Military brutality against the Muslim Rohingya in northern Rakhine State in 2017 garnered unwelcome and unrelenting global attention (Simpson 2017). The response of the NLD leadership did not bode well for the future respect of democracy and human rights in Myanmar. Whether the country ends up getting better or worse, understanding Myanmar's flux will be an ongoing task and one for which this book offers some relevant points of guidance.

References

Farrelly, Nicholas. 2015. 'Myanmar's middle-class bulge'. *The Myanmar Times*, July 27. www.mmtimes.com/index.php/opinion/15675-myanmar-s-middle-class-bulge.html.

Farrelly, Nicholas. 2016. 'Researching Myanmar today—this way please!' *The Myanmar Times*, March 28. www.mmtimes.com/index.php/opinion/19681-researching-myanmar-today-this-way-please.html.

Faxon, Hilary, Roisin Furlong and May Sabe Phyu. 2015. 'Reinvigorating resilience: Violence against women, land rights, and the women's peace movement in Myanmar'. *Gender & Development* 23 (3): 463–479.

Holliday, Ian. 2012. *Burma redux: Global justice and the quest for political reform in Myanmar*. New York: Columbia University Press.

Jones, Lee. 2014. 'Explaining Myanmar's regime transition: The periphery is central'. *Democratization* 21 (5): 780–802.

Kipgen, Nehginpao. 2013. 'Conflict in Rakhine State in Myanmar: Rohingya Muslims' conundrum'. *Journal of Muslim Minority Affairs* 33 (2): 298–310.

Ling, Rich, Elisa Oreglia, Rajiv Aricat, Chitra Panchapakesan and May O'Lwin. 2015. 'The use of mobile phones among trishaw operators in Myanmar'. *International Journal of Communication* 9: 3583–3600.

Pedersen, Morten B. 2008. *Promoting human rights in Burma: A critique of Western sanctions policy*. Lanham: Rowman & Littlefield.

Simpson, Adam. 2017. 'Dark clouds over Rakhine State'. East Asia Forum. 19 September. Accessed 21 September 2017. www.eastasiaforum.org/2017/09/19/dark-clouds-over-rakhine-state/.

Simpson, Adam and Susan Park. 2013. 'The Asian Development Bank as a global risk regulator in Myanmar'. *Third World Quarterly* 34 (10): 1858–1871.

Teerawichitchainan, Bussarawan and John Knodel. 2015. 'Economic status and old-age health in poverty-stricken Myanmar'. *Journal of Aging and Health* 27 (8): 1462–1484.

Than, Tin Maung Maung. 2013. 'Myanmar's 2012 by-elections: The return of NLD'. *Southeast Asian Affairs* 2013: 204–219.

Thant Myint-U. 2011. *Where China meets India: Burma and the new crossroads of Asia*. New York: Farrar, Straus and Giroux.

Turnell, Sean. 2011. 'Myanmar in 2010'. *Asian Survey* 51 (1): 148–154.

Wiles, Ellen. 2015. *Saffron shadows and salvaged scripts: Literary life in Myanmar under censorship and in transition*. New York: Columbia University Press.

PART I

Fundamentals

2

THE STATE

Maitrii Aung-Thwin

The transfer of power from the Union Solidarity and Development Party (USDP) to the National League for Democracy (NLD) in April 2016 marked a significant step forward in the recent history of the Myanmar state (*naingntaw*). For only the second time under the 2008 constitution, control of the state successfully changed hands through the mandate of the ballot box. Many international observers regarded the ascension of Aung San Suu Kyi to the highest echelons of government via the national elections of 2015 as the all-important sign that genuine democracy in Myanmar had arrived. Although the crucial institutional changes actually occurred five years earlier with the arrival of the Thein Sein administration and his celebrated reforms, Aung San Suu Kyi's ardent supporters at home and abroad privileged the outcome of the elections—rather than the institutional process—as the criterion for political transformation. Some commentators reserved judgement until they could determine if the *Tatmadaw* (military) would step aside and assess whether the NLD could manage the transition from activism to governing. In the four months between the November 2015 elections and the handover in April 2016, stakeholders negotiated behind closed doors to manage what was clearly uncharted territory (Clapp 2015).

The success of the transition cannot be overstated considering that the conditions were ripe for a confrontation with the military over Aung San Suu Kyi's eligibility to take office. Determining who would lead the country was up for speculation as it was unclear whether the NLD would challenge the constitutional clause that prohibited her from taking office as president. To their credit, all of the relevant stakeholders were able to avoid dragging the new government through a constitutional crisis. In the end, the procedures managing the appointment of new members to the executive and legislative branches of government held fast and provided the mechanism to see the results of the 2015 election materialise. In effect, the 2008 constitution, despite its acknowledged imperfections and contested beginnings, successfully provided the necessary framework for the peaceful transfer of power in a country beleaguered by nearly seventy years of civil war. Within this context, the current rapprochement between the civilian NLD and the military would seem to be all the more remarkable given the history of the contest for the Myanmar state (Taylor 2009).

The state—defined here as the network of mechanisms through which social and political order is maintained—has been the object of contestation in modern Myanmar history (Mitchell 1991; Taylor 2009). In Myanmar, these mechanisms might refer to those institutions, agencies, officials, governing relationships, or bureaucratic practices that have been associated with or employed on behalf of those wielding power and authority. While the enforcement of laws and interaction with government officials might be the more obvious form through which the state asserts its presence, other everyday forms of the state and its networks of order might be considered as well. The collection of taxes, the establishment of postal codes, the initiation of public health campaigns, the standardisation of education, and the designation of official holidays are some quotidian examples in contemporary Myanmar of how communities might encounter the state, its agents, and its claims of authority.

The uneven presence and capacity of the state throughout Myanmar's history highlights the myriad ways that communities have encountered the state in daily life, influencing in turn how the state has been envisioned (Lieberman 2003; Sadan 2013). In pre-colonial times, state authority was encountered via court appointees, the sangha, or more often, through local elites bearing particular symbols of status bestowed upon them by the Burmese throne. Standards of measurement, attachment, behaviour, writing, language, architecture, and modes of belief reflected 'state' norms that spread from centres into society through personal, commercial, and religious patronage networks (Aung-Thwin 1985). Cycles of administrative, territorial, cultural, and economic integration over time and space affected the degree to which local peoples encountered the state and its corresponding representatives while oscillation between periods of political consolidation and fragmentation created different forms of authority, patronage, and legitimacy that were connected with the state (Lieberman 2003).

In colonial and post-colonial Myanmar, these varying axes of the state were shaped by the official and quotidian experiences of the colonial economy, the disruptions of World War II, Cold War tensions, and Myanmar's broader relationship with members of the international community since 1948 (Taylor 2009). Colonial institutions and personnel reflected the administrative contours and priorities of British Burma—ministries were established to prioritise the effective operations of a colonial economy while local elites (often minorities), Deputy District Commissioners, seconded headmen, and British Indian troops represented the 'face' of the colonial state (Saha 2013). After the Japanese Imperial Army and the Burmese Independence Army brought about the collapse of the colonial state in 1941, various domestic political factions competed for the state, reflecting deep-seated divisions that permeated Myanmar society during and after World War II (Aung-Thwin and Maitrii 2013).

Social fissures informed by class, language, religion, education, ethnicity, locale, history, and ideology produced different political visions amongst competitors for the state. Myanmar social structure, as in much of Southeast Asia, was (and continues to be) organised predominantly along patron–client ties in the absence of strong institutions, creating a political landscape featuring competing networks of association linked by personal loyalty, reciprocity, and obligation to an individual. Competition for control of the state in post-independence Myanmar was often fought amongst elites and their constitutents, who were often connected by education, wealth, genealogy, and access to external resources, travel, and support. The post-World War II civil war that continued for over sixty years was exacerbated by a social structure based on vertical patronage ties, clientalism, and the lack of civic institutions that might have promoted political affiliation beyond the ethnic, religious, or personal networks that continue to divide Myanmar society today (Hicken 2011).

This chapter examines the development of the state in Myanmar since 1948. It suggests that the current republican vision of the state, led by a mixture of civilian and military personnel and organised through liberal-democratic institutions, is part of an older effort to resolve deeply entrenched socio-economic challenges and political debates over how the nation should be defined. Earlier attempts to adopt particular political orientations and pursue different economic goals are considered here as context for Myanmar's recent liberalisation in 2011. Rather than treating the current civilian–military composition of the government as the exception in Myanmar history, this chapter suggests that: (1) this form of institutional partnership has been a signature feature of the state since 1948; (2) each new government recalibrated institutions to either concentrate or disperse state power; and (3) the state has oscillated between connecting the country's economy to the global market and developing its domestic economic infrastructure through more independent means. As discussed below, an ongoing civil war, a destroyed infrastructure, and fractious socio-political divisions amongst political elites have constrained these efforts since 1948.

The independence state, 1948–1962

The new Union of Burma was established in 1948 as a constitutional government, based primarily on the institutional foundations of the colonial administration and a constitution that was written and ratified by a constituent assembly a year earlier. While the colonial state promoted a more laissez-faire economic orientation, the new independent government began to dismantle the colonial economy and reduce foreign influence while continuing to maintain connections to the global market (He and Brown 2012). The replacement of British personnel by local elites was an important change in 1948, though much of the colonial administrative architecture was retained. Key posts were occupied by both Burmese Defence Army and Western-educated local politicians who had served within the former colonial administration. Thus, the current model of a hybrid government, with civilian and military personnel forming the core of the government's staff, has been an important feature of the state since independence.

Nationalisation of key sectors was slated to include the banking, utility, non-agricultural lands, and large-scale manufacturing industries, suggesting a more centralised government operation than what was articulated by the 1947 constitution (Taylor 2009). This mixed economy reflected the liberal-socialist orientation of the country's governing party, the Anti-Fascist People's Freedom League (AFPFL), who were concerned with uplifting their country's economic conditions domestically while remaining connected to the international market economy (He and Brown 2012).

This period in Myanmar's history can be understood differently through the prisms of Rangoon's international and domestic profiles. On the one hand Rangoon was regarded as a cosmopolitan city, full of economic potential and connected to global rhythms of post-World War II Asia. Institutions were designed to complement the power of the state and uplift civil society, a particularly progressive idea in post-colonial Southeast Asia. Rangoon's emergence as a global city, a culturally vibrant society, and a growing economy created a reputation that extended—perhaps too generously—to the rest of the country.

However, the view towards the interior revealed a starkly different picture. Rangoon's relationship to its hinterland was, quite literally, an uphill battle. The architecture of the state did not extend beyond the city limits and certainly not into the highlands, giving the centre little leverage to establish a single governmental system. This situation was particularly acute in regard to ethnically designated territories, whose affiliation to Rangoon and the central government varied considerably. The post-war purge of communists from the AFPFL and the departure of the Karen National Union from the AFPFL-led constitutional process left the central government struggling to maintain the political union it had only recently secured. Within a year, a communist rebellion and a Karen rebellion erupted, threatening the state with disintegration (He and Brown 2012).

The uncertain political situation was also complicated by a broader contest to gain control of the state internally between different political interests. Key stakeholders including the Burma

Defence Army, communists, socialists, former civil services administrators, and a range of political organisations began to compete for control of the state in the name of nationalism (Taylor 2009). State managers, many of them former civil servants, attempted to re-establish the basic structures of governance and bureaucratic procedures that had been in place before World War II. Laws, infrastructure, and state financial operations were reconstituted in an attempt to address the often competing requirements of the new state and the priorities of local stakeholders. Predictably, the expansion of the state, its institutions, and its claims of broad authority lacked relevance and capacity in the countryside while the insurrections prevented the state from collecting revenue (He and Brown 2012).

Many of the political differences that crippled the state were over how to identify and resolve fissures within the new government. With the expulsion of the communists from the AFPFL, many of the unifying principles and key individuals that had bound the party began to dissolve. While broadly liberal-socialist in orientation, differences within the party over policies concerning minorities, religion, and the economy divided politicians and their respective client networks along personal and ideological lines. Ethnic communities in the borderland hills were also distrustful of the new state and threatened to reassert their political autonomy from the central government, reigniting the centuries-old tension between centre and periphery. Splits occurred over whether the state should adopt a stronger socialist orientation in an effort to create a workers' state or whether, given the influence of Cold War concerns, the economy should be more market-oriented and open to foreign capital. The AFPFL would soon divide over the orientation of the state and its ideological priorities. Severely damaged infrastructure, financial deficits, unemployment, capacity shortage, and an armed countryside worsened the situation (Taylor 2009).

The Caretaker Government, 1958–1960

With the eruption of several armed separatist movements, an ongoing communist uprising, and deepening fractures within the AFPFL government, the barely functioning government looked to its military roots to save the Union, resulting in prime minister U Nu inviting the army to temporarily establish Emergency Law and erect a 'Caretaker Government' in 1958 (Taylor 2009). In October 1958, military leadership was installed in the cabinet under General Ne Win who was not encumbered by party politics. Wielding actual power and installing non-military officers in the cabinet answerable only to him, Ne Win was able to tackle corruption, end worker strikes, and launch a pacification campaign to quell a violent and armed countryside.

After conducting the functions of state for eighteen months, the army held national elections and returned power to a civilian government in 1960. The two-year interregnum and handing over of power set a precedent for similar action in the years to come and reinforced the military's belief that its role was to protect and preserve the nation. International partners, especially those in the West, had few concerns about the military's intervention as Cold War priorities and containing communist China were the priorities of the day. By 1962, with the state at the verge of collapse due to communist and separatist insurgencies, the military overthrew the civilian government of Prime Minister U Nu and established a military Revolutionary Council that would introduce a new system of civilian–military governance to replace the last vestiges of the independence state.

The socialist state, 1962–1988

At the time of the coup, the state had little institutional or ideological leverage; it lacked unifying principles and strong institutions while the political elite were hopelessly divided (Taylor 2009).

Most foreign observers at the time regarded the coup as a positive step towards reviving the focused and disciplined governance that Ne Win had introduced in 1958–1960 (Taylor 2009). The adoption of socialist principles and a single-party system was as much a reaction to the constant infighting amongst political parties under the old regime as it was a rejection of a more market-oriented economy. At the same time, the army made it clear that the continued unity of the nation, an objective still echoed today, was the primary rationalisation for seizing power from Nu's civilian-led government.

Socialism had of course been important to anti-colonial thinkers and its ideological appeal was still strong amongst the nation's new leadership for it explained the post-colonial predicament and also provided guidelines for modernisation. The post-independence government had a strong pro-West orientation to it and Rangoon had developed into a cosmopolitan city that was quite different from the rest of the country. Still psychologically raw from colonial occupation and concerned about exposing Myanmar to the instabilities of the market economy, the new leadership decided to align itself with a socialist cosmopolitanism and a neutralist foreign policy as a way of insulating itself from what it viewed as the harmful effects of foreign influence (Aung-Thwin 1989).

Under the Revolutionary Council, a new treatise called 'The Burmese Way to Socialism' was announced as part of a wider campaign to rationalise and explain the state's broader objectives. Drawing ideas from anti-colonial nationalists and former members of the communist movement, the main principles attempted to address anxieties concerning community, economy, and modernity, fundamental issues that had nearly brought down the state at the end of the 1950s. It promoted a coherent Myanmar identity, domestic industrial growth, and a common political trajectory for the new nation. Populist policies were directed to enhance the lives of agriculturalists, local artisans, and labourers in order to reach out to a large segment of the rural population that the previous government had not prioritised effectively (Aung-Thwin and Maitrii 2013).

The Revolutionary Council, made up of military officers, launched its own civilian political party called the Burma Socialist Programme Party (BSPP) in 1975, following a constitutional convention, a national referendum, and a general election that was held one year earlier. These steps, in hindsight, would provide a blueprint for the military government nearly thirty years later when similar steps would be authorised under the 'Roadmap to Disciplined Democracy'. The BSPP was created, in part, to mobilise support from the civilian ranks in 1975 as existing groups with alternative ideologies were eventually dismantled. The BSPP was the civilian counterpart to the military, which had ostensibly handed over power to the new People's Assembly following the ratification of the 1974 constitution (Taylor 2009).

Key features of the BSPP state were its command and planning—a legacy of the strong influence of military management and its organisational character (Nakanishi 2013). While some ministerial structures of the previous regime persisted, along with continuing roles for indispensable civilian personnel, the new state was envisioned by its managers quite differently. The BSPP entered social spaces considered by the former government and liberal democracies to be off limits. Universities, the press, the publishing industry, and various spaces of cultural life were taken over by the state. Communities began to encounter the state through mass cultural and historical campaigns that directed how the state and citizenship were to be understood. Public rallies, commemorations, new holidays, and museums were established to cultivate both a sense of national belonging and affiliation for the state. BSPP-run agencies, development programmes, officials, and media represented the public's encounter with the state. Although the 1974 constitution technically placed the army under the BSPP, in reality the top positions within the party were held by senior army officers, essentially confirming the military's higher status over its civilian counterparts (Nakanishi 2013).

The infighting and division that had been part and parcel of Burmese party politics since the 1920s was addressed by summarily declaring all opposition to the state illegal and by depoliticising ethnicity as a constitutional issue (Taylor 2016). Councils that had been originally designed, under the 1947 constitution, to serve as administrative organs for ethnic groups were dissolved. Further, institutions that might have supported alternative centres of power were dismantled and replaced with bodies that would complement the state, further limiting the potential for the expansion of 'civil society'. Yet divisions still continued within the Revolutionary Council, resulting in unilateral decisions and the purging of rivals. All legislative, judicial, and executive powers were transferred to the Chairman of the Revolutionary Council. Whereas the previous post-colonial state had been more oriented towards an open economy, an international worldview, and a fairly decentralised state, the new manifestation of the Myanmar state emphasised domestic self-sustainability and a limited connection to market economies.

Despite investing resources in the countryside and ambitious multi-year development plans, the BSPP state struggled to achieve its economic goal of self-dependency and political autonomy. The capacity of the state was limited, due in part to the ongoing civil war and to its approach to economic development. As one scholar has put it, the socialist government realised too late that in its attempt to insulate itself from global market forces, the state ended up being almost as exposed to the effects of the market economy as it would have been had it remained connected to international economic networks (Taylor 2009). As a result, the BSPP found itself bankrupt and unable to support the basic functions of the state. Realising the socialist revolution had failed and a total reform of the economy was needed, General Ne Win dissolved the executive council of the BSPP and began calling for economic reforms in 1987, opening the door for groups with different visions of the Myanmar state to enter the conversation.

The military government, 1988–2011

The collapse of the BSPP government and its military–civilian administration left the state in disarray. With the country reeling from a dysfunctional economy and society teetering towards complete disorder, urban protests erupted over a host of socio-economic issues, corruption, and the mismanagement of the state. What began as a series of student protests soon became a larger mass movement, prompting several political elites from the now defunct BSPP government and Aung San Suu Kyi, the daughter of independence hero, General Aung San, to begin campaigning for change through democratic terms and ideals.

In some cases, peaceful demonstrations developed into more wide-spread looting, violence, and vandalism as social order deteriorated. Troops flooded the cities to re-establish order, but in doing so violently suppressed and arrested those on the streets. Soon thereafter, the *Tatmadaw* announced that it had taken over functions of the government and would establish the political, economic, and administrative structures that would guide the state. Leading civilian and military personnel from the previous administration were purged by a younger generation of military officers, prompting the formation of opposition organisations by former generals, including the NLD. While the military authorities promised multi-party elections in the near future, the new government reclaimed the streets through strong coercive measures that left the death toll allegedly in the thousands (Taylor 2009).

Although this might not have been the original intention, the State Law and Order Restoration Council (SLORC), renamed the State Peace and Development Council (SPDC) in 1997, governed Myanmar for the next twenty-two years. There was an attempt to hold constituent assembly elections in 1990 to form a constitutional convention and write a new constitution in a similar fashion to that done between 1962 and 1974. All the participating parties initially agreed to the process as it was thought it would lead to both civilian rule and a market-based economy (Tonkin 2007). Unfortunately the process broke down with elements within the NLD seeking a handover of power before the constitutional convention had been established, resulting in a stalemate and a refusal by the military to move forward with the transition.

The shift from a military–civilian hybrid system under the BSPP to a fully military SLORC/SPDC government resulted in the dismantling of the previous state apparatus, a purge of BSPP military officers, and the replacement of the hybrid system by the *Tatmadaw*'s own structures (SLORC, 1988, No. 2/88 Announcement). Scholars have suggested that the state might be best understood as a 'garrison state' or 'praetorian state' given the dominance by the military in nearly all aspects of governance between 1988 and 2010 (Egreteau and Jagan 2013). Intervention and tight control of the streets of Rangoon, now renamed Yangon, extended into the broader society, as the military extended the apparatus of the state into the everyday lives of citizens.

During this period the *Tatmadaw* focused on ending the nearly fifty-year civil war by securing seventeen cease-fire agreements and by attempting to reach out to Asian economic partners who did not take part in the sanctions regime. The effort to expand the state's presence in territories claimed by ethnic groups has been an ongoing priority of successive states since the late 1940s. These measures were contested by domestic opposition groups, activists, exiles, and ethnically designated armed separatists, who viewed these actions as part of a broader campaign to entrench military rule. The expanded reach of the military into everyday spaces highlighted the danger that 'the army was in danger of becoming the state' (Taylor 2009).

In 2003, Prime Minister Khin Nyunt announced the seven-step 'Roadmap to Disciplined Democracy' that would guide the transition from military rule back to a civilian–military model. A constitutional convention was re-convened; over the next five years, a new constitution was written, and it was ratified in 2008. While this process of constructing the constitution was heavily criticised and dismissed, few observers at the time realised that the Roadmap was in fact establishing the very foundations that would ultimately lead to the return of civilian–military rule in Myanmar (Cheesman, Skidmore, and Wilson 2010).

The republican state since 2011

When elections were held in 2010, most commentators were still unconvinced that the military had any intention of passing power over to civilians. Most media and advocacy groups had only understood Myanmar in the context of the post-Cold War period and therefore interpreted events within an 'authoritarian versus democracy' framing (Aung-Thwin 2001). The liberalisation programme that was initiated by the new Myanmar government in 2011 thus took most observers by surprise. Part of the reason was that the prospect for change was most frequently associated with the efforts of opposition parties, ethnic separatists, and exiled political elites. Many observers did not take the military government's 'Roadmap to Disciplined Democracy' very seriously. As a result, the arrival of Thein Sein's government and the launching of sweeping economic and political reforms were not anticipated.

The new government was dominated by the USDP, the military's civilian party, and the winner of the majority of seats in the 2010 elections. Aung San Suu Kyi and some of her NLD colleagues joined Parliament following a by-election in 2012 after boycotting the 2010 elections. In many respects, President Thein Sein was able to demonstrate to the country and to international partners that Myanmar was indeed on the path to reform. Key policies to liberalise and integrate both the economy and society were quickly enacted, giving both citizens and foreign investment interests some grounds to be optimistic about the country's future.

While the state has retreated from certain social spaces, there has been an expansion of legal, administrative, and financial structures via the new system. Laws concerning telecommunication, banking, education, labour, assembly, and land management are some examples of legislation that was promulgated by the USDP government (Crouch and Lindsey 2014). The role of local voices in the expansion of the state's authority has been a key change, but these interests continue to conflict with broader national priorities. The expansion of local and regional parliaments signals the devolution of power from the centre, an important structural development that provides the mechanism for greater involvement of rural communities in national affairs. At the same time, the establishment of the legislative system in these locales can also be understood as an expansion of the state's legal infrastructure and part of a broader pattern of administrative integration.

Legislation and policies designed to promote direct foreign investment, a key shift from earlier eras, has been recalibrated to ensure that Myanmar's economic future includes partnerships with *both* Asian and Western economies. Some measures, such as the national census in 2014, fell somewhat short in highland ethnic areas where the state had always struggled to establish a foothold. The state's institutional structures were predictably slow to work, not only because the government lacked the technical capacity to implement policy but also because pre-existing resistance to and lack of trust in the state pre-empted these integrative processes (Directorate of Investment and Company Administration 2012).

The 2015 elections represent one of the most important steps towards recalibration of the Myanmar state since the collapse of the socialist government in 1988. Over ninety political parties participated in the election that was praised by international observers for its inclusiveness and credibility, a significant change from the BSPP single-party system. While smaller political parties made only marginal gains, the NLD, the largest opposition party, made considerable progress by winning over 80 per cent of the seats. The successful holding of elections was a welcome development considering Myanmar's long history of expressing political participation through armed conflict, sectarian violence, or civil disobedience since independence in 1948.

Conclusion

The Myanmar state has oscillated along a spectrum of political-economic visions in the history of its development since 1948, punctuated by two distinct periods of military intervention. At one end of the spectrum was a vision of Myanmar defined by the central position of foreign capital and international partners to the nation's domestic policies and development. The lack of political stability in the 1950s with the onset of civil war, a weak government infrastructure, and political infighting amongst state managers made this vision untenable and undesirable for the state's leadership at the time.

Another vision, at the other end of the spectrum, was one that privileged a more centrally planned, self-reliant, and less engaged position with the market economy and its proponents. After denying their communist allies a place in the nation-building process, civilians and the military in the AFPFL were left to articulate a more moderate vision of modernisation through socialist terms and models. From this domestic perspective, the period between 1962 and 1988 was less a period of international isolation than an attempt to articulate the state's trajectory through an alternative model of governance that was being adopted throughout the post-colonial world—socialism. While the country did turn away from its market-oriented trajectory inherited from the British, the adoption of socialism by the Revolutionary Council reflected an awareness of the political models that were circulating internationally and being adopted by a number of post-colonial nations throughout the world. It is important to remember that

Myanmar's leadership was always cognisant of and ready to adopt international models of rationalising the state.

It is worth noting that the current power-sharing arrangement of civilians and military officials in positions of leadership is an enduring trait in the state's history. During the transition from colonial rule to independence, members of the Burmese Defence Army (the later version of the Burmese Independence Army) took on civilian roles as members of the Executive Council during the transfer of power in 1947–1948 and worked side by side with civilians. Under the 'Caretaker' military government of 1958, civilians were appointed to General Ne Win's cabinet but played a more diminished role in state affairs. During the Revolutionary Council years, the military figured more prominently in leadership roles but civilians were also very much part of the state infrastructure via the BSPP. Even the current NLD was founded by a combination of ex-senior military officers who were purged from the service by their SLORC/SPDC counterparts and their activist colleagues. Seen from this perspective, the current state continues to feature political elites drawn from these two communities and their presence in the current government reflects this abiding pattern in Myanmar's political landscape.

How well the state has been able to manage expectations from the periphery, where minority communities and armed-separatist groups fight over their place in the nation-state, complicates the execution and legitimacy of these visions. Some religious minority communities of contested origins have claimed citizenship but are denied recognition by the authorities. Whereas the BSPP state attempted to de-ethnicise politics, the current government has amplified the politics of ethnicity both in rhetoric and function by creating a Ministry of Ethnic Affairs. Foreign investment into these resource frontiers also lubricates differences and can contribute to friction between the state and these peripheral communities. Ethnic minority groups have historically hesitated to recognise the authority of the nation-state over concerns that their political-economic priorities will be marginalised. Direct foreign investment into their communities from external sources may give little incentive to join the state's reconciliation process.

At the same time, overcoming internal divisions within the centre, even amongst majority communities, will continue to be an important challenge for the current government as the lack of civic institutions enables affiliations based on ethnicity, religion, or personal ties to become the default position at the expense of national reconciliation. Unless the mechanisms of the state include civic institutions that can bridge these differences, the organising principles of Myanmar local society—patronage, clientalism, ethnicity, and religion—will continue to take precedence over broader translocal sources of identity.

Rivalries within majority communities stem from the lack of alternative sources of affiliation that might bridge the personal and communal sources of identity that are the root causes of wide-spread division in Myanmar society. Nation-building and the development of a civic identity—while regarded with suspicion by minority groups—are still a priority for Myanmar. With a national cease-fire agreement nearly achieved and the recent transfer of power in 2016, it is possible that we are now witnessing an important period of reconstruction after nearly seventy years of civil war. Some groups have joined the peace and reconciliation process while others, constrained by their own majority and minority interests, have yet to decide their relationship to the state and the nation.

References

Aung-Thwin, Michael A. 1985. *Pagan: The Origins of Modern Burma*. Honolulu: University of Hawaii Press.

Aung-Thwin, Michael A. 1989. '1948 and Burma's Myth of Independence'. In *Independent Burma after Forty Years: Six Assessments*, edited by Josef Silverstein. Cornell University Southeast Asian Studies Program Series No. 4. Ithaca.

Aung-Thwin, Michael A. 2001. 'Parochial Universalism, Democracy Jihad, and the Orientalist Image of Burma: The New Evangelism'. *Pacific Affairs* 70 (4).

Aung-Thwin, Michael A. and Maitrii Aung-Thwin. 2013. *A History of Myanmar Since Ancient Times: Traditions and Transformations*. London: Reaktion Books.

Cheesman, Nick, Monique Skidmore, and Trevor Wilson. 2010. *Ruling Myanmar: From Cyclone Nargis to National Elections*. Singapore: Institute of Southeast Asian Studies.

Clapp, Patricia. 2015. *Myanmar: Anatomy of a Political Transition*. Washington, DC: United States Institute of Peace Special Report No. 369, April.

Crouch, Melissa and Tim Lindsey. 2014. *Law, Society, and Transition in Myanmar*. Oxford: Hart Publishing.

Directorate of Investment and Company Administration. 2012. 'Framework for Economic and Social Reform'. Naypyidaw, Myanmar: Republic of the Union of Myanmar.

Egreteau, Renaud and Larry Jagan. 2013. *Soldiers and Diplomacy in Burma: Understanding the Foreign Relations of the Burmese Praetorian State*. Singapore: NUS Press.

He, Baogang and Kevin M. Brown. 2012. 'An Empirical World of Cosmopolitan Asia'. In *Routledge Handbook of Cosmopolitan Studies*, edited by Gerard Delanty. New York: Routledge.

Hicken, Allen. 2011. 'Clientalism'. *Annual Review of Political Science* 14 (1).

Lieberman, Victor. 2003. *Strange Parallels, Southeast Asia in Context, c. 800–1830: Volume I, Integration on the Mainland*. Cambridge: Cambridge University Press.

Mitchell, Timothy. 1991. 'The Limits of the State: Beyond Statist Approaches and Their Critics'. *The American Political Science Review* 85 (1).

Nakanishi, Yoshihiro. 2013. *Strong Soldiers, Failed Revolution: The State and Military in Burma, 1962–88*. Singapore: NUS Press.

Sadan, Mandy. 2013. *Being and Becoming Kachin: Histories Beyond the State in the Borderlands of Burma*. Oxford: Oxford University Press.

Saha, Jonathan. 2013. *Law, Disorder and the Colonial State: Corruption in Burma c. 1900*. Cambridge: Cambridge University Press.

Taylor, Robert H. 2009. *The State in Myanmar*. Singapore: NUS Press.

Taylor, Robert H. 2016. 'Can Myanmar's NLD Undo the Gordian Knot of Federalism and Ethnicity?' *Trends in Southeast Asia* 3.

Tonkin, Derek. 2007. 'The 1990 Elections in Myanmar: Broken Promises or a Failure of Communication?' *Contemporary Southeast Asia* 29 (1).

3
THE DEFENCE SERVICES

Andrew Selth

Between 1962 and 2011, Myanmar boasted the modern world's most durable military dictatorship. Since then, its armed forces, or *Tatmadaw*, have overseen a managed transition to a more open and democratic system. While the National League for Democracy's (NLD) landslide victory in the 2015 elections dramatically changed the political landscape, the Tatmadaw remains the country's most powerful institution. It is also becoming a more capable military force. However, the evolution of Myanmar society and demands for wider reforms will test the generals' willingness to permit further changes to their status and influence, and their ability to control developments.

The data deficit

Despite its prominence in national affairs since Myanmar regained its independence in 1948, the Tatmadaw's internal workings have long been a closed book. Even basic data have been beyond the reach of researchers. For example, the size of Myanmar's armed forces is a mystery. By the end of the Ne Win era (1962–1988), it was generally accepted that there were about 186,000 men and women in its three services (IISS 1986, 152). The actual number, however, was a state secret. After the 1988 pro-democracy uprising, when the Tatmadaw took back direct political power from the socialist government, the State Law and Order Restoration Council (SLORC) launched an ambitious military expansion and modernisation programme. By 2000, the Tatmadaw had doubled in size to an estimated 400,000, about 370,000 of whom were in the army (Selth 2000, 296). Since then, however, the total number has declined, possibly to 300,000. It could even be lower.

Nor can anyone be sure about the level of Myanmar's defence expenditure. Ne Win's curbs on military spending were abandoned by the SLORC and its successor, the State Peace and Development Council (SPDC), lending credence to claims that the armed forces were routinely allocated 45% of the national budget. A more likely average annual figure was 32%, but this was still more than double the funds formally allocated to the health and education portfolios combined (Selth 2009, 12–13). Also, the budget did not take account of the other ways that the Tatmadaw supplemented its income, from both official and unofficial sources. Since 2011, annual defence spending has fluctuated, but remained high. In 2014/2015, for example, defence was allocated about 23% of total government expenditure, estimated by the Asian Development

Bank to be 4.8% of GDP (DVB 2015). In terms of defence spending per capita, Myanmar still rates below most other regional countries, but the Tatmadaw has enjoyed a privileged position in Naypyitaw's accounts.

How these statistics translated into the Tatmadaw's order of battle and operational capabilities are two more 'known unknowns', to quote Donald Rumsfeld. Under the SLORC/SPDC, Myanmar purchased a wide range of arms and military equipment. Most came from China, but several other countries contributed to the influx of armoured vehicles and artillery, missiles and munitions, fighter and transport aircraft, frigates and patrol boats. Few of these acquisitions were new or state of the art, raising doubts about their reliability and effectiveness. The Tatmadaw's command, control, communications and intelligence capabilities were also largely unknown. Questions hung over its combat proficiency. Under Ne Win, the Tatmadaw was considered an experienced and battle-hardened counter-insurgency force, but its ability to perform in a larger, more conventional and multi-dimensional conflict still cannot be reliably assessed (Selth 2009, 15–18).

Given this level of uncertainty, all reports about the Tatmadaw need to be treated carefully. It has become evident, however, that since the advent of a hybrid civilian–military government in 2011 Commander-in-Chief (CinC) Senior General Min Aung Hlaing has presided over a far-reaching plan to develop the Tatmadaw as a military organisation. The extension of his appointment until 2021 should help it maintain momentum.

The new look Tatmadaw

In an effort to create a better equipped, more professional and more respected force – what former President Thein Sein called a 'world-class Tatmadaw' – the CinC took steps to strengthen its cohesion and unity. He removed several senior officers and rotated others to new positions, in a major generational shift. He trimmed the top-heavy command structure and replaced most of the country's Regional Military Commanders. The infusion of new talent and (potentially, at least) new thinking has been maintained through periodic reshuffles of personnel. Officer cadet intakes have been reduced and child soldiers are being demobilised. There have been large scale transfers of personnel to the Myanmar Police Force (MPF). Pay levels have been increased, new uniforms have been issued and greater control has been exerted over the Tatmadaw's finances. The CinC has introduced new training programmes and revised others, while seeking to diversify the sources of the armed forces' expertise. He has also spoken out against corruption and sought to improve the Tatmadaw's public image.

There have been major equipment upgrades and new arms production programmes. Between 2011 and 2014 Myanmar reportedly purchased arms valued at US$1.6 billion (SIPRI 2015). The main suppliers were China, Russia, Ukraine, India and possibly North Korea. The army has acquired armoured vehicles, ground-based air defence systems, trucks and artillery. The air force is taking delivery of new fighters, combat helicopters, trainers and light transport aircraft. In 2015, it reportedly ordered 16 JF-17 multi-role jets. Since 2011, Myanmar's navy has commissioned five new frigates, three of which were built with foreign technology in local shipyards. Several corvettes and patrol boats are under construction or on order. It has also been widely reported that Myanmar plans to buy two Russian submarines, but no evidence has yet been offered to support such a claim (Selth 2014). In 2015, nearly 35% of the defence budget was earmarked for new warships, fighter jets, armoured and other vehicles, heavy weapons and ammunition, suggesting that Myanmar's order of battle is still expanding.

Myanmar has also continued to develop its defence industries. This has not just been to upgrade and expand its weapons holdings but also to make the Tatmadaw more self-sufficient

(Selth 2015a, 9). There are some 25 factories and other major sites (such as shipyards and research institutes) producing a wide range of arms, ammunition and equipment. For example, Ukrainian BTR-3U and MT-LB armoured vehicles are currently being built in Myanmar. The Tatmadaw is also able to build, and provide ammunition for, truck-mounted 122mm multiple-launch rocket systems. It is likely that most of the 60 K-8 jet trainers ordered from China in 2009 will be assembled at the Aircraft Production and Maintenance Base at Meiktila, in cooperation with a Chinese firm. The Tatmadaw reportedly hopes to build most of its new JF-17 jet fighters in Myanmar. As noted above, it is already constructing a range of major naval vessels in its Yangon shipyards. To facilitate these projects, Naypyitaw has signed agreements with several foreign countries, related mainly to technology transfers and licensed production.

Over the past 30 years, there have been numerous claims that Myanmar has tried to develop, or has even acquired, weapons of mass destruction. Arguably, before the international community embraced Thein Sein's reform programme and developed closer relations with his government, Myanmar had a strategic rationale for the acquisition of such weapons. An invasion was never a real prospect, but the hostility shown towards the SLORC and SPDC by the Western democracies between 1988 and 2011 encouraged military leaders to believe that Myanmar faced an existential threat (Selth 2008). The regime's interest in nuclear technology fell well short of an actual weapons programme, however, and no hard evidence has ever been produced to support reports that the Tatmadaw has developed, tested or used chemical and biological weapons. Accusations that North Korea is helping Myanmar to produce ballistic missiles are harder to refute, but little is known about this programme, its scope, the stage it has reached and the type of missiles possibly involved.

Min Aung Hlaing's military reform programme is still a work in progress, and appears to be encountering obstacles. There are reportedly divisions within the Tatmadaw over the loss of certain powers and privileges, both on active service and after retirement. There are problems of poor recruitment levels, low morale and high desertion rates. There are also concerns about an inflated junior officer corps, which threatens a promotions logjam (Maung Aung Myoe 2014, 233–49). In addition, recent campaigns against non-state armed groups have exposed deficiencies in leadership, tactics, training and equipment. Many officers and men lack combat experience. Confidence in the ability of the Tatmadaw concurrently to pursue counter-insurgency campaigns in different parts of the country is low. Reports of human rights abuses against both combatants and non-combatants in Chin, Kachin, Shan and Karen States have raised questions over discipline, an issue that also arose in Rakhine State in 2012, when the army was called in to help quell widespread sectarian violence (Human Rights Watch 2013). Similar concerns were raised over operations against the Muslim Rohingyas in late 2016 and early 2017.

The Tatmadaw's military doctrine has been revised to 'suit the new political context' and changed strategic circumstances (Callahan 2012, 128; Maung Aung Myoe 2016). However, there are doubts over its ability to reach the levels of professionalism to which Min Aung Hlaing aspires. In Myanmar military circles, 'professional' is often equated with 'mercenary'. Such an approach to soldiering is anathema to many officers, who see themselves as patriots charged with an historical responsibility to protect the country and constitution. This mindset envisages a perpetual role for the armed forces in national politics. At the same time, accusations have been made that 'the Tatmadaw's idealism, professionalism and patriotism have over the years been eroded by nepotism and corruption'. It has been suggested that 'returning to a more disciplined system is not really practical' (Euro-Burma Office 2013). Whether or not that is true, the expansion of Myanmar's polity, economy and civil society since 2011 means that a military career is no longer the only way to obtain an education, technical skills, employment and social status.

The Tatmadaw's political role

One question often asked is: when will the Tatmadaw 'return to the barracks' (ICG 2014)? This reflects a widespread wish for an elected civilian government in Myanmar, but it misses a vital point. The Tatmadaw has never seen itself as having separate military and political roles, with the first naturally having primacy over the second. Rather, it is deeply imbued with the idea that since 1948 it alone has been responsible for holding the Union together, defeating its enemies – both internal and external – and saving the country from chaos. This has given rise to an abiding belief, strengthened by indoctrination programmes, in the importance of 'national politics', as opposed to 'party politics'. It has also led to the conviction that the Tatmadaw has both a right and duty to supersede other state institutions if circumstances demand. It was on this basis that the armed forces took power in 1962 and crushed the 1988 uprising. As Robert Taylor has written, after the latter upheaval the Tatmadaw 'set out on its own to reunify or, as later termed "reconsolidate", the country in order to create the conditions for passing authority to a constitutional government' (Taylor 2015a, 8).

In the 2008 constitution, the Tatmadaw was recognised as an autonomous institution free from civilian control or oversight. It was given the right to administer and adjudicate its own affairs independently, including the management of its personnel. It also has an exclusive right to set its own agenda, particularly with regard to military strategy and operations. In some areas authority is shared, leading to questions over the power of the CinC, relative to the president. However, the constitution specifies that the portfolios of defence, home affairs and border affairs are filled by serving officers chosen by the CinC. If the military-nominated vice president is included, the CinC exercises effective control over 6 of the 11 members of the powerful National Defence and Security Council (NDSC). More to the point, as supreme commander of all 'Defence Services' in Myanmar, the CinC has ultimate control over the MPF (including its 30-plus armed security battalions), Border Guard Forces and all other paramilitary organisations.

Under Thein Sein, Myanmar's executive and armed forces were in broad agreement about the way forward. The Tatmadaw as an institution no longer ran day-to-day politics. It let the government formulate policy in most areas and implement a wide-ranging programme of economic and social reforms. It went from being a 'hegemonic player' to a 'veto player'. As Renaud Egreteau pointed out, the military appointees in parliament did not 'pursue active law-making, but rather a detailed scrutiny of legislations and motions prepared either by the executive branch or the executive bloc of the legislature' (Egreteau 2015, 1). In contrast to their more powerful predecessors, the 14 Regional Commanders tended to exercise their authority only on military matters, deferring on other issues to the local civil authorities. For its part, the government seemed content to let the armed forces manage their own affairs. Complications could arise when military and political factors coincided, as may have occurred over peace talks with ethnic armies and the Tatmadaw's links to North Korea, but these issues were manageable.

The Tatmadaw's attitude to reform, and the extent to which it feels obliged to control the transition process, will be tested by several issues over the next few years. These include the policies of the NLD government, any new attempts to amend the constitution, and negotiations with non-state armed groups over a comprehensive peace agreement.

Before considering these issues, it is worth noting that the paradigm shift from a dictatorship to a more liberal government is taking place because the Tatmadaw has permitted it to do so. Contrary to the claims of some foreign politicians and activists, Myanmar's military leadership was not persuaded to loosen its grip on national affairs by external factors such as economic sanctions. Nor was its hand forced by internal strife or military defeat. The decision to launch a transition to a 'discipline-flourishing democracy' was made on the basis of careful calculations as to the Tatmadaw's status, the political state of the country, its needs in terms of development, and how best to manage its complex security problems. The 2008 constitution was designed to ensure that the armed forces retained overall control of a top-down reform process that met those broad requirements. The pace and degree with which the Tatmadaw steps back further from political power will depend on the nature of the new government and the way in which it manages those issues the Tatmadaw deems most important.

Also, the 2015 elections were held, were relatively free and fair, and produced an accurate result, because the armed forces leadership permitted them to occur and did not interfere. As history attests, it could have intervened at any stage of the process and ensured that the elections were cancelled, postponed or manipulated to give a different outcome. Given their resources and control of Myanmar's internal affairs, the generals must have known that an honest election would result in a decisive victory for the NLD. The final statistics may have come as a bit of a surprise (before the poll some analysts were doubtful the NLD could achieve a landslide) but the outcome could not have been in doubt. This being the case, it can be assumed that, before the election took place, the Tatmadaw's senior leadership, in consultation with Thein Sein, took a collective decision to accept the results. There is no tradition in Myanmar of sharing political power, but they must also have faced the prospect of negotiating the future governance of the country with Aung San Suu Kyi and her party.

This is all encouraging, but the Tatmadaw and the NLD still needed to strike a deal of some kind. The massive show of popular support for the main opposition party in 2015 gave it enormous moral authority and a strong bargaining position, but it did not guarantee a free hand to shape Myanmar's future. That can only be done in cooperation with the armed forces. As Robert Taylor noted before the election, 'Only the army can end its own role in Myanmar's politics, and that decision is dependent on its perception of the civilian political elite's ability to manage the future' (Taylor 2015b). He might have added, 'and protect the Tatmadaw as a national institution'. Neither the Tatmadaw's leadership, nor Aung San Suu Kyi and the NLD, however, would gain anything from a direct confrontation. Such a clash of wills would inevitably slow down the democratic transition process. It could even halt it.

The Tatmadaw and the NLD government

A deal appears to have been struck between Aung San Suu Kyi and Senior General Min Aung Hlaing, but a continuing bone of contention will be the constitution, which is seen by the generals as 'the main or mother law' of Myanmar, protecting their core interests and guaranteeing them a role in national affairs. Any attempt to reduce the status of the armed forces will also be resisted. They have already rejected moves to reduce their guaranteed 25% representation in all national and regional assemblies. Future amendments have not been ruled out, but have been opposed on the grounds that Myanmar is still a 'young democracy'. Concerns have also been expressed that 'Myanmar is still in a democratic transition . . . stability and reconciliation are very important in this period and democratic practices are not mature enough yet' (Hnin Yadana Zaw 2015). The generals also opposed changing the constitution to permit Aung San Suu Kyi to become president. In response, she rejected the notion that the president 'takes precedence over all other persons' in Myanmar (Constitution 2008, 19), and declared that she would 'run the government' and 'make all decisions' (Min Zin 2016).

One message consistently given by the generals is that the Tatmadaw will always act according to the law, in particular the constitution. Given that there is a plethora of restrictive laws already on the books, some dating back to the colonial era, and the 2008 charter was written specifically to safeguard the Tatmadaw's independence, operations and national role, this is rather disingenuous. The generals will always be able to find some formal legal basis for their actions. Under the provisions of chapter 11 of the constitution, for example, the Tatmadaw can return the country to full military control, if such a step is deemed necessary by the president. Given certain triggers, the CinC could simply mount another coup. Some observers have put the likelihood of that happening over the next five years at 20% (Kurlantzick and Stewart 2013). A few have rated the prospect even higher, but these kinds of estimates are highly speculative. A more realistic notion of the Tatmadaw's future behaviour can be gauged by examining factors involved at the national, institutional and personal levels.

At the national level, the Tatmadaw is committed to Myanmar's sovereignty, unity and internal stability, as it judges such matters. These goals were encapsulated in the SLORC/SPDC's three 'national causes' and have been enshrined in the constitution. If they are challenged, military intervention of some kind becomes more likely. Since 2011, perceived external threats have greatly diminished. However, any attempt by the international community to intervene, for example by exercising its 'responsibility to protect' the Rohingyas, would be resisted. There is the potential for civil unrest to erupt over several contentious political, economic and social issues. There are 23 Border Guard Force battalions and about a dozen People's Militia Force units, the reliability of which is suspect. There are also about 100,000 armed personnel in Myanmar, divided among nearly 40 non-state groups (Maung Aung Myoe 2014). Most have resisted efforts to place them under government control, including the estimated 30,000-strong United Wa State Army and the 20,000-strong Kachin Independence Army.

At the institutional level, the Tatmadaw would be concerned at any attempts to deny it a central place in national affairs. This is not only spelt out in the constitution but has been reaffirmed on several occasions by the former president and CinC. Most military officers are intensely nationalistic and take seriously their role as guardians of the country, with its responsibility to step in and 'save' Myanmar, if believed necessary. The military leadership is also likely to act if the Tatmadaw itself was considered under threat. Since 2011, the two military-controlled conglomerates known as the Union of Myanmar Economic Holdings and the Myanmar Economic Corporation have lost profitable monopolies and certain tax exemptions, but the Tatmadaw's leadership seems to have accepted that it will still have the men and materiel necessary to fulfil its duty to 'safeguard the constitution'. Should a future government or parliament drastically reduce the defence budget, however, or seriously try to restrict the armed forces' sources of off-budget income, there is likely to be trouble.

At the personal level, many servicemen would be unhappy about an attempt to remove the constitutional clause that effectively grants them immunity from prosecution for human rights violations committed before 2011. If any local politicians, or members of the international community, tried to put Myanmar military personnel on trial for such offences, that would cause considerable concern within the armed forces. According to one senior officer, the SLORC did not hand over power to the NLD after the 1990 elections because the Tatmadaw feared it would face a Nuremberg-style trial. Yet, such issues continue to arise. In 2014, for example, Harvard Law School researchers accused three senior officers, including the then Home Affairs Minister, of war crimes and crimes against humanity (Harvard 2014). Operations against the Rohingyas in 2016 and 2017 were branded 'genocide' and 'ethnic cleansing'. The US has also cited individual officers for their links to Pyongyang. Another possible scenario that deserves brief mention is an attempt by a faction within the Tatmadaw to slow down the reform process, or to preserve perks and privileges that seem to be slipping away.

All that said, the Tatmadaw is no longer the institution it once was and there are significant constraints on direct action of the kind seen in the past. If it should occur, there would inevitably be a strong reaction, both within the country and outside it. Even Myanmar's traditional friends are unlikely to welcome such a retrograde step. Indeed, it could lead to precisely the kind of external pressure and internal 'chaos' that the military leadership has tried to avoid. The generals would also need to weigh the benefits of such a move against the possibility that it might spark a serious breakdown in military discipline, as there are clearly many NLD supporters in its ranks. A mutiny has always been one of the generals' greatest fears, and a reason for some of the measures taken by Myanmar's security agencies over the past 50 years. In any case, they need not resort to anything as crude as a coup. Thanks to the constitution, and the Tatmadaw's historical legacy, the CinC can exercise considerable influence without actually assuming power.

For example, through its control of the state's coercive apparatus, its monopoly of the means of exercising armed force, its guaranteed ministerial appointments and its domination of the NDSC, the Tatmadaw exercises a powerful influence over Myanmar's internal affairs (Selth 2015b). While the role of the armed forces in the national economy has been declining since 2011, the generals and their capitalist 'cronies' could still exert considerable economic pressure on the new government, if they chose to do so. Also, Aung San Suu Kyi knows that an early resolution of the country's many long-running insurgencies will be one of the NLD's most pressing policy issues. Yet, there is no hope of a more comprehensive ceasefire agreement – let alone a nation-wide peace settlement – without the full cooperation and active support of the armed forces. Talk of a federal system of government, of the kind mooted by the NLD and some ethnic groups, has already made the Tatmadaw nervous.

It is also relevant that 37 of the 46 ministers in Thein Sein's government were from the Tatmadaw, including 5 on active duty. Of the 14 Chief Ministers of the states and regions, all but one were retired military officers (Maung Aung Myoe 2014, 247). The UN estimated that nearly 90% of the national parliament had some affiliation to the former military regime (IBAHRI 2012, 52–3). These numbers have changed dramatically as a result of the 2015 elections, but in all national, state and regional assemblies 25% of the seats are still reserved for military personnel. In addition, 80% of senior civil service positions are currently filled by ex-servicemen and women. Of the 33 permanent secretary positions created in 2015, 23 were held by former military personnel. As Renaud Egreteau and Larry Jagan have written, over decades the officer corps has been socialised into believing that the Tatmadaw is the sole and uncontested embodiment of the state (Egreteau and Jagan 2013). The NLD has resisted purging the public service, but that means many positions of authority will be occupied by former military officers with a strong institutional loyalty to the armed forces.

The Tatmadaw and the international community

While Myanmar continues to attract criticism from governments and organisations, for various reasons, one striking aspect of its re-emergence as an international actor in recent years has been the readiness of foreign countries to renew or strengthen ties with the country's armed forces and police. Before the advent of Thein Sein's reformist government, any relationship with the security forces was politically difficult, if not (in the case of some Western democracies) impossible. Yet, since 2011 several governments, international institutions and private foundations have offered Myanmar aid in this sector. These approaches were enthusiastically welcomed by Naypyitaw and, albeit more cautiously, by Aung San Suu Kyi.

Most of these initiatives have been expressed in principled terms, but broadly speaking they make up two separate, if related, sets of proposals. One is aimed at increasing the professionalism of the armed forces, reducing their direct political role and encouraging them to observe internationally accepted norms of behaviour. The other relates to the modernisation and civilianisation of the MPF. While the latter set has been couched in vague terms, refers to the 'rule of law' in Myanmar, and alludes to the reform of the country's deeply flawed judicial system, most seem to envisage aid to the MPF as a way of 'civilianising' Myanmar's coercive apparatus. The thinking seems to be that, the more the police force accepts primary responsibility for law and order, the less the army needs to be involved. Such programmes also help develop bilateral relationships and exert a positive influence on the government, by encouraging the reform process.

The US has been interested in restoring defence ties with Myanmar since Barack Obama came to office, something he hinted at during his state visit in 2012. In 2013, the Tatmadaw sent two observers to Exercise Cobra Gold in Thailand. Later that year, the State Department announced that the US was looking at ways to support 'nascent military engagement' with Myanmar as a way of encouraging further political reforms. Pentagon officials have since referred to a 'carefully calibrated' plan of engagement that includes Myanmar's cooperation in the search for the remains of 730 US military personnel missing since 1945. Tatmadaw officers have participated in events sponsored by the Asia-Pacific Centre for Security Studies in Hawaii, and the US Defence Institute for International Legal Studies has also become involved. Training places in the US for Tatmadaw personnel and a formal military–military dialogue or 'partnership' with Myanmar have not been ruled out.

Other countries have followed the US's lead. During Thein Sein's 2013 visit to Canberra, for example, Australia's government announced that it was restoring the resident Defence Attache position in Yangon, which was closed in 1979. Then Prime Minister Gillard said that this would permit engagement with the Tatmadaw in areas like peacekeeping, humanitarian assistance and disaster relief, as well as enhancing other forms of dialogue. When Thein Sein visited the UK in 2013, the British government announced that it too was posting a Defence Attache to Yangon. Myanmar was also offered training in human rights, the laws of armed conflict and the accountability of democratic armed forces. Thirty Tatmadaw officers attended a UK-sponsored staff course in 2014 and additional training has been discussed. A European Union (EU) arms embargo remains in place but the EU has provided training in crowd control to the MPF.

The activist community has pointed out that the Tatmadaw still dominates politics in Myanmar, is waging campaigns against armed ethnic groups and is guilty of numerous human rights violations. The MPF has been accused of corruption and other abuses. Another criticism has been that assistance to the security forces gives them a legitimacy they do not deserve and helps them oppress Myanmar society. Some activists have even claimed that foreign training directly helps the army and police to suppress the ethnic minorities, Muslims and the democracy movement. While these accusations have not stopped foreign governments from cautiously providing aid to the security sector, the US Senate has warned of the potential for 'well-intended engagement [to be] misdirected towards a negative result' (Lohman 2013). Should the Tatmadaw make life difficult for Aung San Suu Kyi's government, or fail to curb its excesses in Rakhine State, the attitude of the US and other countries towards bilateral security links would doubtless harden.

Looking ahead

Myanmar's future is unclear, but the Tatmadaw seems to have two main goals over the next decade. The first is the development of a 'world-class Tatmadaw', that is more professional, more capable and more respected, both within Myanmar and abroad. As it has acquired new arms and technology, and built up its defence industries, so defence relations with China, Russia and other arms suppliers have strengthened. The Tatmadaw hopes also to develop closer contacts with the forces of Western and ASEAN countries. As far as can be judged, the military reform programme seems to have been reasonably successful, but many difficult problems remain to be dealt with. As it tackles these issues, the relationship of the CinC and the Tatmadaw with Aung San Suu Kyi's government and the new parliament will be critical. That said, the Tatmadaw will remain a powerful political force. By exercising its considerable influence, both directly and indirectly, it is likely to be able to continue its current modernisation and rearmament programmes.

The Tatmadaw's other main goal seems to be a measured withdrawal from government, while retaining its institutional independence and key national role. It has long been the generals' intention, however, to decide the time frame for Myanmar's transition to a genuinely democratic system. Before 2015, there were signs that they envisaged at least one more term under a military-endorsed president before any real handover of power, and then only if certain conditions were met. It remains to be seen how the modus vivendi negotiated between Aung San Suu Kyi and Min Aung Hlaing fares as the NLD settles into government, policy priorities change and more far-reaching reforms are proposed. The Tatmadaw is unlikely to welcome the constraints on its power and influence that will be required for Myanmar to become a real democracy. Any perceived challenges to the country's unity, internal stability and sovereignty will also disrupt this process. As the International Crisis group has written, 'Tatmadaw backing for the transition is indispensable, but by no means unproblematic' (ICG 2014).

References

Callahan, M.P. 2012. 'The Generals Loosen Their Grip'. *Journal of Democracy* 23 (4): 120–131.

Constitution. 2008. *Constitution of the Republic of the Union of Myanmar (2008)*. Naypyidaw: Ministry of Information.

DVB. 2015. 'Burma Among World's Highest Spending on Military'. Democratic Voice of Burma, April 27. www.dvb.no/news/burma-among-worlds-highest-spenders-on-military-myanmar/50257.

Egreteau, Renaud. 2015. 'Military Delegates in Myanmar's Legislature: What Do They Do? What Will They (Continue To) Do?' *ISEAS Perspective* (21). Singapore: Institute of Southeast Asian Studies.

Egreteau, Renaud and Larry Jagan. 2013. *Soldiers and Diplomacy in Burma: Understanding the Foreign Relations of the Burmese Praetorian State*. Singapore: NUS Press.

Euro-Burma Office. 2013. 'The Tatmadaw: Does the Government Control the Tatmadaw?' Euro-Burma Office Briefing Paper, Brussels, March 2013. https://euroburmaoffice.s3.amazonaws.com/filer_public/bb/2b/bb2ba05e-f7cd-4960-bf19-526dd9d1b73f/ebo_brief_no_3_2013_tatmadaw.pdf.

Harvard. 2014. 'Clinic Investigation: Senior Myanmar Officials Implicated in War Crimes and Crimes Against Humanity'. Human Rights @ Harvard Law, November 7. http://hrp.law.harvard.edu/press-releases/clinic-investigation-senior-mynamar-officials-implicated-in-war-crimes-and-crimes-against-humanity/.

Hnin Yadana Zaw. 2015. 'Myanmar Military Puts Its Case for Hanging on to Political Power'. Reuters, June 24. www.reuters.com/article/2015/06/24/us-myanmar-politics-idUSKBN0P417N20150624.

Human Rights Watch. 2013. '"All You Can Do Is Pray": Crimes Against Humanity and Ethnic Cleansing of Rohingya Muslims in Burma's Arakan'. Washington, DC: Human Rights Watch, April 22. www.hrw.org/report/2013/04/22/all-you-can-do-pray/crimes-against-humanity-and-ethnic-cleansing-rohingya-muslims.

IBAHRI. 2012. *The Rule of Law in Myanmar: Challenges and Prospects: Report of the International Bar Association's Human Rights Institute (IBAHRI)*. London: International Bar Association, December.

ICG. 2014. 'Myanmar's Military: Back to the Barracks?' *Asia Briefing* (143). Yangon & Brussels: International Crisis Group, April 22.

IISS. 1986. *The Military Balance, 1986–1987*. London: International Institute for Strategic Studies.

Kurlantzick, Joshua and Devin T. Stewart. 2013. 'Burma's Reforms and Regional Cooperation in East Asia'. Carnegie Council for Ethics in International Affairs, Summer 2013. www.carnegiecouncil.org/publications/articles_papers_reports/0164.html/:pf_printable.

Lohman, Walter. 2013. 'Hill Concern over US–Burma Military Engagement Grows'. The Foundry, June 27. http://blog.heritage.org/2013/06/27/hill-concern-over-u-s-burma-military-engagement-grows/.

Maung Aung Myoe. 2014. 'The Soldier and the State: The Tatmadaw and Political Liberalization in Myanmar since 2011'. *South East Asia Research* (22) 2: 233–249.
Maung Aung Myoe. 2016. 'Myanmar Military's White Paper Highlights Growing Openness'. *Nikkei Asian Review*, March 28. http://asia.nikkei.com/Viewpoints/Viewpoints/Maung-Aung-Myoe-Myanmar-military-s-white-paper-highlights-growing-openness.
Min Zin. 2016. 'Burma's Puppeteer-in-Chief Takes Charge'. *Foreign Policy*, March 12. https://foreignpolicy.com/2016/03/12/burmas-puppeteer-in-chief-takes-charge-aung-san-suu-kyi/.
Selth, Andrew. 2000. *Burma's Armed Forces: Power Without Glory*. Norwalk: EastBridge.
Selth, Andrew. 2008. 'Burma and the Threat of Invasion: Regime Fantasy or Strategic Reality?' *Regional Outlook* (17). Brisbane: Griffith Asia Institute, Griffith University.
Selth, Andrew. 2009. 'Burma's Armed Forces: Looking Down the Barrel'. *Regional Outlook* (21). Brisbane: Griffith Asia Institute, Griffith University.
Selth, Andrew. 2014. 'Is Burma Really Buying Submarines?' *The Interpreter*, January 29. www.lowyinterpreter.org/post/2014/01/29/Burmas-submarine-dream.aspx.
Selth, Andrew. 2015a. 'Strong, Fully Efficient and Modern: Myanmar's New Look Armed Forces'. *Regional Outlook* (49). Brisbane: Griffith Asia Institute, Griffith University.
Selth, Andrew. 2015b. 'The Realities of Power in Myanmar'. *New Mandala*, November 16. http://asiapacific.anu.edu.au/newmandala/2015/11/16/the-realities-of-power-in-myanmar/.
SIPRI. 2015. Arms Transfers Database, Stockholm International Peace Research Institute, July 14. http://armstrade.sipri.org/armstrade/html/export_toplist.php.
Taylor, R.H. 2015a. 'The Armed Forces in Myanmar Politics: A Terminating Role?' *Trends in Southeast Asia* (2). Singapore: Institute of Southeast Asian Studies.
Taylor, R.H. 2015b. 'Myanmar Military Preserves Its Autonomy, for Now'. *Nikkei Asian Review*, March 16. http://asia.nikkei.com/Viewpoints/Perspectives/Myanmar-s-military-preserves-its-autonomy-for-now.

4
DEMOCRACY

John H. Badgley and Ian Holliday

The process of building democracy in Myanmar is long and convoluted. Launched in the late 1940s during Burmese independence from Britain, democracy was first suspended for 18 months from 1958 to 1960, and then overthrown by General Ne Win's military coup in 1962. In 1988, mass street protests returned the concept firmly to the political agenda, and prompted leaders of the military machine that ultimately crushed the popular uprising to issue a promise of free and fair elections. In 1990, however, the landslide electoral triumph registered by the major opposition party was ignored, and the military junta that had seized power in 1988 continued to rule as before. Only in 2010 were elections again held, though both at home and abroad they were seen as deeply flawed. Nevertheless, they enabled a transition to constitutional rule to take place in 2011, with former members of the junta assuming power under President Thein Sein. Five years later, in 2015, fresh elections were held. Broadly free and fair, they generated a similar result to 1990 and led to the formation in 2016 of a more fully civilian government notionally under President Htin Kyaw, but in fact dominated by Aung San Suu Kyi in the role of state counsellor. In this chapter, we examine the career of democracy in Burma/Myanmar by focusing on context reaching back to the nineteenth century, initial experience from 1948 to 1962, military years from 1962 to 2011, and attempts since 2011 to make a sustainable transition.

Context

Any democracy is an evolving political culture. Once limited to antecedents in ancient Greece, where it was widely seen as an undesirable political model, democracy has become a worldwide phenomenon shaped by diverse cultures and experiences on five continents. In Myanmar, the process of transforming individuals from passive subjects to engaged citizens was intimately linked to British colonization through invasions launched in 1824, 1852 and 1885. Together, these generated formal imperial control of Burma by the start of 1886, and full integration into the Raj. Important steps in the process were the emergence of a handful of liberal newspapers in the mid-nineteenth century, of a circumscribed legislative council at the start of the twentieth century, and of elected town councils, a judiciary, political parties and commercial interests routinely lobbying government two decades later. In place by 1920 were a rudimentary free press, both English and Burmese, limited elections, an executive-controlled legislature, a merit-based civil administration and a legal system framed by an independent judiciary. Rights were not a priority, but a national strike that year demonstrated newfound freedom of political expression.

This foundation for democracy was less than exemplary. In *Burmese Days*, published in 1934, George Orwell, a young colonial police officer in the 1920s, depicted a local magistrate hopelessly corrupted by familial greed in a culture of exploitation. However another Englishman, J. S. Furnivall, who worked as an imperial civil servant for decades in the early part of the twentieth century, saw Burmese society differently through close ties with leaders of the General Council of Buddhist Associations in the 1910s, of the General Council of Burma Associations in the 1920s and of the nationalist student association Dobama Asiayone in the 1930s. He especially admired radical nationalist students, and wrote with authority about the nation's nascent democratic underpinnings. He advised the student *thakins* ('masters') who created the Nagani Book Club, a literary resource for Fabian socialist thought as well as a publishing outlet. He knew personally the new crop of politicians, including cultural icon Saya (sometimes Thakin) Kodaw Hmaing, teacher, poet and activist who in a series of novels depicted a Burmese version of revolutionary democracy (Kyaw and Badgley 2009, 275–276).

However, when independence came in January 1948 it heralded only limited freedom for most citizens. Burma was, and as Myanmar since 1989 has remained, a land of multiple histories shading from idealized liberty into tyranny and abusive governance within diverse ethnic communities. The political settlement written into a constitution adopted in 1947 contributed to this problem because it was based on a union system designed to be revisited and possibly reconfigured within a decade. The lower House of Deputies and the upper House of Nationalities were conceived by lawyers steeped in English political experience but largely ignorant of Burma's diverse societies and cultural norms. They thus failed fully to grasp that Burma's minority ethnic groups had long shared with the majority Burman population conservative political traditions based on kinship, patrimony and patronage. As the imperial Konbaung Dynasty withered and ultimately collapsed under the three British interventions in the nineteenth century, its institutions were replaced by the steel frame of Britain's Indian empire. Initially controlled by the military arm of the imperial state, Burma was ultimately placed under direct civil administration in the heartland and under indirect rule through traditional authorities in the periphery. In ethnic minority areas, this did little to change old norms among communal rulers and chiefs who carried on with minimal interference. In the Burman heartland, however, rapid change took place, with industrial agriculture serving India's commercial interests soon transforming the lives of Burman and Karen villagers living in and around the expansive Irrawaddy delta. Many Tamil labourers and Chettiar money lenders arrived, developing commercial paddy cultivation among smallholders and landless peasants (Adas 1974). Yet even where the economy was transformed, village educational systems built on Buddhist monastic foundations remained essentially unchanged from monarchial days. The constitution implemented at independence on January 4, 1948 sat astride these conservative social institutions, and the democracy launched under Prime Minister U Nu had no option but to operate within this context.

Initial experience: 1948–1962

In the immediate postwar period, British troops and police preserved order in Burma. The security they provided enabled the dominant Anti-Fascist People's Freedom League (AFPFL) to cohere, first under General Aung San and then after his July 1947 assassination under Nu. Dominating politics and governing within a civil code bequeathed by imperial administrators, the AFPFL favoured union over federation, an orientation that most ethnic minorities found unacceptable. Within a year Karen military and police units broke into competing armies, leaving the government in control of only a few dozen square miles around Rangoon. This shabby onset for democracy was but one of a litany of problems threatening a state that within two years had functionally shattered into half-a-dozen mini-states. While the AFPFL rallied around Nu, who completed negotiations with London so that independence could take place on schedule, doctrinaire socialist and communist factions split into insurgent armies, creating a two-government system in many rural districts. The military, administrative and economic consequences of this fragmentation were severe as crisis politics rapidly became more significant than elections. They remain today part of the landscape within which democratic institutions must function.

That Nu became Aung San's legitimate heir during final negotiations with Britain in 1947 demonstrated his capacity to orchestrate politics at the heart of the state, and enabled a form of democracy to find its feet. In the years down to 1962, elections of varying degrees of fairness were held (in 1947, 1951–1952, 1956 and 1960), and were won by increasingly fractured versions of the AFPFL. However, Nu's 'golden democracy' never delivered on its promise. Successive *pyidawtha* four-year plans envisioned networks of health, education, cooperative production and marketing organizations throughout Burma. While foreign advisers competed with wealthier politicians for office space in Rangoon, less affluent candidates toured distant towns and villages seeking votes. Socialist democracy seemed blessed, looking not to the Soviet Union or China but rather to Britain, Scandinavia and Yugoslavia for inspiration. Yet the AFPFL, a people's party claiming several million members, was always short on capacity. Missing during this era was an understanding of how sustainable industry and commerce might work, how an economic environment suitable for entrepreneurs might be created and how a market economy might function. Indeed, capitalism was anathema to most AFPFL leaders, whose vision of progress rested on cooperatives among farmers and fishermen, traders and bus line owners, industry and finance. Taxes on profits were expected to emerge as if by divine response to the speeches of parliamentarians and the prayers of meditating monks. In actual fact, however, the land was plagued by insurgencies, and the Tatmadaw or military arm was rising to clear dominance within the state. Hundreds of villages suffered grievously during those anarchic days, besieged by residual armies after the AFPFL split into a series of distinct parties, 'pocket' armies and bandit gangs (Badgley 1970, Callahan 2003).

Scant funding meant that welfare organizations paid low wages to health workers, teachers and transport officials, who in turn delivered diminishing services. Even though democracy seemed secure in the halls of parliament and among foreign scholars living in Rangoon and Mandalay, government became an easy target for opposition attacks across the countryside. The system started to unravel in 1958, when the AFPFL divided into two dysfunctional factions, 'stable' and 'clean', and party membership evaporated. Parliament became so paralysed that Nu vacated the premiership, inviting Chief-of-Staff General Ne Win to administer civil government. Although elections in February 1960 led two months later to a revival of party government, structural problems remained. Nu's final administration was severely weakened and the services it was able to provide kept declining. In March 1962, Ne Win returned to power as chairman of a new Revolutionary Council (RC) with no invitation and no constitutional authority. A fig leaf of legitimacy came from the RC's amalgam of seasoned senior officers and non-military professionals. Civilian leaders, despairing for the economy and for continued opposition of ethnic minority leaders, gave tacit compliance. At a time when authoritarian interludes were common in democratizing former British colonies, few expected military control to last for long.

Military years: 1962–2011

At the outset Ne Win was respected because he had contained insurgents and kept his 1958 pledge to set democracy back on track and return to the barracks. Although intellectuals and ethnic leaders were sceptical of his avowed lack of political ambition, many Burmese were prepared to give him the benefit of the doubt. Ne Win was known for *joie de vivre*, not politics. However, it soon became clear that while the RC remained committed to the socialist component of the postcolonial political order, it took little interest in restoring democracy. Initially, the Burmese Way to Socialism, unveiled in April 1962, triggered extensive nationalization and rapid economic decline. Subsequently, it spawned the Burma Socialist Programme Party (BSPP), backed by military force, and a governance structure somewhat reminiscent of state socialism in East-Central Europe. In 1974, a fresh constitution was enacted and the RC ceded power to a civilian BSPP cabinet led by retired generals. Although elections took place from time to time, they were only ever able to generate a renewed mandate for the BSPP. In peripheral parts of the country insurgents fought for the cause not of democracy but rather of communism and a variety of ethnic claims to enhanced autonomy or secession.

In these years, the flame of democracy flickered into life no more than sporadically. Looking back to the fledgling independence movement in the 1920s and 1930s and forward to the mass uprising in 1988, students led early opposition to the RC. However, following detonation of the student union building at Rangoon University in July 1962, allegedly with students trapped inside, this resistance faded out. Now and then calls for democracy were revived through guerilla action, notably U Thant disturbances in December 1974 that saw students enraged by shabby treatment accorded to the deceased former UN Secretary-General lead street protests in Rangoon (Selth 1989). It was not until 1988, though, that a movement for democracy spread across much of the country. In a context of deep economic malaise, students again took the lead, building on spontaneous outrage at police brutality in March to spearhead protests that in the 8-8-88 revolt took on the character of a general strike. However, while the 1974 constitution, the BSPP and state socialism were all casualties of the 1988 mass uprising, state power itself was not. Instead, in September 1988 military forces regrouped to form a junta under General Saw Maung and crush the democracy movement (Lintner 1989). At the same time, they promised through President Maung Maung, a civilian jurist with slender political support who remained in office for just 30 days as the BSPP regime collapsed, to hold general elections for a multiparty system. This promise was restated by the incoming junta, quickly named the State Law and Order Restoration Council (SLORC), and implemented through elections held in May 1990. While close to 100 parties registered to contest the elections, the dominant force was the National League for Democracy (NLD) formed in 1988 and led by Aung San Suu Kyi, who had been placed under house arrest in July 1989. The NLD took roughly 60 per cent of the vote and, with help from a majoritarian system, won 80 per cent of the parliamentary seats.

Again, though, military power was undisturbed as SLORC ignored the NLD landslide and continued to govern as before. Once Senior-General Than Shwe emerged as paramount SLORC leader in April 1992, however, the junta decided in the wake of both 1988 and 1990 to create a sustainable political system with which it could feel comfortable. In January 1993, it thus launched a National Convention to devise a framework for discipline-flourishing democracy, a formulation that did not become explicit until the 2000s but was nevertheless implicit in the six major objectives devised for the convention in October 1992. These were: non-disintegration of the Union; non-disintegration of national unity; perpetuation of national sovereignty; promotion of a genuine multiparty democracy; promotion of the universal principles of justice, liberty and equality; and participation of the Defence Services in a national political leadership role in the future state (SLORC 1992).

Discipline-flourishing democracy derives from many sources, but ultimately cannot be grasped without understanding the normative Buddhist prescriptions of *awza* (deep respect) and *pon* (karmatic-derived power). Historically, these mandated that only qualified members of a brotherhood, such as the king's council of ministers, could take full responsibility for the future of the empire. In modern times they have been embraced by the Tatmadaw, generating the belief that it is natural for military leaders to supervise social change. While non-governmental organizations, both domestic and foreign, stepped into the void left by the collapse of socialist doctrine in the late 1980s and typically embraced contemporary notions of democracy, such established notions faded away only very slowly as the conviction remained among military leaders that democracy should be guided from the centre into the periphery. Political authority, for them, is both the duty and the reward generated by ultimate service, such as life-risking combat, to the realm (Badgley 1970).

The attempt to devise a new political settlement proceeded very slowly in the 1990s, and only truly built a head of steam in the mid-2000s. Following fatal attacks on Aung San Suu Kyi's convoy in May 2003, during a brief period when the NLD leader was released from house arrest, she was again taken into 'protective custody'. Responding to the avalanche of international criticism heaped on a junta that in November 1997 had been relaunched as the State Peace and Development Council (SPDC), General Khin Nyunt, then prime minister, in August 2003 unveiled a seven-stage roadmap to discipline-flourishing democracy. Dismissed as a publicity stunt by domestic and foreign observers, it in fact described the major steps subsequently taken by the nation under its military tutors. In May 2004, the National Convention, adjourned in March 1996, was reassembled. In May 2008, a nationwide referendum on a draft constitution implausibly generated 94 per cent support on a 98 per cent turnout. In November 2010, elections were held for a bicameral parliament and 14 regional and state assemblies. They saw the military-backed Union Solidarity and Development Party (USDP) take 259 out of 325 elected seats in the lower house of the national assembly (80 per cent), and 129 out of 168 elected seats in the upper house (77 per cent). Results in the 14 territorial assemblies were broadly similar, though with important local variations. As in 1990, a constituency-based majoritarian electoral system generated a 'winner's bonus', which this time operated to the advantage of the USDP. The NLD, victorious in 1990, chose not to contest the elections, arguing through Aung San Suu Kyi that the laws underpinning them were unjust and that participation was thereby ruled out. In January 2011, the various legislative bodies convened. In March 2011, President Thein Sein assumed office at the head of a notionally civilian government tasked with leading construction of a new democratic state.

Transitional period: since 2011

While it evidently has a lengthy and complex pre-history, Myanmar's current democratic transition is held by most analysts to date from the end of March 2011. This is when Than Shwe's SPDC was dissolved, and Thein Sein took office as president and head of a notionally democratic state. However, the polity created at this time was rather long on discipline and correspondingly short on democracy, chiefly because of military guarantees written into the 2008 constitution. In both houses of the national parliament and in all 14 territorial assemblies, for instance, 75 per cent of members are elected and the remaining 25 per cent are appointed by the military commander-in-chief (Articles 109, 141, 161). In the executive, while two presidential candidates are nominated by elected members of the bicameral legislature, a third is named by military appointees, and all three are required to be well acquainted with military affairs (Articles 59, 60). The commander-in-chief also appoints three cabinet ministers in the fields of internal and external security (Article 232). Moreover, the National Defence and Security Council (NDSC), chaired by the president, has significant powers and a strong military presence (Articles 201, 204, 206, 213, 340, 342 and 410–432). Additionally, there are provisions designed to limit political participation in egregious ways, including the notorious Clause 59(f), widely viewed as written for Aung San Suu Kyi. This states that each candidate for president and vice-president 'shall he himself, one of the parents, the spouse, one of the legitimate children or their spouses not owe allegiance to a foreign power, not be subject of a foreign power or citizen of a foreign country'. Together, these provisions and many others ensure that while in some respects Myanmar's discipline-flourishing democracy builds on global democratic experience, in several key areas it falls well short of established democratic practice (Holliday 2011, 81–86).

These shortfalls notwithstanding, some aspects of democracy developed quite rapidly in Myanmar following the March 2011 shift to constitutional rule. In the executive, President Thein Sein moved within six months of taking office to reach out to opposition forces. In August 2011, he met with NLD leader Aung San Suu Kyi and asked her to become part of the transitional political process. She duly gained election to the lower house of parliament in a set of by-elections held in April 2012. In September 2011, he responded to public protest by announcing the suspension for the duration of his presidential term of the controversial China-backed Myitsone Dam hydroelectric project in Kachin State. In the legislature, confident predictions of little more than a rubber-stamp role were quickly shrugged off as the lower house in particular became a vibrant forum for policy debate, and Speaker Shwe Mann from the USDP (formerly a leading junta member) built a formidable political reputation. In civil society, public protest became common not merely in major cities such as Yangon and Mandalay, but also in small towns and rural areas. Furthermore, the April 2012 by-elections for 45 seats spread across national and territorial assemblies in diverse parts of the country generated widespread interest and participation. The NLD won 43 out of the 44 seats it contested. In civil society, established media outlets flourished as forums for political debate, and even highly sensitive matters such as brutal state treatment of protesters at the China-backed Letpadaung copper mine project in Sagaing Region were widely and critically reported. Moreover, the wildfire spread of social media generated by exponential increases in mobile phone use during the lifetime of Thein Sein's administration served to extend the sphere of civic debate in wholly unexpected ways as internet platforms such as Gmail, Facebook and Viber registered millions of users throughout the country.

These promising signs were reinforced by the November 2015 general election. Leading up to the poll there was again considerable scepticism that the process would be free and fair. Questions focused particularly on the role of the Union Election Commission (UEC), charged with organizing elections, licensing political parties and vetting parliamentary candidates. Appointed by the SPDC in its final weeks in office and chaired by Tin Aye, a retired lieutenant general, the UEC seemed unlikely to embody the degree of impartiality required of such a body, and was also generally held to be lacking in capacity. Devious motives were read into many of its rulings, such as one restricting the official campaign period to 60 days and another disqualifying named candidates from contesting the election. Right up to the last few days, registers of voters in many constituencies were known to be defective, and rumours were widespread that the poll would be flawed for this reason. More broadly, concerns were raised about a policy decision to deny the vote to holders of temporary ('white') identity cards who had been allowed to participate in the 2010 election. Since most of the affected individuals were Rohingya Muslims concentrated in Rakhine State, though, this issue tended to be of far greater concern to foreign than to domestic observers. In the event, however, the 2015 election unfolded smoothly, and was generally seen as being about as free and fair as is possible in a fledgling democracy like Myanmar.

Indeed, some elements of the electoral process were quite remarkably positive. One was the extent of international engagement with technical aspects permitted by the authorities, which was substantial and played an important part in delivering a broadly fair process. Another was the degree of voter support and education offered by a variety of local and international bodies, focused on potentially marginal groups such as women and ethnic minorities. Yet another was the engagement of accredited election observers, both domestic and foreign, tasked with monitoring the poll at stations throughout the country. Putting all this together, thousands of foreigners and tens of thousands of local people engaged in activities such as voter education, party canvassing, political research and, above all, election observation. Perhaps most positive of all was the outcome of the election and the fact that a result viewed as disadvantageous to political forces aligned with the military that had dominated the political scene for more than half a decade was allowed to stand and be implemented.

In overall terms, the result of the 2015 general election was similar to that of 1990. Again the NLD was triumphant, across the two houses of parliament taking 57 per cent of the vote and 79 per cent of the seats. Again the military-backed party went down to a crushing defeat, and ethnic minority parties garnered little more than 10 per cent of the total vote. Again Aung San Suu Kyi was far and away the dominant political figure, with the significant difference that in 2015 she was able to campaign throughout the country and indeed stood for election herself. In 2015, in contrast to 1990, the election generated a transfer of power. In the weeks and months following release of the electoral returns, a delicate dance led by Aung San Suu Kyi for the NLD and by Commander-in-Chief Min Aung Hlaing for the Tatmadaw played out. At issue was the extent to which the country's emergent democracy might be able to push back the frontiers of a privileged political space long occupied by the nation's military forces, and marked out in some detail in the 2008 constitution. Ultimately military leaders refused to countenance constitutional reform, with the result that President Htin Kyaw was nominated by the NLD and selected by parliamentarians to succeed President Thein Sein at the end of March 2016. Days later, however, parliament enacted a law to enable Aung San Suu Kyi to serve as state counsellor for the duration of the legislative term, and thereby deliver on a commitment made just before the election that she would be 'above the president' in an NLD administration. In addition, she held two key portfolios as foreign minister (with a seat on the NDSC) and minister in the President's Office.

Conclusion

Making a transition to democracy in Myanmar has always been a deeply challenging enterprise. 'Even to turn a mango seed into a tree required time and patience,' wrote Nu (1975, 220) in the midst of Ne Win's long period of authoritarian rule. 'The task of raising the tree of democracy was incomparably more demanding.' The country has external and internal boundaries set by Britain that frame bifurcated authorities, with a civil tradition of secular law and civilian parties set against the monarchical self-image of the Tatmadaw, which holds itself in high regard as the preserver of law and order and functions as an armed political party. Ever since the time of Ne Win, leading generals have seen themselves as a central authority cast within the traditions of a thousand-year monarchy, a romantic perspective consistent with the dominant strand of Buddhist nationalism cultivated by writers, artists and politicized monks since the 1920s. While party splits have often characterized civilian politics, military cohesion has long been remarkable.

Tatmadaw treatment of minorities has often been egregious, and the generals' capacity to work with opposition leaders has been no less problematic. In most ethnic communities, authorities are overwhelmingly conservative, with leaders favouring their respective religious heritages over competing systems of knowledge. Most Buddhist monks, Christian pastors, Muslim mullahs and especially *nat* worshippers cleave to authorities that belie commitments to a modernist embrace of democracy. Yet without these wellsprings of traditional morality it is hard to imagine the state of Myanmar sustaining itself. Grafted on to all this in recent years has been a form of crony capitalism that has seen a few thousand families benefit enormously from the shift away from state socialism while most citizens continue to live in a world devoid of state-funded development. In this context of competing centrifugal and centripetal forces, fundamental questions inevitably surface. Can non-military administrators really be allowed to govern? Can a civil society prevail? Can the public commons be protected in the interest of all?

The 2015 general election did clarify the political landscape somewhat. Min Zin (2016, 117) asserts that it reduced the number of veto players in national politics to two individuals and one group: Aung San Suu Kyi from the NLD, Min Aung Hlaing from the Tatmadaw, and a not entirely cohesive amalgam of minority ethnic groups. This increases the possibility that lasting political agreements can be reached, and that in time democracy can be deepened and consolidated. For that to happen, however, it will be necessary for political development to move beyond the focus on individuals that has long been a central feature of the political culture. Although Aung San Suu Kyi, the most prominent individual in the current political firmament, is unquestionably a remarkable and resourceful leader, the long-term prospects for democracy will depend on far more than a single iconic figure. Equally essential is that a fixation on monist values is able to give way to the more pluralist conceptions of the political realm that underpin consolidated democracies. Ultimately, then, the success of Myanmar's democratic transition will be a function of structural reform within the domain not only of democracy itself but also of those social forces that have long operated as barriers to its development.

References

Adas, M. 1974. *The Burma Delta: Economic Development and Social Change on an Asian Rice Frontier, 1852–1941*. Madison, WI: University of Wisconsin Press.

Badgley, J. H. 1970. *Politics Among Burmans: A Study of Intermediary Leaders*. Athens, OH: Ohio University Center for International Studies.

Callahan, M. P. 2003. *Making Enemies: War and State Building in Burma*. Ithaca, NY: Cornell University Press.

Holliday, I. 2011. *Burma Redux: Global Justice and the Quest for Political Reform in Myanmar*. New York, NY: Columbia University Press.

Kyaw, A. and Badgley, J. H. 2009. 'Foundations of Burmese Nationalism'. In *Red Peacocks: Commentaries on Burmese Socialist Nationalism*, edited by J. H. Badgley and Aye Kyaw, 242–288. New Delhi: Readworthy.

Lintner, B. 1989. *Outrage: Burma's Struggle for Democracy*. Hong Kong: Review.

Selth, A. 1989. *Death of a Hero: The U Thant Disturbances in Burma, December 1974*. Nathan: Griffith University.

State Law and Order Restoration Council (SLORC). 1992. *Formation of the Convening Commission for the National Convention*. SLORC Order 13/92.

U Nu. 1975. *U Nu: Saturday's Son*. New Haven, CT: Yale University Press.

Zin, M. 2016. 'Burma Votes for Change: The New Configuration of Power'. *Journal of Democracy* 27 (2): 116–131.

5
ETHNICITY AND IDENTITY

Violet Cho

Myanmar is characterised by ethnic diversity. The government view is that the country is composed of 135 'races', although there are eight major 'races' that are regularly highlighted. This taxonomy serves multiple purposes. One is to unite diverse groups into a single, unified nation to the exclusion of so-called 'alien races', such as Hokkien and Haka Chinese, Tamil, Punjabi and Rohingya. Another purpose is to justify authoritarianism – since 'non-disintegration of the union' has been a central slogan of military rule. 'Bamar' as the majority ethnic category makes up around 60–70% of the population (Smith 1991). However, mainstream usage inside the country does not ordinarily classify Bamar as an ethnic group, as ethnicity is a minoritising discourse in Myanmar. This is unsurprising as majority identities are often taken for granted. The erasure of Bamar ethnic status, and the presentation of Bamar-ness 'as the norm' reflects Bamar privilege, a privilege that is 'invisible to itself' (Walton 2013, 5–6).

Contemporary ethnic politics in Myanmar is framed around conflict between the majority, linked to the panethnic nation, and minority ethnicities. This is largely a legacy of British colonial policies and colonial knowledge production, which involved the classification and enumeration of 'racial' groups, in many instances leading to ethnic consciousness. In Burma, where caste and religious difference was insignificant, 'race' became the primary category of social organisation. At different times, the colonial and postcolonial state and ethnic minority elites have attempted to solidify the notion of racial categories through the spread of vernacular languages, new religious movements, historiography and ethnicised forms of violence. The postcolonial state has invested significant resources into popularising 'Burmese' as a panethnic category and in countering ethnic minority group-making projects that challenge the interests of the state, although there has always been state recognition of diversity. Colonisation marked a profound shift in social organisation. In pre-colonial times, it appears that other social categories were of greater importance, such as whether one is an aristocrat or commoner, land-owner or landless, or under royal authority or outside of it. While different languages and cultural practices obviously existed, they did not accompany (ethno)national sentiment as they do today. This also means that ethnicity was far more flexible. One study of pre-colonial ethnicity found that change to ethnic allegiance was as simple as changing one's clothes (Lieberman 1978, 458). As Leach (1964) observed in his study of Kachin social systems, ethnicity is dependent on and shifts with context.

In this chapter, I will explore ethnicity in Myanmar as socially constructed and process-oriented. Taking Roger Brubaker's approach into account, the following discussion does not equate ethnicity with group as a prior, bounded entity. Brubaker argues that ethnicity does not exist as something substantive and should rather be examined as projects, processes, discourses and events. Ethnic-making projects may aim to form, solidify or disrupt ways of identifying, some successful and others not (Brubaker 2004, 7–27). The politics of ethnic identity-making involves multiple views and discourses that connect and disconnect, that aim to control and resist and that represent a range of interests, sometimes transparent and sometimes hidden. I will look at some of the discursive processes involved in ethnic group-making, involving the state, ethnic elites and subaltern voices through the exploration of texts. Some texts are written in a way that appears scientific, some are literary. Some texts recreate popular myth and, by codifying myth in text, disrupt oral tradition by consecrating a particular telling. Some transform ethnogenesis stories into 'scientific' histories. Taken together and in conversation with each other, these texts provide a brief, partial overview of ethnicity in Myanmar's recent history, from the colonial period onwards. The first section will examine state and allied projects. The second section will examine projects that diverge from and often aim to resist the state from ethnonationalist perspectives. The conclusion will then briefly consider contemporary implications of ethnic identity in Myanmar's democratic transition and beyond.

Ethnicising difference

The state is a key entity involved in ethnic group-building projects. The state is a geographically bounded entity that is constituted by a collection of institutions and actors at multiple levels. State ethnic-making projects have evolved over Burmese history. For the colonial state, 'race' was central to social organisation and colonisation involved the detailed categorisation of colonial subjects. Bernard Cohn describes 'the enumerative modality' as the enumeration, categorisation and codification of the social world in a way that

> objectified social, cultural, and linguistic differences . . . The panoptical view that the British were constructing led to the reification of India as a polity in which conflict, from the point of view of the rulers, could only be controlled by the strong hand of the British.
>
> *Cohn 1996, 8*

Postcolonial states inherited this intricate racial taxonomy, which was incorporated into a national identity, and expanded through postcolonial modes of enumeration. However, the postcolonial state recast ethnicity as a form of kinship, emphasising similarities, unity in diversity and a shared history of anti-colonial struggle rather than difference and inherent conflict.

The classification and enumeration of 'race' was a key project in British rule and set the precedent from which later ethnic-making projects have operated. Classification and enumeration involved a variety of tools, including the census, gazettes, archaeological surveys, dictionaries, grammars and texts describing culture and customs. These tools crossed multiple academic fields – history, anthropology, linguistics, statistics, geology and biology. This immense process of knowledge production made an alien landscape and population knowable and thereby governable. In Scott's (1998) words, it is 'seeing like a state'. Through the gazettes and censuses, the macro taxonomy of 'racial' groups was outlined and enumerated. Biology was a key register and allowed the colonial regime to map 'races' along scales of evolution and create spurious meta-categories, such as 'Sino-Karen'. The biological production of Burmese 'races' is seen in the 235-page volume of anthropometric data, published as part of the Ethnographic Survey of India. It includes detailed cranial measurements, separated by tribe, including different data sets for Lower Burma, Upper Burma, Southern Chin, Chinese Shan, Pwo Karen and S'gaw Karen, with statistics relating to head and nose (Office of the Superintendent 1906). Later work, such as Tildesley's (1921) study of the Burmese cranium, was used to make broader, taxonomical conclusions. One of Tildesley's findings was that the Burman is more similar to the Malayan than the Chinese, the latter having a 'shorter transverse arc . . . [and] a longer sagittal arc . . . due to greater occipital development from lambda to opisthion' (242).

Accompanying the censuses and macro-statistical studies was more localised and detailed descriptive work. One such study aimed to make the Palaung knowable, attempting to create them as a bounded unit and differentiating them from Others:

> The Palaung is peaceable and law-abiding. More reserved and suspicious than the Burman and the Shan, he is capable nevertheless on occasions of expanding. Industrious up to a certain point, he becomes when the limit is passed, hopelessly supine and inert. He has the reputation of being niggardly and extortionate.
>
> *Lowis 1906, 3*

Writing such as this serves to create and solidify stereotypes and essentialise ethnicity. These studies are a central part of colonial governmentality, 'in which power comes to be directed at the destruction and reconstruction of colonial space so as to produce not so much extractive-effects on colonial bodies as governing-effects on colonial conduct' (Scott 1995, 204). Colonial governmentality produces ethnicised ways of being and seeing, which is crucial for colonial (and later, postcolonial) governance.

The colonial period saw an explosion in vernacular literacy and print cultures, which were instrumental in producing ethnic identities. Some, such as 'Karen', did not correspond to a particular linguistic group. 'Karen' is rather a loose umbrella term that linguistically refers to two main language groups, S'gaw and Pwo, with some counts of more than twenty linguistic sub-groups. Others, such as Mon, had a long literary history and vernacularisation popularised Mon, contributing to ethnicisation. Literacy and language have since been tools that minorities have used to raise ethnic consciousness and make demands for self-determination. As in Europe, literacy was first associated with religion for sacred texts and then was subsequently secularised and, in the vernacular form, facilitated national and ethnonational imaginings (Anderson 1983). For the oral cultures of Burma, this involved not only the start of mass media but also the development of new scripts and the introduction of text-based culture. This was done in line with colonial ideas linking writing with civilisation that privileged textuality over orality and Roman script over non-Roman. For instance, in 1873 a Christian missionary in the Kachin region called U Ma Saung created a Jingpaw script based on the Burmese alphabet, in order to translate the Christian Bible. He died before he could complete the script so an American missionary continued the project in 1876 and sent the completed alphabet to colonial officials for permission so as to begin Christian translation. Colonial authorities refused and only approved a later Roman script, purportedly to avoid a link between Burmese and Kachin (Hintha 1993).[1] Roman script and Christianity then became part of Kachin identity, although this was a process that slowly evolved through to the mid-twentieth century (Sadan 2013).

Karen literary movements also started in the nineteenth century with a proliferation of scripts, each attached to competing religious and linguistic Karen ethnic-making projects. While a number of missionary, colonial and Karen Christian writers claim that the origins of Karen literacy were in 1830, when Jonathan Wade created a S'gaw Karen alphabet, this has been criticised by Buddhist Karen and scholars, who claim the Buddhist Pwo alphabet, Leiktoori, pre-dates Wade by hundreds of years and was used in the royal city of Thaton, along with

Mon (Bone Myint 1975). Another Pwo Karen script was created by U Nanda Mala and the first texts were translations of Buddhist literature from Burmese and Mon. The initial aim was religious, but in the following decades it became secularised, used for the dissemination of a range of ideas related to culture, economy and morality (Bone Myint 1975). These literary movements, while influenced by new colonial modes of power and ideas of ethnicity, were also 'organic outgrowths . . . of the union of existing Karen ideas about writing' (Womack 2005, 18). While pre-colonial Karen told myths of a lost alphabet and possibly had earlier forms of writing, Karen literacy exploded and became central to 'modern' forms of Karen nationalism with the arrival of the first printing press in Dawei. While writing was confined to an elite minority, literacy spread rapidly through church networks, and books were also used in rituals as sacred objects, which in turn made Karen language sacred.

Ethnicity in anti-colonial narratives

Creating a common national identity against an external Other was a key aim of postcolonial nation-building. After independence from the British in 1948, Burma went through a decade of political turmoil, in which key political stakeholders fragmented along ethnic and ideological lines, leading to widespread armed conflict. In 1962, the military took power and formed a socialist regime, which stayed in power until the mass protests of 1988. A core preoccupation of the government was to create socialism through the unification of ethnic groups. After the colonial period, this involved the next most expansive period of ethnic classification, enumeration and knowledge production. While methods were similar, objectives sharply differed, the colonial government emphasising division and the Burmese socialist government emphasising unity. Directly and indirectly, the Socialist Party published a number of texts that highlighted the unity of ethnic minorities. One important book is *The History of the Ethnic Nationalities' Resistance*, a compilation of ethnic minority involvement in anti-colonial resistance, from the Anglo-Burman wars onwards. In this book, the pre-colonial society is portrayed as a utopia of peace and freedom where diverse cultures lived together until it was destroyed by British colonisation (Burma Socialist Programme Party 1971). The narrative describes how ethnic groups in Burma, with a united consciousness and desire for freedom, fought against the colonial system (Burma Socialist Programme Party 1971, 11–19). Texts like this articulate a position of unity in diversity – the nation is an amalgamation of ethnic groups who suffered and struggled together, albeit with Bamar in the front.

In contrast to the writing of ethnic anti-colonialism as a unifying force, key texts were also published at that time that were clearly assimilationist – detailing ethnic minority resistance figures without making explicit their presumed ethnic minority status. Instead, they are 'Myanma' – part of a collection of 'Myanma' heroes, who the reader is positioned to identify with, regardless of ethnicity (Ba Maung 1975). For instance, in Thakin Ba Maung's history, ethnicity does not figure. In the section on U Ottama, there is no mention of his Rakhine ethnicity, which is strongly emphasised in other nationalist texts. In that text, all are simply Burmese, fighting against colonial power (Ba Maung 1975). The reader is positioned to identify with 'Myanma' as a common identity, although what it refers to is not made explicit.

Ethnicising unity

Ethnic unity has been a key goal for all Burmese postcolonial governments, exemplified in slogans such as 'union spirit'. In the late 1960s onwards, the socialist government oversaw the production of knowledge on ethnicity, including the identification and categorisation of races, languages and descriptions of cultural forms. While this was methodologically similar to colonial knowledge production, through the use of science and history, the underlying rationality was similarity and unity rather than difference and conflict. One key ethnological project was through a consortium of the universities of Yangon and Mandalay and Moulmein College, called 'ethnic culture and traditions', launched in 1964. Only five ethnic groups were included, Kayin, Kayah, Kachin, Chin and Shan, although it was later expanded.

The aim of this project was also to produce knowledge about ethnic minority groups in Burma, in a way different to work done by foreign influenced researchers. Underlining this was the view that foreign researchers were biased and had a stereotypical and discriminatory view, especially of hill peoples. However, that discourse is reproduced in the book, showing how powerful colonial ethnology is, even to those actively resisting it. For instance in the Karen volume, researchers (quoting Marshall) say that Karen love war and fighting and have a tradition of taking revenge (Burma Socialist Programme Party 1967, 196). The researchers use this as evidence to explain why they are underdeveloped and failing to progress. One of the features of the university consortium project was involvement of ethnic minorities in carrying out the research. Under the Ministry of Culture, each state has a cultural department that was involved in the research. Field interviewers were also supposedly from ethnic minority groups, and were led by university researchers. The project states that ethnic minorities should produce knowledge about themselves and their histories and thus the project is also a form of epistemological decolonisation (Burma Socialist Programme Party 1967, iv). However, this knowledge production was only about Others as Bamar were not included. The exclusion of Bamar, the ethnicity associated with state power, demonstrates the privilege of the ethnic majority. The state could calculate and control who the subjects of anthropology would be, who would be excluded and, by extension, which ethnic groups would be included in the nation.

Part of the postcolonial codification of knowledge involved the production of histories that emphasised commonality. A prominent example is Nai Pan Hla's study of the history of a long war between Bamar and Mon kingdoms. In it, he describes the forty-year war between the kingdoms of Ava and Hanthawaddy, associated with Bamar and Mon ethnicity respectively. Despite the rivalry between them, it is presented more as a problem between siblings rather than enemies. Bamar and Mon kings call each other brothers, the Mon king being an older brother and the Bamar king a younger brother, showing a common kinship (Hla 2005). When Mon king Yazatiri died, the Bamar king cried. Those around him asked him why he was crying for his enemy. The Bamar king replied that they waged war to show how powerful they are and that they need each other to do that (Hla 2005, 360). So rather than one group trying to subjugate the other, they are reliant on each other to project each other's power, with neither the victor. The book also contains a heroic narrative of unity against a mutual Other. A Mon warrior was captured by the Bamar king. During the Mongol invasion, the Mongol king sent a letter asking for a fight between one of the Mongol warriors and a Bamar warrior. If the Mongol warrior wins, the Mongols would take the kingdom. No Bamar warriors dared to join but the Mon warrior volunteered. He is quoted as saying 'now I want to take this responsibility because I want to save the Innwa kingdom. I want Innwa to be strong and successful' (Hla 2005, 10). This is praised within Burmese historiography as an example of 'union consciousness' (ibid.). Even though history writes Mon and Bamar as different ethnic groups and kingdoms, when it comes to foreign invasion, they unite for the greater good, as one nation. This particular story has its origins in royal chronicles and has been translated into vernacular Burmese and thereby popularised.

Identity-making against the state

Much ethnonationalist work is focused on discourses of suffering inflicted by Bamar oppressors, thereby producing a community in common victimhood within a boundary defined largely against Bamar Others. This is notable in Arakan and Mon texts, in which the reader is positioned to grieve the loss of power by successive kings, ethnicised as Bamar. Resistance Arakan history describes how Buddha came to Arakan land (Dhanyawaddy). King Sanda Thuriya met Buddha and made a request to build an image so when Buddha leaves he has something to pay respect to. The Buddha agreed and the king collected huge numbers of gems to build the image of the Buddha. That statue was maintained across generations of Arakan kings, symbolising moral legitimacy and sovereignty. However, in 1784, the Arakan kingdom was occupied by King Bodawpaya. According to one account, the Maha Muni image 'was worse off than the human captives, dismembered before being hauled away' (Hla n.d., 46). This particular text concludes that 'with the monarchy toppled, a terrible fate laid its grip upon the people of Rakhine whose misery reached beyond the limit of endurance' (ibid.), concluding a melodramatic narrative that continues to influence a particular Rakhine ethnonationalist worldview.

Similarly, historic loss is also important in the construction of Mon ethnic identity and nationalism (South 2003). While Nai Hpan Hla's popular history, mentioned above, emphasises similarity between Mon and Bamar kingdoms, Mon resistance history tells of centuries of an advanced and peaceful Mon civilisation that controlled Lower Burma, only disrupted from the eleventh century onwards, by Bamar aggression. This culminated in the destruction of the Mon nation in the mid-eighteenth century, as described in the following nationalist account of the period:

> The Mon have ever since become a people without a country. The conquering Burman leader U Aungzeya persecuted the Mon by massacring over 3,000 learned Mon monks near Rangoon; by burning down holy scriptures and monasteries; by proscribing Mon language and literature; and by genocidal mass execution whereby thousands of Mon were exterminated in several stockade-inferno holocausts. Racial discrimination was rife and hundreds of thousands of the Mon fled to Siam (Thailand) for safe haven. In modern human rights terminology, it was a drastic 'ethnic cleansing' process.
>
> *Mon Unity League 2004*

In this narrative, pre-colonial history is ethnicised and the source of Mon identity is tied to an ethnonation that has been irreparably harmed by the ethnic Bamar Other. As such, historical references to Rehmonya, Ramandesa, Hanthawaddy and Suvanabhumi are prominent within resistance Mon ethnic-building projects. On the one hand they provide a foundation for Mon claims of sovereignty, associated with Mon kings, and on the other they create a link between Mon identity and suffering that continues into the present time, much like the legacy of King Thuryia in Rakhine historical memory. As Michael Gravers has observed, 'in the rhetoric of nationalism, historical memory is used to structure the social practices of the present' (Gravers 1993, 131).

An ethnicised view of loss and suffering under Bamar domination has continued into post-colonial history and become a dominant feature of ethnic minority identity, in the borderlands and exile in particular (Thawnghmung 2012). This suffering is linked to contemporary global human rights discourse that is a feature of ethnic minority media in exile (Brooten 2004). Since 1988, there has been extensive human rights documentation by ethnic human rights groups and journalists of extrajudicial killings, rape, forced labour, the destruction of villages, land confiscation and the suppression of some forms of ethnic minority culture. This is sometimes labelled as genocide, which is a particularly powerful part of claims for ethnic minority in-group unity, as a defensive process, and in claims for recognition and self-determination. Key events in narratives of ethno-suffering, such as battles, dam-building, the destruction of villages and mass displacement, give substance to ethnicity.

Ethnological stereotypes are also brought into ethnonational discourse and used as a way to differentiate the ethnonation from the Bamar Other. This is seen in the work of San C. Po in one of the classic texts of Karen nationalism. San C. Po essentialises Karen 'nature' in opposition to Bamar: 'Burman will quarrel and fly into a passion and when he has cooled down, he will be as good a friend as ever, the Karen will not show his passion but will hold fire for perhaps years' (San 1928, 26). Similarly, within the Karen national anthem, the Karen are described as honest and hospitable, as opposed to Bamar who are mischievous, a trope that is found in colonial writing.

Ethnicity in transition

Ethnic identity, at both an everyday and state level, is a hierarchical means of social organisation and a normative struggle for emancipation. Ethnic identity often takes a mythic and spiritual form, as a way of explaining human existence. Myths explain and legitimate ethnonations. For example, a myth of the beginning of Pao people is that they derived from a dragon mother and *weikza* father. For Pao, this story can be read as a way of making sense of an ethnicised social world and of bringing ethnic categories into a mythological worldview. New religious movements have also been an enduring element in ethnic-making processes. In the context of Karen, they are 'as much expression of religious and localised political identity, as emanations of a self-consciously "Karen" nation-building project' (South 2008, 186).

In Myanmar's current political milieu, ethno-myths and religious movements mix with 'secular' political demands for human rights and power. Holding a minority identity in Myanmar is itself political, and involves navigating the tensions of the cultural and moral expectations of ethnic community belonging and the requisite boundary-maintenance between one's ethno-community and others against cosmopolitan market forces and the state. Ethnic identity involves a claim to particular histories, a demand for citizenship and a share of power and resources. The National League for Democracy (NLD) has thus far only had limited success at easing widespread mistrust within minority groups towards the state, which many continue to associate with the Bamar ethnic group. The Rohingya are an important exception, as the NLD has continued to exclude them from who belongs in the nation, which has intensified the continuing conflict in Rakhine State. Identifying as Rohingya therefore remains a dangerous means of resistance. A liberal state can be culturally hegemonic in a way that a dictatorship, with a much more transparent form of power, cannot be. Religious movements and ethno-myths can militate against cultural hegemony and underpin future ethnic demands.

Conclusion

Ethnicisation has been central to struggles for power in Myanmar, in the colonial and postcolonial states and within resistance movements. The politics of ethnicity is a key element for the state to manage within the current political transition. The ability of the NLD to settle violent forms of ethnic politics and bring former insurgent groups into the political fold is widely seen as a key benchmark of success. However, ethnic division and conflict is also in the interest of elements of the state, as it has been since colonial times. The military has a large stake in Burmese politics and any conflict will justify and further entrench their role for the presumed stability of the state. The legal and peaceful contestation of ethnic politics therefore weakens the military.

The politics of co-option and exclusion of particular ethnicities has been popularised in the political transition and will continue to play out into the future. The renewal and intensification of communal violence based on ethnic and religious identities has strengthened the position of the military and of more extreme forms of ethno- and religious nationalism. Political leaders who were once detested for their authoritarianism can now be recast as protectors of the nation. This is only possible through the discourse of Othering. This, more than any act of military repression, has created a 'union spirit' of sorts, as Bamar and state-sanctioned indigenous people can define themselves and come to belong through the exclusion of a Rohingya or Muslim Other. Through the process of inclusion and exclusion, ethnic identities in Myanmar reconstruct and transform. However, Myanmar is now also contending with the politics of globalisation and the spread of capitalist modernity. To what extend these global trends will shift the politics and culture of ethnic identities remains to be seen.

Note

1 Similarly, the missionary use of Burmese script as a basis for Pwo Karen was criticised as 'perverse' (Brown 1922, 298).

References

Anderson, B. 1983. *Imagined Communities: Reflections on the Origin and Spread of Nationalism*. London: Verso.

Ba Maung 1975. *Wunthanu ayei-taw pon thameing [History of the Wunthanu Revolution]*. Yangon: Tathetta Sa Pe.

Bone Myint, U. 1975. *The History of Buddhist Pwo Karen Literature*. Yangon: Thabyay U Sape Tuik.

Brooten, L. 2004. 'Human Rights Discourse and the Development of Democracy in a Multi-Ethnic State'. *Asian Journal of Communication* 14 (2): 174–191.

Brown, R. G. 1922. 'A Comparative Dictionary of the Pwo-Karen Dialect. By the Rev. WCB Purser and Saya Tun Aung. 16½ × 4, 217 pp. Rangoon: American Baptist Mission Press, 1922'. *Journal of the Royal Asiatic Society of Great Britain & Ireland* 55 (2): 298–299.

Brubaker, R. 2004. *Ethnicity Without Groups*. Cambridge, MA: Harvard University Press.

Burma Socialist Programme Party. 1967. *Tineyintha yin jay mu yoya dale tone san mya Kayin (Karen Ethnic Culture and Traditions)*. Yangon: Sape Beikman.

Burma Socialist Programme Party. 1971. *Tineyintha lu myo mya e nay chait chan kyan re thamine (The History of the Ethnic Nationalities' Resistance)*. Yangon: Sape Beikman.

Cohn, B. S. 1996. *Colonialism and its Forms of Knowledge: The British in India*. New Jersey: Princeton University Press.

Gravers, M. 1993. *Nationalism as Political Paranoia in Burma: An Essay on the Historical Practice of Power*. Copenhagen: NIAS.

Hintha. 1993. *Thway chin tui mre kachin mre (Kachin: A Land of Kin)*. Yangon: Sape Beikman.

Hla, N. P. 2005. *Yazadarit ayedawbon (A Historical Account of King Yazadarit's Campaign)*. Yangon: Ahmann Thit Sape.

Hla, T. no date. 'The Rakhaing'. *Neo Historical Journal* 1: 41–46.

Leach, E. R. 1964. *Political Systems of Highland Burma*. London: Athlone.

Lieberman, V. B. 1978. 'Ethnic Politics in Eighteenth-Century Burma'. *Modern Asian Studies* 12 (3): 455–482.

Lowis, C. C. 1906. *A Note on the Palaungs of Hsipaw and Tawngpeng*. Rangoon: Government Printing.

Mon Unity League. 2004. 'The Mon History'. Mon News. Accessed May 10, 2015. http://monnews.org/mon-people/.

Office of the Superintendent. 1906. *Anthropometric Data from Burma*. Calcutta, India: Government Printing.

Sadan, M. 2013. *Being and Becoming Kachin: Histories Beyond the State in the Borderworlds of Burma*. Oxford: Oxford University Press.

San, C. P. 1928. *Burma and the Karens*. London: Elliot Stock.

Scott, D. 1995. 'Colonial Governmentality'. *Social Text* 43: 191–220.

Scott, J. C. 1998. *Seeing Like a State: How Certain Schemes to Improve the Human Condition Have Failed*. New Haven: Yale University Press.

Smith, M. 1991. *Burma: Insurgency and the Politics of Ethnicity*. London: Zed Books.

South, A. 2003. *Mon Nationalism and Civil War in Burma: The Golden Sheldrake*. London: Routledge.

South, A. 2008. *Ethnic Politics in Burma: States of Conflict*. London: Routledge.

Thawnghmung, A. M. 2012. *The 'Other' Karen in Myanmar: Ethnic Minorities and the Struggle without Arms*. Plymouth: Lexington Books.

Tildesley, M. L. 1921. 'A First Study of the Burmese Skull'. *Biometrika* 13 (2–3): 176–262.

Walton, M. J. 2013. 'The "Wages of Burman-ness": Ethnicity and Burman Privilege in Contemporary Myanmar'. *Journal of Contemporary Asia* 43 (1): 1–27.

Womack, W. 2005. 'Literate Networks and the Production of S'gaw and Pwo Karen Writing in Burma, c.1830–1930'. PhD Diss., School of Oriental and African Studies, University of London.

PART II

Spaces

6
THE CAPITAL

Nicholas Farrelly

Naypyitaw was built five hours' drive north of the former capital, Yangon, as a new physical, political and symbolic centre for Myanmar. Its original goal was to secure the system of authoritarian rule that was, at that time, under sustained pressure from ethnic armies and democratic activists. The colonial city of Yangon had long been judged an inadequate showcase for the glories of the Myanmar military and its leading decision-makers. The inspiration for this lavish investment of national resources came from the top. Former Senior General Than Shwe is widely credited with conceiving the plan to move the country's elite military echelon, and the supporting government agencies, northwards to a well-protected area far from prying eyes. With construction commencing in the early 2000s, Naypyitaw quickly encompassed a sprawling network of buildings, roads, precincts and townships that, taken together, spread across a vast area of central Myanmar, more than 7,000 square kilometres. The making of this grand new capital city required labour from the length and breadth of the country, and technical expertise from beyond its borders, especially from China and Thailand.

From the beginning, Naypyitaw was a monumental and ornamental undertaking. No expense was spared in the plan to construct a new centre to exemplify Myanmar power and prowess. In its early years, foreign commentators were unimpressed: the BBC dismissed Naypyitaw as 'vast and extravagant' (Head 2007), while the *The New York Times* (2008) called the city 'remote, lavish and off-limits'. It is not an easy place to love. The core facilities now include major military precincts; two enormous sporting complexes; the palaces for the President, Vice-Presidents and Speakers; the 31 buildings of the sprawling Union Assembly complex; the Defence Services Museum; and the incredible configuration of other infrastructure required to keep the entire city, with an official population of over 1 million people, accommodated, fed, entertained, wired and on the move (see Naypyitaw Development Committee 2014, 1; also Myint 2011). Its train station, airport and endowment of highways and major arterial roads are supposed to ensure the city is connected to the rest of Myanmar, although it can still feel isolated, even remote.

Yet the development of Naypyitaw is not as inexplicable as sometimes assumed. Former Senior General Than Shwe's vision should be considered in the context of the past two millennia, a period when there have been many capitals in the area now known as Myanmar. Old civilizations built centres for administrative control, even though many struggled to consistently project power at any distance, especially in the wet season. Ordinarily, these centres co-existed, much as the different centres of power in Myanmar today co-exist. So, why did the former military regime opt to make a new capital? From their perspective, Yangon, developed during British rule as the country's administrative hub, carried an unpalatable legacy. For many Myanmar powerbrokers it was too foreign, cluttered and colonial for the purposes of restoring Myanmar national pride, and also potentially vulnerable to foreign incursions and political instability (Dulyapak 2009, xvi; Myoe 2006; Seekins 2009, 63). When the early ambition to construct Naypyitaw was being discussed, there would have been many reasons, both practical and cosmological, for moving the centre of government back to what is widely considered the emotional and logistical heartland (see Steinberg 2013).[1]

From a practical perspective, re-centring the administrative functions of such a diverse and incoherent nation has some logic. That such plans needed to wait until the 2000s to be implemented is also not surprising. This was a period when the Myanmar government appeared anxious about regime survival and worked assiduously to undermine the competing claims for legitimacy from democratic and ethnic forces. It also benefited from new revenue sources, especially the export of valuable resources to China and Thailand. Moving the capital inland no doubt also offered strategic benefit for leaders worried about foreign instigated 'regime change'. The move to Naypyitaw further endorsed the Bamar-centric oriented approach of the leadership, many of whom originally hailed from places like Bago, Mandalay and Magwe in central Myanmar. The new capital was a calibrated retreat from the dissenting politics of Yangon and offered a chance to exert more control over civil servants (Horsey 2008, 19). Naypyitaw signalled a shift of power away from a contested, cluttered, post-colonial city to a region where the machinery of government could begin to stretch its muscles anew.

Logic, layout and design

Naypyitaw only makes sense if its monumentalist ambition is put in a deep historical context. For Myanmar's former military ruler the over-riding purpose of government was to build a proud nation, independent and unique. The senior leaders were not prepared to compromise on what that agenda would mean. It is this exceptionalism that motivated the isolationist streak of the Ne Win era, and it is what strengthened the resolve of the military dictatorship after the 1988 uprising (Farrelly 2013). Former Senior General Than Shwe had, in Naypyitaw, an opportunity to stamp his own ideas about state formation on this fallow terrain. From Yangon, where he was constantly under pressure from the international community, from democratic activists, and especially from Aung San Suu Kyi, he must have considered the move a prudent, even necessary, step. It would allow space for different politics to emerge in a tightly controlled space: one that could be sealed against outside influences as desired, and where movement could, at least initially, be closely controlled.

Nowadays, leaving Yangon by road, as most people travelling to Naypyitaw do, you pass through a number of tollgates. Then, once you are on the highway, which leads eventually to Mandalay, the rhythm of long-distance travel takes over. Every furlong along the road, a marker sets out how far you have come. This means that for every mile there are eight markers. They drag the stream of cars, trucks and buses, and occasional agricultural vehicles, the 200 miles up the road. It is a wide road, although many regular commuters complain that the camber of the corners fails to meet international road engineering standards. To travellers whizzing past villages, many of which still do not have access to mains electricity, Myanmar's agricultural zone is a blur of small-scale farms, plantations and some modest industrialization. At '115 Miles' a famous rest-stop has restaurants offering quick bites. For many of those who use the road frequently, the diversion of a meal at 'Feel' or 'Pioneer' is the only highlight of the journey.

Arriving in Naypyitaw, traffic is diverted off the highway and down a ramp. After passing a military and police checkpoint with automatic number plate recognition technology, and then paying a small fee to enter the city proper, Naypyitaw awaits. Buses and cars then take a long left-hand turn at one of the city's major roundabouts, before heading up into the heart of Hotel Zone 1, and then reaching the Myoma Market or the bus station to the east. Foreign visitors, usually corralled in one of the dozens of major hotels, find a comfy bed. For most Myanmar government staff their next stop is their apartment complex.

For junior, unmarried officials, home is a single-sex dormitory, where they live cheek-by-jowl with others from their Ministry or agency. Life in Naypyitaw is expensive, with many recent recruits forced to spend much of their income just on accommodation. This is partly because in the system of allocating accommodation more senior staff receive preferential treatment. Junior staff are paid around 100,000 kyat per month.[2] This modest income ensures that they have relatively few opportunities for travel or to save. Their life is focused on eating basic meals, at their dormitory and place of work, and shuttling backwards and forwards on the 'ferry' transport provided by the Ministry. The 'ferry' can be a well-appointed bus or just a truck with hard wooden seats in the back. Each morning and afternoon these services rumble along the main thoroughfares, taking groups of officials from home to office and back again.

More senior officials, particularly those of officer rank, still use the shuttles but they will have a better quality accommodation.[3] Unmarried officers usually live in an apartment, which they probably share with others until they make the rank of Director. Before that level, married officers are provided with an apartment graded for their position in the hierarchy. Some officers will keep their families in Yangon and will therefore have quite a spacious allocation. For Deputy Directors, this will usually be a two-bedroom apartment. They are commonly surrounded by colleagues from the same Ministry. In adjacent buildings other Ministries will have taken up residency. For the most senior officials—Deputy Directors-General, Directors-General and Permanent Secretaries—the accommodation is better still. For some it will be higher quality and more lavishly appointed apartments. Many Directors-General and Permanent Secretaries live in standalone bungalows.

Their accommodation is out-ranked, then, by the residences offered to Deputy Ministers and Ministers. Their handsome dwellings, surrounded by fences and with gates that are usually closed, habitually fly the Myanmar flag. Most will have a sentry on duty to keep an eye on the comings and goings. In some of the most sensitive areas of the city there are extra guard posts to monitor the passing traffic. Ministerial residences are often used for functions, although because so much of the entertaining that occurs in Naypyitaw is focused on restaurants, hotels and the convention centres, there are fewer large-scale private gatherings.

The most senior officials, such as the President and the Speakers of the Union Assembly, and a select group of retired officials, live in much more heavily guarded complexes. There are two major clusters of mansions set aside for their accommodation in Naypyitaw. The first is home to the President, the two Vice-Presidents and the two Speakers of the Hluttaw. They live in a cluster of double-storey mansions directly adjacent to the Union Assembly complex. Each of these buildings is heavily guarded, with multiple layers of security. Both uniformed and Special Branch police are entrusted with the safety of these senior leaders and their families. Such dwellings have tennis courts, swimming pools and well-curated gardens. They are also used to entertain dignitaries and have large spaces designated for that purpose, with ornate rooms mimicking the style of the legislative compound's ceremonial spaces. Second, there is a residential complex nestled behind trees just beyond the view of commuters where former Senior General Than Shwe, former Vice Senior General Maung Aye and other senior retired generals have residences. They vary in scale and are not built to identical specifications like the other leadership residences. This area is off-limits to the public, and while there is a three-pronged road that leads towards these mansions, it is not used. Police are often seen patrolling the neighbourhood.

The areas where foreigners congregate in Naypyitaw are also carefully set apart from the rest of the city. Near the three Hotel Zones (Hotel Zone 1, Hotel Zone 2 and the 'ASEAN' zone) there are large shopping centres. With fastfood restaurants, supermarkets and batteries of ATMs, the shopping centres send a strong signal about the style of modernity endorsed by Naypyitaw's planners. In time, the Myanmar government hopes to populate the barren Diplomatic Quarter. No foreign missions have yet moved permanently to the new capital although some, such as Australia and the United Kingdom, maintain offices there. Since the lead-up to the ASEAN meetings there in 2014 a number of foreign diplomats have been based in Naypyitaw. Initially, some were working directly on the planning for the ASEAN events. When the National League for Democracy government took power in 2016 it made sense for foreign officials to spend as much time in Naypyitaw as they could manage, such was the pace of change and the challenge of maintaining strong professional links.

One area that foreigners, including diplomats, only rarely see up close is the military zone, in Zeyathiri township. It is in the far east of the city, wedged against the towering mountains of the Shan Yoma mountain range. The military installations in this part of the city are heavily guarded. There is the parade ground used for Armed Forces Day celebrations each year (Weng 2013). It features the statues of the three historic kings, Anawrahta, Bayinnaung and Alaungpaya, who are considered iconic by many of Myanmar's military leaders. There are also large compounds for senior military officers, and other areas where the tens of thousands of more junior officers who live in Naypyitaw reside. There is another military area, for the Naypyitaw Region Command HQ. It sits right behind the Theintheidi (World Peace) Pagoda, which is on the main road leading through rice paddies towards Pyinmana township, an old settlement that has now been subsumed by Naypyitaw's sprawl.

Indeed it is important to recognize that not everything in Naypyitaw is new. There is Lewe, in the south, which is a well-established agricultural town, famed for its wood working. Then there is Pyinmana itself. This is Naypyitaw's most vibrant urban environment, a bustling and somewhat incoherent place. It has a noticeable Muslim minority, and Islamic prayer facilities fortified with barbed wire. This sets it apart from the townships of 'new' Naypyitaw. By contrast, they are almost devoid of non-Buddhist religious architecture. Each of these towns existed before Naypyitaw, and they are now being rapidly reshaped by the economic and political priorities of the new centre.

Official role

In general terms, Naypyitaw was designed for the convenience of government and to showcase Myanmar's potency. Its more specific purpose is to manage the incomplete transition from long-term military rule towards, in the medium term, a managed form of democracy. It may eventually be the site of a robust and well-consolidated democratic system, but that will take many years of persistent effort. For now, it hoists the machinery of ministries, legislatures, the judiciary, the armed forces command and the executive above the fray of ordinary Myanmar life. Taken together, these institutions, all moved from Yangon since 2005, are part of a great experiment in the mobility of a bureaucratic workforce but also in the evolution of a culture that supports Myanmar's ongoing political and economic transformation. Naypyitaw is a crucial piece in the national puzzle of re-orienting the state and producing a system of control, which while still beholden to military interests, has become increasingly open to democratic instincts.

With Aung San Suu Kyi in a tailor-made position as State Counsellor, the new capital claims the pro-democracy leader as one of its many temporary residents.

With its genesis in military dictatorship, Naypyitaw's spaces are all designed to manage access and discourage any unauthorized activity. Most of the large compounds are fenced and gated. Some gates come with high security. Some facilities require the presentation of credentials, checks are made, vehicles closely inspected. At many other gates, however, a familiar wave or an audacious confidence will ensure that no checks follow. In those cases, and with the right navigation, Naypyitaw can open up. Even with a semi-democratic government, Naypyitaw is a place that has multiple layers of access and inscrutability. Guards tend to be young, uniformed, males, members of the Combat Battalions that have taken over much of the frontline security functions recently abandoned by the army. In other areas it is Special Branch, which maintains a very large operation in Naypyitaw. They will grant passes to enter sensitive locations and keep an eye on suspicious visitors. Many Special Branch wear a uniform, of a sort: they are often identified by their 'Special Branch' designated tracksuits. They will even wear these while off-duty. Naypyitaw is a city where the right uniform matters.

For officials, the standard uniform is a *longyi* (which is Myanmar's traditional sarong) and a shirt or blouse. For men, especially those in more senior positions, it is customary to wear a *taikpyone*, a Chinese-style jacket secured by cloth buttons on the front. Such a jacket is a mark of status. The quality of longyi varies widely. Only the most senior officials wear a silk one. Others will make do with a longyi that fits their status in the hierarchy.

This style of hierarchical dress is especially apparent at the Union Assembly, where everyone wears a uniform of some sort. Legislators are often the best dressed: silk longyi are worn by most Bamar representatives under the former Union Solidarity and Development Party administration. The National League for Democracy have a more low-key style, but almost always wear the same brown coloured longyi and jacket. Those from other ethnic groups usually wear some interpretation of their 'national race' dress. In many cases it is a variation on Bamar-style clothing, although there are some radical departures from the norm. It is difficult for anybody who is Naga or from some of the Chin 'races' to hide their origins. In Naypyitaw, when in uniform, they are distinctive in any crowd.

Since they first convened in 2011, all of the legislators who meet for Union Assembly sessions have been part of Naypyitaw's tentative embrace of more representative government (Egreteau 2012; for more current details see Farrelly (2016a)). Under the government of President Thein Sein, they tended to explain their role as a 'check and balance' on executive excess. With the election of the National League for Democracy in November 2015, the faces have changed but the programme of legislative work has remained on tempo. Legislators spend around five months each year in Naypyitaw. There are usually three parliamentary sessions each year. The first session begins in January, the second in May and the third in October. These sessions, which will last for varying periods, from five to nine weeks, give the legislators a chance to live together at their shared accommodation.

Their accommodation is segregated by party. First, there is the Union Solidarity and Development Party headquarters where almost all of the government MPs lived from 2011 to 2016. Their accommodation, in two-storey blocks, is formal and disciplined. Many USDP MPs were former military officers, government officials, school teachers or local political operatives. They brought a style of living carried over from the socialist era. After the November 2015 election, their party headquarters is a much quieter place, with the number of representatives greatly reduced. Second, there is the Naypyitaw Council guesthouse, a large residential compound where the non-USDP MPs live. From 2011 to 2016, they were drawn from a range of democratic and ethnic political parties. At this guesthouse, many MPs had family members join them for long periods in Naypyitaw. Since 2016, the Naypyitaw Council guesthouse has mainly accommodated the National League for Democracy members elected at the 2015 poll. Third, there is the guesthouse accommodation made available to the military MPs. With 25 per cent of MPs drawn from uniformed ranks, mostly the army, they require accommodation in Naypyitaw. These officers, from brigadier general to captain, are drawn from commands across the length and breadth of the country (Egreteau 2016).

Culture and commerce

Away from the comfortable life enjoyed by Union Assembly members, Naypyitaw is developing a distinctively middle-class economic orientation. As many government officials lament, it is a place to spend money, not make money. This makes it challenging for junior officials who often have few opportunities for developing a diverse economic portfolio, as they do when they are living in Yangon. Stories of very tight household budgets are common. For officials in some Ministries, such as Foreign Affairs, it is only through the extra income that a posting brings that families can stay on top of their commitments in the long term.

At the same time, Naypyitaw also serves as a place where people can seize new opportunities. Some are enticed to join the private sector where their skills in navigating the Myanmar bureaucracy are highly prized. It is common to hear that officials at both senior and middle ranks have accepted jobs that will pay them many times what their government salaries would. There are also those who have managed to take advantage of further educational or other opportunities. Many of the foreign visitors to Naypyitaw are in a position to help facilitate access to graduate education abroad, or to participation in delegations or training programmes. While these may not prove financially lucrative, they can also help to support a wide range of new entanglements for people who have struggled, in the past, for regular foreign connections.

Naypyitaw is also a site of occasional cultural and sporting spectacles. The Southeast Asian Games that were held in the city in December 2013 were an early opportunity for foreigners to have a close look at its design. As Creak (2014, 864) has argued, 'the symbolism of building new stadiums and other infrastructure was especially great in Myanmar's new national capital of Naypyitaw'. As Creak explained,

> [t]he city is itself a paean to high-modernism, with designated 'zones' for hotels, ministries, leisure, and so forth; vast boulevards spanning the enormous distances between these sites; little traffic; and few visible signs of life to upset the pervasive sense of order.

With no further sporting events of the same scale, the 2013 games have left a somewhat incongruous selection of sporting facilities. There are two major complexes for athletics, with substantial facilities for swimming and other sports. There is also a BMX track. It is hard to imagine when some of this infrastructure will be used again.

The city also has two large-scale convention centres. The first was built by the Chinese government and completed in 2013. It was used to host the World Economic Forum for East Asia in June that year. This event brought together senior business figures and the leading lights of the Union Solidarity and Development Party government. Ministers chatted with executives drawn from around the world to see Myanmar's changes for themselves. The second Myanmar International Convention Centre was completed in early 2014, widely judged by Naypyitaw locals as a Myanmar response to the Chinese construction. It is a much larger facility: one that was built to host, in the first instance, the most important meetings of the ASEAN summit season from May to December 2014. These meetings also required new hotel accommodation in the form of jade villas spread across the area between the city's Hotel Zone 1 and the Yangon–Mandalay highway. In the aftermath of this investment, the government sought, but largely failed, to build a tourism economy focused on conference visitors (Eleven 2015).

Across Naypyitaw there are also a number of notable museums. The Gem and Jade Museum, on Yaza Thinghaha Road, is a key landmark. Situated adjacent to the Maniyadanar Jade Hall where the three-times-a-year jade auctions are held, it is a major site for explaining the significance of mineral wealth for the country. Further up Yaza Thinghaha Road are the sites for the National Archives and National Museum. The site devoted to the National Defence Museum, which is set between the Zeyar Thiri Sports Complex and the National Landmark Garden, is perhaps the largest cultural site in the city. It is directly across the road from the National Defence College, where mid-ranking officers receive key parts of their academic and military training. The museum relocated to Naypyitaw in 2012. It is a complex of cavernous buildings devoted to the self-presentation of Myanmar government ideas about the country, its history and, naturally, the role of the defence services. It puts the army at the centre of the national story, with special emphasis on the roles of Generals Aung San, Ne Win and Than Shwe. Other senior figures, such as former Vice Senior General Maung Aye, former President Thein Sein and the serving commanders of the three branches of the armed forces, are each given special prominence. The story of the defence services is largely shaped by the interventions of such senior leaders. Almost every room has a portrait of Senior General Min Aung Hlaing in pride of place.

The National Landmark Garden is another key feature of the Naypyitaw landscape. It is a mini-Myanmar, designed in the shape of the country as a whole. Miniaturized versions of Mandalay Hill, a Kachin Manau ground and the ruins of Mrauk-U in Rakhine State offer visitors a chance to see the entire country from the comfort of a chauffeur-driven buggy. Every step of the way there is a chance to be reminded of the significance of Myanmar's Buddhist culture and of the way that the country has been united. It is reasonable to judge that most of those at the National Landmark Garden have not seen many parts of the country. Distances are too vast and costs too high for most ordinary people to travel far. The National Landmark Garden includes a pavilion that explains the development of Naypyitaw. Curiously it is the only part of this facility, and one of the few places in Naypyitaw, where photography is not permitted. The diorama of the city, replete with illuminated pointers to the key sites, sprawls across a swimming pool sized landscape.

Conclusions

During its construction and consolidation phases, Naypyitaw remained a city in prospect. It was easy to belittle as artificial, inept or incomplete. Over time, however, such criticisms will become hazy. They will be lost in the day-to-day functioning of a strong city where, each day, the mechanics of Myanmar power are put into concrete action. Some will still call for the capital to be returned to Yangon. It is fair to guess that such calls will echo for decades to come. At some stage a future Myanmar government may even decide to abandon the city. They will have ample reasons for reconsidering the site of the capital. For a period, the National League for Democracy had a general intention to return administrative power to Yangon. Yet that prospect now appears less likely than ever before, with the Myanmar government now fully entrenched in its new home.

This means that a generation of children, born and raised in Naypyitaw, will start to think of the city not as an administrative creation but as a place where their own lives and aspirations can take root. They may well resent its size and lack of entertainment options, but they will still come to think of it as home. Their parents, many of whom are in today's rising generation of bureaucrats, will also have different ideas once they are fully settled in the city. It should be a safe place to raise a family and a place that can draw strength from the diversity of Myanmar's many different parts. Whether they are from Magwe, Sagaing, Chin, Yangon or Mon, they may never truly, or really, return home. These new lives will be forged by Naypyitaw as it brings together so much of the youthful creativity that Myanmar can proudly claim.

As a city, Naypyitaw will still need to work hard to be taken seriously. During the early years it has benefited from a novelty value, especially among non-Myanmar people. Some find it charming or exciting to be in a place that was so recently conjured from a supposedly blank canvas of scrubland and paddy fields. The idea that Naypyitaw could become stale is yet to be fully explored. Naypyitaw has yet to cultivate the affection of the Myanmar people. Many still consider the deployment of resources to the new capital an outrageous waste. There is resentment against its origins during the years of military dictatorship. Its sprawling layout also dissuades many from engaging with it beyond a purely functional level. Travelling from apartment or hotel to an office, and back again, with occasional forays to shopping centres or parks does not build loyalty. Naypyitaw will take many years to grow into its role and to build a local culture that provides adequate diversions and stimulation, even for its ardent critics.

Nonetheless, its unpopularity serves a further ambiguous purpose. With some exceptions, those who spend time in Naypyitaw have a specific goal. Once it has been met they are usually prepared to leave. Civil servants take advantage of the regular bus services to Yangon. On a Friday afternoon the exodus of officials from the capital, mostly heading back to Yangon, provides one indication of the ties that bind officials to the rest of society. Many maintain families and lifestyles in Yangon: they do not find Naypyitaw an adequate replacement. For now, this still gives the entire city a transient character; few people are prepared to claim a permanent stake. The exceptions may be the rising generation of Naypyitawrians, a new group of Myanmar citizens, eagerly seeking the middle-class future that the new city could deliver (see Farrelly 2016b). How they fare under future governments will remain a matter of great interest as Myanmar continues its experiment of building an inclusive democratic system in a city first imagined by a dictatorial elite.

Notes

1 It would have helped that Myanmar's senior military decision-makers at that time had experience of visiting Putrajaya, Malaysia's administrative capital since 1999. For discussion, see King (2007).

2 For discussion of the relationship between the move to Naypyitaw and an increase in official salaries see Turnell (2008); also Peck (2007).

3 The distinction between 'officers' and 'staff' in Myanmar's civilian bureaucracy is broadly equivalent to the distinction between officers and enlisted personnel in the armed forces. It is only officers who enjoy a career pathway that may culminate in a senior command position, while staff are usually focused on technical and administrative specialities.

References

Creak, Simon. 2014. 'National Restoration, Regional Prestige: The Southeast Asian Games in Myanmar, 2013'. *The Journal of Asian Studies* (73) 4: 853–877.

Dulyapak, Preecharushh. 2009. *Naypyitaw: The New Capital of Burma*. Bangkok: White Lotus Press.

Egreteau, Renaud. 2012. 'Burma/Myanmar'. *Political Insight* (3) 2: 30–33.

Egreteau, Renaud. 2016. 'How Powerless are Myanmar's Military Legislators?' *Nikkei Asian Review*, June 5.

Eleven. 2015. 'Ministry Aims to Boost Naypyitaw Tourism'. Eleven, March 29.

Farrelly, Nicholas. 2013. 'Discipline Without Democracy: Military Dominance in Post-Colonial Burma'. *Australian Journal of International Affairs* (67) 3: 312–326.

Farrelly, Nicholas. 2016a. 'Subtle Politics to Greet New NLD Legislators in Naypyitaw'. *The Myanmar Times*, January 18.

Farrelly, Nicholas. 2016b. 'Who are the "Naypyitawrians"?' *The Myanmar Times*, February 29.

Head, Jonathan. 2007. 'Burma's New Capital City Unveiled'. BBC, March 27. Accessed January 2016. http://news.bbc.co.uk/2/hi/asia-pacific/6498029.stm.

Horsey, Richard. 2008. 'The Dramatic Events of 2007 in Myanmar: Domestic and International Implications' in *Dictatorship, Disorder and Decline in Myanmar*, edited by M. Skidmore & T. Wilson. Canberra: ANU E Press.

King, Ross. 2007. 'Re-Writing the City: Putrajaya as Representation'. *Journal of Urban Design* (12) 1: 117–138.

Myint, War War. 2011. 'Study on Geometric Design of Naypyitaw–Mandalay Expressway and Possible Improvements; Sagarinn–Myinsain Portion'. *World Academy of Science, Engineering and Technology* (51): 620–624.

Myoe, Maung Aung. 2006. 'The Road to Naypyitaw: Making Sense of the Myanmar Government's Decision to Move its Capital'. Singapore: National University of Singapore, Asia Research Institute, Working Paper No. 79.

Naypyitaw Development Committee. 2014. 'Presentation of the Construction of Naypyitaw'. Naypyitaw: Naypyitaw Development Committee.

Peck, Grant. 2007. 'Myanmar's Remote Capital is Still a Work in Progress'. *The New York Times*, October 5.

Seekins, Donald M. 2009. '"Runaway Chickens" and Myanmar Identity'. *City* (13) 1: 63–70.

Steinberg, David. 2013. *Burma/Myanmar: What Everyone Needs to Know*. Oxford: Oxford University Press.

The New York Times. 2008. 'Myanmar's New Capital: Remote, Lavish and Off Limits'. June 23.

Turnell, Sean. 2008. 'Burma's Insatiable State'. *Asian Survey* (48) 6: 958–976.

Weng, Lawi. 2013. 'In Naypyitaw, Suu Kyi Attends Armed Forces Day'. *The Irrawaddy*, March 27. www.irrawaddy.com/burma/in-naypyidaw-suu-kyi-attends-armed-forces-day.html.

7
URBAN

Jayde Lin Roberts

At the opening of Myanmar's first Urban Research and Development Institute (URDI) in January 2012, the Union Minister of Construction Khin Maung Myint expressed his hope that 'URDI will assist the Government's endeavours of building a new, modern and developed nation' (UN-HABITAT 2012). While this fixation on modernisation and development is not new for Myanmar, it has taken on increased urgency since 2011 as its leaders officially pursued economic integration with ASEAN and adopted a number of international standards including the UN Millennium Development Goals as near-term targets (Htut 2013). In this drive to catch up with its neighbours and reconnect with the global economy, Myanmar's cities are seen as the engines for economic development. However, in this rush to make Myanmar competitive, what is the *urban* and what constitutes development in this particular national context have yet to be discussed. Other cities in the global South and postcolonial countries have encountered similar challenges, leading scholars in urban planning, geography and other disciplines to question the uncritical application of the tenets of development and neoliberal globalisation on so-called developing nations. This chapter focuses on the making of the urban in Myanmar as a contingent and contested process that is increasingly subjected to international circuits of authoritative knowledge. In particular, this chapter asks: What is a city if it is not the production of space undertaken by its inhabitants? What are the roles and functions of cities in a reforming Myanmar? And, what is Myanmar urbanism in a rapidly globalising country?

After UN-HABITAT helped establish URDI in 2012, other international aid agencies such as Japan International Cooperation Agency (JICA), the European Union (EU) and the Asian Development Bank (ADB) provided funding, expertise, capacity building and even master plans for urban development. These multi-million-dollar projects were undertaken in earnest to make better cities in Myanmar, ones that are modern, livable, green, pro-poor and attain other lofty goals that even developed cities have yet to achieve. These are worthy, if aspirational, objectives but the pursuit of them must consider actual urban life in Myanmar's cities and question the equivalence of economic growth with urban wellbeing. Experts and bureaucrats in international aid agencies are cognisant of the spatial, social and economic inequality in international and national development, but that awareness has yet to transform standardised practices dictated by measurable results within the constraints of annual budgets. This work of promoting progress is further complicated by the fact that the history of Myanmar's cities has yet to be investigated in depth. Knowledge to date, however, suggests that development in

Myanmar cities diverges significantly from the histories of cities in the global North. This divergence, discussed below, is significant because theories about how cities function remain rooted in the developed world but prescribe planning practices worldwide (Roy 2005). Trajectories similar to that of Myanmar's might be found in postcolonial cities such as Kolkata and Mumbai but Myanmar's cities have the additional challenge of being the product and subject of the nation-state rather than the creation or incorporation of local merchants and residents.

Whose city?

In much of the literature about the effects of neoliberal globalisation, scholars call attention to the disenfranchisement of urban residents and the privatisation of public institutions. In the case of contemporary Myanmar, neither urban nor rural residents have ever been enfranchised and the definition and function of the public sector remains unclear. These fundamental deviations from the international model must be critically examined if the country is to formulate context-appropriate policies for sustainable growth rather than copy a litany of global best practices or development miracles.

First in this consideration is who has rights to the Myanmar city in the past, present and future. As defined by David Harvey, the right to the city is a common right wherein residents exercise collective, democratic control over processes of urbanisation (Harvey 2008). Similarly, for Henri Lefebvre, this right belongs to urban inhabitants and includes two principal aspects: the right to participation and the right to appropriation (Lefebvre 1996). That is, the right to the city is far more than the individual liberty to access urban resources; it is the power to participate directly in the decisions that produce urban space (Harvey 2008). These are of course unrealised ideals in the global North but the long history of local, self-organised governance that could be traced back to the classical Greek city-state and the medieval town has laid the foundation of participation and enfranchisement that continues to influence the form, function and social lives of cities today. In the context of Myanmar, where rule of law is 'lexically present but semantically absent' (Cheesman 2015, 7–11) and good governance awaits definition, the issues that confront urban residents remain much more rudimentary. They require basic services such as electricity, potable water and sewage treatment. Participatory decision-making, if urban residents are even aware of the practice, is a distant dream.

On 27 December 2014, the Yangon City Development Committee (YCDC), the municipal government, held its first elections since 1962. Although the election was a significant step towards political reform, several problems plagued the process, the most notable of which was the restriction of the poll to about 8 per cent (409,889) of the total urban population of 5.2 million. Only one person per household that possessed government-issued residency documents was allowed to vote.[1] On polling day, a mere 2 per cent (106,089) cast their ballots.[2] Activists and international observers criticised the process, but viewed within the history of Myanmar's cities, this exclusion was only following precedents. The military generals who ruled Myanmar from 1988 to 2011 prized control and security over participation but even before the State Law and Order Restoration Council (SLORC)—later renamed the State Peace and Development Council (SPDC)—took power, the people of Myanmar were not enfranchised. Between 1948 and 1962, the new independent government of Burma struggled to build a sustainable democracy, and before that, the colonial government established constituencies along racial lines to maintain the dominance of the European minority.[3] The colonial population of Rangoon was divided into Europeans, Burmese, Muslims, Chinese, Hindus and Karen constituencies and only 5 per cent of the residents were enfranchised (Pearn 1939, 243). These restrictions and the stringent financial and educational requirements for holding office failed to encourage public participation among non-European residents. Indeed, as J. S. Furnivall has pointed out, municipal committees were seen as a burden on everyday residents because they demanded taxes but failed to provide desired services (Furnivall 1948, 75, 145–151, 155).

In a city produced by the Empire to instigate a British world order, non-Europeans were understandably marginalised. Rangoon was a colonial city dominated by Europeans and Indians. It did not belong to the Burmese.[4] However, to investigate who has the right to the city beyond Rangoon, we must consider the pre-colonial conception of cities in Myanmar. Although limited scholarship only allows for a preliminary analysis, it is nonetheless important to examine the definition and politico-economic structure of the *myo*, the Myanmar word usually translated as city.[5] According to the *Myanmar–English Dictionary*, *myo* is: a wall surrounding an area; stockade; a walled town with a market-place; and a town, city. These definitions for *myo* can be found in other places, such as in China where *cheng* is a walled city officially decreed and taxed by the imperial government, and in medieval Europe where towns were recognised centres of commerce protected by a city wall.[6] However, unlike medieval towns in which local merchants and elite asserted autonomy through liberty charters that guaranteed the freedom of its residents and ensured rights to property and fair taxation, residents within *myo* exercised little or no power. They remained subjects of kings and local rulers: *myoza*, *myowun* and *myothugyi*.

Myoza (town-eaters) were lowland rulers, junior princes and officials who were entrusted by the king with modest territories. They had the right to monopolise taxes and, in return for royal recognition, had to forward tribute, supply troops and pay homage (Lieberman 2003, 155–161). Similarly, *myowun* (usually translated as governors) were invested with power by the king. However, unlike *myoza*, who exercised significant independence from the royal court, *myowun* were centrally appointed to centralise rule (Lieberman 2003, 162–186). They served at the pleasure of the king and could be recalled and replaced at any time without warning (Sein 1973, xii). *Myowun* were responsible for standardising trade, collecting taxes and ensuring the order and security of their *myo*. In a largely complementary role to the centrally appointed *myowun*, *myothugyi*, local hereditary headmen who ruled over a group of villages and hamlets, were duty-bound to 'look after the interest of the government, to collect the revenue and forward it to the *Kathaung myuang* (treasury) at the nearest large town . . . and settle all civil disputes' (Sein 1973, 66). In the lowlands, Burmese people were divided into different orders or regiments and subject to their designated captains regardless of physical location. Even if a captain lived miles away from a member of his regiment, that member was expected to obey and pay taxes to his captain and seek his counsel to settle civil disputes (Furnivall 1957, 34).

The obvious fact that Burmese people lived as subjects under kings and were excluded by the colonial administration would not require mentioning if they had achieved the right to the city after independence. However, after the British left, Burmese people soon became subjects of the Union government. An approximately twelve-year experiment with democracy ended in a military coup in 1962. In the 1950s, when approximately 50,000 squatters camped out on pavements in downtown Yangon and in townships such as Kyimyindaing, Ahlone, Botahtaung, Pazundaung and Tamwe, one could say that Burmese people appropriated urban space. Many of these squatters had fled from rural areas where civil war was raging. Although these informal settlements were seen as a blight on the city, the Anti-Fascist People's Freedom League (AFPFL) was unwilling to clear these slums for fear of losing votes (Nwe 1998). However, the military-led Caretaker Government that assumed power in 1958 did not require popular support and decisively cleaned up the city. The five decades since Ne Win took power for the second time in 1962 have witnessed deteriorating relations between the government and its people, most of whom are citizens who do not exercise the rights of citizenship and many who are not even granted the label of citizen.

From pre-colonial Burma to the present, political power has remained opaque, militarised and highly centralised. This historical fact calls into question a fundamental assumption in modern urban planning that conceptualises urban residents as enfranchised citizens who can work with or against the municipal government to shape their cities. This fact also demands a more context-appropriate investigation into the forces of urbanisation and what constitutes development.

Cities in the national framework

Prior to 2015, former President Thein Sein called for a 'people-centred development'—a notable effort towards decentralisation. Under the new government led by the National League of Democracy (NLD), the rhetoric of placing people first is also present. However, it is unclear if cities and towns will become more than cogs to support national economic development. The history of Myanmar shows that cities and towns have exercised little autonomy. The work of planning for and managing cities is still highly centralised and constrained by the lack of local revenue and expertise. As of 2015, cities in Myanmar were divided into three broad categories: the capital, Naypyitaw, with its unique administration as a Union Territory; the large cities, Yangon and Mandalay, that have their own development committees but are not fully autonomous because they are delegated authority from the Yangon Region and Mandalay Region governments;[7] and cities and towns such as Mawlamyiang and Bago that have gained unprecedented levels of autonomy since 2011.[8] Local Development Affairs Offices (DAOs) manage these second-tier cities without guidance from the Union government because they have been removed from the Ministry of Border Affairs, their former mother ministry. The hundreds of DAOs across the country are 'nascent bureaucracies of the states and regions' that could serve to strengthen subnational and local governance (Arnold et al. 2015, xi).

However, the DAOs, functioning as municipal governments, have no capacity in urban planning. Master plans for all cities with populations above 100,000 are being drawn up at the Union level by staff in the Department of Human Settlements and Housing Development (DHSHD) within the Ministry of Construction. As already noted, Myanmar is severely lacking in planning expertise and the decision to have all of the master plans drawn up at the Union level was probably determined by practical limitations. There are about 20 to 30 urban planning professionals in the entire country of approximately 51 million people.[9] Comprehensive and integrated socio-economic and spatial planning is unquestionably necessary, but given Myanmar's history of authoritarian rule, this continued concentration of power at the Union level could exacerbate long-standing inequalities between the centre and the periphery.

In particular, the urgency, number and complexity of urban problems will likely push the limited pool of planners to adopt universalised planning solutions without adequate consideration for the specificities of each town or city. Master planning is necessarily abstract and relies on rational categories that tend to segregate urban functions into specialised urban zones. Although the Modernist approach that sees cities as machines is no longer the standard in the global North, it remains attractive in Myanmar because scientific order, segregation and specialisation appears to be the antidote for urban ills such as chaotic growth, land-use conflicts and unhealthy living conditions. Abstract universals will also exercise undeserved influence because the numerous sets of quantitative data that are assumed to be the rational basis for planning decisions are missing in Myanmar. Therefore, the unenviable job of the overworked 20 to 30 planners is to produce master plans while gathering data or to produce the plans as if they had sufficient data. Furthermore, the push for national development will likely prioritise the nation over individual cities as the necessary path towards an economically competitive Myanmar.

In the logic of the generals who have and still maintain significant control under the NLD-led government, the unity of the nation is non-negotiable. Furthermore, in securing the territorial integrity of the Union, order is almost synonymous with development, and development is a top priority. We can see this in the two names the military junta chose for their government between 1988 and 2011: 'State Law and Order Restoration Council' and 'State Peace and Development Council'. But again, there is little clarity about what constitutes development in the urban context and this vagueness is evident in the various Myanmar words that are translated as development. In the names of municipal governments such as the YCDC and the Development Affairs Organizations, *si-bin-tha-ya-ye* is translated as development. The word has two parts: *si-bin*, 'to prosper', and *tha-ya*, 'pleasant'; *ye* is a nominaliser. In everyday usage, Burmese people say *to-teq pwint-pyo hmu* for development, which is a combination of *to-teq*, to progress, and *pwint-pyo*, to bring about or realise, and *hmu*, another nominaliser. In Burmese, both the SPDC and DHSHD use *pwint-pyo* as in 'to bring about peace' and 'to bring about housing'. This range of usage and understanding requires careful consideration because the names of municipal governments that are supposed to enable development do not employ the everyday Burmese words for development, and the combination of *si-bin* with *tha-ya* suggests prosperous pleasant neighbourhoods that can only be found in the most exclusive quarters of Yangon and gentrified neighbourhoods in the developed world.[10]

The Burmese word *si-bin* could also be understood as 'to bring in more people'. Urbanisation will undoubtedly make Myanmar's cities more populous. There is a concern that Yangon, the country's former capital and largest city, will become a megacity with its attendant infrastructural, social and political challenges. To prevent chaotic urbanisation and distribute growth, the Union government is following the advice of international organisations such as JICA and UN-HABITAT and adopting a 'concentrated decentralisation development strategy'. This strategy identifies five tiers of cities: 1) capital city; 2) national economic growth centres including Yangon and Mandalay and special economic zones, namely Kyauk Phyu and Dawei; 3) secondary regional growth centres such as Lashio and Pathein; 4) border trading towns such as Muse and Myawaddy; 5) other towns with 'different growth potentials' such as Pyi and Hpa-An (Oo 2015). These cities are mapped out as an integrated network along four economic corridors (North to South, East to West, Northeast to Southwest and Southeast to Northwest) that not only connect cities within Myanmar but also join them with economic centres in Thailand, China and India. Within ASEAN, Myanmar is considered to be a land bridge that will facilitate trade across Southeast Asia and better connect the region with South and East Asia. Construction of the Three Nation Highway Project, a part of the larger Asian Highway Project, began in 2012 and once completed will connect Moreh in India to Mae Sot in Thailand via Tamu, Mandalay and Myawaddy in Myanmar (ASEAN Briefing 2015). This physical integration into ASEAN will increase transnational trade but will also subject the cities along this and other proposed highways to significant socio-economic pressures. Unless Myanmar's municipal governments have sufficient resources and expertise to manage the various challenges brought on by regional integration, the welfare of Myanmar's cities will be overwhelmed by the drive to make the country more economically competitive. The economic imperative of neoliberal globalisation will intensify inequalities between rural and urban populations, between the working class and elite, and could inflame conflicts between different ethnic and religious groups.

Myanmar urbanism

Incremental if inconsistent market reform from the 1990s onward has already spurred informal and unplanned urbanisation, leading Myanmar's elite to fear that globalisation will produce chaotic, faceless cities that are no longer Myanmar in character. However, what is a Myanmar city? Are national and municipal identities synonymous and how do these conceptions intersect with ideas of developed and modern cities? In interrogating the teleology of development, Urban Studies scholars have also called for alternative and indigenous urbanisms that focus on local variations and histories as central characteristics of Asian cities rather than as deviations from the developed norm. As the political and economic reforms initiated in 2011 continue to increase urbanisation, what will become Myanmar's urbanism?

Since the colonial era, Yangon and Mandalay have been the two most prominent cities and represent contrasting images of Myanmar urbanism. Yangon, designed by the British, is often described as a former cosmopolitan gateway that opened Burma to the world. In contrast, Mandalay, built by King Mindon, the penultimate ruler of the last Burman dynasty, is known as the Burman cultural heartland that needs to be defended against foreign encroachment. As national reform ushers in more foreign influences, many cities will have to negotiate a path between embracing modernisation and safeguarding tradition, however ill-defined. In the narrative of urban development, city building is a process of creative destruction and modernity consumes tradition. However, as we see in the built environment of most cities, tradition and modernity are mutually constituted. The urban fabric is almost always a patchwork of old and new, decay and growth. Indeed, Mandalay's tradition is in the form of a fortress wall encircling a replica of the Yadanabon palace complex that was rebuilt in the 1990s. The original was founded by King Mindon in 1857. Yadanabon palace was occupied by the British as Fort Dufferin after the third and final Anglo-Burmese War in 1885 and then destroyed in World War II. Just outside the palace walls are concrete and glass apartments, shopping centres and hotels, standing in stark contrast to the physical remnants of tradition. Similarly, Yangon is Myanmar's most modern city not because of its few glass towers but because of its grand colonial buildings that once represented the height of modernity. In international media, Yangon is usually represented as a former colonial capital and its fading colonial monuments garner the most attention, usually identified as the key asset for renewing the city.

This definition of Yangon as a cultural commodity to be traded in the world market suggests a condition of 'postcoloniality' wherein the city's elite endeavour to generate interest by selling Yangon's aesthetic attributes (Appiah 1991). However, it also makes an inclusive Myanmar urbanism possible. Yangon can be an iconic Myanmar city without being purely Myanmar. The elite promoting the conservation of Yangon's colonial core portray the downtown as a cosmopolitan centre where pagodas, monasteries, churches, mosques, Hindu and Sikh temples, and a synagogue represent the diversity and inter-religious harmony in the city. Anti-Indian riots during the colonial era and the public expression of anti-Muslim sentiments after 2011 both challenge this depiction. However, the approximately 100 years of peaceable coexistence between various ethnic and religious groups in Yangon is proof of the city's historic diversity. Whether this atmosphere of tolerance will continue into the future remains to be seen. In other cities, such as Meiktila and Lashio, explicit anti-Muslim violence has resulted in death and serious injury, and in Mandalay, anti-Chinese sentiments have been simmering for years. The cosmopolitan ideal presented by Yangon will be tested as neoliberal globalisation and urbanisation exerts increasing pressure on the city. In India, Egypt, Lebanon and other countries, religion and ethnicity have been increasingly invoked in urban struggles, particularly over space for housing and livelihood (Roy & Al Sayyad 2004).

Conclusion

Even before the initiation of reform in 2011, Myanmar's cities were not meeting the housing and infrastructural needs of its people. According to DHSHD, the annual demand for housing without factoring in rural to urban migration is 20,000 units, but in 2013, only 7,000 were produced (McVitty 2015). To meet the demand, DHSHD is working with private investors to build an average of 50,000 houses annually, some of them in periurban areas with established informal settlements (Paing 2013). Similarly, the Yangon Electricity Supply Board (YESB) is seeking a public–private partnership to improve their services. The electricity infrastructure is dated, incomplete and inefficient, and according to YESB's vice-chairman Maung Maung Latt, requires a dramatic upgrade. This courting of capital is understandable given the shortage of revenue in the subnational and local governments. However, for a state that has largely failed to work for public good, and where profits from national resources such as natural gas have been channelled into private bank accounts, privatisation further debilitates the public. Privatisation easily becomes neoliberal encroachment on public space and the public itself. In Myanmar where a public has yet to form, privatisation could suffocate the various civil society groups before they can gather together the diversity of people in Myanmar's cities into a coherent public.

Notes

1 This of course excludes anyone who does not have official residency documents. In Yangon, there are significant populations of migrants who live in informal settlements in areas such as Dagon Seikkan and Hlaing Thaya. However, as yet, there is no reliable statistic.

2 This likely reflects the low level of interest among the electorate. Thank you to U Khin Zaw Win, Director of Tampadipa Institute, for pointing this out on 18 August 2016.

3 In the 2015 Asia Foundation report, *Municipal Governance in Myanmar*, municipal elections were held only twice: in Rangoon in 1949 and in other major cities in 1951. However, Donald Seekins states that elections for the municipal council were held every three years until 1958. See Seekins, D. 2010. *State and Society in Modern Rangoon*. London & New York: Routledge, 81. I am currently researching the history of Rangoon but do not have conclusive data.

4 I discuss this in more detail in Roberts, J. 2016. 'Hybrid places in a former colonial capital'. In *Mapping Chinese Rangoon: Place and Nation among the Sino-Burmese*, edited by J. L. Roberts. Seattle: University of Washington Press.

5 Myanmar geographers such as Than Than Nwe and U Win have published studies about the physical structure and growth of Myanmar's cities. See Nwe, T. T. & U. Win. 2011. 'A preliminary review on the urbanization of Bago (Pegu) Division of Myanmar (Burma)'. Research on Urbanization in Burma/Myanmar, 25 September. Accessed November 2015. Available from: http://urban-research-burmamyanmar.blogspot.com.au/. In addition, Naing Oo provided an analysis of urbanisation and economic development in Burma.

6 In the case of *cheng*, the word that has come to mean city in modern Chinese, they began as market towns and, as they grew in economic significance and were deemed worthy of having city walls, came under increasingly direct rule of the emperor; see Johnson, L. C. 1995. *Shanghai: From Market Town to Treaty Port, 1074–1859*. Stanford: Stanford University Press.

7 Thanks again to U Khin Zaw Win for pointing out the following on 18 August 2016: 'The lines of demarcation between these two region governments and the respective mayors is not clear. The chief minister is regarded as senior and in the past pecking order this was accepted. But more assertive and able mayors could change things.'

8 This categorisation is based on form of municipal governance. Alternative conceptions have a four-tiered system: capital city, national economic growth centre, secondary regional growth centre and other towns with different growth potentials.

9 Conversation with Daw Hlaing Maw Oo, Secretary, Yangon City Development Committee, 14 November 2014.

10 I have been enquiring into the naming of municipal governments since 2008 but have yet to uncover documents that discuss the name. Conversations with Burmese friends suggest that the use of

si-bin-tha-ya is unusual and only associated with the names of Yangon City Development Committee and Mandalay City Development Committee. Some even said that *si-bin-tha-ya* would not be used in any other context and did not know about the local Development Affairs Offices.

References

Appiah, K. A. 1991. 'Is the Post in Postmodernism the Post in Postcolonial?' *Critical Inquiry* 17: 336–357.

Arnold, M., Y. T. Aung, S. Kempel & K. P. C. Saw. 2015. 'Municipal Governance in Myanmar: An Overview of Development Affairs Organizations'. Discussion Paper No. 7, Asia Foundation, July. Accessed August 2016. Available from: http://asiafoundation.org/resources/pdfs/MunicipalGovernanceinMyanmarENG.pdf.

ASEAN Briefing. 2015. 'Asian Highway to Link India, Myanmar, and Thailand'. ASEAN, 4 September. Accessed November 2015. Available from: www.aseanbriefing.com/news/2015/09/04/asian-highway-to-link-india-myanmar-and-thailand.html?utm_source=iContact&utm_medium=email&utm_campaign=Asia%20Briefing&utm_content=ab-flyer-sept-08-as.

Cheesman, N. 2015. *Opposing the Rule of Law*. Cambridge: Cambridge University Press.

Furnivall, J. S. 1948. *Colonial Policy and Practice: A Comparative Study of Burma and Netherlands India*. Cambridge: Cambridge University Press.

Furnivall, J. S. 1957. *An Introduction to the Political Economy of Burma*. Rangoon: People's Literature Committee & House.

Harvey, D. 2008. 'The right to the city'. *New Left Review* (53): 23–40.

Htut, T. 2013. 'National Brief Report on the Status of Implementation of the Istanbul Programme of Action (IPOA) for Least Developed Countries for the Decade 2011–2020'. Foreign Economic Relations Department, Ministry of National Planning and Economic Development, Republic of the Union of Myanmar. Accessed October 2015. Available from: http://unohrlls.org/custom-content/uploads/2013/11/Myanmar-Speech.pdf.

Johnson, L. C. 1995. *Shanghai: From Market Town to Treaty Port, 1074–1859*. Stanford: Stanford University Press.

Lefebvre, H. 1996. *Writings on Cities; Selected, Translated and Introduced by Eleonore Korman and Elizabeth Lebas*. Oxford: Blackwell.

Lieberman, V. 2003. *Strange Parallel: Southeast Asia in Global Context, c. 800–1830*. Cambridge: Cambridge University Press.

McVitty, J. 2015. 'An overview of the housing sector in Myanmar: A country in transformation'. *Housing Finance International* 29 (4): 27–32.

Nwe, T. T. 1998. 'Yangon: The emergence of a new spatial order in Myanmar's capital city'. *Sojourn: Journal of Social Issues in Southeast Asia* (13): 86–113.

Nwe, T. T. & U. Win. 2011. 'A Preliminary Review on the Urbanization of Bago (Pegu) Division of Myanmar (Burma)'. Research on Urbanization in Burma/Myanmar, 25 September. Accessed November 2015. Available from: http://urban-research-burmamyanmar.blogspot.com.au/.

Oo, H. M. 2015. 'Regional cities and corridors in Myanmar'. Urban Systems in Southeast Asia I, Naypyitaw and Mandalay, Myanmar, September 7–14.

Paing, M. S. 2013. 'Burma to build 1 million houses in 20 years'. *The Irrawaddy*, 10 January.

Pearn, B. R. 1939. *A History of Rangoon*. Rangoon: American Baptist Mission Press.

Roberts, J. L. 2016. 'Hybrid Places in a Former Colonial Capital'. In *Mapping Chinese Rangoon: Place and Nation among the Sino-Burmese*, edited by J. L. Roberts. Seattle: University of Washington Press.

Roy, A. 2005. 'Urban informality: Toward an epistemology of planning'. *Journal of the American Planning Association* (71): 147–158.

Roy, A. & N. Al Sayyad. 2004. *Urban Informality: Transnational Perspectives from the Middle East, Latin America and South Asia*. Lanham, Maryland: Lexington Books.

Seekins, D. 2010. *State and Society in Modern Rangoon*. London & New York: Routledge.

Sein, D. M. 1973. *The Administration of Burma*. London: Oxford University Press.

UN-HABITAT. 2012. 'UN-HABITAT Supports Establishment of the Urban Research and Development Institute (URDI) in Myanmar'. Regional Office for Asia and the Pacific, Fukuoka, 20 January. Accessed August 2016. Available from: www.fukuoka.unhabitat.org/projects/voices/myanmar/detail01_en.html.

8
RURAL

Ardeth Maung Thawnghmung

Approximately 70 per cent of the population of Myanmar—those living outside the cities of Yangon, Mandalay, and Naypyitaw and several major towns—can be defined as 'rural' residents. They tend to live in thinly populated areas with few paved streets and limited access to electricity, sewerage, and clean drinking water. These residents also have limited access to schools, healthcare, and higher education, and experience higher rates of poverty compared with their urban counterparts (IHLCA Project Technical Unit 2010). Agriculture is the main occupation of rural dwellers, but a minority earn a living as petty traders, shop owners, and operators of transport businesses. This chapter begins with a sketch of the main features that distinguish rural from urban areas in Myanmar. It then turns to general living conditions in rural areas and the challenges faced by rural populations in different regions of the country. Lastly, the chapter dwells on how rural residents use a variety of strategies to help them cope with multiple economic stresses.

For a start, what distinguishes 'rural' from 'urban'? There are no agreed and universal distinctions between urban and rural areas, especially for Myanmar. While each country has developed its own definitions in accordance with its own needs, most assessments employ criteria based on lifestyle, standard of living, and the degree of concentration of the population (UN Stats 2016). Some employ additional criteria such as the proportion of the economically active population employed in agriculture, the general availability of electricity and/or piped water in domestic living areas, and the level of access to medical care, schools, and recreation facilities.

Locating rural Myanmar

Myanmar's rural population includes people from a wide variety of ethnic, religious, and geographical backgrounds encompassing coastal, dry and arid, and mountainous environments. The extensive coastline of almost 3,000 kilometres stretches from the western part of the country to its southernmost tip—from the Rakhine coast (along the Bay of Bengal), to the Ayeyarwaddy Delta and the Gulf of Moattama (Martaban) through to the Tanintharyi coast adjacent to the Andaman Sea. Rakhine State, Ayeyarwaddy Region, Yangon Region, Mon State, and Tanintharyi Region all include substantial areas of coastline. Myanmar's coastal regions generally enjoy fertile soils, abundant rain, and productive fisheries and forests. The majority of residents of coastal areas rely on farming (mainly rice), fishing, aquaculture, and logging for their livelihoods.

Myanmar's mountainous periphery—encompassing areas over 1,000 feet above sea level—includes two-thirds of the country's townships and is home to 42 per cent of the national population (Food Security Working Group 2011, 1). The mountainous areas include the states of Kachin, Shan, Kayah, Kayin, and Chin and parts of the Bago and Sagaing regions. Agriculture is the main source of livelihood, but crops and agricultural practices vary depending on the local conditions and the ethnic and cultural groups that occupy specific 'elevation layers'. For example, in Shan State, Shan people often grow paddy rice in the valleys, Palaung have a reputation for cultivating tea at middle elevations, and Kachin grow millet and maize at higher altitudes (Food Security Working Group 2011, 13). Opium is also grown extensively at high and medium elevations in Myanmar's remote areas, especially in Shan and Kachin states and increasingly in Chin and Kayah states. It is a valuable crop for impoverished farmers because of its high market price, and also because it can be grown, without irrigation or chemical inputs, on slopes at high altitudes (UNODC 2012).

With the exception of Chin State, Myanmar's mountain regions have rich mineral deposits (chiefly jade, gold, and rubies), other natural resources, and what were once dense forests. However, these areas remain relatively underdeveloped due to poor roads and infrastructure and the presence of non-state armed groups fighting for greater autonomy from the central government. Much of the revenue from activities based on resource extraction in these areas is pocketed by state authorities and their cronies at the expense of the local population (see Buchanan et al. 2013).

The 'dry zone' encompasses Mandalay, Magway, and Lower Sagaing in central Myanmar. This region is marked by high temperatures, irregular rainfall, drought and extreme water scarcity, and barren soils. As a result, it suffers from low rates of agricultural productivity and high levels of food insecurity, indebtedness, and poverty. Some dry-zone areas—such as Sagaing and Magway—rely on extensive irrigation networks to produce rice and drought-resistant, edible oil crops such as sesame and groundnut, as well as a variety of dried beans and legumes. Petroleum and natural gas are also produced in Magway.

Livelihood and welfare

Official census data published in 2015 shows that little economic change has occurred in rural areas of Myanmar since 1973, although those changes that are discernible vary from region to region (see Table 8.1). The proportion of urban residents at the national level is 30 per cent, but it is 17 per cent in Sagaing Region and Rakhine State. Generally speaking, rural areas have lagged behind urban areas judging by all socio-economic criteria (see Table 8.2). Agriculture, hunting, and forestry, for instance, employ approximately 64 per cent of rural residents, but only 7.1 per cent of the urban populations.

Table 8.1 Population changes between 1973 and 2014 (census data)

	1973 census	*2014 census*
Population	35,442,972	50,279,900
Rural (%)	76	70
Urban (%)	24	30

Sources: Maung (1986, 9); Ministry of Immigration and Population (2015, 1).

Table 8.2 The rural–urban divide in Myanmar[a]

	% of rural residents	*% of urban residents*	*Total*
Poverty rate	29.2	15.7	25.6[b]
Proportion of population	70	30	—
Infant mortality rate (deaths per 1,000 births)	68	41	62
Life expectancy	65.5	72.1	66.8
Proportion literate	87	95.2	89.5
Household units with bamboo walls	56.3	38.1	51.2
Access to water seal toilets (improved pit latrine)	66.4	87.1	72.2
Electricity as main type of energy for lighting	14.9	77.5	32.4
Electricity as main type of energy for cooking	5.6	44	16.4
Firewood as main type of energy for cooking	86.2	25.6	69.2
Ownership – TV set	39.2	75.8	35.5
Ownership – mobile phone	21	63.5	32.9
Ownership – internet at home	17	2	6.2
Ownership – car/truck/van	8.1	1.2	3.1

Sources: [a]Ministry of Immigration and Population (2015, 23–34).
[b]The United Nations Development Programme (UNDP) (2010, 16).

A nationwide Rural Development and Poverty Alleviation Programme initiated by the government of President Thein Sein (2011–2015) resulted in improvements across the board—from the number of low-interest loans and microfinance packages provided by government, farmers' associations, and local and international NGOs, to an increase in irrigated farmland, electricity coverage, and the provision of mobile phones to a growing number of schools and hospitals. While these changes have improved the welfare of some sectors of the rural population, they have failed to transform the rural economy. Their effects have also been uneven depending on the locality and make-up of a given regional economy. In addition, a number of persistent challenges continue to undermine the welfare of rural people.

Insufficient income

The first common challenge confronting rural populations is their dependence on agriculture—crops, livestock, and fishing—as their main source of income; such activities are usually unable to meet residents' needs and are often unpredictable. This situation can be attributed to the high cost of agricultural inputs, low prices for produce, extreme weather fluctuations, and poor infrastructure (MSU & MDRI/CESD 2013, 10).[1] High input costs result from labour shortages, high-interest agricultural loans, the high cost of fuel, and poor transport and irrigation networks (MSU & MDRI/CESD 2013, 51–55). The continuing outflow of the population from rural areas has resulted in a shortage of daily wage labourers, driving up the cost of planting, harvesting, and clearing the land.

Extreme weather events

The second shared challenge faced by rural communities is a marked increase in the frequency and scale of natural disasters—both droughts and floods—which have destroyed crops on a large scale and seriously undermined the rural economy and the viability of working on the land. The most devastating example was Cyclone Nargis, which killed more than 138,000 people in the Irrawaddy Delta in 2008. In August 2015, rural areas were hard hit by massive floods which affected 1.6 million people across 12 states and regions, displaced 400,000 households, and destroyed nearly 1 million acres of farmland (Myint 2015). In addition to these major natural catastrophes, farming communities frequently suffer the consequences of natural disasters on a lesser scale. For example, an estimated 50,000 acres of coastal aquaculture shrimp ponds were damaged by Cyclone Giri, which hit parts of the Rakhine district in 2010 (Joffre & Moe Aung 2012, 9).

While extreme fluctuations in weather conditions are a global phenomenon, in Myanmar the effects have been exacerbated by large-scale mechanisation of the mining sector, timber extraction, commercial farming, and infrastructural development that has placed additional stresses on the environment (Buchanan et al. 2013, 40). According to the Burma Environmental Working Group,

> mining operations have drained water resources, caused severe soil erosion and polluted rivers with mercury (gold mining) and other chemicals. Intensive logging has also been shown to be directly responsible for floods, soil erosion, landslides, sedimentation, build-up behind dams, river siltation, increased dry season water, stunted farm productivity and declining topsoil fertility.
>
> *Buchanan et al. 2013, 40*

Depletion of natural resources

The third major challenge faced by rural populations is the depletion of natural resources—for example, fresh water, fish stocks, and forest products. The degree and scale of resource extraction intensified after the military regime opened up Myanmar to foreign investment in the 1990s with respect to mining, fisheries, and logging. Fishing ventures, for instance, were intensified following the liberalisation regime introduced in the early 1990s which allowed private investors to exploit Myanmar's relatively unexplored coastal waters. Official figures, which are frequently underreported, indicate that the marine fish catch has increased from 949,000 metric tonnes in 2000 to 2,060,000 metric tonnes in 2009 (Department of Livestock, Fisheries and Rural Development 2010). Although the government stopped issuing new offshore fishing licences in response to a report on the alarming rate of marine resource depletion, it was too little, too late. Freshwater fisheries have also been gradually depleted by intensive harvesting as well as by pollutants from factory waste and from mining. In Kachin State, for example, the runoff from large open-pit gold mines, along with smaller, unregistered mines, has killed off most of the fish species in local rivers. Large numbers of dead fish floating on the surface have been reported from several areas of the country (7Day Daily News 2015).

Large-scale aquaculture, while boosting farmers' incomes in the short term, has also reduced fisheries stocks. One pertinent example is the practice of 'trap and hold' shrimp farming in Rakhine State, an intensive production system which was widely adopted in the 1990s and led to the destruction of large areas of mangrove forest in order to construct large open holding areas—which vary in size between 2 and 100 acres.[2] This practice does not allow shrimp to spawn as they do in their natural environment, as it involves trapping juveniles at sea during high tides in the spring and raising them with little or no feed for a period of around three-and-a-half months. The mature shrimps are filtered and harvested when they make for the ocean, carried on the receding tide, an event that takes place over two cycles per month. Shrimp farming also depletes fishing stocks as a variety of species are no longer able to lay their eggs in protective mangrove forests. Shrimp ponds also destroy rice fields, which become inundated with salt water.[3]

As a consequence of all these developments, the fishery sector—including both marine fishing and aquaculture—experienced a gradual decline in productivity in the early 2000s after experiencing two decades of growth. In an interview with the author in 2011, a cold storage operator from Rakhine State remarked that 'in the past, a fishing boat carrying 100 tonnes of fish was filled up in a week; now it takes forty days to fill the same boat'.[4] The size of fish taken is also getting smaller, and these undersized specimens or 'trash fish' are processed for animal feed. This practice undermines the whole food chain, depriving bigger fish of their natural prey. This situation has led to intense competition among small-scale local fishermen who increasingly rely on prohibited methods such as trawling, poisoning, or fishing out of season.[5] Enforcement measures to stamp out illegal fishing have largely failed, as poorly paid and under-resourced civil servants have frequently engaged in corrupt practices as a means of supplementing their incomes.

Timber and mining extraction carried out on a massive scale by large private operators using heavily mechanised methods has likewise deprived many rural populations of access to basic foodstuffs, forest and other products, and opportunities to make a living. The UN Food and Agriculture Organisation reported in 2011 that, on average, Myanmar has lost just over 1 per cent (or 800 hectares) of its forest cover every year since 1990, or more than 7 million hectares in all (IRIN News 2011). Deforestation also deprives wild animals of shelter and food, leading to frequent incursions of wild elephants, boar, and flocks of birds, which destroy crops and (in the case of elephants) sometimes kill villagers. A flagrant example of such exploitation occurred in the 1990s in northern and northeast Burma, where illegal logging and mining was carried out on a massive scale after the military concluded ceasefire agreements with a number of ethnic armed groups (Facts and Details 2013).

According to a recent study, mangrove forest cover in the Ayeyarwady Delta shrank by 64.2 per cent between 1978 and 2011, due to harvesting wood for fuel and conversion to rice paddies. It is projected that the country's mangroves will disappear by 2044 if the current rate of deforestation continues (Webb et al. 2014). Mangrove loss directly undermines the livelihoods and even the survival of rural residents, as mangroves function as nurseries for aquatic species, a bulwark against coastal erosion, and a buffer lessening the impact of extreme storms.

Although President Thein Sein's government oversaw the building and repair of irrigation networks, they are still inadequate and ill-prepared for severe drought conditions. Massive hydroelectricity dams have also been constructed at various locations without conducting social and environmental impact assessments or obtaining consent from local populations. These projects have generated concerns among activists and local populations alike over their potential to flood and divert waterways, destroy indigenous cultures and devastate their land, and fuel ethnic conflict—most of the projects are located in ethnic minority areas affected by long-running civil wars between the central government and various ethnic groups (Vrieze 2015).[6] A pertinent example is the Myitsone river project in Kachin State, a massive 1,055 megawatt hydroelectric power plant that was constructed with Chinese funding and displaced around 15,000 people in order to supply power mainly to Chinese citizens across the border. Completion of the project was postponed by U Thein Sein in 2011 after he ceded to domestic pressure (Mon 2011).

Land tenure insecurity

Land tenure insecurity is the fourth major challenge faced by rural communities. Until recently, Myanmar farmers were subject to the 1953 Land Nationalisation Act, which recognised the state as the ultimate owner of the country's lands and resources, and prohibited farmers from mortgaging, selling, or transferring their land use rights. In 1991, the government created a new policy to promote public and private investment in agricultural crops, livestock breeding, and aquaculture enterprises under the control of the Central Committee for the Management of Cultivable Land, Fallow Land and Waste Land, which allowed owners to lease a maximum of 5,000 acres for 30 years to private investors (Leckie & Simperingham 2009, 605–607). Investors were exempted from tax collection for a period of two to eight years.

The early 1990s witnessed land grabbing by the army, government ministries, domestic enterprises, and private citizens for economic activities, including the cultivation of commercial crops, extractive industries such as gold and jade mining, oil and gas pipeline construction, and the establishment of special economic zones (SEZs). Crony companies and powerful families with links to the military government were granted titles to large tracts of 'waste' lands, which, however, often contained scattered areas being cultivated by farming communities. Many of these small farmers had been settled on these lands for generations, often without registering their plots for permanent land use rights, and were operating under customary law on lands that were categorised as 'fallow' or 'waste' in the official record. There has not been any reliable data on the percentage of rural households which have land use certificates (LUCs). Andersen estimated that only 15 per cent of farmers in Myanmar have official land use certificates, but official figures revealed that 5.3 million LUCs were issued by the end of 2015 (Andersen 2015, 3). The latter figure accounts for half to two-thirds of households (or 8.5 million households) with an average of six people per household.

In recent times, Kachin State and northern Shan State have witnessed the country's highest incidence of land grabbing by Chinese companies—and local concerns with Chinese backing—in order to grow rubber, cassava, and other cash crops (Woods 2015, 44). In 2006, each of the two Burmese companies with alleged Chinese financial backing—Yuzana and Jadeland—received concessions amounting to approximately 200,000 hectares to grow cassava and other crops in Hukawng Valley Tiger Reserve. This expansive valley—21,890 square kilometres—contains one of the world's most important tiger sanctuaries and provides habitat for an array of other endangered species, most of which are on the verge of extinction due to poaching for the Chinese market and changing patterns of land use (Martov 2012). This project displaced some 600 local families. Yuzana Company had cleared valuable hardwoods and sold them in the local and regional markets and imported workers from Thailand, central Myanmar, and delta regions, but has planted only approximately 20,000 acres of the concession. Jadeland Company has sold part of its concessions to a mainland Chinese company for planting corn and rubber, and ceded 50,000 acre of its concession to the National Progressive Party. The former mainly focused on timber harvesting which was later stopped by the Hukawng Valley Tiger Reserve Police, while the latter has continued to face local villager resistance to clear-cut forests and plant industrial agricultural crops (Woods 2015).

Activists have expressed concerns about further land alienation that would affect the rural poor following the passing of the Farm Land Law in August 2012, which allows for the sale, transfer, lease, and mortgaging of agricultural lands to create a land market in agricultural production and investment; and the Vacant, Fallow and Virgin Lands Management Law of 2012 (the VFV Law), which governs the allocation and use of 'virgin' or abandoned land. In the same year, these two market-oriented measures were complemented by the Foreign Investment Law which offers land use rights to foreign investors for up to a total period of 70 years. In May 2013, official statistics revealed that a total of 377 domestic companies had been allocated 2.3 million acres of 'vacant, fallow, and virgin' land and 822 companies or individuals had been allocated a total of 0.8 million acres of forest land. The Ministry of Agriculture and Irrigation (MOAI) plans to convert 10 million acres of 'wastelands' to commercial agricultural production between 2000 and 2030 (Andersen 2015, 2).

The government has also set up a Farmland Management Committee, chaired by the Minister for Agriculture and Irrigation that will enable individuals to register for LUCs. Although an estimated 5.36 million LUCs were issued between January 2013 and 17 November 2014, many households still do not hold LUCs for the lands they are cultivating (Mark 2016, 7).[7] Farmers thus remain vulnerable to land grabs. In addition, some farmers have sold their land in response to the precipitous rise in land values caused by speculative pressures on farmland, with investors seeking to convert agricultural lands into higher value industrial zones or residential areas, particularly on the outskirts of cities.

In addition to these pressures, five decades of civil war have displaced many farming households and disrupted their livelihood practices. Civilian populations living in minority ethnic and border areas suffered the brunt of civil war in the 1960s, 1970s, and 1980s, and many fled to neighbouring China, India, Bangladesh, and Thailand. Today, most of them are either living as displaced people in areas near their home villages or living in refugee camps. Recent ceasefire agreements with ethnic armed groups have reduced the level of violence directed at civilians, allowed them greater freedom of movement and more humanitarian aid, and facilitated the return of displaced populations (MPSI 2014). However, there are still an estimated 140,000 people in refugee camps in the Thailand–Myanmar border area, and 100,000 Kachin people dispersed around the border with China. In addition, as of June 2016 approximately 150,000 Muslims, previously employed as farmers, fishermen, shopkeepers, trishaw drivers, and construction workers, are living in refugee camps in Rakhine State, with no opportunity to earn a living.

Coping strategies

Rural households use a variety of strategies to deal with man-made and natural disasters. Most take on multiple tasks during the agricultural off-season, while cutting expenditure on food, education for their children, and healthcare. For instance, at some times of year, lowland people move up to the hill areas to work in tea plantations in Shan State and rubber plantations in Mon State, or travel to central Myanmar to pick beans and pulses. They also seek work as rice transplanters on paddy farms in local villages or in Mon State.[8] Some households will seek assistance from local and international NGOs. Collectively, villagers pool resources to build bridges, roads, schools, and irrigation schemes and to buy electricity generators.

They also commonly intensify the use of their land and the extraction of resources. One study revealed that, in upland areas, the average period that land is left fallow to allow the soil to recover after successive mixed cropping of grains and vegetables has reduced from 15 years to between 4 and 6 years today (Food Security Working Group 2011, 13). While the use of chemical fertilisers in Myanmar remains low compared with its Southeast Asian neighbours, particularly Thailand and Vietnam, intensive farming and the over-application of fertilisers to promote productivity and increase production are increasing (MSU & MDRI 2013, 33).[9] Local fishermen also seek to improve their returns by using prohibited methods—including poison and explosives—and fishing during closed seasons. While intensive farming and fishing boosts incomes in the short term, it results in land degradation and loss of fertility, harmful health effects, and impoverishment for producers as well as consumers. In a conversation with the author, a woman in Chin State, in Myanmar's northwestern hill district, said of tomatoes and cabbages grown in her region that 'even flies that rest on them die on the spot'.[10] A fishing boat operator in Rakhine State made a similar remark about the use of chemical preservatives to speed up the drying process during the rainy season: 'Any flies that landed there didn't last long!'[11]

The more open political system introduced after 2010 has changed the configuration and dynamic of power in Myanmar by providing underprivileged populations with multiple venues for expressing their grievances. These channels are expected to be further expanded and improved after the National League for Democracy (NLD) won a landslide victory in the 2015 national elections and took over power in April 2016. The most common and immediate response of farmers to outright land occupation was to negotiate directly with the land grabbers and local authorities. However, since 2011, some farmers have appealed directly to the military Commander-in-Chief if their lands have been taken by the army. Others have approached the local authorities, media, courts, MPs, and even the president of Myanmar to gain a hearing. Some have worked with political parties and influential local leaders to get their land back. Many have made use of newly opened official channels, filing their grievances with the Parliamentary Land Investigation Commission set up by President Thein Sein at both state and regional levels. Although the process is imperfect, there are cases of farmers having their land returned as a result of using one or more of these mechanisms.[12] In 2014, the Land Investigation Commission reported that it had received 35,000 complaints in total. Of that, 6,445 cases of land confiscation were reviewed. Finally, in a report released in February 2014 the commission recommended the return of 512,204 acres of land from 745 cases it deemed to be improperly seized by the military, the government, and individuals over the past two decades (Lwin & Aung 2017).

The commission has recommended that affected farmers should receive adequate compensation from the military in cases where their land has subsequently been developed. At the same time, civil society groups have also successfully lobbied the government to recognise customary land practices through new laws and regulations.

In fighting land seizures, some farmers have initiated out of court negotiations often subsidised by supporters and development agencies. A few affected communities have engaged in negotiations outside the courts, often preventing or delaying threatened land seizures or resulting in monetary settlements. For example, in Rakhine State, civil society groups, supported by an influential Buddhist monk, have taken the lead in negotiating compensation for land taken for the Kyaukphyu SEZ, resulting in increased levels of compensation—from US$1,800–4,000 per acre—for farmers whose lands were confiscated for the SEZ (Mark 2016, 13). In Ayeyarwady, local farmers' associations have petitioned the regional government for the release of 246 farmers in Mawlamyinegyun Township who were imprisoned for resisting land seizures in 2013 and for the return of confiscated land (Mark 2016, 17).

Other farmers have resorted to protest action by refusing to pay the annual tax levied by the military to work on land it has confiscated from them, or by defiantly building houses or ploughing occupied land to challenge actions that they view as unjust (Min 2014).[13] Such protests have occurred in various parts of the country.

Migration is another common strategy adopted in many farming communities by those who find life on the land too challenging. It has been estimated that one in five members of rural households leave their home villages in search of better economic status and job opportunities. Rural migrants make their way to Yangon, Mandalay, or other urban centres seeking employment in service industries—such as domestic staff, or in restaurants, hotels, and the entertainment sector—factories, and construction work. They leave their homes either individually or as family units. Whether a migrant decides to search for work inside or outside Burma depends on a variety of factors—the distance to their intended destination, the nature of their skills, the extent of their financial resources and professional networks, and the experiences of other migrant workers from their village or neighbourhood. For example, it is estimated that 20,000 migrant workers from Ayeyarwaddy and central Myanmar now work on Mon rubber plantations and in other agricultural ventures abandoned by Mon residents who have themselves moved to Thailand in search of work. Many of these migrants, especially from ethnic areas such as Mon, Karen, Shan, Kachin, and Chin states, have crossed Myanmar's borders to take up dirty, dangerous, and demeaning jobs in Thailand, Malaysia, India, and China. In 2010, the International Organisation for Migration (IOM) estimated that 3 million out of Myanmar's total population of 50 million were working in Thailand alone.[14]

Conclusion

It is difficult to make sweeping generalisations about the living conditions, employment opportunities, and availability of resources across different rural areas of Myanmar. However, rural areas can be distinguished from their urban counterparts insofar as they trail the major cities with respect to all socio-economic measures, and they rely heavily on agriculture that is subject to the vagaries of a changing climate, and on natural resources that have been depleted at an alarming rate. They also continue to experience insecurity with respect to land tenure. Rural populations are responding to these economic challenges through recourse to a variety of economic, social, and political coping strategies. However, most of these strategies are piecemeal in character, and have limited transformative capacity.

The NLD Election Manifesto stated that in order to ensure farmers' rights and economic well-being, it would facilitate the return to farmers of illegally lost land, and payment of compensation and restitution; defend against illegal land confiscation practices; amend the existing land laws that are not appropriate for the present era; identify fallow, vacant, and virgin lands that are suitable for agriculture, and distribute these lands to landless people, providing them with legal ownership rights; establish an accurate land registry system; and work to ensure easy access to land records. Immediately after taking power on 1 April, the NLD government stepped up agricultural loans to farmers and accelerated the previous government's move to return confiscated land to individuals. In the first month after the start of the new government, the Central Review Committee on Confiscated Farm Lands and Other Lands was reformed from the earlier National Land Use Management Central Committee. The new Central Committee is headed by the Vice President Van Thio, and it incorporated greater degrees of inclusion into its subcommittees, which reach from national to village tract levels. The Committee on Confiscated Farmlands and Other Lands sent additional orders to regional governments to return lands that had been identified under the Thein Sein government. By June 2016, Parliament had already received 2,000 new land complaints, adding to the 6,000 received by the last parliament. These are positive developments; however, unless the NLD government takes drastic measures, Myanmar's rural areas will remain hostile environments for their most marginalised and vulnerable residents.

Notes

1 Agricultural income per average agricultural worker is lowest in Myanmar (at US$194) compared with its nine Southeast Asian and Asian neighbours. Michigan State University (MSU) and the Myanmar Development Resource Institute's Center for Economic and Social Development (MDRI/CESD), 2013, *A Strategic Agricultural Sector and Food Security Diagnostic for Myanmar.*

2 In 2010, 'trap and hold' shrimp farming accounted for 101,945 acres in Rakhine State.

3 Author's interview with a shrimp farmer, Sittwe, 2011.
4 Author interview, Yangon, 2011.
5 Author interview, Sittwe, 2011.
6 According to Min Khaing, director of the Department of Hydropower Implementation at the Ministry of Electric Power, Myanmar has 24 operating dams, and 7 that are under construction. The government has also signed preliminary agreements on 35 projects, including agreements with Chinese companies for the construction of at least 8 dams on the Irrawaddy River and its tributaries in Kachin State, and with Chinese and Thai firms for the building of at least 6 dams on the Salween River, which runs through Shan, Karen, and Mon States in eastern Myanmar. When completed, these combined projects are expected to increase the nation's hydropower resources from 3,011 to 43,709 megawatts. See Vrieze, Paul. 2015. 'Optimism and Concern: Mark Burma's First Workshop on Hydropower Dams'. *The Irrawaddy*, January 23.
7 *Eleven Myanmar*. 2015. 'Proposal to Help Farmers Obtain Loans'. January 10. See also Mark, Siu Sue. 2015. 'Are the Odds for Justice "Stacked Against" Them? Challenges and Opportunities to Securing Land Claims by Smallholder Farmers in Myanmar', 2016.
8 Author interviews, Mon State in 2012; and Shan State in 2011.
9 According to the 2013 MSU and MDRI report, around two-thirds of paddy farmers in Myanmar apply fertiliser to their monsoon paddy crop, while over 90 per cent apply fertiliser to the irrigated summer season crop. Application rates, however, remain low by Asian standards. See Joffre, Olivier & Moe Aung. 2012. 'Prawn Value Chain Analysis: Rakhine State, Myanmar'. Livelihoods and Food Security Trust Fund.
10 Conversation with the author, Chin State, 2011.
11 Conversation with the author, Chin State, 2011.
12 Land activists have pointed to the restrictive political environment under which the Land Investigation Commission was set up, failure to document all reported claims, and lack of cooperation by local authorities. In addition, the commission has no decision-making powers and is only mandated to investigate land grab cases, which must not date back before 1988 (the year the previous military regime seized power).
13 Land activists and lawyers in Yangon have offered to help farmers who are facing trial or who were imprisoned for joining a 'ploughing protest' in Ayeyarwady Region's Kyaiklatt Township in July 2014.
14 According to *The 2014 Myanmar Population and Housing Census Report: The Union Report*, there are approximately 2 million former nationals living outside of Myanmar. Of this number, around 1.7 million (83 per cent) are aged between 15 and 39—up to 1.1 million of whom are male. Around 70 per cent of those living outside Myanmar were reported to be living in Thailand, while 15 per cent were domiciled in Malaysia. See Ministry of Immigration and Population. 2015. *The 2014 Myanmar Population and Housing Census Report: The Union Report*, Census Report Volume 2. *Naypyitaw*: Republic of the Union of Myanmar, p. 54.

References

7Day Daily News. 2015. 'Kyaingtong Myo Naung Kana Twin Nga amya su thay sone'. *7Day Daily*, July 22.

Andersen, Kirsten Ewers. 2015. 'Analysis of Customary Communal Tenure of Upland Ethnic Groups, Myanmar'. Paper presented at the International Conference on Burma/Myanmar Studies, Chiang Mai, July 24–25.

Buchanan, John, Tom Kramer & Kevin Woods. 2013. *Developing Disparity: Regional Investment in Burma's Borderlands*. Amsterdam: Transnational Institute.

Department of Livestock, Fisheries and Rural Development. 2010. *Ministry of Livestock and Fisheries, Fishery Statistics 2009–2010*. Yangon: Republic of the Union of Myanmar.

Eleven Myanmar. 2015. 'Proposal to Help Farmers Obtain Loans'. January 10.

Facts and Details. 2013. 'Deforestation and Illegal Logging in Myanmar'. Accessed August 2016. http://factsanddetails.com/southeast-asia/Myanmar/sub5_5h/entry-3145.html.

Food Security Working Group. 2011. 'Upland Land Tenure Security in Myanmar: An Overview, Yangon'. Accessed August 2016. www.burmalibrary.org/docs16/FSWG-Upland_Land_Tenure_Security-2011-02-ocr-en-red.pdf.

IHLCA Project Technical Unit. 2010. 'Integrated Household Living Conditions Survey in Myanmar IHLCS (2009–2010)—Poverty Profile, Yangon: Republic of the Union of Myanmar'. Accessed August 2016. www.mm.undp.org/content/myanmar/en/home/library/poverty/publication_1.html.

IRIN News. 2011. 'Deforestation Threatens Breadbasket'. November 14.
Joffre, Olivier & Moe Aung. 2012. 'Prawn Value Chain Analysis: Rakhine State, Myanmar', Livelihoods and Food Security Trust Fund. Accessed August 2016. www.lift-fund.org/downloads/call_for_proposal/Final_Report_VCA_Prawn_Sector_Rakhine.pdf.
Leckie, Scott & Ezekiel Simperingham (eds). 2009. *Housing, Land, and Property Rights in Burma: The Current Legal Framework*. Geneva: Displacement Solutions & The HLP Institute.
Lwin, Ei Ei Toe & Noe Noe Aung. 2017. 'MPs Pressure Government to Return Farmland'. *The Myanmar Times*. Accessed February 2017, www.mmtimes.com/index.php/national-news/10923-mps-pressure-govt-to-return-farmland.html.
Mark, Siu Sue. 2016. 'Are the Odds for Justice "Stacked Against" Them? Challenges and Opportunities to Securing Land Claims by Smallholder Farmers in Myanmar'. *Critical Asian Studies* 48(3): 443–460.
Martov, Seamus. 2012. 'World's Largest Tiger Reserve "Bereft of Cats"'. *The Irrawaddy*, November 16.
Maung, M. Ishmael Khin. 1989. 'The Population of Burma: An Analysis of the 1973 Census'. East West Population Institute, Number 96, East West Center, Honolulu, Hawaii, 9.
Michigan State University (MSU) and the Myanmar Development Resource Institute's Center for Economic and Social Development (MDRI/CESD). 2013. 'A Strategic Agricultural Sector and Food Security Diagnostic for Myanmar, USAID'. Accessed August 2016. http://fsg.afre.msu.edu/Myanmar/myanmar_agricultural_sector_diagnostic_july_2013.pdf.
Min, Thet. 2014. 'Desperate "Ploughing Protesters" to Get Legal Assistance'. *Eleven Myanmar*, October 17.
Ministry of Immigration and Population. 2015. *The 2014 Myanmar Population and Housing Census Report: The Union Report*. Census Report Volume 2. Naypyitaw: Republic of the Union of Myanmar.
Mon, Kyaw Hsu. 2011. 'President Halts Dam'. *The Myanmar Times*, October 9.
Myint, Moe. 2015. 'Civil Society Groups to Cooperate on Flood Rehabilitation Efforts'. *The Irrawaddy*, August 24.
The Myanmar Peace Support Initiative (MPSI). 2014. *Lessons Learned from MPSI's Work Supporting the Peace Process in Myanmar: March 2012 to March 2014*. Yangon: The Myanmar Peace Support Initiative. Accessed August 2016. http://reliefweb.int/sites/reliefweb.int/files/resources/Report_Lessons-learned-supporting-the-peace-process_MPSI_Mar2014.pdf.
UNDP. 2010. *Integrated Household Living Conditions Survey in Myanmar IHLCS (2009–2010) — Poverty Profile*. Yangon: UNDP.
UNODC. 2012. 'South-East Asia Opium Survey 2012: Laos PDR, Myanmar'. Accessed June 3, 2013. www.unodc.org/documents/crop-monitoring/sea/SouthEastAsia_Report_2012_low.pdf.
UN Stats. 2016. 'Population Density and Urbanization'. Accessed August 2016. http://unstats.un.org/unsd/demographic/sconcerns/densurb/densurbmethods.htm.
Vrieze, Paul. 2015. 'Optimism and Concern: Mark Burma's First Workshop on Hydropower Dams'. *The Irrawaddy*, January 23.
Webb, Edward L., Nicholas R. A. Jachowski, Jacob Phelps, Daniel A. Friess, Maung Maung Than & Alan D. Ziegler. 2014. 'Deforestation in the Ayeyarwady Delta and the Conservation Implications of an Internationally-Engaged Myanmar'. *Global Environmental* (24): 321–333.
Woods, Kevin. 2015. 'Commercial Agriculture Expansion in Myanmar: Links to Deforestation, Conversion Timber, and Land Conflicts'. Forest Trends Report Series. Accessed August 2016. http://forest-trends.org/releases/uploads/Conversion_Timber_in_Myanmar.pdf.

9

BORDERLANDS

Patrick Meehan and Mandy Sadan

Myanmar's distinctively shaped mainland borderline encloses a country that stretches from the high mountain peaks of the extended eastern Himalayan massif in the north to a narrow strip of land squeezed between the Titiwangsa mountains and the Andaman Sea in the south. The land borders constitute a near abroad for Myanmar that is politically, economically and culturally diverse, making it also diplomatically challenging for national governments: Bangladesh, India (including some of its least developed northeastern 'tribal' areas), the People's Republic of China (incorporating Tibet), Laos and Thailand are all Myanmar's immediate neighbours. Some parts of this extensive land border in the north have never been fully demarcated and every point along the borderline can be a porous interface. The official crossing points and red lines that are drawn on the large-scale national map are often subverted at a smaller scale by multiple illicit and hidden local pathways, sometimes of considerable historical longevity and significance. These land-based 'cross-border' routes and tracks have long sustained the various armies and militias that have made Myanmar's 'borderlands' synonymous with political violence and resistance in recent decades; they have also provided pathways for the flight of civilians caught in the cross-fire between state and 'non-state' armed groups. Some of the armed ethnic nationalist movements that have emerged in these borderland environments have the dubious honour of having sustained the longest continuous intra-state conflicts seen anywhere in the modern world. The distinctive physical geography of the border regions, in which a horse-shoe of mountain ranges encloses a central Burmese river valley, goes some way to explaining how such movements of resistance could be upheld through decades against a much larger and more highly equipped national army.

In addition to its long land border, Myanmar also has an extensive maritime border. The littoral connects the mainland outwards to a world of sea-borne trade and exchange in goods, people and ideas. Historically, these flows have in turn also contributed to the 'making' of modern Myanmar. Today, however, this maritime border zone, comprising the northeastern side of the Bay of Bengal, which morphs further south into the mainland coastline of the Andaman Sea, is fast becoming a focus of renewed international concern around issues such as resource access and the illegal migration and trafficking of people. Myanmar's land borders clearly do not have a monopoly over demographic crisis and human displacement issues arising from within the country. The recent flow of people entering the Bay of Bengal is testament to that fact, as many hundreds, if not thousands, of refugees and economic migrants have been trafficked down towards the Andaman Sea and beyond in recent years.

With regard to resources, too, the maritime border regions are significant sites of contest. The rivalry in the Bay of Bengal between India and Bangladesh over oil fields has made this maritime border zone an area of regional and global concern. Myanmar has become inescapably implicated by its border proximity to this region as these issues escalate into the international arena. The maritime border continues to draw in 'new' economic and political actors, of which China and the US are the most powerful. In recent years, this has even led to new physical connections being made between Myanmar's land and sea borders. The development of pipelines that link the sea border on the west with the eastern-most land border with China are a key component of contemporary Myanmar's economic 'border integration' approach. Yet the Myanmar government's economic relationship with Chinese resource extraction companies, which desire access to the Bay of Bengal and reflect China's changing role and aspirations from the Bay to the South China Sea, have defined the scope of these developments. In turn, heightened US concerns in recent years about the international relations implications of China's maritime ambitions have meant that Myanmar has acquired a new significance in the international relations of the region as it has emerged from its former 'pariah' status in the West.

China's interest in feeding its energy requirements partly from the Bay of Bengal has contributed to producing a heightened military-economic approach to managing 'border development' in contemporary Myanmar, as shall be discussed more fully later in this chapter. Again, one can see how the sea and land border regions are being brought together by these interests. The head-waters of Myanmar's main rivers, which themselves reside in the borderlands, are also sites of major energy production enterprises capitalised by Chinese companies and have seen both large-scale dams and forced displacement of people envisaged as related components of borderland 'projects'. As the Myanmar government's most recent materialisation of the 'border development' concept, both the sea-to-land-border pipelines and the dams are seen by many living in these areas as having little to do with the development of the border regions in their own right. Unfortunately, the model of centre–periphery interaction that these enterprises demonstrate, in which the borderlands are valued mainly as sites of resource extraction and production, has largely defined the relationship of Burma/Myanmar governments to its margins in the long term, including both colonial and post-colonial regimes. It also does much to explain the volatility of these spaces over many decades.

Myanmar's modern borders, therefore, be they mainland or maritime, produce volatile and fractious spaces. Regional and global players have long played active if often covert and destabilising roles in these border regions, while successive Myanmar governments have failed to unify them in the aspiration towards more complete national integration. Yet none of this description of the dynamics associated with Myanmar's borders is unique to the contemporary situation or condition of Myanmar. The movement of peoples fleeing violence or seeking economic improvement has long been important in the process by which borders have been defined, built up and, in some areas, challenged. The shifting political and economic osmotic balance across borderlines has always made them areas of flux and movement, promoters of heterogeneity rather than homogeneity. Resource access and the movement of people have been the driving forces behind the creation of Myanmar's borders historically. Although it is common to consider 'borderlands' issues through a narrative of political structures, the Panglong Agreement and discussions about constitutional relationships, this chapter will focus on this issue of economic imbalance, constraint and opportunity, which also arises from a long process of historical interaction with different regimes at 'the centre'.

Early colonial influences in the emergence of Myanmar's borderlands

Myanmar's modern borders started to materialise at the end of the eighteenth century and the initial process was also influenced by a humanitarian crisis that saw hundreds of small vessels set out on a journey from the Bay of Bengal transporting people in search of refuge. It is a story that resonates eerily with events at the time of writing. Yet the economic potential of these spaces was what came to define them. Myanmar's modern borders began to take shape following the increasing influence of the British East India Company (EIC) upon the historic Burmese kingdom, particularly from the end of the eighteenth century onwards. The EIC was just one of the powerful, militarised trading companies that had emerged from Europe, which successively carved up the seas and ports of the region into zones of influence and then control. The expansion of the EIC into the Chittagong region of what is today Bangladesh at the end of the eighteenth century was partly a consequence of the wider shifts in geo-politics that had also seen a period of intense military activity under the Burmese Konbaung dynasty monarchs. The Konbaung dynasty's success in war had led to the great expansion of the Konbaung kingdom as the monarchs engaged in wars with Ayutthaya, Chiang Mai and Laos, eventually annexing Arakan and Manipur to the west. The Burmese invasion of Arakan in 1784 led to many years of violence and upheaval, and as a result of this, tens of thousands of Arakanese inhabitants, Hindu, Muslim and Buddhist, fled across the natural boundary line with Arakan into Chittagong. The local humanitarian crisis produced on the Chittagonian frontier led to attempts by EIC officials to delineate peoples, places and resources as being either subject to the 'King of Ava', as they called the Konbaung monarchs, or amenable to incorporation into their own sphere of influence. While there were no formal border demarcation proposals, this humanitarian crisis at the juncture of the Bay of Bengal began a process by which territorially defined spheres of interest entered the arena of international relations in a newly sharpened way and began to determine the EIC's concerns in its engagements with the historical regime of Burma.

Initially, there was no significant subversion of the 'boundary' as already understood in the geo-politics of the region. People were judged to have responsibilities towards a sovereign authority (or a proxy representative in the case of the EIC), and this would be confirmed by the payment of taxes and other dues as required. As a general concept made operational by both parties, the EIC's understanding of these obligations and rights was not too distinct from that by which the local sovereign regimes of the region determined their own, traditional spheres of control, at least superficially. Borders, where they existed, were defined largely by the geography that intervened between kingdoms and states. Borderlines or boundaries often reflected naturally occurring fracture points in systems of power: a mountain range, an estuary or delta system, for example. During this period, the British EIC was as disinclined towards territorial acquisition as an end in itself as was any local ruling authority. The expense of maintaining and protecting tracts of land made this of little appeal unless it could bring economic rewards or security. However, the impetus towards modern border lines began to take shape through the close association that the EIC made with territorial settlement and cultivation as an evidential good. They saw capitation tax rooted in land ownership as morally desirable. Environment could be read as a sign of the moral order, of 'civilisation' in places where taxation and revenue were produced by households with cultivable land. Where such an economic model was not evident, then the environment as a source of resources to be developed and made 'useful' dominated the reading of landscape. In this way, economic sovereignty, which lay at the heart of the EIC's rationale for existence, was exercised through the direct connection between authority over delineated territory and the right to tax its productive output and this was an exclusive right that could not be overlapped by any other national authority. This was the seed out of which Myanmar's modern borderlines were to grow, as British control was extended, formalised and entrenched as a form of political-economic sovereignty over the course of the next century. While the delineation of territory through borderlines was influenced by a wide range of political and other influences that could change over time, resource extraction and production and the management of populations seen as only loosely committed, if at all, to a 'national project' have been central to the thinking of governmental regimes of many varieties in Burma/Myanmar and have influenced the mentality and policy towards border regions throughout.

However, the perpetual conflict that has raged throughout the country's border regions ever since independence has encouraged a tendency to analyse the country's post-colonial borderlands through a binary prism of state versus rebel and to perceive the dominant forces shaping the borderland as a conflict between processes of militarised counterinsurgency versus insurgent resistance. The appeal of such categorisations reflects a broader tendency within the literature on state-building and conflict to draw distinct binaries between state and non-state actors. In the case of Southeast Asia, in recent years the continued use of state versus non-state categories to frame political analysis also reflects the influence of James C. Scott's work on Zomia through which a new generation is starting to take interest in borderlands in this region. Scott's conceptualisation of the region's upland borderland regions as 'non-state spaces' with histories shaped by the binary dynamics of state encroachment versus the arts of resistance has proved enticing (Scott 2009). Although seductive in their apparent ability to rationalise the complexity of Burma's conflicts, these kinds of conceptual binaries are nonetheless deeply problematic. The history of conflict across Myanmar's borderlands has never fitted easily into a single state versus anti-state dynamic. Rather, it has been underpinned by multiple conflict fault-lines and has been shaped by groups and individuals whose actions and interests have often straddled these supposed boundaries. Indeed, the history of post-colonial conflict across the border areas has been one of profound fragmentation and the proliferation of armed groups, often fighting as much against one another as against the central government. The 'motivations' of these actors have fluctuated between the material and the ideational, between predation and protection, and between localised interests and conflicts and attempts to engage with larger-scale dynamics of state encroachment and regional economic development shaping the borderland.

Borderlands during the BSPP era

Attempts by successive governments to assert greater control across the country's vast borderlands, and the forms of contestation and resistance this has evoked, have therefore also been one of the defining features of Myanmar's post-colonial history. Ever since independence, state-building ideologies of political elites have been founded upon aspirations to establish sovereign unitary control across the country's borderland spaces. Idealised notions of creating a territorially homogeneous 'modern' nation-state have, however, come up sharply against pre-existing regional networks of trade, localised structures of political authority and great diversity of cultures and languages across the borderlands. It was in the borderlands that post-colonial governments' attempts to create a territorially defined nation-state were revealed most starkly as problematic and where, as a result, violent coercion often became the dominant strategy for imposing and 'securing' the nation-state. In turn, government fears of disunity, fragmentation and treachery have often served to create 'zones of exception' in the borderlands, and government attempts to consolidate control have diverged most clearly from idealised models of statecraft.

Under General Ne Win's rule (1962–1988), the Burma Socialist Programme Party (BSPP) government's decision to resort to increasingly violent and coercive means to secure authority over border areas invariably served to inspire greater resistance. Within this battleground it was a truism that for borderland populations the region they lived in was not marginal but was the centre of their world. These populations proved unwilling to calibrate their lives to a territorial framework in which they were made peripheral. As a result, some within the borderlands continued to demonstrate greater 'loyalty' to regional economies and trade networks and localised structures of political authority, upon which their livelihoods were dependent, rather than to the nation-state of which they now found themselves to be a part. As opposition to the BSPP government hardened, the country's borderlands became 'privileged' sites of rebellion against the power of the state (van Schendel 2005, 256). They were assisted in this by the natural geography of the borderlands. The terrain of steep hills and dense forests, the lack of road networks and the challenges to travel posed by the annual monsoon rains all served to blunt state penetration. Control of strategic hilltops, river crossings, trade routes and border gates enabled a plethora of groups to generate sufficient income and protection to enable them to hold opposing forces at bay. Access to borderlines conferred further advantages, offering sanctuaries and training sites, enabling even relatively weak rebel groups to wage protracted guerrilla warfare. Cross-border trade networks and resources provided opposition groups with access to weapons, finance, medical services and information. The gross mismanagement of the domestic economy also created a thriving black market for goods illegally entering the country through its insurgent-controlled borderlands, creating further revenue-generating opportunities for those armed groups operating in these areas.

Furthermore, the socialist revolution pursued by Ne Win, the country's strict foreign policy neutralism in the midst of the Cold War and the regime's inability to secure territorial control over its borderlands aroused the self-interested concerns of other countries. This in turn enabled armed groups in the borderlands to establish foreign connections and receive their backing. Throughout the 1960s, 1970s and 1980s, Chinese patronage greatly strengthened the Communist Party of Burma (CPB), based along the China border. In turn, this enabled avowed anti-Communist movements operating along the Thai border to secure US and Thai support. Meanwhile, the country's western borderlands with India became home to a confluence of insurgent groups; those in India opposing the Indian state regularly crossed the border into Burmese territory to evade security forces, and vice versa. All of these processes reflected the fact that while attempts to solidify and 'harden' international borders were used by governments throughout the region as part of nation-state-building enterprises, these processes also acted against them by providing resistance groups with secure spaces 'beyond' the border, which for diplomatic reasons it became extremely difficult to access (van Schendel & de Maaker 2014, 6). Border-based insurgencies had a huge impact upon the trajectory of the Burmese state. Fighting insurgency posed a significant financial drain on the state's already impecunious coffers and also ensured that the Burmese military, or *Tatmadaw*, remained at the very heart of the state.

Borderlands during the SLORC era and beyond

Understanding the *longue durée* of Myanmar's border regions reveals how they have long provided 'ecologies of constraint and opportunity' for national regimes seeking to establish sovereign authority over them (Barkey 2008, 36). Furthermore, the specific spatial dynamics of these regions have been instrumental in shaping political authority far beyond the borderland itself and have played an important role in determining the trajectory of national- and regional-level political and economic developments. Over the past quarter-century these dynamics have undergone significant transformation. By the late 1980s, it was clear that the militantly authoritarian state-building strategies employed by General Ne Win since the 1962 coup were failing. Chronic economic mismanagement had left the state close to bankruptcy, insurgency remained rife throughout the country's borderlands, despite decades of brutal counterinsurgency offensives, and widespread pro-democracy protests in 1988 demonstrated that the government was losing support within the very core of the country. The emergence of Aung San Suu Kyi and the National League for Democracy (NLD) embodied a credible opposition seemingly able to win support across ethnic groups, as evidenced by the party's landslide victory in the 1990 election. Yet in many ways it was in the border regions that the failures of post-colonial state-building initiatives were revealed most starkly. The brutality of military-led counterinsurgency strategies perpetuated the heightened wariness of local populations towards the encroachment of state power; a plethora of armed groups continued to fight against the government; flourishing cross-border trade provided revenue for these groups; and ethno-nationalism and calls for federalism provided robust counter-narratives to the government's own efforts to forge popular sovereignty under a centralised unitary state.

However, new opportunities and motivations to consolidate state power were also emerging, which the State Law and Order Restoration Council (SLORC)—the new military government which had replaced Ne Win's ailing BSPP in 1988—was quick to act upon. For both political and economic reasons, processes of state re-building under the SLORC placed renewed focus upon securing greater control over the country's borderlands, especially those with China and Thailand. This ensured that, in the minds of government elites, the border regions were no longer viewed merely as a frontier to be pacified, but as spaces whose effective territorialisation would definitively determine the outcome of their state-building aspirations (Meehan 2011).

Chief amongst these reasons was the growing emphasis given to regional economic integration as a tool for development following the end of the Cold War. This served to transform the perception of borderlands across Asia from frontier regions or 'buffer zones' to economic corridors, providing greater impetus for states to invest resources in consolidating control over such areas. Since the mid-1980s China increasingly looked to Myanmar as a potentially useful economic ally. At a bilateral level, Myanmar's vast natural resources became highly coveted commodities to fuel China's industrial economy, while access to the Bay of Bengal has become integral to China's efforts to improve its energy, as noted. At a provincial level, increasing cross-border trade was viewed as a cost-effective way to ameliorate the country's coast–interior divide by stimulating economic development in land-locked Yunnan Province. At a more local level, the emergence of casino frontier towns across the border in Myanmar and the influx of tourists and gamblers that this has inspired has been a boon for otherwise remote Chinese border towns, which have provided electricity, water and internet connection to these cross-border settlements (Chenyang & Fook 2009, 272).

Similarly, India, after an initial deterioration of diplomatic ties following the Myanmar government's brutal crackdown against the 1988 pro-democracy protests, increasingly looked to border trade as a means of stimulating economic development in the northeast (Egreteau 2003). In Thailand, the emergence of a powerful business class altered domestic power relations, forcing the military, which had often viewed the presence of insurgency groups on the Thai–Myanmar border as a useful buffer against the activities of the Myanmar Army, to acquiesce to the demands of political and business leaders determined to improve economic relations with Myanmar (Thant 2006, 287, 308). Today, Myanmar's border regions stand at the apex of ambitious regional development plans. Notable examples include India's *Look East* policy in which Northeast India has come to be viewed as an important gateway to economic integration with Southeast Asia, and the Asian Development Bank-funded Greater Mekong Sub-Region (GMS) Initiative, which is designed to stimulate trade between Thailand, Laos, Cambodia, Vietnam, Yunnan Province (China) and Myanmar by establishing 'economic corridors' through borderland regions over which central governments across the region have historically commanded little authority (Swe & Chambers 2011, 6). Within Myanmar, numerous border regions have been designated as 'special economic zones' (SEZs), providing investors with tax breaks and preferential import/export rights.

Consequently, the post-1988 military government increasingly viewed the country's border regions as hugely important sites of accumulation, with resource concessions to foreign companies, primarily for logging, mining and hydropower, and the construction of oil and gas pipelines becoming central to improving the central government's finances. In many cases, the government's quest to transform the border regions into sites of resource extraction and production has led to them becoming the repository of environmentally and socially destructive forms of extraction, some of which have already been banned in neighbouring countries. The vast levels of deforestation that have decimated virgin forests across parts of Kachin, Shan, Karenni and Karen States, for example, were largely inspired by the bans imposed on logging in both China and Thailand in the late 1980s and attempts by foreign companies to move their operations to new regulatory zones across the border. In turn, resource concessions in border regions became increasingly important to central government coffers. Timber concessions granted to Thai companies, for example, generated in the region of US$135–200 million for the military government in 1989/90, amounting to more than 40 per cent of the country's total official export earnings and helping to stave off financial crisis (Bryant 1997, 13; Smith 1994, 13). Similarly, the hydropower dams that have been constructed in border regions along the Irrawaddy, Salween and Shweli Rivers, at huge environmental and social cost to local populations, have been used to generate significant income for the central government through the export of electricity. At the same time border regions have continued to suffer from chronic electricity deficits.

Economic ambitions have been greatly aided by the array of ceasefire agreements forged between the government and the majority of ethnic armed groups in the late 1980s and early 1990s. Although these agreements did not seek to address the more intractable political grievances surrounding the conflict and allowed insurgent groups to retain troops and weapons, they did serve to reduce levels of conflict across many border regions. The ceasefires can be understood as creating a 'kind of post-civil-war-not-quite-peace environment' (Callahan 2007, xiv) in which the military government's actions have been effective at 'managing conflict rather than resolving it' (Kramer 2012). Over the past twenty-five years, reduced threat of insurgency and the government's determination to wrestle economic sovereignty over border regions has precipitated sustained militarisation of these regions by the *Tatmadaw*. Growing stability has also attracted inflows of investment and growing competition not only to extract resources but also for land. In many border regions the landscape is being transformed by large-scale agribusiness concessions for an array of crops including rubber, biofuels and corn, in joint ventures between the government (or private companies closely linked to it) and/or ceasefire groups and foreign investors. Discourses of borderland development continue to be underpinned by top-down, centrally imposed mantras of modernisation which have embraced large-scale commercial enterprises with little interest in supporting smallholder agriculture that remains the backbone of livelihoods throughout the country.

As shown through Kevin Woods' analysis of the Kachin–China border area, these forms of 'ceasefire capitalism' have also been extremely important in reconfiguring the dynamics of conflict and insurgency (Woods 2011, 751). The government's granting of large-scale land concessions to both domestic and international companies has directed transnational finance into areas where state sovereignty has historically been weak. In these militarised borderland areas—where access to land and resources remains highly contested—national and transnational corporations have sought to promote functioning state institutions, especially those able to wield coercive power, viewing these institutions as the most viable way to 'fix, regulate and expand capitalist spaces' and to uphold and enforce their property 'rights' (Woods 2011, 751). Through these new 'geographies of power' the state has spearheaded processes of primitive accumulation and increased state legibility, thus converting the state's de jure sovereignty into de facto control (Woods 2011, 767). This profound reconfiguration of borderland spaces is underpinned by a powerful nexus of inter-dependent military, government and private sector power and an emerging clientele of borderland elites whose political and economic interests are vested in institutionalising, rather than resisting, state control. Amidst these changes, large areas of the country's borderlands can be understood as having transitioned, to borrow Baud and van Schendel's terminology, from 'rebellious borderlands', defined by outright powerful insurrection against the state, towards the emergence of 'unruly borderlands', where organised opposition is weak but in which local populations have continued to challenge and resist 'new social and territorial boundaries and the rules that come with them' (Baud & van Schendel 1997, 227–228)

Reflecting the diverse and complex history of Myanmar's border regions, the dynamics of ceasefires during this period have varied from place to place and over time. The strategic and economic importance of certain regions, notably major border trade gates and large-scale development sites, has inspired heavily militarised and centralised forms of control. In other areas, the financial costs and military challenges associated with securing control have remained prohibitive. This has often inspired more prosaic forms of stabilising border regions through ceasefire arrangements and/or government-by-proxy through the proliferation of government-sanctioned militias (Meehan 2015). Although significantly weakened, the border regions have also remained home to armed groups continuing to fight against the government. The political economy of border regions thus continues to be shaped by a messy and fragmented multiplicity of societal actors (including insurgent armies, ceasefire groups, the military, local militias, Thai and Chinese border security forces, national and transnational investors, and local populations), motivations, and sub-national and transnational political and economic networks. Categorical distinctions between periods of 'war' and 'non-war' are unable to capture the array of non-formal types of violence that borderland populations have continued to face during the 'ceasefire' period, which cannot easily be equated to formal measurements such as counterinsurgency-related battle-deaths. All of these factors have created deeply complex and fragmented mosaics of power and territorial control, which have differed over time.

Conclusion

Although dizzying at times in its complexity, engaging with the history and hybridity within Myanmar's border regions is essential to analysing their contemporary dynamics. Without this kind of fine-grained analysis, our understanding of Myanmar's border regions remains obscured and well-intentioned policies designed to promote development, regional integration and peace-building are likely to have unintended and potentially deleterious impacts. This has become of increasing importance in recent years following the rush of donors and NGOs seeking to support peace-building and poverty reduction in border areas. The prioritisation given to the signing of a nationwide ceasefire agreement by donors and foreign governments, for example, is in danger of obscuring engagement with the sustainability or quality of the 'post-war' peace. Indeed, although previous ceasefire agreements have brought populations significant benefits through reducing active conflict, new forms of impoverishment have coalesced around the dynamics of militarisation, commercialisation and deeply illiberal and inequitable forms of 'state-building' and 'development' during such ceasefire periods. This raises troubling questions about the kind of 'peace' and 'development' that may emerge throughout the country's border regions should a nationwide ceasefire agreement be signed. A historical political economy approach, which helps us to understand the complex local, national and transnational actors and interests surrounding attempts to manage borderland populations and resources, provides important and timely reminders of the challenges which such interventions will need to engage with.

References

Barkey, Karen. 2008. *The Ottomans in Comparative Perspective*. Cambridge: Cambridge University Press.

Baud, Michiel & Willem van Schendel. 1997. 'Toward a comparative history of borderlands'. *Journal of World History* (8): 211–242.

Bryant, Raymond. 1997. *The Political Ecology of Forestry in Burma*. London: Hurst.

Callahan, Mary. 2007. *Political Authority in Burma's Ethnic Minority States: Devolution, Occupation, and Coexistence. Policy Studies (31)*. Washington, DC: East–West Center; Singapore: ISEAS Publishing.

Chenyang, Li & Lye Liang Fook. 2009. 'China's policies towards Myanmar: A successful model for dealing with the Myanmar Issue?' *China: An International Journal* (7) 2: 255–287.

Egreteau, Renaud. 2003. *Wooing the Generals: India's New Burma Policy*. Delhi: Authorspress.

Kramer, Tom. 2012. 'Ending fifty years of military rule? Prospects for peace, democracy and development in Burma'. NOREF Report. Accessed October 2014. www.files.ethz.ch/isn/155015/00a4e800d45def2a0a82e6f0f71eb3c8.pdf.

Meehan, Patrick. 2011. 'Drugs, insurgency and state-building in Burma: Why the drugs trade is central to Burma's changing political order'. *Journal of Southeast Asian Studies* (42): 376–404.

Meehan, Patrick. 2015. 'Fortifying or fragmenting the state? The political economy of the opium/heroin trade in Shan State, Myanmar, 1988–2013'. *Critical Asian Studies* (47) 2: 253–282.

Scott, James C. 2009. *The Art of Not Being Governed: An Anarchist History of Upland Southeast Asia*. New Haven, CT: Yale University Press.

Smith, Martin. 1994. *Paradise Lost?: The Suppression of Environmental Rights and Freedom of Expression in Burma*. London: Article 19.

Swe, Thein & Paul Chambers. 2011. *Cashing in Across the Golden Triangle: Thailand's Northern Border Trade with China, Laos, and Myanmar*. Chiang Mai: Mekong Press.

Thant, Myint-U. 2006. *The River of Lost Footsteps: Histories of Burma*. London: Faber.

van Schendel, Willem. 2005. *The Bengal Borderland: Beyond State and Nation in South Asia*. London: Anthem Press.

van Schendel, Willem & Erik de Maaker. 2014. 'Asian borderlands: Introducing their permeability, strategic uses and meanings'. *Journal of Borderlands Studies* (29) 1: 3–9.

Woods, Kevin. 2011. 'Ceasefire capitalism: Military–private partnerships, resource concessions and military–state building in the Burma–China borderlands'. *Journal of Peasant Studies* (38) 4: 747–770.

10
CYBER-SPACES

Gerard McCarthy

Myanmar is in the midst of a dramatic transformation in how people consume information, maintain relationships, build communities and mobilise social movements. Media dissemination and consumption has long been acknowledged as an essential mechanism in the development of nationalism (see Anderson 1991). Drawing on Walton's argument in this volume that Myanmar has never really been a unified 'nation', this chapter focuses its attention on the role of Myanmar's fastest growing form of media—social media—in (re)formulating notions of citizenship and nation amid Myanmar's transition. This chapter opens with an overview of the history of mobile and internet access in Myanmar. It then explores the new social and political opportunities, tensions and dynamics that are emerging as a result of Myanmar's recent liberalisation, particularly of the telecommunications sector. Focusing on the emergence of low-cost, web-enabled mobile phones in recent years, it explores how these technologies interact with and alter pre-existing social networks, relationships and communication practices, opening up new spheres for activism and advocacy of various kinds including the reforging of civil–military relations and notions of citizenship. It concludes with a call for future research to recognise the interaction between online–offline action, and how this may influence the emergence of a 'national' culture in Myanmar over the coming years.

Historical context and recent reforms

Internet in Myanmar has existed since the late 1990s, though access to it—both through computers and mobile devices—was deliberately limited throughout the authoritarian period to those trusted by the regime. Telecommunications networks were developed in many parts of the country in the 1990s and 2000s through the infrastructure constructed during the successive State Law and Order Restoration Committee (SLORC) and later State Peace and Development Committee (SPDC) periods—especially in some ethnic minority areas on the fringe of the country. Despite this, the price of sim-cards was kept artificially high through regulatory mechanisms that limited access to members or associates of the state apparatus unlikely to challenge the status quo. Sim-cards thus sold for around US$2,500 until the mid-2000s, and retailed for US$100 as late as May 2014—though cheaper sim-cards were issued to members of the military-aligned Union Solidarity and Development Association (USDA)[1] and later to employees of state agencies who entered sim-card lotteries. Despite this access, figures from the

International Telecommunications Union suggests that prior to the commencement of liberalisation in 2011 Myanmar had the lowest mobile penetration rate in the world at 2.6 per cent (Qiu 2014, 381).

Liberalisation of the telecommunications sector ultimately occurred in mid-2014, after a process commenced in 2012 resulted in passage of legislation in 2013 by the USDP-led parliament and subsequent tendering process for operator licences.[2] Two international companies received licences from the Myanmar Government in June 2014, Qatari company Ooredoo and Norwegian operator Telenor. The companies began competing not just for customers but also to acquire sites for the roll-out of thousands of communication towers across the country in order to develop a national network. Throughout this process Myanmar Post and Telecommunications (MPT) upgraded many of their pre-existing towers with new receiving and transmission devices and extended into rural areas, saving the time-consuming and expensive work of developing backbone infrastructure. For Ooredoo the roll-out process has been further complicated by a consumer boycott, urged by Buddhist nationalists on the grounds that it is a 'Muslim company' based in Qatar, which has slowed both their sim-card sales and their roll-out in many Buddhist communities, as key strategic sites have been unwilling to host a tower for the company or its sub-contractors.[3]

By mid-2016, over 43 million sim-cards had been sold by telecommunications companies Telenor, Ooredoo and Myanmar Post & Telecommunications. It was estimated that around half (21.5 million) of these sim-cards regularly used internet data and 39 million had the capacity for internet use, highlighting an extraordinarily rapid uptake of low-cost, web-enabled smartphones in Myanmar, which retail in increasingly ubiquitous mobile phone shops around the country from around US$25 (Aung Kyaw Nyunt 2016).[4] The liberalisation of 2011, the lifting of media censorship and the deregulation of the telecommunications sector in 2014 have caused the rapid transformation of Myanmar's information landscape and were major reforms spruiked by President Thein Sein and parliamentarians during their re-election campaigns at the November 2015 elections.[5]

As noted elsewhere in this volume (see Kean, Chapter 15), these processes have had a particular impact on the development of the media and journalistic sector in recent years. A major part of this shift is that technological developments are facilitating the emergence of new domains of internet-mediated communication—or what I refer to here as 'cyber-space'. As has occurred elsewhere, these are creating new mechanisms to maintain and develop relationships of various kinds (see Miller 2008), and also offer ways to exploit the potential audience of millions or even billions and encourage them to engage in various forms of social, religious and political entrepreneurship essential to cultivating ideas about political community, citizenship and nationalism.

Transforming or intensifying social networks?

One of the major hopes associated with the rise of social media globally is that, with increased access to information, people are likely to be exposed to new perspectives and opinions, potentially facilitating socio-political organisation and democratisation (Diamond 2010; Tufekci & Wilson 2012; Shirky 2011; Deibert & Rohozinski 2010; Goldberg 2011; Stromback & Shehata 2010; Centola & Macy 2007). However, studies of emerging digital political spheres (Sunstein 2008, 2009; Baum & Groeling 2008) have highlighted a long-acknowledged sociological fact—that people tend to herd into groups or 'echo-chambers' where members share the same opinion or interests.[6] Contrary opinions are rarely expressed or relevant for users in these contexts.

In Myanmar, the major beneficiary of the rapid embrace of mobile phones in recent years has been Facebook, which has emerged as the primary platform of internet-based interaction across the country. Events that are of interest to the public now are increasingly encountered—and even occur first—on Facebook, prior to any other traditional media or internet site. This has led InterNews and other analysts to declare that 'Facebook is the internet in Myanmar' (Bourgault 2013).

Facebook is an archetypical example of an 'echo-chamber'. The contents of newsfeeds are determined by the posts of friends and the pages users choose to like or follow, both of which are reflective of the pre-existing social networks, class and interests of the user (see Schissler 2015). The tendency of Facebook to facilitate 'herding' was evident during my doctoral fieldwork in central-east Myanmar throughout 2015. For dozens of my informants, Facebook served as the primary platform to manage and engage with pre-existing social ties and relationships.[7] Whilst many of their newsfeeds featured posts about current events from pages they had chosen to follow such as BBC Burmese or Seven Day News Burmese, by design the vast bulk of posts were images and messages shared by friends, relatives and prominent local contacts. These focused largely on what might be considered 'everyday' events, such as visits to monasteries, lunch with friends or soccer at a local playing field—the staple of social media activity in most contexts and referred to simply as 'phatic' communication aimed at maintaining social ties (see Miller 2008).

Viewing people's Facebook experiences as a formal demonstration of their real-life networks is useful in this regard as it grounds optimistic assessments of social media's implications for 'democratisation' in the fabric of local social life. Myanmar people, and indeed Facebook users in general, rarely access entirely 'new' networks simply as a result of purchasing a web-enabled smartphone. Established social practices, such as swapping rumours and pieces of information in an attempt to construct a narrative of meaning—a deeply embedded cultural practice developed during the authoritarian period of censorship (see Schissler 2015; Fink 2001; Leehey 2012)—similarly do not disappear with the abundance of information offered by social media. Indeed, Facebook's popularity in Myanmar—as in many other social contexts—may derive at least partly from the similarity of the platform to casual, in-person interactions with kin and local community members rather than the extent to which entirely new perspectives are encountered through use.[8]

In a country where a large proportion of families have relatives living and working abroad, maintaining these social ties is made infinitely easier with the increasing availability of smartphones. As Aricat & Ling (2015) have observed, however, many still miss out on these benefits as a result of price and lack of mobile phone coverage—especially in rural and less accessible areas of the country where the telecommunications revolution has been slower to arrive than in large towns in central Myanmar (Aricat & Ling 2015). Increasingly, however, device-sharing practices within families and at communal forums such as tea and betel nut shops—similar to practices in countries such as India (see Jeffrey & Doron 2013)—likely extend the reach and impact of the number of phones, especially web-enabled devices, currently in circulation.

New forums for deliberation or compartmentalisation?

In addition to easing trans-local 'phatic' communication, for the 22 million or so people in Myanmar who, as of early 2017, have regular access to a the internet via a smartphone device, use of Facebook has also opened up new opportunities to engage with information outside friendship and kin networks, albeit mediated through the Facebook pages of prominent local social and religious actors.

For instance, even for those with access to social media, the Facebook pages of local community or religious groups that provide a range of social welfare and public goods in central Myanmar are for many the first profiles they follow outside kinship or friendship networks.[9] In my field-site in central-east Myanmar throughout 2015 and 2016, prominent volunteers with these local groups took it upon themselves to post articles and photos every day to their 5,000 followers, many of whom first came into contact with these groups through the various social services they offer such as complimentary funerals, payment of medical bills, ambulance transportation and blood donations. At various points throughout my fieldwork, the Facebook pages of these welfare groups became the focal point for controversies, rumours and campaigns.[10] On a daily basis, however, around 50 per cent of the posts were images of Buddhist monks, Pali prayers and the promotion of their own social work. The other half were more 'current events' posts, including photos of car accidents from the Yangon–Mandalay highway, national political or electoral developments, and events or occurrences elsewhere in Myanmar or internationally.

Articles about violence committed by the so-called Islamic State (IS), rumours of Al Qaeda cells within Myanmar, or posts detailing alleged 'coerced' conversion of Buddhist women, were especially prominent on these pages throughout my fieldwork in 2015. These sparked comments and processes of narrative-making by other local Facebook users who often drew on the theme of social compassion—an identity which ostensibly animates these Buddhist welfare groups—to clarify a distinction with Muslims: between 'us' and 'them' (see McCarthy 2016). 'Muslim's are evil. They don't value life like we do,' was a sentiment that recurred regularly in the comments of posts about atrocities committed by IS or other so-called Islamist armed groups. Especially in the weeks prior to the Muslim celebration of Eid al-Adha in September 2015, this sentiment was localised to focus on cruelty towards cows, with images of slaughtered bovines in Mandalay circulating online after the festival with the claim that 'Muslim's get good merit for killing animals.'

Echo-chambers, violence and defining the 'Other'

The extent to which individual Facebook networks simply act as an 'echo-chamber' in which pre-existing opinions are reinforced through the views of close social ties is evident when one is able to compare the newsfeeds of everyday Buddhists and Muslims. The rhetoric of posts about animal cruelty during Eid al-Adha stood in contrast to the images of Muslim families sharing beef curry with their neighbours that appeared in the Facebook feeds of Muslim contacts during this period, often with a similarly compassionate frame about Islamic virtues of feeding and helping the poor and needy. Similarly, periods of widespread citizen social action such as the 2015 floods—during which hundreds of thousands of people engaged in fundraising and disaster relief across the country—were regularly cited by Muslims and Buddhists alike as proof of their own virtue and morality, though often with the 'Other' referred to as 'stingy' or selfish in their provision of assistance.

Anxiety about the dehumanising language used on social media to refer to minorities has been a major feature of domestic and international commentary about Facebook in Myanmar since the outbreak of communal violence in Rakhine State in 2012. Defining the distinction between disparaging normative judgements about Muslims—often supported by alleged visual evidence—and 'hate-speech' that is inciting physical violence has proved difficult. The fear of technological advancement driving communal conflict became particularly acute after a rumour about an alleged rape of a Buddhist girl by 'Bengali-Muslim' brothers spread on Facebook in Mandalay in June 2014 after a post by extremist monk U Wirathu. In the days that followed, a seemingly coordinated riot occurred in the surrounding areas of Mandalay where the brothers ran a teashop, resulting in the deaths of two local activists—one Muslim and one Buddhist.[11] During the nights of the riots, the belief that Facebook was driving violence led the Ministry of Information to suspend the platform around the country between the hours of 9pm and 5am (see McCarthy & Menager 2015).

Efforts at controlling the spread of hate-speech[12] and incendiary imagery of violence, as well as promoting education about respectful usage of Facebook, are certainly productive—especially in cooling tempers during moments of acute communal tension. However, it would be irresponsible to suggest they are likely to erode the generalised panic about the decline of Buddhist social morality, and the broader economic grievances embedded within these rumours. As Schissler et al. (2015) have demonstrated, the online popularisation of religious justifications for righteous violence is in fact a reflection of a larger narrative of the decline of Buddhism and allegedly rapid growth of Islam in Myanmar in the context of social transformation. Meanwhile, the aforementioned theme that Muslims 'do not value life' has been popularised at least partly through the work of Buddhist welfare groups which have filled the gap of the absence of Myanmar's thin authoritarian state since the 1990s and now have strong presence both offline and on Facebook (McCarthy 2016).

A key battleground is the images of social work activities and donations taken by volunteers and posted to Facebook, a practice that ensures a large number of people are exposed to their meritorious social activities thereby promoting and inspiring forms of social or moral citizenship amongst others and expanding circuits of merit (see McCarthy 2017). These images are referred to repeatedly by those linked to Buddhist welfare groups as proof of the compassionate virtues that Buddhists live out. 'Look at my Facebook—there are so many images of Buddhists helping each other,' a volunteer and member of the Buddhist nationalist group Ma Ba Tha told me in the weeks following the flood appeals. 'I never see Muslims making donations or volunteering for these kinds of projects,' he said. Facebook photos shared within insular social networks can thus become a one-sided battleground where strong in-group social cohesion and out-group boundaries are rhetorically and visually developed as users disparagingly compare the 'clean and pure' intentions of Buddhists with the allegedly 'stingy' parochialism of Muslims who, it is claimed, offer help 'only to their own kind'. Ironically, the reverse theme recurred in the Facebook feeds of Muslim contacts about Buddhists during the floods.[13] With the increasing ubiquity of Facebook across Myanmar and its potential for visually assisted claim-making, the echo-chamber of pre-existing social networks can help to reinforce and embed social cleavages of various kinds essential to constructing popular conceptualisations of the religious 'Other' and the definition of alleged national and religious virtues and values.

In this context, anxieties about fear of loss of popular religion and morality amid Myanmar's rapid globalisation and social change recur regularly in both online and offline discussions, especially within Buddhist welfare and religious networks. These themes should point researchers, analysts and policy makers interested in communal violence as much to the legacies of authoritarian welfare policy, non-state social protection and the growing securitisation of Buddhism now enshrined in legislation as they do to the emergence of social media and its problematic but comparatively rarer use as a mechanism for propagation of hate-speech and organisation of violence.

Avenues for social and political entrepreneurship

Beyond the 'echo-chambers' that have driven Myanmar's socio-religious polarisation in recent years, the rise of Facebook as a prominent node of information and exchange in Myanmar social life has also allowed a broader spectrum of people, groups and institutions to engage in various forms of social and political entrepreneurship. The trans-local exposure offered by Facebook is increasingly inspiring citizen social action, reformulating civil–military relations and playing an essential role in defining parameters of the national political community.

Facebook and the 2015 floods response

National crises and outpourings of solidarity are now being facilitated and intermediated through Facebook. This was especially evident in a multitude of welfare groups and campaigns that emerged to coordinate a response to the deluge that swept Myanmar in July and August 2015 and affected millions of people in over half of Myanmar's states and divisions. Initial images of the floods posted to Facebook in areas with functioning 3G networks spread rapidly across the country and around the world, especially via diaspora networks. Many people changed their profile pictures to images of flooded villages in an effort to express solidarity, raise awareness and in some cases inspire donations. Exposure to the images of devastation prompted an extraordinary outpouring and mobilisation of civilians, with thousands of people leading local fundraising efforts and many taking leave to travel and provide assistance directly to flood - affected communities.[14] In numerous interviews with volunteers, images of the flooding and its widespread devastation seen on Facebook were repeatedly cited as the inspiration for their involvement.[15]

A stark contrast can be made here between the citizen and government activism that occurred in 2015 and that which was permitted during the devastation of Cyclone Nargis in 2008. Information was sparse during this period as the absence of mobile phones and social media meant most relied on heavily sanitised and censored state-run media. The 2008 devastation certainly saw similar though smaller-scale outpourings of assistance and solidarity (see Jaquet & Walton 2013; CPCS 2009; HRW 2010). However, it is clear that the liberalisation of civil society and volunteering, especially of a trans-local nature, which commenced in 2011 combined with the more recent uptake of social media has enabled groups to fundraise and coordinate their assistance far more freely than was possible in 2008.

The floods also highlighted the increasing role of social media in reinforcing—and forging—new conceptualisations of citizenship and political community. In urban areas with access to mobile phone coverage, images both of the flood victims and of the civilians offering them assistance seen on Facebook or TV helped to mobilise many volunteers to engage in fundraising or offer funds to help their 'fellow Myanmar family' in need. Likely as a result of the poor roads, limited mobile coverage and few linkages to people and communities in Chin and Rakhine States, however, comparatively few images of flooded communities in these areas reached the Facebook newsfeeds of people in Bamar-majority central Myanmar. Most flood assistance teams from this area subsequently travelled via the Yangon–Mandalay highway to more accessible flooded regions such as the Irrawaddy delta, Bago Division, Magway Division and Sagaing Division.

This lack of information and accessibility reinforced pre-existing dynamics of isolation and ethnic exclusion of some of the poorest and hardest hit regions in Myanmar. Meanwhile, in rural areas of central Myanmar with limited mobile phone coverage and more locally-oriented mechanisms of reciprocity, few had seen images of the floods or had in-depth knowledge of their impacts. Perhaps as a result, people in these areas expressed far less concern for flood victims in interviews and were much less likely to participate in fundraising efforts than those with 3G coverage and a higher concentration of smartphones.[16] These varied sentiments of affective national belonging and obligation are intimately tied to Facebook access along with broader media—the essential role social media increasingly plays in emergent notions of nationalism and notions of 'citizenship' in contemporary Myanmar (see Walton in this volume).

Civil–military relations in transition

In addition to enabling civilian humanitarian action, cyber-space has also become one of the primary domains through which civil–military relations are being reforged after decades of authoritarian rule. The successful spread of the 'Black Ribbon' campaign in 2015, which opposed the placement of former military officials into senior positions in the Ministry of Health, highlighted the potential for social media to raise the profile of issues and inspire others to take social action in Myanmar's emerging democratic space.

The campaign was started in August 2015 by nurses in Mandalay Bone Hospital and Taungoo General Hospital who placed a black ribbon on their uniforms in protest against placement of former military doctors into senior positions in the Ministry of Health (see Aung Naing Soe 2015). The motif and campaign then proliferated across the country through a Facebook page, profile pictures and offline demonstrations featuring ribbons, stickers and car decals of the 'Black Ribbon' motif. Within days of the campaign's launch, the Facebook page had received over 40,000 likes.[17] In Taungoo in northern Bago Region, the campaign—which rose to prominence in the weeks following the ousting of Shwe Mann on 13 August from the chairmanship of the ruling USDP by a hard-line faction frustrated by his cooperative relationship with Aung San Suu Kyi and failure to nominate senior members of the Thein Sein government for the 2015 elections[18]—received strong support from local members of the USDP with close links to doctors in the General Hospital. Local candidates for the USDP changed their Facebook profile pictures to the 'Black Ribbon' motif and covered their cars in the movement's stickers.[19] The ribbon campaign began to spread across other sectors including in the judiciary (Nay Aung 2015), Ministry of Education (May Thinzar Naing 2015), Ministry of Electrical Power and Ministry of Energy, all of whom set up their own respective Facebook pages (see Palatino 2015). The campaigns had mixed success, with the 'Black Ribbon' movement initially able to secure a verbal commitment from the Ministry of Health not to appoint unqualified military officers into senior positions in the future (Shwe Yee Saw Myint 2015). The movement and its proliferation via Facebook are indicative of the growing importance of Facebook as a platform through which citizens are asserting their new freedoms and resisting the militarisation of civilian institutions.

Social media is not just the domain of civilian activists, however. The Commander of the Myanmar Armed Forces, Senior General Min Aung Hlaing, now has a Facebook page with over 1.2 million followers on which he posts regularly about civilian meetings and international delegations (see @seniorgeneralminaunghlaing). During the 2015 floods he shared regular updates of military assistance being distributed to deluged communities, as did Minister for Information Ye Htut to his 310,000 followers. In spite of attempts to sponsor posts to boost the reach of these 'official' announcements and images of assistance, more frequently it was the images of individual soldiers and police spontaneously engaging in work perceived popularly as 'beyond the call of duty' that were shared by everyday people and were recalled later by respondents.[20] Images taken by civilian by-standers and loaded online of soldiers and police submerged in flood waters assisting disabled women, children and animals crossing rushing rivers were shared thousands of times during this period. The historically oppressive and extractive role of the Myanmar police and military in civil engagement was evoked by many commenters, who drew a distinction between the institution and the individual: 'This is a real soldier . . . I hate the Tatmadaw, but many of the soldiers have good, compassionate hearts,' exclaimed one comment that received hundreds of likes.[21] Given the limited military assistance lent to communities in the immediate wake of the 2008 Cyclone Nargis (see HRW 2010; Jaquet & Walton 2013), the online and offline actions of the Tatmadaw during the 2015 floods can be seen as part of a broader attempt to 'soften' the image of the armed forces after more than six decades of authoritarian rule using the mechanisms now popularly available with increasing access to web-enabled smartphones.

Karen State pagoda dispute

Local issues and events have also been able to garner extra-local exposure and coalition partners through the platform of social media, as was demonstrated by the case of a pagoda constructed in the compound of a 100-year-old Baptist church in eastern Karen State in September 2015. The dispute began after a prominent monk in Karen State—known locally as the Myaing Gye Ngu Sayadaw—had a dream whilst on dialysis in Thailand that a pagoda should be constructed in the compound of a local Christian church.[22] When construction subsequently commenced and Buddhist Dhamma flags were erected within the church compound by followers of the Sayadaw in September 2015, photos were taken by local Christians and shared to their Facebook accounts. The images were then shared repeatedly across Myanmar's Karen and Christian communities in Myanmar and abroad, frequently with comments imploring people to pray for divine intervention to protect the church, which apparently had roots back to the early twentieth century.

In the weeks that followed, the issue gained traction in international diaspora and domestic activist networks and became a symbol of the increasing assertion of a chauvinistic Buddhist nationalism amid Myanmar's transition. This was especially the case after prominent UK-based Burmese activist Maung Zarni provided his own commentary and shared the case on Facebook. Within a week of the initial images being taken in the remote compound in Karen State and loaded to Facebook, lobbying and exposure had resulted in the intervention of the Myanmar Minister of Religion (Ye Mon 2015a). In interviews I conducted with various Christian Karen politicians and everyday people in central Myanmar and northern Karen State in the weeks after the initial images spread on Facebook in September 2015, the issue was repeatedly raised as a point of concern but also of hope in the government's initial intervention on behalf of the Christian community.[23] The case highlights both the increasing centrality of Facebook and the networks that it has intensified and broadened in attracting attention to localised cases of injustice and in providing mechanisms for citizens to mobilise to highlight contravention of fundamental religious rights. The gradual framing of the case as an example of Buddhist nationalist sentiment which had been mobilised throughout the country in the months preceding the November 2015 elections also indicates the manner in which cases and incidents acquire additional layers of meaning as new actors share and reframe issues both online and offline.

Myanmar's 2015 'Facebook elections'

Political and social entrepreneurship of various kinds online were also evident during Myanmar's November 2015 elections. In many ways the elections occurred first on Facebook, prior to any other media platform. Numerous candidates for the NLD in central Myanmar learned of their nomination to run in the elections after perusing photos of the paper nominations lists from the party's Yangon headquarters posted online by local party members. Facebook also became an essential mechanism for citizen engagement with the electoral process. During the voter registration period prior to November's elections, local activists and citizen journalists visited their local ward and village offices to take photos of dozens of pages of names—loading them to Facebook and tagging the maximum allowable 50 friends and family and encouraging them to check their names. Facebook similarly became the focal point for one of the most dramatic events of the pre-election period—the late-night ouster of Lower House Speaker Shwe Mann from the chairmanship of the USDP.[24]

During the campaign, many expressed—often for the first time—their political aspirations and allegiances by turning their profile pictures to NLD flags or filters, repeating the same practice used during the floods earlier in 2015. Whilst many everyday citizens admitted they were scared of being 'too political' on Facebook, others said that seeing their friends sharing their political opinions online led them to be more public about their own hopes and frustrations with the Myanmar government.[25] The presence of party politics on Facebook is a distinct break from the fear that defined political opposition in Myanmar for decades, highlighting the role of social media in re-engagement of the citizenry with the affairs of the nation. Notably, USDP loyalists rarely showed this same enthusiasm online, potentially out of fear of abuse of regime party and military employees that had occurred elsewhere in the country.[26]

The election campaign itself was also deeply mediated by Facebook. Aung San Suu Kyi released a number of her major speeches as short video clips on Facebook, which were subsequently shared widely. Meanwhile, President Thein Sein posted several professionally produced video clips, including one comparing the bloody revolutions of the Arab Spring with the orderly, regime-led transition of Myanmar (AFP 2015). The clip ended with the ominous phrase: 'Only when peace prevails can democracy be fulfilled.' Unlike in other political contexts, however, candidates rarely engaged in direct Facebook campaigning outside of their pre-existing social networks. Few official pages were set up by candidates, apparently chastened by directives to maintain a focus on the party rather than candidates—especially in the NLD.[27] Meanwhile, the USDP's largely rural-focused campaign meant that strategies were less focused on social media.[28]

One of the most notable moments of the election campaign was the speech given by prominent monk Sitagu Sayadaw at an event by Buddhist nationalist group Ma Ba Tha on 4 October in Yangon celebrating the passage through Parliament of the 'Race and Religion' Laws. Sections of the complex speech struck a conciliatory tone, cautioning against conflict and calling for peaceful co-existence between religions. Within hours, a number of short two-minute excerpts from the speech began to circulate on Facebook, often shared by local NLD supporters and activists. They interpreted the Sayadaw's speech as calling for calm and dismissing the notion that had been popularised by some members of the USDP and Ma Ba Tha at the time: that the NLD was not able or willing to protect the 'Buddhist character of the nation'. After the elections, when asked about whether the incoming NLD government could encounter difficulties navigating nationalist monks, local party activists in Taungoo responded hopefully: 'Ma Ba Tha is no problem, didn't you see Sitagu Sayadaw's speech?'[29] Without the emergence of Facebook as a major platform of trans-local communication it is inconceivable that a speech of this kind would have been so well disseminated in such a short period of time and have such a significant effect on popular political opinion.

The intensified partisanship which occurred both online and offline in the period before Myanmar's 2015 elections also exposed the ability of authorities to pursue citizens under the guise of 'defamation' using of a variety of mechanisms, including those enshrined in the Telecommunications Law passed in 2013.[30] Three particularly egregious cases attracted substantial attention where people were charged under Section 66(d) of the Telecommunications Law for 'insults' made online about senior members of the Thein Sein government (Hern 2015). The section allows the issuance of fines and sentences of up to three years in jail for those convicted of 'extorting, coercing, restraining wrongfully, defaming, disturbing, causing undue influence or threatening to any person by using any Telecommunications Network'.[31] Despite expectations that such prosecutions would be rarer with the election of a democratically-elected government led by Aung San Suu Kyi, this has not proved to be the case.

Section 66(d) under the NLD

Since the NLD took office in March 2016, the number of cases of 'defamation' brought under the Telecommunications Act has increased sharply, especially those involving Section 66(d). As of early 2017 over 40 Section 66(d) cases had been launched against political party members, journalists, human rights activists or charity volunteers across the country for statements, articles or images posted online.[32] The ambiguous and heavy-handed nature of the Act has been criticised by journalists, writers and free-speech advocates as enabling targeted prosecution and intimidation of the press and public (Kyaw Phone Kyaw 2017). The fact that those accused of breaching Section 66(d) can be imprisoned for months during court proceedings has caused significant concern. Despite this, senior NLD members have themselves launched legal proceedings using the Act against critics in the media for statements made on Facebook.

The most prominent case commenced in November 2016 when NLD Yangon Chief Minister Phyo Min Thein took action against the executives of Eleven Media Group in response to Facebook posts suggesting he had received an expensive watch from a military-linked businessman.[33] The case and others like it around the country have prompted a debate about the 'responsibility' associated with free speech online, and also fostered fear—especially amongst those who share devices or accounts—about the possibility of being prosecuted on the basis of social media activity for which they may not be personally responsible (see Kyaw Phone Kyaw 2017).

Despite significant advancements in freedom of the press in Myanmar since 2011, the escalating prospect of prosecution on the basis of statements, comments or jokes—true or false—made online is indicative of the place of Facebook in the popular and political psyche of contemporary Myanmar. Since the case was commenced by Phyo Min Thein, there has been a proliferation of memes, cartoons and satirical articles circulating on Facebook referencing Section 66(d).[34] Despite the replacement of pre-publication censorship with self-censorship under threat of prosecution, increasing digital connectivity allows citizens to continue to creatively and satirically push the boundaries of acceptable speech in the same way many did for decades under military rule (Leehey 2012).

Conclusion

Myanmar is undergoing extraordinarily rapid transformation in the way that information, socio-political events and national identity is mediated, created and disseminated. After decades of authoritarian rule, when it was exceedingly difficult to conduct research exploring the attitude, beliefs and identities of everyday people, the increasingly central role played by social media in Myanmar creates new opportunities and challenges for those seeking insight into a society undergoing rapid social change. As this chapter has shown, for many of those who are one of the rapidly growing number of mobile phone owners in Myanmar—of whom a sizeable proportion are internet users—access to social media has brought with it new mechanisms for the maintenance and deepening of pre-existing relationships as well as the creation of new ties and interests. Opportunities for social, cultural and political entrepreneurship are now offered as various actors seek to utilise the informality and reach of social media to raise the profile of various issues amongst both domestic and, occasionally, international audiences. Through these campaigns new notions of citizenship, politics and 'nation' are being formulated and popularised. At a local level these processes are frequently reinforced by a rich sociology of welfare groups tied organisationally and discursively to religious networks and moral frameworks (see McCarthy 2017). Increasingly, these durable 'informal institutions' are playing a growing role as are Facebook forums where information is shared, narratives are created and local and trans-local events are discussed both online and subsequently offline—frequently as everyday people offer their time for various socially-oriented projects and causes linked to these networks (see McCarthy 2016).

Moving forward, researchers must resist the temptation to conceive of 'cyber-space' as an isolated domain of social action, but rather see it as an extension of pre-existing relationships, networks and cultural practices (see Schissler 2015). On a practical level, this implies studying both the role of various Facebook networks in social phenomena, such as the framing of Rohingya and Muslims more broadly as threats to morality and security (McCarthy 2017; McCarthy & Menager 2017; Morrison 2015; Nyi Nyi Kyaw 2015), and the linkages, disconnects and frequent contrasts between online and offline behaviour. With rates of regular internet use only likely to increase in the coming years—especially in ethnic minority areas—researchers must engage with this evolving domain, enlisting a mixed-method toolbox of both quantitative and qualitative methods. Only through this kind of focused study will we be able to understand the role of social media and the internet more broadly within the rapidly changing contours of Myanmar's evolving social, political and national culture.

Notes

1 The Union Solidarity and Development Association was converted to a regime-aligned political vehicle—the Union Solidarity and Development Party—to compete at the 2010 elections.

2 For a comprehensive timeline of telecommunications reforms since 2012 see *The Myanmar Times*, 2014, 'Telecoms in Myanmar: From tender to launch', 2 August.

3 Interviews with contractors suggest that in identifying sites and erecting towers, urban areas of central Myanmar presented a particular challenge for Ooredoo. In one instance, a monastery in Taungoo requested payment of over US$4,000 in up-front rental payments for the construction of a tower in vacant space within the grounds of a monastic compound. Subsequently, the senior monk claims to have been told by a local committee of monks that it would be 'inappropriate' for the monastery to house the reception tower of a Muslim company. The money was not returned, however, apparently as it had already been spent on the purchase of teak for a new monastic building. Partly as a result of these challenges, as well as differing roll-out strategies, MPT remained Myanmar's largest operator with over 20 million subscribers as of the time of writing.

4 By 2016 Telenor had taken a significant lead between the two new operators, with 15.5 million sim-card subscriptions compared with 6.9 million for Ooredoo. Telenor's initial strategy of offering more basic 2G Internet in more remote areas seemingly allowed the company to pick up large numbers of subscribers outside major cities, whilst Ooredoo focused on offering 3G services in largely urban areas. This helped sort the market so that by July 2015 80 per cent of Ooredoo users connected to the network via smartphone devices while Telenor reported only 80 per cent of its customers as active data users. See Trautwein C. 2015. 'Results reveal Ooredoo falling further behind rival Telenor'. *The Myanmar Times*, 31 July; Trautwein, C. 2015. 'Telenor strides further ahead of Ooredoo'. *The Myanmar Times*, 30 October; and Trautwien, C. 2016. 'Telenor reaches 15.5m users'. *The Myanmar Times*, 28 April. In 2016 a fourth licence was issued to a conglomerate of Vietnamese and Myanmar businesses.

5 Telecommunications reforms were a major feature of the USDPs November 2015 election campaign, both on the local level hustings in central Myanmar (author field notes; 12 and 13 October 2016) and in videos released on Facebook by President Thein Sein's office. See Khan, M. 2015. 'The Arab Spring and the vote'. *New Mandala*, 7 November.

6 This phenomenon of individuals preferring information which confirms existing views or subjectivities is referred to as 'homophily'. See McPherson et al. 2001. 'Birds of a feather: Homophily in social networks', *Annual Review of Sociology*, 27 (1).

7 Often at their instigation, my informants regularly exchanged phones with me for a few minutes after I expressed an interest in how their Facebook newsfeed may be different from my own.

8 Similar arguments about the informal communal atmosphere of Facebook and other applications such as WhatsApp being conducive to the dissemination of gossip are made in other contexts, such as the Pacific where Facebook has emerged as a major forum of social and increasingly political life with some politicians regularly holding Facebook town-hall meetings with their constituents. See Logan, S. 2012. 'Rausim! Digital Politics in Papua New Guinea', State Society and Governance in Melanesia Discussion Paper 19, Australian National University, Canberra.

9 This is a consequence of the fact that Myanmar, one of the weakest welfare states in Southeast Asia, has one of the highest numbers of community-based organisations of any country in Southeast Asia. A 2006 study by Heidel found more than 200,000 operating in almost every corner of the country. See McCarthy (2016 and 2017) for a more detailed exploration of these dynamics.

10 Posts included allegations of corruption in the local Ministry of Electricity Office; rumours of mismanagement of donor funds by a committee constructing a local statue of General Aung San; and leading fundraising of more than US$20,000 for a new blood transfusion machine for the local General Hospital.

11 See RFA. 2014. 'Anti-Muslim riots turn deadly in Myanmar's Mandalay city', Radio Free Asia, 2 July.

12 See Shwe Aung. 2015. 'Government, Facebook to purge hate speech accounts'. Democratic Voice of Burma, 14 September.

13 This was evident in a post during the 2015 flood, which had been shared four times by friends of an informant and thus appeared prominently in his news feed. The posts included six images—five depicting alleged assaults and attacks on Muslims in Myanmar including burning mosques, while the final was a photo of Muslim men wearing religious headwear handing sacks of rice to what appeared to be Buddhists affected by the floods. Above the images was the caption: 'They do this to us . . . And we do this to them.'

14 For analysis of the civilian flood response see Chambers & McCarthy. 2015. 'Amid the deluge, solidarity and leadership emerge', *The Myanmar Times*, 18 August.

15 Interviews with volunteers, Taungoo, August 2015.

16 Author fieldnotes, 15 August 2015.

17 The original page can be found at: @BlackRibbonMM. 'Black Ribbon Movement Myanmar 2015', Facebook. Available at: www.facebook.com/BlackRibbonMM/?fref=ts. [Accessed August 2016.]

18 For greater context and analysis see Zaw, H. & A. Slodkowski. 2015. 'Shake-up in Myanmar as Suu Kyi allies with ruling party boss', Reuters, 18 August.

19 Author fieldnotes, 20 August 2015.

20 Author fieldnotes, 6 July and 18 August 2015.

21 Author fieldnotes, 4 July 2015, Burmese.

22 The pagoda was located in areas under the control of the largely Buddhist Democratic Karen Benevolent Army (DKBA), an armed group which has had a series of ceasefires with Myanmar's military since 1994.

23 The pagoda was in fact completed in early October 2015, with the golden umbrella personally placed atop by the Min Gye Gnew Sayadaw himself—in contravention of orders from the Minister of Religion which went entirely unenforced, seemingly due to the fact that this was a DKBA-controlled area. Many of those who expressed alarm at the initial case had not as of November 2015 heard about the pagoda's completion—indicating the selective and contingent nature of social media virality. The case did factor in the voting judgements of a number of Karen Christian informants in central Myanmar, however, as they perceived the NLD as too reluctant to intervene on behalf of minority Christians. See Ye Mon (2015b).

24 Shwe Mann used Facebook to respond to his dismissal via a series of Facebook posts a few days following. He also used a Facebook post to announce his admission of defeat in the seat of Phyu after the election on 8 November.

25 Interviews with university students in Taungoo, November 2015.

26 See 'Meaning of Myanmar Elections 2015', University of Yangon and ANU Myanmar Research Centre.

27 Interview with NLD activist, 3 June 2015.

28 Interview with USDP activist, 13 September 2015.

29 Interview, 3 November 2015.

30 The legislation also grants expansive powers for surveillance and wire-tapping. See Freedom House. 2015. 'Myanmar: Freedom on the net 2015'. Report for Freedom House, Washington, DC. Available

at: https://freedomhouse.org/sites/default/files/resources/FOTN%202015_Myanmar.pdf. [Accessed December 2015.]

31 For the English translation of the law, see 'The Telecommunications Law'. 2013. Republic of the Union of Myanmar, www.mcit.gov.mm/sites/default/files/Telecom%20Law%20English%20 Version_0.pdf. [Accessed 29 January 2017.]

32 For politically-related cases of prosecution under 66(d) of the Telecommunications Act see Maung Aye. 2016. 'Teen charged over Suu Kyi Fb Post'. Eleven Media Group, 30 October 2016; and DVB. 2016. 'NLD youth leader charged for slandering official on Facebook'. Democratic Voice of Burma, 16 December 2016.

33 For an overview of the case and statements posted on Facebook see Sithu Aung Myint. 2016. 'Eleven Media case puts 66(d) in the media spotlight, again'. *Frontier Myanmar*, 4 December 2016.

34 See for example Moe Thet War. 2016. 'This cartoon pretty much sums up Section 66(d) of the Telecommunications Law'. *Coconuts Yangon*, 8 December 2016.

References

@BlackRibbonMM. 'Black Ribbon Movement Myanmar 2015', Facebook. www.facebook.com/BlackRibbonMM/?fref=ts.

@seniorgeneralminaunghlaing. Facebook. www.facebook.com/seniorgeneralminaunghlaing.

AFP. 2015. 'President warns of Arab Spring-style violence'. *The Myanmar Times*, 4 November.

Anderson, B. 1991. *Imagined Communities: Reflections on the Origins and Spread of Nationalism*. 2nd ed. London: Verso.

Aricat, R. & L. Ling. 2015. 'Mobile phone appropriation and non-adoption at the bottom of the pyramid (BoP): Evidence from the pre-privatized telecommunications era in Myanmar'. Paper Presented at International Conference on Burma/Myanmar Studies. Chiang Maig: Chiang Mai University.

Aung Kyaw Nyunt. 2016. 'Ministry puts mobile penetration at 90 percent'. *The Myanmar Times*, 19 July 2016.

Aung Naing Soe. 2015. 'Myanmar medics wear black ribbons to protest "militarization" of health sector'. *Coconuts Yangon*, August 11.

Australian National University & University of Yangon. 2015. 'The Meaning of Myanmar's 2015 election'. Paper published by University of Yangon Department of International Relations and the Australian National University's Myanmar Research Centre.

Baum, M. & T. Groeling. 2008. 'New media and the polarization of American discourse'. *Political Communication* 25 (4): 345–66.

Bourgault, J. 2013. 'Is Facebook holding Burmese media back?' *The Guardian*, 21 August.

Centola, D. & M. Macy. 2007. 'Complex contagions and the weakness of long ties'. *American Journal of Sociology* 113 (3): 702–34.

Chambers, J. & G. McCarthy. 2015. 'Amid the deluge, solidarity and leadership emerge'. *The Myanmar Times*, 18 August.

CPCS. 2009. 'Listening to the voices from inside: Myanmar civil society's response to Cyclone Nargis'. Center for Peace and Conflict Studies Report, Phnom Penh.

Deibert, R. & R. Rohozinski. 2010. 'Liberation vs. control: The future of cyberspace'. *Journal of Democracy* 21 (4): 43–57.

Diamond, L. 2010. 'Liberation technology'. *Journal of Democracy* 21 (3): 69–83.

Fink, C. 2001. *Living Silence: Burma Under the Military Rule*. Bangkok: White Lotus Press.

Freedom House. 2015. 'Myanmar: Freedom on the net 2015'. Report for Freedom House, Washington, DC. Accessed December 2015. https://freedomhouse.org/sites/default/files/resources/FOTN%20 2015_Myanmar.pdf.

Goldberg, G. 2011. 'Rethinking the public/virtual sphere'. *New Media and Society* 13 (5): 739–54.

Hern, A. 2015. 'Victim of state spying? Facebook will tell you'. *The Guardian*, 19 October.

HRW. 2010. *Burma: After Cyclone, Repression Impedes Civil Society and Aid*. Bangkok: Human Rights Watch.

Jaquet, C. & M. Walton. 2013. 'Buddhism and relief in Myanmar: Reflections on relief as a practice of Dāna'. In *Buddhism, International Relief Work, and Civil Society*, edited by H. Kawanami and G. Samuel. Basingstoke, UK: Palgrave Macmillan.

Jeffrey, R. & A. Doron. 2013. *The Great Indian Phone Book: How Cheap Mobile Phones Change Business, Politics and Daily Life*. London: Hurst.

Kyaw Phone Kyaw. 2017. 'Reform group to deliver Telecommunications Law findings to parliament'. *Frontier Myanmar, Yangon*. 13 February 2017.

Leehey, J. 2012. 'Reading "Saturn": Interpretive practice under censorship in Burma'. *Journal of Burma Studies* 16 (1): 1–25.

Logan, S. 2012. 'Rausim! Digital politics in Papua New Guinea'. *State Society and Governance in Melanesia Discussion Paper 19*. Canberra: The Australian National University.

McCarthy, G. 2016. 'Buddhist welfare and the limits of big "P" politics in provincial Myanmar'. In *Conflict in Myanmar: War, Politics, Religion*, edited by N. Cheesman & N. Farrelly. Singapore: ISEAS.

McCarthy, G. 2017. 'The value of life: Citizenship, entitlement and moral legibility in provincial Myanmar'. In *Citizenship in Myanmar: Ways of Being in and from Burma*, edited by A. South & M. Lall. Chiang Mai and Singapore: Chiang Mai University Press and ISEAS.

McCarthy, G. & J. Menager. 2015. 'Viral rumours and the quotidian cultivation of political identity in Myanmar's transition'. In *Communal Violence in Myanmar*, edited by N. Cheesman. Yangon: Myanmar Knowledge Society.

McCarthy, G. & J. Menager. 2017. 'Gendered rumours and the Muslim scapegoat in Myanmar's transition'. *Journal of Contemporary Asia* 47 (3): 396–412.

McPherson, M., L. Smith-Lovin & J. Cook. 2001. 'Birds of a feather: Homophily in social networks'. *Annual Review of Sociology* 27 (1): 415–44.

May Thinzar Naing. 2015. 'Teachers plan campaign on military appointees'. *The Myanmar Times*, 29 September.

Miller, V. 2008. 'New media, networking and phatic culture'. *Convergence: The International Journal of Research into New Media Technologies* 14 (4): 387–400.

Morrison, M. 2015. '"The new radicals": Social media and communal violence in Myanmar'. Paper Presented at Johns Hopkins University Conference on Asian Affairs. February 2015.

Nay Aung. 2015. 'Yellow ribbon campaign extends'. *The Myanmar Times*, 18 September.

Nyi Nyi Kyaw. 2015. 'Alienation, discrimination, and securitization: Legal personhood and cultural personhood of Muslims in Myanmar'. *The Review of Faith & International Affairs* 13 (4): 50–9.

Palatino, M. 2015. 'Myanmar's ribbon movements challenge militarization'. *The Diplomat*, 10 October.

Qiu, J. 2014. '"Power to the people!"Mobiles, migrants, and social movements'. *International Journal of Communication* 8: 376–91.

RFA. 2014. 'Anti-Muslim riots turn deadly in Myanmar's Mandalay city'. Radio Free Asia, 2 July.

Schissler, M. 2015. 'New technologies, established practices: Developing narratives of Muslim threat in Myanmar'. In *Islam and the State in Myanmar: Muslim–Buddhist Relations and the Politics of Belonging*, edited by Melissa Crouch. Oxford: Oxford University Press.

Schissler, M., M. Walton & P. T. Phyu. 2015. 'Threat and virtuous defence: Listening to narratives of religious conflict in six Myanmar cities'. Report by Myanmar Media and Society Project, University of Oxford.

Shirky, C. 2011. 'The political power of social media'. *Foreign Affairs* 90 (1): 28–41.

Shwe Aung. 2015. 'Govt, Facebook to purge hate speech accounts'. Democratic Voice of Burma, 14 September.

Shwe Yee Saw Myint. 2015. 'Ministry backs down on jobs for soldiers'. *The Myanmar Times*, 13 August.

Stromback, J. & A. Shehata. 2010. 'Media malaise or a virtuous circle? Exploring the causal relationships between news media exposure, political news attention and political interest'. *European Journal of Political Research* 49 (5): 575–97.

Sunstein, C. 2008. 'Neither Hayek nor Habermas'. *Public Choice* 134: 87–95.

Sunstein, C. 2009. *Republic.com 2.0*. Princeton: Princeton University Press.

The Myanmar Times. 2014. 'Telecoms in Myanmar: From tender to launch'. 2 August.

Trautwein, C. 2015. 'Telenor strides further ahead of Ooredoo'. *The Myanmar Times*, 30 October.

Tufekci, Z. & C. Wilson. 2012. 'Social media and the decision to participate in political protest: Observations from Tahrir Square'. *Journal of Communication* 62 (2): 363–79.

Ye Mon. 2015a. 'Minister promises Christians removal of dream-inspired stupa'. *The Myanmar Times*, 8 September.

Ye Mon. 2015b. 'Sayadaw refuses to halt stupa construction'. *The Myanmar Times*, 17 September.

11
ANOMALOUS SPACES

Nicholas Farrelly

In the common description—often repeated in state-sanctioned statements of national geography—Myanmar is divided into seven States and seven Regions, plus the Union Territory of Naypyitaw. The idea of this configuration is that space in Myanmar is carefully balanced between ethnic minorities and the Bamar majority. Yet this set of spatial categories misses the variety of anomalies that exist at the margins of the carefully crafted story of national cohesion and belonging. Exceptions are common, at all scales. They tend to express hesitation about a universal standard for the management of space. The peculiarities of different types of marginal space offer insights about the character of political, economic and cultural control, and the exceptions that exist to help maintain the outlines of what is supposed to be a simple story of integration. Lived experiences across the breadth of anomalous spaces highlight persistent patterns of ambiguity and contestation. Myanmar's uneven terrain—one where governments have been prepared to accept significant local variation where such concessions help to maintain overall stability—encompasses rebel-controlled territories, Special Regions, Self-Administered Zones, military bases and Special Economic Zones.

This tapestry of spaces helps to explain some of the challenges faced by the central authorities in Naypyitaw while also illuminating alternative claims to political and economic authority. Since independence in 1948, vast areas of the country have only ever been under nominal central government control. Even today, important pockets are still held by groups implacably opposed to the agenda for unity that emanates from both democratic and military interests in Naypyitaw. The 2008 constitution has entrenched some of the spatial anomalies, with certain autonomous zones given special privileges to organise local political and cultural administration (Taylor 2009). Other exceptional spaces are managed by Myanmar's armed forces. They still assert ownership of large tracts of land as part of their nationwide network of garrisons and other military facilities. With Myanmar's decades-long history of military rule, local commanders enjoy significant autonomy when it comes to managing their people and the spaces they occupy. At the same time, the government has recently encouraged the development of economic zones that sit outside the ordinary legal and regulatory framework. Three large Special Economic Zones are deemed integral to economic growth and the revitalisation of foreign investment in the manufacturing and industrial sectors. These anomalous spaces are all the product of competing ideas about the best way of managing Myanmar's internal affairs and external relationships. Often, the government has opted to concede ground to groups that may otherwise cause further political grief. Taken together, these exceptions to the Myanmar government's ordinary management of space help to explain the range of centrifugal frustrations, and countervailing forces, that push and pull at the fabric of this unruly nation-state.

Rebel-controlled territories

Throughout Myanmar's long history of inter-ethnic and ideological conflict, rebel groups have controlled large parts of the country. This was most apparent from the 1960s through to the 1980s when up to two thirds of the national territory was controlled by anti-government groups (see Smith 1991; Lintner 1999). The Communist Party of Burma's fixed bases along the border with China were a good example, exerting influence across much of the Shan State and Kachin State. In other mountainous areas, groups like the Kachin Independence Army, Mong Tai Army and Karen National Union also managed large parcels of terrain. For a period in the 1980s the main Kachin armed group held sway across the highlands of the north, and was well-placed to deny access to government patrols. In most cases, the rebel armies had their strongholds in the mountains where they could only be dislodged after ferocious fighting. Where possible, they maintained networks of checkpoints and outposts to guard against unauthorised incursions. Access control, for rebel commanders, was always a top priority.

It helped that, in many cases, regular resupply has remained possible across international frontiers. The borderlands adjacent to India, China and Thailand have proved particularly important for rebel groups who have relied on access to foreign supplies, sometimes including weapons, ammunition and other provisions for their military forces (see Farrelly 2009; Woods 2011). The strongest Myanmar-based rebel groups have levied regular taxes on those undertaking economic activities in their territories. Some of these activities are illicit, with narcotics production and trafficking being a profitable enterprise, especially in parts of the Shan and Kachin States (Chin 2009). Rebel-controlled areas have often supported opium cultivation and heroin refineries and, in more recent years, there has been a spike in the production of synthetic drugs, particularly amphetamines (for details see Meehan 2011). The ambiguity and deniability of rebel-controlled spaces has facilitated what is one of the world's most dynamic narcotics economies. Murky interactions between government and non-government forces have largely precluded effective law enforcement countermeasures, whether from domestic or international agencies.

Over the decades, this patchwork of non-state territories has caused other persistent problems for the Myanmar government. Rebel-controlled areas usually drastically limited the scope and reach of government activities, such as education and health care, while also entrenching long-term militarisation across large parts of the country. Instead of local facilities that might inspire commitment to the central government's rule, effort was generally expended on fortifications to protect military and police personnel. These investments in the security of frontline security forces still mark the landscape where they present a different exception to the ordinary control of space. Such outposts became sites for the expansion of Bamar Buddhist culture, generating disquiet among other religious and ethnic communities. As part of the broader counter-insurgency push, official programmes of aggressive Burmanisation were followed by much slower shifts in the demographics of many ethnic areas (see Holmes 1967; South 2007; Jirattikorn, 2010). Over time, resentment has grown against government initiatives that end up diluting the political or cultural primacy of local ethnic minority populations. In some areas, resentment has led to the further estrangement of rebellious groups that see no future for themselves in Myanmar's centralising political system.

Some rebel-controlled territories have now taken on the character of micro-states, offering ethnically differentiated lifestyles that do not conform to the standards of contemporary

Myanmar society (Dean 2005; Aung 2016). Education and health facilities, while usually basic, offer services in local languages not usually allowed in government-controlled areas where the national lingua franca dominates public discourse. In its time, the Communist Party of Burma, which sought to portray itself as an alternative to the socialist military government of General Ne Win, was formed to offer an ideological contrast to central rule. The same dynamics emerged when ethnic armed groups gained enough military and political strength to maintain stable, fixed populations. Until the fall of Manerplaw in 1995, the Karen National Union claimed a 'capital' which they hoped would embody the goals of an independent Karen nation. The Kachin Independence Army also created its own parallel state institutions and would refer to itself as 'the Kachin government' (see Farrelly 2012). Its headquarters at Laiza are a Christian, Jinghpaw-speaking enclave, where commercial links to China help to sustain relatively vibrant cultural, educational and political alternatives to the Myanmar mainstream. On a smaller scale, various Chin, Naga, Shan, Lahu, Karenni and Pa-O militia groups have succeeded in creating spaces for the maintenance of their own independent political and cultural agendas.

From time to time, like at Manerplaw, rebel-controlled areas were over-run, with cherished towns and villages destroyed in what were often vicious battles. Most of these battles were against government forces, which could rely on superior numbers of fighters and also sometimes on superiority in weapons and training. With air power, artillery and armoured transport, the Myanmar government's armed forces have proved formidable adversaries even in the mountainous terrain that provides advantages to guerrilla forces. Where rebel-controlled territories were over-run, it would often be impossible for government forces to establish full control. Skirmishes and ambushes would usually persist, often for years, requiring representatives of the government, including civilian officials, to bunker down behind trenches and walls. In many cases, government forces eventually withdrew from the most heavily contested areas, leaving behind uneasy stalemates. The push-and-shove of insurgency and counter-insurgency kept peace and security out of reach for most people living in places across Myanmar where rebels sought to exert their will.

Special Regions

In some areas of ethnic conflict it has been possible to reach longer-term ceasefire deals, which helped to create the conditions for other anomalous spaces to emerge. When the Communist Party of Burma collapsed in the late 1980s it splintered into a number of large, ethnic-based armed groups (see Lintner 1990). These groups are still found in parts of the Kachin State and the Shan State. The most important is the United Wa State Army, which, in its quest to defend cherished autonomy, may have around 25,000 fighters (for historical context see Fiskesjö 2010). Other significant groups that emerged from the Communist Party include the Myanmar National Democratic Alliance Army and the New Democratic Army–Kachin. Their heartland areas became known as Special Regions. Each was designated with a number. So, the Wa territories were known as Shan State Special Region No. 2, while the New Democratic Army–Kachin called its territory Kachin State Special Region No. 1. The Kachin Independence Army, after its 1994 ceasefire agreement with the government, took control of an area called Kachin State Special Region No. 2. Over time, other groups also took Special Region status, including the Eastern Shan State Army, which controlled Mong La, a town most famous for its illicit trades, including in animals (Nijman and Shepherd 2014). It is otherwise known as Shan State Special Region No. 4. Eventually there were 12 Special Regions: two in the Kachin State, seven in Shan State and three in Kayah State (Smith 2005, 78).

Under the ceasefires of the 1990s and 2000s, the leaders in these Special Regions had opportunities to build substantial parallel state structures, with their own semi-autonomous economies. Special Regions located in the borderlands enjoyed easy cross-border trade, particularly with China and Thailand. In many cases, local economic activity was focused on mining and logging, although some of the Special Regions also became notorious for their role in the narcotics trade. The United Wa State Army is still regularly referred to as a 'narco-army' (for discussion see Kramer 2007). Its businesses are accused of supplying billions of amphetamine pills to the Thai market and of complicity in a wide range of other illicit activities (for historical context see Ball 2003). In Mong La, the major town in Shan State Special Region No. 4, an anti-drugs museum is one of the local attractions. Other common economic activities in Special Regions are gambling and prostitution, both of which have boomed in frontier towns along the Chinese border. During crackdowns by the Chinese authorities, the flow of visitors subsides, but innovative local businesses still seek to make money. Virtual gaming houses beaming live vision back to gamblers in China have emerged at times when the borders are closed (Black and Fields 2006).

The Special Regions have also helped to generate significant changes on the other side of the frontier, whether in Thailand or China. Both the Thai and Chinese governments have usually been comfortable working with ethnic armed groups, especially where they have been able to develop mutually beneficial economic partnerships. Opportunities for employment and trade have flowed in both directions. This has ensured the Special Regions have been secure places for investment, with substantial new buildings springing up. Hotels, casinos and resorts, drawing custom and technology from across the border, have been built under these anomalous conditions. Back when Internet and mobile phone access in Myanmar was heavily restricted, some of the Special Regions could claim the best telecommunications systems in the country. Inevitably, they were relying on infrastructure sourced directly from across the border. As the Myanmar government seeks to negotiate durable peace agreements with armed ethnic groups that have controlled Special Regions, the political status of these exceptional spaces is particularly sensitive.

Self-Administered Zones

To formalise the relationship between powerful ethnic minority groups and the central government, the 2008 Constitution created five Self-Administered Zones and one Self-Administered Division. The zones are Kokang (centred on the town of Laukkaing), Naga (Lahe), Danu (Pindaya), Pa-O (Hopong) and Palaung (Namhsan), while the United Wa State Army controls a Self-Administered Division. These zones enjoy most of the privileges that were accumulated by the Special Regions, but are further bolstered by their constitutional status. Each local administration is headed by a leading group, which should include members of the state legislature, alongside representatives from local political and military organisations, and from the central government.

These arrangements are not necessarily stable. Since 2009 there have been episodes of significant conflict around the Kokang Self-Administered Zone. The most recent outbreak of serious fighting occurred in early 2015 between the Myanmar National Democratic Alliance Army and the central government's military forces. This intense conflict drew sustained media and public interest elsewhere in Myanmar. In towns and cities across the country, Facebook profiles were adjusted to show support for the Myanmar government forces, using the distinctive shoulder patch of Northeastern Command, which is headquartered in Lashio, as an emblem of national solidarity. As government troops were deployed to battle the Kokang forces, President Thein Sein's administration in Naypyitaw made clear their unwillingness to accept what they considered illegal activities in the Self-Administered Zone. The government presented its offensive as a counter-narcotics operation.

In other Self-Administered Zones, relations with the government have also had moments of tension. The fundamental challenge for both the government and the leaders of these exceptional spaces is that the rules for interaction are re-negotiated on a regular basis. As local military commanders are shuffled around in the country, there are also adjustments to national policy about how to handle ethnic politics. Under the NLD government, the 21st Century Panglong Conference, an omnibus negotiation of majority–minority relations, has become the primary vehicle for managing the overall ethnic landscape. Such national-level agreements are determined far above the primary concerns for those seeking a modicum of extra autonomy at the local level. In a political system where there is little faith in central government agendas the outcome tends to be lingering tension and stalemates about the best framework for managing ethnic political ambitions.

Military bases

Across Myanmar there are countless government military facilities, over 1,000 of which are of battalion size or larger. Each of these bases requires land and in most instances they are surrounded by a fence or wall. It can be difficult to know exactly what goes on inside (Selth 2007). These military bases are a constant physical reminder of the dominance of the military in political affairs. With the Commander-in-Chief of Defence Services at the top of the hierarchy, there is a connection between every military unit and the national defence headquarters in Naypyitaw. Together, these different commanders have inherited protocols for managing military spaces that were first implemented in British colonial times.

In general, these facilities are off-limits to civilians or to anybody who does not have a specific reason for visiting. In some cases, very strict entry procedures are followed. These procedures ensure that, for many people in Myanmar, military compounds are only ever observed from a distance. Their parade grounds, obstacle courses, gardens, offices and countless other facilities are usually kept behind barbed wire. In parts of the country with recent histories of significant fighting with rebel forces, many bases are also heavily fortified. Pillboxes and other defensive infrastructure reinforce a sense that the military stands apart from the rest of society, and that it has become estranged from ordinary civilian concerns.

In some places, particularly in the northern suburbs of Yangon, and the eastern portion of Naypyitaw, the military residential compounds are so large that standalone communities exist that have only limited interaction with civilian populations. During the era of direct military rule, the armed forces sought to present themselves as a caste apart from the rest of society. The military leadership's preference for keeping military personnel in their own compounds only exacerbated this sense of dislocation. With their own shops, schools and leisure facilities, military members and their families were isolated. In Naypyitaw, Zeyarthiri township is still dominated by military families and at the 2015 general election was the only constituency in the capital which endorsed a Union Solidarity and Development Party representative. In the northern suburbs of Yangon, especially past the airport at Mingaladon, are a series of sprawling military bases that date, in some cases, to the Japanese occupation during the Second World War. Few people from outside the military ever see inside these facilities, but there is an increasing sense that the exceptions enjoyed by the armed forces are starting to break down.

For instance, in other parts of the country the relationship between the military and the rest of society has tended to be more flexible. It helps that military facilities are a significant factor in local economies, especially in key garrison towns like Myitkyina, Hpa-an, Myeik and Ann.

These are places where a sizeable proportion of the population has regular contact with military bases and personnel, either through family connections, business relationships or social interactions. In these provincial population centres, the link between military deployments and political power is also clear. Under the State Peace and Development Council government, military commanders in such areas took on responsibilities for leading the civilian administration. In many cases they also seized prominent positions at cultural and sporting events, and anywhere else that would possibly improve the military's battered image. In such towns, business arrangements also helped to consolidate connections between military bases and other local interests. Preferential access to equipment, fuel and labour gave military-aligned commercial activities some advantages if they wanted to collaborate with non-military entrepreneurs. Where such activities bumped against government regulations there was also the prospect that, with the right briefing to the local commander, favourable interpretations would follow.

Special Economic Zones

The development of Special Economic Zones became a priority under the government of President Thein Sein from 2011 to 2016. Three of these zones were designated: at Thilawa outside Yangon; at Dawei in Tanintharyi Region in the south; and at Kyaukphyu, on the coast of Rakhine State (see Walsh 2015; Loewen 2012; Min and Kudo 2012). Each of these vast new economic zones was presented as a space specifically tailored to attract new commercial and trading opportunities. Thilawa, where Japanese conglomerates have supported the early construction phase, is a nascent industrial and manufacturing hub, which its backers hope will become a showcase for the newly liberalised Myanmar economy. Its proximity to Yangon and to port facilities should mean that it offers a new platform for exports. Dawei is a different proposition, nestled on the Andaman Sea coast in southern Myanmar. It is only 252 kilometres from Bangkok. The long-term goal for Dawei is to serve as a link between businesses elsewhere in mainland Southeast Asia and the Indian Ocean. Kyaukphyu has a different model entirely from its location in Rakhine State. It is part of an integrated oil and gas development that has been supported by Chinese investment, alongside significant technical backing from elsewhere in the world. From Kyaukphyu, gas and oil pipelines run across Myanmar, right up to the Chinese border. The goal is to create refining and processing capacities to support the oil and gas sectors servicing off-shore fields. China is committed to creating a supply corridor that avoids the potential hazards of the Strait of Malacca between Malaysia, Indonesia and Singapore.

In all cases, these Special Economic Zones, like their cousins elsewhere in East Asia, offer incentives to investors (see Arnold 2012). Concessional taxation arrangements are the primary way for the government to entice foreign companies to consider the SEZs. It helps that similar methods have a long history in other places, especially in China where SEZs became the boomtowns in the early phases of economic liberalisation. Mimicking elements of those existing models, Myanmar's plans for economic development focus on creating hubs where investors can expect rapid returns through a combination of robust infrastructure, inexpensive labour and proximity to major regional markets like Thailand, China and India. Whatever problems investors anxiously anticipate elsewhere in Myanmar, the hope is that a 'ring-fenced', trade-friendly environment will increase their confidence.

In their early phases of development, inconsistent electricity and inadequate supplies of trained labour have caused frustrations for investors, while there is concern that the concessional tax arrangements may not be sufficient to make businesses competitive. The hope, in the medium term, is that the SEZs will support a wide range of integrated industrial and manufacturing activities, in customised environments. Myanmar's ambitions are well aligned, in these respects, to some of the advice offered by business consultants and international development advisors. In many parts of East Asia, such specially configured commercial zones have proved an important element in the transformation of economies that were previously condemned to low growth and little international interest.

Understandably, many people, especially those displaced by the SEZs, end up criticising this development model. Environmental and human-rights activists have targeted each of these anomalous spaces. There are specific concerns about labour exploitation, the degradation of soil and water resources, and risks to the overall health of fragile local societies unprepared for the changes that will follow the rapid expansion of economic opportunities. Other critics focus on what they perceive is a flawed expectation that Myanmar can thrive by imitating the political and economic structures implemented elsewhere. For them, the risks of the SEZs outweigh any eventual benefits, especially when the agreements for welcoming foreign businesses on concessional terms were supported by figures who prospered under the former military government. For some, this makes the SEZs permanently illegitimate.

In these different ways, the SEZs offer an example of exceptional and anomalous space that is widely contested. Supporters of this model argue that the rest of Myanmar society will be too slow to match international market needs. Special spaces, with fewer rules, are therefore needed to better anticipate the requirements of foreign investors and their local partners. The hope is that while the SEZs prove an anomaly, they may also offer a chance to catalyse sustained economic growth and technology transfer. Training of workers is a further benefit often identified by proponents of the SEZ plans. In the long-term the government's stated goal is to take lessons from Thilawa, Dawei and Kyaukphyu that can be applied elsewhere in society. These spaces are defined by their perpetually unfinished status, and by the need to adequately respond to market demands.

Anomalous futures

Myanmar's anomalous spaces have evolved across decades of changing political, economic and social conditions. Progressions from rebel control to designation as Special Regions or to constitutional recognition as Self-Administered Zones are examples of the different ways that spaces in ethnic areas have been managed over recent decades. The government has usually endeavoured to create frameworks that give sufficient flexibility for local interests to thrive, like with the new SEZs. This has been an imperfect and incomplete process, which has also alienated those whose preferred spaces have been disallowed. Some rebel groups continue to dispute re-designation and the ongoing splintering of ethnic leadership is one of the consequences of such conflict. Tensions become most apparent where independence movements have struggled to create their own autonomous entities. Moves towards ending the exceptions that define these spaces are one of the goals of Myanmar's ongoing peace processes. The anomalies of Myanmar government military bases are a further example of spatial management in a country only slowly emerging from many decades of difficult authoritarian rule.

In this context, Special Economic Zones are relatively recent additions to Myanmar's landscape. These zones make sense while Myanmar has a comparative advantage in low labour costs, readily available raw materials and reasonable access to adjacent regional markets. In a country where industrialisation stalled, to a large extent, during decades of military rule the political ambition to rebuild local economic capacity makes the SEZs politically attractive. They also fit neatly into a global vocabulary of economic and social progress. Critics of these schemes suggest that more caution is required if the best interests of Myanmar people are to be defended. For now, the SEZs remain works in progress and it is unclear whether the existing model will be maintained under more democratic political arrangements.

The ultimate conundrum across Myanmar's anomalous spaces is that they are defined by the same political, economic, bureaucratic and cultural logics that have made the entire country synonymous with military misrule and social disorder. Each of the exceptions clarified in these spaces highlights ways that society has struggled to build cohesive institutions that can maintain consistent expectations among different interests. Concessions and compromises have created spaces that simply do not conform. As vehicles for handling contested and conflicted politics, the various anomalies have a role to play. For Myanmar's government, however, there are lingering questions about the need to insist on greater uniformity across the length and breadth of the country. Anomalous spaces can offer excuses when, as often happens, central government policies do not go to plan.

References

Arnold, Dennis. 2012. 'Spatial Practices and Border SEZs in Mekong Southeast Asia'. *Geography Compass* (6) 12: 740–751.

Aung, Lanau Roi. 2016. 'Laiza: Kachin Borderlands—Life After the Ceasefire'. In *Politics of Autonomy and Sustainability in Myanmar*, edited by W. Tantikanangkul & A. Pritchard. Singapore: Springer.

Ball, Desmond. 2003. *Security Developments in the Thailand–Burma Borderlands*. Sydney: Australian Mekong Resource Centre.

Black, Michael and Roland Fields. 2006. 'Virtual Gambling in Myanmar's Drug Country'. *Asia Times*, August 26.

Chin, Ko-Lin. 2009. *The Golden Triangle: Inside Southeast Asia's Drug Trade*. Ithaca: Cornell University Press.

Dean, Karin. 2005. 'Spaces and Territorialities on the Sino–Burmese Boundary: China, Burma and the Kachin'. *Political Geography* 24 (7): 808–830.

Farrelly, Nicholas. 2009. ''AK47/M16 Rifle–Rs. 15,000 Each': What Price Peace on the Indo-Burmese Frontier?' *Contemporary South Asia* (17) 3: 283–297.

Farrelly, Nicholas. 2012. 'Ceasing Ceasefire? Kachin Politics Beyond the Stalemates'. In *Myanmar's Transition: Openings, Obstacles and Opportunities*, edited by T. Wilson, M. Skidmore & N. Cheesman. Singapore: ISEAS Press.

Fiskesjö, Magnus. 2010. 'Mining, History, and the Anti-State Wa: The Politics of Autonomy Between Burma and China'. *Journal of Global History* (5) 2: 241–264.

Holmes, Robert A. 1967. 'Burmese Domestic Policy: The Politics of Burmanization'. *Asian Survey* (7) 3: 188–197.

Jirattikorn, Amporn. 2010. 'Shan Noises, Burmese Sound: Crafting Selves Through Pop Music'. *South East Asia Research* (18) 1: 161–189.

Kramer, Tom. 2007. *The United Wa State Party: Narco-Army or Ethnic Nationalist Party?* Singapore: Institute of Southeast Asian Studies.

Lintner, Bertil. 1990. *The Rise and Fall of the Communist Party of Burma (CPB)*. Ithaca: SEAP Publications, Cornell University.

Lintner, Bertil. 1999. *Burma in Revolt: Opium and Insurgency Since 1948*. Chiang Mai: Silkworm Books.

Loewen, Elizabeth Mary Ruth. 2012. *States, Capital, and Enclosures: Thailand, Myanmar, and the Dawei Special Economic Zone*. Rotterdam: Erasmus University.

Meehan, Patrick. 2011. 'Drugs, Insurgency and State-Building in Burma: Why the Drugs Trade is Central to Burma's Changing Political Order'. *Journal of Southeast Asian Studies* (42) 3: 376–404.

Min, Aung and Toshihiro Kudo. 2012. 'Newly Emerging Industrial Development Nodes in Myanmar: Ports, Roads, Industrial Zones Along Economic Corridors'. In *Emerging Economic Corridors in the Mekong Region*, edited by M. Ishida. Bangkok: Institute of Developing Economies, Japan External Trade Organisation.

Nijman, Vincent and Chris R. Shepherd. 2014. 'Emergence of Mong La on the Myanmar–China Border as a Global Hub for the International Trade in Ivory and Elephant Parts'. *Biological Conservation* (179): 17–22.

Selth, Andrew. 2007. 'Burma, China and the Myth of Military Bases'. *Asian Security* (3) 3: 279–307.

Smith, Martin. 1991. *Burma: Insurgency and the Politics of Ethnicity*. London: Zed Books.

Smith, Martin, 2005. 'Ethnic Politics and Regional Development in Myanmar'. In *Myanmar: Beyond Politics to Societal Imperatives*, edited by Kyaw Yin Hlaing, R. H. Taylor & Tin Maung Maung Than. Singapore: ISEAS Press.

South, Ashley. 2007. 'Karen Nationalist Communities: The "Problem" of Diversity'. *Contemporary Southeast Asia: A Journal of International and Strategic Affairs* (29) 1: 55–76.
Taylor, Robert H. 2009. 'Myanmar: Reconciliation or Reconsolidation? Isolation or Resolution?' *Asian Affairs* (40) 2: 210–223.
Walsh, John. 2015. 'Thilawa Special Economic Zone and the Single Window'. *International Journal of Services Technology and Management* (21) 1–3: 27–39.
Woods, Kevin. 2011. 'Ceasefire Capitalism: Military–Private Partnerships, Resource Concessions and Military–State Building in the Burma–China Borderlands'. *Journal of Peasant Studies* (38) 4: 747–770.

PART III

Cultures

12
LANGUAGES

David Bradley

In Myanmar, over a hundred languages are spoken among the 135 officially defined ethnic groups. The dominant language is Myanmar language, spoken as a mother tongue by over two-thirds of the population and by most others as a second language. It has been the national and official language since independence in 1948, written in a long-established and now archaic script with the earliest surviving dated inscription from AD 1112. Because of its long written history, the literary language has been stable for centuries and is now quite different from the modern informal spoken language. This difference is institutionalised; the literary language is used in most written and some formal spoken contexts and taught in schools, while the spoken language is used in most informal speech as well as an increasing range of informal written contexts; examples are given below.

There is substantial historical diversity among the languages of Myanmar, with some closely related to Thai in the Thai-Kadai (TK) family, others related to Mon and Khmer in the Mon-Khmer (MK) family, two from the Miao-Yao (MY) family, several from the Indo-Aryan (IA) branch of Indo-European, one Austronesian (AN) language and one Chinese language; all the rest, nearly 80 per cent, are related within the Tibeto-Burman (TB) family, and thus more or less closely related to Myanmar language. There is also structural diversity, with the TK, MK, MY, AN and Chinese as well as some of the TB languages being verb-medial—'man eat rice'—but the bulk of the Tibeto-Burman languages as well as the IA languages are verb-final—'man rice eat'. Among the TB languages, about twenty Karen languages and one language of Rakhine State, Anu/Khongso, are verb-medial.

Most of the languages show many structural similarities; for example, the obligatory use of a separate element after each numeral which indicates something about the meaning of the noun being counted, called a numeral classifier in the linguistic literature; in Myanmar language, for example, ယောက် /yau'/ for counting humans in ကလေးငါးယောက် /khalê ngâ yau'/ 'child five human' meaning 'five children', ကောင် /kaun/ for counting animals in မြင်းရှစ်ကောင် /myîn shi' kaun/ 'horse eight animal' meaning 'eight horses', and so on. Also, apart from the IA languages on the western side of the country, nearly all lack any endings on verbs indicating the subject of the verb, and lack a separate category of adjectives; these are instead a subcategory of verbs. In terms of sounds, Myanmar language and all other TB, TK and MY languages as well as Chinese have tones; that is, the pitch of the voice on a syllable makes a meaning difference, for example

Myanmar language က /ká/ 'dance' with high pitch, ကာ /ka/ 'obstruct' with low pitch and ကား /kâ/ 'spread out' with falling pitch.

Myanmar language group

The literary and historical form of the name of the country and the language is မြန်မာ /myanma/—this has been in every Myanmar language version of the name of the country since independence in 1948. In informal spoken language, a small number of very frequently used words including this word, ဘယ် /beh/ 'which?' and ဘာ /ba/ 'what?' long ago underwent an irregular change from /my/ to /b/, and so the informal spoken form of this name is ဗမာ /bama/, the source of the former English term. During the British colonial period, Burma was used for the country, Burmese for the language and Burman for the majority ethnic group. During the Japanese occupation from 1942 to 1945, the official term for the country was ဗမာ /bama/ in Myanmar language. From 1948, the independent government continued to use the terms Burma and Burmese in English, but in 1989 the SLORC government eliminated various Anglicised place names and introduced Myanmar as the English term for the country and the language, but kept Bamar as the term for the majority ethnic group whose mother tongue is Myanmar language. China has been in contact with Myanmar frequently since the mid-thirteenth century, and Chinese uses the older literary term *Mian*, but nearly all other foreign names for the country are based on the spoken form; this includes Thai *Phamâ* and many others. The NLD and some other popular political groups prefer the informal spoken name and the former English name, so it is possible that these will make a comeback.

Almost every grammatical marker in the language has two different forms in the literary versus spoken language; these are comprehensively listed and compared in Okell and Allott (2001). In some cases, there are extra distinctions in the literary language which do not exist in the spoken form: marked ၏ /í/ after the verb in one of a sequence of real current or past events versus unmarked (and much more frequent) သည် /thi/ where sequence is unspecified or first or last in a sequence, but only a single spoken form တယ် /teh/ after the verb indicating real events, in sequence or not. In some cases, the spoken forms are simplified versions of the literary ones: literary လျှင် /hlyin/, spoken ယင်/ရင် /yin/ 'if', but in most cases they are completely different, for example literary သော့ /tháw/, spoken ကို /ko/ after a noun indicating motion towards that noun. There are also some structural differences; for example, negation is marked in literary style by မ /ma/ preceding the verb, but in spoken by မ /ma/ preceding and ဘူး /phû/~/bû/ at the end of the clause: literary မသွား /mathwâ/ 'go', spoken မသွားဘူး /mathwâ bû/ 'not go'.

The following sentence modified from Allott (1985, 136) illustrates some differences; the literary sentence is given above, and the spoken sentence is below.

သည်	လူ	သည်	သူ ၏	ရည်းစား	နေ	သော့	ရွာ ၌	အလွန်	ပျော်	နေ	သည်
thi	lu	dhi	thu-í	yîzâ	ne	-dháw	ywa-hnai'	alun	pyaw	ne	dhi
ဒီ	လူ		သူ့	ရည်းစား	နေ	တဲ့	ရွာ မှာ	သိပ်	ပျော်	နေ	တယ်
di	lu		thú	yîzâ	ne	-déh	ywa-hma	thei'	pyaw	ne	deh
this	person	SUBJ	his	sweet-heart	live	REL	village-in	very	happy	–ING	REAL

'This person is very happy living in his sweetheart's village.'

In addition to having distinct forms for most of the grammatical markers and some other very frequent words, most verbs have a literary form with an added second syllable, separately often meaningless in Myanmar language: ကောင်း /kâun/ 'good', literary ကောင်းမွန် /kâun mun/ or ငတ် /nga'/ 'starving', literary ငတ်မွတ် /nga' mu'/.

The pronunciation of Myanmar language has been changing relatively rapidly over the past couple of centuries. The first major change was the replacement of the ရ/ြ /r/ sound by the existing /y/ sound, which was completed by the late eighteenth century. Another was the shift of သ from /s/ to /th/ in the early nineteenth century, followed by the simplification of စ /ts/ to /s/, ဆ /tsh/ to /hs/ and ဇ/ဈ /dz/ to /z/ by the mid-nineteenth century. Some current changes include the merger of ဆ /hs/ into စ /s/; of ဝပ်/ဝတ် /wu'/ and ဝမ်/ဝန် /wun/ into ဝစ် /wi'/ and ဝင် /win/; and of -က် /–e'/ into -ပ်/-တ် /a'/ (Bradley 2011). Naturally, as in many languages undergoing extensive phonetic changes, the innovations are most widely used in urban settings, especially in Yangon. Older speakers often dislike the new forms and use them less; and younger speakers use the new forms less frequently in more formal situations. Schools still teach the more conservative forms; the innovations have had no effect on standard spelling, though many younger speakers make spelling errors reflecting the new pronunciations.

In addition to Myanmar language itself, there are seven other recognised ethnic groups whose TB languages derived from old Myanmar language. The largest of these is the Rakhine (also known in English as Arakanese) in Rakhine State in the west of the country, with over a million speakers. This differs from standard Myanmar language in various ways, most notably the preservation of the initial and medial /r/ sound still distinguished in Myanmar writing as initial ရ and medial ြ but not distinguished from the /y/ sound in pronunciation for over 200 years (Bradley 2011), as well as in the vowels; for example, -စ် is pronounced /ai'/ in Rakhine, unlike Myanmar language where it is /i'/ (Bradley 1985; see Okell 1995). Some of the former English place names replaced in 1990 reflect Rakhine rather than Myanmar pronunciation; the British controlled Rakhine from the mid-1820s onwards, and would first have heard pronunciations like /rangoun/ rather than /yangoun/ for Rangoon or Yangon and /irawadi/ rather than /eyawadi/ for the Irrawaddy (Ayeyarwaddy) River, before they had direct contact with Myanmar language from the mid-1850s.

The second largest such group is the Dawei (in English Tavoy for the town, Tavoyan for the speech variety) in Taninthayi Division in the southeast of the country, with about 400,000 speakers. This variety is more different from the standard; it preserves the medial လ /l/ sound in consonant clusters, as was seen in the earliest Myanmar inscriptions from 900 years ago but lost in the standard and most other varieties over 700 years ago, in words such as က္လား /klâ/ 'tiger', standard Myanmar ကျား /câ/ (see Okell 1995). Another large distinct group is the Beik (in English Merguese, derived from the earlier pronunciation Mreik of the name of the town Beik), about 250,000 people in far southern Taninthayi.

All the other regional varieties are spoken by much smaller populations; the best-known are the 90,000 Intha 'children of the lake' who live around Inle Lake in the southwestern Shan State. Like Dawei, Intha keeps medial /l/, which suggests that this is also a very early offshoot of Myanmar language, though separately from Dawei (see Okell 1995). The Danu are a slightly larger group in the same area, and have a Special Administration Zone of two townships. The Yaw and Yabein are small groups in the low hills west of the Ayeyarwaddy, and the Hpon are a group of about 1,500 people in the gorges of the Ayeyarwaddy north of Bhamo, who no longer speak their traditional language at all.

All of these regional varieties derived from early Myanmar language show a strong tendency to converge towards the standard, gradually eliminating regional vocabulary and levelling regional pronunciation differences in favour of the standard. When we compare the Marma sub-variety spoken by descendants of the former Rakhine court who moved to what is now Bangladesh about 230 years ago, we can see how much convergence of Rakhine in Myanmar back towards the standard there has been since the conquest of Rakhine State in 1784. These regional varieties, especially the smaller ones, are likely to continue to contract and may eventually disappear, as the Hpon language already has.

North Burmish languages

The groups who speak the Myanmar language and closely related varieties came from the northeast, probably in the invasion of the Nanzhao Kingdom circa AD 832 which conquered the Pyu kingdoms of the upper Ayeyarwaddy valley and took their territory (Stargardt 1990). Related groups who stayed in western Yunnan and nearby areas which subsequently became part of Myanmar in the northern Shan State and southeastern Kachin State now speak a cluster of languages which includes Maru (own name Lhao Vo), Atsi or Zi (own name Zaiwa), Lashi (own name Lacit) and Maingtha (own name Ngochang). These four groups traditionally intermarry and most individuals are bilingual in two of these languages or in one of these languages and another nearby language. Most are part of the Kachin culture complex and also speak Jinghpaw Kachin; some, especially in China, have undergone profound cultural influence from the local Shan.

Members of the Maingtha ethnic group speak four mutually unintelligible varieties all called Ngochang, including two in Myanmar. One is from Husa valley in northern Longchuan County, western Yunnan, a Buddhist group strongly influenced by the Shan. The Shan term for a valley state is pronounced Maing in Myanmar language; the 's' sound in Myanmar language changed to 'th' about 200 years ago (Bradley 2011). Thus the name Maingtha is a modern Myanmar pronunciation of 'Sa state'. Husa Ngochang or Maingtha also live in Myanmar in small numbers, scattered in Shan villages in the Kachin State, often working as blacksmiths. The main branch of Ngochang in Myanmar, about 35,000 people, often intermarry with the 30,000 Lashi, and so most of them also speak Lashi as well as Jinghpaw Kachin. This close contact has resulted in structural convergence; while the languages keep their distinct sound systems and vocabulary, the meanings have converged so that most words have exact semantic equivalents between these varieties of Ngochang and Lashi, and they are combined in exactly parallel sentence structures. The same kind of local convergence is also seen between the speech of the 100,000 Maru and the 30,000 Atsi in Myanmar, as these two groups also very often intermarry.

Systematic linguistic comparison shows that nearly all of the basic vocabulary of all North Burmish languages is historically cognate with the corresponding vocabulary in Myanmar language.

> 'heavy' Maru *là*, Atsi *lái*, Lashi *laai*, Maingtha *lì*, Myanmar လေး /lê/
> 'horse' Maru *mya*, Atsi *myàng*, Lashi *myang*, Maingtha *hmràng*, Myanmar မြင်း /myîn/
> 'house' Maru *yàm*, Atsi *yúm*, Lashi *yawm*, Maingtha *ín*, Myanmar အိမ် /ein/
> 'ill' Maru *nò*, Atsi *nô*, Lashi *nàaw*, Maingtha *náw*, Myanmar နာ /na/
>
> *Huang 1992: 90, 165, 338, 387*

Ngwi (Loloish) languages

There are five recognised ethnic groups living in the northeast of the country: Kaw (own name Akha), Kwi (own name Lahu Shi 'Yellow Lahu'), Lahu (own name Lahu Na, 'Black Lahu'), Lisu and Pyen (own name Bisu); all live in the Shan State, and the Lisu also live in the Kachin State. The Kwi and Lahu are sometimes classified as one group; they were formerly known as Musur in Shan or မှူဆို Muhso in Myanmar language. Until recently, they shared a single orthography, but they are linguistically distinct; Kwi is another Shan name for the Lahu Shi subgroup. The majority subgroup within the Lahu is the Lahu Na (see Bradley 1979). The Akha were formerly called Ikaw in Thai, and are also called Aini in China, where they are treated as part of the Hani national minority. The Lisu were formerly called Yeren 'wild people' in Chinese, and this was borrowed in the Jinghpaw term for them, Yawyin, sometimes also used in colonial-period sources for the Lisu in the Kachin State. The initial list of 135 ethnic groups of Myanmar included the Lisu twice, as လီဆူး /lihsû/ in the Kachin State and as လီရှော /lishâw/ in the Shan State; the latter is the Shan name for them, and has now been removed from the official list. Lisu, like Lahu, has substantial internal dialect differences; but these are levelled out in the compromise standard written version of the language (see Bradley 2006). All these groups have ABC-based writing systems devised by Christian missionaries during the twentieth century; the Lisu script is an interesting blend of ABC with some features of Myanmar script. There are also smaller unrecognised groups who are classified as part of one of these five ethnic groups but speak distinct languages; for example, the Akeu who are classified as Akha and in fact can also speak Akha and intermarry with the Akha, but have their own distinct language.

These same languages and many other related languages are spoken further east in China, and also spread into Thailand, Laos and Vietnam. Historically, they form the other major component of what is variously called Burmic, Burmese-Lolo or Lolo-Burmese in the linguistic literature; however, the term Lolo or Loloish is now viewed as pejorative and is being replaced by the term Ngwi, based on what was probably their own original name for themselves, cognate with the Myanmar language ငွေ /ngwe/ 'silver'; the point of origin of the Ngwi subgroup of Burmic is in Yunnan, with subsequent migrations, especially to the southwest into Myanmar and neighbouring countries.

Lahu is a minor trade language in the eastern Shan State and nearby in other countries; many of the hill groups including speakers of various MK languages such as Wa as well as speakers of various related Ngwi languages use it to communicate with each other.

As the following words show, these languages are also fairly closely related to Myanmar language, but in some cases with an extra added syllable, replacement of a word and/or more extensive sound changes; for example, words which are *li* in related languages all change to *(h)aw* in Lahu, and Akha has simply replaced the original word for 'heavy'.

'heavy' Lisu *li*, Lahu *hâw*, Akha *yaw kah*, Myanmar လေး /lê/
'horse' Lisu *á mò*, Lahu *í mvûh*, Akha *mah*, Myanmar မြင်း /myîn/
'house' Lisu *hin* Lahu *yeh* Akha *nym*, Myanmar အိမ် /ein/
'ill' Lisu *na*, Lahu *nà*, Akha *ná*, Myanmar နာ /na/

Bradley 1979, 2006; Lewis 1989

Other Tibeto-Burman languages

It is impossible to cover the major internal diversity within the Chin languages of Myanmar in depth here. Chin is a collective Myanmar language name; fifty-two other named groups in the Chin State and three in the Rakhine State speak over thirty distinct languages. These are sometimes referred to by place names such as Tedim, Hakha and Falam, sometimes by clan names, and sometimes by their own group name or a former group name. They are all closely related within the Kuki-Chin branch of TB, in seven distinct clusters: Khumi, Mara, Southern, Central, Northern, Old Kuki and outlier. Many of these groups live only in Myanmar, but others are also or mainly in India and/or Bangladesh. Sometimes the same group goes under different names in different countries. There are also some other more distantly related TB languages,

Tangkhul, Makuri and Para or Jejara, spoken further north; and additional groups who may have distinct languages but who are included within another recognised ethnic group, such as the Akyaung Ari and Koki within the Tangkhul.

Karen is another English name which shows Rakhine influence; the Myanmar pronunciation of this collective name is ကရင် Kayin. This is also seen in the old term Karenni 'red Karen' which is now replaced by the newer Myanmar collective term ကယား Kayah. The twenty-one Kayin and Kayah ethnic groups speak twenty distinct languages. The three largest groups, S'gaw, Pho, Shu or Pwo and Pa-O, all use writing systems which are based on Myanmar script but substantially modified to cater for the different sound systems of these languages; these were developed more than a century ago. Some other groups use ABC writing systems, and some have chosen to share an orthography with another Karen group. For example, the Zayein and Lahta use the Kayan script. Many Karen, especially S'gaw and Pho, have moved into the delta region, and in these areas the languages are being replaced by Myanmar language. S'gaw, Kayah and Pho have indigenous writing systems as well, neither ABC nor Myanmar, but these are not widely used.

There are various groups whose TB languages are distantly related within the Sal subgroup. This includes the large Kachin group—own name Jinghpaw, with numerous dialects—whose standard language serves for interethnic communication in the Kachin State; the scattered Sak group, with Kadu, Kanan and Sak (all calling themselves 'Atsa') as well as extinct Taman and Malin; the Mru group in Rakhine State including Mru and Anu/Hkongso; and the Northern Naga group including four distinct groups within the Naga ethnic group: Tangshang (a new collective ethnic name, various former subgroup names such as Rangpan, Haimi and Moshang appear in the older literature), Konyak, Lainong and Khiamnyungan (also Nauk-Aw in Myanmar language).

In the far north of the Kachin State there are three groups of distinctive TB languages: the Rawang—and some small related unrecognised groups—speaking Nungish languages, the Taraon speaking a Digarish language, and some Tibetans.

Other language groups

There are nine recognised ethnic groups who speak seven distinct TK languages, all rather closely related to standard Thai of Thailand. These are sometimes collectively known as ရှမ်း /shân/ in Myanmar language, and as Shan in English, but are distinct ethnic groups. They have a long history; they were in conflict with the Bagan dynasty during its final stages over 750 years ago, and were probably already living in what is now the Shan State before that. All of them have traditional writing systems; the Shan language itself, known to its speakers as Tai Yay 'big Tai', borrowed its writing system from Myanmar language about 700 years ago, with some minor modifications, while other TK languages have distinct systems, all derived from similar nearby sources and all ultimately derived from the same Indic source as the Myanmar script: Tai Mao, Tai Lue, Tai Khyn, Tai Khamti, Tai Lai and Yuan (the last nearly identical to Northern Thai as spoken in Chiang Mai, which was under Myanmar rule for many centuries). These scripts have been used primarily as a medium for Theravada Buddhism and are usually learned by male children in monasteries, but are also sometimes used for non-religious purposes. The various TK languages also serve as local market languages in the valleys of the Shan State, and are spoken to some extent by many of the smaller ethnic groups living nearby.

Historically the most important MK language of Myanmar is Mon as spoken in the Mon State; it was formerly more widely spoken throughout the delta region as well as in central Thailand. There are many smaller groups in the Shan State who speak a wide range of distinct MK languages which can be grouped into four clusters: Palaungic (from the Myanmar language term for the largest of these groups, who call themselves Ta-ang; the vast majority of the population of speakers of Palaungic languages is in Myanmar), Waic (from Wa, the Myanmar and Chinese language terms for these groups, who use various names; the largest group calls themselves Puroik; about half of the total Wa population lives in China) and also Angkuic and Khmuic (smaller groups, much more numerous and diverse in China and Laos). Other Palaungic groups include the Danaw near Inle Lake (not to be confused with the nearby Danu, whose language is closely related to Myanmar language), the Riang groups—with two recognised ethnic groups, Yinnet or Black Riang, own name Rianglang, and Yinkya or striped Riang, own name Rianglai—and the Pale group; within the Myanmar collective category Palaung there are at least two distinct languages, Ruching and Rumai, also known in Myanmar language as Ngwe Palaung 'silver Palaung' and Shwe Palaung 'gold Palaung'. The sole Angkuic group which has been recognised as an ethnic group is the Tai Loi (which literally means 'hill Tai' in Shan); they call themselves Mok and speak a very wide range of quite distinct varieties spread across southwestern Yunnan in China. The Khmu are likewise a very small group in Myanmar; there are many more Khmu in Laos and surrounding areas, with much more linguistic diversity.

The two MY languages of Myanmar are relatively recent arrivals from China.The IA languages of Rakhine State reflect the fact that the border in this area shifted many times over the centuries, with many periods when the Rakhine ruled over substantial populations of IA speakers, some of whom converted to Buddhism: the Daingnet (better known as Chakma) with their distinctive Ojhopath script modified from Bengali script and the Maramagyi. Others remained Muslim, and these are the Rohingya, to whom the Myanmar government currently denies citizenship and other rights. How long they have lived in Rakhine State is a matter of dispute; some may be recent arrivals, as the Myanmar authorities claim; others may have come in since British rule started there in 1825; others may have come during one of the periods when Rakhine ruled parts of what is now southeastern Bangladesh centuries earlier. Apart from these groups, there are many more immigrant groups speaking other IA and Dravidian languages of South Asia who came during British colonial rule. The sole AN language of Myanmar, Saloun (known as Moken to its speakers), is fairly closely related to Malay but is written with Myanmar script. The Kokang ethnic group of northeastern Shan State speak a Yunnanese variety of Chinese and write it with Chinese characters, as do the many urban Chinese who speak the same variety or other varieties of Chinese.

Written languages and language in the media

Myanmar language has been written with Myanmar script since AD 1112; this was originally derived from the southeastern Indian Brahmi script as used by the Mon, and was adapted for Myanmar language after the Bagan dynasty conquered the Mon in the delta region during the eleventh century. Early stone inscriptions used a square form, but a rounded form appropriate for use on palm leaves (which could be pierced by straight lines) has long been in general use, and is now universally used. The spelling was standardised in the late twelfth century, with very minor reforms in the 1880s and 1970s. Other languages using this script include of course Mon, as well as more or less modified scripts used for Shan, several Karen languages, and so on.

The modern pronunciation is clear and unambiguous from the written form of the Myanmar language; however, pronunciation does not distinguish the spelling of some contrasts that have been lost over the past 900 years, such as between final ပ် /p/ and တ် /t/, between final မ် /m/ and န် /n/, between initial ရ /r/ and ယ /y/ and consonant clusters with medial ြ /r/ versus ျ /y/ and so on; speakers simply need to learn the historically correct spelling for each word.

There are several genres of written Myanmar language. One is Nissaya, which is used for translating Pali Buddhist texts word by word; this adopts various particles which are added after a noun to indicate its grammatical case and after a verb to indicate its tense, categories which are often absent from other genres. The Nissaya style has to some extent influenced formal literary Myanmar language, for example in the use of the particle သည် /thi/ after the subject noun in a sentence, which is normally unmarked or marked by other kinds of particles which indicate topicality or focus in the earliest written language of inscriptions and in the spoken language. Pali influence has also led to the much more frequent use of a plural marker များ /myâ/ after nouns; this is an obligatory category of Pali, but is only rather infrequently marked in spoken Myanmar by the particle တွေ /twe/.

Literature in informal spoken Myanmar language has been appearing for over forty years, notably the work of the late Ludu U Hla; this has also been used in comic strips and other informal sections of some popular magazines. As outlined in U Thaw Kaung Sithu (2014), there was strict government censorship of all print media from 6 August 1964 until 10 June 2011, which was gradually relaxed until 28 August 2012 when all censorship was removed. Since then, the media in Myanmar has expanded enormously and its language style has shifted substantially, with much greater use of informal spoken language in many new non-government newspapers and on television, notably for chat shows and light entertainment such as quiz shows; of course contemporary drama has been in informal spoken style for some time. However, government newspaper and broadcast media news and other formal content remain primarily in literary Myanmar language.

Conclusion on language policy

The 1948, 1974 and 2008 constitutions all specify that Burmese or Myanmar language is the official and national language, though the 1948 and 2008 constitutions make provision for some use of English, and the 2008 constitution further recognises and authorises the use of ethnic minority languages, and requires the government to assist in developing the languages, literatures and culture of the ethnic minority groups.

Until recently, all government schools conducted all classes in Myanmar language, and all examinations for progress within the education system have been centrally administered. As a result of the 2014 National Education Law and the 2015 Ethnic Rights Law, ethnic minority languages are able to be taught in early years of government schools, and with the assistance of UNICEF and the Ministry of Education, over a hundred ethnic groups across the country have developed materials which have started to be introduced into school use. Teachers with relevant language background are being encouraged to return to their own communities to teach in their own ethnic languages. Ethnic languages also continue to be taught in a variety of non-government settings, especially in Buddhist monasteries and Christian churches.

At the tertiary education level, government institutions teach mainly in Myanmar language, though many of the textbooks are in English. There are also many Buddhist and Christian seminaries which have expanded their offerings in recent years and now teach popular courses in business, computer science, communications, English and other areas, and some use English as a teaching medium. The 2014 National Education Law officially permitted the use of English as a language of instruction, alongside Myanmar language or alone. Standards of English declined steadily from 1948 onwards, but are now starting to improve again. In addition to English, various other foreign languages are also taught at the tertiary level and in private language schools.

In the legal system, literary Myanmar language has been the norm since 1948. The 1974 constitution provided for interpretation for members of ethnic minorities when necessary, not explicitly mentioned in the 2008 constitution and in reality never widely implemented.

In government administration, literary Myanmar language is used, notably in all government forms. Most public signage is also in literary style; but spoken style is extensively used in advertising.

Myanmar is fortunate to have a long-established, well-developed and widely-used national language. The government and its formal and adult education systems have long fostered literacy in Myanmar language, both among the Bamar majority and among the other ethnic groups. Myanmar language is normally used for communication between the Bamar majority and the other 134 ethnic groups. Myanmar also has a rich heritage of other indigenous languages, most of which are historically related to it. Many of these also have long written history and large numbers of speakers.

References

Allott, A. J. 1985. 'Language Policy and Language Planning in Burma'. In *Language Policy, Language Planning and Sociolinguistics in South-East Asia*, edited by David Bradley, 131–154. Canberra: Pacific Linguistics.

Bradley, David. 1979. *Lahu Dialects*. ANU Press, Canberra.

Bradley, David. 1985. 'Arakanese Vowels'. In *Linguistics of the Sino-Tibetan Area: The State of the Art*, edited by Graham Thurgood, James A. Matisoff & David Bradley, 180–200. Canberra: Pacific Linguistics C-87.

Bradley, David. 2006. 'Lisu Orthographies and Email'. In *Lesser-Known Languages of South Asia: Status and Policies, Case Studies and Applications of Information Technology*, edited by Anju Saxena & Lars Borin, 125–135. Berlin: Mouton de Gruyter.

Bradley, David. 2011. 'Changes in Burmese Phonology and Orthography'. Keynote, Southeast Asian Linguistics Society 21, Kasetsart U, Bangkok, Thailand. www.academia.edu/1559757/Changes_in_Burmese_Phonology_and_Orthography.

Huang, B. F. (ed.). 1992. 藏缅语族语音词汇. 北京: 中央民族学院出版社 *[Zang-Mian yuzu yuyin cihui], 'A Tibeto-Burman Lexicon'*. Beijing: Central Institute of Nationalities Press.

Lewis, Paul W. 1989. *Akha–English–Thai Dictionary*. Chiang Rai: Development and Agricultural Project for Akha.

Okell, John. 1995. 'Three Burmese Dialects'. In *Studies in Burmese Languages*, edited by David Bradley, 1–138. Canberra: Pacific Linguistics A-83.

Okell, John, & Anna Allott. 2001. *Burmese/Myanmar Dictionary of Grammatical Forms*. London: Curzon.

Stargardt, Janice. 1990. *The Ancient Pyu of Burma. Vol. 1 Early Pyu Cities in a Man-Made Landscape*. Singapore: PACSEA Cambridge, Cambridge and Institute of Southeast Asian Studies.

U Thaw Kaung Sithu. 2014. 'Media Control and Relaxation in Myanmar'. *Minpaku Anthropology Newsletter* (38): 5–6.

13
RELIGION

Charles Carstens

Golden pagodas and saffron-clad monks are among the most common visuals associated with Myanmar. Buddhism has fundamentally shaped the country's cultural history and is unquestionably recognised as its predominant religious tradition. Much of religion in Myanmar could be captured through an overview of Buddhism; however, three complexities challenge such an approach. Most obvious is the presence of religious traditions that are differentiated from Buddhism. Forms of animism (i.e., nat religion) and worship of Hindu gods are nearly ubiquitous.[1] Christianity is identified as the majority religion of major ethnic groups such as the Kachin, Chin, and Kayin.[2] Islam has been present in Myanmar's territories for over a millennium and currently stands as the country's largest non-Buddhist religion.[3] Beyond pluralism, the beginning and end of religion is nearly impossible to discern. History, politics, education, and the law have all been intimately entwined with religion.[4] Myanmar lacks what we might call a robust distinction between religious and secular domains.[5] Third and perhaps most troublesome, the very definition of religion in Myanmar is actively contested. What counts as religion? How is religion related to other forms of identity (e.g., race or citizenship)? Which religions belong to Myanmar? Debate over such questions has generated multiple and often conflicting conceptions of religion by persons and institutions in unequal positions of power.[6]

These complexities illuminate the limitations and contingencies intrinsic to any survey of religion. Since a definitive account of religion is not only problematic but could even result in unintended political consequences, I propose a bottom-up approach. Selecting three occasions on which I encountered religion outside of religious settings, I analyse how the words of persons and public documents both articulate diverse notions of religion and sketch out broad features of Myanmar's religious climate. This climate, I argue, is currently inflected by discourses that evoke the looming threat of a non-Buddhist minority described in terms that blend religion, race, ethnicity, citizenship, and national belonging.

The census

Standard encyclopaedia entries on 'religion' present demographic statistics: often a nation's population distributed among various religious traditions. The CIA World Factbook, for instance, lists the following statistics for 'religion' in Myanmar: 'Buddhist 89%, Christian 4% (Baptist 3%, Roman Catholic 1%), Muslim 4%, Animist 1%, other 2%'.[7] In 2014, Myanmar's

Ministry of Immigration and Population and the United Nations Population Fund (UNPFA) jointly conducted a national census. This survey included assessment of religion. Preliminary census reports were published in late August 2014; however, release of data about religion was delayed. Curiosity about the motives behind this decision roused speculation. Rumours alluded to concerns about violence in response to evidence of expanding numbers of 'ku lā″', a pejorative racial term for a person of South Asian descent.[8]

Casually discussing the census over dinner at a restaurant in the city of Magway in central Myanmar, Soe San,[9] the restaurant's owner, broached the subject of religion:

> I have no idea why [census data] was postponed. It doesn't really matter anyway. Let me tell you a funny thing about the census. There were seven choices for religion: Buddhist, Christian, Islam, Hindu, Animist, other religion, and no religion. I joked to my friends: 'What's the right answer?' You know, my mother is Buddhist and father Christian. I studied English at church. I ordained as a Buddhist monk. I've gone to nat festivals and Hindu temples like anyone else. Which one am I? I'm not a Muslim. That's for sure. But you know, none of this is relevant to 'the right answer'. Who is conducting the census? I don't know what they're going to do with this information. They come, ask questions, and write things down. The right answer is the one that avoids trouble: Buddhist. That's what I said. You know, I bet that even some ku lā″s would say the same.
>
> *Soe San 2014*

As Soe San explains, his comment is humorous because of the absurdities it reveals. The census calls for Soe San to disclose a single religious tradition with which he identifies. He contrasts this notion of religious exclusivity with his multidimensional encounter with religion, one that gives rise to a plural religious identity through parentage, education, rites of passage, and even leisure activities. Soe San's joke exposes how assumptions embedded in the census format undermine the very possibility of a truthful answer.

Soe San's gesture to the 'right answer' introduces a second absurdity. The census is not experienced as neutral data collection but as a precarious encounter. Expressing uncertainty about the use and purposes of the collected information, Soe San views the census as an occasion that calls for cunning, especially when it comes to religion, a domain he marks as potentially dangerous. Soe San's 'right answer' does not pertain to any of the various facets of religion listed above. Rather, it is a matter of personal safety. His cunning is not a lie. A truthful response is impossible after all. However, his final words do allude to the possibility of others deploying deception intentionally. 'Even some ku lā″s' insinuates that persons of South Asian descent are not Buddhists and would feel insecure to disclose this non-Buddhist religious identity to the state. For Soe San, religion is both politically sensitive and tied to race.

Buddhist-ethnicity

The fraught politics of claiming a religion are not confined to the census. Calls for religious identification are commonplace such as in moments of personal introduction. On one such occasion, I became aware of a hybrid term for ethnicity: 'Buddhist-ethnicity' (Buddha-bhā-thā -lū-myui″). Links between religion and blood are not without historical precedent. For example, historical texts such as the Glass Palace Chronicles place the Buddha's Sakya race at the head of the lineage of Myanmar kings (Tin and Luce 1960). Such statements certainly make no claims about ethnic identity; however, memory of the past may introduce new interpretations.[10]

Despite such antecedents, the term Buddhist-ethnicity appears to be new. During an early encounter with the term, I confessed lack of familiarity to my interlocutor, Thiha. Asking how long he had been using the term, he responded:

> 'Buddhist-ethnicity' is *not really* an ethnicity. I am actually Rakhine. There are many ethnic groups in Myanmar with various customs and traditions. While some may be very different from one another, others are quite close. The Burmese, Shan, Arakanese, and Mon peoples all have Buddhist traditions. They all worship the Buddhist religion. That's the main point. When I say 'Buddhist-ethnicity', I am referring to these ethnic groups as one, united.[11]

Clarifying who was excluded from the group, he readily replied: 'ku lā″s. All Buddhists have problems with ku lā″s these days. The authorities do nothing about this. We need to unite to remain vigilant of this danger' (Thiha 2015).

Buddhist-ethnicity is not a widely circulated term, most claiming to have never heard of it. Its mention did, however, elicit comments that further texture this review of religion. Consider Htun's, Sithu's, and Aung Kyaw's responses to the question: 'Have you ever heard of Buddhist-ethnicity?'

> Htun:
> I have never heard of 'Buddhist-ethnicity'. You know, these terms—religion and ethnicity—are really tangled up. Take me for example. What is written on my national identity card? When I applied, I wrote Islam as my religion. What must I write for ethnicity? My family has been living in this country for generations. My ethnicity is Myanmar of course. I applied with Myanmar as my ethnicity, but when I received my card, I find Pakistan. I am not from Pakistan. My family is not from Pakistan. They forbid me from writing 'Myanmar' because I am a Muslim. What you see written on that card is not me.[12]

> Sithu:
> I don't know anything about 'Buddhist-ethnicity', but it does not seem especially strange. Look at my identity card. For ethnicity, 'Hindu', under religion, 'Buddhist'. I worship at Hindu temples and Buddhist temples. Buddhists, too, come to Hindu temples. How are Hindus and Buddhists any different? We worship together, unlike Muslims. So I am Hindu and a Buddhist. That is why you see both on my identity card.[13]

> Aung Kyaw:
> 'Buddhist-ethnicity'? That is incorrect. Look here. [He pulls out his national identity card]. My name, ID number, date of birth, ethnicity, religion. Do you see? 'Bamar' is written there for ethnicity and 'Buddhist' there for religion. Ethnicity and religion are not the same. Ethnicity is your blood, your family. Religion is what you believe. Whoever said 'Buddhist-ethnicity' is uneducated or just crazy.[14]

Articulating explicit religious affiliations, these remarks appear to diverge from Soe San's plural and shifting notion of religious identity. Instead of taking Soe San as an exception, these assorted views jointly illustrate a spectrum of religious affiliation. At one extreme are those who identify with a single religious tradition such as Aung Kyaw. At the other are those like Soe San who do not exclusively commit. Between these extremes are those like Sithu who identify with multiple religious traditions, but not all. As Soe San describes, movement along the spectrum may shift depending on one's context. Thiha, Sithu, Htun, and Aung Kyaw do not indicate such movements. However, this may reflect the different contexts in which these words were spoken, the census prompting a unique set of conditions.

Beyond matters of affiliation, each respondent delineates distinct boundaries between outsider and insider as well as a conceptual relationship among religion, race, ethnicity, citizenship, and belonging. Thiha identifies with Buddhist-ethnicity and then Rakhine, qualifying that the former term is 'not really' an ethnicity. This qualification does not invalidate Buddhist-ethnicity, but acknowledges its limited currency in comparison with Rakhine, one of the eight major state-authorised ethnic classifications. Self-identifying with Buddhist-ethnicity makes a political intervention. According to Thiha, his home state—Rakhine State—is beset with a foreign, non-Buddhist threat, which is growing through rapid reproduction and religious conversion of Buddhist bodies. In the absence of a responsive state, Buddhist-ethnicity marshals private citizens to stand in unity and security. Bound by a common religion, ethnic differences among Buddhists are made irrelevant. This group is set against a racialised non-Buddhist outsider.

Thiha's usage of Buddhist-ethnicity shuffles not only persons but also the very concepts of religion, ethnicity, race, and citizenship. In the abstract, these concepts remain separate. But as instantiated human attributes (e.g., Buddhist or Rakhine), they express elective affinities or configure specific sets of identity markers. In other words, certain types of religion, race, and ethnicity go together. For example, linking Buddhism, Rakhine ethnicity, and belonging, Thiha configures one set of attributes: Buddhist-Rakhine-Myanmar citizen. Another configured set is composed of ku lā" race, Islamic religion, and foreign citizenship.[15] The elements of each set are not necessarily categorically equivalent. These two sets contain religion and belonging, but ethnicity and race are not interchangeable. For Thiha, religion is conceptually separate from, but is practically connected with race, ethnicity, and belonging.

This notion of configured sets of identity markers is also found in Htun's narrative. According to his explanation, his failed application is the result of the state perceiving an impossible set. 'Muslim' and 'Myanmar' do not match. This dissonance is resolved by reassigning an ethnicity compatible with Islam: 'Pakistan'. This term—shared with a foreign country—renders him an outsider, invalidating his claims to belonging based on family history. This ethnic designation has a direct impact on Htun's status as a member of the nation. Religion thus does not just have political implications, but is foremost a matter of politics.

Sithu highlights similarities between Buddhists and Hindus. Comparison yields a notion of religion that is constituted through his points of comparison. According to Sithu, religion is about practice and sacred space. Selection of these two points is no neutral act. Hinduism and Buddhism are brought together whereas Islam is set apart. Different points of comparison could position religions alternatively. For instance, if notions of divinity were compared, Hinduism may express a stronger resemblance to Islam than Buddhism. Appreciating how comparison affects distances between religions, we see that definitions of religion matter.[16]

According to his identity card, Sithu is ethnically Hindu and religiously Buddhist. Religion and ethnicity are conceptually distinct and Hindu is an ethnic classification. His words, however, assign no such distinctions. Hinduism and Buddhism are religions and ethnicity receives no mention. The identity card's label of ethnicity is effaced, becoming an empty placeholder for another religion. Limiting conversation to the register of religion is also evident in his word choice of 'Muslims' and not the racial term ku lā". Religion is the only category of importance. Ethnicity and race are either irrelevant or folded into religion. Unlike Htun and Thiha, Sithu's words do not evoke configured sets.

While Sithu attributes no special significance to his Hindu identity being ethnic, recall Soe San's allusion to ku lā"s self-identifying as Buddhist. Is Sithu making himself Buddhist to avoid trouble? Sithu is of South Asia descent, which puts him at risk of being perceived as an outsider in the current political climate. If he were to designate Hinduism as his religion, he might be forced to accept a foreign ethnicity like Htun. Also, by making Hinduism ethnic, the religion category becomes open. Inserting Buddhism as his religion would allow him to attain an insider attribute that offsets his outsider race. Maintaining discussion only on the level of religion strengthens 'Muslim' as an outsider attribute and dilutes the significance of race. Race is not defended, but redefined. Ku lā" becomes 'possibly Buddhist' and not always foreign.[17] I do not evoke Soe San's remark to cast doubt on Sithu's Buddhist affiliation. Rather, Soe San shows us how Sithu's Buddhist identification could be called into question.

Outright rejecting the term Buddhist-ethnicity, Aung Kyaw stresses conceptual boundaries between religion and ethnicity. Religion is defined as beliefs and religious affiliation is determined through personal preference. Aung Kyaw makes no reference to conflict, divisions between insider and outsider, and political implications of religious affiliation. Aung Kyaw's position may seem exceptional, but he may also be the exception that proves the rule. Recall his identification as a Bamar Buddhist. As a member of the ethnic and religious majority, he may be less susceptible to forms of racial, ethnic, and religious discrimination. His claims to belonging are less likely to be suspected. Without such experiences, connection among these domains may appear less pronounced. This is undoubtedly speculation, but it is important to remember that notions of religion are not just personal opinions, but develop in a world where power and vulnerability are unequally distributed.

Similar to religious affiliation, conceptual relationships among religion, ethnicity, race, and citizenship are diverse and fall along a spectrum. At one extreme these concepts are radically separate and at the other boundaries overlap. The middle encompasses positions that acknowledge conceptual differences, yet linkages as configured sets. Amidst their diversity, these words also shade in different, but overlapping, segments of a common picture. This picture displays Buddhists who perceive threats from non-Buddhist minorities who are designated as outsiders and described through varying combinations of race and ethnicity. Among those adversely affected, some put forward religious identifications which place themselves within spaces of belonging. This is exhibited in Sithu's emphasis of religious practice and Thiha's promotion of pan-ethnic religious unity. Others like Htun submit to conceptions of religion imposed by those in a greater position of power.

Legislating religious freedom

Each account thus far bears traces of the state. Some portray the state as a coercive force that constrains religion whereas others show how the state creates the very conditions in which religion is articulated. According to the 2008 Myanmar Constitution, the state is a secular institution, meaning religiously neutral.[18] This secularity is theoretically maintained by prohibiting religious discrimination and banning certain forms of political participation by members of the clergy, such as voting. Religion is located in the domain of private individual rights: 'Every citizen is equally entitled to freedom of conscience and the right to freely profess and practise religion subject to public order, morality or health and to the other provisions of this Constitution.'[19] The open-ended language of this right poses a potential challenge to state secularity. What constitutes freedom of conscience and religious practice? If these rights are guaranteed to every citizen, how must the state respond when non-state actors interfere with other non-state actors' freedom of religion? Must the state maintain a stance of non-involvement, allowing infringements of religious freedom by non-state actors? Or must the state intervene and police religious freedom?

These questions have been answered in legislation known as the 'Race and Religion' laws passed in 2015.[20] These laws seek to regulate inter-faith marriage, polygamy, religious conversion, and population growth. In the conversion bill, freedom of conscience is elaborated as the free choice of one's religion. Religious choices are deemed free if made without inducement, intimidation, undue influence, or pressure.[21] To ensure that religious choice remains unhindered, the bill outlines the following state administered procedure for conversion: The aspiring convert applies to a registration board with a document containing the applicant's background information as well as reasons for conversion. The board interviews the applicant to ascertain whether he or she truly believes in the religion. The aspiring convert must demonstrate knowledge of the religion's essence and various customs such as marriage, divorce, and inheritance. He or she must also show no intent of insulting, degrading, destroying, or misusing religion. If the board approves of the application, the applicant is awarded a certificate of conversion. Conversion outside of these procedures is regarded as invalid and illegal.

The right to freely profess and practise religion is detailed in the marriage law. The bill presents a hypothetical non-Buddhist male obstructing his Buddhist wife's freedom to worship, his children's pursuit of their own religious preferences, and all family members' abilities to freely venerate religious icons. Religious freedom is also violated through denigration of his Buddhist family members' religious faiths. Examples of denigration include tactics designed to cause abandonment of religion, to defile sacred places and objects, or to cause bitterness in the religious spirit of Buddhism through spoken words, written words, symbols, or gestures. Various legal penalties for these violations are listed.[22]

By defending religious freedom as a private individual right, the Constitution theoretically commits the state to religious non-interference, thereby delineating separate domains for religion and politics. However, through interpretation of the Constitution's language of religious freedom, these laws place the state in a position of direct administration of religious life. This is well exemplified through the conversion procedures. The bills' language also establishes principles of religion. For example, the definition and process of conversion presumes that religious traditions are separate and their memberships are exclusive. In devising measures that safeguard religious freedom, these bills define conditions of religious injury, presuming what is and is not essential to religious life. Also prominent is its attention to gender. Buddhist women are portrayed as religious victims and points of vulnerability in the religious community. Women thus become a broader religious issue, their supervision a matter of public religious concern.[23] Lastly these hypothetical confrontations between Buddhists and non-Buddhists imply religious difference at sites of potential confrontation. For instance, prohibiting non-Buddhists from interfering with Buddhist icon worship insinuates that interference is a matter of religious difference. These points of difference are again points of comparison. As discussed in Sithu's case, points of religious comparison create concepts of religion, which have significant consequences for how various groups are seen as similar or different, insiders or outsiders.

Scale

Whether designated as ku lā″, Muslim, or non-Buddhist, references to religious threat have been consistent throughout this chapter. Growing circulation of this rhetoric has paralleled a resurgence of violence against Muslims starting in 2012. International organisations and foreign governments have placed demands on the state to contain this violence by reining in so-called Buddhist 'nationalists' or 'extremists'. The 969 movement and its affiliated organisation, Ma-Ba-Tha, have been held primarily responsible. Not only did Ma-Ba-Tha draft the 'race and religion' laws, but U Wirathu—the popular figurehead of the group—is notorious for making such comments as: '[Muslims] are breeding so fast and they are stealing our women, raping them' (Beech 2013).

While Ma-Ba-Tha may be the most conspicuous source of this rhetoric, the scale is certainly much larger than this group alone. Myanmar's rapidly expanding telecommunications industry has created technological conditions to allow rapid dissemination of images and stories of violence perpetrated by Muslims. Public figures have also echoed this language of religious threat and confrontation. Leader of the National League for Democracy, Aung San Suu Kyi, has explained:

> The fear is not just on the side of the Muslims, but on the side of the Buddhists as well . . . Muslims have been targeted but Buddhists have also been subjected to violence . . . I think we'll accept that there's a perception that Muslim power, global Muslim power, is very great. And certainly that is the perception in many parts of the world and in our country too.
>
> *BBC News 2013*

Suu Kyi's final comment introduces an important observation. This religious threat is not perceived as simply a local problem, but a local manifestation of a global problem. This is reflected in circulating digital materials. The majority of featured events and actors are international, not local. Ways of speaking about religious threat are also congruent with those of the Western media such as characterising Islamic as an expansionary, singular, and aggressive force.[24] The formidable influence of the Western media may not be surprising. As a fledgling, aspiring democracy, the people of Myanmar are being urged to adopt leadership recommendations and expertise of the West.[25] Nevertheless, if the impact of the Western media is taken seriously, religion in Myanmar must be understood on the scale of not merely the local but also the global.

Conclusion

In this chapter, I have drawn attention to some of the ways in which religion is deployed in Myanmar. Religion is constituted as beliefs, worship, sacred space, entertainment, and even the protection of women. Religious affiliation shows varying degrees of exclusivity as well as stability. Matters of race, ethnicity, citizenship, and belonging are variously fashioned in connection to religion. This diversity is expressed by persons and institutions of unequal power in a climate where religion is politically sensitive. Discourses of religious threat pervade the current religious climate. This threat takes shape within international norms of speaking about religion and is articulated in religious, ethnic, racial, and political terms.

Recognising these global and extra-religious dimensions, religion in Myanmar must be studied in ways that relax conventional assumptions about its boundaries and involve new forms of scholarly collaboration. This is a call for not only interdisciplinarily but also extending boundaries beyond area studies. Myanmar is not best studied within the confines of its boundaries but within a complex web of global discourses and power. At stake in developing such collaboration is a better scholarly treatment of not merely religion but also identity, citizenship, rights, and public administration in Myanmar today.

Notes

1 A 'nat' is a spirit-like being that is commonly worshipped in Myanmar. Nats and Hindu gods are both incorporated into and excluded from Buddhism depending on the context. For more on nats, see Spiro,

Melford E. 1967. *Burmese Supernaturalism*. Englewood Cliffs: Prentice-Hall; Brac de la Perrière, Bénédicte. 2009. 'An overview of the field of religion in Burmese studies'. *Asian Ethnology* (68) 2: 185–210.

2 Secondary scholarship about Christianity in Myanmar is in short supply. For more, see Bigandet, Paul Ambrose. 1887. *An Outline of the History of the Catholic Burmese Mission from the Year 1720 to 1887*. Rangoon: Hanthawaddy Press; Pearn, Bertie Reginald. 1962. *Judson of Burma*. London: Edinburgh House Press.

3 The size of the Muslim population is a topic of dispute. Estimates range from 4% to 20%. For more on Islam in Myanmar, see Yegar, Moshe. 1972. *The Muslims of Burma*. Wiesbaden: O. Harrassowitz; Berlie, J. A. 2008. *The Burmanization of Myanmar's Muslims*. Bangkok: White Lotus Press.

4 For more on religion and political discourse, see: Jordt, Ingrid. 2007. *Burma's Mass Lay Meditation Movement: Buddhism and the Cultural Construction of Power*. Athens: Ohio University Press; Houtman, Gustaaf. 1999. *Mental Culture in Burmese Crisis Politics: Aung San Suu Kyi and the National League for Democracy*. Tokyo: Tokyo University of Foreign Studies, Institute for the Study of Languages and Cultures of Asia and Africa; Smith, Donald Eugene. 1965. *Religion and Politics in Burma*. Princeton: Princeton University Press. For more on the Buddhism and history writing, see: Kirichenko, Alexey. 2009. 'From Ava to Mandalay: Toward charting the development of Burmese Yazawin traditions'. *Journal of Burma Studies* (13) 1: 1–75; Leider, Jacques. 2005. 'The emergence of Rakhine historiography: A challenge for Myanmar historical research'. In *Myanmar Historical Commission Conference Proceedings, Part 2*. Yangon: Myanmar Historical Commission; Berkwitz, Stephen. 2004. *Buddhist History in the Vernacular: The Power of the Past in Late Medieval Sri Lanka*. Boston: Brill. For more on religion and education in Myanmar, see Turner, Alicia. 2011. 'Religion making and its failures: Turning monasteries into schools and Buddhism into a religion in colonial Burma'. In *Secularism and Religion Making*, 226–42, edited by Markus Dressler & Arvind-Pal S. Mandair. Oxford: Oxford University Press; Scott, Sir James George. 1882. *The Burman, His Life and Notions*. New York: Norton and Co.; Kaung, U. 1963. 'A survey of the history of education in Burma before the British conquest and after'. *Journal of the Burma Research Society* (46) 2: 1–125. For more on religion and law in Myanmar, see: Huxley, Andrew. 2014. 'Pāli Buddhist law in Southeast Asia'. In *Buddhism and Law: An Introduction*, 167–82, edited by Rebecca R. French & Mark R. Nathan. New York: Cambridge University Press; Lammerts, Christian. 2014. 'Genres and jurisdictions: Laws governing monastic inheritance in seventeenth-century Burma'. In *Buddhism and Law: An Introduction*, edited by Rebecca R. French & Mark R. Nathan, 183–97. New York: Cambridge University Press; Maung, E. 1970. *Burmese Buddhist Law*. Rangoon: Daw Than Tint Mya Sapay.

5 Although notions of secularism do exist in Myanmar, they are neither pervasive nor uniform. For more on secularism in Myanmar, see: Turner, Alicia. 2014. *Saving Buddhism: The Impermanence of Religion in Colonial Burma*. Honolulu: University of Hawai'i Press.

6 Such questions are relatively new since the concept of religion in Myanmar emerged only in the nineteenth century. For more, see: Turner, *Saving Buddhism*; Houtman, Gustaaf. 1990. 'How a foreigner invented Buddhendom in Burmese: From thathana to bok-da' ba-tha'. *Journal of the Anthropological Society of Oxford (JASO)* (21) 2: 113–28.

7 These statistics originate from the 1983 Myanmar Census. See The World Factbook. Washington, DC: Central Intelligence Agency. [Online]. Available from: www.cia.gov/library/publications/the-world-factbook/geos/bm.html. [Accessed August 2016].

8 All Burmese words are transliterated according to Library of Congress conventions of romanisation of Burmese. See: 'ku lā″', Mran′ mā-'Aṅgalip′ 'abhidhān´. 1993. Ran′ kun′: Dept. of Myanmar Language Commission, Ministry of Education, Union of Myanmar. p. 10.

9 All names are pseudonyms due to the potentially controversial nature of the comments.

10 Differences between race and ethnicity are complex and difficult to convey within the confines of this footnote. For the purposes of this chapter, race refers to physical attributes such as skin colour. Ethnicity refers to cultural attributes such as dress, music, etc.

11 Thiha. Buddhist ethnicity. March, 2015.

12 Htun, Buddhist ethnicity, May, 2015.

13 Interview with Sithu, Buddhist ethnicity, June, 2015.

14 Interview with Aung Kyaw, Buddhist ethnicity, March, 2015.

15 A prominent example of linking attributes of ethnicity and religion may be found at Yangon's National Races Village. In this village-scale representation of the peoples and geography of Myanmar, each major ethnic group is represented through a collection of archetypical features such as architecture, clothing, and household objects. Each group is identified with a predominant religious tradition. These traditions

are displayed through iconography, religious objects, and the construction of religious space within the home (e.g., shrine room).

16 More examples of religion-making through comparison can be found in early missionary work. Early Baptist missionaries, for instance, identified theological divergence between Christian and Buddhist notions of God. Through repeated comparison between Buddhist and Christian positions on God, the conception of God became a feature of religion. As a result, the Buddhist position on God became a characteristic of Buddhism, despite this theological claim having little importance prior to comparison. For more on the politics of religious comparison, see Smith, J. Z. 1990. *Drudgery Divine: On the Comparison of Early Christianities and the Religions of Late Antiquity*. Chicago: University of Chicago Press.

17 This parallels how Muslims in Myanmar often respond to questions about Buddhist aggression. Buddhist aggressors are not denounced and Islam is not defended. Rather, Muslims as a whole are redefined as good Muslims and bad Muslims. The threat becomes refocused to a specific kind of Islam.

18 The Constitution, indeed, recognises the 'special position' of Buddhism in Article 361. However, this special position is not detailed and the belonging of non-Buddhist traditions is acknowledged in Article 362. See Praññ' thoṅ' cu Sammata Mran' mā Nuiṅ' ṅaṃ to' Phvai′ caññ'″ puṃ 'a khre Upademū kram'″(2008 khu nhac'). www.burmalibrary.org/docs09/Myanmar_Constitution-2008(bu)-red.pdf.

19 See Article 34, Praññ' thoṅ' cu Sammata Mran' mā Nuiṅ' ṅaṃ to' Phvai′ caññ'″ puṃ 'a khre Upademū kram'″ (2008 khu nhac'). www.burmalibrary.org/docs09/Myanmar_Constitution-2008(bu)-red.pdf.

20 See 'Mran' mā Buddha bhāsā vaṅ' min'″ ma myā″ 'A thū″ thim'″ mrā″ khraṅ'″ chuiṅ' rā Upade kram'″', *The Light of Myanmar (Mran' mā 'A laṅ″)*, December 3, 2014; 'Kui″ kvai' ra Bhā sā kū″ proṅ'″ khraṅ ″chuiṅ'ra Upade (mū kram'″) nhaṅ'′ cap' lyañ'″ r* Ra han'″ rhaṅ' lū praññ' sū myā″ e* 'a kraṃ pru khyak' myā″ pe″ pui′ ran' phit' kho'', *Mirror (Kre″muṃ)*, May 27, 2014.

21 See Article 15, 'Kui″ kvai' ra Bhā sā kū″ proṅ'″ khraṅ″ chuiṅ' ra Upade (mū kram'″) nhaṅ'′ cap' lyañ'″ r* Ra han'″ rhaṅ' lū praññ' sū myā″ e* 'a kraṃ pru khyak' myā″ pe″ pui′ ran' phit' kho',' *Mirror (Kre″muṃ)*, May 27, 2014.

22 Such penalties include sufficient grounds for divorce; forfeiture of jointly owned property and rights to custody of the children; payment of child support for underage children; three years, imprisonment; and a fine of 500,000 kyat.

23 The role of women in matters of religious controversy has been consistent throughout religious clashes in Myanmar. It is not uncommon for anti-Muslim mobs to be mobilised in response to rumours of aggression against Buddhist females.

24 For more, see: Schissler, Matthew, Matthew J. Walton & Phyu Phyu Thi. 2015. 'Threat and virtuous defence: Listening to narratives of religious conflict in six Myanmar cities'. Report by Myanmar Media and Society Project, University of Oxford.

25 For instance, an article in *The New York Times* considers the impoverishment of democratic vocabulary and concepts in contemporary Burmese language. These inadequacies are to be rectified through the importation of education and capacity building from the West. For more, see Fuller, Thomas. 2015. 'Those who would remake Myanmar find that words fail them'. *The New York Times*, July 19.

Bibliography

BBC News. 2013. 'Suu Kyi blames Burma violence on "climate of fear"'. *BBC News*, October 24.

Beech, Hannah. 2013. 'The face of Buddhist terror'. *Time Magazine*, July 1.

Berkwitz, Stephen. 2004. *Buddhist History in the Vernacular: The Power of the Past in Late Medieval Sri Lanka*. Boston: Brill.

Berlie, J. A. 2008. *The Burmanization of Myanmar's Muslims*. Bangkok: White Lotus Press.

Bigandet, Paul Ambrose. 1887. *An Outline of the History of the Catholic Burmese Mission from the Year 1720 to 1887*. Rangoon: Hanthawaddy Press.

Brac de la Perrière, Bénédicte. 2009. 'An overview of the field of religion in Burmese studies'. *Asian Ethnology* (68) 2: 185–210.

Dayan, Alain. 2012. 'Irrawaddy: Fleuve sacre de Birmanie'. Directed by Alain Dayan (Paris: Seven Sept), video. Accessed August 2016. www.youtube.com/watch?v=Fk6j1JsBaow.

Fuller, Thomas. 2015. 'Those who would remake Myanmar find that words fail them'. *The New York Times*, July 19.

Houtman, Gustaaf. 1990. 'How a foreigner invented Buddhendom in Burmese: From thathana to bok-da' ba-tha'. *Journal of the Anthropological Society of Oxford (JASO)* (21) 2: 113–28.

Houtman, Gustaaf. 1999. *Mental Culture in Burmese Crisis Politics: Aung San Suu Kyi and the National League for Democracy*. Tokyo: Tokyo University of Foreign Studies, Institute for the Study of Languages and Cultures of Asia and Africa.

Huxley, Andrew. 2014. 'Pāli Buddhist law in Southeast Asia.' In *Buddhism and Law: An Introduction*, edited by Rebecca R. French & Mark R. Nathan, 167–82. New York: Cambridge University Press.

Jordt, Ingrid. 2007. *Burma's Mass Lay Meditation Movement: Buddhism and the Cultural Construction of Power*. Athens: Ohio University Press.

Kaung, U. 1963. 'A survey of the history of education in Burma before the British conquest and after'. *Journal of the Burma Research Society* (46) 2: 1–125.

Kirichenko, Alexey. 2009. 'From Ava to Mandalay: Toward charting the development of Burmese Yazawin traditions'. *Journal of Burma Studies* (13) 1: 1–75.

Lammerts, Christian. 2014. 'Genres and jurisdictions: Laws governing monastic inheritance in seventeenth-century Burma'. In *Buddhism and Law: An Introduction*, edited by Rebecca R. French & Mark R. Nathan, 183–97. New York: Cambridge University Press.

Leider, Jacques. 2005. 'The emergence of Rakhine historiography: A challenge for Myanmar historical research'. In Myanmar Historical Commission Conference Proceedings, part 2. Yangon: Myanmar Historical Commission.

Maung, E. 1970. *Burmese Buddhist Law*. Rangoon: Daw Than Tint Mya Sapay.

Mran' mā-'Aṅgalip' 'abhidhān'. 1993. Ran' kun': Dept. of Myanmar Language Commission, Ministry of Education, Union of Myanmar.

'Mran' mā Buddha bhāsā vaṅ' min'" ma myā" 'A thū" thim'" mrā" khraṅ'" chuiṅ' rā Upade kram'"'. 2014. *The Light of Myanmar (Mran' mā 'A laṅ")*, December 3, 2014.

Pearn, Bertie Reginald. 1962. *Judson of Burma*. London: Edinburgh House Press.

'Praññ' thoṅ' cu Sammata Mran' mā Nuiṅ' ṅaṃ to' Phvai' caññ'" puṃ 'a khre Upademū kram'" (2008 khu nhac')'. www.burmalibrary.org/docs09/Myanmar_Constitution-2008(bu)-red.pdf.

Tin, Pe Maung & G. H. Luce, trans. 1960. *The Glass Palace Chronicle of the Kings of Burma*. Rangoon: Rangoon University Press.

Schissler, Matthew, Matthew J. Walton & Phyu Phyu Thi. 2015. 'Threat and virtuous defence: Listening to narratives of religious conflict in six Myanmar cities'. Report by Myanmar Media and Society Project, University of Oxford.

Scott, Sir James George. 1963 [1882]. *The Burman, His Life and Notions*. New York: Norton and Co.

Smith, Donald Eugene. 1965. *Religion and Politics in Burma*. Princeton: Princeton University Press.

Smith, J. Z. 1990. *Drudgery Divine: On the Comparison of Early Christianities and the Religions of Late Antiquity*. Chicago: University of Chicago Press.

Spiro, Melford E. 1967. *Burmese Supernaturalism*. Englewood Cliffs: Prentice-Hall.

The World Factbook. 2016. Washington, DC: Central Intelligence Agency. Accessed August 2016. https://www.cia.gov/library/publications/the-world-factbook/geos/bm.html.

Turner, Alicia. 2011. 'Religion making and its failures: Turning monasteries into schools and Buddhism into a religion in colonial Burma'. In *Secularism and Religion Making*, edited by Markus Dressler & Arvind-Pal S. Mandair, 226–42. Oxford: Oxford University Press.

Turner, Alicia. 2014. *Saving Buddhism: The Impermanence of Religion in Colonial Burma*. Honolulu: University of Hawai'i Press.

Yegar, Moshe. 1972. *The Muslims of Burma*. Wiesbaden: O. Harrassowitz.

14
ARTS

Charlotte Galloway

There is a thread that runs through all early Western accounts of Burma, namely that the richness and visual splendour of Buddhist temples and the Burmese royal courts was something not seen before. Whether approaching a city and being overawed by golden and silver spires glistening with tinkling bells or during an audience with a king so laden down with gold and rubies he could not stand straight, the writer's words always seem to struggle to adequately capture the complexity and depth of Burmese visual culture (Abbott 1998, 5). Today, visitors are also overwhelmed by the visual cacophony of temple complexes and the seemingly random appearance of visual culture whether small *nat* (spirit) shrines found in trees on street corners, flashing neon halos behind Buddha images or the eclecticism of colours that happily coexist with each other. Appreciating Myanmar's arts can be a challenge to foreign eyes, with many of these new innovations seemingly out of place, yet when seen in historical context, the present is a continuum of artistic practices that are deeply embedded in Burmese culture.

Throughout Burmese history virtually all of Myanmar's visual repertoire existed for the purpose of supporting Buddhism and the royal courts. There was little art for art's sake, and artistic practice occurred within prescribed workshop environments. With the introduction of Western art training in the late nineteenth century and a growing foreign presence, Burmese artistic traditions expanded to meet a market demand that favoured Western aesthetics. The establishment of the Burma Art Club in Yangon in 1918 provided a focus for teaching in Western-style art techniques, and with colonial patronage, a small number of Burmese artists were sponsored to train in Europe. The advent of World War II and subsequent upheaval in Myanmar effectively cut off the steady trajectory of Myanmar's rising artistic talents. Throughout the 1960s to 1990s, with little access to foreign contemporary art practices, and virtually no local market for Western-style art, the arts faltered. Economic struggles saw many traditional arts and crafts workshops that had up until then survived for centuries through their work of decorating Buddhist temples and monasteries for patrons, simply become unviable. There was for a period a real threat that traditional arts and crafts skills and techniques would be lost. As access and freedom of movement in Myanmar has increased since the mid-2000s an initially tentative reinvigoration of the art scene has now exploded into a vibrant and exciting artistic subculture. In parallel with a Western-style art world, the traditional arts and crafts of Myanmar that have underpinned their visual culture since earliest times are also undergoing a resurgence.

Modernisation of techniques and changes in decorative forms are a fundamental requirement for the survival of traditions and this is now happening. The arts of visual culture in Myanmar are not simply decoration, they are adaptive and responsive and indicators of social change. All of this is based in a history that stretches back millennia. Appreciating the place of Burmese arts in the past offers an understanding of what this imagery can tell us about the present.

From the second century CE onwards Buddhism became a major influence through Southeast Asia and it brought with it the traditions of Indian art from which it originated. City centres emerged in Arakan, central and southern Burma. The richest sources of early visual culture come from the Pyu Ancient Cities of Halin, Beikthano and Sri Ksetra which were inscribed on UNESCO's World Heritage List in June 2014 (UNESCO 2014). While these three cities are definitely all linked culturally through Buddhism and organisation, the visual links are less clear with each city having commonalities and differences in visual culture. At Beikthano, for example, funerary vessels display complex bird-like elements and decorative devices, all hand modelled and without regional precedent. In contrast, decorative glass and stone beads, some inlaid with gold, and gold jewellery have been found across the regions indicating a shared interest in personal adornment (Moore 2012). The artefacts so far found at Sri Ksetra, near Pyay, have yielded a complex array of imagery that is only now being systematically assessed (Galloway 2015). What we can surmise, however, is that as far as visual culture goes, there was a genuine acceptance of diversity, a telling foundation for Myanmar's art history.

Sri Ksetra was a sophisticated walled city, with a central palace, moats and complex irrigation systems, and diverse religious practices which, while essentially Buddhist, were not uniform. There is evidence of a Hindu Vishnavaite presence, and indigenous spirits, called *nats*. Sri Ksetra reached its zenith around the sixth–ninth century before slowly declining, and by the eleventh century Bagan had become the capital of the first great Burman empire. With so few textual sources about the Pyu, visual culture offers insight into their lives and history. Visual analysis of Buddhist artefacts confirms connections between India and Burma, particularly with Nagarjunakonda and Amaravati in Andhra Pradesh. There are stylistic connections to the early Buddhist art of the Wei Kingdoms in China, and many interregional connections extending across mainland and maritime Southeast Asia. Sri Lankan and northern Indian links are also mooted (Galloway 2011, 72). With such a richness of external imagery contributing to the Pyu visual repertoire it is little wonder that there is such diversity in styles and themes. While the Pyu adapted these new forms and created images that were distinctly their own, there is still no chronological uniformity in artistic style. This is in contrast to later developments in Myanmar history as Buddha images became defined by dynastic or ethnic terms.

The archaeological excavations at Sri Ksetra are in their infancy. There is much to be discovered, yet it is already possible to see the origins of the Ten *Pan* (flowers), the arts that are integral to Burmese visual history:

- *Panbe* (blacksmithing)
- *Panbu* (sculpture in wood and ivory)
- *Pantain* (gold- and silversmithing)
- *Pantin* (bronze casting)
- *Pantaut* (floral stucco work)
- *Panyan* (bricklaying and masonry)
- *Pantamault* (stone sculpture)
- *Panpoot* (wood turning)
- *Panchi* (painting)
- *Panyun* (lacquerware)

Iron held a special place in Pyu culture and was believed to have special protective and auspicious powers. Large iron pegs up to 1 metre long are found at the corners of the palace walls at Sri Ksetra, placed in a way that indicates a ritual rather than structural purpose. Blacksmiths forged iron nails and fasteners, and likely weapons and cart wheel straps. *Panbu* is the art of sculpture in wood and ivory rather than stone. While we have little evidence of wooden or ivory sculpture or *Panpoot*, wood turning, from the first millennium, we surmise that artefacts were produced using these techniques and mediums just as they were in other materials. There is almost no first millennium evidence of lacquerware and painting, referring to temple wall painting in this case, due to the relative fragility of these mediums. The role of the remaining arts and crafts in Pyu culture is illustrated through the Khin Ba Gon trove, the most significant intact relic chamber found from the period. The temple and relic chamber were excavated in 1926 by archaeologist Charles Duroiselle under the auspices of the Archaeological Survey of India (Duroiselle 1930, 171–82). The centre piece was a silver gilt reliquary with imagery of the four Buddhas of the recent past, with their disciples. There were many images of the Buddha in silver, gold and lead, other reliquaries, metal plaques with guardian figures in relief, bowls and offering containers, large silver lotuses, silver stupas, coins, a cast bronze of a bodhisattva, gold rings set with gems, and terracotta votive tablets. One of the most important finds was a set of gold manuscript leaves inscribed with Pali text, using Pyu script. Epigraphic research suggests a late fifth-century date (Stargardt 2000, 24–7). The relic chamber covers are large stone slabs carved with reliefs of the five Buddhas of the current eon placed along the base of a stupa, complete with imagery of the sun and moon, streamers cascading from the *hti* (umbrella) at the top of the stupa, flanked with an attendant figure on each side holding a parasol aloft, imagery that has been repeated through the centuries. In addition to showcasing the role of Ten *Pan* in Myanmar's visual culture from early times, excavation revealed extensive use of decorative terracotta reliefs. The imagery is creative and dynamic, with figures of horses and lions, rishis, dancing figures and standing Buddha images. There are also wonderfully elaborate architectural reliefs of balustrade columns, featuring Buddhist elements such as kalasa pots and lotuses. The art of *Panyan* is evident in the complex brick profiling, with rounded and stepped levels all coming together to create a sophisticated and creative visual experience.

The stone sculptures from Sri Ksetra follow through on the theme of dense decoration. Throne backs behind Buddha images are full of figures and foliate motifs and hardly an unadorned space can be found. Terracotta votive tablets follow through in this as well with many being like miniature paintings, so detailed is the imagery (Mya 1961). Made for the purpose of donation and merit-making, it is likely the more ornate the imagery, the more significant the donation. This is the first sense we get of Myanmar's kammatic Buddhism, whereby merit is earned through patronage and support of the three jewels of Buddhism: support of the Buddha through temple buildings and donations, study of the dhamma, and support of the sangha or local monks, the last also often manifesting itself through donations for building monasteries and the giving of Buddhist texts and manuscript chests. At Sri Ksetra, single finds of hundreds of small terracotta votive tablets attest to the significant role of donation in Buddhist practice.

While we can only surmise what drove this aesthetic preference for elaborate decoration during the Pyu period, this 'busy-ness' comes to characterise the visual manifestations of Buddhism and is seen in its fully developed form through the extraordinary monuments of Bagan (Stadtner 2005). Bagan came to prominence under the rule of Anawrahta (r.1044–1077). Acknowledged as the first great Burman rule, Anawrahta's role in history is as the unifier of the kingdom and upholder of the Theravada Buddhist tradition. It is likely that Bagan was a small village inhabited by Pyu people or, at very least, with strong links to the Pyu as evidenced by some of the artistic finds which include Pyu votive tablets, Pyu-style stupas and other Buddhist imagery. It is during the reigns of Anawrahta, Sawlu (r.1077–1084) and Kyanzittha (r.1084–1113) that artistic expression starts to coalesce into a distinctive Burmese style. The Buddhist imagery associated with temples attributed to Anawrahta is quite mixed. For example, in the Shwesandaw, likely built around the 1050s, the Hindu elephant-headed god Ganesha is brought into the service of Buddhism as a guardian figure, terracotta plaques of the jatakas, the stories of the previous lives of the Buddha, adorn the exterior and large votive tablets are found inside the stupa, the structure itself being evidence of a formative phase of Theravada Buddhism.

The monuments of Bagan are a case study for the development of Burmese Buddhism. Through their ornamentation, selection of iconography and sheer size we can relate these features back to external influences and gain insight into the aspects of the canon favoured by the local rulers. As kammatic Buddhism became entrenched in Burmese society the act of donation became part of everyday life. Building temples and stupas became a very visual and prominent notice to the populace of the elites' support for Buddhism and their deservedness to be re-born in a privileged position. This attitude ensured that art in the form of Buddhist visual culture flourished. At its peak temple decoration left almost no surface spared. Glazed terracotta plaques featuring jataka scenes were integrated into the exterior of temples and stupas. Tiles in bright turquoise, cream, green and yellow were used to decorate lintels, terraces and temple roofs. In conjunction with high relief stucco depictions of guardians, animals, makaras, nagas and deities, likely coloured, and golden spires, the temples of Bagan must have been a miraculous sight. This visual extravaganza extends to temple interiors with walls usually completely covered in paintings depicting Buddhist scenes with some secular elements. Sculptures of the Buddha, while by necessity quite consistent and simple in their form, were supported by complex narrative imagery telling viewers about the great events of the Buddha's last life. Known as the Eight Great Events, these, along with additional scenes specific to the Buddha's life, offered the populace a focus for their meditations that would hopefully lead them to an accumulation of kamma.

At Bagan the significance of the Ten *Pan* is all apparent in these elaborated adorned monuments. Again there appears to have been a willingness to adopt and integrate external artistic forms into local style. Pala India's influence is readily apparent in Kyanzittha's temples, especially the Ananda and Nagayon. Given the rapid pace of building and lack of prototypes it is thought artisans from the Pala kingdom made their way to Bagan where their skills were in demand, in contrast to the waning support for Buddhism in Bengal and India. Images of the Buddha were typically in the Pala style, with the classical slim-waisted torso and sheer garments, static poses and characteristic parrot-beak noses. During the twelfth century the imagery changed to become distinctly Burmese. Buddha images had short necks, and took on a youthful appearance. There is great uniformity in this visual culture which coincides with the strengthening Burmese empire. A singular identifiable style allowed for a visual statement that differentiated the kingdom from its neighbours. Such uniformity only seems to become apparent when there are expansionist policies or external threats. At Bagan, as the empire grew, consistent visual symbols spread throughout the kingdom particularly in the form of votive tablets and the architectural features of stupas.

The craftsman's role was now entrenched in Burmese social structure with much of the community's economic support coming through Buddhist patronage. The secular realm also offered work but only for the elite. The country fragmented as Bagan fell into decline in the late 1200s. Under the Taungoo kingdom (1510–1752) the country was once again mostly under central rule, at one point the extent of the kingdom forming the largest known in Southeast Asian history. Court records reference elaborate ceremonies, donations to monasteries and temple building. In 1600 an order declared that mining of amber, gems, gold, gums and iron were now royal monopolies (Tun 1983).

These materials were effectively for exclusive use of the king and the court. In 1633, 500 artists were commissioned to paint the enclosure walls of the Maha Myat Muni pagoda with the 547 jatakas and in 1637 an order was passed to gild the Shwedagon pagoda (Tun 1983, 36, 81). In 1638 copies of the *Tipitaka* on ivory, gold and silver were commissioned (Tun 1983, 98). Over the next centuries sumptuary laws were enforced dictating that only kings and members of the court could use gold, and only in quantities ascribed to rank. Performance art was codified. The range of marionettes and plays that could be performed was decreed. Each rank was accompanied with a prescribed set of courtly possessions. Such strictures necessitated vast numbers of artisans who were paid by the court. Unfortunately, there are few objects that can be reliably dated prior to the 1700s.

The Konbaung dynasty (1752–1885) continued this extravagant court patronage and new art styles emerged. After the sacking of Ayutthaya in 1767 the Burmese brought Siamese artisans back to the court at Inwa (Ava). The Burmese court embraced the Siamese use of glass mosaics. Nowadays, glass mosaic inlay is considered quintessentially Burmese. In hindsight adoption of a Siamese style by the Burmese kings can be interpreted as an act of cultural domination. Using a visual form that was intimately associated with Ayutthaya art and using it themselves effectively diminished the significance of this art form for the Siamese and shored up the dominance of the Burmese in a very powerful way. The Siamese never fully regained ownership of this technique.

By all Western accounts the Konbaung court was splendid. Perhaps it was fortunate that British Emissary Michael Symes was kept waiting for royal audiences, as his diary included extensive observations of court buildings, temples and, importantly, secular visual culture in the form of references to costumes and domestic objects. Symes's detailed notes provide insights into artistic practice and offer some considered opinions on the quality of the Burmese artisans' workmanship. He states that 'gilding is forbidden to all subjects of the Birman empire: liberty to even lacker [*sic*], and paint the pillars of their houses is granted to very few' (Symes 1800, 186). At the Shwemawdaw pagoda at Pegu, Symes remarked on wooden pavilions (saloons) being erected, 'they are made entirely of wood; the carving on the outside is laborious and minute; we saw several unfinished figures of animals and men in grotesque attitudes, which were designed as ornaments for different parts of the building' (Symes 1800, 189). He notes with interest the sumptuary laws that ensure clothing and associated accoutrements such as betel boxes, water containers drinking cups and even horse 'furniture' reflect, through their quality and shape, 'the precise station of the owner' (Symes 1800, 244). In a more discursive account:

> It has already been noticed, that almost every article of use, as well as ornament, particularly in their dress, indicates the rank of the owner; the shape of the beetle-box, which is carried by an attendant after a Birman of distinction wherever he goes, his earrings, cap of ceremony, horse furniture, even the metal of his spitting-pot and drinking-cup are made (which, if of gold, denote him to be a man of high consideration), all are indicative of the gradations of society; and woe be unto him that assumes the insignia of a degree which is not his legitimate right.
>
> *Symes 1800, 310*

There are numerous references to gilding of court architecture and furniture, with gilding only being allowed for court use and for Buddhist buildings. The use of glass mosaics is noted, in reference to the Prince of Thaton's royal sofa. An alabaster Buddha was seated on a gilded pedestal, and manuscript chests 'curiously ornamented with gilding and japan . . . the contents of each chest, were written in gold letters on the lid. Very beautiful writing on thin leaves of ivory, the margins of which were ornamented with flowers of gold, neatly executed' (Symes 1800, 383).

Until then most foreign commentary addressed the visual splendour of the courts, and observations on secular life focused on customs rather than providing any detailed visual analysis of cultural artefacts. Symes was generally more appreciative of the unusual decorative tastes of the Burmese. When at Mandalay visiting the Mahamuni image he remarked that:

> Several gigantic images of Rakuss, the Hindoo demon, half beast, half human, made of brass, were shewed to us, as composing a part of the spoils of Arracan. From these we were conducted to a magnificent temple which is erecting for the image of Gaudama, that was brought from the same country. The idol is made of polished brass, about 10 feet high and sitting in the usual posture, on a pedestal within an arched recess: the walls are gilded, and adorned with bits of different coloured mirrors, disposed with much taste.
>
> *Symes 1800, 391*

Symes also remarked on the Burmese attitude towards rebuilding, a topic that is now at the forefront of international discussion as Myanmar moves towards proposing Bagan as a World Heritage Site, noting that the focus was not on rebuilding or maintaining but on letting things go to ruin and building new pagodas (Symes 1800, 208).

The second event was the increasing presence of the British. It was through the British that Western-style art for art's sake was popularised and Myanmar's first museum was established. The Phayre Museum, named after British Envoy Sir Arthur Phayre, opened in Yangon in 1871 and it became a storehouse for antiquities gathered by the British. By 1892 it was in a poor state, as architect F. O. Oertel wrote: 'the present accommodation in the Phayre Museum appears, however, to be very limited and it no doubt be found necessary to add to it if it is to serve a useful purpose' (Oertel 1995 [1894], 10). He also notes the paucity of provenance information, making the object practically useless for research purposes.

The collapse of the Konbaung dynasty and subsequent British rule upset the centuries-long hereditary workshop system and the artisan–patron relationship. With few large-scale temple commissions, stucco skills were particularly affected. Smithing was in decline due to industrialisation. Workshops closed simply because of a lack of demand. The British showcased Burmese lacquer at international exhibitions, giving some support to this sector. Indeed, the importance of authorship in Western art saw artisans sign their lacquerwares for the first time, instilling a Western-style art hierarchy of 'quality' into the system. Myanmar-based British citizens offered artisans new markets, and styles were adapted to suit demands. The skill of woodcarvers found new form in lifelike sculptures of Burmese citizens in poses representing daily life such as a chinlon player, or woman smoking a cheroot (Tilly 1903). Souvenir art became a new outlet for craftsmen and helped sustain traditional crafts.

British rule also brought Western drawing and painting techniques. First, it was architectural drafting and mapping through Army officials. Later, the Burma Art Club was established in Yangon in 1918 by a group of interested British officials and Burmese artists. The Club served as a gathering place for group painting, both indoors and outdoors. Two outstanding local artists were sponsored to travel to London for formal training, U Ba Nyan (1897–1945) in 1921 and U Ba Zaw (1891–1942) in 1927. Both achieved critical praise and returned to Yangon in 1930. Together they can be considered the founders of Modernism in Myanmar, with U Ba Nyan a major influence in Yangon and U Ba Zaw in Mandalay, his home town (Ranard 2009, 91–2). In 1930, the government opened an art and music school. Western-style art was embraced by a new generation of artists though there were divides between the Mandalay and Yangon schools and both followed different trajectories. The outbreak of World War II had a devastating impact on art practice. Against an already troubled political backdrop formal art training was severely compromised during Japanese occupation and no art exhibitions were allowed to be held. The Japanese set up an art department to produce propaganda-related material and this offered some opportunities to develop commercial art skills. Post-war these skills became particularly important as Myanmar gained independence and sustained a number of artists during the years of isolation from the West (Nyunt 2006; Ranard 2009).

In 1946 the Associated Artists of Burma was founded and in 1952 and 1953 the Burmese government established the State School of Fine Arts in Yangon and Mandalay respectively. Focusing on fine art, traditional art, design and sculpture these secondary level high schools supported continuity of knowledge in these fields. Traditional dance, performance and music were taught at a separate state school in Mandalay. The National Museum was established in 1953, an accoutrement required of a developing nation wishing to showcase its cultural credentials. It acquired works by Myanmar's leading Modernist painters. However, while there was active support of the arts no Burmese artists followed the paths of U Ba Nyan and U Ba Zaw and exhibited in Europe. The 1950s was a period of cultural upheaval for Myanmar with internal ethnic divides working against the formation of a united independent Myanmar ready to face the world as an emerging post-war nation. Artists had virtually no opportunities to engage with the dramatic shifts that were occurring in Western art such as the radical abstract expressionism of the New York schools.

It is not surprising that once Ne Win formed a government in 1962, national order required uniformity and compliance in all creative fields. In a country where visual culture is everywhere artists were well positioned to promote anti-government messages through cartoon illustrations in popular press and magazines, and in public posters. Yet dissent was short lived and art practice, like all aspects of cultural life, became strictly controlled. The State Schools of Fine Art trained artists in painting and drawing in a prescribed traditional Western model. Public art exhibitions displayed traditional landscapes in oils and watercolours. Interestingly, propaganda art never reached the levels of exploitation seen in neighbouring countries. Indeed, finding a purpose for 'art' outside the traditional Ten *Pan* seemed of little interest to government. Private galleries did open and offered opportunities for artists to develop local markets. Lokanat was the first private gallery in Yangon, opening in 1971, and provided a much needed display space where artists could gain critical reception even if the style of works exhibited was limited (Lokanat 2014).

While secular art was stagnating, traditional arts and crafts suffered a further blow as the demand for tourist-related artefacts virtually collapsed. Private and government commissions were all that sustained these enterprises and both of these were slowly contracting as the economy shrank. Woodcarving workshops in Yangon, which in 1900 boasted many high quality carvers, virtually disappeared. Stone carving, bronze casting, gold- and silversmithing and wood carving workshops consolidated around Mandalay which had long been a major centre for these activities. Likewise, lacquerware production contracted with the principal production area at Bagan (Than Htun (Dewaye) 2013).

Traditional and Western-style art practice remained stuck in a time warp leading up to the uprising of August 8, 1988. Western-style art became a platform for public criticism of the government. While public art had taken a conservative and singular political voice, artists had clearly been expressing alternative views away from the public eye. With the first rumblings of anti-government voices, artists were at the forefront of public dissent; however, this dissenting voice, like many others that were heard by the military government, was rapidly shut down. Artists were faced with the choice of either censoring their own work or continuing to push the reform agenda in visual mediums. This included visual artists, actors and writers. Many were arrested, others had works seized. More would paint but hide away their works that were deemed subversive. With subsequent sanctions, artists had even simpler problems such as sourcing canvases and paints. The market for contemporary art was cut off, and what followed was more than a decade of virtual stagnation in the art scene. It was against this backdrop that in 1993 the government founded the National University for Arts and Culture in Yangon, and in 2001 its counterpart opened in Mandalay. The official website records the stated aims as keeping dynamic patriotism, strengthening of national unity and preservation of national culture. The objectives and strategies were:

- To preserve, promote and disseminate Myanmar Cultural Heritage.
- To conduct research and training with the aim of bringing about the progress of Myanmar fine arts and visual arts turning out outstanding artistes and artists.
- To contribute to the teaching of traditional cultures and customs of indigenous national races at the universities, institutes, colleges and schools.
- To help strengthen the spirit of nationalism and patriotism.
- To turn out good artistes and artists with refined morality and integrity.

Ministry of Culture and Tourism 2013

Little indication is given as to 'what end'. That said, it can be taken as an acknowledgement of the integral role traditional arts and crafts play in Myanmar culture.

Supporting tradition in the arts at the expense of creativity quashed artistic freedom. Censorship of Western-style painting was enforced in a heavy-handed and unclear way. What was deemed unacceptable in the visual arts was simply anything that was seen by the censor, usually a military official, as potentially inciting civil unrest or commenting negatively on the government. In the early 2000s there were some active local galleries, such as Lokanat and New Treasure Gallery and the works shown were always under government scrutiny. A few artists who were, through circumstance, able to gain some international access emerged. In the late 1990s to early 2000s Win Mae Aung's (1960–) paintings of monks walking away from the viewer, now much copied, passed the censor but could be interpreted as subversive, a commentary on the constancy of Buddhism within society and its independence from government rule. Po Po (1957–) is considered the founder of performance art in Myanmar, and is now internationally known for his installation works. However, both stand amongst a small group of artists and tightening of international sanctions, and travel in the late 2000s further restricted artistic freedom at a time when Southeast Asian art was attracting worldwide interest.

With a limited market, making a living out of contemporary art was virtually out of the question for most. What is notable about artists who were practising and exhibiting during the 2000s is the subject matter of their paintings. Censorship offered clear options – push boundaries and risk police attention or choose safer subjects that would allow artists to exhibit their works. While first glance suggests a lack of originality in paintings produced at this time, many works need to be viewed through a much more nuanced frame. Landscapes and rural scenes can be interpreted as reflections on Burmese traditional life, cityscapes become documentary images of decay and, later, rapid change, and Buddhist themes represent strength and endurance. What is also unseen in these works is the simple struggle to access painting materials. Indeed, simply being an independent artist at this time is representative of strength and resilience.

The randomness of censorship has recently been addressed in the exhibition 'Banned in Burma: Painting Under Censorship' held in Hong Kong late in 2014. Showcasing fifty paintings that were censored between 1962 and 2011, curator Melissa Carlson notes in interview the multifaceted approach to censorship that saw paintings viewed through lenses such as colour, subject and abstraction that were beyond the comprehension of censors (Sokol 2014). In 2013 censorship laws were relaxed. With many international sanctions removed, the art scene in Myanmar has expanded exponentially. The influx of tourists and ex-patriate workers has fuelled a demand for contemporary art. In a twelve-month period from 2014 to 2015 at least twelve new art galleries opened in Yangon. This number is still increasing. Public dialogue about art practice is now possible without imminent fear of arrest. Pansodan Gallery and Scene, for example, offer spaces for discussions about art practice. Artist and gallery owner Aung Soe Min's works of early 2015 'Crisis of Buddhism' featured works that would never have passed the censor even eighteen months before (Aung Soe Min 2015). Art practice is also changing. Performance and installation art are now fixtures in contemporary art exhibitions. Yangon's Gallery 65 'Art + Plug season Five (Metamorphosis), held in January 2017, was dominated by installations and multi-media works. While the exhibition's title refers to the artists' own self-discovery and experimentation, it also signifies the major socio-political changes that have occurred to allow artists room for such exploration, and a public venue to share their ideas. Engagement with international artists is also invigorating the contemporary art scene. In January 2017 German artist Wolfgang Laib's exhibition in the Secretariat Building, Yangon, showed the power art can have in bringing fractured societies together (Kalish 2017). Holding such an exhibition in one of the most symbolic buildings in Myanmar is a positive sign for artists and artistic freedom. Yet there is still an undercurrent of unease amongst the art community. Government trust has to be earned, and until there is a sustained period of artistic freedom, art practice in Myanmar will remain tethered, even if ever so slightly.

In parallel to contemporary art, the traditional arts that have underpinned Myanmar's rich visual culture are also undergoing a renaissance. With more money circulating and an emerging middle class, patronage of temples and monasteries is increasing. Throughout the country new temples are being constructed, and the demand for traditional craftspeople is increasing. Workshops in Mandalay are bustling with activity as works are made for both local and export markets. Heritage interest is also driving demand for high quality traditional craftspeople, though this is proving challenging. As skills were lost following independence, it will take time to reinvigorate the traditional crafts to the skill levels that were in evidence during Myanmar's dynastic history. The government continues to support traditional arts and crafts through the State Schools, though their relevance will depend on continually moving the curriculum forward.

It is a challenging time in Myanmar history, but that in itself is a constant. Throughout centuries of change, an enduring feature of Myanmar is its visual culture. From the Pyu settlements of the first millennium we discern the importance of artistic language through complex and eclectic imagery that indicates regional creativity blended with foreign concepts. At Bagan we see a transformation from eclecticism to uniformity as the empire expands and visual culture functions to assist unifying imperatives. The constant aesthetic is one of density and diversity which is also inherently linked to Buddhist merit-making enterprises. This 'busy-ness' is sustained throughout the dynastic period, with courtly patronage an assurance of keeping craft traditions alive and invigorated. Burmese artistic practice was transformed under colonial rule. Traditional patronage systems broke down and craftsmen adapted their repertoire in response to new market demand. The introduction of Western art practice saw a stream of visual culture evolve that spoke to a new audience and offered artists the opportunity to engage in an international visual dialogue. Independence brought with it more change. All spheres of artistic practice contracted as markets all but disappeared. The establishment of government-run schools of traditional art practice focused on maintaining the status quo and inevitably this has led to a decline in creativity and quality. While not harnessing modern art practice for propaganda use, artistic output was so effectively censored that innovation was publicly invisible. Today, it is another period of rapid change. Across the country the traditional arts are flourishing as there is a new generation of Buddhist patrons. Refurbishment and renewal along with new constructions have reinvigorated this artistic sphere. For contemporary artists, critical foreign buyers are facilitating their creativity by demanding works that are beyond the simply decorative. Relaxation of censorship laws is giving artists more confidence to express publicly what many of them were doing privately. Yet there is a tenuous undertone as Myanmar moves into a new era. In the artistic arena experimentation is burgeoning but there is still a degree of hesitancy. Craftspeople are taking advantage of expanding markets while they can. How long this frenetic activity surrounding visual art practice can be sustained is uncertain. However, as history has shown, it will always endure.

References

Abbott, G. 1998. *The Traveller's History of Burma*. Bangkok: Orchid Press.

Aung Soe Min. 2015. 'Crisis of Buddhism'. Facebook. Accessed March 2016. www.facebook.com/aungsoeminn/posts/10153411067518322.

Duroiselle, Mons. Charles. 1930. 'Excavations at Hmawza'. In *Annual Report of the Archaeological Survey of India*, edited by Sir John Marshall. Calcutta: Government of India, Central Publications Branch.

Galloway, Charlotte. 2011. 'Ways of seeing a Pyu, Mon and Dvaravati artistic continuum'. *Bulletin of the Indo-Pacific Prehistory Association* (30): 70–8.

Galloway, Charlotte. 2015. 'Sri Ksetra Museum Collection Inventory Version 1.0'. Self published. Accessed February 2016. https://archive.org/details/InventorySriKsetraMuseum1.0.

Kalish, Lillian. 2017. 'Yangon's Secretariat re-opens for art exhibit'. *The Myanmar Times*. Accessed February 2017. www.mmtimes.com/index.php/lifestyle/24528-yangon-s-secretariat-re-opens-for-art-exhibit.html.

Nyunt, Khin Maung. 2006. *Myanmar Paintings. From Worship to Self-Imaging*. Ho Chi Minh City: Education Publishing House.

Lokanat. 2014. 'Truth, Beauty, Love: The Lokanat Gallery of Art'. Lokanat Galleries. Accessed August 2015. www.lokanatgalleries.com/about_us.php.

Ministry of Culture and Tourism. 2013. 'National University of Arts and Culture (Yangon)'. Union of the Republic of Myanmar. Accessed August 2015. www.culture.gov.mm/Universities/NUAC_YGN/default.asp?id=35.

Moore, E. 2012. *The Pyu Landscape: Collected Articles. Myanmar Archaeological Series*. Myanmar: Ministry of Culture, Republic of the Union of Myanmar.

Mya, T. 1961. *Votive Tablets of Burma*. Yangon: Department of Archaeology, Rangoon University Press.

Oertel, F. 1995 [1894]. *A Tour in Burma in March and April 1892*. Reprint Bangkok: White Orchid Press.

Ranard, Andrew. 2009. *Burmese Painting: A Linear and Lateral History*. Chiang Mai: Silkworm Books.

Sokol, Zach. 2014. '"Banned in Burma" showcases the best of Myanmar's censored art'. *Vice*. Accessed August 2015. www.vice.com/read/banned-in-burma-is-exhibiting-the-best-of-myanmars-censored-art-122.

Stadtner, Donald M. 2005. *Ancient Pagan: Buddhist Pain of Merit*. Bangkok: River Books.

Stargardt, Janice. 2000. *Tracing Thought Through Things: The Oldest Pali Texts and the Early Buddhist Archaeology of India and Burma*. Amsterdam: Royal Netherlands Academy of Arts and Social Sciences.

Symes, Michael. 1800. *Account of an Embassy to the Kingdom of Ava, Sent by the Governor-General of India, in the Year 1795*. London: W. Bulmer & Co.

Than Htun (Dewaye). 2013. *Lacquerware Journeys: The Untold Story of Burmese Lacquer*. Bangkok: River Books.

Tilly, Harry L. 1903. *Woodcarving of Burma*. Rangoon: Superintendent Government Printing.

Tun, Than. 1983. *The Royal Orders of Burma, AD. 1598–1885: AD. 1598–1648 Part 1*. Kyoto: Center for Southeast Asian Studies, Kyoto University.

UNESCO. 2014. 'World Heritage List, New Inscribed Properties'. http://whc.unesco.org/en/newproperties/date=2014&mode=table.

15
PUBLIC DISCOURSE

Thomas Kean

Myanmar's media has been at the forefront of government-led reforms initiated since 2011. Pre-publication censorship has been lifted for print media, controls over internet access have evaporated and government officials are more accessible and accountable than ever. Reporting is probing and provocative, and publications enjoy a level of independence that would make many of their peers in the region jealous.

Bucking the global trend, Myanmar's private print media industry—decimated under socialist and then military rule—has grown dramatically over the past decade, with hundreds of weekly and monthly publications and nearly ten daily newspapers now in circulation.[1] Online audience reach has also taken off, thanks to a liberalisation of the telecommunications sector that has put internet-enabled SIM-cards within reach of most of the country's population. A number of independent industry bodies have been established, including a press council, a training institute and journalists' association and union.

Yet the relaxation of controls on print media and journalists' aggressive pursuit of stories have also brought about increased conflict with the authorities, and resulted in reporters from several publications being imprisoned or fined between 2014 and 2015. While not indicative of the general state of the industry, the cases highlight the shortcomings of the legal framework and the limits of tolerance for criticism and provocative reporting, particularly from the military.

Reforms have also been uneven and concentrated primarily on the print media sector, which will form the basis for this chapter on public discourse. The broadcast media industry remains concentrated in the hands of the state, the military and a few powerful companies. State media still has the largest audience reach and is heavily subsidised, arguably at the expense of the private sector. Colonial and military era laws that can be used to imprison journalists and other media professionals remain in force. While editorial freedom has increased, privately owned print media still face a range of challenges. Intense competition makes financial viability an impossible dream for most and newsrooms are often badly under-resourced. Circulation growth is constrained by poor infrastructure, limiting the possibility for expansion of print readership. The advertising market is limited, with the majority of spending funnelled into broadcast media, particularly television. Mirroring the shift in most other countries, print advertising is also increasingly shifting online as more people gain access to the internet.

However, the future remains largely bright. Comparisons in coverage of the 2010 and 2015 general elections provide a dramatic illustration of how far editorial freedom has come during President Thein Sein's tenure. Examples abound as to where media coverage has played an important role in shaping decision-making and public opinion. This will undoubtedly bring journalists into conflict with the authorities on a regular basis, yet most will be able to go about their work relatively unimpeded. Finally, there is a belief—or at least acceptance—from all stakeholders that a vibrant, independent media sector is essential for the development of Myanmar's emerging democracy.

Myanmar's independent media: destruction and slow recovery

Myanmar enjoyed a vibrant press environment during the colonial and early post-independence years. Yangon was home to dozens of daily papers in a range of languages and journalists enjoyed a level of prominence on the political stage. The downfall of Burma's press industry was rapid. Less than six months after the military coup in March 1962, General Ne Win enacted the Printers and Publishers Registration Act, which required all publications to renew their licence annually. Many were refused permission, and a number of prominent journalists were imprisoned. By 1965, there were no private publications left, with some of the more prominent titles nationalised by the socialist regime.

By the early 1990s, a handful of private publications had been established—mostly monthly literary magazines. The first private news publications appeared in about 2000 and by the end of the decade there were around a dozen large weeklies, and a plethora of smaller ones. Also in the 1990s, the first exile media organisations were established. These operated beyond the reach of the Myanmar government's censorship process, although there were sometimes complaints that coverage was anti-government rather than impartial, reflecting the activist roots of these publications.

Licensed publications inside Myanmar were all subject to pre-publication censorship by the Press Scrutiny and Registration Division (PRSD), the successor to the Press Scrutiny Board. Every page of content—even advertisements and classifieds—was vetted closely before printing. PSRD would return the proposed content to the publication with mark-ups showing what had to be removed. Editors would then replace the censored material with other approved content. Censorship was extremely strict; in any given edition, more than a dozen articles could be censored in their entirety and replaced.

The first signs of a relaxation of censorship came in mid-2010. To this point, coverage of opposition political parties had been largely banned from publication. Now the censors began to allow reports on these groups, including the backgrounds of their founders, their reasons for contesting the election and the challenges they faced in competing with the military-backed Union Solidarity and Development Party. This enabled many of the key issues surrounding the election to be discussed, albeit sometimes indirectly (Kean 2015). For many journalists, it was the first time they had covered domestic politics or met members of the opposition movement.

Journalists used this opening to 'reclaim the area they had relinquished . . . in order to appease or to avoid problems with the censor' (Pe Myint 2012). It was a limited opening, though; there was little portent of the rapid changes to come. A further hint emerged in President Thein Sein's inaugural speech, however, when he said, 'We also need to respect the role of the media, the fourth estate . . . and appreciate positive suggestions from the media.' It was the first time in decades the role of the media had been acknowledged in this way by the government (Nwe Nwe Aye 2012).

Media reforms: a 'quick win' from a long-term plan

The liberalisation of the print and online media environment was one of President Thein Sein's first major achievements after taking office in March 2011. This did not always make life easy for the government—it meant closer scrutiny of ministers and officials, for example, and publicity for the opposition movement—but was crucial for building its legitimacy following the deeply flawed 2010 election. While their reports have often been critical of the government, the domestic print and exile media sectors have largely accepted the political system established by the military, despite its undemocratic features.

The media liberalisation process has been carefully managed by the government, particularly the Ministry of Information. Planning for reforms began shortly after the purge of Military Intelligence in 2004, when ex-military officials such as Tint Swe and Ye Htut were transferred to the Ministry of Information. With assistance from German and Asian NGOs, they began planning for the end of state censorship. This was not necessarily endorsed by all within the military regime. 'The framework for media reform had from the very beginning the aim to abolish censorship but in 2007 that could not be pointed out,' said Paul Pasch of Friedrich Ebert Stiftung, which worked with the ministry.

Reforms to the media landscape—while concentrated in the period 2011–13—have essentially taken a decade to deliver. Changes have often been implemented step by step, with the authorities always maintaining a high degree of control. They have also been subject to political turbulence, including the need to maintain strict control during periods of uncertainty and change, and the management styles and tolerance levels of individual ministers. Since 2011, two ministers for information—Kyaw Hsan and Aung Kyi—have been replaced for failing to adhere to the government's vision for media reform.

As a result of the changes, journalists have been able to exert a degree of influence over the reform process. Because of their advocacy and ability to shape the debate, reforms have come faster and been broader in scope in print and online media than in other areas of public discourse, such as broadcast media or filmmaking. The government's willingness to heed their demands highlights their importance to the transition process.

The reforms have received widespread international recognition, including by press freedom groups. In 2010, Freedom House gave Myanmar a 95 out of 100 Press Freedom Score—where zero is the best and 100 the worst—but this had improved to 70 out of 100 by 2014. Meanwhile, Myanmar rose from 174 (out of 178 countries) in 2010 to 143 (out of 180) in 2016 on Reporters Without Borders' World Press Freedom Index. It is important to recognise that the picture on press freedom varies significantly depending on where one is standing in Myanmar, however. In Yangon, and to a lesser extent Mandalay and Naypyitaw, journalists can operate largely unimpeded. In border areas, the personal risks are heightened due to conflict (Htun Khaing 2016). Similarly, in rural areas civil servants and security forces are less likely to accommodate the probing of journalists.

The most significant policy change has been the complete removal of pre-publication censorship, which followed a gradual relaxation of control. By the time censorship was lifted for all publications in August 2012, the tone and scope of coverage in the domestic media had shifted dramatically, with articles critical of the government appearing regularly. Since then, newsrooms have been able to operate and publish with virtually no government interference. In a similar manner, restrictions on online content were removed in September 2011. The government previously operated an unsophisticated filter to block users from accessing banned websites, including those of exile and some international media. While the lifting of these restrictions was symbolically important, the decision to liberalise the telecommunications sector was far more significant on a practical level, as it gave tens of millions the opportunity to access the internet for the first time.

With publishing restrictions lifted in both the print and online spheres, journalists have also had much better access to the corridors of power. The government began actively engaging private sector journalists, appointing spokespersons—most notably Ye Htut, who would become an important voice for the administration—and holding semi-regular press conferences. Journalists had been banned from the first session of parliament, convened in January 2011 by the military regime, but were allowed to watch proceedings when the second session convened in August 2011. This has become an important means of improving access to information, such as detail on draft laws, government performance and budget spending.

Also in August 2011, the government issued an appeal to exiles to return home and work for Myanmar's transition. This offer was extended to exile media journalists, who had previously been labelled 'axe handles'—a quaint term for traitor—by state media. In the later months of that year, staff from exile media began making their first legal reporting trips to Myanmar; by 2013, exile media outlets had shifted most of their operations into the country. This was in part a response to changing conditions and press freedom improvements, but also to a shift in donor priorities away from groups operating on the country's borders, particularly in Thailand.

For almost 50 years the state media enjoyed a monopoly on daily publishing. In December 2012, the government announced it would grant daily newspaper publishing licences to the private sector. The first four of these newspapers began printing on 1 April 2013. In subsequent years, around a dozen more—nearly all in the Myanmar language—were launched. In such a crowded market, some lasted just a matter of months. By late 2016 around half a dozen Myanmar-language dailies had become well established, with daily print runs approaching or exceeding six figures. Two English dailies have been launched, with one still in operation. Many new weekly and monthly publications have also appeared.

Importantly, licences have been granted to virtually all comers, with preference no longer given to applicants considered friendly to the government. The exception to this has been foreign publishers. Investment rules ban foreign or joint venture publishing operations in the Myanmar language, and foreign investors require Ministry of Information permission to publish in a foreign language.

The state media has not been exempt from reforms under Thein Sein's government. The government announced its intention to transform state mouthpieces into what it termed 'public service media'—semi-independent publications and broadcasters that conveyed important information to the public in a non-partial manner. Results to date have been modest. There is still, for example, no coverage of opposition political parties, while information about government activities is conveyed uncritically.

Finally, journalists have been able to establish credible industry bodies, albeit following some initial missteps. In September 2012, the Myanmar Press Council (Interim), comprising journalists, publishers, academics and legal experts, was formed. The council subsequently played an important role in the print industry's development, including mediating disputes, drafting codes of conduct and lobbying on draft media legislation. Similarly, a Myanmar Journalists Association was formed the same year, along with a union and network. These latter two organisations have been strong advocates for media freedom, and have not been afraid to speak out publicly when they feel that freedom is potentially at risk (International Media Support (IMS) 2013).

There have been fewer developments in the media sector under the National League for Democracy administration, which has largely continued the status quo. State-owned newspapers are still used to disseminate pro-government propaganda, for example, and the government rarely holds press conferences or responds to requests for information from journalists. Aung San

Suu Kyi, who holds the position of state counsellor, she has done limited press conferences alongside visiting dignitaries inside Myanmar since her election victory, and is known to be personally distrustful of journalists and the media. Some even argue that the promises that the party made in its election manifesto—for example, to 'ensure that the media has the right to stand independently in accordance with self-regulation of matters relating to ethics and dignity, and the right to gather and disseminate news'—are not being upheld (Sithu Aung Myint 2017).

Legislative changes: hotly contested

Policy changes have been complemented by reforms to the legal framework. However, this process has been much more contested and fraught. A plan to replace the Printers and Publishers Registration Act was announced in early 2012 but the draft was scrapped after Kyaw Hsan was sacked in August of that year. A new version, known as the Printing and Publishing Law, was submitted to parliament in 2013 but provoked protests from the industry, particularly over licensing provisions.

The ministry conducted further consultations with the interim press council but instead of amending the version being considered by parliament it submitted the council's draft law as a separate bill, titled the News Media Law. In March 2014, both laws were approved by parliament and enacted by the president. Bylaws for the Printing and Publishing Law were enacted in October 2014, while bylaws for the News Media Law were introduced the following year.

The Printing and Publishing Law focuses on the issuing of publishing licences and the terms under which they are issued. Some types of content—such as pornographic material or content likely to incite violence—are banned, but punishments are minimal. While a 'step forward' from the old law, media freedom groups have questioned whether it is necessary at all (Article 19 2014a). An important change under the bylaws is that publishing licences only need to be renewed every five years, rather than annually (Sandar Lwin 2014a).

The News Media Law focuses on regulation of print and online media. It specifies the composition and responsibilities of the News Media Council (which replaced the Myanmar Press Council (Interim) and guarantees 'media workers' the right to criticise the government). Those found guilty of violating the law face only a fine and not a custodial sentence. The imprecise language and lack of definitions for key terms have been criticised, as well as the perceived lack of independence of the Press Council (Article 19 2014b).

In August 2015, the government also enacted a Broadcasting Law. Two other planned pieces of media-related legislation, focused on public service media and libraries, were not approved before the Thein Sein government left office and their status is now unclear. Since the transition, the NLD administration has focused its attention on a Right to Information Law, although its introduction is considered unlikely before 2018.

Broadcast sector: largely overlooked

Broadcast media in Myanmar remains closely controlled by the Ministry of Information. Under the 1989 State-owned Economic Enterprises Law, only the state can run a broadcast media operation. While this law has not been repealed, since the mid-2000s a number of joint venture operations have been established, along with one wholly private operation. The nature of these agreements has ensured that the government can maintain control over content, but for the most part they have focused on entertainment rather than sensitive questions of national politics (Sandar Lwin 2014b).

In 2006, the Ministry of Information signed a 12-year agreement with Forever Media Group to set up MRTV-4, a joint venture terrestrial network. In 2010, five private FM radio stations were licensed as joint ventures with the ministry. Most of the private partners are linked to major business, including Htoo Group, Shwe Than Lwin and Zaykabar (Pyae Thet Phyo 2013).

The largest broadcaster is Skynet, which in 2010 was given a 33-year licence to run a satellite broadcasting service that is now available in many parts of the country. This service features mostly foreign channels—including CNN, BBC and other news services—but also several local news lines. One of these, Up To Date, covers a range of news events, including those arranged by opponents of the government. However, editors have said that they receive pressure from the Ministry of Information not to cover certain topics. In recent years these agreements have come under close scrutiny in the media. The government has been forced to release the terms of the arrangements, prompting accusations that the ministry received far less from its private partners than it should have. The deals have been re-negotiated to apparently bring them into line with the terms of the Broadcasting Law, but the new contracts have not been made public.

The Broadcasting Law was adopted following around two years of negotiation and debate, including extensive consultation with civil society that some argue resulted in significant improvements (Article 19 2015). The law has been praised for allocating spectrum between state, private and community media, and for providing a basis for independent regulation of the sector. However, it does not enshrine freedom of expression and gives the president the right to appoint and remove members of the regulator, the Broadcasting Council. It also does not contain provisions on digitalisation or convergence and is therefore likely to require amendment in the near future.

In late 2016, the NLD government responded to pressure to liberalise the broadcast sector by calling a tender for private broadcasters. The five winning bidders were to each receive one terrestrial channel from the state broadcaster, Myanma Radio and Television. In April 2017, the government announced the winners: a mix of big businesses with no publishing experience (Kaung Myanmar Aung, Fortune International and Young Investment Group) and former exile media (DVB and Mizzima).

There are already some independent voices in the broadcasting sector, however. These operate through short-wave radio and satellite television, and include the BBC, VOA, RFA and DVB. These are important sources of unfiltered information for many in Myanmar, particularly in areas outside the reach of independent print media.

Tatmadaw and the media: an uneasy truce

President Thein Sein's media reforms were initially acknowledged as an important signal of progress towards democratisation. In the latter years of the Thein Sein government, the narrative began to shift, with warnings that the government was backtracking on its commitment to media freedom. The prosecution of dozens of journalists in 2014–15, the death of a reporter while in military custody and self-censorship on particular issues offered grounds for concern and provided indications of the limits on freedom of expression in Myanmar.

Much international attention has focused on the 'Unity Five'—four journalists and the chief executive officer from weekly publication *Unity* who were arrested in January 2014 under the State Secrets Act for publishing an article alleging that the military was running a chemical weapons factory in rural Magwe Region. In July of the same year, they were sentenced to ten years' imprisonment with hard labour, later reduced to seven years on appeal. While they became something of an international cause celebre, the case was more complicated. The article was obviously flawed, and possibly designed to gain attention for a struggling publication.

The response, however, was clearly disproportionate to the alleged crime and prompted public protests from journalists.

Another incident that generated a local and international outcry was the death of Par Gyi, a freelance reporter who was shot while in military custody in October 2014. The Tatmadaw only informed the Press Council that he had died almost three weeks after the fact, and four weeks after he had disappeared while covering conflict in Mon State. After much lobbying from his wife and other human rights advocates, a township court held an inquest into his death. Towards the end of this hearing it was revealed that a military court had already cleared the soldiers who killed Par Gyi of any wrongdoing.

There is a common thread through these cases, and a number of others that occurred in 2014 and 2015: the involvement of the military. There is a clear divergence between how the Thein Sein government and Tatmadaw view the media. For the government, independent print media is an unavoidable reality and needs to be engaged on some level, even though information is also disseminated through state-run outlets. The Tatmadaw as an institution, however, remains wary of journalists. Its few attempts to systematise and improve the sharing of information have failed. Individual officers fear being quoted by name and as a result are reluctant to provide any information (Yee Mon and Lun Min Mang 2015). Often, the best outcome that most journalists can hope for is an off-the-record comment. Officers understand that this leaves the Tatmadaw at a major public relations disadvantage—particularly vis-à-vis the more nimble and media-savvy armed ethnic groups—but currently perceive non-engagement as the safest option.

Everyday challenges

The *Unity* and Ko Par Gyi cases are largely outliers; the majority of journalists go about their work without fear of arrest or death. Yet they are also indicative of some of the everyday challenges that journalists in Myanmar face. The legal framework and judicial system are largely stacked against journalists if they are subject to a criminal complaint. While the Electronic Transactions Law has been amended to remove provisions that could potentially be used against journalists, several colonial- and post-colonial-era laws—not least the criminal code—that can be used against journalists remain in force. These include sedition, incitement and defamation sections of the criminal code, the Unlawful Associations Act, the State Secrets Act and the Emergency Provisions Act. The government's use of the judiciary and legal framework to maintain 'law and order' rather than uphold 'rule of law' has been well documented (Cheesman 2015).

New laws that threaten freedom of expression have also been enacted, most notably the 2013 Telecommunications Law. Section 66(d) provides for a prison term of up to three years for anyone found guilty of 'extorting, coercing, restraining wrongfully, defaming, disturbing, causing undue influence or threatening to any person by using any Telecommunications Network'. The section was first applied in 2015 by the military to prosecute Facebook users for satirical posts. However, its use has since expanded dramatically; under the Thein Sein government, seven cases were opened by police under the section, but in the first nine months of the NLD government 42 people were prosecuted. Facebook users have faced charges for abusive language against public figures, including President Htin Kyaw and State Counsellor Aung San Suu Kyi, while businesses have filed complaints against ordinary people who criticised their products or services. Media workers have not been exempt; in November 2016, the Yangon Region Chief Minister Phyo Min Thein filed a complaint against the chief executive officer and chief editor of Eleven Media after an article suggested he was corrupt. The pair were arrested and only granted bail nearly two months later, after issuing a public apology; the case was continuing at the time of writing. Amendments to the law were finally passed in August 2017, but these were relatively minor and are unlikely to stop journalists being prosecuted (Hein Ko Soe and Kean 2017).

Personal safety remains a concern in some circumstances. Journalists covering armed conflict or public protests know there is a degree of risk involved, from both state forces and other actors. Shortly after the Kokang conflict broke out in February 2015, two Myanmar Red Cross Society workers were killed when their convoy was ambushed by unidentified soldiers; a number of journalists and photographers were in the same convoy, but were unharmed. During the police crackdown on student demonstrators at Letpadan, Bago Region, in March 2015, officers made no distinction between journalists and demonstrators as they wielded their truncheons (several were briefly detained). In December 2016, an Eleven Media journalist in Monywa, Sagaing Region, was killed while investigating organised crime. At the time of writing, the case remained unsolved.

However, only a fraction of the reporting conducted by Myanmar-based publications would potentially be subject to either legal or physical threats. In contrast, the problem of access to information affects the majority of journalists. Although transparency in the government and business spheres has improved markedly, gaining access to and verifying information is difficult. Little government data is publicly available and most of that which is has not been digitised or put online.[2] Officials regularly request reporters come and take information in person rather than provide it by email or phone—in some cases, when they are on the other side of the country.[3] As a result, journalists often struggle to find evidence to support a contested allegation. Combined with a lack of resources this can lead to substandard reporting. Another outcome is that journalists tend to over-rely on comments from sources rather than data or other forms of evidence, such as government documents or records.

This is not helped by the fact they typically enter the industry with little training. A legacy of the destruction of independent media was that, when private publications resumed from 2000, there were few experienced journalists to lead the way. In recent years there has been a major push from the government, the industry and international donors to improve journalism training opportunities. Working journalists benefit from a range of donor-funded short programmes, while in May 2014 the independent Myanmar Journalism Institute was set up with donor support.

Self-censorship and bias exist, but are inevitably difficult to measure. There are clearly a number of issues that journalists struggle to cover adequately, for different reasons. Two of the most prominent are religious conflict, particularly in Rakhine State, and national politics (Nyein Ei Ei Htwe 2015). On the first, journalists face pressure—from the government, Buddhist leaders, readers and even advertisers—not to write articles that could be perceived as sympathetic to the cause of Muslims and particularly the Rohingya. On national politics, the majority of journalists have in the past been personally sympathetic to the NLD, or for other reasons felt unable to criticise Aung San Suu Kyi. However, this has changed to some degree as the NLD has shifted from opposition to government office.

Economic challenges

To some extent, the tastes of readers and advertisers dictate the tone and coverage of media in any competitive market. However, this is amplified in Myanmar, where most print publications struggle to break even, let alone make money. Daily newspaper publishing is particularly competitive. One year after daily private newspapers were permitted in April 2013, about half that launched had stopped publishing (Aung Shin 2014); by early 2017, there were around five Myanmar-language dailies still operating. Most print publications rely on sales rather than advertising for revenue; ad spending in Myanmar is heavily concentrated in the broadcast sector, with just 30 per cent going towards the print sector, and 7 per cent for daily newspapers (Aung Shin 2014).

However, this low slice of the ad pie reflects the relatively limited reach of Myanmar's newspapers. The challenges of distributing in a country with such limited road infrastructure are immense. Only the state newspapers can claim to have a truly national reach. As a result, print runs are modest; the largest papers print only around 100,000 copies a day. Low levels of disposable income and widespread poverty, particularly in rural areas, make daily and weekly papers unaffordable. The difficult economic environment for independent media results in under-resourced newsrooms. Some smaller weeklies cannot even afford to provide PCs to new reporters or cover taxi fares. Larger newsrooms are still not adequately staffed to cover the breadth of the country, with journalists concentrated in Yangon, Naypyitaw and Mandalay. Instead, they rely on regional stringers or freelance contributors, many of whom have no formal training.

In this context, economic consolidation could bring benefits. Fewer newspapers would mean those that exist grab a larger slice of the advertising and circulation pie. Larger revenues would result in better-staffed newsrooms, broader coverage and better quality reporting. On the other hand, it would also concentrate media in the hands of a few owners. Big business has already begun moving into the sector and there are concerns among journalists that this represents state control by stealth. Such ownership changes are unlikely to result in newspapers becoming mouthpieces for political or business interests, as that would make little economic sense in a market where independence is prized. But they may shy away from sensitive topics that could arouse controversy and potentially harm the interests of their owners. Such accusations have been levelled against *The Myanmar Times* since it was bought by businessman Thein Tun, owner of distribution company Myanmar Golden Star, in early 2015 (Gleeson 2017). In October 2016, the special investigations editor of the English edition of *The Myanmar Times* was fired for her reporting of military operations in Rakhine State; the English daily was also forced by management to halt all coverage of Rakhine State due to the perceived sensitivity of the issue (Gleeson 2016).

Reach and relevance

Most of the shackles on the print media have been removed. But a number of recent surveys suggest that because of the limited reach of print media organisations—and their online presences—and political indifference, the impact of doing so will have been limited. From December 2013 to February 2014, Myanmar Survey Research conducted polling for the International Republican Institute (IRI) on a range of political questions, including media usage. Just 10 per cent of respondents said they were most likely to get news and information from daily newspapers or weekly journals. Meanwhile, 35 per cent listed radio and 23 per cent televisions as their most likely source. Barely 30 per cent read a newspaper, journal or magazine once a month, but 42 per cent watched TV or listed to the radio almost every day.

The internet appears to have had a limited impact on how people access information. Just 1 per cent of respondents in the IRI survey listed the internet as their most likely source of news and information. From May 2014 to March 2015, more than 1,600 people from 36 randomly selected townships were interviewed for the Asian Barometer Survey (ABS). More than 80 per cent did not use the internet or social media networks to get information on politics or the government, while 87 per cent never engaged in political discussion on such platforms.

This in part reflects low levels of political engagement, particularly in rural areas and among women and those who have not completed high school. In the ABS survey, 41.6 per cent of respondents reported that they 'practically never' followed news about politics and the government. Two-thirds never discussed politics with family and friends, while 54 per cent were 'not at all interested' or 'not very interested' in politics. In contrast, just 11.4 per cent said they followed news about politics and the government every day.

The internet: a whole new ball game?

The greatest opportunities for the development of media organisations in Myanmar stem from the introduction of new communications technologies, particularly mobile-phone-based internet. A state monopoly meant that for more than a decade SIM cards were expensive—about US$1,500 in 2010—and provided poor network coverage. This has been liberalised in stages. Following a highly competitive tender, the government awarded Telenor and Ooredoo mobile operator licences in 2013. The licences set high benchmarks for population reach and geographic coverage for 3G internet services within five years. The increased competition has reduced SIM-card prices to the equivalent of just a few dollars and led to dramatic expansion in network coverage. By the end of 2016, there were an estimated 48 million registered SIM-cards, with a high proportion—at least 50 per cent—using data.

Increased access and download speeds and lower costs have already brought millions of new potential readers into the orbit of private news media organisations. This will eventually end the state media monopoly in rural and remote areas. While many remain reluctant to read or engage in debate on political issues, news will inevitably be thrust upon them through their use of social media—for example, when articles are shared by their Facebook friends and appear in their newsfeeds. Media organisations in Myanmar have terrific reach through Facebook and are spending money to give their posts extra prominence. At the same time, the internet, particularly Facebook, has created opportunities for new, previously unknown voices to gain influence. Additionally, with everyone from the former president's spokesman, Ye Htut, to the Yangon traffic police force on Facebook, citizens now have more opportunities than ever to engage with people of authority. Despite the dangers, Facebook gives the government the opportunity to share information and views directly with the public, without its message being filtered by the mainstream media.

The Ministry of Information has made clear that licensing will remain a central plank of its media regulation policy. However, the internet and social media networks enable new operators to circumvent the government's licensing process and potentially attain substantial influence. This represents both an opportunity and a threat. There is a degree of transparency around those who hold publishing licences that does not exist for websites and Facebook pages. For years a number of sites have been accused of publishing material aimed at discrediting the opposition and anti-government figures.

Like publications around the world, those in Myanmar will face challenges in stopping already-meagre advertising revenues from migrating online. Few currently make any money from online advertising or subscriptions. The late development of the sector, however, offers opportunities to learn from what is working elsewhere around the world. Because Myanmar's print media has never enjoyed the 'rivers of gold' that their counterparts in Western countries did for much of the twentieth century, they have not over-expanded or become bloated. Modest advertising revenues, an awareness of the looming challenges and a culture of working on tight budgets mean newsrooms are likely to be kept relatively lean. Meanwhile, electronic payment systems that use mobile technology will make the sale of print and online products to customers easier than ever.

Those who arguably stand to benefit the most from reform of the licensing process and the spread of the internet are ethnic minority communities. For years, ethnic language publications were banned by the government, but in many regions of the country there are now weekly and monthly newspapers for these communities. Due to government controls, a number of these started out online then migrated into print—a reverse of the normal trend. Community newspapers have also become established in regional, ethnic Burmese cities, providing information on events overlooked by the Yangon-based media.

Conclusion

Public discourse in Myanmar is still largely led by its print media industry, which is among the most vibrant and free in the region. A number of important reforms were initiated by the Thein Sein government, for which it received international recognition. The expansion of the internet has only heightened the opportunities for influence and also allowed new voices into the debate. The broadcast media sector, in contrast, remains tightly controlled by the Ministry of Information. The direction it will take in the coming years remains unclear, although the NLD government has begun a partial liberalisation. The print media also still faces substantial challenges, however—including some that may threaten its position at the forefront of public discourse. Much will depend on future governments' tolerance for critical voices. Inevitably, there will continue to be conflict, particularly with the military. While some new media laws have been enacted, there has been little progress in removing the existing statutes that threaten media freedom. These continue to remain a threat.

Economic constraints and trends will also affect the work of the country's journalists. Heavily subsidised state media will continue to play an outsized role in the sector for years to come. Consolidation among private players could lead to larger and better-resourced newsrooms but with a more conservative outlook.

Nevertheless, a culture of independence has been established within the print media industry. New technologies and distribution platforms give the government fewer levers for controlling the spread of information. Rather than restrict private sector media, it has shown a willingness to adopt new approaches in order to get its message out to the public. Rolling back the reforms would not only provoke conflict with the now sizeable private sector media industry but also damage the credibility of the transition both at home and abroad.

Notes

1 As of mid-September 2015, 32 daily, 381 weekly and 284 monthly publishing licences had been issued, according to the Ministry of Information. However, in many cases the licence-holder is not publishing.

2 The Directorate of Investment and Company Administration is a notable exception to this. It has established an open register of companies that is fully searchable online.

3 In one case, a reporter at *The Myanmar Times* was forced to travel to Muse, on the Chinese border in Shan State, to get the latest information in a murder investigation.

References

Article 19. 2014a. 'Myanmar: Printing and Publishing Law'. www.article19.org, 11 November. Accessed September 2015. www.article19.org/resources.php/resource/37765/en/myanmar:-printing-and-publishing-law.

Article 19. 2014b. 'Myanmar: News Media Law'. Accessed September 2015. www.article19.org/data/files/medialibrary/37623/News-Media-Law-Myanmar-EN.pdf.

Article 19. 2015. 'Myanmar: Broadcasting Law'. Accessed March 2017. www.article19.org/data/files/medialibrary/38199/15-11-24-Myanmar-Broadcasting-analysis.pdf.

Aung Shin. 2014. 'Daily papers struggle to reshape the media landscape'. *The Myanmar Times*, 23 March.

Cheesman, Nicholas. 2015. *Opposing the Rule of Law: How Myanmar's Courts Make Law and Order.* Cambridge: Cambridge University Press.

Gleeson, Sean. 2016. 'Journalist's sacking after MoI complaint raises concerns over press freedom'. *Frontier Myanmar*, 10 November.

Gleeson, Sean. 2017. 'Troubled times'. *Frontier Myanmar*, 2 March.

Hein Ko Soe & Kean, Thomas. 2017. '66(d): The defamation menace'. *Frontier Myanmar*, 5 January.

Htun Khaing. 2016. 'Journalists under pressure'. *Frontier Myanmar*, 21 July.

International Media Support (IMS). 2013. 'Journalist unions in Myanmar in joint campaign for press freedom'. Accessed August 2016. www.mediasupport.org/journalist-unions-in-myanmar-join-forces-in-campaign-to-curb-restrictive-media-laws/.

Kean, Thomas. 2015. 'Election reporting in the dark days of 2010'. *The Myanmar Times*, 16 September.

Nwe Nwe Aye. 2012. 'Role of the media in Myanmar: Can it be a watchdog for corruption?' In *Myanmar's Transition: Openings, Obstacles, and Opportunities*, edited by Cheesman, Nicholas, Monique Skidmore & Trevor Wilson. Singapore: Institute of Southeast Asian Studies.

Nyein Ei Ei Htwe. 2015. '"Some can't decide whether they are activists or journalists": U Myint Kyaw'. *The Myanmar Times*, 16 September.

Pe Myint. 2012. 'The emergence of Myanmar weekly news journals and their development in recent years'. In *Myanmar's Transition: Openings, Obstacles, and Opportunities*, edited by Cheesman, Nicholas, Monique Skidmore & Trevor Wilson. Singapore. Institute of Southeast Asian Studies.

Pyae Thet Phyo. 2013. 'Broadcasting deals in line with the law: ministry'. *The Myanmar Times*, 10 October.

Sandar Lwin. 2014a, 'New rules for publishing licences to open up sector'. *The Myanmar Times*, 17 October.

Sandar Lwin. 2014b. 'An ownership dispute with a twist'. *The Myanmar Times*, 20 October.

Sithu Aung Myint. 2017. 'Questioning the government's commitment to media freedom'. *Frontier Myanmar*, 16 February.

Yee Mon & Lun Min Mang. 2015. 'Tatmadaw press club dinner party proposal'. *The Myanmar Times*. 2 January.

16
EXILES

Inga Gruß

For many years, Myanmar's diaspora has played a crucial role in shaping the perception of the international public on Myanmar's political situation and its protracted conflicts. Arguably, the Myanmar diaspora was a key player in drawing attention to the country when many people had rarely ever heard about it. The influential media and information network that was constructed in exile was a main source of information about the country and its people. The Myanmar diaspora as a whole was characterised by a focus on the strong involvement in political activities on different levels—grassroots activities, political education, or lobbying on an international stage. The strong focus on the activism of the diaspora, on the one hand, reflects the desire of exiled populations to stay involved in the affairs of their homeland. On the other hand, the focus on activism resonates with the emphasis on human rights violations, the paradigm through which many Myanmar-related developments have been analysed.

This chapter looks at research on Myanmar's diaspora and exiled populations. The purpose is to provide a discussion of the distinct trajectories of different groups of people in the diaspora and to point to themes that have been highlighted across the different populations. I argue that the human rights paradigm and its resulting implications have narrowed the topics for analysis and exploration by interested scholars. As a result, the demographic and geographical diversity of the diaspora has been perceived as limited. This chapter aims to broaden the perspective on the Myanmar diaspora and point to current and emerging concerns of those living outside Myanmar's border.

Categorising people—shaping perceptions

Any discussion of the Myanmar diaspora is implicated in the construction of labels that are imposed upon people and in important ways guide the perception of outsiders about the categorised. As an inevitable practice, categorisation is a powerful tool that evokes specific life trajectories and conjures up imagined challenges or opportunities of said populations. The predominance of categories and labels in everyday life often glosses over the fraught nature of constructing categories and imposing labels which always deny difference and construct sameness among people that might only be superficial, as Malkki (1995) reminds us. This insight reverberates with discussions of pertinent terminology in the scholarly writings on the Myanmar diaspora.

The most commonly employed terms to describe those living outside Myanmar are migrant and refugee. To most scholars, the difference between those categorised as migrant or refugee lies in their reasons for leaving Myanmar: migrants have left Myanmar for mostly economic reasons while refugees have left Myanmar for mostly political reasons (Arnold 2013). Dudley (2010) has followed the same reasoning for categorising people as migrants or refugees, but uses a different label for refugees (forced migrant). Some scholars have suggested alternative interpretations. Brees (2008) introduces the categories of the self-settled refugee versus the camp refugee. In her analysis, camp refugees live within the confinement of a refugee camp and have limited opportunities to generate income. Self-settled refugees live outside refugee camps and are usually engaged in occupational activities. Brees argues that camp refugees and self-settled refugees both leave Myanmar due to a pervasive climate of insecurity and limited livelihood options and therefore should not be treated separately in analysis. Following the same line of argument, Caouette and Pack (2002) similarly blur the distinction between refugees and migrants. These alternative interpretations, though, that point to the often conflated nature of the political and economic have not replaced the predominant mode of categorisation. A term less frequently employed, but nevertheless relevant in relation to the Myanmar diaspora is the label immigrant (Lu 2008).

The debate over whom to categorise as migrant or refugee is rooted in an emphasis on previous experiences—learning more about the past of those to be categorised is considered crucial in creating appropriate labels to describe their current condition. In contrast, when labelling a person as immigrant, their reasons for leaving their home countries are rarely of interest, but their future trajectories as permanent residents in a country different from their homeland are highlighted. The disagreement about the more appropriate categorisation of exiled populations obscures other important temporal connotations that the terms migrant, refugee and immigrant carry. The term refugee creates an orientation towards the past. It situates the subject in a continuous relationship with a traumatic event or series of events that cause displacement. Once categorised as refugee, contemporary lives are continuously assessed in relation to the series of traumatic events irrespective of their current relevance. The term migrant holds a more neutral temporal position and predominantly is interpreted as describing the current condition of a subject. In contrast, the word immigrant is mostly directed towards the present and future. It recognises that a subject has relocated permanently to a society that is different from their home country. Difference of origin is acknowledged and marked indefinitely. At the same time, the subject is positioned vis-à-vis the current society they live in, rather than their place of origin. These temporal connotations are also reflected in the topics that have been selected for analysis of the Myanmar diaspora.

In a similar vein, the terms exile and diaspora carry temporal connotations. Malkki (1995) argues that exile is often used to describe a self-imposed displacement that can be ended upon one's own terms and is rarely associated with refugees. Diaspora, in contrast, describes groups of people who have taken root elsewhere and maintain connection to their home countries (Clifford 1994). Irrespective of these interpretations, exile and diaspora have often been used interchangeably in relevant Myanmar scholarship and rarely delineate a strict temporal separation as suggested by Malkki and Clifford. The usage of the terms refugee, migrant, immigrant, diaspora and exile in this chapter reflect common usage in the Myanmar literature as explicated above. With a short note of caution, I would like to point out that all these labels serve descriptive purposes imposed by me and do not necessarily reflect self-identification of people categorised as belonging to either label.

Crossing the border—the Myanmar diaspora in Thailand

Thailand is home to the largest contingent of the Myanmar diaspora, and hence the majority of scholarship engages with those living there. Estimates about the size of the Myanmar population there vary as the discrepancy between the documented and undocumented populations is significant. In addition to the two million documented people, some scholars suggest that there are as many as two to six million undocumented workers (Hall 2011). The 2,400 kilometre long shared border has made it possible for thousands of people to enter Thailand travelling by foot. The Myanmar diaspora in Thailand is a medley of people from all walks of life: daily commuters who live in border towns; long-term migrants living in economic centres in Thailand; refugees who are seeking protection from persecution; activists whose lives are dedicated to positively impacting lives and livelihoods in Myanmar; armed resistance fighters; and political representatives of ethnic nationality governments. In the scholarly literature, though, not all these groups are equally discussed or represented at all.

The diversity of the Myanmar diaspora and its differing experiences at times is glossed over by the narrow emphasis placed on some topics that in turn are discussed in great detail. Factors that contribute to distinct experiences include, for example, geographical location; whether one lives in close proximity to the border in Mae Sot or Mae Sai, in and around Bangkok, along the Gulf of Thailand or the Andaman coast creates vastly different experiences of exiled life. Furthermore, socio-demographic backgrounds of exiled peoples that, for example, influence their access to housing, work and networks of people can play an important role in creating a more positive or negative diaspora experience.

International attention to the Myanmar diaspora in Thailand and the country in general was drawn on a large scale after the violent crackdown of student demonstrations in 1988 (Lintner 1990). In the aftermath of the crackdown, the international public learned about the fraught political situation and the decades-long civil war that had displaced thousands of people. Feeling no longer safe in Myanmar, many student activists fled to Thailand. During their flight from Myanmar, they were aided by armed resistance groups whose decades-long struggle against the central government had equipped them well with survival skills in the jungle; skills dearly missing among many student activists. The All Burma Student democratic front was born, an alliance of students who took up arms to voice their discontent with the Myanmar government (Zaw Oo 2006).

The fully-fledged ongoing civil war between insurgents fighting for autonomy and self-governance of their lands and the *Tatmadaw* (Armed Forces) was at the expense of civilians living in the contested regions. Thousands were forced to leave their homes and embarked on arduous journeys through a war zone to Thailand. These contrasting groups—urban, middle-class students and dispossessed peasants—became emblematic of exiled populations from Myanmar in Thailand for at least two decades. Having suffered abuse at the hands of the Myanmar government was the common theme highlighted time and again that constructed commonalities between these otherwise vastly different populations. Their presence and activism in Thailand were to shape the public image of Myanmar, its political struggles and its diaspora for decades to come. The lives of other exiled peoples—such as migrants—despite outnumbering refugees and activists by far remained until recently largely unnoticed.

From student activists to media professionals

The successful creation of the international news and information network by Myanmar activists is well documented (Brooten 2008). As Brooten (2004) has argued, the rise of activist-led news outlets was aided by the rise of human rights discourses on an international platform in the early 1990s. Governments promoting human rights increased access to funding for those echoing their discourses. The exiled student activists were able to use available funding to voice their political concerns through emerging information technology: the internet. Thus, the transformation of these student activists to media professionals was aided by the global ascent of human rights as an ideological tool, the related availability of funding, growing popularity of the internet, a motivated body of young, energetic activists and, finally, the near impossibility of circulating uncensored information in print in Myanmar.

The enmeshed relationship between ideological convergence and access to funding enabled student activists to widely share their political points of view (Brooten 2004). Duell (2014) has pointed out that the mature identities of activists were mostly built around dissent and opposition to the Myanmar government. Combined with a conflation of professional and personal identities and opinions, it was not always possible to tell whether personal points of view or larger political positions were promoted in news outlets. The strong reflection of personal beliefs in news reporting stood in opposition to professed professional standards of objectivity in journalism, as Brooten (2006) has pointed out. Until the ascent of these young professionals, English language reporting about Myanmar was rare and the motivation of these students to bring change to Myanmar resulted in their almost monopolistic control over public Myanmar discourses. In addition to professional media channels such as the Democratic Voice of Burma, Mizzima and The Irrawaddy, these student-turned-publicity-professionals were crucial in kick-starting global movements that advocated democratic change in Myanmar—for example, the BurmaNet and the Free Burma campaigns.

There is little agreement as to how these professionals have actually contributed to their initial goal of bringing political change to Myanmar (Duell 2013). Egreteau (2012) argued that their political influence in Myanmar has been less powerful than the impact remittances have had in bringing forth political change. Zaw Oo (2006), though, argued that a lot of their work was clandestine in nature and activists were not able to take credit for their achievements. In summary, their status as heroes of democratic change and influential sources of information is largely unrelated to an assessment of their actual achievements or positionality.

The conundrum that characterises the work of many exiled activists worldwide has caught up with many of these advocates of change. The campaigns promoted by activists promoted political change in Myanmar which in the end would make their work in exile no longer necessary since they helped to create a more open society in which dissent can be voiced publicly. While there is disagreement about the sincerity of the reforms by the Myanmar government, in the eyes of many donors priorities have now shifted to support work in Myanmar, leaving many activists fearing for their livelihoods (Duell 2014). For many activists, the decades-long engagement meant that the centre of their lives shifted—they started families and raised children in Thailand or elsewhere. Few funding organisations are still willing to make long-term commitments for additional projects. Aside from a few high-profile cases of activists returning to Myanmar, the future of many exiled activists is unclear.

The trajectory of the other high-profile exiled population from Myanmar—refugees—was incomparably different from that of the activists discussed above. Despite a similarly high degree of self-organisation, involvement in activism and political lobbying, refugees have not been able to transform their public image from victimhood to self-empowerment. Rather, refugees and the remaining refugee camps in Thailand have become the living testament to the abysmal human rights record of the Myanmar government.

Activist lives—from refugee camps to transnational campaigns

Lang (2002) provides one of the most comprehensive overviews of the presence of Myanmar refugees in Thailand. Since 1984, there have been permanent refugee camps in Thailand. Before 1984, people regularly crossed the border into Thailand seeking shelter from armed conflict, but usually were able to return after a period of waiting. A change to this pattern of flight and return was marked with the loss of autonomously governed territory by the Karen National Union in 1984. Many Karen people fled from the intruding Myanmar army and the growing number of people required more permanent infrastructure that could accommodate a larger number of people. From the beginning of the permanent settlement in Thailand, refugees relied on their own initiative to construct shelter and to create access to food. The Thai government was reluctant to get involved in supporting the construction of refugee camps, but also did not prevent refugees from settling permanently. Although the Thai government is not a signatory to the 1951/1965 UN Convention on Refugees and does not adhere to a formal framework to accommodate requests for asylum, they have cooperated with refugees and their representatives in maintaining the camps, as Lang (2002) points out.

At the peak of the refugee crisis in 1997, the UNHCR categorised 170,035 people of concern from Myanmar residing in Thailand. In 2002, 113,669 people of concern from Myanmar were registered and in 2015, 130,238 (UNHCR 2015). The most recent numbers suggest that there has been an increase in refugees again. This is true, but these refugees do not continue to arrive from Myanmar's eastern border regions, but from the western coastal region as will be explained in greater detail below. In general, the numbers of refugees from Myanmar's east are decreasing mostly due to international resettlement programmes. Resettlement programmes were the solution to the stalemate that developed around the stagnant situation of refugees. The term refugee camp barely adequately describes the permanent fixtures that these sites have become. With return to Myanmar appearing less and less likely, resettlement to other countries has become the solution to enabling refugees to continue their lives outside the perimeters of the camps. Resettlement has been in place since the early 2000s, and more than 88,000 refugees have been relocated to the US since (Vang and Trieu 2014).

The presence of refugees from Myanmar's eastern states and provinces in Thailand has been documented well (Grundy-Warr 2004). Analysis has focused on reasons for displacement (Burma Ethnic Research Group 2000), health and related humanitarian concerns (Beyrer 1999), legal and security issues (Brees 2008) and an almost uncountable number of policy reports (see for example Martin 2007). Some of the many human rights organisations that have published relevant reports include Amnesty International; Human Rights Watch; Thai–Burma Border Consortium; Burma Ethnic Research Group; Karen Human Rights Group; Shan Human Rights Foundation; and the Karen Women's Organisation. These publications have effectively communicated the urgency of addressing the conflict in Myanmar and finding long-term solutions for displaced peoples. They also have reiterated the position that refugees are trapped in an enduring conflict that leaves them largely helpless.

Despite the image of helplessness and victimhood that many of the writings above have contributed to creating, it has amply been demonstrated that refugees continued to remain active agents in their own lives. Governance, administration and all other day-to-day affairs, including education in refugee camps, have been in the hands of refugees (Bowles 1998). Others have demonstrated how refugee camps have become creative sites of self-invention, renewal and community development (Dudley 2007, 2011). Furthermore, refugee camps have played a crucial role in raising political awareness that has resulted in the more explicit creation of politicised identities (Dudley 2007).

The will and interest to organise have not only been expressed in self-governance but also in founding of and participating in the activities of countless grassroots and non-governmental organisations. Participation in these movements is not restricted to people living in camps, but includes others residing in Myanmar, people in the borderlands outside the camps. Brooten (2004) highlighted that the funding mechanism in place that benefited political activists has not been as advantageous for ethnic minorities. Ethnic minority activists have mostly received funding to document human rights abuses in Myanmar, rather than funding that would enable them to promote their own political agendas that often include advocacy for self-determination. Furthermore, the intense focus on reporting mostly about human rights abuses has continuously stereotyped ethnic nationality groups into roles of victimhood (Brooten 2013, 2015). This, however, has not prevented activists from forming broad social movements. Simpson (2013) sees in the social movement that has gathered around environmental concerns an example of a pan-national movement that has overcome ethnic factionalism that otherwise continues to play an important role in interactions among people from Myanmar. Embracing activism is not only a commonality between refugees and media professionals but also between migrants (Williams 2012). Labour activism is an important concern for migrant workers (Arnold 2013). Campbell (2012, 2013) highlights how solidarity among labour activists has the potential to bridge differences that in an otherwise ethnically tense country often arise.

The lives of refugees, migrants and others living outside the borders of Myanmar often intersect, as has particularly been illustrated by borderland studies (see Meehan and Sadan in this volume). The border region has historically been home to a medley of people and this diversity has only increased with more frequent border traffic (Ropharat 2009). Early approaches in which border zones were portrayed as marginal spaces have been left behind (Grundy-Warr and Wong 2002). While the border continues to be recognised as a potential dividing line that can provide security (Soe Lin Aung 2014), it also is portrayed as a tightly knit zone that fosters cross-border religious alliances that sustain religious communities on either side (Horstmann 2014).

Working for change: Myanmar migrants in Thailand

People from Myanmar have sought employment in Thailand for decades. The failing Myanmar economy combined with poor domestic infrastructure has acted as a push factor for many migrants. In turn, Thailand's proximity, the higher salaries, a range of employment opportunities and better infrastructure have acted as important pull factors. Over the decades, witnessing improvements in the living conditions of extended families of migrant workers in Myanmar and stories that positively describe work and living conditions in Thailand have further influenced the decisions of people to migrate. Thailand now is home to large Myanmar communities, which has further lowered the threshold for others to join existing communities of migrants.

The presence of migrants in Thailand has often been analysed within the human rights paradigm that gained prominence through the works of activists. Topics such as trafficking, (sexual) exploitation, reproductive rights, general gender-related concerns and workplace precarity have been analysed in detail (Arnold and Hewison 2005). It has been pointed out, though, that as deplorable as some of these experiences might be, they only represent a small segment of the overall situation of Myanmar migrants in Thailand (Farrelly 2012). Some studies have moved beyond this paradigm and followed trajectories common in transnational studies and discussed questions of belonging (Faucher 2010) and access to education (Lee 2014; Zeus, 2011).

Concerns about legal status have arguably impacted the lives of all migrants in Thailand (Hall 2012; Sai Latt 2011). The national verification (NV) process, which is the term for the mechanism that has been implemented to allow migrants to obtain temporary passports and work permits, has entangled migrants in unforeseen ways with bureaucratic structures in Thailand and Myanmar. The NV process has created bureaucratic machinery that financially benefits the Myanmar and Thai states, as well as others such as brokers (Myat Mon 2010). It has been pointed out multiple times that the registration process is fraught and subjects migrants to further discriminatory policies (Amporn 2015; Hall 2012). These works explicate the legal pitfalls of the process, but the NV process also has influenced the ways in which migrants have made a place for themselves in Thailand beyond legal conundrums (Gruß 2015). The NV process has enabled the Myanmar state for the first time in decades to collect information about their citizens on a large scale.

Despite the many drawbacks of the NV process, at this point it is the most promising avenue in providing migrants with access to existing legal infrastructure. Speculations about the return of thousands of migrants to Myanmar are largely unfounded and providing migrants with standardised access to legal papers will become more and more important in the future. Many migrants are eager to return to Myanmar, but only once salaries have been raised and the general infrastructure improved such that it enables a less burdensome life. Current economic reforms in Myanmar will not have tangible results in rural areas—where most migrants are from—for decades. Therefore, the Thai economy that has come to rely on Myanmar migrant workers will continue to offer employment to thousands of migrants over the coming years.

Living in the shadow: Rohingya refugees

The discussion so far has ignored the presence of another group of refugees in Thailand: Rohingya, originating from Myanmar's west coast (Cheung 2012). The Rohingya refugee crisis is not a recent phenomenon and their presence is not limited to Thailand, but includes Bangladesh and Malaysia (Abrar 2003). Their displacement has mostly been caused by violent conflicts in Myanmar. Rohingya, who are Muslim, have repeatedly been rejected by the Myanmar state as citizens. Religious riots flared up for the first time during the Second World War and since then have intermittently returned and caused further displacement. The conflict has further escalated in recent years and accusations of ethnic cleansing of Rohingyas by the Myanmar army have been raised (Al Jazeera 2017). Aung San Suu Kyi and the NLD-led government have notably remained silent about the continued persecution of Rohingya in Myanmar.

The Rohingya crisis has historically stood in the shadow of the conflict in Myanmar's eastern states. Christian groups have played an important role in drawing attention to the displacement of peoples in eastern Myanmar as many of the displaced are Christians (Horstmann 2011). Christian groups have not only played an important role in bringing attention and financial support to Christian refugees but also played a crucial role during the resettlement by acting as sponsors on behalf of Christian refugees (Kenny and Lockwood-Kenny 2011). One is only left to wonder how the situation of Rohingya refugees might be different if they had a powerful ally like the Christian church at their side.

Global networks

The Myanmar diaspora in Thailand has thrown a long shadow over the more geographically and demographically diverse Myanmar diaspora worldwide. The US has been home to a Myanmar diaspora for at least fifty years. Immigration from Myanmar to the US was documented after 1967 when, in Myanmar, tensions about wearing Mao badges ensued between students of Chinese descent and the Myanmar government (Fan 2012). Resulting riots caused many people of Chinese descent to leave Myanmar and to settle in the US, mostly in California and New York. Scholars have illustrated the ways in which these Sino-Burmese immigrants have maintained a unique hybrid cultural profile in which Buddhism and Burmese language transmission are crucial markers of identity (Cheah 2002). More immigrants from Myanmar followed after the 1988 clashes. By 2000, according to the US census bureau, officially there were 16,720 people from Myanmar in the US (US Census Bureau 2015). This number, however, is unreliable since between 1977 and 2000, 25,229 people from Myanmar alone immigrated to the US (Cheah 2008). There are stark ideological cleavages between the different generations of immigrants, mostly embodied by different notions about political engagement with Myanmar (Zaw Oo 2006).

The resettlement of refugees mostly started after 2004, resulting in a striking growth of the US Myanmar diaspora; by 2010, 100,000 people from Myanmar were estimated to reside in the US (US Census Bureau 2015). With a few notable exceptions, scholarly interest has been slow to emerge in this rapidly growing population. MacLachlan (2008, 2012, 2014) analysed the role of music among resettled refugees and how it aided renegotiation of explicitly transnational identities. Others have interrogated work environments (Vachon 2012) and educational circumstances (Isik-Ercan 2012).

Although there has been an emphasis on the US, the documented global diaspora spans further than North America and includes Myanmar people in at least Japan (Banki 2006), South Korea (Mee 2012), Taiwan (Lu 2008), Norway (Yee Yee Swe 2013) and Singapore (Sarojini *et al.* 2005). Worldwide, there has been vast interest in mental health and health care circumstances more generally among resettled refugees (Allden *et al.* 1996). The broad interest in mental health reflects the past-oriented paradigm that often guides the analytical framework within which people once categorised as refugees are perceived.

In addition to these populations that might be understudied, but recognised as part of the Myanmar diaspora, there are others whose belonging to the diaspora is not recognised as widely. Post-colonial policies of nationalisation disenfranchised Indian populations who had migrated to Myanmar under British colonial rule (Egreteau 2011). Their ensuing return to India might be considered a return to their official homelands by some. Egreteau (2014), though, has illustrated how a diasporic longing for Myanmar continues to remain an important aspect of the transnational identities of these Indian returnees.

In a similarly strained relationship to Myanmar stands the Myanmar-Nepali diaspora. Many Nepalis came as part of the Gokhalis under British rule to Myanmar (Joshi 2011). Although few have returned to Nepal, many have moved from Myanmar to destinations such as Thailand or Singapore, but maintain ties with their families in Myanmar (personal conversation). Notably, the silence around Nepali or Indian-Myanmar transnationals as part of the Myanmar diaspora has not applied to Sino-Burmese people. These three populations have developed unique positions in contemporary Myanmar society based on factors such as intermarriage, language and religious affiliation. Their position in Myanmar society in turn may have influenced the ways in which the respective populations are considered part of the Myanmar diaspora.

Myanmar diaspora in 2017 and beyond

This chapter has illustrated the diverse nature of the Myanmar diaspora. It has highlighted the persistent analytical focus on the Myanmar diaspora in Thailand and the influence of global discourses on topics chosen for exploration by scholars interested in the Myanmar diaspora. Human rights have played an important role in scholarly inquiries among scholars interested in the Myanmar diaspora and those focusing on domestic populations. The historical trajectory pointed out in this chapter indicates that recent studies increasingly have focused on topics prominent in transnational studies rather than Myanmar studies: for example, the analysis of transnational networks or questions of belonging.

The economic policies presented in July 2016 by the NLD-led government explicitly addressed the importance of job creation to support the return of migrants and displaced peoples to Myanmar. It will be long before reforms halt and reverse the economic marginalisation that so many experience and that plays an important role in encouraging the ongoing migration across Myanmar's border. Meanwhile, the government lacks a framework to address migration management and to support migrants overseas in effective ways.

The changing nature of the Myanmar diaspora in Thailand and elsewhere where migrants and resettled refugee populations form the core of the diaspora offers countless opportunities for scholarly inquiry. Existing studies provide a strong foundation for interrogating, for example, transnational networks that the resettlement of refugees from Myanmar has created, not unlike the resettlement of Vietnamese, Hmong and Khmer refugees has in the past. In a similar vein, the global expansion of Myanmar migrant workers to, for example, the Middle East provides fertile ground for analysing, for example, the vast brokerage system that has evolved around global labour. Last but not least, the relationships between populations in Myanmar and the diaspora are sorely lacking from the otherwise solid Myanmar diaspora scholarship and invite an overcoming of the separate treatment that the two so far often have experienced.

References

Abrar, C. R. 2003. 'Still waiting for a better morrow: A decade of Burmese refugees in Bangladesh'. In *Missing Boundaries: Refugees, Migrants, Stateless and Internally Displaced Persons in South Asia*, edited by P. R. Chari, Mallika Joseph & Suba Chandran, 87–98. New Delhi: Manohar Publishers.

Al Jazeera. 2017. '"Hundreds of Rohingyas" killed in Myanmar Crackdown'. Accessed March 2017. www.aljazeera.com/news/2017/02/rohingyas-killed-myanmar-crackdown-170203101817841.html.

Allden, Kathleen, Charles Poole, Supang Chantavanich, Khin Ohnmar, Nyi Nyi Aung & Richard F. Mollica. 1996. 'Burmese political dissidents in Thailand: Trauma and survival among young adults in exile'. *American Journal of Public Health* 86 (11): 1561–1569.

Amporn, Jirattikorn. 2015. 'Managing migration in Myanmar and Thailand: Economic reforms, policies, practices and challenges'. *Trends in Southeast Asia* 09. Singapore: Institute of Southeast Asian Studies.

Arnold, Dennis 2013. 'Burmese social movements in exile: Labour, migration and democracy'. In *Social Activism in Southeast Asia*, edited by M. Ford, 89–103. London: Routledge.

Arnold, Dennis. & Kevin Hewison. 2005. 'Exploitation in global supply chains: Burmese workers in Mae Sot'. *Journal of Contemporary Asia* 35 (3): 319–340.

Banki, Susan. 2006. 'Burmese refugees in Tokyo: Livelihoods in the urban environment'. *Journal of Refugee Studies* 19 (3): 328–344.

Beyrer, Chris. 1999. 'The health and humanitarian situation of Burmese populations along the Thai–Burma border'. *Burma Debate* 6 (3): 4–13.

Bowles, Edith. 1998. 'From village to camp: Refugee camp life in transition on the Thailand-Burma border'. *Forced Migration Review* 2: 11–15.

Brees, Inge. 2008. 'Refugee business: Strategies of work on the Thai–Burma border'. *Journal of Refugee Studies* 21 (3): 380–397.

Brooten, Lisa. 2004. 'Human rights discourse and the development of democracy in a multi-ethnic state'. *Asian Journal of Communication* 14 (2): 174–191.

Brooten, Lisa. 2006. 'Political violence and journalism in a multiethnic state: A case study of Burma (Myanmar)'. *Journal of Communication Inquiry* 30 (4): 354–373.

Brooten, Lisa. 2008. 'Media as our mirror: Indigenous media of Burma (Myanmar)'. In *Global Indigenous Media: Cultures, Poetics and Politics*, edited by Pamela Wilson & Michelle Stewart. Durham, NC: Duke University Press.

Brooten, Lisa. 2013. 'The problem with human rights discourse and freedom indices: The case of Burma/Myanmar media'. *International Journal of Communication* 7: 681–700.

Brooten, Lisa. 2015. 'Blind spots in human rights coverage: Framing violence against the Rohingya in Myanmar/Burma'. *Popular Communication: The International Journal of Media and Culture* 13 (2): 132–144.

Burma Ethnic Research Group. 2000. *Conflict and Displacement in Karenni: The Need for New Approaches.* Chiang Mai: BERG.

Campbell, Stephen. 2012. 'Cross-ethnic labour solidarities among Myanmar workers in Thailand'. *SOJOURN: Journal of Social Issues in Southeast Asia* 27 (2): 260–284.

Campbell, Stephen. 2013. 'Solidarity formations under flexibilisation: Workplace struggles of precarious migrants in Thailand'. *Global Labour Journal* 4 (2): 134–251.

Caouette, Therese M. & Mary E. Pack. 2002. 'Pushing past the definitions: Migration from Burma to Thailand'. Refugees International and Open Society Institute.

Cheah, Joseph. 2002. 'Cultural identity and Burmese American Buddhists'. *Peace Review* 14 (4): 415–419.

Cheah, Joseph. 2008. 'The function of ethnicity in the adaptation of Burmese religious practices'. In *Emerging Voice: Experiences of Underrepresented Asian Americans*, edited by Huping Ling, 199–217. New Brunswick: Rutgers University Press.

Cheung, Samuel. 2012. 'Migration control and the solutions impasse in South and Southeast Asia: Implications from the Rohingya experience'. *Journal of Refugee Studies* 25 (1): 50–70.

Clifford, James. 1994. 'Diasporas'. *Cultural Anthropology* 9 (3): 302–338.

Dudley, Sandra. 2007. 'Reshaping Karenni-ness in exile: Education, nationalism and being in the wider world'. In *Exploring Ethnic Diversity in Burma*, edited by Mikael Gravers, 77–106. Copenhagen: NIAS Press.

Dudley, Sandra. 2010. *Materialising Exile: Material Culture and Embodied Experience Among Karenni Refugees in Thailand*. New York: Berghahn Books.

Dudley, S. 2011. 'Feeling at home: Producing and consuming things in Karenni refugee camps on the Thai–Burma border'. *Population, Space and Place* 17 (6): 742–755.

Duell, Kerstin. 2013. 'Local perceptions of returning exiles and their roles in shaping Myanmar's future'. In *Myanmar in Transition: Polity, People and Processes*, edited by Kerstin Duell, 67–81. Singapore: Konrad Adenauer Stiftung.

Duell, Kerstin. 2014. 'Sidelined or reinventing themselves? Exiled activists in Myanmar's political reforms'. In *Debating Democratization in Myanmar*, edited by Nick Cheesman, Nicholas Farrelly & Trevor Wilson, 109–135. Singapore: Institute of Southeast Asian Studies.

Egreteau, Renaud. 2011. 'Burmese Indians in contemporary Burma: Heritage, influence, and perceptions since 1988'. *Asian Ethnicity* 12 (1): 33–54.

Egreteau, Renaud. 2012. 'Burma in diaspora: A preliminary research note on the politics of Burmese diasporic communities in Asia'. *Journal of Current Southeast Asian Affairs* 31 (3): 115–147.

Egreteau, Renaud. 2014. 'The idealization of a lost paradise: Narratives of nostalgia and traumatic return migration among Indian repatriates from Burma since the 1960s'. *Journal of Burma Studies* 18 (1): 137–180.

Fan, Hongwei. 2012. 'The 1967 anti-Chinese riots in Burma and Sino–Burmese Relations'. *Journal of Southeast Asian Studies* 43 (2): 234–256.

Farrelly, Nicholas. 2012. 'Exploitation and escape: Journeys across the Burma–Thailand frontier'. In *Labour Migration and Human Trafficking in Southeast Asia: Critical Perspectives*, edited by Willem van Schendel, Lenore Lyons & Michele Ford, 130–148. Milton Park: Routledge.

Faucher, Carole. 2010. 'Capturing otherness: Self-identity and feelings of non-belonging among educated Burmese in Thailand'. *The Copenhagen Journal of Asian Studies* 28 (2): 54–81.

Grundy-Warr, Carl. 2004. 'The silence and violence of forced migration: The Myanmar–Thailand border'. In *International Migration in Southeast Asia*, edited by Aris Ananta & Evi Nurvidya Arifin, 228–272. Singapore: Institute of Southeast Asian Studies.

Grundy-Warr, Carl & Elaine Siew Yin Wong. 2002. 'Geographies of displacement: The Karenni and the Shan across the Myanmar–Thailand border'. *Singapore Journal of Tropical Geography* 23 (1): 93–122.

Gruß, Inga. 2015. 'Waiting for elsewhere: Place, temporality and Myanmar migrants in Thailand'. Unpublished PhD dissertation, Cornell University.

Hall, Andy. 2011. 'Thailand's low skilled migration policy: Progress and challenges'. Nakhon Pathom: Mahidol Migration Center.

Hall, Andy. 2012. 'Myanmar and migrant workers: Briefing and recommendations'. Nakhon Pathom: Mahidol Migration Center.

Horstmann, Alexander. 2011. 'Sacred spaces of Karen refugees and humanitarian aid across the Thailand–Burma border'. *Aktuelle Südostasienforschung/Current Research on South-East Asia* 4 (2): 254–272.

Horstmann, Alexander. 2014. 'Stretching the border: Confinement, mobility and the refugee public among Karen refugees in Thailand and Burma'. *Journal of Borderlands Studies* 29 (1): 47–61.

Isik-Ercan, Zeynep. 2012. 'Education of young Burmese refugees in the midwestern United States'. *Oxford Monitor of Forced Migration* 1 (1): 26–30.

Joshi, Sushma. 2011. 'The Gorkhalis of Myitkyina'. Kathmandu: Himal Southasian, October.

Kenny, Paul & Kate Lockwood-Kenny. 2011. 'A mixed blessing: Karen resettlement to the United States'. *Journal of Refugee Studies* 24 (2): 217–238.

Lang, Hazel J. 2002. *Fear and Sanctuary: Burmese refugees in Thailand.* Ithaca, NY: Southeast Asia Program Publications, Southeast Asia Program, Cornell University.

Lee, Sang Kook. 2014. 'Migrant schools in the Thailand–Burma borderland: From the informal to the formal'. *Asia Pacific Journal of Education* 34 (1): 125–138.

Lintner, Bertil. 1990. *Outrage: Burma's Struggle for Democracy.* London: White Lotus.

Lu, Hsin-chun Tasaw. 2008. 'Festivalizing Thingyan, negotiating ethnicity: Burmese Chinese migrants in Taiwan'. *Journal of Burma Studies* 12: 29–62.

MacLachlan, Heather. 2008. 'Innovation in the guise of tradition: Music among the Chin population of Indianapolis, US'. *Asian Music* 39 (2): 167–185.

MacLachlan, Heather. 2012. 'Creating pan-Karen identity: The wrist tying ceremony in the United States'. *Asian and Pacific Migration Journal* 21 (4): 459–482.

MacLachlan, Heather. 2014. 'Singing, dancing, and identity in the Karen diaspora'. *Asian Music* 45 (2): 58–83.

Malkki, Liisa, H. 1995. 'Refugees and exile: From "refugee studies" to the national order of things'. *Annual Review of Anthropology* 24: 495–523.

Martin, Philip. 2007. *The economic contribution of migrant workers to Thailand: Towards policy development.* Bangkok: International Labour Organization.

Mee, Kim Hyun. 2012. '"Life on probation": Ambiguity in the lives of Burmese refugees in South Korea'. *Asian and Pacific Migration Journal* 21 (2): 217–238.

Myat Mon. 2010. 'Burmese labour migration into Thailand: Governance of migration and labour rights'. *Journal of the Asia Pacific Economy* 15 (1): 33–44.

Ropharat, Aphijanyatham. 2009. *Perceptions of Borders and Human Migration: The Human (In)Security of Migrant Workers in Thailand.* Bangkok: IRASEC.

Sai S.W. Latt. 2011. 'More than culture, gender and class'. *Critical Asian Studies* 43 (4): 531–550.

Sarojini, Sooi Foong Mak, Chin Pin Choo, Ting Ting Nge & Edward Poon Wing Hong. 2005. 'The expectations and experiences of Myanmar nursing aides working in an inpatient hospice in Singapore'. *Singapore Nursing Journal* 32 (3): 44–50.

Simpson, Adam. 2013. 'Challenging hydropower development in Myanmar (Burma): Cross-border activism under a regime in transition'. *The Pacific Review*, 26 (2): 129–152.

Soe Lin Aung. 2014. 'The friction of cartography: On the politics of space and mobility among migrant communities in the Thai–Burma borderlands'. *Journal of Borderlands Studies* 29 (1): 27–45.

UNHCR. 2015. 'Thailand 2015 UNHCR Country Operations Profile'. Accessed August 8, 2016. www.unhcr.org/pages/49e489646.html.

US Census Bureau. 2015. '2010 Census Data'. Accessed August 10, 2016. www.census.gov/2010census/data/.

Vachon, Christyne J. 2012. 'Burma just around the corner: When US corporations employ refugees'. *Wisconsin Journal of Law, Gender & Society* 28 (2): 159–180.

Vang, Chia Youyee & Monica Mong Trieu. 2014. 'Invisible newcomers: Refugees from Burma/Myanmar and Bhutan in the United States'. Washington, DC: Asian & Pacific Islander American Scholarship Fund.

Williams, David C. 2012. 'Changing Burma from without: Political activism among the Burmese diaspora'. *Indiana Journal of Global Legal Studies* 19 (1): 121–142.

Yee Yee Swe. 2013. 'Mobility encounter: The narratives of Burmese refugees in Norway'. *Norsk Geografisk Tidsskrift—Norwegian Journal of Geography* 67 (4): 229–238.

Zaw Oo. 2006. 'Exit, voice and loyalty in Burma: The role of overseas Burmese in democratizing their Homeland'. In *Myanmar's Long Road to National Reconciliation*, edited by Trevor Wilson, pp. 231–259. Singapore: Institute of Southeast Asian Studies.

Zeus, Barbara. 2011. 'Exploring barriers to higher education in protracted refugee situations: The case of Burmese refugees in Thailand'. *Journal of Refugee Studies* 24 (2): 256–276.

17
YOUTH

Jacqueline Menager

Young people in Myanmar are growing up in a period of social transformation, faced with an influx of foreign goods, including music, cars, clothes, art and alcohol. Underlying this profusion of goods are more significant considerations: identities, morals and values. Where previously Myanmar was isolated and insulated from foreign influences and cultures, since 2010 the outside has flowed in. Young people are largely embracing change and choice. Older generations are less unanimously welcoming. Young people have less reason to distrust the country's elite-led political transition: they have not lived during the country's brutal and violent repression. Instead of facing an omnipresent and controlling state—as their parents and grandparents did—they confront the wider Myanmar population. Through decades of military rule, the Myanmar population grew increasingly distrustful, suspicious and intrusive. In the context of pervasive scrutiny from their parents and communities, young people in Myanmar are navigating the transition to adulthood. Despite burgeoning opportunities for young people to redefine themselves, the ways young people are adapting alternative identities and lifestyles reveals some persistent features in Myanmar that endured through the social transformation of Myanmar: virgins, virtue and vice.

Myanmar's youth are dismantling decades of tradition and conservatism. The opportunities open to young people are no longer defined and controlled by the military. A democratically elected political party, the National League for Democracy (NLD), led by Nobel-prize laureate, Aung San Suu Kyi, has replaced the military government. Since 2010, the government has been embracing the outside and change. Now repression and confinement lie with older generations, who are suspicious of difference and resistant to change. During decades of military control, a devolution of repression from the state into the wider public occurred. At one time repression in Myanmar was the responsibility of the state and the military, until they instilled qualities of self-censorship and mistrust in the population. Cautionary tales of dissenters disappeared, families punished and communities ostracised bolstered civilian vigilance and community policing (Fink 2009). Overcoming these survival mechanisms is a long and arduous process faced by Myanmar's young people.

Their parents, communities and peers judge young people in Myanmar. Judgement takes place overtly and subtly, online and offline, in public and in private. Sometimes it is just a withering look from their elders when they dress provocatively, sometimes it is from journalists refusing to televise heavily tattooed young people, sometimes it is from peers disapproving of perceived sexual looseness. Judgement is ever present, and young people choosing to challenge and controvert it face the emotional toil of constant vigilance and disapproval.

A 2009 Democratic Voice of Burma report titled 'The "Victim" Treatment: A self-fulfilling prophecy' voiced frustration regarding foreign ignorance of young people in Myanmar, saying, 'We like hip-hop and breakdancing, and we are on Facebook and Hi5. We know Paris Hilton and have seen her sex-tapes online, and we love The Simpsons' (Ye Thu 2009). The author, Ye Thu, goes on to identify the locus of oppression not at the censor board, who he says young Myanmar artists are adept at working around and who 'turn a blind eye' to underground hip hop artists. Instead he asserts, '[w]e live in a country where older generations desperately cling on to "traditional values" while youths rush to grab hold of the Western world's finest exports, and it creates conflict.' Interestingly, Ye Thu wrote the piece in 2009, prior to the liberalisations of 2010. He identified a movement already underway, with the introduction of the internet (albeit slow and restricted) in 2000, and what has occurred in Myanmar since his article largely confirms his observations.

Young and educated Myanmar people interpret the entrance of the 'inexorable force of cultural imperialism' as agency and not victimisation by the Western capitalist hegemony (MacLachlan 2011, 175). Myanmar people have not had access to these systems and, despite any socialist or nationalist military rhetoric justifying the country's isolation, the population does not perceive their insulation from foreign systems as protection, but rather as deprivation. Accordingly, many young people are perceiving the entrance of foreign culture as freedom and agency from their decades of isolation, rather than some aggressive drive by foreigners (for impassioned opposition to this view see Aung-Thwin 2001–2002).

Generational differences in Myanmar are more significant than in less rapidly transitioning societies. Where other countries have the luxury of slowly exposing the older generation to new systems and styles gradually, Myanmar has experienced a more sudden shock to the existing generation's entrenched conservatism. The tempo of social change in Myanmar does not allow for a mere adaption or modification of traditional systems; instead a new generation is forming. The development of a new generation is not unilinear or successive, with co-existing generations constantly in dialogue with one another. Further, opponents to a new generation style mainly consist of those who 'because of their "location" in an older generation, are unable or unwilling to assimilate themselves into the new entelechy growing up in their midst' (Mannheim 1972 [1927/1928], 318).

The role of Buddhism for the older Myanmar generations cannot be overlooked, but should also not be overstated (Houtman 1999).[1] Older generations speak of accepting the military's oppression and deserving their unfortunate lives as a result of past karmic actions, and say that they are happy to work off the karma in this lifetime in order to earn a better rebirth. This fatalistic worldview is not as common amongst the young people of Myanmar. Perhaps they are less pessimistic and downtrodden simply by virtue of youthful optimism and lack of experience. More likely, however, it is because they have grown up in a different era to that of their parents, best demonstrated by the political excitement and hope of 2015 culminating in the electoral victory of democracy icon Aung San Suu Kyi's opposition party, the NLD. These young people are not as embittered or suspicious of the democratic process as previous generations. The appeal of Buddhism under the military junta may have been as a way for the population to explain their country's hermit status, their imprisonment in their selves, and to justify their mundane existence (Houtman 1999, 36, 196). But with the end of the military's rule, so the appeal of Buddhism appears to be less certain. A perceived diminishment of Buddhism's significance in young people's lives adds to the older generations' perception that their way of life and ideas of nationalism are under threat (Walton 2015).

There are different types of young people in Myanmar's new generation, who are experiencing the same social change and yet reacting in different ways according to their social positions (Furlong, Woodman & Wyn 2011, 357). Spearheading the influx of foreign systems are a group of transnational elite young repatriates to Myanmar and cultural leaders (Menager 2014). Negotiating these systems for wider consumption are the popular culture artists, predominately made up of K-Pop influenced artists and formerly-underground hip hop crews. And finally, and most importantly for the longevity and intransience of the new generational consciousness and cultural transition, are the wider urban and rural young people seeking out new trends and cultures online, replicating what they find, dubbing them into their circumstances (Boellstorff 2003) and confronting older generations with their choices.

Virgins

Myanmar society values ideas of feminine purity and sexual conservatism. The female comes into play in the political realm frequently, particularly during recent communal violence between Buddhists and Muslims since 2012 (McCarthy & Menager 2017). This is not particularly surprising, with the feminine body established as symbolising nationhood and social reproduction (Das 2008). What is more interesting is the way young women are engaging with the social mores surrounding gender. There are those who challenge cultural boundaries while still continuing to self-regulate according to the virgin complex. Young women may choose to dress provocatively but they will often refrain from going to nightclubs, or publicly fraternising with young men, or violating their curfews for fear of having their purity questioned and damaging their reputations.

Young women lament the double standards for men and women in Myanmar. The perception is that young men can do almost whatever they want without having their reputation jeopardised. Young women have to be very careful to protect their reputation. Young women are challenging the double standard very gradually, most overtly by dressing in Western and Korean style clothing. Despite outward appearances, however, most continue to adhere to parentally enforced curfews and self-regulate the frequency with which they go out at night. For young women who value and strive for marriage and family, they recognise the necessity of maintaining their reputation and begrudgingly abide by the rules.

In contrast to these young women are another type of young women who are actively disregarding all of Myanmar's conservative standards of decency. Many of these more liberal young women are in Yangon away from their family for university or work. At the extreme end of the spectrum are young women such as Zune Thinzar, a Myanmar model, who intentionally and very publicly flouts convention. Zune Thinzar's Facebook is full of almost-pornographic photos of her in lingerie posing on beds and cars, often dripping in oil. While the majority of comments on the photos are from adoring young men, there are many who criticise her. At a recent performance, members of the audience threw stones and food at Zune Thinzar until she was forced to leave the stage (*Coconuts Yangon* 2016).

Since 2011, the rise of Myanmar beauty pageants and fashion shows has also polarised domestic audiences. Beauty pageants were banned in 1962 following the country's first coup by Myanmar's first dictator, General Ne Win. On 3 October 2013, Moe Set Wine was crowned Miss Universe Myanmar, the first time Myanmar had entered a contestant into the Miss Universe pageant since 1961. Allegedly, ensuring Miss Myanmar was indeed a 'Miss' was of tantamount importance. Moe Set Wine was purportedly inspected by Myanmar authorities to confirm her virginity. Miss Myanmar's participation in the swimsuit category also split social commentators and the wider public in Myanmar (Chit Win 2014).

In addition to the rigours of the competitions, beauty pageant contestants are subjected to personal attacks and vicious rumours. Rumours of a relationship between Moe Set Wine and former-dictator Than Shwe's grandson, Nay Shwe Thway Aung, sparked aggressive social media attacks and even calls for Moe Set Wine to give up her Miss Universe Myanmar crown (Zarni Maung 2013). Moe Set Wine also had her ancestry scrutinised by Myanmar Facebook users, with some questioning her citizenship status and asking whether a Myanmar citizen with Chinese ancestry should be allowed to represent the country (Myo Zaw Linn 2013). In another pageant in 2014, controversy ensued after May Myat Noe was crowned Miss Asia Pacific World in South Korea, and then absconded with her crown. She claimed organisers had falsified her age from 16 to 18, restricted her contact with her mother, pressured her to have breast implants and suggested funding a music album by providing escort services to Korean businessmen (Thin Lei Win 2014).

Myanmar's participation in domestic and international beauty pageants reveals several fault lines of Myanmar society: gender standards, wealth disparity, ethnic divisions and international influence. Ultimately, as Chit Win has argued, Myanmar's beauty queens are public figures who promote women's empowerment and progressive moral values. As Chit Win says, through Myanmar's engagement with pageants, Myanmar 'society will learn to differentiate between modernity and indecency' (Chit Win 2014). Generational differences are made visible in the opposing labelling of the same act, as either 'modern' and acceptable, or 'indecent' and unacceptable. Indeed, the disparity between generations' moral standards may be such that only time and the eventual demise of the older generation will achieve a degree of consonance.

In spite of the manifold difficulties, a growing number of Myanmar women are working to challenge repressive and unequal norms surrounding women. Pyo Let Han, a feminist author, is encouraging women to 'break out of the norms' and question sexist attitudes in Myanmar. Myanmar feminists often highlight the impact of the Theravada Buddhist conception of *hpone* in their gender narrative. *Hpone* is the idea that men are on a spiritually higher level than women (Droulers 2016). Khin Mar Mar Kyi says that *hpone* was 'one of the things that was recreated [by nationalist leaders] to give a sense of unity and identity' to the Myanmar people, and that in the construction of gender relations nationalisation and militarisation are key in all societies and 'the military is always a patriarchy' (quoted in Droulers 2016).

Women in Myanmar often engage with their religious and cultural circumstances in a nuanced way. Matthew Walton, Melyn McKay and Khin Mar Mar Kyi point to women's support for the 'Religious Protection Laws', which are discriminatory to women, as evidence of women embracing a role in protecting Buddhism 'as a way of claiming or asserting a religious identity and achieving the religious objectives that are limited by their role within lay and monastic society' (Walton et al. 2015). In a society which has done little to address issues of violence against women, real and perceived, Buddhist actors including MaBaTha (or the Organisation for the Protection of Race and Religion) and the 969 Movement are giving voice to women's concerns—albeit in a way which many claim discriminates against women (European Union 2015; Lee 2015).

What is apparent is that young women in Myanmar are not adhering to the conservative standards of their parents. They are living in a liberalising society and are actively engaging with discourses seeking to dictate how they should and can behave. Ways of doing this range from the confrontational shock of the promiscuous model to the internationally engaged beauty queen to the revolutionary feminist. The very existence of these options and the emergence of voices so different from the older generation are evidence of the development of a new generation of young women.

Virtue

An analysis of the complexity of Myanmar gender relations expressed through young people's relationships reveals that ideas of virtue, fidelity and trust are paramount. Courtships begin as very sweet and innocent, ratcheting up to very serious and demanding rapidly. Proof of devotion and commitment is expected early in a relationship, sometimes on first dates or during initial conversations before a couple has even met in person. In young people's relationships there is interplay between Myanmar's existing social mores and foreign systems. Where previously expressions of relationships and devotion were confined to personal declarations and proofs, they are now expected to be publicised on social media and in tattoos for a much wider audience.

Facebook is a key site of relationship establishment, expression and maintenance, as well as a new avenue for infidelity. Within days of beginning a new relationship young men and women will exchange passwords to their Facebook accounts. Prior to this, they will undertake a meticulous 'friend cull' removing their more lascivious friends or previous love interests and delete conversation histories with other potential suitors. After the password exchange young men and women will continue to monitor each other's Facebook activity. Many fights in relationships are caused by Facebook activity, for indiscretions ranging from having private conversations with others young men or women, 'friending' other young women or men, and liking a photo or activity of other young men or women. Myanmar relationships can be quite volatile and dramatic, explained by one young woman as 'if your girlfriend does not get more psychotic about you every day, she does not love you'.

Further proof of devotion and fidelity is enabled through the availability of apps such as Skype and Viber. The proliferation of smart phones with reliable internet connections allows young people to sleep through the night with an active video link to their partners (Aung Kyaw Nyunt 2016). This is taken as apparent proof that both parties are faithfully at home in their beds and not out drinking and fraternising with others. The ability to be in constant contact has made this the standard of the Myanmar relationship with anything less than almost incessant contact interpreted as suspicious. Young people have developed ways around this. Many young men are quite adept at maintaining multiple relationships, or some combination of one stable girlfriend, various more casual flirtations, one-night-stands and encounters with prostitutes.

Another foreign practice that has become a popular Myanmar trend is the couples tattoo. Couples will often get tattoos of each other's names, matching symbols (e.g. a lock and a key), or young men will sometimes get a portrait of their girlfriend. This tattooing often occurs in the first months of dating. The popularity of the couples tattoo early in a relationship speaks to the naivety and hopefulness of relationships in Myanmar. While similar innocence also characterises young love elsewhere, it seems to pervade Myanmar relationships well beyond adolescence. With trust so elusive, rendering a partner's name into skin for life is just one way to prove love. However, even this permanent mark does not earn young men or women much reprieve from suspicion. While tattooing has a long history in Myanmar, this style of tattooing is relatively new. The proliferation of these tattoos can be attributed to the way the foreign practice of the couples tattoo appeals to the Myanmar desire for continual proof of loyal devotion and commitment.

Interestingly, when couples tattoo their names, they tend to choose the Romanised versions of their Myanmar names. A possible explanation for this practice is because Facebook, Viber and phone contacts often use the Roman script for Myanmar names so this is the way young people actually visualise their names. They rarely write their names in Myanmar script, but instead constantly see and write them in the Roman script. The integration of this foreign practice clarifies young people's willingness to adapt new systems of meaning and expression to their ends.

Further animating young people's trust and commitment preoccupation is the atmosphere of distrust heightened by the pervasive level of scrutiny amongst young people. Many young people in Myanmar do not work during their school or university years. This allows plenty of free time to fixate on their private lives: creating online identities, forging friendships, gossiping and monitoring one another. It is common for 'popular' young people to reach the 5,000 Facebook friend limit. Young women often spend considerable amounts of time confined to their homes on the phone and social media. Young people have seemingly exhaustive knowledge of others in their age group and demographic as a result of hours spent gossiping and stalking each other online.

In keeping with the expectations of female virginity, many young women maintain that they do not have sexual relations with their boyfriends before marriage. Young men on the other hand admit that they have sexual relations with their girlfriends after they have established the relationship as 'serious'. While there is of course no single truth to be uncovered here, what can be accepted is that some young men and women are having sex before marriage, though it is impossible to accurately establish how common the practice is. With no reliable historical information on sex before marriage rates in Myanmar it is impossible to say with certainty, though it is generally accepted, that with relaxing moral standards sexual relationships are, if not more common, at least increasingly more socially acceptable and visible. Prostitution has a long history in Myanmar, and is increasingly evident on the streets and in clubs (Talikowski & Gillieatt 2005; Si Thu Thein, Tin Aung & McFarland 2015).

There has not been a comprehensive study into the sexual behaviour of young people in Myanmar, but some tentative observations are possible.[2] Firstly, sex education is very poor. Even well-educated sexually active young men in Yangon have little to no knowledge of sexually transmitted diseases, though encouragingly many get tested regularly. Secondly, condom use is very low and heavily stigmatised (Nyi Nyi Htay et al. 2013). While young men may use condoms with prostitutes, there is considerable opprobrium surrounding condom use with other sexual partners. It is often considered offensive to wear, or even suggest wearing, a condom as it implies the young woman involved is a prostitute and/or that the young man is having sexual relations with others.

Instead of using condoms young couples predominately rely on emergency contraception, such as the morning after pill. Without reliable statistics it is difficult to quantify the potential abuse of the morning after pill, but initial observations have suggested it is used to dangerous excess by young couples (Macgregor 2015). In 2015, the government demonstrated state-level birth control misdirection when they enforced a contraception ban ahead of the water festival (*Thingyan*). Shops were forced to remove the morning after pill, erectile dysfunction medication and condoms from shelves in anticipation of heightened drinking and casual or irresponsible sexual relations during the festive period. State efforts to discourage sexual relations have been shown elsewhere to be less effective than pragmatic public health campaigns which treat pre-marital sex as the norm amongst young people (Furstenberg 2009).

Accordingly, Myanmar's young people engage in relationships that tend to be fixated on ideas of devotion and trust, while often plagued by infidelity and duplicitous conduct. These relationships occur under intense online and offline public scrutiny. Avenues for relationship expression and conduct are quickly shifting with improving communications, social media proliferation and new sites of expression such as tattooing. Sexual education is lagging and risky sexual behaviours are increasingly common amongst young people in Myanmar.

Vice?

The new generation of Myanmar's youth are experiencing lives which have become individualised and are increasingly focused on non-traditional methods of political participation. It is possible to see young people's political consciousness expressed at the informal level of consumption and leisure. The political goal for young people, in Myanmar and elsewhere, is increasingly touted as 'self-determination and sovereignty over oneself' achieved and expressed through their social lives (Riley, Morey & Griffin 2010). In Myanmar, popular culture and young people's leisure activities show increasing diversity and prominence. Hip hop has become a popular music of choice, and increasingly creativity and ingenuity are encouraged. Hip hop artists are leading a cultural movement in Myanmar, and while they are performing at an elite level of society, ultimately their reliance on popular support from young people means they negotiate with and express the sentiments of many young people in Myanmar.

Myanmar rap is focused on place and is inherently political. Raps may not directly speak about politics (Keeler 2009), but there is no escaping the politics of the struggle they describe. Their struggle is inextricably linked to their country, but it is not the government or the military they decry, it is the conservatism and repression meted out by the wider population. Myanmar hip hop is also working to bring musical originality and authenticity to Myanmar. Leading their country out of musical duplication and public aversion to difference is a stated aim, and the first site they have dismantled is the practice of copy songs.

Myanmar's hip hop artists are undoing the legacy of the country's popular music dominated by copy songs (*copy thachin*) (Ferguson 2013; 2016). Hip hop artists almost unanimously lament copy songs and their impact on Myanmar music and culture. Ye Naung, of hip hop group PBD Hood, says outright that copy songs 'suck' and that 'you need to create [music], because it's art'. Ar-T, Myanmar's self-proclaimed first electro-pop artist, goes almost so far as to connect copy songs with the population's repression, saying the country needs 'more opportunities that encourage children to dance and sing and create' and less repetition. Hlwan Paing, a popular hip hop artist, released an album in June 2014 which included one cover song. Other artists expressed disappointment that the song was included on the album, including comments such as 'I thought we were past that'.

In Myanmar previously-underground hip hop has cultural cachet for its perceived subversiveness. While artists rapping and dressing in a confrontational way is nothing new, the ability to include them in official song releases is. Underground music in Myanmar referred to any music which was not passed through rigorous censorship processes, but instead released online or performed live. With the Press Scrutiny Board disbanded in 2012, these artists can now release music officially. While there are underground artists now releasing their own music, more mainstream artists continue to draw on the cultural cachet of these artists by using young people with confronting tattoos, including neck, arm and face tattoos, in their video clips and paying underground artists to feature on their tracks.

Official recognition of the popularity of hip hop was displayed in the promotional material for the SEA Games, which included an album of songs and accompanying music videos which assembled an impressive array of previously-underground hip hop artists. Further, when Coca-Cola conceived their marketing campaign in Myanmar, they chose two musicians who deploy hip hop fashions, dances, rap lyrics and slang to further their popular appeal: female artist Bobby Soxer and male pop star Sai Sai Kham Leng. From a marketing perspective, they were an excellent choice for Coca-Cola's campaign. They are both young, famous, attractive and have well established and significant fan bases. They are cool and yet they are relatively safe and conservative.

Similar to the generational challenge of sexual freedoms and relationship developments, hip hop and popular culture continues to face opposition and some barriers to its free expression. In music videos, for example, young hip hop artists continue to face difficulties finding models willing to dress scantily or to wear bikinis in pool party videos. To overcome this issue, rather than dull down their videos, many shoot their videos in Singapore. In 2013, Ar-T overcame the problem by recruiting his close friends to perform in a video with him. He made what was possibly the most scandalous music video of 2013, with young women in cut-off denim shorts and topless young men. The music video received a strong backlash with some denouncing him and his friends as 'prostitutes'. Ar-T said although the response was personally hurtful, he would continue to push the boundaries.

In addition to enjoying hip hop culture, increasing numbers of young people in Myanmar are drinking and smoking cigarettes to pass the time. While young men in particular have been drinking and smoking for a long time, more recently, illicit drug use has increased to become a serious issue for Myanmar society. With increasing domestic consumption of methamphetamine, the social costs are rising (Lintner & Black 2009). Where previously drugs were primarily a security and economic problem in border areas, they are increasingly wreaking havoc amongst the wider domestic population. Further, methamphetamine use can slide into heroin addiction and social oblivion for some. In the music industry, drug use is widespread, though carefully hidden as known drug-addicts will struggle to find work as they are considered unreliable and untrustworthy. Again, government initiatives to combat substance abuse have been ineffective and punishment focused.

Accordingly, the new generation of young Myanmar are creating new cultures and challenging the boundaries of past generations. Popular music represents a new avenue for the expression of political consciousness and standards of music and music videos indicate the music industry is internationalising. Accompanying new leisure pursuits are some vices, namely drinking, smoking and drug taking. While these may be socially damaging, the overall cultural shift of popular culture amongst young people represents a positive move for Myanmar, into creative outlets and freer expression. Young people are crafting their identities and generation in new and exciting ways for Myanmar.

Conclusion

Generational change is a tumultuous process, whose outcome is far from inevitable. Young people in contemporary Myanmar are facing rapid social change and are responding with the creation of a distinctively new generational consciousness. Young people cannot use their parents' experiences as a guide; instead they must 'renegotiate core values' as an 'ongoing project largely devoid of explicit markers' (Furlong, Woodman & Wyn 2011). Youth studies, broadly conceived, have changed the parameters of 'youth', acknowledging the deficiencies of appraising youth as a discrete period of transition to 'adulthood'. Accordingly, young people in Myanmar are appraised here as a generation rather than a discrete similarly aged cohort. While the majority are 17 to 35 at present, these young people will continue to be Myanmar's youth generation until some future period of rapid social change marks the creation of a new generation.

Myanmar's young people are forging ahead into their future without a roadmap and into unchartered territory for the country. They are calling on foreign and international systems for guidance, while adapting them into the Myanmar context. The older conservative generation are sceptical and wary of the transition, but ultimately they are no longer in the position to determine the generational consciousness. Now is the time for Myanmar's young people to craft their own morals and determine the realities of their country. Inevitably there will be damaging elements in the new generation, but hopefully the state will develop to be able to effectively regulate and provide the necessary education to assist in addressing these challenges. Overall, the youth of Myanmar are growing up and shaping their world full of hope and optimism and, so far, they have created a more liberal system, which still respects many of the redeeming qualities of Myanmar. These young people are the new generation, and they are not only here to stay, but they are here to shape the future.

Notes

1 Gustaaf Houtman's exploration of the involvement of Buddhism in political discourse and processes is useful for its thorough collation of available literature.

2 Research in the field tends to focus on HIV/AIDS, sex workers, men who have sex with men (MSM) or migrant Myanmar people in Thailand rather than any quantitative studies of young people.

References

Aung Kyaw Nyunt. 2016. 'Ministry puts mobile penetration at 90 percent'. *The Myanmar Times*, July 19.

Aung-Thwin, M. 2001–2002. 'Parochial universalism, democracy jihad and the orientalist image of Burma: The new evangelism'. *Pacific Affairs* (74) 4: 483–505.

Boellstorff, T. 2003. 'Dubbing culture: Indonesian "Gay" and "Lesbi" subjectivities and ethnography in an already globalized world'. *American Ethnologist* (30) 2: 225–242.

Chit Win. 2014. 'Miss Myanmar helps shape a society in transition'. *Nikkei Asian Review*, August 19.

Coconuts Yangon. 2016. 'Racy model Zune Thinzar pelted with stones during performance'. January 20.

Das, V. 2008. 'Violence, gender, and subjectivity'. *Annual Review of Anthropology* 37: 283–299.

Droulers, A. 2016. 'Meet the Burmese women tackling tradition and taboo'. Democratic Voice of Burma, January 25.

European Union. 2015. 'Statement by the Spokesperson on the Legislative Passage of the "Buddhist Women's Special Marriage Bill" in Myanmar'. Accessed January 31. http://eeas.europa.eu/statements-eeas/2015/150708_01_en.htm.

Ferguson, J. 2013. 'Burmese super trooper: How Burmese poets and musicians turn global popular music into copy thachin'. *The Asia Pacific Journal of Anthropology* (14) 3: 221–239.

Ferguson, J. 2016. 'Yesterday once more: Tracking (un)popular music in contemporary Myanmar'. *Journal of Burma Studies* (20) 2: 229–257.

Fink, C. 2009. *Living Silence in Burma: Surviving Under Military Rule*, 2nd edn. Chiang Mai: Silkworm Books.

Furlong, A., Woodman, D. & Wyn, J. 2011. 'Changing times, changing perspectives: Reconciling "transition" and "cultural" perspectives on youth and young adulthood'. *Journal of Sociology* (47) 4: 355–370.

Furstenberg, F. Jr. 2009. 'Early childbearing in the new era of delayed adulthood'. In *Handbook of Youth and Young Adulthood: New Perspectives and Agendas*, edited by A. Furlong. Abingdon: Routledge, 226–231.

Houtman, G. 1999. *Mental Culture in Burmese Crisis Politics: Aung San Suu Kyi and the National League for Democracy*. Institute for the Study of Languages & Cultures of Asia and Africa Monograph Series, no. 33. Tokyo: Tokyo University of Foreign Studies.

Keeler, W. 2009. 'What's Burmese about Burmese rap? Why some expressive forms go global'. *American Ethnologist* (36) 1: 2–19.

Lee, Y. 2015. Statement by Yanghee Lee, Special Rapporteur on the Situation of Human Rights in Myanmar at the 70th Session of the General Assembly, Third Committee, Item 72 (c), October 28, New York.

Lintner, B. & Black, M. 2009. *Merchants of Madness: The Methamphetamine Explosion in the Golden Triangle*. Chiang Mai: Silkworm Books.

McCarthy, G. & Menager, J. (2017). 'Gender rumours and the Muslim scapegoat in Myanmar's transition'. *Journal of Contemporary Asia* (47) 2: 396–412.

Macgregor, F. 2015. 'Time for new thinking on contraception'. *The Myanmar Times*. April 24.

MacLachlan, H. 2011. *Burma's Pop Music Industry: Creators, Distributors, Censors*. New York: University of Rochester Press.

Mannheim, K. 1972 [1927/1928]. 'The problem of generations'. In *Karl Mannheim: Essays*, edited by P. Kecskemeti. Abingdon: Routledge, pp. 276–322.

Menager, J. 2014. 'Law fuckers, cultural forgers and the business of youth entitlement in Yangon, Myanmar', *South East Asia Research* (22) 2: 201–212.

Myo Zaw Linn. 2013. 'Chinese controversy surrounds Miss Universe Myanmar'. Democratic Voice of Burma (DVB), October 11.

Nyi Nyi Htay, Maneesriwongul, Wantana Phuphaibul, Rutja Phuphaibul & Pisamai Orathai. 2013. 'A causal model of condom use among people living with HIV/AIDS in Myanmar'. *Pacific Rim Internaional Journal of Nursing Research* (17) 3: 234–246.

Riley, S., Y. Morey & C. Griffin. 2010. 'The "pleasure citizen": Analyzing partying as a form of social and political participation'. *Young: Nordic Journal of Youth Research* (18) 1: 33–54.

Si Thu Thein, Tin Aung & W. McFarland. 2015. 'Estimation of the number of female sex workers in Yangon and Mandalay, Myanmar'. *AIDS Behaviour* (19): 1941–1947.

Talikowski, L. & Gillieatt, S. 2005. 'Female sex work in Yangon, Myanmar'. *Sexual Health* (2) 3: 193–202.

Thin Lei Win. 2014. 'Beauty pageants expose dreams and dangers in modern Myanmar'. Yangon: Reuters, September 26.

Walton, M. 2015. 'The post-election future of Buddhist nationalism in Myanmar'. East Asia Forum, November 19.

Walton, M., M. McKay & Khin Mar Mar Kyi. 2015. 'Why are women supporting Myanmar's "Religious Protection Laws"?' East Asia Forum, September 9.

Ye Thu. 2009. 'The "victim" treatment: A self-fulfilling prophecy'. Democratic Voice of Burma (DVB), April 7.

Zarni Maung. 2013. 'Bumpy start for Burma's divisive Miss Universe'. *The Irrawaddy*, October 11.

PART IV

Living

18
POLITICAL ECONOMY

Lee Jones

This chapter provides a basic, general overview of the main features of Myanmar's political economy to help contextualise the more specific chapters that follow in this section. Myanmar's economy today contrasts starkly with those of its more developed Southeast Asian neighbours like Thailand and Malaysia. While the latter underwent rapid industrialisation from the 1970s, becoming middle-income economies, Myanmar remains one of the world's poorest countries, with socio-economic indicators slightly worse than Southeast Asia's other post-'socialist' economies and comparable to underdeveloped African states (see Table 18.1).

Beyond these headline data, Myanmar is also struggling to reform an economy characterised by severe capital scarcity; atrocious infrastructure; a rapacious, extractive and predatory mode of development; rampant corruption; and the concentration of economic power in a small elite clustered around the military (Jones 2014b). While these arrangements staved off state collapse in the face of economic crisis and Western sanctions, they have perpetuated patterns of violence, poverty and exclusion that have changed little since the installation of an electoral regime in 2010–2011.

The following sections explore the two major dynamics shaping this outcome: the failure of Cold War-era 'socialist' development, which retarded the development of class forces and locked Myanmar into a resource-exporting, capital-importing model; and the post-Cold War, politically-constrained moves towards marketisation, which concentrated economic power in a small elite. The implications for Myanmar's contemporary political economy and the 'reform' process are then considered before the conclusion.

The failure of 'socialist' development

Myanmar's post-colonial development – under civilian rule (1948–1962), the military-dominated Revolutionary Council ([RC] 1962–1974), and the Burma Socialist Programme Party ([BSPP] 1974–1988) – involved a quest for 'nationalisation, Burmanisation and industrialisation' (Brown 2013). Attempting to overcome colonial legacies and secure Myanmar's independence, successive regimes pursued an increasingly autarkic mode of import-substituting industrialisation (ISI). As in other developing countries, this failed due to structural weaknesses: inadequate exports to finance industrial development, producing growing dependency on external finance that proved disastrous when commodity prices collapsed in the 1980s. In Myanmar, this was

Table 18.1 2014 GDP (estimated, constant 2005 prices and exchange rates) and Human Development Index data

Country	*GDP (US$bn)*	*GDP per capita ($)*	*HDI (rank)*
Malaysia	220.2	7,294	0.78 (62)
Thailand	248.3	3,705	0.73 (93)
Philippines	165.1	1,650	0.67 (115)
Vietnam	92.8	1,003	0.67 (116)
Laos	5.4	781	0.58 (141)
Cambodia	11.5	745	0.56 (143)
Tanzania	33.1	652	0.52 (151)
Myanmar	26.3	490	0.54 (148)
Mali	11.6	490	0.42 (179)

Source: UNCTAD (2016); UNDP (2015: 208–211).

Note: Myanmar's statistics are notoriously unreliable. They are used herein to indicate broad patterns, rather than provide precise measures.

exacerbated by the total exclusion of foreign investment and cost of counter-insurgency operations against communists and ethnic-minority separatists. Ultimately, 'socialist' development failed to change the sectoral composition of Myanmar's economy, leaving it heavily reliant on basic commodity production and low-level industry, while weakening or destroying key economic classes and concentrating power among state-based actors.

At independence, the modern sectors of Myanmar's economy were controlled by foreigners: Europeans dominated foreign trade and large-scale industry; Indians, credit, domestic trade and intermediate industry; and Chinese, urban retailing. Economic nationalism – which remains a powerful ideological current – drove the Bamar-led independence movement to reverse this effect of British colonialism and develop an independent, Bamar-dominated industrial economy. As in many post-colonial countries, this involved nationalising economic assets and the state-led nurturing of domestic industries to substitute foreign imports (Brown 2013).

However, also like similar countries, ISI faced fundamental structural impediments. Developing domestic industry requires mobilising capital to purchase machinery and necessary inputs. This can be financed through domestic or foreign investment, loans or aid; the earning of export surpluses; and/or government revenues. However, developing countries typically lack adequate domestic savings and their states struggle to collect taxes. Furthermore, colonial underdevelopment left their economies largely producing primary commodities while relying on imports from developed countries for capital goods and intermediate industrial inputs. Consequently, even if the necessary finance is available, developing industry typically involves increasing imports, which erodes the surplus of exports over imports used to finance capital purchases. In order to restore the surplus, governments must often suppress imports, which dampens economic growth by starving the economy of necessary resources.

Myanmar has experienced this classic underdevelopment 'trap' for its entire post-colonial history, except perhaps after 2005, since when booming hydrocarbon exports have finally produced a structural trade surplus (though this is now again being eroded). Myanmar's main opportunity to generate export surplus was through commercial agricultural development. However, successive regimes, embroiled in counter-insurgency in Myanmar's borderlands, instead prioritised socio-political stability in the Bamar heartlands. To avoid peasant unrest, the state avoided consolidating large, industrial farms, and barred private lenders from agriculture; yet, it could not finance adequate infrastructural investment or inputs itself. Forced rice purchases at below-market prices appeased urban consumers, but disincentivised peasants to improve output. Accordingly, agricultural output actually fell (Brown 2013, ch. 4). Meanwhile, counter-insurgency campaigns sucked scarce resources into unproductive military spending. Consequently, Myanmar failed to generate the surplus necessary to finance ISI. As early as the late 1950s, as the state invested in factories, power generation and infrastructure, dependence on imported inputs rose, and production became constrained by chronic shortages of foreign exchange required to purchase inputs and equipment (Taylor 2009, 21; Larkin 2012, 10).

This structural problem persisted under RC and BSPP rule, prompting more radical measures that did not spur growth but did substantially alter patterns of economic ownership and control. An exodus of European and Indian capitalists after World War II had already shifted ownership into the hands of local merchants. However, the RC went further, abolishing agrarian tenure and nationalising all internal trade and 15,000 private firms, driving up to 300,000 ethnic-Indian entrepreneurs to emigrate, and excluding foreign investors (Taylor 2009, 342, 317). Far from solving ISI's fundamental contradictions, these measures only exacerbated capital shortages. However, they also entirely eliminated the domestic bourgeoisie and the remnants of the landlord class, and drove much of the petit-bourgeoisie into the black market (further reducing tax revenue). Consequently, by the mid-1980s, while some 34,596 private firms remained, they were almost exclusively small-scale, with only six employing over 100 people. The state monopolised large-scale industry, funnelling what scarce resources it could mobilise for ISI into state-owned enterprises, and controlled 39 per cent of domestic output (Taylor 2009, 346). Thus, the main impact of nationalisation was to concentrate economic power in the hands of state-based actors, eliminating independent, legal centres of power and wealth. ISI's failure also retarded the development of a working class: by 1985/6, only 8.3 per cent of the population worked in industry, lower than in 1931 (Taylor 2009, 345). This suppression of socio-economic forces beyond the state is a crucial legacy of RC/BSPP rule which continues to shape Myanmar's development.

The chronic shortage of capital needed for ISI, and growing economic stagnation, led the BSPP to try to stimulate commodity exports and accept foreign aid and loans after 1971. Again like many developing countries, Myanmar was encouraged to borrow heavily after the oil crises and subsequent petrodollar glut. By 1987, its foreign debt was US$5.7bn (Taylor 2009, 376). Loans were initially used to increase agricultural commodity and natural gas production, boosting export revenues, and to expand industrial output. However, with foreign investment still banned, Myanmar's exports did not grow sufficiently to cover the growing cost of imported capital and intermediate goods needed to fuel this growth, generating persistent trade deficits after 1978. Subsequent efforts to suppress imports merely retarded growth, further depressing government revenues. To cover the shortfall, the government began printing money, generating hyperinflation, and borrowed more, increasing its indebtedness (Tin Maung Maung Than 2005, ch. 6).

In the early 1980s, most developing countries, including Myanmar, suffered a massive collapse in export revenues as global commodity prices fell, leaving them unable to service their foreign debt. Myanmar's capitalist neighbours in Southeast Asia escaped their debt crises via the 1985 Plaza Accord, which inflated the yen, encouraging Japanese firms to outsource production to their economies. This consolidated their successful turn to export-oriented industrialisation, financed by foreign investment and export revenues. However, since Myanmar remained closed to foreign investment, the Plaza Accord merely increased the cost of servicing its yen-denominated debts (Steinberg 2001, 22). By 1988, Myanmar's debt-to-GDP ratio was 75 per cent, and debt repayments were absorbing 55–91 per cent of its dwindling export revenues (Steinberg 2001, 6). The ISI development model had utterly failed; the state was on the verge of bankruptcy. Belated interventions, including two disastrous currency demonetisations designed to quash the black market, helped precipitate mass unrest that toppled the regime in 1988, prompting the military to seize power.

Given ISI's failure, the basic sectoral composition of Myanmar's economy had remained basically unchanged since colonialism, notwithstanding significant shifts in ownership and control. By 1985/6, two-thirds of the population remained engaged in unproductive, mostly subsistence agriculture, comprising about 28 per cent of GDP. Only 10.5 per cent worked in industry, contributing just 8.3 per cent of GDP, while the state employed 10.6 per cent of citizens (Taylor 2009, 344–346). Myanmar's military regime thus inherited a bankrupt state and a backwards economy heavily dependent on basic commodity production and lacking an indigenous bourgeoisie. This legacy significantly shaped Myanmar's subsequent development trajectory.

The constrained turn towards marketisation

Rather like other developing countries faced with structural adjustment imposed by International Monetary Fund intervention, Myanmar's new rulers had to significantly liberalise the economy to avert state collapse. As elsewhere in Southeast Asia, however, this process was heavily shaped by political imperatives: the need to restore socio-political order, particularly in Myanmar's insurgency-prone borderlands. Constrained marketisation thus generated a new economic elite, but one tied closely to the military: army generals-cum-businessmen; former borderlands smugglers and drug lords; and crony capitalists. Economic development was further constrained by Myanmar's balance-of-payments trap, the legacy of socialist underdevelopment, and dependence on Asian markets and investors. Combined, these trends channelled Myanmar's economy towards rapacious natural resource exploitation, generating an uneven and often violent mode of development.

Although Myanmar's military regime (1988–2011) initially embarked on crash liberalisation, this was curtailed in the late 1990s, partly for structural reasons inherited from the BSPP era. Initially, foreign investment was welcomed; trade in agricultural commodities, timber and fisheries was liberalised to generate export revenues; and oil contracts were signed with Western companies. The regime also committed itself to expanding the private sector and began privatising state assets. This averted total state bankruptcy and restored economic growth, though it was not until 1995/6 that per capita incomes recovered to pre-crisis levels (Brown 2013, ch. 5). However, liberalisation slowed then reversed in the late 1990s. Reflecting Myanmar's underdevelopment trap, as the economy recovered, imports exceeded exports, generating a persistent balance-of-payments crisis and foreign exchange shortages – exacerbated by the 1997–1998 Asian financial crisis (see Figure 18.1). Yet again, the government had to suppress imports, retarding growth. Structurally, the state remained incapable of mobilising resources for investment. Rising government spending vastly exceeded revenues, prompting the regime to print more money, causing hyperinflation until spending, like imports, was suppressed in the late 1990s (Myat Thein 2004, 215, 220). Privatisation also foundered due to a BSPP legacy: the absence of an indigenous business class capable of purchasing and managing state-owned enterprises (SOEs), which generated fears that buyers would simply asset-strip SOEs and fire workers (Abel 2012).

The constraints on liberalisation were not merely structural, however; they also stemmed from the military regime's political strategy, which prioritised socio-political stability and 'state-building' over economic liberalisation (Mya Maung 1998). The junta confronted a restive Bamar population that had revolted in 1988 and kept simmering following the military's refusal to transfer power to civilians after multiparty elections in 1990. Privatisation was partly curtailed due to fears of renewed unrest if unemployment rose further (Khin Maung Nyo 2012). An even more serious threat was the widespread ethnic-minority insurgency in Myanmar's borderlands.

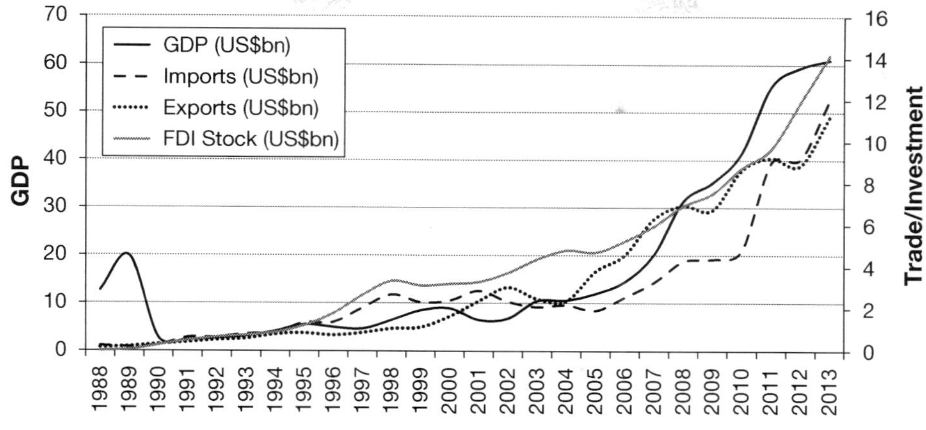

Figure 18.1 Myanmar's macroeconomic indicators

Source: UNCTAD (2016).

Although the regime wanted economic growth to pacify the population, its willingness to embrace liberalisation was heavily constrained by these security imperatives, coupled with the traditional Bamar-nationalist disdain for foreign investors and capitalists in general. Rather than allowing markets free rein, the military thus sought to channel economic flows so as to strengthen forces loyal to the state over their enemies.

First, the military shaped economic liberalisation to augment the economic base of itself and the wider state apparatus that it dominated. It established two large, military-run conglomerates to absorb state assets and attract foreign investment. Union of Myanmar Economic Holdings Limited developed interests in banking, trade, gems, tourism and real estate, and joint ventures with foreign firms in garment and consumer goods factories, gems, wood products and trade, transportation, cement, construction and real estate. Myanmar Economic Corporation acquired interests in heavy industry, foodstuffs, trade, banking, tourism, gems, minerals, natural gas, electricity, telecoms, construction, and transportation (Steinberg 2001, 178, n17–18; Brown 2013, ch. 5). The state channelled 81 per cent of foreign investment for joint ventures (comprising 25 per cent of total foreign investment) towards such entities (Myat Thein 2004, 256).

Secondly, and more innovatively, the regime fostered the emergence of so-called 'national entrepreneurs': indigenous big businesspeople who would be loyal and useful to the state. They mostly emerged from the black market – the only domain where people had been able to accrue capital and business experience – supplemented by those who successfully exploited the early liberalisation of border trade to earn small fortunes. Marketisation was a significant capitulation to these forces, reflecting the regime's desperate need for capital. However, the junta sought to encourage their 'return to the legal fold' on its terms insofar as possible. Thus, for example, individuals who had reaped fortunes from cross-border smuggling and drug trafficking were invited to create private banks – after paying a 25 per cent 'whitening tax' – and invest in the national economy (Turnell 2009, 260–265). Others were allowed to found major business enterprises and given privileged access to finance, licences and government contracts. The state had strategically retained legal monopolies in key industries like timber, hydrocarbons, gemstones, communications, metals, and air and railway transportation. Yet, with SOEs unable to run these effectively, their activities were often subcontracted to favoured private businesspeople or carried out as joint ventures. These concessions generated what are now

Myanmar's dominant private conglomerates, headed by leading 'crony capitalists' like Tay Za, Zaw Zaw, Kyaw Win, Thein Tun, Eike Htun, Htay Myint, Aung Ko Win and the late heroin kingpin Lo Hsing Han (succeeded by his son, Steven Law). In exchange, these individuals were expected to provide services to the state, such as mediating between the regime and their respective ethnic-minority groups, donating funds to regime activities and undertaking construction work. Significant assets were also 'privatised' into the hands of the United Solidarity and Development Association, a military-organised mass organisation that later became the basis for the Union Solidarity and Development Party (USDP) under President Thein Sein (2011–2015) – which was partly bankrolled and staffed by crony capitalists (Jones 2014b, 149–151). Although some independent businesspeople were able to flourish under military rule, none could do so without close connections to army patrons.

Importantly, this development strategy now encompassed ethnic-minority leaders, as part of a strategy dubbed 'ceasefire capitalism' (Woods 2011b). From 1989, the regime signed ceasefires with war-weary ethnic-minority insurgents, promising their leaders development spending and business opportunities in exchange for halting their armed rebellions and tolerating expanded military deployments in their domains. Regional military commanders subsequently mediated extensive business deals – particularly around timber, mining, hydrocarbons, hydropower and, more recently, agribusiness – tying borderland elites into increasingly centralised patronage networks (MacLean 2008; Woods 2011a, b; TNI 2011; Jones 2014a). Again, state-mediated foreign investment cemented these ties: by 2011, two-thirds of Myanmar's total foreign investment was concentrated in the resource-rich borderlands (TNI 2011, 12).

Implications: Myanmar's contemporary political economy

The legacy of the failure of 'socialist' development, coupled with the military regime's development strategy, yields four important outcomes that fundamentally shape the contours of Myanmar's contemporary economy and polity. Growth has occurred, consolidating forces loyal to the state. However, this growth has been concentrated in extractive sectors, cementing Myanmar's structural position as a producer and exporter of raw commodities. This has generated a rapacious, uneven and often violent mode of development, and a configuration of socio-political forces that is less amenable to genuine democratisation than to violent unrest.

First, the military succeeded in strengthening the state vis-à-vis those capable of disrupting socio-political order. The military regime presided over significant economic expansion, a point overlooked by those primarily concerned to criticise the junta (see Figure 18.1). Although its 'achievements' fell well short of total victory, one simply cannot understand the military's decision to cede formal power to an electoral regime in 2011 without the realignment of forces that this strategy helped bring about (Jones 2014a).

Secondly, however, this strategy clearly failed to generate broad-based economic development, notwithstanding a significant shift of ownership and control to the private sector. The regime's retention of extensive economic regulation – partly for structural reasons and partly to help control Myanmar's emerging capitalist class – produced a climate inhospitable to market-led growth. Western investors were deterred by the regulatory climate and mounting international economic sanctions (see Jones 2015, ch. 3). Accordingly, despite investment commitments of US$7bn by 1998, less than a quarter of this actually materialised (Rüland 2001, 151). Apart from a short-lived boom in low-value-added garments manufacturing – curtailed after 2003 by sanctions – private industry remained underdeveloped. It remained hamstrung by structural problems, notably capital scarcity, exacerbated by the regime's regulatory policies and funnelling of resources towards state-linked enterprises; and poor infrastructure, which, as noted, the government could not muster enough resources to fix. Similarly, agriculture remained stubbornly underdeveloped. Notwithstanding the emergence of some large-scale agribusinesses in the regime's final years, the junta continued to prioritise maintaining rural social order and low rice prices for urban consumers over the structural reorganisation of agriculture. Some output improvement, as before, private capital largely remained barred from agriculture, yet the state could not finance additional infrastructure and inputs (Brown 2013, ch. 5).

Thus, internal and external structural constraints, coupled with the regime's strategy, channelled Myanmar's development towards the extractive sectors and primitive accumulation. Otherwise starved of capital, the regime became dependent on Asian investors primarily interested in accessing Myanmar's largely untapped natural resources – an approach that gelled with the regime's 'ceasefire capitalism'. In the 2000s, while Western investors fled, Indian, Thai and especially Chinese investors funded large-scale oil, gas, mining, timber and hydropower projects. This entrenched Myanmar's structural position as a primary commodity producer, exporting raw and semi-processed natural resources and importing capital goods, inputs and complex manufactures (see Tables 18.2 and 18.3, and chapter by Caillaud and Bissinger). Apart from a boom in oil, gas and gemstone production, which comprises most of the apparent rise in 'industry', Myanmar's economic structure and employment patterns remain essentially unchanged since BSPP rule – indeed, since independence. The rest of the modern economy remains underdeveloped, with most people reliant on subsistence agriculture or the informal economy (see chapter by Okamoto).

The third, related implication is that Myanmar's mode of development – particularly in the borderlands – is extractive, rapacious, highly uneven and often violent. Failed ISI, coupled with military state-building, has constructed an economic system centred on subsistence agriculture and low-value-added, menial services in the non-tradable sector, and the rapid extraction and export of natural resources in the tradable sector. The latter involves what Harvey (2004) calls

Table 18.2 Share of value added and employment by sector

	Share of value added (%)[a]		*Share of employment (%)*	
	1985	*2013*	*1990*[b]	*2010*[c]
Agriculture	48.2	33.2	56.5	52.4
Industry	13.1	29.9	15.1	12
Services	38.7	36.9	28.4	35.5

Sources: [a] UNCTAD (2016); [b] Government of Myanmar (1990); [c] Government of Myanmar (2011: 38).

Table 18.3 Composition of Myanmar's trade

Top 2011/12 exports (%)		*Top 2011/12 imports (%)*	
Gas	38.3	Petroleum products and chemicals	25.8
Grains and pulses	18.0	Machinery	10.9
Jade	8.5	Iron, steel and products thereof	11.3
Wood and timber products	6.7	Motor vehicles	8.5
Fish and crustaceans	6.5	Palm oil	4.3

Source: WTO (2014: 14).

'accumulation by dispossession': the often violent grabbing and enclosure of natural resources, including land, from local inhabitants and users, and the monopolisation of rents by powerful groups. Crucially, these sectors are effectively 'enclaves', providing massive export revenues but very little employment or spill-over benefits to the wider economy (Brown 2013, ch. 5). For example, in 2010, hydrocarbons and gemstones comprised 63 per cent of Myanmar's exports (US$4.8bn), but the entire mining and quarrying sector employs just 1.6 per cent of the population (UN Data 2013; Government of Myanmar 2011, 38). Chinese-backed extractive projects are particularly notorious for failing to benefit locals, sometimes even using migrant Chinese labour and imported food to feed them. Moreover, revenues are often appropriated by ceasefire groups, military units or crony companies controlling the trade. According to Global Witness (2015, 35), up to US$6bn per year is being misappropriated in the jade industry alone.

Although some proceeds have flowed through the state, enabling recent increases in government spending, there is little sign that this is being reinvested in productive activity. The military still takes the lion's share, absorbing around 20 per cent of the formal government budget since 2011, plus extensive off-budget income. Rents have been funnelled into extremely unproductive uses, such as military spending and vast construction projects, like the new capital at Naypyitaw, which have further fuelled inflation. While this may have benefited some workers, and military families dependent on the army for basic sustenance (Callahan 2000, 31–32), the wider population has not benefited. Plans for development led by small and medium sized enterprises have seen little realisation, while agriculture remains hamstrung by the longstanding problems identified above (see chapter by Okamoto). Crony capitalists have gradually expanded their empires, monopolising business opportunities and extracting rents from the population. While their banking interests are booming in the reform era, dominant groups continue to receive most credit (see chapter by Förch). In the borderlands, widespread hopes for post-ceasefire development have been dashed in most areas as ceasefire group leaders and their allies have monopolised economic opportunities, fuelling extensive popular resentment (see chapter by Sadan and Meehan). Military, capitalist and ethnic-minority elites have generally failed to energise Myanmar's productive forces, instead purchasing luxury goods, funnelling money offshore and fuelling a domestic real-estate bubble (Saw Yan Naing 2013; Mahtani 2014; Ko Ko Aung 2015). Although the lifting of Western sanctions and the initiation of economic reform raised hopes of change, dominant forces have so far steered much of the reform process to benefit themselves. Foreign investment remains concentrated in the extractive sectors, while industrial and commercial investors are mostly partnering with established crony conglomerates (Jones 2014b, 156–163).

The final noteworthy outcome of Myanmar's developmental trajectory is the socio-political forces and conflicts it has generated. *Ancien régime* forces are deeply entrenched in the political economy. The main social entity to have consolidated is the now 450,000-strong army. Retired and serving generals have extensive business interests, and neither they nor their civilian crony capitalists could be easily dislodged from their dominant economic position; indeed, their capital and business skills are in more demand than ever. Even Aung San Suu Kyi has courted the cronies (Aung Zaw 2013). Under her post-2015 government, reform has stalled, while military and crony-capitalist firms continue to be prime beneficiaries of economic liberalisation (Peel 2017). The dominance of such forces, and the illicit nature of their wealth, means that corruption and associated poor governance is likely to persist (see chapter by Tin Maung Maung Than). Conversely, alternative social forces remain weak. Given the failure of industrial development, the petit-bourgeoisie is still overwhelmingly small-scale and fragmented, while the working class is small and – despite the recent legalisation of enterprise-level trade unions – remains relatively disorganised and subject to continued violent state repression. Most of the population are impoverished peasants, fragmented by severe ethnic divisions. Put bluntly, this configuration is unfavourable for the consolidation of genuine democracy, or even serious economic reform (Jones 2014b). Coupled with the National League for Democracy's own weaknesses, this helps explain why the post-2015 government has so far failed to deliver significant economic change. Its economic 'policy', announced in July 2016 – seven months into its tenure – covered just three pages. More substantive policies have not materialised. Changes to foreign investment rules, for instance, have been repeatedly promised but, as of early 2017, remain forthcoming.

The political economy context is also rife with conflict. Rapacious resource grabs and extraction in the borderlands have generated widespread popular resentment among ethnic-minority populations and are understood to have directly prompted the resumption of the Kachin insurgency since 2011 (Brenner 2015). Much of the subsequent fighting has occurred around the massive Sino–Myanmar oil and gas pipeline traversing Kachin state. The failure of borderlands development means that drug cultivation and trafficking – often the only source of income for rural populations – remains endemic; indeed, despite recurrent crackdowns, it is increasing (UNODC 2014). Popular Bamar-nationalist resentment of extensive Chinese involvement in extractive investments has also prompted protests, resulting in the postponement of the US$3.6bn Chinese hydropower project at Myitsone in 2011. The state violently suppressed demonstrations against the joint Myanmar military–Chinese Letpadaung copper mining project in 2013, then renegotiated the deal to favour Myanmar – backed by Aung San Suu Kyi, who instructed protesting farmers to relent. Farmers are increasingly protesting other forms of land-grabs by military and crony companies, again often facing harsh state repression. Since anti-military, anti-crony and anti-Chinese protest clearly remains dangerous, growing Bamar economic nationalism has also apparently been channelled into a viciously xenophobic, anti-Muslim boycott movement led by Buddhist monks. This has intersected dangerously with anti-Muslim communal violence in Rakhine state.

Conclusion

The main features of Myanmar's post-colonial development have been the failure of state-led industrialisation before 1988, followed by politically-constrained economic liberalisation. Combined, these dynamics have barely altered the basic structure of Myanmar's political economy, which – despite considerable growth in the past two decades – remains heavily agrarian and reliant on exporting basic commodities and raw materials, and importing capital goods and inputs. Myanmar has thus never escaped the 'underdevelopment trap' afflicting many developing countries. Indeed, Figure 18.1 shows that, even today, as Myanmar's economy booms in the so-called 'reform' era, imports are once more outstripping exports. While foreign investment is partially plugging the gap, currently, the government's ambitious spending plans are yet again being financed by arguably unsustainable overseas borrowing – US$1bn from 2011–2013 alone (Eleven Media 2015). These failures – stemming from the political constraints and strategies of successive regimes – explain Myanmar's dismal performance relative to Southeast Asia's export-oriented, industrialising neighbours.

Myanmar's mode of development is also highly uneven, exploitative, rapacious and often violent, generating a narrow economic elite, widespread corruption and deep social conflicts. Essentially, capital accumulation occurs primarily in lucrative, cartelised/monopolistic and tradable sectors dominated by the state, the military and their corporate allies. The rest of the population remains largely mired in low value-added activity: subsistence agriculture, petty trading, basic service provision and small-scale, labour-intensive manufacturing and processing.

This structure has empowered and enriched forces close to the previous regime, and has been functional in avoiding state collapse and allowing the army to superintend a transition to what it calls 'discipline-flourishing democracy'. But it has also entrenched poverty, underdevelopment and corruption, and bred widespread resentment and social unrest. So far, the National League for Democracy government has done virtually nothing to challenge these structural dynamics. Unless it moves rapidly to leverage growing resource export revenues and foreign investment to rapidly generate broader-based growth, the prospects for Myanmar's economy and social stability look dim.

References

Abel, D. 2012. Former Minister of Finance and Planning. Interview with Lee Jones, Yangon, July 6.

Aung Zaw. 2013. 'Rehabilitating Burma's Cronies'. *The Irrawaddy*, January 28.

Brenner, D. 2015. 'Ashes of Co-optation: From Armed Group Fragmentation to the Rebuilding of Popular Insurgency in Myanmar'. *Conflict, Security and Development* 15 (4): 337–358.

Brown, I. 2013. *Burma's Economy in the Twentieth Century*. Cambridge: Cambridge University Press.

Callahan, M. 2000. 'Cracks in the Edifice? Military–Society Relations in Burma since 1988'. In *Burma Myanmar: Strong Regime, Weak State?*, edited by M. B. Pedersen, E. Rudland & R. J. May, 22–51. Adelaide: Crawford House Publishing.

Eleven Media. 2015. 'Myanmar's Irresponsible Borrowing'. *Eleven Myanmar*, March 3.

Global Witness. 2015. 'Jade: Myanmar's Big State Secret'. October.

Government of Myanmar. 1990. 'Distribution of Employed Population by Occupation and Industry, 1990 (Labour Force Survey, 1990)'. Accessed June 28, 2017. www.mmsis.gov.mm/sub_menu/statistics/statDbList.jsp?vw_cd=MT_ZTITLE&self_id=195_006.

Government of Myanmar. 2011. *Integrated Household Living Conditions Survey in Myanmar (2009–2010): Poverty Profile*. Yangon: IHLCA Technical Unit, Ministry of National Planning and Development.

Harvey, D. 2004. 'The "New" Imperialism: Accumulation by Dispossession'. *Socialist Register* 40: 63–87.

Jones, L. 2014a. 'Explaining Myanmar's Transition: The Periphery is Central'. *Democratization* 21 (5): 780–802.

Jones, L. 2014b. 'The Political Economy of Myanmar's Transition'. *Journal of Contemporary Asia* 44 (1): 144–170.

Jones, L. 2015. *Societies Under Siege: Exploring How International Economic Sanctions (Do Not) Work*. Oxford: Oxford University Press.

Khin Maung Nyo. 2012. Economist and Former Official in the Prime Minister's Office. Interview with Lee Jones, Yangon, July 11.

Ko Ko Aung. 2015. 'Market Slows But No Bursting Bubble'. *The Myanmar Times*, February 22.

Larkin, S. 2012. 'Myanmar at the Crossroads: Rapid Industrial Development or De-industrialization'. Accessed August 5, 2012. www.burmalibrary.org/docs12/Stuart_Larkin-Myanmar_at_the_Crossroads.pdf.

MacLean, K. 2008. 'Sovereignty in Burma After the Entrepreneurial Turn: Mosaics of Control, Commodified Spaces, and Regulated Violence in Contemporary Burma'. In *Taking Southeast Asia to Market: Commodities, Nature, and People in the Neoliberal Age*, edited by J. Nevins & N. L. Peluso, 140–157. Ithaca: Cornell University Press.

Mahtani, S. 2014. 'Meet the New Rich . . . in Myanmar'. *Wall Street Journal*, September 4.

Mya Maung. 1998. *The Burma Road to Capitalism: Economic Growth versus Democracy*. Westport: Praeger.

Myat Thein. 2004. *Economic Development of Myanmar*. Singapore: ISEAS.

Peel, M. 2017. 'Myanmar: The Military-Commercial Complex', *Financial Times*, February 1.

Rüland, J. 2001. 'Burma Ten Years After the Uprising: The Regional Dimension'. In *Burma: Political Economy under Military Rule*, edited by R. H. Taylor, 137–158. London: Hurst.

Saw Yan Naing. 2013. 'Burma Govt Denies Reports That It Holds $11B in Singaporean Banks'. *The Irrawaddy*, September 13.

Steinberg, D. I. 2001. *Burma: The State of Myanmar*. Washington, DC: Georgetown University Press.

Taylor, R. H. 2009. *The State in Myanmar*. London: Hurst.

Tin Maung Maung Than. 2005. *State Dominance in Myanmar: The Political Economy of Industrialization*. Singapore: ISEAS.

TNI. 2011. *Financing Dispossession: China's Opium Substitution Programme in Northern Burma*. Amsterdam: TNI.

Turnell, S. 2009. *Fiery Dragons: Banks, Moneylenders and Microfinance in Burma*. Copenhagen: NIAS Press.

UN Data. 2013. Myanmar. Accessed April 24, 2013. http://data.un.org/CountryProfile.aspx?crName=myanmar.

UNCTAD. 2016. UNCTAD Stat. Accessed April 4, 2016. http://unctadstat.unctad.org.

UNDP. 2015. *Human Development Report 2015: Work for Human Development*. New York: UNDP.

UNODC. 2014. *Southeast Asia Opium Survey 2014: Lao PDR, Myanmar*. Bangkok: UNODC Regional Office for Southeast Asia and the Pacific.

Woods, K. 2011a. 'Conflict Timber along the China–Burma Border: Connecting the Global Timber Consumer with Violent Extraction Sites'. In *Chinese Circulations: Capital, Commodities, and Networks in Southeast Asia*, edited by E. Tagliacozzo & W.-C. Chang, 480–506. Durham, NC: Duke University Press.

Woods, K. 2011b. 'Ceasefire Capitalism: Military–Private Partnerships, Resource Concessions and Military–State Building in the Burma–China Borderlands'. *Journal of Peasant Studies* 38 (4): 747–770.

WTO. 2014. Trade Policy Review: Myanmar, Report by the WTO Secretariat, WT/TPR/S/293, January 21. Accessed April 4, 2016. www.wto.org/english/tratop_e/tpr_e/s293_e.pdf.

19
AGRICULTURE

Ikuko Okamoto

This chapter examines the current status of and challenges in Myanmar's agricultural sector. Agriculture commands the largest share of Myanmar's economy, comprising about 40 per cent of its GDP. More than 70 per cent of Myanmar's population live in rural areas, and the majority of the people depend on agriculture for their livelihood. This rural population is generally the country's poorest, and transformation in agriculture will therefore determine the direction of Myanmar's economy and the extent of poverty reduction for the coming decades. Thus, it is no surprise that the National League for Democracy (NLD) government, which took office in March 2016, prioritises the agricultural and rural sectors in its policies.

Because of agriculture's perennial importance, agricultural policies—especially those related to rice—have been critical for successive governments. This remained the case even after Myanmar's 1988 transition to a market economy. Because of the vulnerability of a regime with weak political legitimacy, the government made every effort to avoid food (rice) shortages and price hikes for fear of political and social instability. Consequently, government interventions ignoring the market forces were maintained under the military government throughout the 1990s until 2011.

However, the situation dramatically altered after President Thein Sein took office in March 2011. Defying generally pessimistic expectations, the government first launched political reforms (mostly through national reconciliation) followed by fundamental economic reforms, all of which were long overdue. In this process, agricultural policies and regulations that had long dragged down Myanmar's agricultural sector were finally reformed as well.

This chapter proceeds as follows. First, the characteristics of Myanmar's agricultural sector and policies since the Socialist period and the military regime will be reviewed, because the sector's long-term stagnating performances as well as emerging current problems have deep roots in policies from those periods. Then the major agricultural reforms under the Thein Sein government, followed by challenges that emerged in the process of reforms, will be discussed. Challenges for the new NLD government for achieving sound agricultural development will conclude the chapter.

Beginning of rice-centred policy under the Burmese Way to Socialism (1962–1988)

The basic pillars of Myanmar's agricultural policy, namely, land nationalisation, cropping regulations and agricultural marketing regulations, were formed and strengthened during the

Socialist period starting in 1962. The Socialist government aimed at developing yet controlling the agricultural sector with a strong socialistic orientation (Perry 2007).

First, the government intervened in domestic and export markets to control both the supply and price of agricultural produce, especially rice. To ensure nationwide rice rationing for consumers, a compulsory delivery system was introduced. Under this system, paddy was procured by the government to an extent that almost absorbed any surplus after deducting an amount for home consumption. In addition, the prices offered were generally below the free market or export price. Total paddy procured by the state accounted for 26–30 per cent of total output during the 1980s (Okamoto 2009). Exports were permitted only after meeting domestic demand; thus, it was important for the government to maintain an export monopoly over rice. Under these circumstances, it is not surprising that the compulsory delivery system became a disincentive for rice-cultivating farmers, and that farmers were generally reluctant to undertake effort to cultivate more rice. They knew that, even if a higher yield was achieved, the producers' benefit was small because the extra crops had to be sold at an unfairly low price. Thus, some farmers started to evade the procurement obligation by planting crops other than rice, such as bananas.

To suppress such evasive moves by farmers, the government needed to enforce rice production to feed the increasing population and also maintain rice rationing. A cropping plan was utilised for this purpose. The government formulated a cropping plan every year, which was allocated to each individual farmer.

The land tenure system, or tillage right system, became an important policy tool to enforce these marketing and cropping regulations. Land nationalisation was first attempted in 1948 and then in 1953, aiming to return to the Burmese land which had been in Indian money lenders' hands in the colonial period. The tillage right system was initially meant to protect Burmese farmers, but it eventually strengthened role of the state as the absolute owner of farmland. Under this system, farmers were given only 'tillage rights', which were renewed every year. As a tenant of the state, farmers were not allowed to transfer, mortgage or inherit this right freely. The government could threaten to revoke farmers' tillage rights if they disobeyed either the cropping plan or procurement obligations.

Continuation of rice-centred policy under the military regime (1988–2011)

From 1988 to 2011, agricultural policy under Myanmar's military regime continued to be 'rice-centred', the prime aim being to secure a stable supply of low-price rice for consumers. In this context, despite the government's call for a transition to a market economy, three major agricultural policy imperatives—cropping, marketing and land tenure policies—firmly remained in force with only minor modifications (Fujita and Okamoto 2009).

To increase the supply of rice, the government started to push double cropping of paddy aggressively from 1992 (Ardeth Maung Thaunghmung 2004). However, given the suppressed domestic price of rice, ranging between 40 and 60 per cent of the international price on average during the 1990s and early 2000s, together with the higher cost of cultivation, the summer paddy cultivation did not yield sufficient profit for the cultivating farmers, even compared with the first crop, i.e. the monsoon paddy (Fujita and Okamoto 2009). Thus, most farmers were reluctant to launch double cropping of paddy. Rather, they wanted to produce pulses and beans, which were free from government intervention and yielded much higher profits (Okamoto 2008). Given this unpopularity of double cropping, enforcement of the crop plan came to play the central role in meeting the target for rice production.

In contrast to cropping and land tenure policies, which remained unchanged, agricultural marketing policies underwent gradual revisions. First, in 1987, a partial liberalisation occurred and the procurement burden of rice was reduced to about one-third of that in the previous era, responding to changes in rice rationing given only to public servants. Then, in 2003, the government abolished state procurement completely, most likely because the cost of maintaining the system became larger than the benefit for the government (Okamoto 2009).

However, exports remained in the government's grip until quite recently. With the liberalisation of domestic marketing in 2003, the government was even more pressed to maintain an export monopoly for domestic price control. For this reason, it halted permission for private exports in 2003. Only in 2007 were private companies once again allowed to export rice, but this, too, was only on quota bases. By then, the government gradually felt comfortable loosening its grip on rice exports because production had risen sufficiently.

These rice-centred policies yielded several 'distortions'. For example, the government focused only on statistical increases in production and ignored the economic conditions of farmers themselves. Further, to promote double cropping of rice once irrigation water became available, farmers had no choice but to cultivate summer rice, even though they preferred more profitable crops such as pulses and beans. Such was the situation that farmers were disappointed when irrigation facilities were set up in their area. In the late 1990s, to increase production, the government promoted a regional self-sufficiency policy even in the areas without suitable lands for rice cultivation.

In addition, when farmers could not meet the requirements of the compulsory delivery system for various reasons, such as crop failure, they were forced to purchase the required amount in the market. Moreover, private traders were sometimes forbidden to buy paddy or rice from farmers until the target for government purchase in the area was met.

The Myanmar government's pressure on farmers to cultivate according to their plan also distorted land markets. Prices for tillage rights in informal transactions, which normally occurred based on mutual understanding among villagers, were lower for land near primary roads because these areas were easily subject to official inspections, and farmers had less chance to evade the cropping plan.

The government's regulations and enforcement accrued various transaction costs on the farmers' part and eventually inhibited the development of Myanmar's agricultural sector for almost 50 years. Production remained dependent on labour and bullocks, and farmers continued to suffer under low productivity and heavy debt.

Reforms under the Thein Sein government

The Thein Sein government's economic reform had two main objectives: industrialisation by promoting foreign direct investment, and reduction of poverty. Developing the agricultural sector was indispensable for both objectives for three reasons. First, it was necessary to suppress wages to promote industrialisation, especially in the early phases, because food commands a large share of labourers' consumption. Thus, the agricultural sector was expected to provide it at low prices. Second, improving the rural population's purchasing power was critical to expanding markets for domestic industrial goods (Fujita 2016). Last, reducing poverty nationwide entailed reducing it in rural areas, where most of the country's poor live.

After 2011, the Thein Sein government proceeded with several long-overdue reforms. The unification of multiple foreign exchange systems in 2012, which were a major constraint in economic transactions for almost three decades, presents a good example of one such reform. In the agricultural sector, the Thein Sein government abolished or deregulated the three pillars supporting longstanding previous policies. We will examine these changes in detail.

Strengthening land rights via new farmland laws

In March 2012, the government enacted the Farmland Law and the Vacant, Fallow and Virgin Lands Management Law. Under these new laws, farmers still have only tillage rights, but these rights are akin to property rights in several respects. First, farmers can legally sell, purchase, mortgage, lease, exchange, donate and inherit tillage rights. Second, land certificates would be issued to prove ownership of the right. Third, farmland could be used as collateral to borrow money from formal financial institutions.

Despite these changes, there still remained some restrictions on production. Farmers still needed permission to plant non-rice crops on paddy land, or use land for non-agricultural purposes or leave land fallow. These restrictions were intended to regulate land in a gentler manner while strengthening farmers' rights. The Vacant, Fallow and Virgin Lands Management Law, on the other hand, was expected to foster large-scale agriculture and livestock development. It permitted an individual or a company to apply for up to 50,000 acres of vacant land for 30 years. Foreign companies could apply if they formed joint ventures with Myanmar companies and received government recommendation. Although intended to promote large-scale land development, the law raises concerns about land-grabbing and speculation, as will be discussed later.

Free choice of crops

The military regime enforced its crop plan solely by administrative pressure. Thus, no new laws, rules or even official announcements granted free crop choice. However, two important phrases in a report by the Ministry of Agriculture and Irrigation—'farmers have freedom in crop choice' and 'adopting the cropping patterns best suitable to each area' (MOAI 2011, 19)—indicate the Thein Sein government's inclination to guarantee crop choice.

It is still difficult to measure the actual impact of a free choice of crops. However, official statistics reveal that paddy-sown acres, which had shown no yearly declines since the 1990s, fell for the first time in 2011(CSO 2016). Paddy yield also declined in 2011, and production was about the same as that in 2005. Abnormal weather in 2011 might explain the decrease, but it is reasonable to assume that township administrative bodies faced less pressure to increase paddy-sown areas, i.e. they could report less acreage than the previous year.

Liberalisation of agricultural exports

In 2012, the government relinquished its 50-year monopoly on rice exports that had been introduced in 1962 to help restore the country's status as a major rice exporter. Export quotas were gradually rescinded and fully liberalised in the same year. The government's initial plan was to export 2.6 million tonnes by 2014 and 4.3 million tonnes by 2019 (Myanmar Rice Federation n.d.). Rice exports exhibited high fluctuation (15 to 360 thousand tonnes) till 2007/08 when the export quota system was introduced, but it jumped to over a million tonnes after full liberalisation in 2012/13.

In 2008, Rice Specialising Companies (RSCs) were established—a scheme initiated by the government to promote private exports, starting in 2008 (Dapice et al. 2010). This scheme was formulated to construct a comprehensive production-to-export supply chain for rice. RSCs were established to introduce contract farming, which provides credits and inputs for cultivation. By the year 2015, the number of RSCs reached 59 in total, located mainly in Ayeyarwady, Bago and Yangon regions. The major benefit for companies to register as an RSC was the preferential export quotas of rice given to RSCs. However, as rice exports were fully liberalised by 2012, most RSCs lost their incentive and stopped operations as RSCs (Okamoto 2015).

Furthermore, other agricultural trade restrictions were also removed. For example, palm oil is now free to be imported from Malaysia to meet Myanmar's demands as it is indispensable to the country's diet. The Union of Myanmar Economic Holdings Limited (UMEHL), the army-backed shareholding company, monopolised those imports until April 2011, when all private companies became eligible for import licences. Reducing the export tax in 2012 and liberalising export licences also aided increase in exports. Export tax reduction was a response to lobbying by private exporters whose competitiveness eroded after Myanmar's currency began to appreciate in 2010. Such liberal economic policy changes show that the Thein Sein government had a more flexible stance and was ready to listen to the voices of the private sector, which was inconceivable under the military regime.

Emerging issues under the Thein Sein government

Removing policy distortions that had long constrained agriculture meant that Myanmar's agricultural sector had entered a new phase devoted to increasing productivity as well as improving farmers' welfare. Specifically, the Thein Sein government emphasised three areas: protecting farmers' rights and benefits; modernising agriculture; and reducing poverty. Its economic development strategy was a 'people-centred approach' that sought to resolve regional and demographic economic disparity. Policy shifted from 'quantity of agricultural produce' to 'quality of farmers' lives'. The Thein Sein government's specific measures to modernise agriculture included the introduction of quality seeds, mechanisation and improved farming practices. Agriculture commercialisation was also emphasised, along with infrastructure development for small- and medium-scale industries and the promotion of foreign direct investment in agriculture.

The government initiated its rural development and poverty-reduction efforts at an official meeting in May 2011. It formulated action plans in eight areas, i.e. agriculture, livestock and fishery, agro-industries, microfinance, cooperatives, socio-economic development, energy and environmental conservation. It determined to reduce the poverty rate from 25.6 per cent in 2010 to 16.1 per cent in 2015, the first poverty-reduction goal set by the Myanmar government.

Improving rural access to financial services via microfinance was one concrete action to reduce poverty, raise agricultural productivity and relieve farmers' dependence on loans with usurious interest rates. MADB has increased lending yearly since 2009 to 100,000 kyat per acre in 2013/14. A loan of that size covers a half to two-thirds of a farmer's cultivation costs—a substantial improvement over the lending that did not cover the cost of one bag of fertiliser.

Besides crop loans, the rural population needs small-scale loans for consumption, education or health expenses (IFC 2013). Again, the Thein Sein government promoted microfinance to reduce dependency on expensive informal loans. Although microfinance began under the military regime (Turnell 2009), it was not completely considered as an official financial institution, and some microfinance organisations faced obstacles in expanding their operations. However, after the enactment of the Microfinance Law in 2011, microfinance institutions gained official status. International and local NGOs, cooperatives and private companies have registered as microfinance organisations and are expanding their operating areas and number of clients.

Among efforts to strengthen farmers' rights, the Protecting Rights and Enhancing Economic Welfare of Farmers Law attracted considerable attention. Initially titled the Farmers Protection Act, it aimed at increase in supply of agricultural credit, providing agricultural inputs and technology and price supports for agricultural products. The concept of price supports was borrowed from Thailand's paddy pledging scheme. Following several years of sluggish agricultural prices, the Thai government in 2011 strengthened price supports through a pledging system designed to win farmers' support. Thus, Myanmar lawmakers also believed that introducing a price support system would lead to greater support from farmers in the 2015 general election.

Prominent economists were concerned about the possible negative impacts of price support because it would generate budget deficits and could impede rice exports. They argued it was not feasible given Myanmar's weak financial capacity (U Myint 2013) and pointed out that funds for a scheme would be better spent on long-term improvements in agricultural productivity (Hla Myint 2013). Moreover, the compulsory delivery system under the previous regimes had demonstrated how difficult it is for the government to control agricultural prices.

Farmers themselves also objected to the bill because the legislation ignored emerging issues of land rights—thereby generating conflicts in rural areas—and favoured private companies over small-scale farmers.

Despite these criticisms, the Myanmar parliament passed the law in October 2013, changing its name by adding 'Protecting Rights and Enhancing Economic Welfare of Farmers' to the original title to emphasise protection of farmers' rights and rewording provisions for price supports to read 'only according to necessity'. Even the initial enthusiasm towards the law among the policy makers gradually lost its momentum, and no concrete measures were taken in line with this law during President Thein Sein's term.

Emerging challenges

The Thein Sein government's agricultural reforms were characterised by a shift of policy emphasis, guided by the precepts of 'protection of farmers' rights', 'modernisation of agriculture' and 'poverty reduction'. All three concepts had never reached the policy agenda under the Socialist and military regime. However, a shift in emphasis does not necessarily imply concrete impacts. New challenges have emerged regarding the implementation of these concepts, and these are also the challenges that the new NLD government needs to tackle.

Land issues

As stated earlier, there was no room for Myanmar farmers to demand their land rights for a long period. However, with the enactment of new land laws together with an emerging consensus—supported by NGOs and political organisations—that the right holder should claim his/her own right, cases of land conflicts became major land issues in Myanmar: previous and current confiscations of farmland by the army or private companies; encroachment, i.e. years of cultivation of lands not officially categorised as farmland (e.g. forest land); and increases in land prices and speculation, which is related to the other two issues.

Land confiscation by the military or companies tied to the regime were frequent when farmers were not given land rights and the means to resist (LCG 2013, Global Witness 2015). Protests against land confiscation spread nationwide after July 2012. The exact number of land confiscation cases is not available, but in 2013, a specially convened parliamentary committee reported 745 cases of confiscation, of which 565 involved the military. In 2014, because of low prospects for legal resolution, farmers launched 'plough protests', occupying land with bullocks and ploughs, to appeal to the public about their problems through the media. Another problem related to land confiscation was that the majority of the land was not utilised for economic activities, which meant a significant waste of economic resources. Again, the exact geographical areas are unknown, but in 2013, the Minister of Agriculture and Irrigation admitted that of 4 million acres leased to private companies, only one-quarter had been used or developed. However, the formulation of procedures to return these lands to the rightful owners has been progressing slowly and is far from resolved.

In response to the second land-related problem, i.e. long-term agricultural encroachment, the Ministry of Environmental Conservation and Forestry removed forest registration restrictions in some areas and allowed 1,231 villages having more than 50 households to remain on 'forest' land. At the same time, participation in 'community forestry programmes' was encouraged for those engaged in agriculture in the forest land as a sort of policy compromise, so that those farmers could continue farming if they plant trees in line with the programme.

The two problems discussed above—confiscations and encroachment—originated under the Socialist and military regimes, but speculation in land is more recent. Some buy farmland to resell at a profit, whereas others divert it illegally towards other purposes. For example, land prices in an area where an industrial zone was planned increased tenfold within two years. Surging land prices fuel further speculation and land confiscation. In fact, it is reported that large-scale agricultural concessions increased by 170 per cent between 2010 and 2013 (Scurrah et al. 2015, 12).

To tackle these problems, the government issued an initial draft of 'the National Land Use Policy' in 2014, which was finalised in early 2016. This was Myanmar's first comprehensive national land use policy, and, in this sense, it is a notable step forward. It includes customary land rights for ethnic minorities, temporary suspension of state land concessions and provisions for gender equality in owning land. Institutional building and implementation will definitely be the key for the policy to be effective.

Hurdle for agricultural mechanisation

Mechanisation has been one of the key strategies to modernise agriculture, but the Thein Sein government advocated it with inadequate measures. Rather, farmers themselves grew keen to introduce machines to offset a rural labour shortage, especially during peak seasons. Labour shortage has been evident for the past five or six years, mainly because of an increase in domestic and overseas migration in search of better earnings. Labour shortages would be expected to be more serious upon the completion of large-scale urban industrial zones such as the Thilawa Special Economic Zone in Yangon. Apart from labour shortage, unstable weather patterns or the impacts of climate change in recent years have forced farmers to use machines to avoid harvest damage. Farmers want to accelerate harvesting operations and reduce vulnerability to weather damage.

However, promoting mechanisation on a wider scale is not an easy task. After Cyclone Nargis in 2008, small-scale power tillers became common as a result of the damage suffered by bullocks. However, this is not the case with mid- and large-scale machineries. The main hurdle is the lack of infrastructures such as farm roads or land consolidation. For example, the cost of harvesting paddy using combine harvesters is almost the same or even lower than that for harvesting by manual labour as the labour wages were increasing. For instance, in the Ayeyarwady delta in 2013, using a combine harvester cost 33,500 kyat per acre, whereas labour harvesting cost 30,000 kyat per acre. Similarly, in the Shwebo area in 2014, prices rose to 45,000 kyat per acre for the combine harvester and shot up to 65,000–70,000 kyat for labour harvesting. However, not every farmer was able to use a combine harvester because of inadequate land consolidation and the state of farm roads. Thus, it is critical to develop appropriate infrastructure to promote agriculture mechanisation.

Hurdles in expansion of agricultural exports

Increasing export stops Myanmar's agricultural policy agenda, but problems in production and milling hinder progress, especially of rice exports (World Bank 2014a, 19–24). The major reasons for the low quality are that high-quality seeds are in short supply, most rice mills are outdated and inefficient. Since too many varieties (more than 200) are cultivated, standardisation is difficult. Moreover, since rice is marketed in categories defined by shape, different varieties can be included in the same category. This also makes it difficult to stabilise the quality for sale. Consequently, the majority of Myanmar's exported rice mostly falls in the category of 25 per cent broken, relegating it to the export of low-grade grains. Further, even with the same quality, Myanmar rice tends to fetch a lower price—US$10–15 lower per ton than the price of the same grade of rice exported by its neighbouring countries such as Thailand, Vietnam and India—because of its poor reputation in the international market.

Logistical problems also hinder exports. Underdeveloped roads increase transportation costs significantly. The fact that transporting produce such as rice to the Chinese border costs more (US$80/tonne) than sending it to Africa (US$65/tonne) indicates the appalling condition of domestic roads. In addition, the various costs incurred in the export process are also high compared with those in neighbouring countries. According to an estimate by the World Bank (2014a, 26), Myanmar's export cost (licence fee, inspection fee tax, etc.) for rice is US$8.49 per tonne, whereas it is US$0.05 for Vietnam and US$0.10 for Thailand. All these high logistical costs negatively affect the competitiveness of Myanmar's produce.

Extreme price fluctuations plague agricultural exports, and Myanmar's export destinations are undiversified (World Bank 2014b, 24–25). For example, its rice exports have exceeded a million tonnes since 2012, primarily resulting from more exports to China through the border, the destination for 60–70 per cent of total rice exports. Until November 2014, however, China had declared rice import from Myanmar illegal and was seizing shipments and arresting importers. The Chinese government decided to strictly regulate any rice import from Myanmar from September 2014. Then, in October 2014, the price of paddy plummeted 17.5 per cent from levels three months earlier because of China's actions. The problem of concentration of export destination also applies to the case of pulses and beans, Myanmar's biggest agricultural exports. India is their major export destination, especially for black gram and pigeon pea, and Indian market conditions influence domestic prices greatly. In 2012, Myanmar pulses' prices fell 50 per cent compared with those of 2011 because of the decrease in demand in India. These cases suggest that it is important to diversify the export markets to avoid price risks and to stabilise farmers' income.

Challenges for poverty reduction

Even though there are some variations, about half of Myanmar's rural population is landless (MDRI/CESD 2013). The landless population is economically vulnerable since such people depend on agricultural wage labour, do not have any economic assets and suffer from low education levels. However, no concrete poverty-reduction policies targeted this poorest segment of the rural economy under the Thein Sein government. Fujita (2016) suggests the possibility of changing this class from wage labourers to tenant farmers under the new farmland law, as it allows more freedom for land right transactions. If this happens, one channel would open for the poorest people to move up in the economic classes.

As noted earlier, microfinance has been one of the major policy tools for poverty reduction in Myanmar. However, its actual impact on rural poverty remains unclear. For example, MADB's much-welcomed increase in lending was accompanied by unexpected defaults in 2013. The cause remained undetermined, but it was suggested that farmers used some of the loans for consumption or purchase of durable goods (such as motorbikes) and not for revenue-generating activities. This suggests an increase in supply alone would not necessarily lead to a favourable result. Closer investigation of the rural credit market as well as borrowers' behaviour patterns is necessary to design an effective rural financial service.

Conclusion

The agricultural sector will remain the key sector for Myanmar in the foreseeable future, both economically and politically. Large populations still reside in rural areas, and the majority of them still do not enjoy the fruits of the economic reforms; they continue to suffer from severe poverty and feel disadvantaged compared with the urban population. The Thein Sein government was right to remove the long-term agricultural policy distortions in place since the Socialist period and shift the policy focus to more adequately address the welfare of rural-area residents, aiming to promote 'protection of farmers' rights', 'modernisation of agriculture' and 'poverty reduction'. However, the regime failed to make any visible impact during its term. This failure is highly likely to have been one of the major reasons for its loss in the 2015 general election.

Understanding the unchanging importance of the sector, the NLD government considers the development of the agriculture sector to be an immediate priority. Its 2015 election manifesto clearly stated that economic improvement and poverty reduction in rural areas need special attention. The NLD argues that farmers would greatly suffer from limitations to their agricultural activities and from an insecure land tenure system if appropriate measures are not taken. In this sense, the agricultural policy direction itself does not significantly differ from that of the Thein Sein government, whereas the emphasis is more on the protection of the rights of farmers, especially in land-grabbing cases.

Nevertheless, significant impact is yet to be observed even after one year since the NLD administration took office. Farmers are suffering from low productivity and income, land disputes are yet to be solved, and there has been little increase in agricultural exports and FDI. Whether the NLD government is able to produce tangible achievements that allow people to feel the benefit of reform in a relatively short period will be crucial to garnering continuous public support. Very high expectations of the new NLD government can indicate that people may quickly become disappointed if anticipated improvements do not materialise. Therefore, the key for the NLD government will be policy implementation, as was also the case for the Thein Sein government.

Having said this, policy makers should be aware that no short cut exists in agricultural productivity improvement and rural poverty reduction. Short-, mid- and long-term goals should be systematically outlined and shared among all stakeholders. Proper and efficient institutional setting for policy implementation is absolutely necessary. In that sense, the merger of three different ministries in the area of rural development (agriculture, livestock and cooperatives) undertaken by the NLD government may be a good first step. However, intensive investment in human resources to support necessary institutions is also indispensable. At the same time, in the long run, as the country aims to promote industrialisation, the issue of smoothly evolving the agricultural sector in line with the overall economic development process is important. This is the challenge that Myanmar has come to face for the first time in its history.

References

Ardeth Maung Thaunghmung. 2004. *Behind the Teak Curtain: Authoritarianism, Agricultural Policies and Political Legitimacy in Rural Burma*. London: Kegan Paul.

Central Statistical Office (CSO). 2016. *Statistical Yearbook 2015*. Naypyitaw.

Dapice, D. et al. 2010. *Revitalizing Agriculture in Myanmar: Breaking Down Barriers, Building a Framework for Growth*. Cambridge, MA: Harvard Kennedy School, Ash Center for Democratic Governance and Innovation.

Fujita, K. 2016. 'Agricultural and Rural Development Strategy in Myanmar: With a Focus on the Rice Sector'. In *The Myanmar Economy: Its Past, Present and Prospects*, edited by K. Odaka and F. Mieno, 97–129. Tokyo: Springer.

Fujita, K. and Okamoto, I. 2009. 'Overview of Agricultural Policies and Development in Myanmar'. In *The Economic Transition in Myanmar after 1988: Market Economy versus State Control*, edited by K. Fujita, F. Mieno and I. Okamoto, 169–215. Singapore: NUS Press in association with Kyoto University Press.

Global Witness. 2015. Guns, Cronies and Crops: How Military, Political and Business Cronies Conspired to Grab Land in Myanmar. www.globalwitness.org/documents/17852/exec_summarygunscroniescrops.pdf.

Hla Myint. 2013. 'Comments on: Farmers Protection Act and Minimum Guaranteed Rice Price'. *New Light of Myanmar*, July 12.

International Finance Corporation (IFC). 2013. Microfinance in Myanmar: Sector Assessment. www.cgap.org/publications/microfinance-myanmar-sector-assessment.

Land Core Group of the Food Security Working Goup (LCG). 2012. 13 Case Studies of Land Confiscations in Three Townships of Central Myanmar. www.mylaff.org/ document/view/2967.

Michigan State University and the Myanmar Development Resource Institute's Centre for Economic and Social Development (MDRI/CESD). 2013. A Strategic Agricultural Sector and Food Security Diagnositic for Myanmar. https://ideas.repec.org/p/ags/midiwp/161372.html.

Ministry of Agriculture and Irrigation (MOAI). 2011. *Myanmar Agriculture in Brief 2011*. Yangon: MOAI.

Myanmar Rice Federation. n.d. *Myanmar Rice Federation*. Yangon: Myanmar Rice Federation.

Okamoto, I. 2008. *Economic Disparity in Rural Myanmar*. Singapore: NUS Press.

Okamoto, I. 2009. 'Transformation of the Rice Marketing System after Market Liberalization in Myanmar'. In *The Economic Transition in Myanmar after 1988: Market Economy versus State Control*, edited by K. Fujita, F. Mieno and I. Okamoto, 216–245. Singapore: NUS Press in association with Kyoto University Press.

Okamoto, I. 2015. 'Rice Export and Contract Farming: Lessons from the Rice Specializing Companies'. In Japan International Cooperation Agency 'Report for Economic Reform' (Agricultural and Rural Working Group), prepared for Japan International Cooperation Organization. http://libopac.jica.go.jp/images/report/12238812_01.pdf.

Perry, P. 2007. *Myanmar (Burma) since 1962: The Failure of Development*. Aldershot: Ashgate.

Scurrah, N., Hirsh, P. and Woods, K. 2015. *The Political Economy of Land Governance in Myanmar, Mekong Region Land Governance*. http://mrlg.org/wp-content/uploads/2015/12/Political_Economy_of_Land_Governance_in_Myanmar_FA.pdf.

Turnell, S. 2009. *Fiery Dragons: Banks, Moneylenders and Microfinance in Burma*. Copenhagen: NIAS Press.

U Myint. 2013. 'Comments, Views and Suggestions on "Draft Law on Enhancing the Economic Welfare of Farmers"'. Mimeo.

World Bank. 2014a. Myanmar: Capitalizing on Rice Export Opportunities. www.bankinformationcenter.org/wp-content/uploads/2014/10/Myanmar-Capitalizing-on-Rice-Export-Opportunities.pdf.

World Bank. 2014b. Myanmar: Rice Price Volatility and Poverty Reduction. www.lift-fund.org/myanmar-rice-price-volatility-and-poverty-reduction-world-bank.

20

BANKING AND FINANCE

Thomas Förch

The peculiar history of Myanmar's financial sector is not glamorous. Having held the top position in the region in the 1950s, the sector has experienced nationalization, multiple financial crises, including three demonetizations, in 1964, 1985, and 1987, as well as a severe banking crisis in 2003. As a result, banking in Myanmar remains at an infant stage with little public trust in the Myanmar kyat as a currency of value and little faith in the soundness of the formal banking sector (True 2015, 1). The financial sector of Myanmar can far too often be found at the bottom end of most rankings, performing poorly in both regional and international comparisons. Examples of this unsatisfactory performance are the ratio of credit to the economy (a widely used metric for the development of a financial sector) of about 12% – of all Asian countries only Afghanistan has a lower ratio and hence a less developed financial sector – or a mere 5% share of the population with a bank account. Up until today, Myanmar predominantly remains a cash economy. The fundamental weakness and underdeveloped state of the financial sector threaten to undermine the existing reform processes (Skidmore and Wilson 2012, 16). Currently, the financial sector cannot adequately take over its role as financial intermediary, failing to support and facilitate the growth of the real economy.

The troubled past of the banking and financial sector

Changes in the economy and the financial sector in Myanmar have historically coincided with political change, given the close ties of the government and the banking sector (True 2015, 1).

Indian moneylenders, called Chettiars, arrived in 1826 after the first Anglo-Burmese War, when parts of Burma came under British colonial rule. They introduced many lending and bookkeeping innovations and employed the hundi system of informal remittances. The Chettiars dominated the financial sector up until World War II, financing Burma's emergence as the 'rice-bowl' of the British Empire (Turnell 2009, 13). In the colonial era proper in Burma, the cooperative credit system experienced spectacular growth, since it was favoured by the British Empire as a device to marginalize moneylenders. Though seemingly of great promise, the cooperative credit system accounted for relatively little of the credit needs in the country and even collapsed entirely in the decade following 1925 due to lax lending practices and the collapse of paddy prices (Turnell 2009, 64). The banking sector also dates back to the colonial era proper, as the Indian Presidency Bank of Bengal opened its Rangoon branch in 1861

(Tin 2013) and the first central bank emerged between the years 1939 and 1947 out of the Rangoon branch office of the Reserve Bank of India. Towards the close of the British colonial era in Burma, by the end of 1941, a total of 20 banks operated in the country, most of them with their headquarters elsewhere.

The Japanese occupation between 1942 and 1945 brought with it the flight of the Indian diaspora in Burma, including the Chettiars (Turnell 2009, 49). The Japanese, in cooperation with the local puppet-government, created a number of symbolic financial institutions with the purpose of supporting the extraction of resources from Burma without cost to the Japanese financial system (Longmuir 2002). After the defeat of the Japanese in Burma in April 1945, the foreign banks returned, the Union Bank of Burma took over the role as central bank and a currency board was introduced, which tried to re-establish a working financial sector.

Being put forward as scapegoats for the misfortunes that heralded the breakdown of Burma's colonial economy, the Chettiars were not allowed to return to their lives and livelihoods after Burma's independence in 1948 (Turnell 2009, 49). The banking sector, including domestic and foreign banks, developed quickly under the parliamentary democracy and went on to account for more than one-third of Burma's gross domestic product (Tin 2013). Hence, Burma's banking sector was the most developed one in the region at that time.

The Revolutionary Council Government seized control of the country in 1962. It nationalized all banks in 1963 and before too long agglomerated them into the Peoples Bank of the Union of Burma. Nationalization and agglomeration of those 10 domestic and 14 foreign banks did not stop at the insurance sector either, which suffered the same fate in 1964. Subsequently, three major demonetizations occurred in 1964, 1985, and 1987. In the latest 1987 demonetization, the military-socialist regime effectively declared about 75% of the cash in circulation illegal and eliminated three banknote denominations without exchange or compensation (Nehru 2014, 7). Sporadic protests broke out among students unable to pay their university fees and, by 1988, these had become widespread, ultimately forcing General Ne Win to step down and triggering a bloody army crackdown on 8 August 1988 (Lintner 1995; Egreteau 2009).

The succeeding military regime, the State Law and Order Restoration Council, abolished the socialist path of development and chose a more market-oriented one. In the financial sector, several laws wiped away the remnants of the socialist area in 1990: the Banking Law liberalized the financial sector, resulting in the re-emergence of private banks starting from 1992; the Central Bank was given a certain degree of authority over the monetary policy via the Central Bank Law; the Myanmar Agriculture and Rural Development Bank Law aimed at supporting the credit deprived rural population. Furthermore, other characteristics of a modern financial sector were introduced to Myanmar in the 1990s, such as a primary government bond market, cash machines, and credit cards. Also a microfinance programme, sponsored by the United Nations, started its operations in 1997. However, the Myanmar banking industry experienced, after a decade of stellar growth (inflation adjusted, deposits grew by 2,100% and loans by 1,600% from 1992 to 2002), a severe crisis in early 2003 (Turnell 2009, 271). This crisis originated in the collapse of a number of trading companies that were acting as informal financial institutions. The contagion spread to banks, which were subsequently instructed to pull back all their loans to increase their own liquidity. This, in turn, created a real sector depression that further eroded the value of financial sector assets (Nehru 2014, 7). This crisis was aggravated further by sanctions of the United States due to Myanmar's continuing failure to address major deficiencies in its anti-money-laundering regime. After three major banks (Asia Wealth Bank, Mayflower Bank, and Myanmar Universal Bank) had been closed down and the crisis eventually subsided, the Central Bank issued stringent prudential measures, such as a high capital-to-deposit ratio and strict collateral requirements, which impeded credit growth for the next decade (True 2015, 1; Turnell 2009, 302f).

After the quasi-civilian government under Thein Sein took office in 2011, Myanmar and the financial sector embarked on a comprehensive set of reforms. With respect to the financial sector, the main thrust of the government reform measures has focused on relaxing controls over private banks and legislating the Central Bank into an autonomous body (Than 2014, 168). New licences were awarded to establish private banks while prudential regulations were eased. Reforms did not stop there. They rather resulted, among other things, in the establishment of the legal basis for a microfinance sector, a new banking law, the breakup of the state insurance monopoly, the unification of the exchange rate regime, and the establishment of the Yangon Stock Exchange. The reform emphasis of the government gave rise to an easing of international sanctions and the re-integration of Myanmar in the global economy. International financial institutions have started to re-engage with the country, foreign banks started operations, and international payments and credit cards came back to Myanmar.

In April 2016, a newly elected government, under the National League for Democracy and headed by President Htin Kyaw, came into power. According to the party's election manifesto, the continuing liberalization of the financial sector is a cornerstone of their political agenda. However, the government still has not published detailed reform plans for the financial sector. Furthermore, the speed and depth of reform measures fell below expectations. As a result, the financial sector is still at a rudimentary level and has a long way to go to meet international standards.

A closer look at the banking sector

When talking about the financial sector in Myanmar, the focus mainly is on the banks. Similar to other developing countries such as Cambodia, Laos, or Vietnam, the banking sector constitutes more than nine-tenths of total financial sector assets. In 2014, the banking sector held 30 trillion Myanmar kyat (about 24 billion US dollars) in assets, equalling less than one-hundredth of the size of the HSBC. Growth rates of credits and deposits have consistently been over 20% each year since 2011 (Central Bank of Myanmar (CBM) 2014).

Four state-owned banks control about three-fifths of the total banking sector assets, while the remaining share is spread out among quasi-governmental and private banks, which form a highly heterogeneous group. Among them are, for example, two banks affiliated to the military, eight banks partially owned or controlled by individual ministries, six public (non-listed) banks, and ten private banks. Furthermore, in 2014 and early 2016, a total of 13 foreign banks were given a licence. The operations of the foreign banks are, however, strictly regulated and limited. For example, foreign banks are limited to one branch only, restricted to US dollar business, and banned from retail banking.

Banks in Myanmar are very diverse, not only with regard to ownership but also with regard to their operations and aspirations. The state-owned banks are mainly channelling subsidized government funds to specific target groups. They rather see themselves as departments of their respective ministries and not as fully fledged, independently operating, financial institutions. The largest state-owned bank, the Myanma Economic Bank, has accumulated substantial losses over the past few years. Since 1990, the bank has been operating at loss; in the fiscal year 2012 to 2013 alone, 79 billion Myanmar kyat of government funds have been needed to cover these losses. Detailed data on the other three government banks are not available. Aggregate data nevertheless show that the state-owned banks are losing market share (CBM 2014) and are struggling to keep pace with the modernizing efforts of their private sector peers. Despite the large share in assets, the state-owned banks only contribute less than 10% of total lending by banks, highlighting their inefficiency. The responsible ministries (the Ministry of Finance, MoF, and the Ministry of Agriculture and Irrigation) are now evaluating restructuring options for the state-owned banks in order to guarantee their sustainability. Out of the 19 quasi-governmental and private banks, the 2 biggest (Kanbazwa Bank and Co-operative Bank) account for half of the total assets. The smallest 14 banks, in turn, only account for a quarter of the assets.

About half a dozen banks work very actively and aggressively to seize the existing opportunities in the sector. They are improving and upgrading their physical infrastructure, internal operations, IT systems, and customer relationships. For example, the first core banking systems have been installed in the past few years, efforts towards the compliance of International Financial Reporting Standards have been made, and internal training schools have been set up. Also, more and more banks have professional websites. Advertisements, an unknown marketing tool for banks up until very recently, are starting to pop up on the web and throughout the cities. Banks are developing their brand identities and are increasingly trying to differentiate themselves from their competitors. Differentiation by products and prices remains limited, as existing regulations set clear limitations on the operational freedom of banks; for instance, interest rate caps are set for deposits and credits, the types of acceptable collaterals are strictly defined, and the maturity of credits is limited to one year. Banks currently try to stand out through an extensive branch network. A total of 1,300 bank branches, i.e. three branches per 100,000 adults, exist in the country – compared with almost 13 branches per 100,000 adults in neighbouring Thailand. The two biggest private banks alone are each opening approximately one new branch every week. Brick and mortar branches are expensive and the low population density of the country poses additional challenges for the profitability of these branches. Several local banks see mobile banking solutions as an opportunity to leapfrog their business. The provision of payments and savings via mobile phones could significantly accelerate financial inclusion, especially in rural areas. The CBM paved the way for the further development of these mobile banking solutions by issuing rules on these services in April 2016. The rules create an enabling framework and regulatory clarity for efficient and secure mobile financial services in Myanmar.

Nonetheless, these significant changes in the country seem to be too fast for some banks. Some are not able or even willing to keep up with the investments and improvements of the top group of banks. Some of the low performing banks are likely to be taken over or disappear from the market in the coming years. The number of banks (28) is rather disproportionally high for an economy and country of Myanmar's size. This large number of banks limits the possibilities for economies of scale. Consolidation of the number of banks could indeed be a healthy process for the sector.

The rest of the financial sector is catching up

The various other sub-sectors of the financial market, namely capital markets, insurance, microfinance and finance companies, are still all at a very early stage of development. While these sub-sectors are likely to grow rapidly and catch up to some extent, the banking sector will continue to dominate the financial sector in Myanmar over the next decade.

Myanmar currently lacks most features integral to a modern capital market. The bond market is restricted to an over-the-counter primary market for government bonds. The Yangon Stock Exchange opened in early December 2015, but remains accessible only to Myanmar entities and individuals. With 'First Myanmar Investment', the first company was listed on the stock exchange in March 2016. The underdeveloped bond market and stock exchange restrict corporates in their access to capital and furthermore limit options for investors. This leads to a misallocation of capital, resulting, for example, in the fuelling of the Yangon real estate market.

For the first time since the nationalization of the insurance business in 1959 (life insurance) and 1964 (all insurance companies), 12 licences were eventually awarded to private companies in 2014, bringing to an end the monopoly of the state-owned Myanmar Insurance. Currently, the range of offered services remains limited, as does their outreach. At present there are merely basic insurance products, such as life insurance or fire insurance, available. The duration of all types of insurance is limited to one year and pay-outs take the form of lump sum payments. In 2014, only about one million people, i.e. slightly more than 2% of Myanmar's population, had formal insurance.

Ever since the establishment of a legal framework in 2011, the microfinance sector has been growing rapidly – albeit from a very low starting point. The estimated unmet demand for microcredits amounts to one billion US dollars (UNCDF 2014). Less than one-eighth of this potential market is currently tapped by the approximately 250 licensed microfinance institutions. The development of the microfinance sector is still inhibited by overly prohibitive regulatory restrictions in the form of the cap on the maximum lending amount of 5 million Myanmar kyat (about 4,000 US dollars) or a recondite case-by-case permission process for refinancing from foreign sources.

While regulations for microfinance institutions and banks are comprehensive and prohibitive, the regulatory and supervisory framework for finance companies is vague. This niche in the regulatory and supervisory framework opened up business opportunities. Finance companies are not allowed to accept deposits from the public. Their asset side focus is on hire purchase services. The number of finance companies rose from only one company in January 2013 to as many as ten in mid-2015. Ten more companies are currently awaiting their licences. Unfortunately, no official data on these companies exist as of now. The finance companies, however, seem to be rather small and limited in their geographical outreach.

Given the decade-long failure of the licensed providers to satisfy the existing needs for financial services in Myanmar, informal providers have stepped in and filled that niche. People in rural areas especially, but by far not exclusively, rely on these providers when it comes to short term loans, paying interest rates of 60% to 120% per annum. An estimated nine million people are indebted to informal service providers (Chamberlain et al. 2014). In addition, informal money transfer services are widely used throughout Myanmar and seem to be largely tolerated by the authorities.

How resilient are the banks?

The standard approach to analysing the resilience of individual banks, and of a banking sector as a whole, is to look at the data. The financial reports of banks, namely their balance sheets, cash flow statements, and income statements, are to provide a true and fair view of the financial situation of an institution. This standard approach, however, does not work in the case of Myanmar. While Myanmar has adopted international accounting and auditing standards, active enforcement is not practised (Nehru 2014, 24). Most banks do not disclose their financial reports at all. If they do, the reports do not satisfy international or even the national reporting standards – neither in quantity nor quality. Most financial reports available do not even exceed two pages in length. Another source of information is the aggregated industry data published irregularly by the CBM. The last data available of that sort cover the fiscal year of 2012 to 2013. Hence, neither the quantity nor the quality of the available data allows for the standard approach in analysing the resilience of banks. This is in fact already the first and most important challenge. This lack of transparency, as well as the unavailability of reliable data, creates uncertainties. Widespread uncertainty, coupled with the troubled past of the sector, makes it very difficult for trust to be developed. Trust, in turn, is the most important 'currency' in the financial sector, which is in short supply in Myanmar. The cautious behaviour of the Myanmar public towards banks is evident, particularly in the recent bank runs. Rumours about liquidity problems of the largest private bank, the Kanbawza Bank, led to massive withdrawals by depositors in autumn 2012. In November 2014, the United Amara Bank suffered a bank run after the owner's father was included in the United States' specially designated nationals list. The sacking of the ruling party's chairman, Mr Shwe Man, in August 2015 led to sizeable withdrawals at several banks. In turn, the perceived insecurity of the parliamentary elections in October and November 2015 led to a shift in deposits from private to state-owned banks, tripling, for example, the deposit base of the largest state-owned bank, the Myanma Economic Bank. All four incidents were eventually resolved, partly with the rigorous support of the CBM. Nevertheless, these highlight the vulnerability of the banking sector in Myanmar. This vulnerability mainly derives from a lack of transparency and trust. This way, mere rumours have the potential to become self-fulfilling prophecies. Shocks to the sector or to individual banks are most certainly going to occur and will be difficult to manage without the confidence of the depositors, creditors, and supervisors. In the event of such a shock, deposits will be withdrawn, the interbank market will run dry and banks will find themselves in a very uncomfortable position.

Related to this lack of trust, the existing mismatch of assets and liabilities poses another challenge to the resilience of Myanmar's banks. The regulatory framework to date only allows for credits with a maturity of up to one year. These credits can be rolled over up to two times, for one year each. The refinancing side, in turn, cannot mirror these credit maturities and leaves the banks vulnerable to changes in interest rates or bank runs. Deposits are to a vast extent, in fact to more than 90%, demand deposits and hence can be withdrawn anytime. Thus, customers rarely commit their savings for fixed, longer periods of time. This existing asset liability mismatch would already pose challenges for banks in the case of sizeable withdrawals, such as in the case of a bank run. In the near future, this mismatch could even intensify further. The new banking law was enacted in January 2016. Most related regulations are still outstanding but are expected to liberalize the credit modalities. Part of this might be the liberalization of the current limit of credits to one year. The increase of the maturities of the banks' assets would have to be accompanied with the increase in the maturity of the banks' liabilities in order to avoid the mismatch increasing even further.

Consequently, for the time being, the lack of public trust combined with an asset liability mismatch leaves the Myanmar banking sector in a vulnerable position.

Standing at the crossroads

Current decisions and reforms are paving the way for the development of the financial sector in the short, medium, and long term. Academic research and experiences gained from other countries have shown the importance of an efficient financial sector for an economy (Havranek et al. 2013, 18). On the upside, the financial sector is a facilitator of economic development. Its function as financial intermediary allows for the channelling of savings into investments and the productive allocation of these investments. This way, the financial sector promotes economic growth and is a prerequisite for modern market economies. On the downside, an inefficient financial sector can hamper real sector growth. Furthermore, financial crises can easily lead to economic crises.

Myanmar's banking sector is waking up from decades of intentional suppression, but how can policy makers ensure that the banking sector will become an asset and not a liability to the development of the country? How can the outreach and depth of the sector be supported while at the same time strengthening its resilience?

Is the current situation of Myanmar's banking sector unique? Yes, and no. Yes, as there is no one perfect blueprint for the development of a country's banking sector. The life of policy makers would be so much easier if there were such blueprints. However, as each country has a unique set of socio-economic framework conditions, the solutions to the challenges in the financial sector also have to be tailor-made to suit these starting conditions. On the other hand, one could also argue in another way: no, the situation is not unique, as other countries have also gained experience in opening up their banking sectors after a period of isolation. Lessons can clearly be learned from these experiences – not only from the success stories but also from the failures.

One main lesson Myanmar can learn from other countries that opened up after times of isolation is that it has to thoroughly prepare for times of stress in the banking sector. As soon as the economic boom displays any signs of slowing down or even reversing, the banking sector will be tested. Vietnam, for example, had this experience in 2011 and 2012 and is still suffering from the backlash. The housing and securities bubble had burst, and Vietnam was faced with rising inflation, a depreciating currency, and an economic growth rate that slowed down to 5% in 2012 – the lowest growth rate in 13 years.

Alongside the experiences of other countries, there are certain international good practices and recommended standards from which Myanmar can benefit. Compliance with certain international standards is compulsory in order to be accepted in the international world of finance. Violation of these standards will immediately and automatically lead to the isolation of Myanmar, as international financial institutions will not be allowed to deal with its domestic financial institutions. One example is the standards on money laundering and financing of terrorism. As recently as 2006, Myanmar was the only country to be flagged up by the inter-governmental Financial Action Task Force (FATF) for having failed to cooperate in the fight against financing of terrorism and money laundering. In June 2016, Myanmar was eventually removed from that list, thereby avoiding the counter-measures that are currently in place against Iran and North Korea, de-facto isolating the respective country from international financial flows. Other standards, while not compulsory, are nevertheless seen as prerequisites for an efficient banking sector. Examples include International Financial Reporting Standards, International Standards on Auditing, and the Basel Standards on Banking Supervision. For many international business partners and investors, compliance with these standards is a de-facto condition for intensive engagement with financial institutions from a country. Therefore, a systematic reform process focusing on compliance with the most important international standards would facilitate and strengthen the further development of Myanmar's banking sector.

The main challenges ahead

Myanmar banks have a number of weaknesses, and they lag well behind regional and global banks in terms of capitalization, application of banking technology, scale of operations, staff skills, scope, and financial products (Nyo 2012, 130). Given these weaknesses and the lessons learned from the experiences of neighbouring countries, there are a number of challenges and issues Myanmar decision makers need to tackle. These entail: i) establishing and implementing a transparent development strategy for the financial sector; ii) developing trust in the banking sector; and iii) building up human resources.

The key stakeholders (notably the MoF, as regulator and supervisor of the stock market, insurance, and microfinance, as well as the CBM as regulator and supervisor of banks and finance companies) neither have a joint strategy nor explicit individual strategies on how the sector should develop further. The government has to give the financial sector more guidance in steering it in the preferred direction. Coordination among the relevant government institutions, the MoF, and the CBM, seems difficult, partly because the CBM used to be a quasi-department of the MoF and these institutions now have to learn how to work as equal partners. Another issue complicating the guidance of the sector and the inter-governmental coordination is the prevailing influence of third parties. For example, in spring 2015, the President's Office announced that it would take over the coordination of monetary policy aspects in spite of the CBM being an independent body. Although clearly authorized by the law, the CBM also seems to have limited powers to object within the process of licensing banks. In 2014 and 2015, a number of banks (politically guided private banks and banks linked to corruption-inflicted business sectors) received their licence. Political influence and lobbying is likely to have facilitated these licences. In order to assure a systematic development of the financial sector, the relevant government institutions need to develop a joint strategy. The links between the sub-sectors of the financial sector, and hence of the responsibilities of the MoF and the CBM, are too extensive to allow for separate strategies. This joint strategy should be developed through a consultative process, involving the financial institutions and also international development partners.

The second challenge is to enable and facilitate the development of further trust and confidence in the banking sector. Trust cannot be imposed upon the people from the outside; it has to be gained and earned over time. The foundations for this development have to be shaped and honed proactively, which especially includes transparency and good governance. Both aspects require stricter regulations as well as rigorous and meticulous enforcement. One example of the improvement of the regulatory framework is the regulatory requirement on audit committees. The domestic banking law stipulates that banks have to form such a committee. As it does not prescribe the details on the modus operandi of the committees, however, some banks in fact have an audit committee only on paper, without a single meeting having taken place in the past year. The improved application of international standards, especially financial reporting standards, is a crucially important element for the development of transparency as this is the only way the published data can gain credibility. In 2012, the government of Myanmar established a deposit insurance scheme to combat the longstanding lack of public trust. This scheme is merely rudimentary by international standards (Turnell 2014, 230f), only covering deposits up to 500,000 Myanmar kyat (about 400 US dollars). In order to gain positive effects, the scheme should be continuously improved and expanded. In addition to the legal and regulatory requirements as well as their enforcement, a change of mind-set among the banks is required. Without more transparency and good governance, the banks will not be able to gain trust from their customers and the banks will ultimately not be able to compete in the increasingly international arena of the banking business in Myanmar. Therefore, it is in the banks' own interest to proactively leave behind the past of the secluded banking sector in Myanmar, and to emerge from the shadows and embrace the concepts of transparency and good governance. Some banks have understood this and are, for example, already investing and preparing to publish financial reports in accordance with international standards in the near future, although this is not yet required by national regulations.

The third challenge is that of human resources. After years of isolation and with a banking sector still in its infancy, Myanmar finds itself deprived of experienced bankers. In mid-2014, Myanmar banks employed in total as few as c.50,000 members of staff – a fifth of the number of employees of HSBC. Local banking experts expect this number to double by 2018. Including the regular retirement process, this would result in about 14,000 new staff joining the banking sector each year. Currently, centralized training providers are training a mere 300 graduates to work in the financial sector per year. It is, however, not only the quantity of required staff that poses challenges to the banks. Banks need specialists in various functions and positions, ranging from IT experts to trade finance experts. Moreover, the CBM is struggling to hire, train, and retain adequate and capable personnel. There is, for instance, not a single certified public accountant employed by the Central Bank. The CBM has only limited influence on the recruitment process, as this process is managed by the Union Civil Service Board. Remuneration is in no way competitive with the private sector. Other than the initial one day training when joining the CBM, all training is currently conducted on the job. In order to keep pace with or even to be a step ahead of the commercial banks, the CBM needs to heavily invest in its human resources.

Reforms – getting the basics right before it is too late

The financial sector is only in the centre of public and political interest when it is in trouble and subsequently negative effects for the real economy begin to emerge. It seems that only then the necessary discourse can take place and major reforms can be undertaken. However, this may come too late as the negative effects have already materialized. Furthermore, these measures often fall short of their stated objective. On the whole, instead of systematic reforms, it appears that sheer trouble-shooting tends to prevail. During good times, the sector largely operates outside of the spotlight.

Hopefully, this general observation will not hold true for Myanmar. The financial sector with its troublesome past is already catching the attention of policy makers and the public. So far, reforms, and especially their implementation, fall short of expectations and the rhetoric used. The newly elected government already announced that it will make the financial sector a top priority. It is now up to them to follow up these words with actions. Next to the communication of a clear vision and strategy for the financial sector, the new government should take a strong political stance in order to send a signal to the population and the sector. The new Minister for Planning and Finance, Kyaw Win, and the Governor of the Central Bank, Kyaw Kyaw Maung, have key roles to play.

Greater and more concentrated efforts geared towards compliance with international standards and the building up of trust are needed by regulators, parliament, and banks in order to allow the banking sector to become an asset, and not a liability, for the development of Myanmar's economy.

References

Central Bank of Myanmar (CBM). 2014. *Annual Report 2012–2013*. Yangon: Central Bank of Myanmar.

Chamberlain, D. et al. 2014. *Making Access Possible (MAP): Myanmar Country Diagnostic Report*. Cenfri, Finmark Trust: UNCDF.

Egreteau, R. 2009. 'The Repression of the August 8–12 1988 (8-8-88) Uprising in Burma/Myanmar'. Online Encyclopaedia of Mass Violence. Accessed December 28, 2015. www.massviolence.org/The-repression-of-the-August-8-12-1988-8-8-88-uprising-in.

Havranek, T., Horvath, R. and Valickova, P. 2013. 'Financial Development and Economic Growth: A Meta-Analysis'. Czech National Bank Working Paper Series, No. 5.

Lintner, B. 1995. *Outrage – Burma's Struggle for Democracy*. Germtore: Kiscadale Publications.

Longmuir, M. 2002. *The Money Trail: Burmese Currencies in Crisis, 1937–1947*. DeKalb, Illinois: Southeast Asian Publications.

Nehru, V. 2014. Banking on Myanmar: A Strategy for Financial Sector Reform. Carnegie Endowment for International Peace. June 2014. Accessed July 15, 2015. http://carnegieendowment.org/2014/06/05/banking-on-myanmar-strategy-for-financial-sector-reform/hcvo.

Nyo, K. M. 2012. 'Taking Stock of Myanmar's Economy in 2012'. In *Myanmar's Transition – Openings, Obstacles and Opportunities*, edited by Nick Cheesman, Monique Skidmore and Trevor Wilson. Singapore: Institute of Southeast Asian Studies, 119–136.

Skidmore, M. and Wilson T. 2012. 'Interpreting the Transition in Myanmar'. In *Myanmar's Transition – Openings, Obstacles and Opportunities*, edited by Nick Cheesman, Monique Skidmore, and Trevor Wilson. Singapore: Institute of Southeast Asian Studies, 3–22.

Than, T. T. M. 2014. 'Myanmar's Economic Reform'. *Journal of Southeast Asian Economics*, 31 (2): 165–172.

Tin, S. 2013. *Financial Development in Myanmar*, 2nd ed. Yangon: Yan Aung Literature.

True, L. 2015. 'Burma – Paving the Road to a Modern Banking System', Asia Focus – Federal Reserve Bank of San Francisco. June 2015. Accessed August 20, 2015. www.frbsf.org/banking/publications/asia-focus/2015/june/burma-modern-banking-financial-sector-legislative-reforms/.

Turnell, S. 2009. *Fiery Dragons: Banks, Moneylenders and Microfinance in Burma*. Copenhagen: Nordic Institute of Asian Studies.

Turnell, S. 2014. 'Banking and Financial Regulation Reform in Myanmar'. *Journal of Southeast Asian Economics* 31 (2): 225–240.

United Nations Capital Development Fund (UNCDF). 2012. *UNDP Formative Strategic Review of Microfinance Investments in Myanmar: Issues and Recommendations for the Future*. New York: UNCDF.

21

FOREIGN DIRECT INVESTMENT AND TRADE

Jared Bissinger

The growth in Myanmar's trade and foreign direct investment (FDI) has been one of the defining characteristics of the country's political and economic transition since 2011 from military dictatorship to 'discipline flourishing democracy'. The interest of international investors in Myanmar, from not only proximate Asian countries but also Western nations, has increased dramatically. Official trade has nearly doubled in the past half-decade. These changes are not an altogether surprising response to the liberalisation of a formerly oppressive and isolated economic system of a comparatively populous and well-positioned country. Rather, they signal Myanmar's move towards becoming a more normal developing Asian country.

Despite significant increases in Myanmar's internal economic engagement, liberalisation has not been wholesale. Instead, liberalisation in some areas such as telecommunications and exchange rate policy has been juxtaposed with policy intransigence in other areas, notably finance. Changes have created a host of new opportunities, but also challenged vested interests and exposed shortcomings in a domestic private sector that has been shaped by a half-century of perverse incentives. Along with National League for Democracy (NLD)–military relations and the future of ethnic conflict, the ability of the domestic private sector to survive and thrive in a rapidly changing environment will be critical to keeping Myanmar's transition on track.

This chapter covers the key areas of Myanmar's international economic engagement – trade and FDI. It starts with a review of recent developments, including facts and figures to quantify changes in trade and investment. It also documents the key policy reforms introduced under the Thein Sein administration. It then addresses the integral role political determinants play in shaping the country's economic prospects, and the capacity of the state to manage key economic issues.

Engaging the world economy

During the Thein Sein government, Myanmar's economy saw significant growth (albeit from a low base), in large part due to increasing trade and FDI. These gains were driven by a host of domestic reforms, including the harmonisation of the official and market exchange rates, ending of the export first policy (which linked export receipts to import licensing), removal of a range of trade licences, and improvements in the FDI process. They were also catalysed by changing perceptions of investment security locally, and by changing international approaches to

Myanmar, which came largely in response to domestic political changes. Almost all international sanctions on Myanmar were removed, clearing the way for a greater volume of trade and FDI. Domestic reforms and the removal of sanctions also helped to dramatically rehabilitate Myanmar's international reputation, reducing reputational risk for foreign businesses considering trade and investment.

Before undertaking a brief analysis of Myanmar's trade and investment, it should be noted that these data suffer from shortcomings. Investment data come from the Myanmar Investment Commission and represent the number and approved value of investments, not actual investment. There are suspicions among some in the private sector that many foreign businesses which had been operating in Myanmar for some time submitted a new foreign investment application to the MIC under a different name in order to access tax holidays. This would artificially inflate the number and value of new FDI. The other significant shortcoming with the investment figures is that they represent only approved investment, while figures for actual investment come only from international sources such as the IMF. On trade, the major shortcoming is the prevalence of smuggling, especially in high value items such as jade, gemstones, and teak.

Trade

During the Thein Sein administration, both imports and exports grew significantly, though import growth was especially strong, increasing more than two-and-a-half–fold (see Figure 21.1). This growth was driven in part by a more liberal trading regime, including a reduction in the number of products that need import licences, removal of the export first policy, and harmonisation of official and market exchange rates. Demand for imported goods also grew significantly. One catalyst of this growth was an increase in domestic demand for capital goods, such as machinery, electric machinery, and transport equipment, which together comprise 35% of total imports (Rahardja et al. 2016). This significant share of capital goods is notable, because they are essential for Myanmar's industrialisation. Growth of imports is also driven by the release of pent-up demand for some products, such as cars, whose import was long restricted under the previous government. Increasing domestic asset prices, such as property, may also encourage consumers to spend more, as may the decreasing inclination to conceal wealth

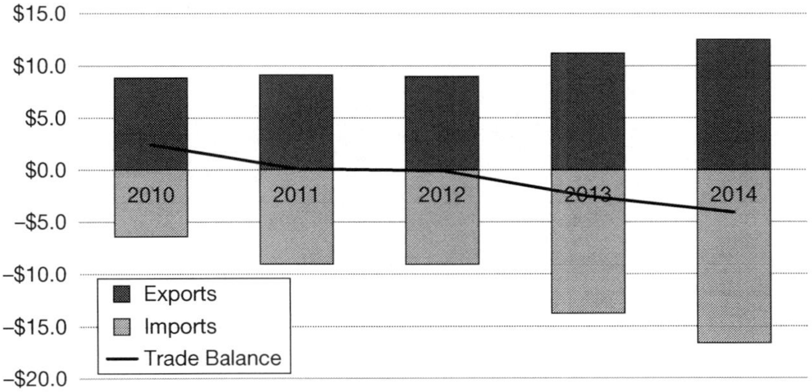

Figure 21.1 Myanmar's imports, exports and trade balance, $US billions

Source: Myanmar Central Statistical Organization, http://mmsis.gov.mm.

among Myanmar's elite. While exports have grown as well, they have not kept pace with import growth. Exports grew by just over 41%, driven primarily by growth in natural gas and, in FY2014, 'miscellaneous manufactured articles'.

Myanmar's major trading partners have historically been proximate Asian countries, and despite the country's newfound openness, they remain its major trading partners. China is the major source of Myanmar's imports and in 2014 became the country's primary export market as well (see Figures 21.2 and 21.3). Thailand had long been Myanmar's largest export market, as it was up until 2014 the sole foreign destination of Myanmar's natural gas. However as of 2015, Myanmar is also exporting natural gas to China through the recently completed pipeline from Kyaukphyu in Rakhine State to China's Yunnan province. Myanmar's imports are less concentrated than exports, though China remains the largest source. Singapore is another important source of imports, being a key regional hub and transshipment port for goods entering Myanmar by sea. A notable inclusion on the list of top sources of imports is the United States, the only Western country to appear on the list of key import and export partners. Myanmar's imports from the United States have increased significantly since 2010, from just under \$60 million to nearly \$500 million in 2014.

Myanmar has long been and largely remains an exporter of primary products, namely agricultural goods and natural resources. Natural gas has long been the country's top export, though in 2014 'miscellaneous manufactured articles' was the top export, at over \$5.2 billion. It is likely that the majority of this was worked jade, based on cross references with Chinese

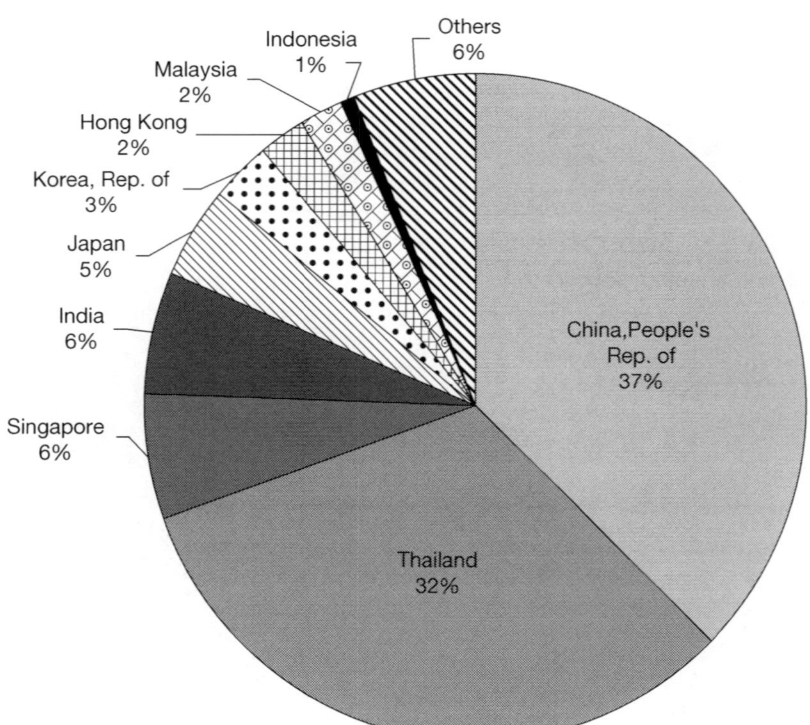

Figure 21.2 Destination of Myanmar exports in FY2014, by share of total US\$ value by country

Source: Myanmar Central Statistical Organization, http://mmsis.gov.mm.

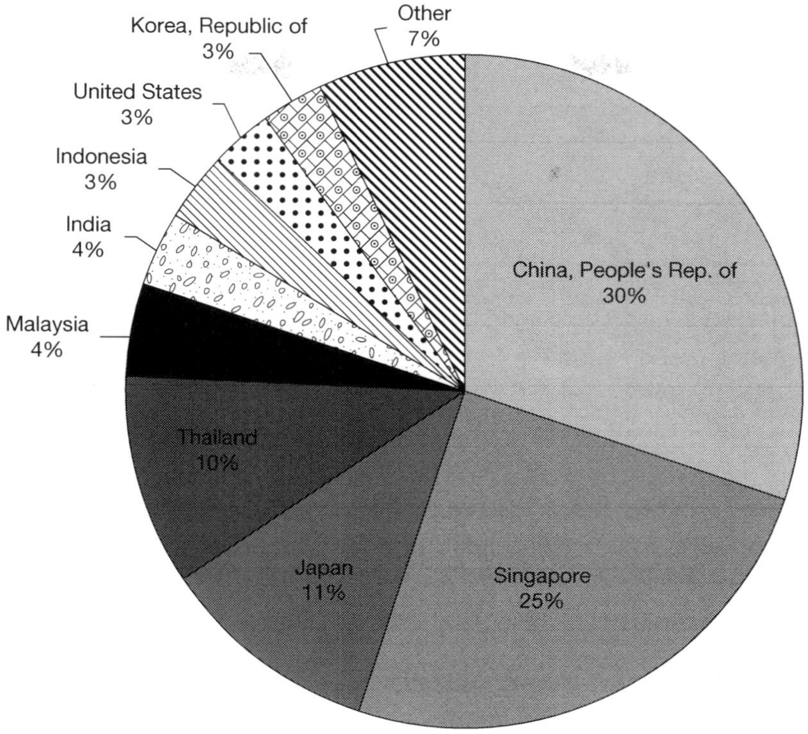

Figure 21.3 Source of Myanmar imports in FY2014, by share of total US$ value by country

Source: Myanmar Central Statistical Organization, http://mmsis.gov.mm.

trade data. 'Mineral products', which comprise mostly natural gas, make up the second largest category, at $3.859 billion. These two resources combined account for over $9 billion of Myanmar's $12.5 billion of exports in FY2014, signalling a dangerous concentration of exports in a few select categories of natural resources. Myanmar's informal exports (e.g. smuggling) of jade may be even greater, according to a 2015 report by Global Witness, which estimated the total value of the country's jade production in 2014 at up to $31 billion (Global Witness 2015). Myanmar's imports are far more diversified, though that is due in large part to the underdeveloped domestic manufacturing base, which necessitates importing a wide range of consumer goods and machinery. Mineral products, which include fuels, were Myanmar's top import, valued at $2.86 billion. This was followed closely by machinery and mechanical products ($2.73 billion) and miscellaneous manufactured articles ($2.60 billion) (Myanmar Central Statistical Organization 2016).

Foreign investment

Foreign investment growth during the Thein Sein administration was significant, and by most measures the largest amount of FDI received in Myanmar's history. During the socialist years, Myanmar was closed to new foreign investment, though a very small number of foreign business interests remained active there through the socialist years. After the political upheaval and the ascension of the State Law and Order Restoration Council (SLORC) in 1988, the new government prioritised the passage of a new FDI law, which was seen as a signature move away from the socialist era towards more international economic engagement. Though Myanmar did experience some bursts of FDI during the era of SLORC/State Peace and Development Council (SPDC), notably in the run-up to the Asian Financial Crisis in 1997, FDI performance overall remained lacklustre. Especially after 1997, Myanmar regressed back towards greater 'self-sufficiency and self-reliance' (Tin Maung Maung Than 2007, 363). FDIs that did come were generally targeted at the extractive industries and sourced from nearby Asian countries (Bissinger 2012, 24). Though there were few investments, some had very large dollar values, given the significant sunk costs of dams and extractive projects such as mines and natural gas wells. Myanmar's extractive and hydropower projects are export-oriented, have significant environmental consequences, and generate large revenues for the state (little of which goes back to affected communities).

Since 2012, there has been a significant and broad-based increase in incoming FDI to Myanmar. The number and dollar value of approved investment projects, especially those in non-extractive sectors, has increased markedly (see Figure 21.4). In FY2014, approved FDI was over $8 billion, though this year was somewhat extraordinary because of major telecommunications and oil and gas investments that resulted from liberalisations in the years immediately prior. Notably, the number of individual projects approved has grown from only 13 in FY2011 to 211 in FY2014, signalling that a significantly greater number of investors are willing to commit money to projects in Myanmar. Actual investment, as recorded by the IMF, also shows steady growth over the past five years, though the actual investment figures remain significantly lower than the approved investments in most years (International Monetary Fund 2015, 30). Note that the year-to-year comparison of approved and actual investment should be taken with some caution, as approved investments may take some time before they enter the country and are recorded as 'actual' investment, due to the time needed between approval and project implementation.

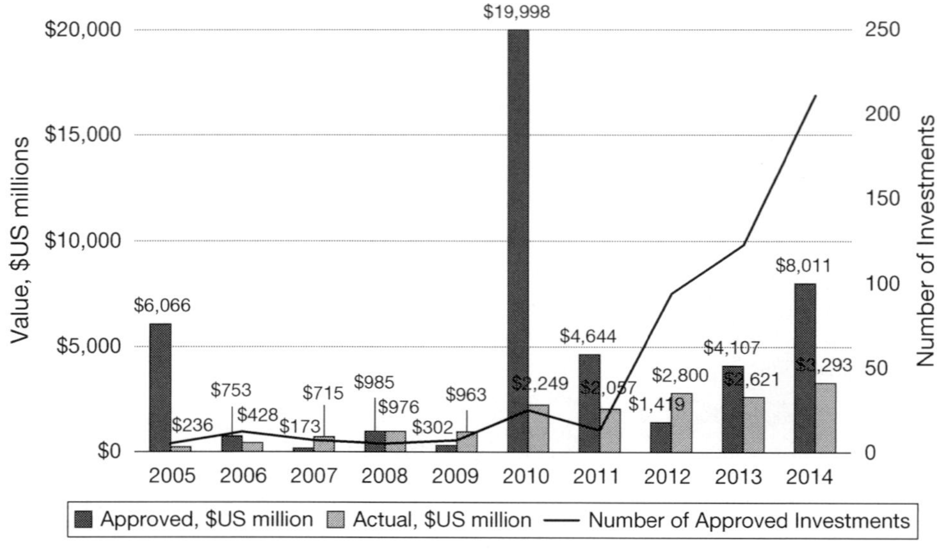

Figure 21.4 Approved and actual foreign investment in Myanmar

Source: Myanmar Central Statistical Organization, http://mmsis.gov.mm and IMF (2015).

As noted earlier, one of the defining changes in FDI in Myanmar has been the overall move away from extractive industries towards economy-wide investment. During the SPDC era, extractive industries (which include mining, oil and gas, and power) comprised the vast majority of Myanmar's FDI, and there was little investment outside these sectors. However investment in manufacturing, communications, and other non-extractive sectors such as real estate and hotels and tourism have grown significantly during the Thein Sein era (see Figure 21.5). There has also been significant growth in the number of countries which have invested in Myanmar. Concurrently, the number of billion-dollar plus extractive investments has decreased significantly. Some previously agreed projects, notably the Myitsone dam, have been suspended, likely adding to the perceived risk of large-scale extractive investments agreed in less-than-transparent deals.

While Myanmar's trade has been growing significantly, this growth has brought about a significant deficit in the current account, which has put pressure on the government's foreign exchange reserves. These reserves shrunk to dangerous levels on at least two occasions in 2015. This, as well as high single-digit inflation for the past half-decade, has been a key contributor to the relatively significant depreciation of the kyat, from 818 kyat/US$ when the new floating exchange rate system was launched in April 2012 to 1,275 kyat/US$ four years later, a decline of nearly 56%. This depreciation, while beneficial for Myanmar's manufacturers and agriculturalists, will increase inflation and present significant challenges for the urban poor, who spend much of their income on food.

Policy reform

Growth in Myanmar's trade and investment has been driven in large part by reforms, not just to the country's political structures but also to economic policy framework, that shape the country's business environment. During the SLORC/SPDC era, disincentives for productive economic activity were many. In some sectors such as teak extraction, banking, and airlines,

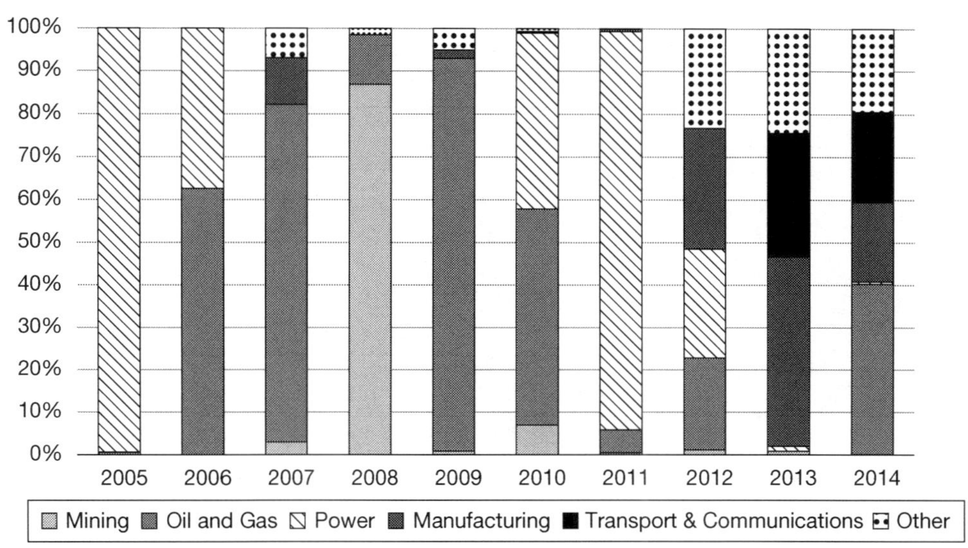

Figure 21.5 Share of approved FDI, by sector

Source: Myanmar Central Statistical Organization, http://mmsis.gov.mm.

private enterprise was prohibited from operating unless they had a joint venture with, or operated under a licence from, the government (Government of the Union of Myanmar 1989). In other sectors private enterprises had to compete with state-owned enterprises (SOEs), which had access to funds from the state budget as well as foreign exchange (in limited amounts) at official rates. Private enterprises faced a business environment with underdeveloped market-supporting institutions, policy uncertainty, a weak financial system, and an exchange rate regime that stunted the growth of domestic manufacturing (World Bank 1995, 48). Foreign investors also faced a host of challenges, including a lack of investment protection and issues repatriating profits. It was a business environment that disincentivised investment and productive activity, and instead favoured trading and extraction. From 1993 to 2010, gross domestic capital formation averaged just 13.7% of GDP, indicating that a very small share of Myanmar's GDP was due to investment (Asian Development Bank 2011, 3). This is especially acute when compared with neighbours in ASEAN. For example, Vietnam had a gross domestic capital formation rate of 34.4% over the 2000s, and Laos had a gross domestic capital formation rate of 24.4%.

Liberalising the policy framework around trade and investment was a priority of the Thein Sein administration. Numerous reforms to the trade and investment framework were cited in the 2013 Framework for Economic and Social Reforms as important 'quick wins' for the Thein Sein government (Government of the Republic of the Union of Myanmar 2013). This policy statement noted a number of reforms that had already happened, including the exchange rate unification and the adoption of a managed float for the kyat. It also noted many other potential areas of reform, including the elimination of the export first policy, the removal of 'all exchange and other non-tariff restrictions on imports', and the development of clear procedures and guidelines for FDI (Government of the Republic of the Union of Myanmar 2013, 3).

Trade reforms

Under the former military government, Myanmar's trading system was encumbered by a myriad of restrictions, some of which were removed by the Thein Sein administration. Myanmar has made some legislative moves to address issues in the trading sector, such as the passage of the Export and Import Law; however, more reform has taken place in the administrative rules and processes. Myanmar's trading system had been previously characterised by significant licensing requirements, and reducing those requirements has been an important area of reform. In 2011, the government took some early steps to relax import restrictions on select products, including cars, palm oil, fuel, soft drinks, and a number of pre-packed food products. In early 2013, the government removed import licence requirements for another 166 types of goods, and eliminated export licence requirements for 152 types of goods. In July 2015, the Ministry of Commerce went further and issued a negative list, which is a list containing all goods which require import or export licences (Ministry of Commerce 2015, 20). All goods not on the negative list were allowed for import and export without a licence. The government also removed taxes on export earnings in 2015.

While there have been some reforms to trade policy, problems remain both in policy and in the facilitating infrastructure. There have been a few reforms to Myanmar's financial system, for example in the improved ease of using letters of credit for trade transactions; however, trade financing remains a problem. It is still not possible to receive trade financing from a bank outside of the normal lending procedures, which include restrictions such as full collateralisation. Improvements in trading infrastructure have been modest, with congestion in ports, roads, and waterways creating logistics problems for businesses. Myanmar's customs administration is in the process of adopting an automated customs clearance system, which should help improve the cumbersome manual processes. Previous research found that imports and exports in Myanmar require nine different documents, more than double the OECD average (OECD 2014, 212).

New foreign investment laws

One of the earliest economic policy reforms of the Thein Sein government was the passage of a new Foreign Investment Law (FIL) in 2012 (Government of the Republic of the Union of Myanmar 2012). The law, while similar in content to the 1988 law, had important symbolic value, to 'demonstrate that Myanmar is once again open for business' (OECD 2014, 88). It left many questions unanswered, including details on investment restrictions in select sectors, investment protections, and procedures for approving foreign investment (OECD 2014, 84). In early 2013, Myanmar's government released the FIL rules and a notification which contained further details about prohibited sectors, investment application procedures, employment regulations, land use rules, and other areas. The rules and notification contained numerous restrictions on foreign investment and required mandatory joint ventures in some sectors. Restrictions often were in sectors in which activities could be dangerous (to the environment or otherwise), or those that were considered sensitive, for example munitions production. The law, while a step forward, evidenced the reluctance to fully liberalise the foreign investment regime. The joint venture requirements, for example, were especially common in sectors in which the local business community had interests. There was greater liberalisation in sectors that involved greater sunk costs or technological complexity that was beyond the reach of the local private sector.

The Myanmar Citizens Investment Law was passed in July 2013, not long after the FIL. It was very similar in structure and content to the FIL of late 2012, and was passed in part due to feedback from the local business community that tax exemptions in the FIL should also be available to domestic investors.

In October 2016, the new NLD Parliament adopted a new foreign investment law which merged the 2012 FIL and 2013 Citizens Investment Law. While this law contained similarities with the previous legislation, there were notable changes including some modifications to tax incentives, the introduction of a new 'Approval Order' process, the addition of some compensation requirements for workers, and new exemptions for inputs for goods that are later exported.

Sectoral and other reforms

There have been a few sector-specific reforms that have helped catalyse sector-specific trade and FDI growth. None has had a more tangible impact than reforms to the telecommunications sector, where the state operator Myanma Posts and Telecommunications (MPT) had a monopoly until 2014, when two foreign telecoms operators, Qatar's Ooredoo and Norway's Telenor, began operating networks under newly established licences granted in 2013. The introduction of the foreign telecommunications operators reduced the prices of SIM cards dramatically, from 200,000 kyat in 2013 to 1,500 kyat in 2014. It also led to improved service and a dramatic increase in mobile penetration rates. In 2012, only 5.5 million people in Myanmar had a mobile phone. By early 2016, the largest telecoms operator, MPT, had 19 million subscribers alone, while new entrants Telenor and Ooredoo had 15.5 million and 6 million subscribers respectively. Military-linked Myanmar Economic Corporation, which also operated a telecommunications network before the liberalisation, received a licence in 2017, with joint venture partner Viettel and a local consortium, making it Myanmar's fourth telecoms provider.

Telecoms is the shining example of a strong private sector response to reforms which has yielded sizeable benefits for government (tax dollars), businesses (profits) and consumers (better services). However, many other sectors have remained largely stagnant due to the lack of reforms, for example mining, which saw FDI of only US$6 million in FY2014. Myanmar's government has also passed other economic reforms, including annual Union Taxation Laws, a Foreign Exchange Management Law, and others. However, many integral business environment issues, notably land and finance, still lack an appropriate legislative framework to encourage economic growth.

Economic prospects and their political determinants

The bureaucracy: reform and continuities

Many factors will play a role in shaping Myanmar's economic trajectory, including the international macroeconomic environment and the country's demographics. However, the ability of Myanmar's leaders to control the bureaucracy and reshape the country's economic institutions will be paramount to sustained growth of trade and investment. The structure of Myanmar's bureaucracy still closely resembles that under the socialist and military governments, when the institutional framework was hostile to private sector development and competition. While there have been some reforms, there is significant institutional inertia that continues to hinder Myanmar's growth prospects.

The Thein Sein and NLD governments have both undertaken some administrative reforms. The Thein Sein government rebranded some departments or ministries to give the appearance of significant change, for example by changing the name of the State Land Records Department to the Department of Agricultural Land Management and Statistics. They also moved some departments, as well as merging Ministry of Industry I and Ministry of Industry II. In 2016, the NLD reduced the number of ministries significantly, by appointing a single minister to cover the portfolios of two or more previous ministers. However, these 'reforms' have not resulted in significant functional change.

The government has also decentralised the decision-making authority of a small range of administrative matters to state/region governments, a notable change in the functioning of the government structures. While these changes have little bearing on trade and investment to date, decentralisation of investment approvals for smaller investments has been floated. While states/regions have control over some administrative matters, their influence over the business environment is limited. This is a missed opportunity to encourage states and regions to compete for FDI and local investment through locally-driven reform programmes.

Despite changes to some bureaucratic structures, many of the longstanding problematic characteristics of state institutions remain. These include:

- *Heavy emphasis on licensing and control*: Licensing of economic activities is a key function of the state, a characteristic which derives from the socialist and military eras. Many union-level ministries engage in business licensing, from Ministry of Industry to Ministry of Finance to Ministry of Agriculture. Requirements for licensing vary considerably, with some types of licences (large-scale mining, banking) being immensely difficult to obtain. Licence renewal is often used by the state as a way to ensure compliance with the law or exert other types of pressure on the private sector.

- *Lack of regulatory capacity*: Much of the country's regulatory apparatus was dismantled during the socialist era, as it was no longer needed in a state-run economy. This has largely not been rebuilt, with government instead relying on licensing as the key mechanism to control private business. The lack of adequate regulatory capacity is a key constraint in some sectors, for example in the financial sector, where a competent regulator is needed to help ensure stability of the financial system.
- *Arbitrary policymaking*: Numerous instances of snap decisions by the Thein Sein government evidenced the continued inability of the state to provide predictability for economic actors. For example, the announcement of the minimum wage in August 2015, despite years of process, gave private businesses three days before the law came into effect. It was characterised by immense confusion over working hours, weekend payment rates, and other problems. Arbitrary application of the law is also common, as evidenced by the targeting of foreign-connected restaurant chains for failure to comply with tax laws, in an environment where tax fraud is commonplace.
- *Lack of authority and delegation*: The civil service in Myanmar remains heavily hierarchical. Lower level staff have little decision-making authority, even over mundane matters. Even simple requests often require high level approval. For example, approval in some states/regions to erect a billboard must come from the state/region Chief Minister, while permission to visit a government-owned factory slated for privatisation may be required from the relevant minister.
- *Lack of capacity*: Many civil servants, including higher-level transfers from the military, lack the technical capacity to implement their assigned portfolios. Though international assistance to Myanmar has focused heavily on improving government capacity, it remains a serious challenge.

Challenges and risks

Building economic institutions that engage with the private sector and enable trade and investment is a fundamental challenge for the NLD. To date, however, the reforms to the civil service have been superficial. The first major move of the NLD, as noted earlier, was to reduce the number of ministerial portfolios. However, many of the newly appointed ministers, as well as state/region Chief Ministers, lack civil service experience. This will only increase the challenge of bringing reforms to a bureaucracy which has long placed a heavy emphasis on monitoring and control. While trade and investment are likely to continue to grow over the short term, bureaucratic reform will be a notable medium to long term challenge. It is vital that the NLD effectively manages and reforms the bureaucracy so that it contributes to a more predictable and efficient business environment, which will have important benefits for sustained growth in trade and FDI.

Another major challenge for the NLD is the successful management of its relationship with the military, so as to ensure that the government retains the space to lead policy reform. The reaction to an unfavourable election result evidences that the military is willing to allow the NLD to take on a greater role in governance of the country. Despite this, the military retains a set of important interests, including its current privileged position from the 2008 constitution and a range of business interests. However, the initial stages of the NLD administration have not seen significant reforms that challenge military economic interests. Economic concerns seem to have taken a back seat in NLD–military relations, with the peace process and security concerns taking precedence.

Another major risk to the continued liberalisation and reform of trade and investment is the maintenance of internal order and cohesion in the NLD. At present, the party remains heavily centred around Aung San Suu Kyi, and it is not clear whether the party has succession plans. Similarly, while the party has largely fallen in line behind Suu Kyi during its first months in office, it is possible that some elements of the NLD may become more vocal about policy directions in the future. This certainly raises the risk that instability within the party could distract attention from the reform of trade and investment policies.

Though the former government concluded a 'nationwide' ceasefire with eight ethnic groups, conflict and ethnic tensions remain a key risk for the continued growth of Myanmar's trade and FDI. The direct risk is most evident in the potential of conflict to inhibit overland trade development, as Myanmar's major overland trading corridors pass through conflict-affected areas. Without greater stability it is unlikely that many improvements will be made in trade-related infrastructure in these areas. Conflict will limit access to natural resources in conflict-affected areas, though given the relatively poor state of public financial management and environmental regulation of resources, as well as their ability to sustain conflict, it is likely a perverse benefit that these resources stay in the ground.

While the risks of conflict dampening trade and FDI growth across the country are moderate, they are acute in areas controlled by ethnic minority groups and the major barrier that prevents some ethnic people from benefiting from the liberalisation. Without increased trade and investment in these areas, the risk of further economic divergence between the centre and periphery is great, which could further fuel tensions between the Burmese government/military and ethnic minority groups. Ethnic tensions, notably with the country's Muslim and South Asian populations and especially the Rohingya, are unlikely to be resolved in the near future. This may have some consequences for trade and FDI, especially if they increase the reputational risk of investing in Myanmar.

A final risk for trade and investment is the continuing desire of many in government and the private sector to retain Bamar control over the economy. A cursory review of the country's colonial history shows that much of the impetus for greater state involvement in the post-colonial economy was due to the country's colonial experience, in which foreign business dominated the economy. Burma rejected free trade and capitalism once before, because it had become 'synonymous with imperialism and exploitation' (Fenichel and Huff 1975, 329). Recent evidence, notably the visceral reaction to the spurt of Chinese resource and hydropower investments in 2011–12, shows that a similar sentiment remains. While present-day Myanmar has much to gain from reforming trade and allowing FDI, there is a risk in reforms creating a perception that foreign businesses once again have an outsize role in the domestic economy. Given this tumultuous history, it is incumbent upon all stakeholders – especially the international community – to understand how the Myanmar private sector and the country generally view reforms. For example, some international institutions, including the OECD and the World Bank, have made calls for Myanmar to ensure a level playing field between foreign and domestic investors (OECD 2014; Rahardja et al. 2016). Calls for a 'level playing field' in one area – e.g. investment legislation – should not be removed from a context in which domestic enterprises face greater hurdles in other areas, not least access to finance. While the domestic private sector can benefit from both cooperation and competition with foreign enterprises, it is essential that the overall enabling environment does not disadvantage one to the benefit of the other.

Conclusion

Growth in Myanmar's trade and investment has been impressive, and while it has brought some much needed benefits to the economy and the people, it also raises a host of challenges moving forward. The perception of foreign dominance over the economy, and the fervent nationalism it fed, was a key driver of the country's move towards greater government control of the economy and eventually a socialist-style economy (or at least the pretence of one). Myanmar's liberalisation to date reflects this historical experience, with reforms in some areas complemented by intransigence in others. Vested interests continue to play an important role in shaping the economic transition. More difficult reforms will come for Myanmar. Some of the low-hanging fruit, for example the removal of the former multi-tiered exchange rate policy, provided so few benefits and such egregious distortions that its removal was a political non-event. Yet harder reforms must be forthcoming, in areas like land and finance, which may challenge vested interests or create significant groups of economic losers. Given the perverse incentives that shaped economic activity for much of the past half-century, such deeper reforms are unavoidable.

References

Asian Development Bank. 2011. *Key Indicators for Asia and the Pacific 2011*. Mandaluyong City, Philippines: Asian Development Bank.

Bissinger, Jared. 2012. 'Foreign Investment in Myanmar: A Resource Boom but a Development Bust'. *Contemporary Southeast Asia* 34 (1): 23–52.

Fenichel, Allen, and Gregg Huff. 1975. 'Colonialism and the Economic System of an Independent Burma'. *Modern Asian Studies* 9 (03): 321–335.

Global Witness. 2015. *Jade: Myanmar's Big State Secret*. London: Global Witness.

Government of the Republic of the Union of Myanmar. 2012. Foreign Investment Law. Yangon: Government of the Republic of the Union of Myanmar.

Government of the Republic of the Union of Myanmar. 2013. Framework for Economic and Social Reforms. Naypyitaw, Myanmar: Government of the Republic of the Union of Myanmar.

Government of the Union of Myanmar. 1989. State-owned Economic Enterprise Law. The State Law and Order Restoration Council Law No. 9/1989. Yangon, Myanmar.

International Monetary Fund. 2015. Myanmar: Staff Report for the 2015 Article IV Consultation. Washington, DC, Country Report No. 15/267.

Ministry of Commerce. 2015. Myanmar Trade Development Landscape. 5th NIU Exchange Program, Session 1, Trade and Development Program Updates. Siem Riep, Cambodia.

Myanmar Central Statistical Organization. 2016. http://mmsis.gov.mm/statHtml/statHtml.do

Organization for Economic Cooperation and Development. 2014. *OECD Investment Policy Reviews: Myanmar 2014*. OECD Publishing.

Rahardja, Sjamsu, Artuso, Fabio, Cadot, Olivier and Rahardja, Sjamsu. 2016. Main report. Washington, DC: World Bank Group. http://documents.worldbank.org/curated/en/899541467002864601/Main-report.

Tin Maung Maung Than. 2007. *State Dominance in Myanmar: The Political Economy of Industrialization*. Singapore: Institute of Southeast Asian Studies.

World Bank. 1995. Myanmar: Policies for Sustaining Economic Reform. Washington, DC: World Bank Group.

PART V

Governance

22
THE EXECUTIVE

Ian Holliday and Su Mon Thazin Aung

When Burma gained independence from Britain in January 1948, it was fitted out with a Westminster-style system of parliamentary government in which prime minister and cabinet formed the most significant parts of the executive. This system remained in place for nearly a decade and a half, even surviving an 18-month period of caretaker military government from 1958 to 1960 that saw General Ne Win assume the premiership and appoint his own cabinet, but leave intact the basic structure of government. It was destroyed, however, by a full-blown coup performed by Ne Win in March 1962, which replaced the governance model created at independence with a military-backed Leninist control apparatus focused originally on an eight-member Revolutionary Council (RC) (Taylor 2009, 296), and from January 1974 on the Burma Socialist Programme Party (BSPP). In turn, this regime collapsed during Burma's 8-8-88 uprising for democracy, and in September 1988 a 19-member military junta took its place (Lintner 1989). Initially called the State Law and Order Restoration Council (SLORC), the junta was known from November 1997 as the State Peace and Development Council (SPDC). In March 2011, a new path was taken when a transition was launched from direct military rule to quasi-civilian government focused on an indirectly elected president authorized to make a wide array of executive appointments. When the opposition National League for Democracy (NLD) won the November 2015 general election and took office in March 2016, a special position of state counsellor was established to enable long-standing leader Aung San Suu Kyi to direct the business of government despite a constitutional provision barring her from the presidency. The new polity remains a work in progress.

Within the executive, the past 70 years have witnessed considerable continuity with many structures carried over from one era to the next, not least because resource limitations have required incoming rulers to make do with existing institutions. At the same time, however, each successive political regime has seen new features come to the fore that, cumulatively, have altered the executive quite significantly. First, the focus on a dominant individual, visible even in a 'first among equals' system of prime minister and cabinet, became increasingly pronounced as the decades passed. In the RC from 1962 to 1974, and also under the BSPP from 1974 to 1988, Ne Win was the dominant figure (Taylor 2009, 367–73). Similarly, in the SLORC, and still more in the SPDC, Senior General Than Shwe established significant control following his rise to the top in April 1992. In the current NLD administration, Aung San Suu Kyi is clearly preeminent, despite having had to permit one of her close associates to assume the presidency.

Second, the deconstruction of British modes of cabinet government, and the creation of a command and control structure, evident in 1962 and fully codified in 1974, was also maintained by the junta from 1988 to 2011 and continued to echo thereafter. Still today, the political system remains highly centralized. Third, the militarization of the executive sphere, through the appointment to elite positions of individuals with current or recent military experience, was also a practice brought forward from 1962 (or 1958). Even though the NLD administration that took office in 2016 sought significantly to reduce the military presence in the upper echelons of government, this remains a feature of the system.

This chapter seeks both to contextualize the attempts made since 2011 to build a functioning executive and to explore how the system currently operates. First, it looks briefly at the executive from 1948 to 2011. Second, it turns to the underpinnings of the present system by examining provisions written into Myanmar's 2008 constitution. Third, it analyses the executive in transitional Myanmar from 2011 to 2017, focusing on the major policymaking bodies. Fourth, it presents three case studies of Thein Sein's executive in operation. Finally, in conclusion, it considers the major challenges facing the Myanmar executive under President Htin Kyaw and State Counsellor Aung San Suu Kyi.

The executive from 1948 to 2011

Burma's first post-colonial constitution was enacted by a constituent assembly in September 1947, and became effective at independence in January 1948. Drawing on an eclectic mix of American, British, French and Yugoslavian practice (Cady 1958, 560), it contained a series of checks and balances and enunciated a clear commitment to social progress. Furnivall (1960, 31) described it as 'a liberal Constitution with socialist aspirations'. The 1947 constitution provided for democratic national elections to a bicameral Union Parliament comprising a lower Chamber of Deputies and an upper Chamber of Nationalities (Chapter VI). In joint session, the two chambers were empowered to elect by secret ballot a president to serve as head of state (Chapter V). Furnivall argued that the president was more than 'merely an ornamental figurehead', for alongside several specified powers he or she had the right to be consulted, to encourage and to warn (Furnivall 1960, 35). Nevertheless, in the 1947 constitution most executive authority was vested in a Union Government made up of a prime minister plus a series of cabinet ministers nominated by the premier for appointment by the president (Chapter VII). This system, led by U Nu as prime minister for most of its 14-year existence, was somewhat compromised by Ne Win's interim premiership from October 1958 to April 1960, which had the ambiguous character of a constitutional coup. It remained intact, however, and resumed normal operations when Nu again served as prime minister in the early 1960s (Thompson 1960, 133–4). Throughout, it was designed to follow the core conventions of the British cabinet system (Cady 1958, 560).

Supporting the executive was a civil service secretariat, modelled on British colonial practice and housed mainly in the distinctive building in central Rangoon where Aung San and several members of his provisional cabinet were assassinated in July 1947 (Furnivall 1960, 63; Tinker 1967). The personnel staffing the civil service were very different, however, from the administrative elite developed under British colonialism. In just six months from October 1947 to April 1948, for instance, nearly 58 per cent of top-grade civil servants resigned (Taylor 2009, 268). The result was that the executive rarely functioned smoothly, partly because of difficulties in adapting a Westminster-style system to Burmese conditions, partly because of a significant lack of capacity, partly because it was overwhelmed by the tasks faced after independence, and partly because of widening fissures within the governing party (Cady 1958; Furnivall 1960; Trager

1966; Tinker 1967). Indeed, in the democratic interlude from 1948 to 1962, the most dynamic period of executive government came during the 18-month military interregnum from 1958 to 1960 (Thompson 1960).

Ne Win's March 1962 coup abrogated Burma's 1947 constitution, did away entirely with liberal-democratic parliamentary practice and set in place the RC (Trager 1966). Socialist in aspiration and provided with forceful military backing, the RC sought to create a Leninist political system with centralized command and control structures (Charney 2009, 108–11). The district level of administration that was essential to colonial governance was thus replaced by a system of security and administration committees stretching from the core down through each territorial level to the village tract or ward (Taylor 2009, 315). In March 1972 the colonial-style civil service secretariat was abolished, and ministers gained the ability to communicate directly with their own departments, rather than having to work through a tier of permanent secretaries (Taylor 2009, 313). Moreover, many top civil servants were replaced by serving military officers reporting directly to the more senior military officers appointed to the RC (Taylor 2009, 313–14). Ultimately, this system was embodied in a new constitution adopted in January 1974, which placed at the heart of a single-party state the BSPP, formed in July 1962 as a small cadre party and turned in the 1970s into a mass party (Taylor 2009, 316–27). Crouch (2014, 43) writes that this constitution 'signalled the overt rejection of the separation of powers'. Throughout the polity, strong executive oversight was established. Inside the executive, however, there was also some continuity. The 1974 constitution brought into being a Council of State whose chairman served as president and head of state (Chapter V). It established a Council of Ministers, designated the highest executive organ of the state, elected by a unicameral parliament (Pyithu Hluttaw) and led by a prime minister (Chapter VI). The key changes introduced by the RC, and by no means dispelled by the advent of a BSPP regime after 1974, were the emergence of a dominant leader around which an entire system of military-style control revolved (Williams 2014, 119). Built to some extent on Burmese political practice in the late 1950s, this nevertheless ran directly counter to the provisions of the 1947 constitution.

Under SLORC from 1988 and the SPDC from 1997, there was no constitution, no parliament and no attempt to codify national governance (Crouch 2014). Instead, ad hoc forms of command and control operated through structures inherited from the BSPP's one-party state, many of which slowly atrophied under direct military rule (Englehart 2005). After April 1992, the entire polity focused increasingly on the dominant figure of Than Shwe. Moreover, with the switch from SLORC to SPDC in November 1997, four individuals carried over from the first junta to the second formed a central executive. Alongside SPDC Chairman Than Shwe, the most important individual until his ouster in an October 2004 purge was General Khin Nyunt, SPDC Secretary 1 and head of the Office of Strategic Services, a powerful and shadowy intelligence organization. Also significant was SPDC Vice-Chairman Vice-Senior General Maung Aye (Taylor 2009, 476–85). The National Security Council (NSC), chaired by Maung Aye until 2007 and by Shwe Mann from 2007 to 2011, operated as a super cabinet and took important political, security and latterly economic decisions. One task overseen by the junta during more than two decades in power was the writing of a constitution for a new political system.

The executive in the 2008 constitution

Myanmar's current constitution, drafted by military leaders and endorsed by citizens through a sham May 2008 referendum, provides for a formal executive focused on an indirectly elected president. This part of the executive consists of the president, two vice-presidents, a series of cabinet ministers and the attorney general (Article 200). It is formed after a general election has taken place for the two chambers of the national legislature (Pyidaungsu Hluttaw): the lower House of Representatives (Pyithu Hluttaw), and the upper House of Nationalities (Amyotha Hluttaw). Within 90 days of the general election, the legislature must convene (Article 123). Alongside the elected members, each house is given a 25 per cent complement of serving military officers appointed by the commander-in-chief of the defence services (Articles 109, 141). In something of an echo of the 1947 constitution, the legislature then creates a Presidential Electoral College with three components: elected members from the lower house, elected members from the upper house and members from both houses appointed by the commander-in-chief. Each sector nominates a vice-president from within parliament or outside. The Presidential Electoral College then elects a president, and the remaining two nominees continue as vice-presidents (Article 60). All serve for five-year terms, and for a maximum of ten years in total (Article 61). The president has wide powers of appointment, choosing cabinet members from within parliament and outside and making other executive appointments with little legislative oversight (Williams 2014, 127). No member of the formal executive can simultaneously be a member of the legislature (Articles 62, 232). The president is given a 14-day power of delay over legislation, but no formal veto (Article 105). This too reflects provisions in the 1947 constitution (Furnivall 1960, 34).

An additional feature of Myanmar's executive is that, in common with the legislature, it has direct military representation and engagement. Three top cabinet members, heading the security-related Ministries of Defence, Home Affairs and Border Affairs, are selected not by the president, but rather by the commander-in-chief, and remain serving military officers (Article 232). The Minister for Home Affairs directs the General Administration Department (GAD), which oversees public administration all the way down to the grassroots level. Beyond that, the constitution creates a National Defence and Security Council (NDSC) chaired by the president and containing the two vice-presidents, the two speakers from the houses of parliament, the commander-in-chief and his deputy, the minister for foreign affairs, and the three cabinet ministers selected by the commander-in-chief (Article 201). Formally, this generates five serving military officers out of eleven members: the three cabinet ministers, plus the commander-in-chief and his deputy. However, the influence of the military spreads further than this, since one individual among the triumvirate of president and two vice-presidents was the military nominee to the Presidential Electoral College (Williams 2014, 121–2), and others may retain close military ties from previous stages in their careers. The constitution vests important executive functions in the NDSC, thereby placing clear limits on the authority of the formal core of the executive, represented by the president and cabinet. Although the president is authorized to appoint the commander-in-chief of the defence services, it is the NDSC that proposes a candidate and approves the president's decision (Article 342). Similarly, the NDSC is authorized to approve the creation of people's militia by the defence services (Article 340). Additionally, should the president wish to declare a state of emergency, this must be done in coordination with the NDSC (Article 410). Moreover, the NDSC assumes executive, legislative and judicial power in the period between the holding of a general election and the creation of the relevant bodies (Article 427). In these ways, constitutional provisions ensure that Myanmar retains a military-weighted executive.

The transitional executive, 2011–17

Since the return to constitutional government in 2011, Myanmar has had executives formally headed by President Thein Sein (2011–16) and President Htin Kyaw (since 2016). Each has respected the constitutional provision requiring that three top security-related ministries be led by serving military officers chosen by the commander-in-chief. In other respects, though, the executives formed under the two presidents have been rather different.

Thein Sein initially created an executive of 30 ministers, most of whom were retired military officers, to oversee 34 ministries. In August 2012, the number of ministers without portfolio in the President's Office, originally set at two, was boosted to six, and the total number of ministries was increased to 36. The ministers without portfolio were tasked with coordinating the activities of clusters of line ministers, thereby generating a kind of super cabinet. In September 2013, five major cabinet committees were created with vice-presidents and senior ministers in the chair, and the rhythm of regular cabinet meetings was changed from once a week to once every two weeks. Mostly, however, Thein Sein dealt bilaterally with line ministers and then took an agreed policy decision to cabinet for endorsement. This ensured that cabinet, serviced by a Cabinet Office located at 18 Naypyitaw, operated as little more than a passive and formal part of the executive. Similarly, the NDSC met roughly once a month throughout Thein Sein's term. Against expectations, however, it was also of only limited policy significance. In April 2015, the president created a raft of permanent secretaries to serve under the ministers and chairmen of central offices, and began to appoint close cadres to these positions.

Under Thein Sein, the super cabinet that coalesced into being in August 2012 took the place of the junta's NSC as the main executive policy forum. Two ministers without portfolio were close to the president throughout his administration: Aung Min charged with security policy and policy related to the peace process, and above all Soe Thein charged with economic and financial policy. Both were based at 14 Naypyitaw, though most of their staff members were located in the President's Office. Nevertheless, 14 Naypyitaw became a key office for transacting executive business. Supporting the work of these senior ministers was the Myanmar Peace Centre (MPC), a highly influential semi-governmental agency led mainly by civilian former exiles.

Complementing the executive functions of the super cabinet, and often overlapping with it, was a set of officials and advisers working directly to the president. Under Thein Sein, the President's Office contained roughly 350 officials serving the president and the six ministers without portfolio. Among these, some 160 officials were based in the presidential palace in Naypyitaw, and the rest were distributed around buildings within the city, including the Cabinet Office. Inside the presidential palace, the key offices were the directorate office of the president (26 officials), the directorate offices of the two vice-presidents (46 officials), the research and development unit (13 officials) and the advisory team (19 individuals). Around 20 officials, mostly from the directorate office of the president and the research and development unit, had key policy functions, undertaking coordinating roles across the whole range of government business, and also engaging with the president to take ad hoc decisions. The 19 individuals appointed to presidential advisory boards within the presidential palace covered broad policy areas such as political, economic, social, legal, religious, education and health matters. The three-member political committee was headed by Ko Ko Hlaing, a retired army colonel with experience in the research department of the War Office. The four-member economic committee was headed by U Myint, formerly professor of economics at the University of Yangon (and known to be close to Aung San Suu Kyi). The four-member legal committee was headed by Sit Aye, a retired police colonel with extensive administrative experience. Most members of these boards had close personal ties to the president.

When the NLD formed an executive in March 2016, formally under Htin Kyaw, it cut the number of ministers in half, removed all deputy minister positions and moved away from Thein Sein's heavy reliance on individuals with a strong military pedigree. Aung San Suu Kyi headed 4 ministries, and 17 other ministers took charge of 17 other ministries. Within a week, however, the State Counsellor Bill was approved by parliament, and Aung San Suu Kyi assumed the position. She quickly relinquished control of the Ministry of Education and the Ministry of Electric Power and Energy, keeping within her portfolio the Ministry of Foreign Affairs (and a seat on the NDSC) and the position of Minister of the President's Office (and a supervisory role at the heart of government business). Kyaw Tint Swe was appointed to the position of Minister of the Office of the State Counsellor, and the office soon amassed a significant staffing complement. Cabinet thereby expanded to 21 mostly civilian ministers, with the state counsellor effectively becoming head of government in a prime ministerial role and the president becoming a somewhat titular head of state. From the outset all major cabinet committees were chaired by Aung San Suu Kyi, who was also the only female cabinet minister. Cabinet itself continued to meet once every two weeks, and remained a largely insignificant policy forum in comparison with cabinet committees. In the first year of NLD government, the NDSC did not meet at all.

On taking office, the NLD made a number of structural changes to the executive. Reflecting the special position of Aung San Suu Kyi, the Office of the State Counsellor, located at 20 Naypyitaw, emerged as a key component working in close collaboration with the President's Office. In something of a compensating reform, Thein Sein's six President's Office ministries were consolidated into one, also headed by Aung San Suu Kyi. As has already been noted, the number of ministries was considerably reduced. Just outside the executive, the MPC, a critical government think tank under Thein Sein, was recast in July 2016 as the National Reconciliation and Peace Centre (NRPC). Comprising 11 senior figures from the executive, the legislature and the military forces, and again chaired by the state counsellor, the NRPC was established as an official government body rather than a semi-governmental organization. It thereby acquired the potential to become even more influential than its predecessor. Beyond these reforms, many of which were triggered by the particular circumstances of a government in which the state counsellor operates 'above the president', much of the executive domain remained largely unchanged.

Case studies of Thein Sein's executive in operation

Beyond the clear dominance of Aung San Suu Kyi, and the significance of her bilateral and multilateral dealings with cabinet ministers and officials, the inner workings of the NLD government are not yet well understood. By contrast, we do have considerable information about how the USDP administration functioned. Among many critical policy issues that surfaced during Thein Sein's presidency, three were the 2011 decision to suspend for the remainder of his term work on the Myitsone Dam project, the 2014 public service media bill designed to move the country decisively beyond state censorship and control of the media, and the 2014 decision to accept use of the word 'federalism' in peace talks with ethnic armed groups. Each sheds light on the workings of his executive.

The Myitsone Dam hydropower project was deeply controversial throughout Myanmar because of its environmental impact, its destruction of communities in Kachin State and its association with a Chinese investor committed to channelling most of the electricity generated by the project to China. The decision to suspend construction work came in September 2011 at the end of the first six months of Thein Sein's term, and was widely seen as confirming his commitment to political reform. For many weeks leading up to it, the Myitsone controversy had dominated national politics and been covered extensively by global media. It became especially sensitive when Aung San Suu Kyi joined widespread civil society mobilization. The issue was thereby placed firmly on the executive's policy agenda. Initially it was addressed by the president and his advisory team, the responsible minister Zaw Min, senior members of the USDP and the NDSC. At that stage, the option of suspending construction work had least support. On September 17, the government organized a workshop in Naypyitaw to discuss Myitsone's environmental impact. Senior ministers, civil society leaders and representatives of the Chinese investor were invited to attend. Instead of pointing the way to resolution of the issue, however, the workshop generated deep division and heated argument among ministers. Zaw Min therefore sketched a series of options, of which the most viable appeared to be inviting parliament to take a decision. On September 27, he submitted to Thein Sein a draft to this effect. On September 29, though, Thein Sein surprised the ministers assembled in cabinet by stating that he intended to announce that the project would be suspended. On September 30, he communicated this decision to parliament and, through it, to the people. Key players involved in earlier discussions, including Zaw Min, only learned about Thein Sein's announcement at the very last minute. In this case, then, the president took control of the policy process at a late stage and, operating largely in isolation from other key actors within the executive, engineered a dramatic policy change.

The public service media bill was less controversial than Myitsone, and did not generate an equivalent wave of public protest. Rather, it was one of a number of reformist measures undertaken to move the country away from authoritarianism towards liberalism and democracy. The context was 50 years of state censorship and control. Initial steps taken by the Thein Sein government included deregulation of the media, and in an August 2012 cabinet reshuffle replacement of Minister of Information Kyaw Hsan, known to be a hardliner, by Aung Kyi, thought to be more conciliatory. With Thein Sein's backing, Aung Kyi took a public service media bill to cabinet for endorsement in April 2013. Thereafter, however, executive support for the bill began to drain away as the president and a series of senior ministers led by Soe Thein began to feel the negative effects of Myanmar's more pluralistic media environment. Such pressures were heightened as the country moved closer to the 2015 general election. At the same time, media professionals argued that the bill did not go far enough. Although Aung Kyi secured cabinet endorsement of a revised bill in March 2014, increasingly hardline measures taken against journalists undermined his credibility within the government and in wider society. Thein Sein's response in July 2014 was to remove him from office. In March 2015, Minister of Information Ye Htut withdrew the bill from parliament, thereby killing it off. Again, the president had operated decisively to trigger a significant policy shift (in favour of inaction).

Use of the term 'federalism' in peace talks with ethnic armed groups was a sensitive issue because, for decades reaching back at least to Ne Win's 1962 coup, military leaders had recoiled from a political direction thought likely to lead to fragmentation of the entire country. By contrast, ethnic communities had long been committed to federalism as the only workable political solution for a polity marked by considerable ethnic diversity. During peace talks led for the government by Aung Min, the issue inevitably surfaced as a critical roadblock on the path to the nationwide ceasefire agreement sought by negotiators on both sides. Over time, it became clear to Aung Min and the MPC team working closely with him that the government would have to agree to discuss the issue of federalism in talks with ethnic armed groups, and in August 2014 he gained the president's permission to do so. However, it appears that this decision was not taken by any formal committee, and that when it was presented to the NDSC on August 14 it was merely to inform members of a policy switch that had already been made. Again, the president was able to act largely in isolation from the rest of the executive he headed.

Together, these three cases indicate the considerable room for manoeuvre exercised by Thein Sein within the Myanmar executive. In the Myitsone and federalism cases, he operated as sole policymaker, taking advice on an ad hoc basis and reaching strongly presidential decisions. In the public service media case, he allowed the mechanisms of cabinet government to function until this no longer suited him, and then stopped the policy process in its tracks.

Conclusion: major challenges facing the Myanmar executive

Myanmar's November 2015 general election resulted in a landslide victory for Aung San Suu Kyi and the NLD, and at the end of March 2016 saw Htin Kyaw take over from Thein Sein as president. Aung San Suu Kyi soon assumed the position of state counsellor. Many challenges face the current government, the country's first truly civilian-led administration in 55 years. First, the pivotal position of state counsellor has no constitutional foundation, and is viewed with suspicion by military MPs and the wider military command structure. If not handled carefully, there is a chance it could one day trigger a constitutional crisis. Second, the degree of executive focus on Aung San Suu Kyi generates significant problems for the smooth running of government business, with problems of isolation, overload and a failure to coordinate policy across the deep silos established by government departments already evident in the first year of NLD government. Third, the dramatic reduction in the number of government ministries, while a necessary and welcome step, poses coordination and workload issues for the newly appointed civilian cabinet ministers. Moreover, many senior bureaucrats at the permanent secretary and director general levels are former military officers, again pointing to potential problems. Additionally, control of the GAD by the Ministry of Home Affairs ensures that the entire state bureaucracy falls under military oversight, making it difficult for the NLD to implement reform. Fourth, many aspects of executive business, notably those focused on internal and external security, require the NLD to work together with military figures, and generate considerable tension. In particular, the ongoing peace process embracing ethnic groups and inter-communal conflict and violence in Rakhine State generate real challenges for this delicate relationship. It is thus possible that the NDSC, unused during the first year of NLD government and not particularly influential during Thein Sein's term, could emerge as a key forum in which NLD and military elites come together within the executive. If that does happen, its inbuilt military majority could generate deep controversy. Fifth, the sheer size of the policy agenda facing the government and the weight of public expectation borne by it inevitably place great stress on the executive branch.

The executive inherited by the NLD administration under President Htin Kyaw and State Counsellor Aung San Suu Kyi fully reflects the power sharing between civilian and military elites written into Myanmar's 2008 constitution. It also lacks basic capacity and has long operated in informal ways. In addition to implementing reform in the wider society, the current government thus needs to restructure and retool the major instrument at its disposal. This is the greatest challenge currently facing the Myanmar executive.

References

Cady, J. F. 1958. *A History of Modern Burma*. Ithaca, NY: Cornell University Press.

Charney, M. W. 2009. *A History of Modern Burma*. Cambridge: Cambridge University Press.

Crouch, M. 2014. 'The Layers of Legal Development in Myanmar'. In *Law, Society and Transition in Myanmar*, edited by M. Crouch and T. Lindsey, 33–56. Oxford: Hart.

Englehart, N. A. 2005. 'Is Regime Change Enough for Burma? The Problem of State Capacity'. *Asian Survey* 45 (4): 622–44.

Furnivall, J. S. 1960. *The Governance of Modern Burma, 2nd ed.* New York: Institute of Pacific Relations.

Lintner, B. 1989. *Outrage: Burma's Struggle for Democracy*. Bangkok: White Lotus.

Taylor, R. H. 2009. *The State in Myanmar*. Honolulu, HI: University of Hawai'i Press.
Thompson, J. S. 1960. 'A Second Chance for Burma: The Interim Government and the 1960 Elections'. In *The Governance of Modern Burma*, 2nd ed., edited by J. S. Furnivall, 133–54. New York: Institute of Pacific Relations.
Tinker, H. 1967. *The Union of Burma: A Study of the First Years of Independence*, 4th ed. London: Oxford University Press.
Trager, F. N. 1966. *Burma, from Kingdom to Republic: A Historical and Political Analysis*. Westport, CT: Greenwood Press.
Williams, D. C. 2014. 'What's So Bad about Burma's 2008 Constitution? A Guide for the Perplexed'. In *Law, Society and Transition in Myanmar*, edited by M. Crouch and T. Lindsey, 117–39. Oxford: Hart.

23
LEGISLATURE

Renaud Egreteau and Cindy Joelene

One of the most surprising illustrations of political change at work in 'post-junta' Myanmar was the resurgence of parliamentary affairs after general elections were held on November 7, 2010. Representative assemblies and the development of legislative activities are key components of political change (Fish 2006; Arter 2009). Several parliaments in Asia have recently shown how legislative institutions can foster democratization in the region (Ziegenhain 2008; Case 2011; Zheng et al. 2014). While the legislative branch has not yet become the nodal centre of Myanmar's public life, it has nonetheless played a critical role in the transitional process engaged after the disbanding of the State Peace and Development Council (SPDC) in 2011.

The Constitution ratified in 2008 has outlined the reinstatement of a bicameral Union parliament (*Pyidaungsu Hluttaw*), a first since the 1947 Constitution, as well as fourteen subnational assemblies – one for each of the seven regions and seven states of the Union. The first 'post-junta' national legislature, convened between January 2011 and January 2016, has rapidly gained a heightened political status (Kean 2013; Egreteau 2014b; Fink 2015). Efforts to bring about political pluralism and contradictory debates in parliament, while at the same time conferring a certain degree of legitimacy on the ongoing military-led transition, have proved resilient. This has been particularly obvious since Aung San Suu Kyi and 40 other members of her National League for Democracy (NLD) entered the Union parliament in April 2012, and even more so with her party's thundering victory in the second round of post-SPDC elections held on November 8, 2015. However, still in its infancy, Myanmar's new legislature remains vulnerable, especially at the provincial level (Holliday et al. 2015). This chapter proposes to shed light on the complexities of Myanmar's re-emergence of national and local legislative politics since 2010.

A backgrounder to legislative affairs in Myanmar

The development of representative institutions in Myanmar was a rather slow and quite erratic process during the course of the twentieth century. Since independence, the country has held only six competitive multiparty elections: in 1951, 1956, 1960, and then 1990, 2010 and 2015. The formation of the first representative assembly preceded independence, though. In 1923, the British established a unicameral Legislative Council for Burma, replicating a set of reforms implemented in their other Indian colonies in 1919. Of the Council's 103 members, 80 were elected, including 58 by the ethnic Bamar majority; 45 seats were allotted to communal groups (such as the European, Anglo-Burman and Indian communities) and various business organizations or labour movements (Trager 1966, 48). After the holding of the first elections to this assembly in 1922, three other nationwide polls followed in 1925, 1928 and 1932. These elections were, however, characterized by low turnouts and widespread boycott campaigns, all inspired by rising anti-colonial forces (Taylor 1996, 166–7). The Government of Burma Act 1935 ensured the political separation of Burma from the rest of British-controlled India. It came into effect after a new round of elections was held in 1936. The Legislative Council was then redesigned as a bicameral legislature composed of a 36-member Senate and a 132-member House of Representatives (Trager 1966, 52). The principle of separate communal and appointive representation was maintained and even extended (Taylor 1996, 168).

As the Burmese started to march towards independence after the end of the Second World War, a constituent assembly was elected in April 1947. Five months later, a decisive meeting of the 255-member body disclosed a new constitution. Postcolonial Myanmar was thereafter to operate under an independent, republican and parliamentary system of government. Subsequently, competitive legislative elections were held in 1951, 1956 and 1960 to form the successive post-independence parliaments and governments of the Union (Maung Maung 1956, 1960; Srinivasan 1958). Voting was, however, never held in all constituencies during these polls; many areas of post-independence Myanmar remained unstable and plagued with armed insurgency. Beyond inter-ethnic conflicts, factional politics and ideological infighting also expanded dramatically over the course of the 1950s. The deep distrust of civilian politics which past and present Burmese military leaders have routinely nurtured certainly seems to stem from the divisive politicking observed during the first post-independence legislatures (Singh 1977; Callahan 1998; Kyaw Yin Hlaing 2008). This indeed propelled the Tatmadaw into power as early as 1958.

While the parliament was not disbanded after the first 'caretaking' military intervention between 1958 and 1960, the bicameral legislature was made irrelevant by the coup d'état staged by General Ne Win four years later, in March 1962. The Tatmadaw's second intrusion into state politics ended the country's early experiment with parliamentary democracy. In 1964, all political parties but one – the Burma Socialist Programme Party (BSPP) – were banned. In the early 1970s, however, Ne Win engaged in a re-civilianization of the national polity and a new constitution was adopted in 1974. The latter created a unicameral 'People's Assembly' (or *Pyithu Hluttaw*), which was meant to become the highest organ of the state. Its first 451 members, though elected by universal suffrage, were all members of (or closely affiliated with) the BSPP and the armed forces. Tightly-controlled parliamentary elections were arranged in January 1974, January 1978, October 1981 and October 1985. The People's Assembly's basic role remained that of a mere rubber-stamp parliament controlled by the single state party and, in the end, by Ne Win himself (Nakanishi 2013).

When General Saw Maung's newly formed junta – the SLORC – seized power in September 1988, it dissolved the legislature elected in 1985 and abrogated the 1974 Constitution. The new military regime promised the organization of multiparty elections designed to form a new 492-member legislature and ease the transfer of power back to civilians. The polls were held on May 27, 1990 and overwhelmingly won by the NLD. Instead of honouring the results, the SLORC proposed the convening of another constituent body, or National Convention, to draft a new constitution. Denounced by many observers as a sham assembly under full military control, the National Convention convened twice, from 1993 to 1996 and from 2004 to 2007 when it finally proposed an original constitutional text. The third constitution of the country was controversially approved by national referendum in May 2008. This adoption paved the way for the organization of a new round of multiparty elections – scheduled for November 2010 – and the formation, eventually, of a new legislature.

The renaissance of the legislature

The 2008 Constitution – in its chapter four, dealing with the legislature – provides for a bicameral national legislature (Union parliament, or *Pyidaungsu Hluttaw*), which is headquartered in Naypyitaw. It combines a 440-seat lower chamber (House of Representatives, or *Pyithu Hluttaw*) and a 224-member upper chamber (House of Nationalities, or *Amyotha Hluttaw*). Only three-quarters of the Union-level parliamentarians (or 498 seats) are elected by universal suffrage. The remaining quarter of each assembly is reserved for non-elected military representatives: a maximum ('not more than' or *ma po thaw*) of 110 seats for the lower house (article 109b) and 56 seats for the upper house (article 141b). Military legislators are directly appointed by the commander-in-chief of the armed forces. Pyithu Hluttaw's 330 constituencies are based on Myanmar's 330 townships, which include five newly crafted townships in Naypyitaw, Myanmar's capital city since 2005. In Amyotha Hluttaw, each state and region has an equal share of twelve elected seats (or a total of 168 seats). The two houses are meant to enjoy equal powers. The lower house, however, tends to be dominant, if only because the number of its legislators gives it an advantage whenever there is a decisive vote of the two houses gathered in congress (or *Pyidaungsu Hluttaw*).

The 2008 Constitution also created fourteen state and region legislative bodies: one parliament for each of the seven states (*Pyinae Hluttaw*) and the seven regions (*Tine Dae Tha Gyi Hluttaw*). Each of the country's 330 constituencies provides 2 seats to these subnational bodies, save those located in Naypyitaw (Holliday et al. 2015). Additional constituencies reserved for ethnic minorities are created if any of Myanmar's 135 recognized ethnic group represents more than 0.1 per cent of the country's total population in a given region or state. There were 29 of them available in both the 2010 and 2015 polls. The number of seats reserved to military officers in each of the latter must constitutionally correspond to a third of the total number of their elected civilian legislators – or mathematically speaking, about a quarter of the seats in each assembly (article 161b). When the fourteen state and region parliaments first convened in early 2011, 222 military representatives were seconded in all of them. In 2016, there were 220.

The first elections to these sixteen post-SPDC legislative bodies were held on November 7, 2010. With its leader still under house arrest, the NLD opted for a boycott. The results were widely condemned as a mockery, at home and abroad (Englehart 2012). The Union Solidarity and Development Party (USDP) won a substantial majority. A political platform made of retired military officers, ex-junta bureaucrats and powerful local businessmen, the SPDC-backed party secured 76 per cent of the elected seats as well as all sixteen speakerships (see Table 23.1). This was meant to ensure a controlled transition from direct military to semi-civilian administration. The legatee of Ne Win's BSPP, the National Unity Party (NUP), came in second with 5.4 per cent of the seats gained in the Union parliament. The Shan Nationalities Democratic Party (SNDP) followed, along with the Rakhine Nationalities Development Party (RNDP), the All Mon Regions Democracy Party (AMRDP) and the National Democratic Force (NDF), a breakaway faction of the NLD (see Table 23.1).

The second post-junta vote was held on November 8, 2015, exactly five years after the electoral controversies of 2010. It, however, proved among the freest, if not fairest, that Myanmar has known in decades (ICG 2015). About 10,000 Burmese and international observers, diplomats and journalists were allowed by the state-controlled Union Election Commission (UEC) to closely monitor the process in more than 40,000 polling stations throughout the country. Startlingly, the political parties that chose to compete in the 2010 elections – and which were key members of the so-called 'Third Force' positioned between the NLD and the army-backed elites – were wiped out five years later. Only 13 parties out of 92 in competition in 2015

Table 23.1 Seat composition of the Union parliament and fourteen region and state hluttaws after the 2010 elections

Political parties	*Pyithu hluttaw*	*Amyotha hluttaw*	*State and region hluttaws*	*Total*
USDP	259	129	495	883
Tatmadaw	110	56	222	388
NUP	12	5	46	63
SNDP	18	3	36	57
RNDP	9	7	19	35
AMRDP	3	4	9	16
NDF	8	4	4	16
CPP	2	4	6	12
PNO	3	1	6	10
CNP	2	2	5	9
PSDP	2	3	4	9
KPP	1	1	4	6
WDP	2	1	3	6
TPNP	1	1	4	6
INDP	1	0	4	5
UDPKS	1	1	2	4
DP-M	0	0	3	3
NDPD	0	0	2	2
KNP	0	0	2	2
KSDDP	0	1	1	2
88 Youths	0	0	1	1
LNDP	0	0	1	1
Independent	1	1	4	6
Vacant	5	0	0	5
Total	440	224	883	1,547

Source: Authors' own compilation.

secured a place in the new Union parliament (2016–2021). The incumbent USDP, as well as many incumbent ethnic Shan, Mon, Chin and Karen legislators, were all but crushed. On the other side, the NLD won a thundering victory: about 77 per cent of all seats available in the sixteen assemblies (see Table 23.2).

Initial functioning

The first session of the first post-SPDC Pyidaungsu Hluttaw (2011–2016) convened on January 31, 2011, at a time when the ruling junta still controlled all political structures. Dubbed the '*15-minute parliament*' by opposition media, the newly formed parliament attracted strong criticism. The low quality of the initial debates and the utter domination of the USDP might explain the blame (Horsey 2011). Ex-generals drawn from USDP ranks were chosen as speakers in both houses: Thura Shwe Mann in the lower house and Khin Aung Myint in the upper house. Most of the parliamentary committees were chaired by USDP legislators. A year later, however, the triumphant parliamentary entrance of Aung San Suu Kyi and 40 other politicians from the NLD greatly enhanced the prestige of the parliament. By-polls were indeed held on April 1, 2012 to replace the forty-odd USDP parliamentarians who had joined a ministerial cabinet or the UEC in early 2011, or were nominated as Chief Minister of one of the fourteen state and region governments.

Table 23.2 Seat composition of the Union parliament and fourteen state and region hluttaws after the 2015 general elections

Political parties	*Pyithu hluttaw*	*Amyotha hluttaw*	*State and region hluttaws*	*Total*
NLD	255	135	496	886
Tatmadaw	110	56	225	391
USDP	30	11	76	117
ANP/RNP	12	10	24	46
SNLD	12	3	26	41
TPNP	3	2	7	12
PNO	3	1	6	10
ZCD	2	2	2	6
Lisu NDP	2	0	3	5
KSDP	1	0	3	4
Independents	1	2	1	4
MNP	0	1	2	3
WDP	1	0	2	3
TNDP	0	0	2	2
Lahu NDP	0	0	2	2
NUP	0	1	0	1
AMRDP	0	0	1	1
KPP	0	0	1	1
KDUP	1	0	0	1
Akha NDP	0	0	1	1
SNDP	0	0	1	1
DP-M	0	0	1	1
UDPKS	0	0	1	1
WNUP	0	0	1	1
Vacant	7	0	14	21
Total	440	224	898	1,562

Source: Union Electoral Commission and ICG 2015, pp. 15–16.

Union level

Session after session, a sense of bold optimism emerged among the Union-level parliamentarians, including those belonging to the opposition to the ruling party (Moe Thuzar 2013; Egreteau 2014b). From the second plenary session which convened in August 2011, public questions began to be raised by elected MPs on matters once deemed too sensitive to deal with, such as the continuing incarceration of political prisoners, and illegal land-grabbing by local and state authorities as well as the denunciation of alleged human rights abuses carried out by the armed forces. Legislators have gradually started to challenge draft bills put forward for parliamentary discussion by President Thein Sein's cabinet (Fink 2015). Foreign and Burmese journalists have been allowed to follow internal workings, and many a legislator has proved eager to appear live on TV at the end of each daily session. As a matter of fact, news coverage of legislative activities has increased substantially since debates in both chambers are now recorded. Daily briefings on topics debated have been included in evening TV news broadcasts and – since 2015 – the state-run *Global New Light of Myanmar*, which devotes its second page to legislative affairs.

Only four standing committees are projected in each chamber by the 2008 Constitution. All other committees have to be framed *ad hoc*, according to the whims of the speakers. Forty-one standing parliamentary committees were formed in the Union parliament during the first post-SPDC legislature, including five joint committees gathering MPs from both houses. Joint committees are formed at the Pyidaungsu Hluttaw level by combining representatives from Pyithu Hluttaw and Amyotha Hluttaw when more coordination between the two hluttaws is needed. All committees comprise fifteen members each. In the NLD legislature, all include one woman MP and one military MP, which was not the case in the previous USDP legislature. They regularly gather to discuss drafts, vet budget papers and debate public complaint letters, including when the parliament is not in regular session. After her first election in 2012, Aung San Suu Kyi was asked to chair Pyithu Hluttaw's Rule of Law, Peace and Tranquillity Committee. A new parliamentary life that had disappeared when the last democratically elected parliament was dissolved in 1962 seems to have resurfaced (ICG 2013; Kean 2013). Between January 2011 and January 2016, the USDP parliament enacted, repelled or amended 232 pieces of legislation (*The Myanmar Times* 2016). In its first three sessions held in 2016, the NLD-led parliament only adopted nineteen laws.

It did not come without flaws, though. Legislative expertise and knowledge about annual budget preparation, the drafting of proposals and more broadly 'lawmaking' were almost completely absent when the bodies first convened. Consequently, domestic and external assistance has been sought. The United Nations Development Programme joined hands with the Inter-Parliamentary Union and various development partners to set up capacity-building projects to strengthen the internal functioning of the legislature. The US-based National Democratic Institute set up a Parliamentary Resource Center in Naypyitaw. Australia, India and the European Union have also organized monitoring workshops for MPs and parliamentary staff.

Regional level

The assemblies of the seven states and the seven regions are also elected by universal suffrage – for three-quarters of their seats though, the remaining quarter being filled up by military appointed delegates. Except in the Kayah state parliament and the seven regional hluttaws, ethnic and region-based parties fared relatively well in the 2010 elections and were thus more substantially represented in six of the state hluttaws than in the Union parliament (Nixon et al. 2013; Holliday et al. 2015). This dynamic was particularly manifest in the Rakhine and Shan state parliaments. However, all fourteen speakers elected in early 2011 were drawn from the ranks of the USDP. After the 2015 polls, eleven of the fourteen assemblies fell under the direct control of the NLD. Only the Shan and Rakhine parliaments were in a position to elect a non-NLD speaker.

On March 1, 2011, the first fourteen post-SPDC regional and state assemblies convened in their respective state capitals to appoint members to their respective bill committees and national race affairs committees (*The New Light of Myanmar* 2011, 5–8). The subnational bodies have the power to enact laws concerning the territory their respective state or region is responsible for, but limited to matters mentioned in Schedule Two of the 2008 Constitution – mostly issues related to local finance and commerce, agriculture and forestry, transportation, housing and culture. State and regional lawmakers have since mostly construed their role as that of a 'voice of local grievances'. Unlike in the Union parliament, the military representatives do not enjoy any veto rights in state and regional bodies.

During the first six years of existence though, state and region parliaments have often tacitly fallen under the dominance of the subnational executive power, headed by a chief minister who remains constitutionally appointed by the president of the Union – regardless of the results of provincial elections.[1] The regular sessions of the subnational bodies are meant to be constitutionally aligned with that of the Pyithu Hluttaw; but in practice they convene for shorter plenary sessions. Among them, only five or six have proved moderately active venues for local policy debates during the USDP legislature. The most dynamic certainly seems to be the regional parliament of Yangon, Myanmar's former capital. Its first speaker (2011–2016), a former army colonel, has relentlessly defended the activity of its 122 elected and appointed members, who have discussed relatively significant legislation on social, economic and technical matters. The regional assemblies of Mandalay, Bago and Ayeyarwaddy have also regularly convened to debate socio-economic and cultural issues between 2011 and 2015. The parliaments of the Chin and Rakhine state hluttaws have conducted surveys on poverty reduction. The Mon state hluttaw has discussed the use of the Mon language on official signboards throughout the state. Others have remained rather passive. In particular, the Kachin state hluttaw has proved unable to earnestly address the renewal of armed conflict between Myanmar's central authorities and the Kachin Independence Army (KIA) since war broke out in June 2011. The NLD's resounding victory in the 2015 elections has brought more representativeness into the fourteen assemblies. Yet, the constitutional order still does not allow much policy influence to these local bodies.

Representation and sociological background

A crucial link between society and polity, parliamentary representation is a core element of modern democracy (Best and Cotta 2000; Löwenberg et al. 2002). During Myanmar's early experiment with parliamentary democracy in the 1950s, the Burmese people were construed as the source of all sovereignty and power, and most Burmese postcolonial elites agreed on the fact that the act of representation was to be accomplished by a parliament and a government regularly elected by universal suffrage (McLennan 1967). Moreover, in transitional societies backing away from extended periods of dictatorship, the formation of new representative elites is expected to bolster social mobility and, in doing so, strengthen (re)democratization processes. Changes in the social composition of state leaders are thus to be considered as indicators of the degree of democratization of a society in transition. The investigation of the differences and similarities in the social composition of Myanmar's upcoming legislatures may thus indicate whether there are patterns of fundamental change in the structure of power in Myanmar beyond the 2010s.

The social composition of the first two post-junta legislatures (2011–2016 and 2016–2021) has revealed unsuspected features. It has shown that there has been, to a certain degree, a remarkable diversity of profiles in both chambers of the Union parliament (Egreteau 2014a). By late 2015, the average age of the elected MPs of the USDP-led Union parliament was 57 years old. The NLD-led parliament that convened in February 2016 was on average three years younger. A substantial majority of the elected MPs registered in both USDP-controlled chambers were ethnically Bamar: about 68 per cent of them in the lower house, and 56 per cent in the upper house. In 2016, their share was respectively 69 per cent and 55 per cent. This appears to be in line with the conventional acceptance that Myanmar's population consists of a two-third majority of ethnic Bamar individuals. Furthermore, 88 per cent of the civilian representatives in both successive legislatures have declared Buddhism as their personal faith. Even more notable is the fact that all 166 military representatives were Buddhist, in both parliaments (Egreteau 2015). By comparison, there were only 52 Christian MPs in the USDP parliament and 56 in the NLD-controlled one. The first post-SPDC legislature welcomed three Muslim legislators. Not a single Muslim candidate was elected to office in November 2015. Women have also been sorely underrepresented: only eighteen female candidates were elected in the 2010 polls, but twelve NLD female legislators joined them after the 2012 by-elections. In January 2014, two female army lieutenant-colonels were appointed as military representatives. However, the number of female MPs increased twofold in February 2016 to reach 10 per cent of the full Union assembly.

In both successive parliaments, more than three-quarters of the legislators were university graduates, holding at least a bachelor's degree in arts, law or science, or a medical graduate degree (MBBS) from one of Myanmar's higher education institutions. Setting aside the military appointees – who are professionals – one of the most interesting features of the socio-professional profiles declared by all the Union-level civilian MPs in the USDP and NLD parliament was that, contrary to the widely held stereotype, only a minority of parliamentarians boasted a military background: less than 12 per cent in the first post-junta legislature and less than 5 per cent in the second. A substantial number of the civilian representatives in both houses of the Union parliament are involved in trade, business, banking and other commercial activities. They are followed by professionals from the education sector: teachers, school headteachers, university lecturers and private tutors, and by other civil servants and lawyers.

A significant, yet controversial, new piece of legislation designed to enhance the capacity of Union-level MPs to 'deliver' services to their constituents – the Constituency Development Fund – was proposed by Thura Shwe Mann in 2013. Inspired by an Indian law, the bill purported to grant funds to the Union-level lawmakers for the development of their own constituency and allowed them to open bank accounts for that purpose. The total block grant was 33 billion kyats – thus allocating 1 million kyats equally (and annually) to each of the 330 townships. The first draft raised concern among international and national experts because of the extensive opportunities for vote buying and corruption. President Thein Sein refused to sign the first draft, which was amended three times but finally enacted in March 2014. Recent studies and interviews have illustrated how a substantial number of MPs have used this new legislation, making constant efforts to respond to the constituents they represent while conveying their grievances during plenary sessions – regardless of their own background or party affiliation (Fink 2015, 333).

Lawmaking

Making laws is one of the core functions of a legislative body. According to the 2008 Constitution, the legislative power is shared among the Pyidaungsu Hluttaw and the regional and state assemblies (article 12a). Three annexes to the Constitution (Schedules One, Two and Three) prescribe the respective competence of each level of legislative power (Union, state and region, and self-administrative zones). At the Union level, a law is passed when the two houses approve the same draft bill by a simple majority vote (article 95a). If the two chambers disagree on a draft, it is either channelled back and forth between the two assemblies for further discussion, or the Union joint legislature is convened to settle the disagreement by a single vote. Bills can be submitted to either Pyithu Hluttaw or Amyotha Hluttaw by parliamentarians, as well as by any other Union-level institution such as the Union government, the Office of the Attorney General or the UEC. Only in matters of national plans, annual budgets and taxation must draft bills be submitted directly to the Pyidaungsu Hluttaw (article 100). A bill must first be vetted by the Bill Committee of the house in which it is first discussed, or by the joint legislature. Once passed by the Union parliament, the bill must be signed into law by the president within fourteen days. If the president does not take any action, the law is nonetheless promulgated on the fifteenth day (article 105).

Between 2011 and 2016, the Union parliament worked on 232 pieces of legislation. Of these, most were originally prepared by the executive branch or other Union-level bodies such as the UEC. Only a minority of bills discussed at the Union level were proposed by parliamentarians themselves, due to either a lack of expertise and time or because most agreed to leave the lead policymaking role to the government, as allowed by the Constitution (Fink 2015, 340). Evaluating the legislative performance of the first post-SPDC legislature, however, remains a complicated business (Arter 2009). Were the resurgent hluttaws effectively 'lawmaking' institutions in the first years of the re-emergence? Did they gain enough legislative autonomy vis-à-vis the post-SPDC executive branch and the armed forces?

During the first plenary sessions, the Union legislature gave priority to the amendment, revision or repeal of existing legislation, including some dating back to the colonial era. This included the Peaceful Assembly and Peaceful Procession Law No. 15/2011, the Association Registration Law No. 31/2014, and the Printing and Publishing Law No. 13/2014, which confirmed the end of the age-old state censorship (ICG 2013, 9–13). Then, original draft bills started to be discussed according to the new policies Thein Sein's government had outlined, particularly in economic and developmental matters. Chief among them were the Foreign Investment Law No. 21/2012 and the Social Security Law No. 15/2012. Hotly debated between the two chambers, they were eventually passed in the Pyidaungsu Hluttaw in 2012. Also aimed at boosting Myanmar's economic resurgence, the Special Economic Zone Law No. 1/2014 and the Minimum Wage Law No. 7/2013 were adopted. Several other new laws nevertheless proved controversial. The Village and Tract Administration Law No. 7/2012 maintained severe restrictions on personal liberties. The Anti-Corruption Law No. 32/2014 fell short of expectations as it laid out extremely weak mechanisms to prevent and condemn graft. Four bills purported to protect 'race and religion', including a Monogamy Law and a Buddhist Women Special Marriage Law, were debated in 2015 in the midst of an intense campaign denouncing their anti-Muslim bias. The NLD-controlled legislature pursued from early 2016 the dismantling of the extant repressive legal arsenal, but at a slower pace. In particular, it revoked in October 2016 the Emergency Provisions Act of 1950, which has long been used to stifle dissent. It also revised for the fourth time since 2010 the country's election laws, illustrating a high degree of amateurism in the legislative process.

Oversight

Experts in comparative politics have examined at length how legislatures in a wide range of political systems have exercised oversight procedures and crafted more or less meaningful controls of other state institutions, starting with the executive (Case 2011). Myanmar's 2008 Constitution has installed a hybrid presidential system, an institutional arrangement that logically confers a lead policymaking role on the executive. Yet it leaves the legislative power with a potential for oversight (article 11a), a function more routinely promoted as 'check and balance' by Burmese parliamentarians (Kean 2013, 53). Among the forty-odd parliamentary committees of both chambers of the first post-SPDC legislature, the Public Accounts Committees are crucially tasked with vetting all expenditures ordered and made by the Union government. Their members work closely with the Auditor General, whose office regularly audits and reports on the state budgets and revenues. Other committees are also ordered to audit the budgets of the ministries they are associated with. Only the ministries under the direct control of the military have escaped thorough oversight of their annual budget proposals (Fink 2015, 344–5).[2]

Interviews with Union-level MPs have shown that most have proved particularly confident – even eager – about developing the checks and balances the parliament is meant to perform (Egreteau 2014b, 70). As a matter of fact, government ministers and deputy-ministers have often seen bills their bureaus had drafted being rebuffed by parliamentary committees – a type of open criticism highly improbable in Myanmar before 2011. In March 2012, the recently appointed National Human Rights Commission (NHRC) saw its first annual budget proposal rejected by the Union parliament. Arguing that the formation of the NHRC did not conform to the 2008 Constitution, legislators willingly snubbed a presidential resolution. In August the same year, the upper house initiated a procedure to impeach all nine members of the Constitutional Tribunal, a body appointed at the sole discretion of the president. Legislators from both the NLD and USDP supported the impeachment process in stark opposition to the president's office – which was supposedly aligned with the USDP majority (Nardi 2012).

Above all, a core element of the relatively successful 'check and balance' function performed by the first post-SPDC legislature was the influence of two powerful speakers, both keen on monitoring what the executive under President Thein Sein was proposing for the post-junta political future. Thura Shwe Mann in particular – until his removal from the head of the USDP in August 2015 – had been using the legislature as a strong power base for his own political ambitions. However, the NLD-led parliament has proved less politicized since it convened in February 2016. Instead of a conspicuous monitoring of the executive branch, now under the aegis of Aung San Suu Kyi, it has favoured a quieter scrutiny of budget papers and annual reports.

Lastly, if parliamentarians have proved keen on scrutinizing what other branches of power have done or intended to do, most were less enthusiastic about facing checks and balances themselves (Kean 2013, 53). According to the Constitution, the parliament cannot be dissolved – even by the president – and the procedure for recalling MPs still had not been, as of early 2017, codified and approved by the Union parliament after five years of debate. Nevertheless, a year after the NLD national and provincial legislatures were first convened alleged cases of corruption and nepotism emerged and judicial and parliamentary investigations were launched in February 2017 against 150 new lawmakers.

Conclusion

The renewal of parliamentary activism in Myanmar since the 2010 general elections has drawn significant praise. The national legislature that re-emerged after decades without meaningful parliamentary debates proved, at least in the first five years of its existence (2011–2016), that it was not a mere rubber-stamp body. The assemblies have since 2011 expanded political pluralism and created new opportunities for participation. Despite enduring restrictions on the political rights of minorities and continuing self-censorship observed among legislative ranks, the Union parliament has crafted a new space for political debates and dialogue, even between military and civilian elites. This has not, however, necessarily translated into effective and meaningful law-making. Among the 230-odd draft bills passed between January 2011 and January 2016, only a handful have proved to be of a high standard.

Raising the performance and strengthening the institutionalization of Myanmar's post-junta legislative branch will require time, political stability and colossal transformational efforts. As the case of Indonesia at the end of the 1990s illustrates, the affirmation and empowerment of the legislative power is a core element in consolidating a democratic transition. As long as the 2008 Constitution is not thoroughly amended, the executive branch, and in particular the armed forces, will continue to concentrate power and influence. The maintenance of a certain degree of legislative autonomy will demand determination from not only the future elected legislators but also the upcoming leaderships of the executive branch. Furthermore, as the scholarship on comparative legislatures has shown, after an acclaimed resurgence during a transitional period, newly formed parliaments often tend to return to the failings of factional and clientelistic politics that prevailed in the previous regimes. Patrimonial political culture and corruption tend to resurface and dominate electoral competition and legislative politics after an acclaimed legislature or two. If history is any guide in Myanmar, upcoming Union and subnational legislatures run a high risk of seeing a progressive drop in the optimism they have raised in their first five years of post-junta existence, even after the resounding victory of Aung San Suu Kyi in the 2015 elections.

Notes

1 A proposal for amending this constitutional provision was submitted in parliament in June 2015 but failed.

2 The annual budget of the defence services is, however, publicly debated in session, even though figures and proposals have so far never been bluntly opposed by MPs (ICG 2014, 15–16).

References

n. a. 2008. *The Constitution of the Republic of the Union of Myanmar*. Yangon: Printing and Publishing House, Ministry of Information.

Arter, David, ed. 2009. *Comparing and Classifying Legislatures*. London: Routledge.

Best, Heinrich and Maurizio Cotta, eds. 2000. *Parliamentary Representatives in Europe, 1848–2000*. New York: Oxford University Press.

Callahan, Mary P. 1998. 'On Time Warps and Warped Time: Lessons from Burma's Democratic Era'. In *Burma: Prospects for a Democratic Future*, edited by Robert Rotberg, 49–67. Washington, DC: Brookings Institution Press.

Case, William. 2011. *Executive Accountability in Southeast Asia: The Role of Legislatures in New Democracies and Under Electoral Authoritarianism*. Honolulu: East–West Center Policy Studies No. 57.

Egreteau, Renaud. 2014a. 'Legislators in Myanmar's First Post-Junta National Legislature (2010–2015): A Sociological Analysis'. *Journal of Current Southeast Asian Affairs* 33 (2): 91–124.

Egreteau, Renaud. 2014b. 'Emerging Patterns of Parliamentary Politics'. In *Myanmar: The Dynamics of an Evolving Polity*, edited by David I. Steinberg, 59–88. Boulder, CO: Lynne Rienner.

Egreteau, Renaud. 2015. 'Who Are the Military Delegates in Myanmar's 2010–15 Union Legislature?' *Sojourn* 30 (2): 338–70.

Englehart, Neil A. 2012. 'Two Cheers for Burma's Rigged Elections'. *Asian Survey* 52 (4): 666–86.

Fink, Christina. 2015. 'Myanmar's Proactive National Legislature'. *Social Research* 82 (2): 327–54.

Fish, M. Steven. 2006. 'Stronger Legislatures, Stronger Democracies'. *Journal of Democracy* 17 (1): 5–20.

Holliday, Ian, Maw Htun Aung and Cindy Joelene. 2015. 'Institution Building in Myanmar: The Establishment of Regional and State Assemblies'. *Asian Survey* 55 (4): 641–64.

Horsey, Richard. 2011. *The Initial Functioning of Myanmar Legislatures*. New York: SSRC Conflict Prevention and Peace Forum Briefing, May 17.

ICG. 2013. 'Not a Rubber Stamp: Myanmar's Legislature in a Time of Transition'. Brussels/Yangon: Asia Briefing No. 142.

ICG. 2014. 'Myanmar's Military: Back to the Barracks?' Brussels/Yangon: Asia Briefing No. 143.

ICG. 2015. 'The Myanmar Elections: Results and Implications'. Yangon/Brussels: Asia Briefing No. 147.

Kean, Tom. 2013. 'Myanmar's Parliament: From Scorn to Significance'. In *Debating Democratisation in Myanmar*, edited by Nick Cheesman, Nicholas Farrelly and Trevor Wilson, 43–74. Singapore: ISEAS Publications.

Kyaw Yin Hlaing. 2008. 'Power and Factional Struggles in Post-Independence Burmese Governments'. *Journal of Southeast Asian Studies* 39 (1): 149–77.

Löwenberg, Gerhard, Peverill Squire and D. Roderick Kiewiet, eds. 2002. *Legislatures: Comparative Perspectives on Representative Assemblies*. Ann Arbor: The University of Michigan Press.

McLennan, Barbara. 1967. 'Evolution of Concepts of Representation in Burma'. *Journal of Southeast Asian History* 8 (2): 268–84.

Maung Maung. 1956. 'Portrait of the Burmese Parliament'. *Parliamentary Affairs* 10 (2): 204–9.

Maung Maung. 1960. 'New Parliament in Burma'. *India Quarterly* 16 (2): 139–44.

Moe Thuzar. 2013. 'The Role of Parliament in Myanmar's Reforms and Transition to Democracy'. In *Myanmar in Transition: Polity, People and Processes*, edited by Kirsten Duell, 19–32. Singapore: Select Books.

The Myanmar Times. 2016. 'Trepidation, Speculation as Commission Gets to Work'. February 24.

Nakanishi, Yoshihiro. 2013. *Strong Soldiers, Failed Revolution: The State and Military in Burma, 1962–88*. Singapore: NUS Press.

Nardi, Dominic J. 2012. 'After Impeachment, A Balancing Act'. *The Myanmar Times*, October 1.

The New Light of Myanmar. 2011. March 2.

Nixon, Hamish, Cindy Joelene, Kyi Pyar Chit Saw, Thet Aung Lynn and Matthew Arnold. 2013. *State and Region Governments in Myanmar*. Yangon: MDRI-Asia Foundation.

Singh, Uma Shankar. 1977. 'Parties and Politics in Burma during the Period 1948–1962'. *India Quarterly* 11 (3): 99–120.

Srinivasan, R. 1958. 'A Decade of Parliamentary Life in Burma'. *Indian Journal of Political Science* 19 (3): 291–304.

Taylor, Robert H. 1996. 'Elections in Burma/Myanmar: For Whom and Why?' In *The Politics of Elections in Southeast Asia*, edited by Robert H. Taylor, 164–83. Washington, DC: Woodrow Wilson Center Press.

Trager, Frank N. 1966. *Burma: From Kingdom to Republic. A Historical and Political Analysis*. New York: Praeger.

Zheng, Yongnian, Lye Liang Fook and W. Hofmeister, eds. 2014. *Parliaments in Asia: Institution Building and Political Development*. London: Routledge.

Ziegenhain, Patrick. 2008. *The Indonesian Parliament and Democratization*. Singapore: ISEAS Publications.

24
JUDICIARY

Melissa Crouch

The courts in Myanmar have been subject to much criticism in the post-2011 environment. Yet in contrast to many other areas of governance and administration, the courts are one sector where reform has been less evident or obvious. In fact, while many have been calling for greater judicial independence, the current framework pulls in the opposite direction towards centralisation and executive-military control over the courts.

This raises the broader question: what is the role of the courts in Myanmar post-2011? The three top parallel courts in Myanmar are the Constitutional Tribunal, the Courts Martial and the Union Supreme Court. The Constitutional Tribunal is a new institution introduced in 2011, but has heard only about 14 cases, has been marginalised and lacks political influence. The Courts Martial are a black hole in terms of academic research, given the difficulties of obtaining access to information on these courts. The Supreme Court is the most active, dealing with hundreds of cases per year.

This chapter focuses on the role and function of the Supreme Court, and the courts below it in contemporary Myanmar. The literature around the role and politics of courts, and of courts in authoritarian regimes, is vast and complex (see for example Ginsburg and Moustafa 2008). In this chapter I unpack the role of the courts in Myanmar and their relationship to the other institutions of governance. First, I show how the composition of the Supreme Court points to the influence of the executive over the courts. Second, the authority of the Supreme Court in terms of its original and appellate jurisdiction, and its reporting, law-making and supervisory functions are focused on keeping the lower courts in line. Third, the new authority the Supreme Court has to hear cases concerning complaints against government decisions is a form of procedural authoritarianism to keep lower courts in check. The court's jurisdiction is subject to change by parliament, and the plethora of new legislation will raise difficult social and legal questions for the courts.

Centralisation of the courts

The Union Supreme Court is the most powerful court in Myanmar, having supervisory jurisdiction over all lower courts. Located on the outskirts of Naypyitaw, the new capital city, the Supreme Court's geographic remoteness is one symbol of its inaccessibility and its removal from everyday life. As the backbone of the judicial system in Myanmar, the Supreme Court has several unique characteristics in terms of its composition, selection, tenure and removal that demonstrate the explicit hold the executive retains over the court and its leadership. I demonstrate this by contrasting the current overt limitations on courts against the implicit, highly discretionary judicial system under the military regime prior to 2011.

Myanmar has endured drastic change to its court system, most notably during General Ne Win's socialist regime (1962–1988) when a system of specialist tribunals and People's Courts replaced the existing common law judiciary (Cheesman 2012a). The Supreme Court as it exists today was formed in 1988, in the wake of the takeover by the former military regime and the abolition of the socialist-era People's Councils. At that time, five judges were appointed to the Supreme Court by military order. Law No. 2/1988 on the judiciary was introduced, and it set out some of the basic judicial principles that today are found in the 2008 Constitution. The Supreme Court's jurisdiction was wide-ranging and included the power to transfer cases to itself. It had full supervisory jurisdiction over the lower courts and had the power to regulate the jurisdiction of the State and Region Courts (then known as Divisions), and Township Courts. The Supreme Court also had full power to select and appoint judges to the lower courts, with no public selection criteria or process. From 1988 to 2010, all details regarding the appointment, removal and tenure of judges were left ambiguous. Judges therefore had no security of tenure. At times there were even overt campaigns against individual judges under the banner of combating corruption (Cheesman 2012b; 2015, 165–166).

Small changes were made to the structure of the judiciary during this era. In 2000, a new Judiciary Law No. 5/2000 amended the number of court personnel by expanding the bench to a minimum of 7 and a maximum of 12 judges. The law introduced a process of special appeal from decisions of the Supreme Court. It also established District Courts as another level in the judicial hierarchy between Township Courts and State/Region Courts. Minor amendments were made through Law No. 2/2003 to expand the number of Deputy Chief Justices from two to three. But again there was no mention of the selection process or tenure for judges, elements that are considered to be crucial to guarantee the independence and impartiality of the courts. This changed post-2011 with provisions in the Constitution and the Union Judiciary Law No. 20/2010 setting out the process for the selection, tenure and removal of judges of the Supreme Court and of judges of the State and Region High Courts. Yet rather than enhance the independence of the courts, the legal framework allows for overt executive control over the courts.

The contemporary legal structure grants the President significant powers over the courts. The President nominates the Chief Justice of the Supreme Court and the Union Parliament cannot object to the nomination unless the candidate does not meet the selection criteria. The current Chief Justice, U Tun Tun Oo, was nominated in February 2011, having previously served as Deputy Chief Justice. In this regard, there has been no change in the leadership of the court. Judges of the Supreme Court are appointed by the President and the Chief Justice, and 7 judges currently sit on the bench, although there can be up to 11 appointed. Among these, several judges are known to have military backgrounds, including the Chief Justice. For legal practitioners in Myanmar, this knowledge alone is one indication of the close relationship between the courts and the military, as well as evidence of continuity in terms of interference with judicial independence. In a similar way, the President also has power to appoint the Chief Justices of the 14 State and Region High Courts in collaboration with the Chief Minister of the State and Region (who is also appointed by the President). Nominations for judges of the High Court are made by the Chief Minister and the Chief Justice, and the State or Region Hluttaw must approve the nomination, unless the nominee does not meet the criteria. A presidential order is usually issued as notification of the appointment of judges. In this way, the President has complete power to determine the composition of the bench of the Supreme Court and all

14 State/Region High Courts, providing candidates meet the selection criteria. This structural advantage in favour of executive control over the courts leaves little room for judicial independence.

The President's decision in terms of the selection of judges is open to significant discretion as the selection requirements for Supreme Court judges and High Court judges are broad. Nominees must be between 50 and 70 years old. The requirements for judges are also linked to the requirements for legislative candidates. They must be loyal to the Union and cannot be members of the Hluttaw or of a political party. They must be a lawyer or judge with years of experience depending on their position, or an 'eminent jurist' in the opinion of the President.

It is widely acknowledged that the courts are not independent of the executive nor of the military, yet there have not yet been efforts to remove judges of the Supreme Court or State/Region High Courts through the new constitutional process. Removal proceedings can be initiated by the President, or the Pyithu Hluttaw or Amyotha Hluttaw. The grounds for removal include high treason, misconduct, breach of the Constitution or inefficiency in office, a broad catch-all concept. The process requires an investigation body to be established with members of parliament at either the national or State/Region level, and amounts to exclusive legislative/executive oversight of the judiciary. The President or the Chief Minister of the Region/State essentially has the power to act as the prosecutor against the accused judge by bringing evidence and witnesses before the investigation body. If the motion relates to a judge of the High Court of the State/Region, the process requires the support of one quarter of the members of the State/Region Hluttaw, which essentially means that military officers who occupy 25 per cent of seats in parliament determine the outcome of an impeachment motion.

Although the tenure of judges is set in the Constitution, this has been subject to discussion as part of the broader process of constitutional amendment. In 2015, two bills on constitutional amendment were discussed and voted on in parliament. Part of the proposal was to limit the terms of the judges of the Supreme Court to five years so that they were tied to the term of the government, although the proposal was ultimately unsuccessful. Nevertheless this suggestion for reform is one indication of the fact that while many people in Myanmar are talking about the need for judicial independence, in fact parliament has attempted to take measures to further limit the capacity of the court. Ironically, the current measures that keep the courts captive to the executive – from the selection criteria to the nomination process – are perceived by parliament to be necessary. This is because parliament sees itself as a 'check' on the power of the courts, rather than the courts as a legitimate check on the power of the executive and legislature.

The realm of judicial authority

The authority of the Supreme Court is used in turn to reinforce its control over the lower courts. The Supreme Court has exclusive authority to hear certain matters; appellate authority; a supervisory function over the State/Region High Courts; a reporting function in terms of the publication of case law; and a law-making function that brings it into interaction with parliament.

In its exclusive or original jurisdiction, it can hear matters arising from bilateral treaties, from disputes between the Union Government and State/Region Governments, or disputes among State/Region Governments that are not of a constitutional nature. It also has authority to issue the writ of habeas corpus, mandamus, prohibition, quo warranto and certiorari as remedies against unlawful government decisions. Excluded from its authority is the power to retrospectively hear penal cases, which conveniently functions to protect the military and former government from prosecutions for past crimes. The Supreme Court also cannot hear matters of constitutional law, although it can refer these matters to the Constitutional Tribunal (Myint Zan 2012).

In its appellate jurisdiction, the Supreme Court can hear appeals from the State/Region High Courts. It has discretion to review a court decision under its revisional jurisdiction (although, unlike in an appeal, it cannot take into account new evidence). It is the final court of appeal and its decisions are said to be final, yet the Constitution allows for several possible appeal mechanisms. There is a right to appeal in all cases concerning the death penalty. There is also an avenue of special appeal for cases heard in the Supreme Court. In short, there are multiple possibilities for appeal in most cases. Shapiro has argued that the appellate function of a court, rather than dispensing individual justice, means that these courts are closely connected to the political agenda of a regime (Shapiro 1981, 52). This is evident in the case of Myanmar, where multiple opportunities for appeal to a higher court channel the discontent of the losing party to bolster the legitimacy of the system. Cheesman has suggested that appeals in Myanmar are in part a result of corruption and the practice of double cropping, where judges at both the original and appellate level can take a cut of bribes (Cheesman 2012b; 2015, 189). I would add that corruption alone does not explain the tendency to appeal, but that the provision of multiple opportunities to appeal also operates to justify and reinforce the authority of the legal system itself.

The appellate function of the Supreme Court is related to its supervisory function. The Supreme Court has oversight of all 14 High Courts (one in each Region or State). Each High Court in turn overseas the District Courts and Self-Administered Zones or Divisions; Township Courts; and other specialised courts below it, such as the Children's Court. The supervisory role of the Supreme Court also extends to prisons and it can inspect prisons or prison camps in order to check that an individual's rights are being upheld while in detention. However, its role in supervising prisons has existed since its inception in 1988, yet the scale of political prisoners and the concerns of multiple human rights organisations about prison conditions suggest it has not actively exercised this authority.

In its law-making function, the Supreme Court has the power to submit bills to parliament and assist in the drafting of legislation. For example, the Supreme Court was instructed to draft the Anti-conversion Law and the Monogamy Law that were passed in 2015, as well as the bill to amend the Penal Code that remains on the legislative agenda. In addition to its role in drafting legislation, the Supreme Court has the power to issue regulations on court practice and procedure. Further, because the Supreme Court is classified as a 'Union-level organisation', the Pyidaungsu Hluttaw has the power to summon judges to parliament (2008 Constitution, s 77(c)). This operates as a way for the overpowerful legislature to call to account judges of the Supreme Court. For example, judges of the Supreme Court have been called to parliament to report on constitutional writ cases. This reinforces suspicions that the judiciary is neither independent nor separate from the executive and the military.

There have been several laws passed or amended by parliament in relation to court procedures and practices, such as the Contempt of Court Law No. 17/2013. While the prior Contempt of Court Act 1926 was initially used in a limited way, Cheesman has identified that in 1992 the Supreme Court significantly widened the ambit of contempt and therefore the operation of the law (Cheesman 2015, 243). The revised law passed in 2013 is a significant deterrent for lawyers and applicants to bring cases to court, and for the media to cover court proceedings. For example, in 2015, the Ministry of Information brought a case for contempt against 17 senior figures of the Daily Eleven news group (Kyaw Phone Kyaw, *The Myanmar Times*, June 22, 2015), who were accused of defamation for alleging that the Ministry had misused government funds. This is in addition to a defamation case brought against them in relation to the coverage of the court trial of five other members of the same media outlet. The excessive use of the Contempt of Court law to target political opponents remains a real way in which the courts actively discourage applicants from bringing cases, and punish applicants who bring a 'wrong' case.

Finally, the Supreme Court plays an important role in cooperation with the Attorney General's Office in the selection and reporting of cases for publication in the annual Myanmar Law Reports. Somewhat ironically, while many of the past restrictions on the media and publications have been lifted since 2011, the process of reporting and publishing court decisions has not changed. The Myanmar Law Reports only include cases of the Supreme Court (not any lower courts), and only a very small number of cases are published per year. Unreported cases are generally not made available to the public. On one hand, the cases are said to be selected on the basis of whether there are any former rulings on the topic; whether the ruling is in the public interest; and whether the ruling is one that is useful for the guidance of the lower courts. Yet it is noticeable that the Myanmar Law Reports have not published any high profile political cases. The accessibility and availability of court decisions may potentially change in the future, depending on the responsiveness of the court to calls for greater transparency.

Courts in the public realm: the Supreme Court and the constitutional writs

A significant part of the caseload of the Supreme Court concerns criminal cases on appeal, and the work of Nick Cheesman has significantly expanded our understanding of the history and political function of criminal law in Myanmar (Cheesman 2012a; 2015). There are no accurate statistics on the caseload of the Supreme Court. A preliminary analysis by Nardi and Lwin Moe of its caseload from 2007 to 2012 found that most decisions concerned matters of inheritance, contracts and criminal procedure (Nardi and Moe 2014), although this data was drawn from the highly selective Myanmar Law Reports. As a way of exploring the caseload of the courts further, I focus on two new or emerging areas for the courts: the first is the constitutional writs, and the second is legislative changes to personal law.

Since 2011, a remarkable addition to the Supreme Court's jurisdiction is its authority to hear complaints against the government by way of the constitutional writs (Crouch 2014). This is important because during the socialist and military era there were few avenues to challenge government decisions. Between 2011 and 2015, several hundred writ cases have been filed directly with the Supreme Court. This has led to growing interest from legal practitioners in this area of law as a means to protect constitutional rights, and several books by Burmese authors have been published on the subject (Tin Win 2012; Win Maung Htet 2013; Yi Sein 2014; Mar Hlar Aung 2011). The constitutional writ cases that have been taken to the Supreme Court primarily concerned issues of property ownership, tenancy, labour rights and employment disputes, compensation, inheritance and also some cases of fraud and divorce. Many cases are brought against decisions of the General Administration Department. Many have been rejected at the preliminary stage and not given a hearing, although it is difficult to determine whether the substance of the application was given fair consideration. Anecdotal evidence suggests cases against the military or police are rarely heard.

What can explain the purpose and operation of the Supreme Courts' writ jurisdiction? While many scholars have argued that such a system of administrative review may play a 'fire alarm' role in terms of alerting the administration to breaches of its rules by subordinates (McCubbins et al. 1989), I suggest this is not the case in Myanmar. Rather, the Supreme Court uses the writs to keep a check on the lower courts (rather than the executive) as a form of procedural authoritarianism.

The picture of writs cases depends on where you look. If you look to the Myanmar Law Reports, you will find very few cases published. In fact, all reported writs cases from 2011 to 2013 concern the review of decisions of a lower court and all were unsuccessful. The cases concern general procedural issues unrelated to administrative law, such as time limitations, and basic issues of court procedure. The cases do display some effort to explain the role of the courts and the purpose of the writs. Yet the court decisions are silent on many other common elements of writs cases. For example, there is no discussion of who has the right to apply for the writs. It therefore appears to be untested whether, for example, an environmental group could bring a case against a government decision that raises environmental concerns, such as a decision to grant a licence for the construction of a dam or a gas pipeline. Nor is there any discussion of the reason the administrative decision is being challenged. This suggests that one of the main roles of the Supreme Court at present is to supervise decisions of lower courts, rather than decisions of the executive.

Yet it is only by looking at unreported cases that the significance or potential of the writs can be appreciated. One unreported case stands out because it appears to be the first case in which the Supreme Court found in favour of an applicant against a government official. In 2013 an economics professor from Yangon University Distance Education brought a writ case to the Supreme Court (Court documents on file with author 2013). The professor claimed she had been forced to retire from her position by the former Minister of Education (all university staff in Myanmar are civil servants). She argued that the decision of the Minister of Education to force her to retire should be cancelled because it was beyond his power according to the Civil Servant Law No. 5/2013. The case was brought on the basis of two constitutional rights claims: equal rights before the law and equal opportunity in public employment (2008 Constitution, ss 347 and 349). The Civil Servant Law lists a wide range of punishments that can be given if a civil servant violates the regulations, including a warning letter, a reduction in salary, a demotion or being fired, among other things. Yet the list does not include the power to force a civil servant to retire. On this basis the applicant was successful. This is the first major case in which the Supreme Court has declared the decision of a government minister to be unlawful and it sent ripples of excitement through the legal profession. Backlash from the government appears to have been serious, with government departments being warned to be careful about not triggering further writs cases. This demonstrates that far from using a successful writs case as a demonstration that the government is willing to be accountable and that the courts can help promote lawful decision-making, instead the government has perceived writs cases as a threat to its legitimacy and a criticism of its performance.

Courts in the private realm: parliament and personal law

In Myanmar the courts, rather than the legislature, have historically played a crucial role in the determination of family law disputes. These cases usually begin in the lower courts and then, if the parties appeal, the case may make its way up to the Supreme Court. The Burma Laws Act 1898 remains in force as the law that acknowledges religious personal law for Buddhist, Muslim and Hindu communities (Crouch 2016a). Myanmar is unique among Buddhist-majority countries in that it has a special system known as 'Burmese Buddhist law' that determines family law for Buddhists (Crouch 2016b). This body of knowledge is based on the *dhammathats* from the time of the Burmese kings, compiled by colonial officials and adapted and interpreted by courts. Burmese Buddhist law became important in determining inter-religious marriage claims. There is no right to testate according to Burmese Buddhist law in Myanmar (Huxley 2014, 69) and so disputes over inheritance are often brought before the courts. The case law on Islamic personal law has followed similar lines as Anglo-Muhammadan jurisprudence, typified in volumes such as *Mulla's Principles* (Crouch 2016a). Hindu law is likewise heavily influenced by the English-language compilations on Hindu law that emerged from British India.

These systems of personal law are primarily based on case law made by judges. Myint Zan spoke too soon in suggesting that legislative reform on matters of family law was unlikely to take place (Myint Zan 1999, 202). Legislative reform in 2015 significantly altered family law in Myanmar, and this is likely to lead to new legal issues for the courts to resolve. Four draft laws were originally proposed by *Ma-Ba-Tha*, a radical Buddhist group, in an attempt to restrict inter-religious marriage, prohibit polygamy, restrict conversion and put in place birth control measures. I focus here on the two laws most likely to change the current makeup of family law for the courts in Myanmar: the Buddhist Women's Special Marriage Law No. 50/2015 and the Monogamy Law No. 54/2015.

In Myanmar, the assumption has been that the Monogamy Law was introduced to target Muslims, and this may be partly true. But it also appears to alter Burmese Buddhist law. That is, up until the passage of this law, Burmese Buddhist law specifically allowed polygamy (although it prohibited polyandry). There is extensive case law discussing the position of a second or so-called 'parallel' wife and her rights in terms of inheritance in particular (Myint Zan 1999). The Monogamy Law fundamentally alters Burmese Buddhist law in this regard, although it remains to be seen how the courts will interpret this. The Monogamy Law 2015 makes it an offence to take a second husband or wife, or to commit adultery. If either of these offences is committed, the wronged partner has the right to divorce. In a twist that I call the 'revenge clause', the guilty partner who has committed the offence must forfeit all their matrimonial property rights to their partner. Further, the law appears to punish a second wife in the sense that she no longer has any rights to inherit from her husband, which she had previously under certain circumstances according to Burmese Buddhist Law. A person found guilty under this law may be convicted of polygamy or of deceiving their partner about their marital status under the Penal Code (ss 494–495). Polygamy is still practised by some Buddhists in Myanmar (though there is a need for contemporary empirical research). For example, in 2012 the Supreme Court heard the case of *Daw Mi Mi Tun* v. *U Maung Maung Lwin* (2012) concerning whether a first wife in a Buddhist marriage had the right to divorce her husband given that he had married a second wife without her consent. The Monogamy Law is likely to lead to new prosecutions in the lower courts. But it is also likely to cause disputes that will require the courts to interpret and consider to what extent the Monogamy Law affects existing family law.

The second law that has altered the role of the courts and may create more work for the courts is the Buddhist Women's Special Marriage Act 2015. This law is largely based on the Buddhist Women's Special Marriage and Inheritance Act 1954, although confusingly the 2015 law does not replace the 1954 law but states that it continues to operate where its provisions do not conflict with the 2015 law. The essence of the 2015 law is not new in its focus on regulating the procedure if a non-Buddhist man and a Buddhist woman intend to marry (see Crouch 2016a). The law requires a man and woman to be 18 years old, although if the woman is less than 20 years old she must also obtain the consent of her parents. The process allows time for any objections to be filed concerning the proposed marriage, which are to be dealt with by a court. The final decision whether to allow the inter-religious marriage or not rests with the court. A couple married and registered according to this law are required to be governed by Buddhist law in terms of possession and property, guardianship and divorce. This means that if a Muslim man married a Buddhist woman and they had a dispute over inheritance or divorce, he cannot bring a case under Islamic law. If the husband later seeks a divorce, the woman has the right to have custody of the children and the husband must still provide financial support. The law contains numerous stipulations on what the husband can or cannot do, such as that he must allow his Buddhist wife to keep statutes of the Buddha at home and he must not insult Buddhism.

These legislative changes to family law are an example of how the Union Parliament under Thein Sein (2011–2016) shaped the agenda and jurisdiction of the court. Given that the Monogamy Law and Buddhist Women's Special Marriage Law contain ambiguities, these legal questions may make their way in cases on appeal to the Supreme Court. These cases will require the court to consider the extent to which these laws affect Burmese Buddhist law, and by implication ideas about the role and freedoms of women.

In addition, parliament over the past six years has passed a wide range of legislation in relation to corporate and commercial law, contracts, employment law, and so forth. This is a new and emerging area of law, but given the increase in foreign investment and greater freedoms for businesses, it may lead to more commercial disputes being resolved by the courts.

Conclusion

The Union Supreme Court remains under the centralised control of the executive and plays a key role in supervising and keeping the lower courts in line. This reinforces a culture of procedural authoritarianism, where there is little room for substantive justice in individual cases. To conclude I want to end with a reflection on some of the broader implications of the current state of the courts. While current scholarship on courts often focuses on the trends in the globalised or comparative nature of judicial discourse, Myanmar's legal system has been shaped by decades of isolation. In addition, since 1974 the courts were required to operate in Burmese language, rather than English. Court decisions in Myanmar are focused on a local audience and have effectively been isolated from the common law world of comparative jurisprudence. Courts rarely cite cases from other jurisdictions, although this may be one area of change in the future, particularly for the Supreme Court in its new-found authority to hear writ cases against the government, because this power bears similarities to other common law countries like India.

The post-2011 environment has also generated new debates over key issues such as how judges should be appointed, whether the Supreme Court should have the power to hear cases for constitutional review, how to create greater judicial independence and how the courts relate to the parliament. These ongoing discussions have been frustrated by the hostile attitude of parliament towards the courts, rather than the practical difficulty of constitutional amendment. The current transition to a quasi-civilian government in Myanmar has generated significant uncertainty for the apex courts, and may potentially lead to major efforts at court reform in the years to come.

References

Cheesman, Nick. 2012a. 'How an Authoritarian Regime in Burma Used Special Courts to Defeat Judicial Independence'. *Law and Society Review* 45 (4): 801.

Cheesman, Nick. 2012b. 'Myanmar's Courts and the Sounds Money Makes'. In *Myanmar's Transition: Openings, Obstacles and Opportunities*, edited by M. Skidmore and T. Wilson. Singapore: ISEAS.

Cheesman, Nick. 2015. *Opposing the Rule of Law: How Myanmar's Courts Make Law and Order*. Cambridge: Cambridge University Press.

Crouch, Melissa. 2014. 'The Common Law and the Constitutional Writs in Myanmar'. In *Law, Society and Transition in Myanmar*, edited by Melissa Crouch and Tim Lindsey. Oxford: Hart Publishing, 141–158.

Crouch, Melissa. 2016a. 'Personal Law and Colonial Legacy: State–Religion Relations and the Practise of Islamic Law in Myanmar'. In *Islam and the State in Myanmar: Muslim–Buddhist Relations and the Politics of Belonging*, edited by Melissa Crouch. Oxford: Oxford University Press. 69–98.

Crouch, Melissa. 2016b. 'Promiscuity, Polygyny and the Power of Revenge: The Past and Future of Burmese Buddhist Law in Myanmar'. *Asian Journal of Law & Society* 3 (1): 85–104.

Daw Mi Mi Tun v. *U Maung Maung Lwin*. 2012. MLR (civil case) 48. [in Burmese].

Ginsburg, Tom and Tamir Moustafa. (eds). 2008. *Rule by Law: The Politics of Courts in Authoritarian Regimes*. Cambridge: Cambridge University Press.

Huxley, Andrew. 2014. 'Is Burmese Law Buddhist? Transition and Tradition'. In *Law, Society and Transition in Myanmar*, edited by M. Crouch and T. Lindsey. Oxford: Hart Publishing.

McCubbins, M, R. Noll and B. Weingast. 1989. 'Structure and Process, Politics and Policy: Administrative Arrangements and the Political Control of Agencies'. *Virginia Law Review* 75: 431–482.

Mar Hlar Aung. 2011. Reported Cases of Writs Application with Judgment Summary 1948–1971. Yangon.

Myint Zan. 1999. 'Of Consummation, Matrimonial Promises, Fault and Parallel Wives'. *Columbia Journal of Asian Law* 14 (1): 155–176.

Myint Zan. 2012. 'The New Supreme Court and the Constitutional Tribunal: Marginal Improvement or More of the Same?' In *Myanmar's Transitions: Openings, Obstacles and Opportunities*, edited by Nick Cheesman, Monique Skidmore and Trevor Wilson. Singapore: ISEAS.

Nardi, Dominic and Lwin Moe. 2014. 'Understanding the Myanmar Supreme Court's Docket: An Analysis of Cases from 2007 to 2012'. In *Law, Society and Transition in Myanmar*, edited by Melissa Crouch and Tim Lindsey. Oxford: Hart Publishing, 95–116.

Shapiro, Martin. 1981. *Courts: A Comparative and Political Analysis*. Chicago: University of Chicago Press.

Tin Win, U. 2012. Sachundaw Lut-tone Shauk-ta-bone Siyintone. December 2012. Mandalay.

Win Maung Htet, U. 2013. Pyidaungsu Thamada Myanma Nainggandaw, Pyidaungsu Hluttaw hma atipyu pya htana thi 2013 ku-hnit, Sachundaw Amein Shauk-ta-hmu sain-ya Ubade hnin Ni Ubade-mya. July 2013. Yangon.

Yi Sein, U. 2014. Sachundaw-E Ahnit Tha-ya-mya. Yangon. *Court case*.

25

CIVIL SOCIETY

Christina Fink and Adam Simpson

Since the reform process was initiated in 2011, the legal space for civil society organisations (CSOs) has expanded. This has enabled CSOs to play important, and newly visible, roles in educating and informing citizens, galvanising national attention to critical issues of concern to citizens – including those who are less than liberal – and engaging with the government in certain policy and legislative arenas. Nevertheless, the Thein Sein government's authoritarian lineage and its concern over public criticism led it to constrain the emerging sector. After the NLD won a landslide election victory in 2015, CSOs looked forward to more inclusive policy-making but found that the NLD leadership tended to make decisions on its own. Mindful of the fragility and limitations of the democratic transition, civil society actors were muted in their critique of the new government but continued to voice concerns and promote policy reform by linking their agendas to the NLD government's stated commitment to the rule of law, peace and national reconciliation.

This chapter begins with an exploration of what constitutes civil society in the Myanmar context and then discusses the historical development of civil society in Myanmar. The third section examines the reforms that have enabled CSOs to take on new mandates and considers the roles CSOs played in engaging the Thein Sein government. The final section analyses the opportunities and tensions that may influence the relationships between civil society and the NLD government, which remains constrained by the military's on-going central role in Myanmar's politics and economy.

Defining civil society in the Myanmar context

Civil society can be defined as the space outside the family, the state and the market in which people come together to pursue shared interests. CSOs are non-profit organisations usually drawn from social movements and may include recreational clubs, religious and social welfare organisations, business associations and specialised policy groups. The arena in which CSOs operate is not predetermined but must be created through the actions of individuals, organisations and institutions (Mati et al. 2010, 19). The system of government, and the degree to which civil and political rights are recognised, and specific legal guarantees for CSOs are in place, can foster or constrain civil society. Authoritarian regimes, which all attempt to repress dissent, may either seek to smother or co-opt civil society depending on what they see as the most efficacious route to dominance (Doyle and Simpson 2006).

CSOs can be differentiated from other types of independent organisations, but in practice, the boundaries are often imprecise. Political parties also bring unrelated people together around a common cause, but they are typically not considered part of civil society, because their members seek political office. The 'civil' in civil society implies that organisations engaging in violence should be excluded; however, members of some CSOs around the world do not rule out the use of violence in certain situations (Labigne and Nassauer 2012). Adherence to nonviolence, in relation to either physical objects or people, is largely dependent on the philosophical pedigree of the social movement from which a CSO emerges.

Within Myanmar there is a wide range of social movements with both domestic and international influences that represent this spectrum. Environmental groups that adhere to universalised 'green' values generally adopt nonviolence as a defining principle and may therefore be considered 'emancipatory governance groups' (Simpson 2017). On the other hand, other more illiberal groups, some of which have drawn inspiration from hardline Buddhist nationalist groups in Sri Lanka, have incited violence against Muslim minorities through their use of hate speech. In addition, the boundaries between CSOs, political parties and armed groups in Myanmar are often fuzzy, as many members of political parties have played active roles in CSOs, and many ethnic CSOs have had close ties to both ethnic political parties and ethnic armed groups, as they share the goal of securing greater rights for ethnic nationalities.

In Myanmar there is also a division between what Ottaway (2011, 192) terms traditional civil society, which is composed of informal, loosely structured community-based or larger-scale popular organisations, and modern CSOs, which are more specialised and professional (Lorch 2008; McCarthy 2015). The distinctions between these types of organisations are reflected in the challenges modern CSOs faced in coming up with an appropriate term for themselves in Burmese: *lu mu yay a pwe asi*, or social affairs organisations, is typically used but more aptly refers to traditional CSOs. Nevertheless, some of the more traditional associations have transformed into more modern organisations as space for civil society activity has widened and policy engagement with the government has become possible.

Within the field of democratisation and development, modern CSOs are generally considered to be positive and progressive, but it is important to recognise that CSOs can also be exclusive, conservative and reactionary. Indeed, as Alagappa (2006, 33) has asserted, CSOs are heterogeneous and the realm of civil society is characterised by struggle and competition. In Myanmar, there have been cleavages over ideological positions, the degree of closeness to the government and modes of operating. There has also been competition for funding. Organisations in smaller towns often feel disadvantaged as most foreign donor money goes to more accessible Yangon-based organisations which generally have English-speaking members.

The relationship between civil society and government can vary but tends to take on certain characteristics depending on the type of government in power. Under authoritarian regimes, CSOs with policy-oriented agendas that challenge the government are typically suppressed. They must choose whether to align with the government, dissolve, or operate underground or from outside the country. In well-established democracies, on the other hand, policy-oriented CSOs may engage constructively with the government, providing policy recommendations, input on legislation and, in some cases, general services to the public under the auspices of the government. In countries such as Myanmar where political reform is underway, roles and relationships are constantly being re-negotiated as government, CSOs and society as a whole undergo momentous transformations.

The development of civil society in Myanmar

Civil society organising has a long history in Myanmar, originating with informal Buddhist associations, and followed in the colonial period by other religious organisations such as the Young Men's Christian Association, and Hindu and Muslim organisations (Kyaw Yin Hlaing 2007; Kramer 2011). Some Buddhist organisations became politicised in the colonial period when the protection and promotion of Buddhism became associated with the nationalist struggle for independence. Business associations, professional organisations, trade unions and organisations based on ethnicity or hometown also arose, primarily in urban areas. Student organisations became key players in the nationalist movement. While the authorities took action against members of politicised organisations who participated in anti-government activities, the colonial government, unlike later military regimes, did not disband such organisations or impose restrictions on them (Kyaw Yin Hlaing 2007, 145).

In the parliamentary period in the 1950s, the number of CSOs increased, especially in urban areas, but the ruling Anti-Fascist People's Freedom League (AFPFL) also nurtured mass organisations whose members were expected to vote for the AFPFL. After the military coup in 1962, independent politically-engaged CSOs were, as Steinberg (1999, 8) put it, 'murdered'. Most such organisations were compelled to dissolve and committed members could only meet informally (Kyaw Yin Hlaing 2007, 159), although some professional organisations continued under state control. Mass organisations linked to the Burma Socialist Programme Party predominated; nevertheless, apolitical religious, cultural and social welfare organisations were able to operate at the local level (Kramer 2011).

Beginning in the early 1990s, the military government established new types of government-sponsored associations, such as the Union Solidarity and Development Association (USDA), a nation-wide organisation, which the majority of civil servants and students were compelled to join, and the Myanmar Maternal and Child Welfare Association, which was led by the wives of senior generals (International Crisis Group 2001). Members of such groups were expected to attend pro-government rallies in which 'destructive elements' such as the NLD were denounced. USDA groups in some instances attempted to take over activities performed by independent social welfare organisations that were becoming popular, while small numbers of USDA members were given military training and engaged in violent attacks on the NLD (Fink 2009).

Nevertheless, a surprisingly large number of independent community-based organisations were formed during the 1990s and 2000s, focusing primarily on the many education, health and social welfare needs of the populace. An independent survey conducted in 2003–4 revealed that there could be as many as 214,000 community-based organisations, the vast majority of which were local parent–teacher organisations, social organisations and religious-based groups (Heidel 2006, 42). Many formed to address gaps in the state's provision of services, particularly in terms of education (Lorch 2008). Over 200 more formalised NGOs also carried out development-related work and were tolerated by the state as long as they remained apolitical. They could not publicly call for policy changes or political reform, although some did try to engage in closed door advocacy with government officials. With a small but growing number of international development organisations in the country, greater opportunities emerged for members of domestic organisations to engage with international counterparts.

Meanwhile, as the regime encouraged foreign businesses to invest, more domestic business-related associations, which generally maintained good working relationships with the authorities, formed. These included the Union of Myanmar Federation of Chambers of Commerce and Industry as well as Myanmar Egress, which was founded by well-established business people and intellectuals with a vision for gradual political change. Using the limited space that had opened up for apolitical educational courses, Myanmar Egress gradually developed into an influential reform-oriented institute providing training in social sciences and leadership to socially-engaged young adults and advice on a range of policy reforms to the government (Lall 2016, 22–8).

Immediately following Cyclone Nargis in 2008, in which over 130,000 people died and over 2 million people were affected, dozens of ad hoc groups formed and existing groups set aside their primary missions to focus on collecting and delivering food and whatever other supplies they could gather. Because the regime did not allow international relief workers to enter the country for the first three weeks after the cyclone, and the government could not manage the scale of the devastation, such groups played a key role in alleviating the suffering of the survivors (Kramer 2011, 12–13). Other community-based groups were formed after international organisations came into the country and often sought to provide assistance through such groups rather than through pre-existing government-instituted village committees. Many groups dissolved once the crisis had passed, but a number continued, albeit often without registering.

According to the Law Relating to Forming of Organizations, which was promulgated by the military regime in 1988, CSOs could not operate legally without being registered, and anyone affiliated with an unregistered organisation could be sentenced to three years in prison. However, in the 2000s, it could take two years for an organisation to obtain registration, and registration was only possible if the organisation had a clearly apolitical mission and board members whom the government trusted.

Meanwhile, in some of Myanmar's ceasefire areas and in neighbouring countries, starting in the 1990s, new CSOs were formed by exiled activists, refugees from civil war in the ethnic states, and interested migrant workers (Duell 2014; South 2008; Kramer 2011); these groups formed an 'activist diaspora' (Simpson 2013a). Generally supported by foreign donors, the organisations were often ethnically-based and focused on the provision of humanitarian assistance, women's rights, human rights, youth concerns and the environment. Many of these organisations became involved in transnational advocacy efforts focused on documenting abuses by the Myanmar government and military and calling for international pressure to bring about change. They also sought to inform and educate members of their communities along the borders or inside Myanmar about international norms and Myanmar's failure to live up to them. Nevertheless, not all ethnic armed groups were enthusiastic about independent civil society groups emerging in their areas of control; like the regime, they did not appreciate public criticism, nor did they like having to compete with civil society groups for new recruits (South 2008, 37–8).

Openings and constraints under the Thein Sein government

Soon after Thein Sein became president in 2011, the legislature passed two laws drafted by the executive branch that signalled greater tolerance for civil society. The first was the labour association law which allowed independent labour organisations to form. The second was the Peaceful Assembly and Peaceful Procession Law which made it possible for groups to hold demonstrations if they applied for and received permission from the police first. In addition, international development organisation staff were permitted to visit Myanmar freely and to develop working relationships with local organisations. In 2012 the government removed from the blacklist over 2,000 names of Burmese dissidents in exile as well as foreigners whom previous regimes had deemed as threats to peace and stability. This enabled members of Myanmar CSOs based outside the country or in ethnic ceasefire areas to travel throughout Myanmar and connect with other CSOs; many had been absent from Myanmar-proper for almost a quarter of a century. The lifting of media pre-censorship and the emergence of private daily newspapers in April 2013 also led to much wider coverage of CSOs' activities. As a result of all these factors, members of Myanmar CSOs began to feel more emboldened.

While actions taken by various branches of the government indicated that there could still be constraints on civil society activities, a new openness to civil society critique was also evident. Draft legislation for the registration of associations prepared by the Home Ministry in 2013 was very restrictive, imposing prison sentences on members of all types of organisations who engaged in activities before their organisations' registration had been approved. As a result, 275 CSOs banded together to lobby lawmakers to make changes to the bill, and the following year, a much more liberal version of the Association Registration Law was passed (Fink 2015b). Only organisations receiving foreign funding had to register and the process was made much easier by allowing organisations to register locally rather than in Naypyitaw.

Despite being an improvement on previous laws, a significant challenge for CSOs under the Peaceful Assembly and Peaceful Procession Law was that the police frequently denied permission for demonstrations to take place. This was particularly true for land rights protesters, student activists and peace marchers. Those who defied the police and carried out their public activities were often charged and, in a number of cases, imprisoned for breaking the law. Parliamentarians amended the law in 2014 so that police could not deny permission without reasonable cause and sentences for protesting without a permit were cut in half from one year to six months. Activists had called for eliminating the sentences altogether and for a requirement only to inform the police of their planned activities.

These examples indicate that while the Thein Sein government was willing to grant a degree of legitimacy to CSOs and to allow greater scope for their activities than before, the former military generals' traditional suspicion of civil society remained. Parliamentarians tended to go along with the executive branch's restrictions until challenged by CSOs, at which point they agreed to temper draft bills and existing laws to a certain extent. However, the judiciary remained beholden to the executive branch in politically-sensitive cases, showing no leniency for activists from CSOs who protested without permission.

Beginning in 2011, a number of existing and new CSOs sought to expand the mandate of their organisations to include formally engaging with the government on policy matters, giving interviews to the media and informing and mobilising the public on a range of previously sensitive issues. In working with the government, they aimed at both widening and institutionalising space for civil society and effecting policy changes. However, members of some of the more political organisations with roots in the democracy movement resisted close cooperation with the Thein Sein government. They considered his administration to be only superficially different from the previous regime and did not want to accord legitimacy to the government or act in ways that they felt might taint their own reputations. At the same time, authorities' attitudes toward CSOs ranged from interest in drawing on their expertise to considering them as adversaries. Some in the government recognised that certain CSOs had greater knowledge and access to resources or deeper connections to communities than they did, and that working together could advance development in that area. Others, however, continued to take a top-down approach towards policy-making and saw the involvement of non-state actors as unnecessary and undesirable.

In some cases, international NGOs and UN agencies were able to facilitate the bringing together of government officials and Myanmar CSOs during military rule and these processes were consolidated and deepened after 2011. The Gender Equality Network's collaboration with the Ministry of Social Welfare and Relief and Resettlement is a good example. International agencies engaged in relief operations after Cyclone Nargis formed the women's protection technical working group to ensure that women's needs were being adequately addressed. The group included a growing number of national NGOs and less formal civil society groups working on women's issues, and it was later renamed the Gender Equality Network (GEN). In 2010, GEN began quietly working with the Ministry of Social Welfare to develop a national strategic plan for the advancement of women, providing international expertise and knowledge of community concerns. The plan, which covered the period from 2013 to 2022, was completed in 2013 and set out actions for both government ministries and CSOs to take.

Other examples include organisations working to both inform citizens about the electoral process and ensure that the 2015 elections were free and fair. Election Education and Observation Partners and the People's Alliance for Credible Elections are two such groupings. They engaged with the Union Election Commission to revise the relatively restrictive draft rules for election monitors in order to ensure they could carry out their mandate. This included being able to conduct independent exit polls and being able to release their data on the election process and results before the government did.

Education policy

A key area where CSOs engaged with the Thein Sein government was education policy, although the relationship was often fraught. In 2012, the government initiated a Comprehensive Education Sector Reform process to develop a master plan for the overhaul of the national education system and to pass a law formalising the overarching framework. The government organised consultative meetings; however, some officials were uncomfortable with the participation of the National Network for Education Reform (NNER), a body formed in 2012 to draft an alternative set of national education policies (see Chapter 26). NNER brought together NLD Education Working Group members, student organisations, teachers' unions and ethnic-based organisations advocating for ethnic language rights and decentralisation of the education system. Members of NNER held consultation sessions around the country and drafted their own policy, which they sent to the Ministry of Education and the legislature. They were frustrated when those in power ignored their proposals, particularly for greater university autonomy, independent student and teacher unions, ethnic language instruction and the earmarking of 20 per cent of the state budget for education.

After the parliament passed the National Education Law in 2014 without incorporating NNER's key demands, student activists put pressure on the legislators to amend the law by organising marches from various towns to convene in Yangon. The parliament agreed to reconsider the law, but the students were irked by the slowness of the process and proceeded with the march. Government officials feared the protesters could end up mobilising the broader public. In March 2015, they used barricades to block a contingent of 200 students from advancing beyond Letpadan, a town 135 km north of Yangon. After inconclusive negotiations, the students decided to break through the barricades. The police attacked them with batons, inflicting numerous injuries. Over 70 students were charged and jailed.

Land rights and environmental justice activism

Land rights are another area where CSOs and the government came into conflict, although the government was responsive to some citizen demands. In the decades before Thein Sein came to power, government departments, the armed forces, businesses and ethnic armed groups appropriated land throughout the country. After 2011, farmers' groups, rights groups and citizens began appealing to government officials and members of parliament for the return of their land or fair compensation (Fink 2015a). Many farmers in Myanmar do not have land titles, but they do have annual land tax receipts, which were commonly used in place of titles in the past. After parliamentarians repeatedly urged the government to resolve the cases, government departments and the military returned some undeveloped land. Other cases were ignored, while new confiscations took place. Farmers and land rights activists responded with demonstrations and ploughing protests, in which they reoccupied their land. Dozens were charged with trespassing and vandalism.

This land rights activism is part of a broader emerging livelihood - and justice-focused environment movement within Myanmar that seeks to both protect the environment and tackle longstanding injustices dealt out to Myanmar's ethnic groups and other marginalised peoples. On-going rent extraction throughout the country's economy has stimulated the growth of oppositional civil society (Prasse-Freeman 2012), and since 2011 many environmental activists from the activist diaspora have returned to Myanmar with their internationally-honed skills to continue their campaigns inside the country against large-scale development projects, particularly hydropower dams (Simpson 2013b). Partly in response to this activism, the Thein Sein government suspended the enormous Chinese-backed Myitsone Dam in Kachin State in September 2011, one of its most significant decisions. While there was undoubtedly a range of motives for this policy, it became emblematic of the Thein Sein government's more amenable approach to civil society actors, despite the on-going restrictions and periodic crackdowns that characterised its term in office (Simpson and Smits 2018).

The increased activities of local environmental groups built on the transnational activism that had developed over large-scale development projects since the 1990s, including the Yadana Gas Pipeline to Thailand and hydropower dams on the Thanlwin (Salween) River in the east and the Shwe Gas Pipeline and Myanmar-China Oil Pipeline that crossed the country to China from Rakhine State in the west. This form of activist environmental governance shifted, from a form that focused on international actors and ignored the ruling military regime prior to 2011, to one far more domestically engaged (Simpson 2017). A representative shift in the domestic operating climate was the establishment of the internationally mediated Multi-Stakeholder Group (MSG) of the Extractive Industries Transparency Initiative (EITI) (see Chapter 39). President Thein Sein committed to joining the EITI in 2012 and the MSG eventually formed and met in early 2014. Despite limited cooperation from some parts of government regarding the EITI, the MSG represented a revolutionary shift in state–civil society relations. Within the MSG – which makes in-country decisions relating to EITI implementation – government, civil society and industry have equal voting rights. The role of civil society in the process is overseen by the International EITI Board, which in 2015 removed Azerbaijan's compliant status due to restrictions on civil society activities.

Despite the EITI being primarily about revenue transparency, CSOs within the MSG have attempted to broaden its remit to address human rights violations, and in January 2015 called an emergency MSG meeting to discuss the shooting of a protester at the Letpadaung Copper Mine. The activists link the lack of human rights in the country to the corruption inherent in the natural resources sector, particularly the jade industry (Simpson 2018). They see complicity between industry, the military and the state in the multitude of rights breaches throughout the country and view the EITI MSG as a key forum for addressing a wide range of related concerns.

The EITI has also become intertwined with CSO demands over natural resource revenue sharing and federalism. Rakhine groups, including the Shwe Gas Movement, have been particularly vociferous on this issue, as they see the central Union government extracting the revenues from their rapidly depleting offshore natural gas reserves while their state remains one of the poorest in the country. This issue has become more acute in Rakhine State since 2012 when violence flared up against Muslim minorities, principally the Rohingya. The competition over resources in the state between Buddhist and Muslim communities has been exacerbated by the Rakhine community's longstanding grievances over its historical exploitation by the predominantly Burman (Bamar) central government and, as a result, has been a key driver in the development of Myanmar's more illiberal civil society.

Buddhist organisations

The newly opened space for civil society in Myanmar has allowed for both liberal and illiberal organisations to grow and spread their messages. In particular, members of Buddhist nationalist organisations and Rakhine nationalist organisations have had significant influence on law-making and public behaviour. The countrywide Association for the Protection of Race and Religion, known by the acronym Ma Ba Tha in Burmese, was founded by monks in early 2014. A number of prominent monks in the organisation are known for their anti-Muslim preaching and for stoking fears of a Muslim takeover of the country. Ma Ba Tha leaders also pushed for the passage of four bills that would put restrictions on marriages between Buddhist women and men of other faiths, make religious conversion more difficult, require monogamy and enable the state to impose birth spacing on particular populations. Over 90 women's, human rights and ethnic minority organisations circulated a joint statement in opposition to the bills, but they were harshly criticised by Ma Ba Tha members, and leading rights activists received death threats (Snaing 2014). Although some parliamentarians from the NLD and other parties voted against the bills, all four passed and were signed into law by President Thein Sein in 2015. This reflected the influence of the nationalist monks, parliamentarians' perception that most citizens supported such laws, and, presumably, their personal views in many cases.

In Rakhine State, the Emergency Coordination Committee, comprising of Rakhine State and central government representatives, together with members of local civil society groups and international humanitarian agency representatives, was formed in 2014 to vet UN and INGO relief and development projects and to stop UN agencies and INGOs from operating in the state if they were acting in ways the committee deemed inappropriate. Local CSOs then banded together to form watch committees in various townships to more directly monitor international humanitarian assistance programmes. Members of such groups accused foreign aid agencies of neglecting the Buddhist Rakhine while supporting Muslim residents, whom they consider illegal immigrants, and giving the Rakhine community a bad name (Lone 2014). Extremist nationalist organisations stirred up feelings of mistrust and antipathy towards other groups in Myanmar, drawing on historical narratives, economic woes and people's feelings of insecurity in a period of change. This created fertile ground for acts of violence against Muslims in several locales and the long-term internment of over 100,000 Muslims in internally-displaced camps in Rakhine State.

Renegotiating relations under the NLD government

With the transition to the NLD government in April 2016, hopes were high that space for civil society would widen and the rights of civil society activists would be more secure. In its first month in office, the NLD government issued an amnesty resulting in the release of most imprisoned activists, including the students arrested for their march against the education law. The administration also initiated a process to withdraw charges against many of the 400 activists awaiting trial. In addition, the NLD-dominated parliament began rescinding or amending laws that had been used to prosecute activists and opposition politicians in the past. This included the 1975 Law to Safeguard the State against the Dangers of Those Desiring to Cause Subversive Acts and the 2011 Peaceful Assembly and Peaceful Procession Law.

Nevertheless, tensions emerged over how the government balances expedience in decision-making with inclusiveness, which is important to CSOs and marginalised communities. Some CSOs worry that the NLD leadership disregards CSOs since the party won a landslide election victory and sees itself as representing the will of the people. Moreover, ordinary folk who voted for the NLD have put their faith in Aung San Suu Kyi's leadership abilities and are still waiting to see changes that will lead to improvements in their standards of living. If engaging with civil society is perceived as needlessly delaying policy reforms, there may be government resistance.

The existence of a wide range of CSOs, often with competing agendas, may also serve as a justification for limiting interaction with civil society. The NLD government is treading a fine line between those supporting Buddhist and Burman nationalism and those advocating for equal rights and interfaith and interethnic harmony. In addition, some business associations and farmers' groups call for diametrically opposed policies regarding agriculture and rural development. Land rights and environmental activists argue for the protection of the environment and local communities while the NLD attempts to placate neighbouring governments, such as China, and woo international investors. In its first year the NLD government has received significant latitude from civil society actors who, after decades of military-backed rule, acknowledge the fragility and limitations of the democratically elected government and recognise the risk of military intervention if social conflict flares up.

The quality of engagement between the NLD government and CSOs in the future will likely be shaped by the ways in which CSOs advocate for their causes. Various CSOs may be able to persuade the government that they have much-needed expertise and their policy prescriptions should be taken into account. Yet, some activist CSOs have little or no experience with the time-consuming process of lobbying and building relationships with members of government, and they may rely on protests and marches as the primary means for asserting their demands. Should protest movements grow substantially, the administration, and particularly the security forces, may act decisively to restrict activities. Given that the military still holds extensive powers in the government, its attitude towards civil society engagement and activism will also be critical in determining the degree of space available to civil society.

Conclusion

Authoritarian governments in Myanmar have long suppressed civil society. Since 2011 the political reform process has gradually opened political space for CSOs to operate, and sometimes protest. Nevertheless, progress was halting under the Thein Sein government, with human rights, student and environmental activists regularly detained. There is hope throughout the country and the international community that civil society freedoms will increase under the NLD government and that established fora, such as the EITI MSG, will provide meaningful mechanisms for influencing government policy. During the NLD's first year in power some restrictions were lifted, although, overall, progress was limited. Nevertheless, civil society criticism of the government was muted, with progressive and liberal activists wary of providing the military with an excuse to intervene. Over time, CSOs may become more vocal if the elected government cannot deliver on its promises. While the potential exists to strengthen protections for civil society and institutionalise civil society engagement in public affairs, the process may be uneven, with the military continuing to influence the parameters for civil society activity for some time to come.

References

Alagappa, Muthiah. 2006. 'Civil Society and Political Change: An Analytical Framework'. In *Civil Society and Political Change in Asia: Expanding and Contracting Democratic Space*, edited by M. Alagappa, 25–60. Stanford: Stanford University Press.

Doyle, Timothy and Adam Simpson. 2006. 'Traversing more than speed bumps: green politics under authoritarian regimes in Burma and Iran'. *Environmental Politics* 15 (5): 750–67.

Duell, Kerstin. 2014. 'Sidelined or Reinventing Themselves? Exiled Activists in Myanmar's Political Reforms'. In *Debating Democratization in Myanmar*, edited by N. Cheesman, N. Farrelly and T. Wilson, 109–36. Singapore: Institute of Southeast Asian Studies.

Fink, Christina. 2009. *Living Silence in Burma: Surviving under Military Rule*. London: Zed Books.

Fink, Christina. 2015a. 'Re-envisioning Land Rights and Land Tenure'. In *Myanmar: The Dynamics of an Evolving Polity*, edited by D. Steinberg, 243–66. Boulder, CO: Lynne Rienner.

Fink, Christina. 2015b. 'Myanmar's proactive national legislature'. *Social Research* 82 (2): 327–54.

Heidel, Brian. 2006. *The Growth of Civil Society in Myanmar*. Bangalore: Books for Change.

International Crisis Group. 2001. *Myanmar: The Role of Civil Society*. Bangkok/Brussels: Asia Report No. 47.

Kramer, Tom. 2011. *Civil Society Gaining Ground: Opportunities for Change and Development in Burma*. Amsterdam: Transnational Institute. Accessed May 17, 2016. www.tni.org/sites/www.tni.org/files/download/tni-2011-civilsocietygainingground-web2.pdf.

Kyaw Yin Hlaing. 2007. 'Associational Life in Myanmar: Past and Present'. In *Myanmar: State, Society, and Ethnicity*, edited by N. Ganesan and Kyaw Yin Hlaing, 143–72. Singapore: Institute of Southeast Asian Studies.

Labigne, Anaël and Anne Nassauer. 2012. 'Violence in Civil Society: Insight from the CSI Databases'. In *Civil Society, Conflict and Violence: Insights from the CIVICUS Civil Society Index Project*, edited by R. List and W. Dörner. London: Bloomsbury Academic. Accessed May 17, 2016. www.bloomsburycollections.com/book/civil-society-conflict-and-violence-insights-from-the-civicus-civil-society-index-project/ch7-violence-in-civil-society.

Lall, Marie. 2016. *Understanding Reform in Myanmar*. London: Hurst.

Lone, W. 2014. 'Rakhine Civil Society Forms Groups to Monitor INGO Activities'. *The Myanmar Times*, May 28. Accessed May 17, 2016. www.mmtimes.com/index.php/national-news/10513-rakhine-civil-society-forms-groups-to-monitor-ingo-activities.html.

Lorch, Jasmine. 2008. 'The (Re)-emergence of Civil Society in Areas of State Weakness: The Case of Education in Burma/Myanmar'. In *Dictatorship, Disorder and Decline in Myanmar*, edited by M. Skidmore and T. Wilson, 151–76. Canberra: ANU E Press.

McCarthy, Stephen. 2015. 'The limits of civil society in militarised regimes: evidence from the Asia-Pacific'. *Australian Journal of International Affairs* 69 (6): 711–28.

Mati, Jacob M., Federico Silva and Tracy Anderson. 2010. Assessing and Strengthening Civil Society Worldwide. Johannesburg, CIVICUS. Accessed May 17, 2016. www.civicus.org/view/media/Assessing%20and%20Strenghtening%20CS%20Worldwide%202008-2010.pdf.

Ottaway, Marina. 2011. 'Civil Society'. In *Politics in the Developing World*, 3rd Edition, edited by P. Burnell, V. Randall and L. Rakner, 182–201. Oxford: Oxford University Press.

Prasse-Freeman, Elliott. 2012. 'Power, civil society, and an inchoate politics of the daily in Burma/Myanmar'. *The Journal of Asian Studies* 71 (2): 371–97.

Simpson, Adam. 2013a. 'An "Activist Diaspora" as a Response to Authoritarianism in Myanmar: The role of Transnational Activism in Promoting Political Reform'. In *Civil Society Activism under Authoritarian Rule: A Comparative Perspective*, edited by F. Cavatorta, 181–218. London and New York, Routledge/ECPR Studies in European Political Science.

Simpson, Adam. 2013b. 'Challenging hydropower development in Myanmar (Burma): cross-border activism under a regime in transition'. *The Pacific Review* 26 (2): 129–52.

Simpson, Adam. 2017. *Energy, Governance and Security in Thailand and Myanmar (Burma): A Critical Approach to Environmental Politics in the South*. Updated Edition. Copenhagen: NIAS Press.

Simpson, Adam. 2018. 'Corruption, Investment and Natural Resources'. In *International Natural Resources Law, Investment and Sustainability*, edited by S. Alam, J. Bhuiyan and J. Razzaque. London: Routledge.

Simpson, Adam and Mattijs Smits. 2018. 'Transitions to energy and climate security in Southeast Asia? Civil society encounters with illiberalism in Thailand and Myanmar'. *Society and Natural Resources* doi: 10.1080/08941920.2017.1413720.

Snaing, Y. 2014. 'Activists Face Violent Threats after Opposing Interfaith Marriage Bill'. *The Irrawaddy*, June 4. Accessed May 17, 2016. www.irrawaddy.org/burma/activists-face-violent-threats-opposing-interfaith-marriage-bill.html.

South, Ashley. 2008. *Civil Society in Burma: The Development of Democracy amidst Conflict*. Washington, DC: East–West Center.

Steinberg, David. 1999. 'A Void in Myanmar: Civil Society in Burma'. In *Strengthening Civil Society in Burma*, edited by Burma Center Netherlands and Transnational Institute, 1–14. Chiang Mai, Thailand: Silkworm Books.

26
EDUCATION

Marie Lall

Myanmar's education system went from being one of the most admired across Asia to one of the weakest and poorest systems in the region over a span of 70 years. Decades of underinvestment and civil strife resulted in the slow and steady decay of the state education system across the country. In 1964 under the socialist regime, all private schools and universities were closed. It was also at this time that Burmese was made the medium for teaching at all schools, abolishing the colonial legacy of English schools for the elite, and instigating ethnic strife as ethnic languages were no longer allowed to be used in schools.

Politics and education were always linked. After the students' protest of 1988, all universities were closed for 2 years. Another series of student strikes in 1996 and 1998 resulted in further closures. In Yangon, the University was closed for 10 out of 12 years. After the re-opening of universities and colleges in 1999, the government relocated universities to different regions and the undergraduate programmes were moved to campuses far away from any urban centre so as to avoid further student protests. Education then stayed out of the news and, with the notable exceptions of JICA and UNICEF, was kept away from international agencies.

The reforms initiated by President Thein Sein's government in 2011/12 changed things quite dramatically, with education again dominating the headlines. After the new education law was submitted to parliament in 2014, student protests rocked the streets of Yangon and other cities in Myanmar. In a twist of fate, the National League for Democracy (NLD) distanced itself from the protesting students by removing Dr Thein Lwin from the party. He is the head of the National Network for Education Reform (NNER) and was a member of the NLD executive committee. The fact that the NLD, then still in opposition, was against the new education law but would not endorse student protests shows how complicated the issue of education reform had become. Pitted against each other were the Ministry of Education (MoE), the President's Office, the Parliamentary Committee, civil society and student groups. The battle centred mainly on who would get to control what and how far the centre would release power to both the state and region governments as well as individual institutions in the wider decentralisation policy debate. In the midst of this were a series of international organisations and development partners such as UNICEF, the World Bank and national government aid agencies that have been pushing their own reform agendas with the help of selective financing.

As the post-2015 NLD government policies take shape and former rector of West Yangon University Dr Myo Thein Gyi, a hardliner during the 2014 student protests (*The Myanmar*

Times, 5 April 2016), has become Minister of Education, the battles around education priorities are set to continue.

Background

Chapter 8 of the 2008 Constitution – 'Citizens, Fundamental Rights and Duties of Citizens' – describes the right of all Myanmar citizens to education. According to Article 366, every citizen shall have the right to education; shall be given basic education which the Union prescribes by law as compulsory; shall have the right to conduct scientific research, explore science, work with creativity and write, to develop the arts, and conduct research freely with other branches of culture. In Chapter 1 of the Constitution, the obligations of the Union are laid out. The Union shall: a) earnestly strive to improve the education and health of the people; b) enact the necessary laws to enable the Nation's people to participate in matters of their education and health; c) implement a free compulsory primary education system; d) implement a modern education system that will promote all-around correct thinking and a good moral character, contributing towards the building of the Nation.

Government schools

At the time of writing the Myanmar education sector is one of the largest government services. In 2012/13 government-run basic education served 8,364,081 students (Ministry of Education 2012) The Net Enrolment Ratio (NER) for primary, lower secondary and upper secondary education shows much improvement in the past decade and a half: In 2011–2012, the NER for the three levels of education was 84.6 per cent, 47 per cent, 30 per cent respectively, but in 1998–1999 it was 74.7 per cent, 23.6 per cent and 10.1 per cent, respectively (Ministry of Education 2012). The dropout rate is high overall, but it is particularly high in the final year of primary school (year 5) where it stands at 23.2 per cent, as poverty drives parents to take their children out of school to help with earning the family income, especially in rural areas where the cost of sending children to school is high. Dropout rates continue to be high throughout lower and upper secondary school, often linked to the direct costs of buying books and uniforms as well as having to pay for 'mandatory' tuition. In sum, problems across the sector exist with regard to access, quality and retention despite the high primary enrolment ratios.

Public education expenditure as a share of GDP has been lower than the ASEAN average. Accurate figures are hard to come by, but seem to hover around 0.6 per cent of GDP. According to a UNICEF study conducted in 2013/14, community funding of education is estimated at 70 per cent of total education expenditure (UNICEF 2013). The largest expenditure of the government budget is salary payments estimated at around 90 per cent, leaving little for maintenance or the goods and services that schools need to function. There is a separate capital expenditure budget where construction expenditure takes up over 90 per cent, leaving little for equipment. Since school budgets are centrally determined based on uniform formulas, they do not meet actual school needs. Township Education Officers (TEOs) and head teachers have little or no discretion over school budgets, making them more reliant on community funds to deal with any emergency and even standard expenses. At the time of writing, teacher hiring is being reviewed to allow TEOs some say in what was till now a highly centralised system of teacher placement run out of the ministry in Naypyitaw. This had resulted in teacher shortages in rural and primary schools, disadvantaging schools that are already serving the poorest sections of Myanmar society.

Monastic schools

Although schooling is free in principle, the parental contributions discussed above are important. Those who cannot afford to go to state schools go to monastic schools or forgo their education altogether. Monastic schools were outlawed during the socialist period as of 1962 and were only allowed to return in 1993. In the early 1990s monastic schools were encouraged to open and allowed to register so as to gain a certain legal status. This was a window that allowed some of the biggest monastic networks to establish themselves. The sector has been growing ever since. The official numbers for 2009/10 – although difficult to verify – were 1,066 monastic schools catering for 167,551 children at primary level, 331 catering for 32,741 at middle school level and 2 officially recognised monastic schools catering for 4,552 children at high school level. However monastic schools operate as networks, and there are more schools that are 'affiliated' to the recognised schools. It is therefore difficult to estimate the total number of children accessing the monastic system.

As Myanmar has signed the international 'Education For All' (EFA) declaration, monastic schools today are seen as part of the solution to provide education across all sections of society and across the country. More recently monastic schoolteachers have been allowed to access in-service teacher training with their government counterparts, and in a drive to increase teacher numbers a government scheme allowed government schools to hire experienced monastic schools teachers.

Private education

The state education system has been inadequate for a number of years, and from the early 2000s civil society jumped in to offer patches where possible; however, these efforts did not manage to replace the state in any significant way. One particular section of civil society, the private sector, has used this business opportunity to turn education into a private and profitable good. Today, the education landscape across Myanmar has totally changed with private schools at pre-elementary, elementary, secondary and higher education level catering to the popular demands of the market in English language, computing, accounting and business related training. Some institutions offer a full curriculum, some focus only on a few subjects. Most private schools have only recently been allowed to operate as an alternative to the state system, and children who graduate from these schools cannot join Myanmar higher education. The government has also started to offer 'private' education (in this case recognised by the ministry because the government curriculum is used). The Private School Law of 2 December 2011 allowed around 46 private schools to be set up officially in Yangon, Mandalay and Pyin Oo Lwin.

Higher education

In 2015 there were 168 higher education institutions in Myanmar under the jurisdiction of 13 different ministries. All the higher education institutions are state-financed and accept students after matriculation depending on their grades. Those who cannot afford to live away from home study in the world's largest but very poor-quality distance education programme. They do so at a comparatively young age, as they finish school at the age of 16. Due to the declining quality of the state education system, students and parents have been craving better qualifications and study opportunities abroad. This is, however, only an option for the rich and upper classes who can afford to send their children abroad. As a result the demand for private higher education has been growing, leading to fierce political debates across government and society.

As Myanmar's state universities start to link with foreign universities, it is hoped that the quality of what is being taught will improve, satisfying the majority of the population who would not be able to take up private higher studies.

Education reforms

In light of the Millennium Development Goals, and the international push for 'Education For All', the MoE developed a 30-year Basic Education Development Programme for 2001–2031. The priorities were to ensure access to good quality, free education. When power was handed over by the State Peace and Development Council (SPDC) to the civilianised government, President Thein Sein developed a 10-point education policy, and a 20-year plan called the 'Basic Education Sector National Education Promotion 20-Year Long-Term Plan 2011–2031'. The new plan was in line with the previous 30-year basic education development programme, but was more specific on policy measures that would improve access to education, such as a stipend programme for students from deprived families. In addition a schools grant programme was proposed. Education reform was the president's fourth priority after national reconciliation with the NLD, peace with the Ethnic Armed Groups (EAGs) and economic reforms (Lall 2016). Education reform was certainly necessary; however, right from the start different stakeholders had very different ideas of what such a reform would encompass and what was needed to bring Myanmar's education system up to speed with the outside world (Lall et al. 2013).

CESR, EPIC and the Parliamentary Committee

In the summer of 2012 Myanmar embarked on a Comprehensive Education Sector Review Programme (CESR). The CESR was in three phases, producing a comprehensive education plan by the summer of 2014. UNICEF led the education consortium, working together with the Multi Donor Education Fund (MDEF). The MoE invited all interested development partners (DPs) to take part, and many, in particular AusAID, the EU and the World Bank, took the opportunity to engage with the ministry for the first time. Their focus was mostly on reviewing state education and the formal sector around the country.

The CESR's responsibilities encompassed all sectors of teaching and learning, from early childhood education to higher education and involved a wide range of ministries and departments that had a stake in education. After the first phase of work, proposals under consideration by the CESR included increasing basic education from 11 to 12 years, and changing teachers' career structures. The former could resolve the time-crunch teachers face in covering the curriculum, although the practicalities of such a transfer are complex. The latter is particularly important as teachers who want to get promoted move to secondary schools, resulting in large student–teacher ratios in primary schools with the least experienced teachers teaching these classes. The CESR also reviewed language policies (including the teaching of English) and recommended the translation of textbooks into ethnic languages. The CESR completed its Phase-1 review in early 2013. The CESR Phase-1 working committee then prepared the Comprehensive New Legal Framework for the Education Sector (2014).

Unfortunately the CESR had little political support from the outset, even the Minister of Education (who died in at the end of 2013 and was first replaced by an acting minister and later by Dr Khin San Yi in February 2014) remained sitting on the fence, ostensibly leaving the running of the CESR to more junior staff. Daw Tin Tin Shu, head of the CESR, was left to coordinate with the development partners and to fend off criticism that came from all quarters, including from inside the government and the opposition parties. The opposition NLD was at first categorically opposed to the CESR. Shortly after the start of the CESR, the NLD and associated civil society and activist groups started to undertake a national education review of their own led by the NNER. Their argument was that the MoE did not have the moral authority to lead the education reform process, that everyone knew what was wrong with the education system (and therefore no review was needed) and that a bid to reform needed to be inclusive of all groups, including ethnic education providers (Interview with Dr Thein Lwin, Head of NNER, 2013). Although the NNER was more inclusive in its approach, allowing for voices from ethnic education systems to be heard, ethnic education groups have also found that the NNER has a very particular agenda. Inclusiveness has not necessarily meant that other viewpoints are taken on board (Interviews with various ethnic education stakeholders 2013/14). The NNER proposal focused mainly on free education, decentralisation and freedom of institutional decision making. Many of their very progressive ideas are simply not implementable given the state of the education infrastructure, the lack of teachers and the cost of fixing basic faults within the system, and the available funding.

At first the CESR process and the NNER operated in parallel without much contact; however, after a few months there was some limited collaboration as each review team invited the other to events and shared limited amounts of information. This was largely due to the great diplomatic skills of Daw Tin Tin Shu who was open to suggestions and ideas from all quarters. However, in the end the NNER officially declared that it had lost faith in the government and in the MoE's reform process. The relationship between the NNER and the NLD soured and Dr Thein Lwin, who had led the NNER since its inception, was removed from the NLD in February 2015. The NLD released a statement saying that neither he nor the NNER was speaking for the party and threatened legal action against him as he had violated party rules by not obtaining permission from the committee to become involved in a separate organisation (*The Irrawaddy*, 2 February 2015).

However, other matters further complicated the working of the CESR. Given the fact that the CESR was the main window through which the development partners were able to exert influence on the thinking around education reform, the process quickly became dominated by the various agencies sending in experts for areas close to their heart. The British Council, for example, paid for a specialist to advise on English language teaching in schools, and others such as AusAid (now DFAT), the EU, etc. also sent in their people to help with issues from early childhood development to higher education. Whilst the help and good intentions were appreciated, the CESR was largely over-run by foreign experts. There was only limited time available for the actual review and to construct a coherent education plan, so the MoE people were rather overwhelmed. This also led to criticisms from inside the government in that the development partners were seen as too influential in setting the course of education reforms. The situation was not helped by the fact that the two resident experts in the posts coordinated by UNICEF to help run the ESRC (technical advisor and coordinator) kept changing. None of these experts had any prior experience of Myanmar and whilst they had worked on education reviews and reforms in other countries previously, each new appointment took a certain time to catch up and understand the workings of the CESR and the complicated political context it was evolving in. This was certainly a strain on the CESR team. Despite this the CESR ploughed on and produced its second set of reports largely on time early in 2014.

Finding that the CESR process was taking too long to feed into the legislative process, and wanting to secure a set of education laws well in time for the 2015 elections, the President's Office constituted the Education Promotion Implementation Committee (EPIC). To the surprise of all the development partners who were called at short notice to Naypyitaw on 7 October 2013, the President's Office convened a National Seminar on Pragmatic Reforms for Education to announce that this new body would take the lead on education. The development partners were assured that this was not to replace the CESR or to do similar work twice, but that EPIC and the CESR were to complement each other. In reality, however, this was a move to retake control of the process without having to shut the CESR down or make the development partners' work redundant. EPIC took up residence only a few hundred metres away from the CESR in the Diamond Jubilee Hall on the Yangon University Campus. The three components included a task force of deputy ministers from the 13 ministries directly involved in education supported by their director generals; an advisory group consisting of retired MoE officials, academics and other national experts; and 18 working groups covering specific areas of education reform, with two co-leads – one from government and one from the group of experts totalling over 200 people. EPIC had limited contact with the CESR teams and the involvement of development partners was severely reduced, not least because all meetings were held in Burmese. The EPIC reports were submitted by the end of January 2014. EPIC was clearly supported by the President's Office and was the answer not only to what was seen as an inefficiently led MoE process that had accepted too much international interference but also as a riposte to the Parliamentary Education Promotion Committee (PEPC) that had been promoted by the speaker of the parliament U Shwe Mann and Daw Aung San Suu Kyi (DASSK). The PEPC was composed of ten Union Solidarity Development Party (USDP) members, three NLD members and two MPs from the Shan Nationalities Democratic Party and was tasked to develop an overarching education 'mother law' to provide a framework for education reforms. The powerful speaker of parliament U Shwe Mann teamed up with DASSK to push the legislative process in parliament (held quite separate from the CESR work). Parliament had started to challenge government ministries, and parliamentary committees quickly learnt to use their new authority to summon officials and hold ministries to account. This has increased as legislation is developed and seems to have been the modus operandi when it came to education reforms. U Shwe Mann and DASSK started by calling the acting Minister of Education and other officials in November 2013 to criticise the pace of the education reforms and demand a greater involvement of parliament in the process. The Parliamentary Guarantees, Pledges and Undertakings Vetting Committee then also criticised the MoE for failing to deliver on 220 of its commitments (Pyoe Pin 2014). As a result U Shwe Mann and DAASK decided to take the lead in parliament with regard to the education reform process.

The President's Office also tried to remain in control of the legislative process by removing hardliners, and putting presidential allies in the right place. Key actors of the executive branch in education included the Vice President Dr Sai Mauk Kham, who allegedly was close to EPIC and attended many of the policy planning sessions, the ministers of the President's Office (also known as the 'super cabinet'), mainly U Tin Naing Thein, who was responsible for social affairs. There were also other advisors including Dr Aung Tun Thet (a former lecturer at the Yangon Institute of Economics and former Director General in the Ministry of Health) and Dr Yin Yin Nwe (a former Country Representative for UNICEF and a former geology lecturer at the University of Yangon).

The new education law and deciding on a course for reforms remain political problems the new government has had to take up. One of the key issues that was not addressed sufficiently is what power would be held at what level across the government education system.

Problems in decentralising education

Myanmar's constitution and policy environment indicate that decentralisation is on the cards; however, the legislative side of decentralisation in the education sector remains ambiguous.

During the Thein Sein government there were some announcements about re-distributing decision-making authority to the local, state and township levels, but they were ad-hoc, incomplete and tentative. In education there were some policy directives relating to decision-making capacity being put in place at the local level on local setting of curriculum, hiring of primary school teachers, the role of the newly appointed district education officers, and responsibility for school construction contracts. However, no one at the local level seemed to be confident as to what these transfers of power actually meant.

The November 2012 Draft Framework for Social and Economic Reforms (FESR), the first document that gave some indication of a possible decentralisation framework, indicated that the Government of Myanmar (GOM) planned to work with a distributed (or deconcentrated) model of education management, although retaining 'the budgetary controls over health and education expenditure for transitional adjustments, which may be a future subject of decision for fiscal decentralisation' (Government of Myanmar 2012, 34). It was also unclear as to how far the deconcentrated education management model envisaged a role for non-state actors and stakeholders in achieving the GOM's key goals in basic education.

During the Thein Sein goverment the budgetary process proved to be an impediment to decentralisation as the funding made available to each school remained centrally controlled and the control of how the funds were spent was also determined at ministerial level, regardless of local circumstances or needs. This has led to a unique and strange situation where schools have to rely on local communities to provide the bulk of resources for financing expenditures within the centralised public school system.

School grants and stipends programme

One way forward in a limited decentralisation or 'deconcentration' programme has been the establishment of two Union Government funded direct grant programmes to schools: Student Stipends and School Grants. The grants were required to be administered locally, and TEOs and head teachers were expected to take local decisions. The first set of school grants, however, were provided to schools with defined expenditure categories, and the TEO's responsibility was to audit these, potentially restricting the development of local decision-making capacity. Research in 2014 showed that schools could not necessarily meet their actual needs with the new money, although many hoped that in time things would become more flexible. Given that these direct grant programmes were the first foray of the GOM into decentralisation, the World Bank decided to get involved in supporting, expanding and deepening the programme (World Bank 2013).

The second programme for stipends was small both in terms of financing and the number of beneficiaries, although it was rolled out across the country. The beneficiary population were about 11,000 students nationally, only 2–6 students per township. The numbers were to be doubled in the 2013/14 school year. The stipend amounted to only US$5 per month over 10 months for primary students, US$6 per month for lower secondary students and US$8 per month for upper secondary students. Schools were asked to select one or two of the poorest or most disadvantaged students of their school and submit these to the township education office for final selection. Priority was given to orphans or children who only had one parent, who was not able to work. Conversations with head teachers in the first year of the project revealed how frustrating some of them found the process as it was a lot of paperwork, and there was a very low chance of their students actually receiving the money. They felt there were many deserving students that could qualify and that the money on offer was simply a drop in the ocean. However, it was the very first time that schools, head teachers and TEOs were able to take some limited decisions without ministerial approval, and this in itself felt like some limited empowerment. The WB then pledged to support both the direct grant programmes by channelling the funding through government coffers. Both programmes have been expanded with WB support since 2015.

Decentralisation, though controversial, was not the most controversial issue in education. In the end it was the passing of the new education law that stole the headlines.

The education law and student protests

In March 2014, EPIC drafted the National Education Bill. The bill was submitted to parliament in July 2014. It then needed presidential approval, and Thein Sein sent the bill back to parliament with 25 suggested changes. On 30 September 2014 the law was enacted, accepting 19 of the proposed changes.

During the whole process, momentum for protest increased as civil society organisations and student and teacher unions accused the government of not taking into account the advice from the relevant stakeholders. The NNER held meetings that decried the law as cementing the centralisation of Myanmar's education system. The meetings resulted in a set of detailed suggestions that had been submitted to parliament. The main issues that sparked unhappiness included the teaching of ethnic languages and cultures at universities, the independence of universities, including private universities, and the legality of students taking part in political activities (*The Myanmar Times*, 20 October 2014).

The Action Committee for Democratic Education (ACDE), comprising members of the All Burma Federation of Students' Unions (ABFSU), the Confederation of University Student Unions and the University Student Union, started to campaign for the amendment or redrafting of the National Education Law. Demanding a quadripartite meeting between ACDE, NNER, the government and parliament, they held a 4-day demonstration between 14 and 17 November 2014 at various locations in Yangon and other parts of the country. They threatened nationwide demonstrations if the government did not respond within 60 days. Once the 60 days expired, more than 100 people started to march from Mandalay to Yangon on 20 January 2015. Other protesters joined the march from places across the country including Pakokku, the Delta, Dawei and Mawlamyine. The 11-point demand issued by the ACDE on 24 January demanded a meeting with the government and for the law to be amended. The government agreed to meet with the students in February to discuss their demands. Three quadripartite meetings took place, during which time the student protests continued. As Dr Thein Lwin had been thrown out of the NLD, the NLD was not seen to be on the side of the NNER and the students. Students maintained that their protests would only stop after the new or amended law had been passed by the parliament. At the last meeting an agreement was struck, with the government promising to take into account the 11 demands. The government repeatedly asked the students to suspend their protests, and even a head monk endorsed this position and asked the students 'to go back to their studies'. However, the tensions grew and, as police tried to stop the protesters from marching on to Yangon from Latpadan, things started to become violent. Solidarity protests by students and civil society organisations near Sule Pyia in Yangon were violently broken up by the police in March 2015. The government not only used police but also civilian thugs who were recruited from poor areas, or who had recently been released from jail, to control the protesters and manhandle them. The riots resulted in the arrest of 127 students.

On 26 March 2015 the Upper House voted to accept amendments to the National Education Law, but with a number of changes to the 11 points that the students had protested for (*The Irrawaddy*, 26 March 2015). Whilst the students had insisted that 20 per cent of national spending should go to education, the law vowed to increase spending year on year, yet without the 20 per cent explicitly guaranteed. Part of the problem in agreeing the amendments of the law was the various competing drafts that had been sent to parliament. The students accused the government of dishonesty as a draft that had allegedly been discarded at one of the quadripartite meetings was presented to the legislature. In June 2015 the revised bill was voted into law, leaving many disillusioned and disappointed as they felt the government had broken its promise (*Radio Free Asia*, 19 June 2015).

Conclusion and ways forward for the NLD government

Clearly education is seen as a prime political consideration for the new NLD government. Politics and education in Myanmar have always been linked, and students have been the hallmark of protests against repressive and reformist governments. As Myanmar embarks on the next stage of its journey of reforms in 2016, getting education right for all will be a key challenge for politicians, practitioners and the supporting development partners.

For almost the first year in office the NLD's education policy was unclear and no official policy documents were in the public domain. On the 23 February 2017 the government launched the new National Education Strategic Plan[1] (*Frontier Myanmar*, 23 February 2017). However, despite being launched, it was impossible to get hold of a copy of the document until the summer of 2017. Based on conversations with relevant officials and development partners, it looks like the plan builds on the CESR process and that there are few if any fundamental changes to the original national education plan that had been developed by the Thein Sein government. This continuity is of course a good thing as it has meant that the effort and resources poured into the CESR process were not wasted. It is hoped that the new strategic plan will adapt teacher training to match the curricular and structural reforms envisaged. It was known that the NLD was rethinking teacher training, wanting to integrate it with HE. The interaction between teachers and academic departments at universities is certainly to be commended; however, care needs to be taken to ensure that teacher training is not seen as a 'second class' option within universities.

Although the NLD still needs to clarify its position with regard to the new education law so as to improve its relationship with the NNER and the student unions that have been protesting against this law since its first enactment, it now looks unlikely that the law will be changed in the short term.

There has been some concern across Myanmar regarding how autonomous universities should be. Autonomy for Higher Education Institutions is now part of the strategic plan and official government policy. Whilst devolution is a good way forward, the institutions need government support to develop after such a long isolation. As discussed above, the centralised budgetary impediments to decentralisation also need to be addressed.

The NLD's focus has been on Yangon and Mandalay Universities. Now that undergraduates are being reintegrated on the main campuses, it would be time to look at all the other, less prestigious, universities, so that it is not only urban elites who are served but others as well. The main issues faced by the HE sector are the quality of what is taught and the teaching methods as academic teaching staff are not research active in an international sense and courses need updating so as to meet international standards. The teaching language is theoretically English; however, this is rarely the case because the academic staff do not necessary speak English well enough. Solid academic language training needs to be a necessary part of academic training, both for students and teachers. At the time of writing various development partners are preparing to supporting the transformation of Higher Education as well as the reforming teacher training in light with the strategic plan. Myanmar's distance higher education needs a total overhaul, as its quality is so low so that its degrees are not worth much, even within Myanmar. HE needs to equip all students with the necessary skills for employment – something current HE in Myanmar fails to do.

The upgrading of the universities is unlikely to reduce the demand for private sector training, especially with regard to IT and languages. The role of civil society and non-government sector training needs to be acknowledged and ways of accreditation and recognition need to be found, as not all Myanmar citizens, especially adults whose student days are over, will be able to study at an HE institution. Adult further education is, however, a crucial pillar for the reforms to embed across society.

Relationship with development partners and donors

The international development partners have funded the CESR and therefore see the agreed developments as a part of their work. The new curriculum is being written with JICA's help. It is important that the NLD clarifies what role it wants funders to take as education reform is taken forward. As a part of this, the Myanmar government needs to take care that it does not adopt too much of a decentralised neoliberal model too quickly. Whilst allowing individual institutions to take local decisions is very positive, the withdrawal of the state seen in some reforming developing countries has resulted in poor results of access and quality across the board. The issue of social justice is crucial and the education reforms need to ensure that all parts of society are served equally.

Ethnic education and the peace process

Decades of ethnic conflict fuelled by Ne Win's Burmanisation and forced assimilation programme have led to Ethnic Armed Groups (EAGs) developing their own education departments. These departments and their dependent schools are supported by ethnic citizens across ethnic states who want to access education in their mother tongue. The NLD needs to revisit the education provision in ethnic states and look at the medium of instruction. The Thein Sein government's support to teach the ethnic language as a second language in schools did not go far enough (South and Lall 2016). Only if international good practice of mother-tongue based education is rolled out across Myanmar's ethnic states will all children be able to have an equal chance in life. This also means reassessing the relationship between government and non-state – i.e. EAG or ethnic civil society funded – schools and working out flexible transfer options for the children for secondary and HE education. This is also essential for families who would like to return to Myanmar from the refugee camps in Thailand.

Overall, there has been a lack of connection between education issues and the politics of the peace process. As the government decides what shape the peace process and the political dialogue should take, education needs to be on the agenda.

Note

1 There had been an event in early December 2016 at Oxford University, where the plan was discussed and informally unveiled by MoE officials on a UK visit.

References

Government of Myanmar. 2012. Framework for Economic and Social Reforms (FESR). November 2012 Draft.

Lall, M. 2016. *Understanding Reform in Myanmar, People and Society in the Wake of Military Rule*. Hurst Publishers, London.

Lall, M., Thei Su San, Nwe Nwe San, Thein Thein Myat and Lwin Thet Thet Khaing. 2013. *Teachers' Voice – What Education Reforms Does Myanmar Need?* Myanmar Egress and FNS, Yangon and Bangkok.

Ministry of Education. 2012. *Access to and Quality of Education: Education for All in Myanmar*. The Government of the Republic of the Union of Myanmar.
Pyoe Pin. 2014. The Political Economy of Basic Education in Myanmar Pyoe Pin, Yangon. March 2014.
South, A. and M. Lall. 2016. *Schooling and Conflict: Ethnic Education and Mother Tongue Based Teaching in Myanmar*. The Asia Foundation, San Francisco.
UNICEF. 2013. Mon State Situational Analysis (SITAN), unpublished report.
World Bank. 2013. School Grants and Student Stipends, unpublished documents.

27
HEALTH

Céline Coderey

Entering the Yangon General Hospital in early 2016, one faced a scene that was inconceivable just 3 years earlier. Hundreds of patients and their families sat here and there on the floor in the halls, the corridors, the stairs, waiting their turn to see a doctor. A place which was traditionally avoided, used as the very last resort, was becoming popular and was even chosen by patients as the first option in the health seeking process.

At the source of this change were the improvement of the hospital's equipment and staff and the introduction of the free of charges policy in the emergency department. These were initiatives that epitomised the reforms of the health care system launched by the former Thein Sein government as part of a broader project of social and economic development of the country in tune with the democratisation process (Aung-Thwin 2014, 207). These reforms represented a crucial step for the country given that, due to many years of neglect on the part of previous governments and the international community, the Myanmar health system became one of the weakest in the world (Skidmore 2008; Coderey 2015). The results of these reforms have formed the basis on which the new NLD government is now implementing its own policy of eventual universal health care.

This chapter describes these reforms and the way they were implemented in order to assess what was new in these reforms and what was not, what improvement they brought, what were their weaknesses and whether or not they are progressing in the direction initially planned. In order to better appreciate the weight of these reforms it is necessary to contextualise them by describing the historical evolution of health policies as well as the structure, the functioning and the weaknesses of the health system at the moment these reforms were launched. I will thus start by providing this contextualisation before turning to outline the reforms themselves. I will describe how they are affecting the country overall but I will also use the Thandwe region in Rakhine State as an example of a peripheral area historically particularly disadvantaged in terms of health care provision (also see Coderey 2015). I will end by providing some brief comments on the way the NLD – as the current ruling party – is pursuing these reforms and the challenge it faces.

A history of neglect

In the first years (1961–1971) of Ne Win's socialist period, government expenditures on medical establishments was up to 10 per cent of the government expenditure (Grundy et al. 2014, 183), leading to a significant increase in the number of hospitals, health centres, medical staff and also an improvement in the population's life expectancy and health condition. Throughout the rest of independent Burma's history, the health sector has always occupied a secondary position in the interest of rulers, resulting in a significantly deteriorated health system. The persistence of the military regime prevented external aid from supporting the system, due to both the protectionist attitude of the state and also the economic sanctions regime developed by many Western countries. The military regime's governance has particularly damaged the health situation in rural areas and even more in peripheral states inhabited by minority ethnic groups. In 1993 a health policy which encouraged an increased role of cooperatives, joint ventures, the private sector and NGOs in delivering health care was drafted with the intent to find a way to inject money into the sector and hence compensate for the government's low contribution. The final aim of the policy was to grant 'Health for All' by 2030. Yet the policy was not implemented and the situation did not improve. By 2000, the contribution of the government to the health sector had dropped to 1.2 per cent of the GDP and the user-fees rocketed to the highest levels. In 2000 WHO ranked Myanmar 190th out of 191 countries for the performance of its health system (WHO 2014). The perpetuation of this situation in a country where 70 per cent of the population dwells in rural areas and nearly 32 per cent lives below the poverty line had deleterious consequences on the health of people. The under-5 child mortality rate and maternal mortality rate were, and still are, among the highest in Southeast Asia (WHO 2012) with particularly high rates in conflict zones and other areas with low levels of socioeconomic development. Malaria, tuberculosis and HIV/AIDS are significant public health problems, in particular in the border areas with Thailand and China as well as in Rakhine and Chin States (Grundy et al. 2014).

The situation has persisted almost unaltered up to the present, yet some signs of change have appeared since the year 2000. The outcome of the abovementioned WHO's ranking acted as 'a galvanizing force for the reconsideration of the health policy' (Grundy et al. 2014, 183) and towards the adoption of a more open attitude concerning the collaboration with international and global actors. Particularly important in this sense was the fact that in 2000 Myanmar agreed to work towards the achievement of the eight Millennium Development Goals, including MDGs 4, 5 and 6 relative to the reduction of the rate of the three diseases (malaria, TB and HIV), the rate of child mortality and the rate of maternal mortality. This said, the change has become more evident only with the economic opening in 2008 and the transition from a military dictatorship to a semi-civil government presided over by Thein Sein in 2011 (Grundy et al. 2014, 184). These two events have set the basis for the health reform I will outline below after describing the situation before these reforms came about.

Structure, functioning and weaknesses of the health care system

The Myanmar health system is composed of biomedicine and indigenous traditional medicine,[1] with the former occupying a dominant position. This system is directed by the Ministry of Health which works in collaboration with WHO, the UN agencies and other international organisations, under the direct control of the National Health Committee, created in 1989 by the military government.

For both medicines there are services in both the public and private sector. Public services consist of hospitals and health centres. For biomedicine, hospitals focus on treatment while health centres focus on primary health care, that is, prevention with much emphasis on hygiene and mother and children health care.

These services are present all over the territory, organised according to a pyramidal structure which goes from state hospitals to regional hospitals and down to quarters and village health centres. Yet in peripheral areas which hold out against the central government such as Kachin, Kaya (Karenni) and Kayin (Karen) State and which are controlled by ethic armed groups (Coderey 2015), they do not exist or they are inoperative (Grundy et al. 2014, 180). Here the local authorities have developed their own health services, which remain nevertheless highly inadequate. Public services are also absent from the Northern Rakhine areas inhabited by the Muslim community of Rohingya, who are not considered citizens.

A first weakness of the system to highlight is the shortage in terms of staff, particularly specialists, equipment and medicine and the important unequal distribution of those that are available. This is a problem especially in the biomedical sector where there are only 17 doctors, 28 nurses and 23 midwives per 100,000 people (Soe Htet et al. 2014); well equipped secondary and tertiary health care is largely concentrated in Yangon and Mandalay, letting the rest of the country depend on scarce regional hospitals and health centres. For instance, for many years and up to 2013, Thandwe hospital only had two paediatricians, one surgeon, one orthopaedic, one anaesthetist, one dentist and one obstetrician-gynaecologist. In terms of instruments the hospital is provided with an operating theatre for simple operations, some basic tests instruments such as an X-ray machine and a dentist chair donated by the French NGO Association Médicale France Asie (AMFA). In contrast, analysis of tissues, ultrasound imaging, CT (computerised tomography) and MRI (magnetic resonance imaging) scans, blood banks, important operations and complex treatments are not available. Health centres are lacking: the main centres are operated by a health assistant and a midwife, the sub-centres only by a midwife. This is particularly challenging especially when one sub-centre operates for several villages of considerable dimensions or highly populated such as Giaiktaw and Myabin where only one midwife has to take care of the 3,000 houses of both villages.

A common complaint about public services of both biomedicine and traditional medicine is that 'staff are often absent, careless and lacking in medical skills' but also that 'patients are treated differently depending on their economic condition' and that 'doctors always try to redirect the patients to their own private clinic so that they can earn more money'.

Another major problem concerning public services is the cost. In 2000 the government introduced a cost-sharing policy, where patients and government are expected to share medical fees. Yet in fact, as stated by Saw et al. (2013), it is the patient who pays almost the totality of expenses out of pocket, going from 99 per cent in 2005 to 92 per cent in 2010, the highest percentage in the world. The situation is also exacerbated by the fact that the government supplies the services with medicines intended to be given free to the patients, but these being very limited, the staff is compelled to buy other products from outside shops and charge them to the patients.

Because most private staff also work in public services, the distribution of private services largely reiterates the (unequal) distribution of public services. The most common form of private service for biomedicine and the only existing for traditional medicine is the clinics that public staff open at home or nearby and which are generally equipped to treat only minor cases. However, for biomedicine in recent years some new polyclinics have emerged. A law allowing the opening of private hospitals was introduced in 2007 and, since then, several biomedical hospitals have emerged in Yangon and Mandalay. These services, particularly those run by doctors, are considered much better than the public services especially because patients are provided with medicines, and doctors are said to take much more care of the patients regardless of their economic status, yet not everyone can afford them (Coderey 2015, 284).

Also part of the private sector are some national and international NGOs that try to fill the gaps with public services by providing ambulatory or institutional care in several places around the country (Coderey 2015, 267). They operate primarily in the biomedical sector. Their number and mobility have always been largely limited by the protectionist attitude of the government. Only after the disaster of Cyclone Nargis in 2008, and the reduction in political control from 2010, has the government allowed more NGOs to operate in the country. Yet, with very few exceptions, they were seldom allowed to work outside Yangon, Mandalay and the area of the Delta hit by Nargis.

The perpetration of the dictatorship has largely limited the number and quality of medicines available on the local market. The majority of biomedical products – 80–85 per cent – is imported from abroad, mainly from India (about 45 per cent) and China, but also from Bangladesh, Thailand, China, South Korea and the Philippines, and, more recently, from Germany, Switzerland, France and the USA. Most medicines are imported through companies after having been tested by the US Food and Drug Administration (FDA) and having been granted a licence. Yet, the weakness in FDA as well as in trade and sales controls combined with a high level of corruption have facilitated the illegal import of medicines through the borders and the production of counterfeits (Coderey 2015, 268).

The production of traditional medicines is regulated by the department of traditional medicine which provides a licence only to products it has tested and proved to be natural, non-toxic and produced according to the Good Manufacturing Practice. However, controls are accomplished neither regularly nor efficiently, giving manufacturers the opportunity to add some pharmaceuticals or some heavy metals to their products that are mainly analgesics.

The reform of the health system

After Thein Sein's government took power in 2011 it launched reforms intended to remedy some of the shortcomings of the health system just described. With this aim it restored the National Health Committee and, by its means, and in collaboration with WHO, it established a 20 year National Health Plan divided into four 5 year plans, of which the first was drafted for the years 2011–2016. This plan was formulated by taking into consideration the prevailing health problems of the population and the need to achieve the MDGs set for 2015. Yet the final goal on the horizon (to be reached by 2030) remained the one formulated in the health policy of 1993, of ensuring that quality health services are accessible and equitable for all citizens. The main strategies stated in the plan were the strengthening of the health system, the extension of the health care coverage in rural, peri-urban and border areas, and the expansion of human resources and infrastructure (WHO 2014, 2–13), to be implemented through an increased role given to cooperatives, joint ventures, the private sector and NGOs, and the strengthening of collaboration with other countries and the encouragement of external aids and investment.

To inaugurate the reform and make it possible, the government increased the budget allocated to health by about 3 or 4 times and kept increasing it in the following years. The most significant growth was in 2013, when the health expenditure went up to 3.9 per cent of GDP (Risso-Gill et al. 2014, 2). According to a doctor from Yangon at the time, 'the budget for 2014/15 is around 705 billions *kyats*, and for 2015/2016 it will be even more, around 756 billions *kyats*'. Considering that since 1988 the expenditure has never exceeded 2 per cent of the GDP, this change was a significant one, although compared with other countries in the region and according to the WHO guidelines it remains largely insufficient. Another initiative on the part of the government has been, in November 2012, the provision of US$5.3 million to administer pentavalent vaccine[2] to 1.4 million children (Saw et al. 2013, 6).

In response to these initiatives, which they saw as a proof of the government's commitment to improve the health system, international actors have themselves increased their contribution.

The Global Fund has increased, and in 2012 the provision of a $300 million Millennium Development Goal Health Fund was announced (Grundy et al. 2014, 184). On the other hand, other sorts of foreign aid and investment the government hoped to attract did not prove significant, with the rules on foreign investment still unclear and reduced activity due to uncertainty surrounding the 2015 elections.

One of the main initiatives of the reforms was the improvement and expansion of medical facilities: hospitals and centres. Intending to ensure adequate coverage of hospital services in every region and state, the government has engaged in building new hospitals and in improving the existing ones by increasing the number of beds in those services located in highly populated areas and by replacing and adding new equipment (such as X-ray and ultrasound machines), by increasing the medicines supply and by appointing new staff. This initiative has been funded partly by the Ministry of Health and partly by external donors and foreign investors (Ministry of Health 2014, 42–44).

The project initially focused on infrastructure and equipment much more than on staff, which remained severely lacking. More importantly, the change focused primarily on Yangon and Mandalay. Two new hospitals have been built in Yangon and in both places the existing ones – General Hospitals, Children Hospitals and Central Women's Hospitals – have been largely improved in terms of equipment and medical supply. These improvements have been made possible through external funding and mainly thanks to the support from the Japan International Cooperation Agency (Ministry of Health 2014, 44) and, according to one informant, for the Yangon General Hospital, a financial contribution from the UK obtained by Daw Aung San Suu Kyi.

However, there are reports of opening and uplifting of hospitals also elsewhere. For instance, new hospitals have opened in Southern Rakhine – two in Gwa and two in Thandwe area – and many have been improved. The Thandwe district hospital has significantly improved since 2011, partly with the help of the French NGO AMFA. As some respondents commented: 'now we have 24 hour electricity and air conditioning'; 'now there is an ultrasound machine, a dental chair and also a consultation room'. Nevertheless, people stress that despite the improvements the equipment is still far from being satisfactory. Moreover, in terms of staff, with the exception of the appointment of an eye specialist, no change has been made.

With the intent of extending the health care coverage especially in rural and difficult-to-reach areas and of strengthening the primary health care sector in order to reach the MDGs 4 and 5, the government planned to establish more grassroots level centres such as Regional Health Centres, sub-centres and station hospitals, to renovate and upgrade the existing ones and to increase basic health staff by recruiting and training voluntary health workers as community health workers and auxiliary midwives (Ministry of Health 2014, 42). This project has been mainly realised through a 4 year Health System Strengthening programme supported by the vaccine alliance, GAVI, and conducted by stakeholders under the Ministry of Health, in collaboration with WHO, UNICEF and the Myanmar Red Cross Society (Ministry of Health 2014, 47–48). This project covered 20 townships in the first year, 60 in 2013 and 180 in 2015. Because of this focus on a restricted area, however, the rest of the country has remained largely unchanged.

A second initiative taken by the government was the reduction of medical costs. Thanks to the increase of the state budget allocated to health, the patients' expenditure has declined from about 80 per cent to 60 per cent. Several informants affirmed that this was not enough, as one doctor from Yangon stated: 'this contribution is still very low, actually the lowest in the ASEAN region. According to WHO, a fair contribution would be a minimum of 50 dollars per capita.'

Although small, this contribution has brought a significant change directly and indirectly, through the foreign support raised in response to the government's change of attitude. Since 2012/13 public hospitals have provided free of charge medicines, tests (for instance blood tests, X-rays) and operations, especially for emergencies and delivery of babies; other medicines and services have to be paid for but the cost is much less than it used to be. A doctor comments that 'now 80, 90 percent of the medicines are given for free, even in rural areas'. That said, so far this change seems to be restricted to the hospital setting: in the health centres and especially the sub-centres the supply of medicines is still insufficient to allow free services.

The main problem highlighted by all informants is that the medicines provided free of charge are of low quality. As a doctor from Yangon explained, 'the government relies on cheap medicines, which means low quality medicines. Medical staff thus explain to patients that they can get those medicines free of charge, but if they want good medicines they have to buy them themselves.' Moreover, a villager from Myabin commented, 'they give medicine free of charge but just a little bit, for a few days; if you need the medicine for longer they give you a prescription letter to buy the medicine in a shop'. Another sign indicating that the system has not yet evolved much is the fact that some people give doctors and medical staff monetary donations in order to get better treatment.

In addition to the free of charge policy, the government claimed that new social security legislation was introduced that would require employers to contribute 6.5 per cent of salaries to health and welfare costs. None of my informants were aware of this; this system, which was already supposed to exist, seems to be ineffective or non-existent.

A third field on which the reform has focused is the achievement of MDGs 3, 5 and 6, that is, reduction of the rates of TB, malaria and HIV and the reduction of maternal and child mortality. Since 2011 a major improvement has been achieved in the treatment of HIV. Up until a few years ago, the provision of HIV treatment in the public sector was restricted to two public hospitals in Yangon and this was due to a lack of resources but it was also in order to monopolise and control the management of this sensitive issue. In 2015 the government decided to amplify and decentralise the treatment by allocating this task to district hospitals all over the national territory. These hospitals distribute the medication only to patients living in that area.

This change has been possible thanks to the increased national and international funding but also to the collaboration with NGOs. In the past NGOs tended to work independently from the government, providing parallel or supplementary services; they have now started working in partnership with it, supporting the public services through the supply of staff and sometimes also medicines and equipment that the systems lack. Another important change has occurred in the private sector. The government has allowed more NGOs to provide HIV treatment, including in remote and borders areas.

In relation to the reduction of mother and child mortality, several strategies have been implemented. The Ministry of Health has stated that it recruited volunteers trained to work as assistant midwives and appointed Public Health Supervisors Grade II in order to reduce the burden carried by midwives and let them focus on their main task, which is mother and child care (Ministry of Health 2014, 40); but according to my survey, this appointment has been limited to a limited number of places. What instead has been done is the improvement of the training. Groups of nurses, midwives and obstetrician-gynaecologists from every state and region and townships are sent to Mandalay, Naypidaw or Yangon where they receive special training on mother and child health. When they return to their workplace they, in turn, have to train the staff working under them. A third level of strategies concern the financial support to pregnant women: 'Myanmar has initiated plans to introduce a Maternal and Child Health Voucher Scheme in one pilot township and a Township-Based Health Protection Scheme in another such pilot township' (Saw et al. 2013, 6).

Another important component of the reforms has been the adoption of a more open attitude toward civil society and the NGOs, numbers of which have since considerably increased. For instance, inspired by a popular local singer who has created an organisation supporting blood donation and providing transportation for funerals, many people around the country have created a network which takes care of these duties. In Thandwe area, Lintha, Myabin and Giaiktaw have such an organisation which also provides free transportation to the hospital for those who need it.

Concerning INGOs, it is very significant that the new government has allowed them to work in more remote places to which they had been denied access for a long time. The main exception to this geographical freedom is the northern part of Rakhine State, where inter-religious conflicts between Buddhists and Muslims have soared since 2012. The presence of some INGOs in that area and their involvement in humanitarian actions in support, at least for some of them, of the Rohingya, have inflamed the situation, reactivating scepticism towards INGOs. After some accidents occurred in 2013 all INGOs were expelled from the state. Only several months later were they able to resume their activities. Nevertheless Rakhine State remains a very sensitive zone for INGOs. INGOs have also started working in association with local NGOs which are well positioned to reach the local community but also to collaborate with government services, providing them with the staff, equipment and medicines they lack, as mentioned in the case of HIV.

Another sector which has largely benefited from the reforms but also from the economic opening of the country is the pharmaceutical market, which is indeed seeing a certain expansion. On the one side, pharmaceutical demand is growing, fuelled by the increase of the per capita income, the emergence of a middle class willing to spend more for better medicines, and the government plan to provide free medicines in public services. On the other side, the opening of the market in 2010, the decrease in the economic sanctions and the economic growth of the country are providing new opportunities for local and foreign investors. Old companies are raising their imports; new companies are established mainly as joint ventures between foreign investors and local actors; several international pharmaceutical companies are exploring business opportunities. Yet many potential investors are still pondering their decision, given the uncertain political landscape, the opacity of the regulatory system, the complexity of the market and the fragmented nature of the sales network. This said, between 2011 and 2012 the overall pharmaceutical market in Myanmar grew by almost 19 per cent (Shobert 2013) and it is expected to expand further in the future, especially with the new NLD government assuming power. If the market is still much dominated by foreign products, the outlook is likely to change. Indeed in 2012 the government has allowed private factories to open in the country.

In terms of quality control, a doctor from Yangon reports that

> in August–September 2015, the FDA created a 'network committee for drug, food and cosmetic safety'. This joint force, which includes FDA personnel, patients' associations and others partners, tries to cope with unofficial drugs, including counterfeits. They check pharmacies and shops and try to educate vendors about the problem.

As a component of the national health system, traditional medicine too has been allocated a part of the increased budget. This said, the improvement in this sector seems to be minor in comparison with that affecting Western medicine, and is unequal among the different services and regions, thus suggesting that the power hierarchy between biomedicine and traditional medicine as well as centre and periphery is still strong.

In this case too, the main change concerns the infrastructure, the building of new services and the upgrading of the old ones. A doctor from Yangon commented that, starting from 2012, the two main hospitals, of Yangon and Mandalay, were upgraded from 200 to 250 beds. On 4 November 2015 a new hospital was opened in the capital Naypyitaw, and all around the country new hospitals and clinics have been built or are under construction. The Thein Sein government aimed to have clinics in every township within 20 years. Concerning Rakhine, a 25 bed hospital is under construction in Thandwe area, which currently has only a 16 bed clinic, and a 16 bed hospital is under construction in Ciauktoo. Informants from Yangon hospitals affirm that 'thanks to the government's support we treat free of charge' while informants from Mandalay affirm that 'the progress has been minimal' and those from Thandwe that 'nothing has changed and the treatment is still under payment'.

What has certainly expanded in recent years is the medicines market. Given the economic growth of the country and the ongoing demand for traditional medicine products, new products have been launched and new factories have emerged. According to government statistics, in 2014, there were 2,578 registered manufacturers and 12,712 registered drugs (Ministry of Health 2014).

Conclusion

Asked whether the Myanmar health care system has improved since 2011 and, if yes, how, a district medical officer replied with a hearty laugh. That 'reply' perfectly encapsulated the explanation which followed and which echoed similar answers I received from many other informants. It can be summarised as 'Yes, there have been some improvements but they are not enough' – certainly not enough to achieve a reliable and accessible health system, not to mention reaching the 2030 goal of health coverage for all.

One of the main weaknesses of this reform is that it is not in tune with the aims stated in the 1993 and 2011 health policies. If the official intention was to focus on the expansion of health care in difficult-to-reach areas and on primary health care, the actual improvement is highly concentrated in the main cities of Yangon and Mandalay and on secondary and especially tertiary health care, places and sectors which have always been privileged. This results in strengthening – instead of reducing – the unequal access to health care.

Moreover, the fact that medicines provided free of charge are of low quality does not really represent a progression towards 'equality of access to health care' and 'health for all'. If it is true that now also poorer people can receive some treatment, the inequality remains because good quality medicines are still accessible only to the wealthy. Moreover, because no improvement has been made in terms of quality and safety checks, all medicines do remain potentially dangerous. Also, the quality of education must be improved in order to produce doctors who are not only more skilful but also, according to a doctor from Yangon, 'more open to dialogue with the patients instead of simply dictating to him/her what s/he has to do'.

Gratuity is certainly important but it is not the priority. All my informants stress the importance of being able to access good quality medicines, equipment and staff. Similarly Shobert (2013) reports that 'in March, 47 percent of people in two cities – Yangon and Bago – said their highest preference for improved healthcare was improved quality'. This said, for several people the price is still crucial, all the more so given that the recent economic development of the country is not affecting everybody and many people still live in poverty. The social security system, which is claimed to have been introduced, needs to be efficiently implemented.

The year 2015 has passed yet the MDGs have not been achieved. If, overall, much progress has been made, the maternal mortality rate is still 282 per 100,000, the highest in the whole ASEAN region; it was expected to be reduced to 145. The fact that, with the exception of training, the different initiatives have not reached remote areas has certainly contributed to hinder the achievement of the goal. Moreover, the inefficient execution of the public health programmes, the low education level on reproductive health, the mistrust in the public health system and the general level of poverty remain largely unchanged, thus contributing to perpetuate the situation.

Assuming power in early 2016, the NLD inherited not only this health care scenario but also the responsibility to improve it by pursuing the reforms initiated by Thein Sein. As Dr Kyaw Zwe, a central committee member of the NLD health network, commented just before the NLD formally took its mandate, the party's aim is to go beyond what the previous government had accomplished – mainly updating hospitals – and to focus on improving the accessibility of public health (Shwe Yee Saw Myint 2016). The challenge – at least initially – was that the incoming ministry was given limited room for action given that the budget for the first year was already allocated – and low. Future plans had already been drafted and previous officers, including from the military, were still very influential in the health sector. The situation is nevertheless likely to change in the following years, at least in terms of budget. 'We plan to increase the health budget by 3 percent every year. So according to our policy, by 2020 the government is going to allocate 12 percent of the budget for health and achieve Universal Health Coverage by 2040,' said Dr Kyaw Zwe. Yet the way the money will be used to reach this goal is still unclear.

From two recent visits to the country, one in November 2016 and the second one in February 2017, and discussions with several health care actors as well as urban and rural dwellers, it is clear that not much has changed during the past year, especially in rural areas. Driving me to the Thandwe airport at the end of my last trip, the driver pointed at a building at the side of the road. 'See? They built this hospital two years ago . . . it is empty . . . no medicines, no doctors, nothing. This is Rakhine State, no change here.' Like him, many people express their frustration at an extremely slow and still unequal development. Others, on the contrary, like a restaurant owner from Myabin village also interviewed in February 2017, state that 'we have only had democracy for one year and, after so many years of military and neglect, how can the change be immediate? They need time; it is coming, but slowly.' Unfortunately not many hold this opinion.

The main challenge for the new government, besides the more logistical, technical and bureaucratic ones, is a matter of building trust, which can be done only by proving to the population that the (health) care is now addressed to everyone, regardless of where s/he lives and that the gap and the hierarchy between centre and periphery are eventually starting to fade.

Notes

1 The traditional medicine which is part of the national health system is a modernised and simplified version of a much more complex form of medicine combining Indian Ayurveda, Buddhist medical knowledge, astrology and other esoteric practices. This new version mainly emphasises herbal medicine.

2 The pentavalent vaccine is a combination of five vaccines in one: diphtheria, tetanus, whooping cough, hepatitis B and haemophilius influenza type b.

References

Aung-Thwin, Michael. 2014. 'Myanmar in 2013: Integration and the Challenge of Reform'. *Southeast Asian Affairs*: 203–223.

Coderey, Céline. 2015. 'Accessibility to Biomedicine in Contemporary Rakhine State'. In *Metamorphosis. Studies in Social and Political Change in Myanmar*, edited by Renaud Egreteau and François Robinne, 260–287. Singapore: NUS Press.

Grundy, John, Peter Annear, Shakil Ahmedb and Beverley-Ann Biggs Deakins. 2014. 'Adapting to Social and Political Transitions. The Influence of History on Health Policy Formation in the Republic of the Union of Myanmar (Burma)'. *Social Science & Medicine* 107: 179–188.

Ministry of Health. 2014. The Republic of the Union of Myanmar. www.moh.gov.mm/.

Risso-Gill, Isabelle, Martin McKee, Richard Coker, Piot Peter and Helena Legido-Quigley. 2014. 'Health System Strengthening in Myanmar During Political Reforms: Perspectives from International Agencies'. *Health Policy and Planning* 29: 466–474.

Saw, Yu Mon, Khine Lae Win, Laura Wen-Shuan Shiao, Moe Moe Thandar, Rachel M. Amiya, Akira Shibanuma, Soe Tun and Masamine Jimba. 2013. 'Taking Stock of Myanmar's Progress toward the Health-Related Millennium Development Goals: Current Roadblocks, Paths Ahead'. *International Journal for Equity in Health* 12 (78) doi: 10.1186/1475-9276-12-78.

Shobert, Benjamin. 2013. 'Healthcare in Myanmar'. Accessed 31 April 2014. www.forbes.com/sites/benjaminshobert/2013/08/19/healthcare-in-myanmar/#6f1558bd6142.

Shwe Yee Saw Myint. 2016. 'NLD Aims for Health Sector Shake-up'. *The Myanmar Times*, 14 March. Accessed 17 February 2017. www.mmtimes.com/index.php/national-news/yangon/19446-nld-aims-for-health-sector-shake-up.html.

Skidmore, Monique. 2008. 'Contemporary Medical Pluralism in Burma'. In *Dictatorship, Disorder and Decline in Myanmar*, edited by Monique Skidmore and Trevor Wilson, 193–207. Canberra: ANU E Press.

Soe Htet, Fan Victoria, Alam Kurshid and Mahal Ajay. 2014. 'Financial Risks From Ill Health in Myanmar'. *Asia-Pacific Journal of Public Health* 27 (4): 418–428.

World Health Organization. 2012. 'Myanmar'. Accessed 31 April 2014. www.who.int/countries/mmr/fr/index.html.

World Health Organization. 2014. 'Myanmar'. Accessed 31 December 2014. www.who.int/countries/mmr/fr/index.html.

PART VI

International

28
THE WORLD

David I. Steinberg

Neutralism as nexus

The quintessential orientation of Myanmar foreign policy since independence has been neutralism. Originally driven by the Cold War and the Sino–Soviet rivalry in the context of the geo-strategic position of Burma, it was also a product of its fissiparous internal political spectrum. Its critical strategic location, effectively sandwiched between China and India, demands a relatively small state pursue such a policy. As U Nu said, 'We are a tender gourd amid the cactus.' But aboveground and underground communist and leftist parties, together with a more Western oriented trained elite, subjected the democratically elected government of U Nu to competing tendencies and loyalties that required deft balancing in both foreign affairs and domestic economic policies. Socialism has since been discredited in Myanmar by inept management, if *dirigiste* tendencies have not. But if such balance in international relations has been perceived by much of the outside world to have been lost in the past half century, it is likely to once again resume its salience in Myanmar's foreign policy in the near future. Whether characterised by some Western concerns of a 'rising China' influence in Myanmar, or Chinese anxiety over Western 'containment' policies coupled – even coordinated – with Japanese economic assistance there, Myanmar will evolve its own 'rebalancing' policies to ensure its national interests are maintained and its international equilibrium restored.

That policy was as much active as it was passive, even if so perceived as the latter by many of the states in the West. The state actively guarded that neutrality and avoided the Vietnam War, abstained from joining ASEAN when it seemed to be an anti-communist force, and in 1979 dropped out of the Non-Aligned Movement when it was to meet in Havana at a period when the Chinese were fearful of Soviet 'hegemony' in the region. U Thant was chosen to be Secretary General of the United Nations in 1961 because the state's perceived political balance – the most neutral in Asia – was recognised by both Eastern and Western blocs. The value of Burma to the United States in that period reflected its centrality: it was not interest in trade, economics, human rights, or even strategic considerations, but rather it was a highly useful listening post on both Soviet and Chinese activities and attitudes in the region. Burma was a centre of diplomatic intrigue.

This neutrality was characterised in the 1950s by both China and the United States as immoral – one could not be neutral in the supposed sweep of socialist historical inevitability (as China supported the rebellion of the Burma Communist Party) nor in the moral democratic movement of the 'free world', with Western information agencies and non-profit organisations assisting the spread of those values. The US clandestinely supported the Chinese Nationalist (KMT-anti-communist) remnants that had retreated into Burma in 1950 and thereafter in their ineffectual forays into Yunnan Province. But after the coup of 1962, to much of the Western media and even to some governments, Myanmar was characterised as having cut itself off from the outside world until the 2010 elections. This simplistic analysis had multiple errors. The Ne Win period (1962–1988) did indeed for most of that time effectively avoid close contacts with the West (the United States was asked to resume its modest foreign assistance programme, cut off after 1962, only in 1979). But it relied on Japan for economic assistance, and those relations were quite close.

US–Myanmar relations and 'regime change'

Following the coup of 18 September 1988, however, Myanmar tried, rather ineptly, to open up. It passed a foreign investment law that year, signed economic pacts with Thailand on timber and fisheries, issued regulations encouraging civil society, internally considered joining ASEAN, and officially – and with considerable fanfare – invited tourists to visit. These were attempts, however poorly administered, to rejoin the international world order but on its own, Burmese or Burman (Bamar), terms that would also help perpetuate military domination of aspects of that complex set of ethnic societies known as Myanmar.

It was the US that attempted to close the country off from the West. Seriatim, it stopped economic, military, and anti-narcotics assistance in 1988; US regulations require the closing of foreign aid if an elected government is overthrown by a coup. Although the BSPP administration was not originally elected but came to power in the 1962 coup, the US modest economic aid programme, anti-narcotics activity, and the military training programme (IMET) were stopped after the riots and coup of 1988. It later imposed sanctions; discouraged investment; prohibited trade; stopped the import of jade and rubies; and encouraged other states, such as those in the European Union (EU), Canada, Australia, and Japan, to join the sanctions regimen. Myanmar's traditional neutralism was compromised by the West, led by the US, which had as its unstated, but quite obvious, policy 'regime change' – rule by the National League for Democracy (NLD) following the May 1990 elections swept by that opposition group. Whether those elections were for a new constitutional convention or a new government is disputed, but it is clear that the West believed it was for the latter, and the NLD acted as if it were. Burmese neutralism had also earlier been compromised by China in 1967, when the 'cultural revolution' was encouraged to spread to Rangoon (Yangon), resulting in anti-Chinese riots, dozens of deaths, and withdrawal of ambassadors for a period.

US policy towards Myanmar, still anachronistically officially called Burma in the US during the Thein Sein government, was in essence determined by the real and purported views of Aung San Suu Kyi who had captured the imagination of the public, the Congress, and the US government by 1989, and was reinforced by becoming the Nobel Peace Prize laureate in 1991. Her views, expounded vociferously by human rights adherents and dissident expatriates and extrapolated by them when she could not communicate to the outside world, favoured a sanctions and exclusion set of policies, denied any semblance of legitimacy to the military regime (including its change of name in 1989), and advocated stoppage of the human rights abuses in that state and termination of her house arrest. They were extremely effective in mobilising supportive sentiments and influencing US policy, and had high-level access throughout the various components of the US executive and legislative branches. In essence, the views of Aung

San Suu Kyi became US policy towards Myanmar. These views strongly influenced the EU, and especially the UK, where she had lived. Her husband and her two sons were British citizens.

Yet, at least by 2007, it had become apparent to knowledgeable observers on both sides of the US political fence that the policy of regime change through sanctions, exclusion, and moral denigration had failed to achieve its goal and was unlikely to succeed (Green & Mitchell 2007). As Selth (2012) noted:

> For 20 years, the United States (US) pursued a policy toward Burma that was never going to achieve its stated aims. Indeed, Washington's unremitting hostility to the military government in Rangoon (and, after 2005, the new capital of Naypyitaw) was in many respects quite counter-productive. It also flew in the face of strategic developments in the wider Asia-Pacific region. No foreign government or international organisation can take credit for the wide-ranging reform program introduced by President Thein Sein after his inauguration in March 2011.

The melding of neutral imperatives

In the earliest period of President Obama's administration, and certainly by March 2009, both the Burmese and the US were sending quiet signals that policies of both states needed adjustment (Steinberg 2015a, 427–452). The Myanmar administration's motivation may have been prompted by the perception of the too strong and penetrating influence of China, which was counter to Myanmar's balanced foreign policy stance, and a rising popular Burmese impression of its undue economic influence; the need for foreign economic and technical assistance, especially though the multilateral economic institutions such as the World Bank and the Asian Development Bank – denied by the US; the appalling low standard of living compared with other ASEAN and regional states that before were far behind Burma/Myanmar, which had once been predicted half a century earlier to be the wealthiest country in Southeast Asia; fears of potential US aggressive action; and perhaps a sense that the reputation of the *tatmadaw* had to be resuscitated through progress by greater international involvement. The argument, articulated at very high government levels, that Myanmar, with sufficient food and natural resources, could continue its policies that cut its population off from the outside world was no longer valid. Internet, television dishes, ubiquitous international radio broadcasting, and the smuggling in of printed materials deprived the military of the continued luxury of political intellectual isolation.

A new US administration perhaps believed that a policy shift in Myanmar could bring a foreign policy success in Asia at little cost. It may also have been in part motivated by a desire to improve relations with ASEAN, which were most difficult as long as Myanmar was deemed a pariah and was in that group, which it had formally joined in July 1997 in spite of strenuous efforts by the US to prevent it (Haacke 2015, 292). A full-scale policy review was undertaken in the spring of 2009, and the policy announced in September of that year. Whether the US shift on Myanmar was linked to, and an intentional precursor of, the later 2011 Obama 'pivot', later termed 'rebalancing', of US policy to East Asia is questionable, although the Chinese regarded the overall US policy shift in emphasis on, as well as the increases in Japanese assistance in, that region as part of the US 'containment' policy to prevent the 'rise' of Chinese influence in Southeast Asia. There is no evidence, however, that these policy shifts were 'in direct response to the policies of any foreign government or international organization' (Selth 2012, 13; Steinberg 2015b). The US 'rebalancing' policy was simply a restatement of its 150-year-old position in Asia, aimed at preventing the rise of any hegemonic power in East Asia.

A United States 'action-for-action' policy of what was called 'pragmatic engagement' was instituted. It called for high-level dialogue, and gradually improving bilateral relations as reforms were instituted within Myanmar. Most important was the release of political prisoners and freeing of Aung San Suu Kyi from house arrest. This pragmatic engagement was a political compromise – an inchoate recognition by the US administration that it could only go so far in improving relations because of the aura and sway that Aung San Suu Kyi commanded; her advocacy of policies to deny legitimacy to the Myanmar government and the thrall in which she held the US Congress were paramount. So sanctions had to continue, as some had been instituted by the Congress and others by the executive branch, while high-level dialogue began (Steinberg 2010).

Until January 2010, Aung San Suu Kyi was mentioned in the *Congressional Record* 1,598 times, of which mentions Senator Mitch McConnell (R, Kentucky), an influential figure, contributed 340 mentions. Myanmar was a 'boutique' issue – a bipartisan political one exciting attention among a small number, and on which no administration was prepared to use up any considerable degree of political capital. High-level dialogue in Myanmar started with the visit of Senator Jim Webb (D, Virginia) who saw both Senior General Than Shwe and Aung San Suu Kyi.

Although the constitutional referendum of May 2008 on the proposed Myanmar constitution was clearly manipulated, and the elections of November 2010 obviously lacked any objective standard and were boycotted by the NLD (because approving that election and participating in it would automatically void the NLD victory in the May 1990 election and Aung San Suu Kyi was still under house arrest), freeing her a few days after the elections, together with progressive liberalisation of the press, labour legislation, and other factors, were sufficient justification for the visit of Secretary of State Hillary Clinton to Myanmar. In effect, the process of gradual reform and liberalisation led to the appointment of a US ambassador, a post that had been vacant since 1991, although an embassy had been maintained and diplomatic relations continued, but at considerable distance from and with coldness towards the Myanmar government. Some executive branch sanctions were eliminated, although a wide swath of individuals were personally continued on a sanctions register, and certain military-dominated institutions could not receive US support. Although the US had provided humanitarian assistance through non-governmental organisations, it opened a USAID mission in Yangon, and began programming in law, democracy, assisting the peace process, and economic development. By September 2015, USAID had committed US$276 million in support, although expenditures were perhaps a quarter of that total at this writing. Aside from some modest programmes in military law and non-lethal training, military-to-military relations were eschewed by the US because of congressional concerns. President Obama visited Myanmar twice following Secretary Clinton's visits, and the US supported Myanmar's efforts to chair ASEAN with technical assistance and training.

The European Union and beyond

The US's officially changed and improved position resulted in an outpouring of Western and Japanese economic assistance. The World Bank and the Asian Development Bank established offices and began reprogramming after a long hiatus. The EU had imposed sanctions under its 'common position' of 1996 that had called for the withdrawal of all military attachés from Myanmar, an embargo on provision of 'arms, munitions, and military equipment', suspension of non-humanitarian economic assistance, denial of visas for SLORC and high-level military, and the prohibition of senior EU officials from travel to that country (see Steinberg 2006, 282–283). Less stringent than the US, these prohibitions were lifted, and states began to relocate individual European military attachés back in the country. The US had kept its attachés in Yangon during that period. Japan restarted its economic aid programme, which the US had strongly pressured it to stop, although it had continued debt relief and humanitarian assistance under a broad definition of such support that was at variance with more restrictive US policies.

In April 2012, the EU suspended its restrictions, except for the arms embargo, and began high-level contacts. The High Representative of the Union for Foreign Affairs and Security Policy/Vice-President of the Commission in April 2012 marked a new beginning in bilateral relations. An EU Office in Yangon was opened, and as of September 2013, the EU had a full-fledged delegation in Yangon. The EU's ongoing development assistance portfolio was over €200 million, and for the period 2014–2020 it was planned to maintain similar high levels of aid (European Union 2013).

The reforms in Myanmar reversed the policies of some European states. Norway, which had since 1992 supported the Democratic Voice of Burma, an opposition radio station in Oslo, began assistance to the internal Myanmar peace process. The UK engaged in a large foreign assistance effort, as did other states as well.

Australia, which had been the centre of much international academic focus on Myanmar during the junta period, lifted its modest sanctions and in 2013 established a resident military attaché in Yangon and opened a trade office there. It provided assistance in health and education, and agriculture, and had a large scholarship programme to train Burmese in Australia, a place that had been a primary focus of political exiles. In March 2016, after ambivalent use of the state's name, Australia decided officially to call the country Myanmar.

Canada in April 2012 eased its economic sanctions on Myanmar (the 2007 'Special Economic Measures (Burma) Regulations'), and by 2012 announced that it would establish a resident embassy in Yangon, which opened in 2014. It provided humanitarian assistance to Myanmar.

As Western policies towards Myanmar were effectively formed in response to Aung San Suu Kyi's actual and purported views while she was under house arrest, when she was released in November 2010 she began a series of travels to many of the countries that had honoured her, resulting in much acclaim in those states. In addition to receiving a number of honorary degrees, she addressed a joint session of the UK parliament in June 2012 and a joint sitting of Congress in the United States in September 2012, where she accepted the Congressional Gold Medal. She travelled to Canada in 2012 and Australia in November 2013. In October 2013, she travelled to Europe and received the Sakharov Prize from the European Parliament, which had been earlier awarded when she could not travel. She saw the Pope and received the Rome Citizens' Award that same month. In addition to these trips, she also has been variously welcomed in Thailand, India, Japan, and China.

These trips had a major focus of concentrating international attention on the positive role of the opposition in Myanmar, and the need for democratic elections in 2015. They also served as platforms for Aung San Suu Kyi to lobby for constitutional reforms in Myanmar that would allow her to run (in an indirect election) for the presidency or vice presidency, from which she was excluded because of the citizenship of her deceased husband and her children. Although the US, UK, and some other states had early stipulated that for the 2015 elections to be considered free and fair they must be 'inclusive', indirectly in the case of the US, and directly in the case of the UK prime minister, these statements indicated that she should be allowed to run for those indirectly elected positions. This was not to be the case.

Burmese international perceptions

The influence of the US abruptly improved since the Thein Sein government began its reforms. But the preeminence and widespread acceptance of the US position in Myanmar since about

2012 was a historic anomaly in the history of their bilateral diplomatic relations since independence in 1948 (Clymer 2015, passim). US interactions with the newly independent Burma were subject in that civilian period to the suspicions and vagaries of an important and vocal left-wing element. US clandestine support for anti-communist Chinese Nationalist (KMT) forces that had retreated into Myanmar caused indignation and prompted Burma to stop the US economic assistance programme in 1954 (it was restarted two years later). The US had effectively blocked Burma's appeal to the United Nations for support against the KMT.

Relations with the US after the coup of 1962 had been going downhill since General Ne Win expelled US and Western non-profit aid organisations from the country, and the US assistance programme quickly ceased. The worst period of relations, however, was in the SLORC–SPDC era when US policy was, effectively, regime change. The US, through publicly appropriated funding and through private resources, supported dissident elements in Thailand and elsewhere with the goal of fostering and eventually moving that state towards 'democracy'. The stated US policy and funding resulted in strong Burmese fears of potential US aggression against the regime. During the Nargis cyclone of 2008, the US navy was refused permission directly to deliver relief supplies to the devastated Irrawaddy Delta area because of the suspicion that the US would not leave. The improved relations with North Korea and the secret trip (later leaked) of the commander-in-chief of the *tatmadaw* there in 2008 prompted US concerns of North Korean supply of military equipment, including missiles, because this both violated UN sanctions against North Korea and strengthened the regime in Naypyitaw. Some dissidents within Myanmar advocated military action, although Aung San Suu Kyi continuously called for non-violent means of regime change through acknowledging the victory of the NLD in the May 1990 elections.

Fear of the US role resulted in suspicions of a potential US invasion, probably launched from Thailand, a treaty ally of the US, and may have been one reason for Burmese reliance after 1989 on Chinese support to the Burmese military. Even though the suspicions of the Burmese were palpable, there was never any likelihood of the US engaging in another war after its Middle Eastern experience, as US national interests were not perceived to be at stake even though, to adhere to internal US legal regulations, the executive branch annually had to maintain that Burma was 'an unusual and extraordinary threat to the national security and foreign policy of the United States' in order to maintain in force the renewable sanctions. Indeed, critical observers sometimes noted that because the US had no vital national interests at stake in Myanmar, it had the luxury to engage its human rights and democracy agenda that it was unable to do in other regional countries (e.g., China, Vietnam). Yet even as China became the predominant supplier and trainer of the *tatmadaw*, Myanmar sought to diversify its military procurement and to mollify reliance on China. It bought arms from eastern European states, Pakistan, and North Korea (in spite of UN sanctions against such activities), and may even have considered the development of a nuclear deterrent to potential US aggression on a misinterpreted North Korean model. North Korea's nuclear capacity, however limited, did not deter the US from action against the North. The capacity of Pyongyang to destroy Seoul (25 per cent of the state's population) with conventional artillery, and the possible reactions of China, were the real reasons for caution.

Significant numbers of Burmese were trained in various nuclear related studies in Moscow, which also supplied attack helicopters and separately MIG fighters after the US sold advanced fighter jets to Thailand. The fear of a US invasion, however unlikely from a Washington perspective, perhaps in part prompted the movement of the capital from Yangon to Naypyitaw in central Myanmar, and likely the transfer of its air command from Mingaladon near Yangon to Meiktila near Mandalay, and its naval command from Sittwe on the coast of Rakhine to Ann, in the interior of that subnational state.

President Obama in May 2014, in reference to 'Burma', took credit for a 'diplomatic initiative' and 'American leadership' (while also crediting the 'enormous courage' of the Burmese) that changed an 'intractable dictatorship hostile to the United States' (White House 2014). Hyperbole at best, it left unstated US hostile regime-change policies towards that government and the mutuality of negotiations to seek a better relationship.

The feelings of vulnerability, manifest in the fear of invasion and foreign cultural inroads, have likely increased the ever-present emphasis on nationalism that is a critical component of the military's view of international conditions, and thus their own responsibilities and role in preserving the state and its culture. The fear of being overwhelmed by Chinese public and private businesses and vastly exaggerated concerns about being swallowed by Muslim demographic expansion and conversions have raised increasing apprehension within the more traditional elements of Burman society as well as among the military. As Western culture, tourists, businesses, and popular music and fashions inundate Myanmar, however, a reaction to the prominence of the West, and especially the United States, as a threat to what are called 'traditional Myanmar values' may become evident.

The pivotal 2015 elections and beyond

The national elections of 8 November 2015, swept by the NLD with some 80 per cent of the electable seats, increased Western support for the continuing liberalisation of governance in that state. The results, which had been observed by a broad array of internal and foreign observers, were an encouraging surprise in many Western circles. Western leaders congratulated Aung San Suu Kyi on a clear victory that will enable her party alone to form a government without a coalition with others. Whether the vote was for 'democracy' as internationally defined, against continued military authority, or for the history and charisma of Aung San Suu Kyi is unclear, although it is probably a combination of the three. Yet the dominance of the military in the constitution, its coercive power including the police and intelligence, its control over critical cabinet posts, national security affairs, and in the administration of the state at all levels, will create a set of extremely delicate issues that all sides in the struggle for power will have to negotiate. The need to build trust, now so evidently lacking in that complex of societies, is an existential requirement. How much federalism, now promised, will be allowed and how various ethnic groups react to the partial 'national' cease fire is in question. The 'peace process' is a decades-long effort to reach some appropriate understanding of the sharing of power and resources in that highly complex ethnic state. Myanmar demonstrated its capacity for administering a reasonably fair election, and the period of installing a new administration after March 2016 is critical. The prospect for increased foreign investment seems improved by the election and its management, but is dependent on continuing cooperation by all parties, and, at least for the United States, the remaining sanctions.

The West was overall pleased, but there was continuing concern that the transfer of power between a legislature dominated by the opposition and a bureaucracy extensively controlled by the *tatmadaw* was fraught with potential problems. There probably was in the United States a sigh of administration political relief, for if the elections had been clearly manipulated or violent, the single East Asian foreign policy 'success' of the US would have been used as a political tool against President Obama's record.

The new administration led by Aung San Suu Kyi and her NLD, which she completely dominates, has formed a new government of 21 ministries, in which she alone will hold two critical portfolios, while the constitution stipulates that active-duty military will head those of defence, home affairs (including the police, intelligence, and administration down to the local level), and border affairs. She has said that she will govern above the president, whom she has chosen. She will be minister for foreign affairs, giving her immediate and extensive overseas relations, and State Counsellor, with a new ministry attached. This latter position, not included in the constitution, will allow her to dominate both legislative and executive branches, and in protocol terms is directly below the president (whom she effectively controls) and above the two vice presidents, one of whom she also chose, with the other picked by the *tatmadaw*. The commander-in-chief of the military is eighth in the hierarchy – a ranking presumably at odds with the armed forces' effective power. Aung San Suu Kyi has also created a ministry of ethnic affairs, which may put her influence through it in competition or conflict with the military's border ministry.

She will dominate the new administration with a workload of immense proportions and with little higher level administrative support and little previous evidence of interest in delegating authority. Prospects for relations with the West, therefore, seem promising, given her role as foreign minister, but she will be forced to concentrate on a myriad of major tasks and problems that would be daunting even to seasoned administrators. At the start of the new administration, any potential and obvious points of contention between the Aung San Suu Kyi and the military have not been publicly aired, although some are obvious, but compromises on both sides are necessary for effective governance and evolving solutions to the state's myriad problems.

In the US, however, concerns remain. The US foreign appropriations legislation of 2015 contain restrictive conditions on US official assistance to Myanmar, including extensive reporting to the US Congress. The new US ambassador to Myanmar was approved with the understanding that some of the existing sanctions on individual and military entities would remain – some were eased in May 2015. Prohibitions continue against military training and assistance except in humanitarian areas. The US Congress explicitly notes the problem of repression of the Rohingya Muslim minority as a factor in its relations with Myanmar. The Congress, under this legislation, will closely monitor developments in that country and the US aid effort. It seems somewhat more ambivalent about prospects than the executive branch.

The dilemma for the Western world, including or perhaps especially for the US, will be how to maintain some appropriate level of public or private influence in encouraging continued reforms but not appearing domineering. The NLD should understand, and the West should appreciate, that a degree of distance between them is essential in a nationalistic environment. A delicate balance may be required.

Under such circumstances, a return to the traditional Burmese foreign policy balance – a new form of neutralism adapted to the post-Cold War era – is likely. The regime in Naypyitaw will recognise the need to have good relations with China. Modern technology, international trade and interdependence, and the free flow of ideas have meant that Myanmar will need friendly ties with the West. The openings internationally have led to greater academic and policy knowledge of, and interest in, Myanmar. As more Burmese are trained abroad and as standards of research internally rise, Myanmar's integration into international intellectual focus will grow, offering opportunities for all to assume greater contacts and relations. The growing sophistication of the Burmese themselves, as well as those Western governments that interact with Myanmar, gives rise to hopes that the foreign policy of Myanmar will respect its international commitments and the salience of its geopolitical role in Southeast Asia.

References

Clymer, Kenton. 2015. *A Delicate Relationship. The United States and Burma/Myanmar since 1945*. Ithaca: Cornell University Press.

European Union. 2013. *European Union and Myanmar/Burma – a New Chapter in Bilateral Relations*. Brussels.

Green, Michael and Derek Mitchell. 2007. 'Asia's Forgotten Crisis: A New Approach to Burma'. *Foreign Affairs* 86: 147–155.

Haacke, Jürgen. 2015. 'US–Myanmar Relations: Development, Challenges, and Implications'. In *Myanmar. The Dynamics of an Evolving Polity*, edited by D. I. Steinberg. Boulder: Lynne Rienner.
Selth, Andrew. 2012. 'United States Relations with Burma: From Hostility to Hope'. *Regional Outlook* 36. Brisbane: Griffith Asia Institute, Griffith University.
Steinberg, David I. 2006. *Turmoil in Burma. Contested Legitimacies in Myanmar.* Norwalk: EastBridge.
Steinberg, David I. 2010. 'Aung San Suu Kyi and US Policy Toward Myanmar'. *Journal of Current Southeast Asian Affairs.* Summer, 29 (3): 35–59.
Steinberg, David I. 2015a. 'Myanmar and the United States, Closing and Opening Doors: An Idiosyncratic Analysis'. *Social Research* 82 (2): 427–452.
Steinberg, David I. 2015b. 'Walking the Tightrope: Implications for America's Rebalancing Policy in Asia'. In *America's Role in Asia. The Implications of America's Rebalancing Policy to Asia*, edited by John Brandon . Seoul: The Asia Foundation.
White House. 2014. Text of President Obama's Speech at West Point, May.

29
REGIONAL

Jürgen Haacke

This chapter examines Myanmar's relations with its regional neighbours: Japan and the ASEAN states. Its principal objective is to briefly situate these two relationships historically and to outline how they have been rebuilt and strengthened after the government of President U Thein Sein embarked on reforms in 2011. As the chapter will demonstrate, following several years during which bilateral relations had suffered, the Japanese state enthusiastically re-engaged Myanmar as a major provider of ODA. On the back of the political transition, Myanmar's ties with other ASEAN members have also expanded and improved. The transition has also allowed Naypyitaw to stand within the Association as a moral equal, even though the complex issue of the self-identifying Rohingya Muslims has proved a sensitive one, especially in bilateral relationships with Muslim majority ASEAN states.

Past relations with Japan and ASEAN

Japan's wartime involvement in colonial Burma looks ambivalent, and not entirely dissimilar to other Southeast Asian countries. On the one hand, Japan played a part in hastening political independence. The father of modern-day Burma, General Aung San, famously received military training in Japan, alongside other Burmese revolutionaries making up the 'Thirty Comrades'. On the other hand, Japan's later occupation and the Allied re-occupation of Burma effectively brought the country to its knees. The war also accentuated political fissures among ethnic communities that played out in domestic politics for years to come. Japan and Burma agreed war reparations in 1954 and subsequently also agreed 'mini-reparations' (Seekins 2007). Under the Burma Socialist Progress Party rule, Japan was a primary source of Official Development Assistance (ODA) for the Ne Win-led regime. Even after the violent suppression of demonstrations in 1988 and the refusal of the State Law and Order Restoration Council (SLORC) to transfer power to the opposition National League for Democracy (NLD) despite the latter's victory in the 1990 elections, Japan remained the largest donor of aid.

Indeed, unlike the United States or the European Union, and notwithstanding ODA rules Tokyo released in 1992 that made assistance dependent on democratisation, Japan not only did not impose unilateral sanctions against Myanmar's military government but instead made available US$33.2 million in Yen loans in the period of 1995–2005. Significantly, Tokyo also provided around US$600 million in debt relief between 1991 and 2003 (Strefford 2006, 159).

This debt relief involved turning debt repayments into grants. It prevented Myanmar from going into arrears, a state of affairs which would have proscribed Tokyo from promising new ODA loans in return for political progress that was encouraged by Japan for many years in a critical but mostly quiet form of diplomacy towards the military regime (Strefford 2006, 164). Japan's quiet dialogue is considered to have played a part in the 1995 release from house arrest of Daw Aung San Suu Kyi. However, the SPDC's subsequent failure to work for political reconciliation with the NLD prevented new Japanese ODA from being disbursed, and when Myanmar eventually did go into arrears in 1997, Japan's particular carrot and stick approach finally came undone (Edström 2009). However, Tokyo maintained humanitarian aid despite the military regime's resistance to political change. As the domestic political antagonism between the military regime and Aung San Suu Kyi worsened and Western pressure on the regime grew, Myanmar drifted more and more into the Chinese economic and political orbit. Cooperative ties with China lessened Myanmar's need for Japanese ODA.

Given both the SPDC's unwillingness to compromise with Nobel Peace Prize laureate Aung San Suu Kyi and especially the 2003 Depayin incident, which involved an attack on an NLD car convoy in which Daw Suu's life was apparently threatened (see, for instance, Popham 2011), the balance of Japan's Myanmar policy ultimately shifted. Whereas business-related and geopolitical arguments in favour of economic engagement could still account for some of the ambiguity in Japan's Myanmar policy especially in the 1990s, the growing chorus of countervailing domestic voices and international pressures, not least from the United States, led Tokyo to become a more resolute critic of the SPDC in the 2000s (Seekins 2007). While still concerned about Chinese influence in Myanmar, Tokyo thus made improvements in bilateral ties dependent on the junta doing more to accommodate Daw Aung San Suu Kyi. The SPDC's disappointment with Tokyo seems to have been considerable as indicated by Myanmar's diplomatic support in the mid-2000s for India's efforts to secure a place on the UN Security Council and the reluctance to offer similar endorsement to Japan's campaign. The growing estrangement with Japan continued more or less unabated throughout the remainder of SPDC rule. From Tokyo's perspective, it was further accentuated by the shooting of Japanese photo-journalist Kenji Nagai during the protests of the so-called 'Saffron Revolution' in September 2007.

Myanmar in ASEAN

Burma was invited to join ASEAN at the time of its establishment in 1967. But the Ne Win regime did not take up the offer, preferring instead to pursue a particularly isolationist brand of non-alignment and neutralism. However, following the end of the Cold War and given the deterioration of relations with Washington and other Western countries as a consequence of the suppression of the democracy movement in 1988, the incoming SLORC soon re-evaluated its position in relation to ASEAN membership. Notably, ASEAN then was understood as a diplomatic community, and even a kind of limited security organisation, that insisted fairly obdurately on non-interference and in many ways thus helped protect ruling regimes within Southeast Asia (Leifer 1989).

These credentials of the Association were important for Myanmar's then incoming military SLORC government, in so far as ASEAN membership seemed to offer Myanmar several opportunities: to deflect the growing international pressure, to enhance its international legitimacy and to avoid becoming overly dependent on China. ASEAN members eager to see Myanmar join the Association also emphasised the last argument. In the event, ASEAN came to be seen by analysts as pursuing vis-à-vis Myanmar a policy of 'constructive engagement' that built on Thailand's pro-business approach towards Yangon pursued by several prime ministers: Chatichai Choonhavan, Anand Panyarachun, during whose administration the term was introduced, and Chavalit Yongchaiyudh (Chachavalpongpun 2005). The basic idea was that regional cooperation and economic engagement would also serve to gradually bring about political reforms in Myanmar.

In the event, however, Myanmar's military government refused to enter into a 'meaningful' dialogue with Aung San Suu Kyi and the NLD, and to move towards 'national reconciliation' (Taylor 2008). Significantly, the 2003 Depayin incident, which led to Daw Suu's renewed house arrest until 2010, marked a decisive moment also in relations between the SPDC and other governments among ASEAN members. Above all, the less authoritarian ASEAN countries increasingly felt challenged by Naypyitaw's political recalcitrance (Haacke 2006). In 2005, external pressure on the Association not least by Washington and frustration at the political situation in Myanmar consequently prompted fellow members to persuade the military government to pass over the ASEAN chairmanship (Ganesan 2006).

For several years that followed Myanmar also consented to limited but symbolic diplomatic censure in ASEAN's formal interactions and outputs, but continued to defy calls by fellow members for the release from house arrest of Daw Suu or national reconciliation. ASEAN countries only occasionally opted for harsh public criticism of the SPDC as happened in the context of the so-called Saffron Revolution. Yet neither quiet nor public diplomacy led ASEAN to obtain greater influence over Myanmar's domestic political situation even as concerns about in-country developments grew and, at least from an academic viewpoint, Myanmar's domestic problems and conflict made for myriad transnational challenges that represented a serious danger for ASEAN community building (Roberts 2010). Only in relation to Cyclone Nargis did ASEAN play an effective role, but this concerned mediating between Naypyitaw and the international community to provide international assistance (Haacke 2009). Even after this success, however, the Association's members failed to persuade the SPDC leadership to deviate from the final steps of the roadmap to a 'discipline-flourishing' democracy, originally outlined by the military regime in 2003; nor could they persuade the military leadership to release Daw Suu before the November 2010 elections.

Japan's support for Myanmar during the reform period

Japan's government was enthusiastic about the reforms undertaken by the U Thein Sein government. Tokyo encouraged these reforms through a combination of high-level diplomacy, economic assistance and other targeted support to develop Myanmar's economic and social capital. High points of related diplomatic activity included the Japan–Myanmar summit of April 2012 and the follow-up summit which saw Prime Minister Abe visit Myanmar in May 2013. This led the two sides to outline a 'new foundation' for mutual friendship. In this context, Myanmar and Japan agreed to enhance their dialogue on regional issues, and to promote cooperation and exchange between their defence authorities. Tokyo, for instance, explained to Naypyitaw its position in relation to China not only in general terms but also with respect to the South China Sea and the Chinese-declared Air Defence Identification Zone. Notwithstanding considerable tensions Myanmar has been experiencing in its ties with China (Aung Myoe 2015; Haacke 2015), these have not translated into Naypyitaw publicly taking sides between China and Japan in relation to the above issues.

The interest in developing their security relationship moreover led Tokyo and Naypyitaw to focus on military diplomacy and cooperation. In September 2013, for instance, Japan undertook a port call involving two Japanese Maritime Self-Defence Force training vessels and an escort destroyer. Also, in the first high-level military exchange for many years, the Chief of

Staff of the Joint Staff Council of the Japan Self-Defence Forces, General Shigeru Iwasaki, visited Myanmar in May 2014. Commander-in-Chief Senior General Min Aung Hlaing undertook a return visit the following September. Discussions about education and training in the area of peacekeeping subsequently took place when a Myanmar delegation visited Japan's Joint Staff College in December 2014. Notably, Prime Minister Abe himself spoke about Japan's expectation to see Myanmar military personnel study at Japan's National Defence Academy. Though growing defence cooperation and exchanges were welcomed by the Tatmadaw, none of these important developments raised any questions about Myanmar's preference for a non-aligned foreign policy.

Strides in bilateral economic cooperation have naturally been much more rapid, extensive and significant. At the April 2012 summit, Japan helped clear Myanmar's arrears with the World Bank and Asian Development Bank and also agreed other significant debt relief measures, including quite considerable debt cancellation. Eager to move Myanmar towards a higher level of development, Tokyo formulated priorities for cooperation that focused on improving livelihoods, capacity building, including rule-of-law assistance, and infrastructure development. Tokyo also made available a significant amount of grant aid to grassroots and NGO projects. It moreover approved a number of high-profile economic projects that stood to raise Japan's presence in Myanmar. In 2014, for instance, Japan authorised funding for improvements to the Greater Yangon water supply, for the second phase of the Thilawa Special Economic Zone (SEZ) and for the Yangon–Mandalay railway line. Other mandated funding projects concerned improvements to Myanmar's communication network, the development of the national power transmission network and the creation of finance for small- and medium-sized enterprises. Critical appraisals of Japan's substantial assistance during this stage of the reform period include the point that it was not leveraged to induce the Thein Sein government to embrace those reform measures the opposition called for, which the military in particular found difficult to countenance.

Japan's role in the development of the Thilawa SEZ, which has been backed both by Japan's government and Japanese businesses, quickly became particularly visible (Mahtani 2015). Notably, Japan also signed a Memorandum of Intent with Myanmar and Thailand to develop the Dawei SEZ as part of the New Tokyo Strategy 2015 for Mekong–Japan Cooperation. Japan is slated to provide both technical and financial support for this project, which for many years seemed almost stillborn. The Dawei SEZ is to include a deep-sea port as well. Whether Dawei will ever become a strategically important gateway for the Mekong Region's trade with India, the Middle East and Africa remains to be seen, however. Japanese companies also succeeded in winning some tenders, such as the building of a $1.4 billion new airport near Yangon (as part of a Singapore-led consortium) and the renovation and running of Mandalay airport.

Japan also sought to make a notable supporting contribution to Myanmar's peace process. Tokyo fostered a role for the Nippon Foundation, which has longstanding contacts in Myanmar, as one of the foreign stakeholders in the country's peace process. The foundation became the first foreign NGO permitted to deliver direct humanitarian aid to populations of ethnic armed groups inside Myanmar. It also emerged as an observer to the peace negotiations upon the request of members of one of Myanmar's ethnic coalitions – the United Nationalities Federal Council (UNFC) in late 2012. UNFC representatives subsequently even travelled to Tokyo to discuss the nature of assistance that Japan could provide. Despite opposition from Beijing, Japan's Special Envoy for National Reconciliation and Nippon Foundation chairman, Yohei Sasagawa, was a witness to the Nationwide Ceasefire Agreement signing that the government of U Thein Sein undertook with eight armed (ethnic) groups in October 2015.

After the NLD-led government came to power in March 2016, Tokyo remained intensely interested in supporting Myanmar, a message conveyed in no uncertain terms by Foreign Minister Kishida when he visited the country in May. Japan also looked forward to an early visit to Japan by Daw Aung San Suu Kyi. In the event, however, the State Counsellor opted to make China her first port of call among the major powers, followed by visits to India and the United States, before also travelling to Japan in November 2016. Having already pledged further assistance on the sidelines of the ASEAN Summit meetings in September, Prime Minister Abe held out the prospect of future ODA and private investment engagements totalling Yen 800 billion over five years to help Myanmar achieve its goal of a balanced development of states and regions, with Yen 40 billion earmarked for ethnic minority areas. Other priority objectives, which reflect the NLD's policy agenda, have included the expansion of employment and human resource development. Emphasising common values such as democracy, human rights and the rule of law, the Abe administration suggested in addition extending bilateral defence cooperation and exchanges and also proposed to Daw Suu that Myanmar should strengthen its connectivity with the Mekong Region and India, address the situation in Rakhine State, and cooperate on issues such as the South China Sea and North Korea's development of nuclear weapons and missile technology. While the State Counsellor pragmatically accepted Japanese assistance and noted Special Envoy Sasakawa's efforts to promote national reconciliation, she remained non-committal in particular in relation to regional security issues.

Support from ASEAN

The support extended by ASEAN states to the Thein Sein government focused initially on political encouragement. Even before Myanmar's incoming president embarked in the summer of 2011 on key gestures of political accommodation with Daw Aung San Suu Kyi and on practical steps to achieve a nationwide ceasefire arrangement with ethnic armed organisations, the ASEAN foreign ministers promised to render their full support to the Thein Sein government for national reconciliation and reconsolidation. And it was not long before ASEAN also acceded to Myanmar's request to award the grouping's chairmanship to Naypyitaw, from which the latter hoped to gain international recognition and legitimacy. In the event, ASEAN's positive decision on the chairmanship was no foregone conclusion. With Jakarta then in the Chair, it was made only after Indonesian Foreign Minister Marty Natalegawa undertook a trip to Myanmar to convince himself of the political progress achieved. By that time, President U Thein Sein and Daw Suu had established an initial personal rapport and the US was already involved in a supporting role to promote political accommodation between the post-SPDC regime and the NLD. From the perspective of several fellow ASEAN states meanwhile, the decision to allow Myanmar to take over the ASEAN chairmanship served to prevent any backtracking on reform (Moe Thuzar 2013). ASEAN states also issued repeatedly a call for Western states to end sanctions against Myanmar.

Throughout the initial period of domestic political transition, Naypyitaw generally played a constructive role in moving forward the ASEAN Community project, including by implementing relevant agreements. Indeed, Myanmar under Thein Sein was keen to demonstrate a capacity to work for shared regional objectives and to do ASEAN proud. This positive attitude was possibly most clearly on display when Myanmar finally assumed the role of ASEAN chairman in 2014. Judging by various appraisals, Myanmar's government and bureaucracy not only pulled off professionally organised meetings that seemed to satisfy ASEAN's gold standard but also addressed with aplomb tricky diplomatic spats involving regional powers. Indeed,

Naypyitaw received widespread plaudits for managing well the South China Sea conflict, especially when compared with Cambodia, which in 2012, as ASEAN Chair, presided over the grouping's only ever failure to issue a joint communiqué after insisting that positions put forward by Hanoi and Manila could not be accommodated.

That stark diplomatic failure, widely viewed as a case of China having used its influence with the Hun Sen government, had prompted Jakarta to rally the other members around a six-point statement which in substance also offered little in terms of a solution to the intractable territorial dispute but restored the notion that ASEAN members should demonstrate unity of purpose. In marked contrast to Cambodia, Myanmar proved unambiguously that its relationship with China was no obstacle to a considered consensual viewpoint that left all claimants broadly content or at least unperturbed. Indeed, in reacting to the oil rig-related incident that rather badly impacted on China–Vietnam relations in early May 2014, Myanmar oversaw what was taken to be a satisfactorily strong response by the ASEAN foreign ministers (ASEAN 2014) expressing 'serious concerns' about developments that were said to cause increasing tensions in the area, yet without being unduly provocative to China (ASEAN 2014).

While Myanmar has no longer been subject to routine collective criticism from within the Association, as was the case under the SPDC, the situation in Rakhine State has been regarded by some within the Association as an issue in need of a collective position given its perceived regional dimension. Following the outbreak of communal violence in Rakhine State in June 2012, the then ASEAN Secretary-General Surin Pitsuwan approached ASEAN foreign ministers in writing with a view to organising a special foreign ministers meeting to discuss the crisis. The 2012 ASEAN Chair, Cambodia, thereupon called for such a meeting, but Naypyitaw objected strongly – whereupon ASEAN in turn relented. Though the Association did release a substitute four-point statement on the situation in Rakhine State (ASEAN 2012), this referred to the killings as 'incidents', made no direct mention of the self-identifying Rohingya, yet offered humanitarian assistance.

Following the second wave of attacks in Rakhine State in October 2012, the ASEAN Secretary-General warned that the further radicalisation of the Rohingya could potentially destabilise Southeast Asia given the possible negative strategic and security ramifications for the region. This attempt to collectively securitise the situation by ASEAN also failed and Myanmar continued to resist perceived interference on the issue. The following year, references to the situation in Rakhine State were not included in the major ASEAN statements issued by foreign ministers and leaders. Not surprisingly, the Rohingya issue also was kept off the ASEAN agenda in 2014 when Myanmar was ASEAN Chair. As presidential adviser Ko Ko Hlaing said:

> The Bengali issue is not a regional issue, just a local issue. No one will try to raise this issue at the summit because, in keeping with ASEAN practice, it will not be discussed if a member opposes the issue.
>
> *Bangkok Post, 5 May 2014*

The 2015 Bay of Bengal migrant crisis that saw thousands stranded on boats in the Andaman Sea, and in relation to which Myanmar's authorities correctly pointed out that many of those involved were economic refugees from Bangladesh, was also not dealt with in an ASEAN context first and foremost. Generally, the limitations of ASEAN's collective endeavours with regard to the situation in Rakhine State demonstrated the ability of the Thein Sein administration to clearly delineate the boundaries of perceived legitimate external involvement in its internal affairs.

Evolving bilateral ties

With the political and economic reforms undertaken by President U Thein Sein and the many opportunities for more cooperation created, it is not surprising that Myanmar's relations with fellow ASEAN countries moved forward. The Thein Sein government was certainly interested in strengthening bilateral relationships with regional states, not least given its calculated focus on achieving greater foreign policy diversification. Its embrace of substantial domestic political reforms notwithstanding, the military-backed government of U Thein Sein remained beholden to its foreign policy principles; a projection of a value-laden foreign policy associated with some democratising states was eschewed. Indeed, comparing the political situation in Thailand with that in Myanmar in 1988, Senior General Min Aung Hlaing publicly voiced understanding for the assumption of power by the present Thai military junta, the National Council for Peace and Order, which was installed by virtue of the May 2014 coup.

Myanmar's relations with Thailand have historically and even in relatively recent times been testy (see Chapter 29), but they again improved after 2011. An important factor underlying this improvement was the efforts by the U Thein Sein government to forge a nationwide ceasefire that paved the way for Thailand to facilitate meetings with ethnic representatives and for the two militaries to build confidence. As in previous instances, the strength of bilateral ties between Naypyitaw and Thailand seemed to partially also rest on personal relationships. The trust ostensibly developed between President U Thein Sein and the current Thai prime minister, General Prayuth Chanocha, was particularly relevant here, as was the relationship between Myanmar's Commander-in-Chief Senior General Min Aung Hlaing and Prem Tinsulanonda, the retired former general and prime minister who served as president of the Privy Council under King Bhumibol Adulyadej. General Min Aung Hlaing in 2012 reportedly asked Prem to adopt him, making for a 'godfather–godson' relationship (Chachavalpongpun 2014).

Under President Thein Sein, government-to-government relations with other ASEAN countries also improved or remained stable including with Muslim majority states such as Indonesia, notwithstanding the Rohingya issue (see below). Beyond Naypyitaw's participation in ASEAN-centred regional security discussions involving foreign and defence ministers, the Thein Sein government slowly also worked on developing security partnerships with individual Southeast Asian countries. Senior General Min Aung Hlaing in particular became engaged in military-to-military diplomacy by undertaking goodwill visits to other ASEAN states. Some reciprocated Myanmar's interest in developing security relations. For instance, shortly after making his introductory visit to Singapore in January 2013, where Min Aung Hlaing visited various military installations, the RSS *Endurance* paid a port call to Yangon, reportedly the first Republic of Singapore Navy vessel to do so for a decade. Thereafter, a growing web of bilateral defence contacts developed, involving defence ministers, senior defence officials and military officers, with meetings taking place also on the sidelines of multilateral events. Singapore also offered a training opportunity for Myanmar on the Command and Staff course (Executive) at the Goh Keng Swee Command and Staff College.

An additional focus seemed to set apart the regular security dialogue at the level of deputy ministers between Naypyitaw and Hanoi. Institutionally this relationship during the Thein Sein years involved Vietnam's Ministry of Public Security and Myanmar's Ministry of Home Affairs, with discussions apparently focusing on the maintenance of domestic social order as well as non-traditional security issues. Interest in military-to-military exchanges also became visible: for instance, two Myanmar navy vessels transferred from China, UMS *Mahar Bandoola* and UMS *Mahar Thiha Thura*, paid a visit to the Vietnamese city of Da Nang in March 2012, which – purposefully or not – coincided with talks then also held by the two countries' foreign ministers. Previously, Senior General Min Aung Hlaing had made Vietnam the destination of his first official visit abroad in November 2011.

Further evidence of Myanmar's growing security ties with other ASEAN member states was Malaysia's invitation for Naypyitaw to become an observer to the Malacca Strait Sea Patrols, in which Singapore, Indonesia and Thailand are also participants. With US affirmation, Thailand had earlier invited Myanmar to attend parts of the Cobra Gold exercises, also as an observer. While cooperation with respect to non-traditional security concerns was thus initially foregrounded, more traditional security cooperation may still follow.

Economic linkages

With the introduction of political and economic reforms, Myanmar's economic ties with other ASEAN states also expanded further, especially with Thailand, Singapore, Malaysia, Indonesia and Vietnam, Naypyitaw's five most important trading partners in ASEAN. Notably, the percentage share of Myanmar's intra-ASEAN trade thus remained higher than that of any other ASEAN country except Laos, although it dropped from more than half to about 40 per cent (CMB ASEAN Research Institute 2015).

On account of the reforms, several ASEAN countries boosted their investments in Myanmar. Singaporean-based investors became particularly active in Myanmar, with some companies scouting for opportunities even before the US eased economic sanctions. On a cumulative basis, among the ASEAN countries Thailand continued as the top investor in Myanmar, but having become Myanmar's main investor in hospitality in 2013 and then the biggest foreign investor in 2014, Singapore has been closing the gap. That said, by the end of the Thein Sein era other ASEAN countries also realised or considered major investments in Myanmar: for instance, Vietnamese investment in Myanmar included a US$300 million property development in Yangon, and PT Semen Indonesia was apparently interested in building a US$200 million cement plant. In Singapore's case, a second wave of investment was said to be under way, targeting the lifestyle niche associated with demand from Myanmar's growing middle class. Meanwhile, Thailand's energy-dependence on Myanmar was set to increase. With the newly producing Zawtika gas field, the largest offshore field to be operated by PTTEP (Petroleum Authority of Thailand Exploration and Production), coming on stream, a reported 25 per cent of Thailand's annual gas consumption was to be sourced from neighbouring Myanmar. Notably, the Thai energy giant was also involved in a range of further offshore and onshore exploration projects in Myanmar.

The impact of the 'Rohingya issue' on bilateral relations

While Myanmar under President Thein Sein was able to avoid unwanted ASEAN involvement and censure in relation to the situation in Rakhine State, the discrimination and violence experienced by Muslim communities there was an important matter for Jakarta and Putrajaya to raise in their respective bilateral dialogue with Naypyitaw. Governments in both Indonesia and Malaysia had come under some considerable pressure from their publics and local media over developments in Myanmar's southwestern borderlands. On occasion, these developments even provoked attacks in Indonesia. For example, in apparent retaliation Buddhist temples were vandalised in the course of pro-Rohingya demonstrations against Myanmar's communal violence. In May 2013, a plot was revealed, the purpose of which was to blow up Myanmar's embassy in Jakarta. Soon afterwards, a bombing occurred at a Buddhist Centre in West Jakarta that was explained by perpetrators with reference to the Rohingyas' struggle in Myanmar.

Jakarta and Putrajaya both registered concerns about the communal violence in Myanmar, the segregation and restrictions applied in Rakhine State, and the broad-based humanitarian suffering and denial of citizenship rights endured by the Rohingya Muslims. However, Indonesia and Malaysia adopted what appeared to be fundamentally different foreign policy strategies to bring about positive change in Rakhine State. Relying largely on quiet diplomacy of a bilateral nature, Jakarta for instance offered insights to the Thein Sein government on how to deal with communal conflict. In Malaysia, the UMNO-led government of Premier Najib Tun Razak decided to draw on its diplomatic weight in the Organisation of Islamic Cooperation (OIC). For instance, Malaysia's deputy foreign minister visited Myanmar in November 2013 as a member of the OIC Contact Group Fact Finding Mission to Rakhine State. Malaysia's government also supported and relied on the subsequent work of former Foreign Minister Syed Hamid Albar as OIC Special Envoy for Myanmar.

As thousands of new migrants, both from Bangladesh and Rakhine State, were abandoned by smugglers in the Andaman Sea in May 2015, pursuant to a Thai crackdown on camps used by smugglers to ferry their human cargo to Malaysia, Indonesia and Malaysia in particular were faced with a new dilemma. Neither country was keen to accept the refugees and illegal migrants and boats were thus pushed back out to sea. However, both Jakarta and Putrajaya then took in significant numbers of the stranded migrants on the condition that they would be repatriated or resettled within a year. In the event, the issue was played up politically more in Malaysia than in Indonesia. Although the Malaysian authorities also announced finding a significant number of mass graves near multiple trafficking camps on the Malaysian–Thai border, some Malaysian politicians thus used the 'boat people' crisis to embarrass and undermine the government of Prime Minister Datuk Seri Najib Razak by suggesting a more forceful diplomatic approach vis-à-vis Naypyitaw was required. With Malaysia holding the ASEAN chairmanship in 2015, former Prime Minister Mahathir Mohamed for instance accused Myanmar of perpetrating atrocities against Muslims and suggested that Myanmar should leave ASEAN if its leaders wanted to 'commit genocide'. Notwithstanding the domestic political sensitivity of their respective publics to the so-called 'Rohingya issue', both Jakarta and Putrajaya nevertheless maintained what basically remained a cordial political relationship with Myanmar under President Thein Sein.

Myanmar's relations with ASEAN under the NLD-led government

When Daw Suu became foreign minister and also State Counsellor in the spring of 2016, it was not immediately clear whether the closer ties between Myanmar and other ASEAN countries would in some ways be tested again. As this chapter noted above, ASEAN leaders did not support the cause of democracy in Myanmar during the 1990s and decided to ignore Daw Suu's appeal not to admit a military-run Myanmar to the Association. For her part, Daw Suu was known to have been critical of 'constructive engagement' even though at least from 2003 ASEAN regularly called on the junta to end her detention. After being released from house arrest in November 2010, her visits to other parts of Southeast Asia were only few in number and stood in marked contrast to her extensive visiting programme to Europe and the United States, suggesting a relative lack of interest on her part in building relations with Southeast Asian governments at the time.

Under Daw Suu's leadership, Myanmar's relations with the other ASEAN countries initially developed smoothly. Fellow ASEAN governments accepted – apparently without question – that as State Counsellor she, and not President Htin Kyaw, would represent Myanmar at the September 2016 ASEAN summit meetings in Laos. However, the situation in Rakhine State following the attack by a group calling itself Harakah al-Yaqin ('Faith Movement') on three border guard police posts in October 2016 has made for grit in the gears of intra-ASEAN relations as far as Myanmar and some fellow members are concerned. The heavy-handed security operations following the attacks not only caused the significant displacement of local community members across the border with Bangladesh as well as internally but also led to a considerable number of detentions and deaths (the exact number of which has been disputed). In the face of official Myanmar denials of allegations of abuse, Malaysia's government in particular grew increasingly indignant over these developments, which it considered to constitute ethnic cleansing, and in December 2016 Prime Minister Najib Tun Razak severely criticised Myanmar at the UMNO assembly as well as at a public Rohingya solidarity rally attended by officials from UMNO and the opposition Parti Islam SeMalaysia – despite being cautioned by Myanmar that this would be seen as a violation of ASEAN's non-interference principle. Significantly, Najib rejected this advice, unequivocally condemned the security operations in Rakhine State, and offered what he labelled a defence of 'humanitarian and universal values', telling Daw Suu that 'enough is enough'. Not least from Myanmar's perspective, this move was attributed to domestic political motives because of the 1MDB corruption scandal in which the prime minister is embroiled.

That said, in December Daw Aung San Suu Kyi did invite fellow ASEAN foreign ministers to Yangon for an informal retreat to explain her government's viewpoint on Rakhine State. This decision was apparently taken as a result of a meeting between the State Counsellor and Indonesia's visiting Foreign Minister Retno Marsudi just days before the invitation. In the event, Malaysia's Foreign Minister Anifah Aman reportedly asked ASEAN to coordinate humanitarian assistance to affected parts of Rakhine State and to establish an independent group of experts or eminent persons to investigate alleged atrocities committed. For her part, Daw Suu appealed for 'time, space and understanding' in dealing with the crisis in Rakhine State. In the event, there was no ASEAN consensus on establishing a separate regional process investigating the matter. But agreement was reached that Myanmar would grant the necessary humanitarian access in areas in which 'clearance operations' had been conducted. Also, the foreign ministers agreed that Myanmar would continue to brief the other members on the evolving situation in Rakhine State. As such, Daw Suu's government conceded a point on which her predecessor had sought to hold a firm line. Notwithstanding the consensus established in Yangon, Malaysia continued to pursue the issue in other fora. In January 2017, for instance, Putrajaya organised an extraordinary meeting of the OIC Council of Foreign Ministers to discuss multiple aspects of the crisis faced by Rohingya Muslims. Myanmar meanwhile received an Indonesian delegation to disseminate its conclusions on how a peace deal was reached between Muslim and Christian communities in Maluku. Notably, Jakarta made clear it shared international concerns about the humanitarian and security situation in Rakhine State, not least because of possible implications for regional stability. An initial assessment would suggest that Myanmar's relations with Malaysia have taken more of a hit than relations with Indonesia because of the situation in Rakhine State. Meanwhile, ASEAN's involvement in the crisis remains limited for the time being.

Conclusion

Following President Thein Sein's political and economic reforms, the Japanese government re-engaged Myanmar with much verve and made significant use of the economic and financial means at its disposal to propel Myanmar's economic development and to boost livelihoods in particular. As a consequence, relations between Myanmar and Japan moved again beyond the alienation that had crept into the bilateral relationship when the former was under SPDC rule. The nature of the support provided suggested that geopolitical considerations relating to China rather than a dedicated democratisation agenda made for the main undercurrent of Japan's Myanmar policy. For Naypyitaw, Japan assumed considerable importance in the foreign policy diversification drive pursued under President Thein Sein. Irrespective of any personal views Daw Suu might hold about Japan's contribution to democracy building in Myanmar, the State Counsellor recognises the benefits of Japanese support. However, judging by the timing of her visits to various regional and international capitals, Japan's considerable assistance has not translated into priority or particularly warm relations between the NLD-government and Tokyo.

In comparison, ASEAN's collective support for Myanmar during the Thein Sein years primarily remained political in nature even though it was complemented by considerable interest among regional businesses in exploring and exploiting business opportunities in Myanmar. With its political transition under way, Myanmar was no longer regarded as a serious problem in the grouping's relations with external powers, and as such Myanmar became subject to far fewer efforts at collective ASEAN involvement than was the case during the SPDC years. To the extent that governments in fellow ASEAN states have continued to target Myanmar for serious criticism and advice because of domestic circumstances, the issue at stake has been the situation in Rakhine State. Notwithstanding the difficulties that the NLD-government has experienced in this regard above all in its ties with Malaysia, Myanmar's bilateral relationships with ASEAN states have generally deepened since the onset of the political transition.

References

ASEAN. 2012. Statement of ASEAN Foreign Ministers on the Recent Developments in the Rakhine State, Myanmar. Phnom Penh, 17 August.

ASEAN. 2014. ASEAN Foreign Ministers' Statement on the Current Developments in the South China Sea. 10 May.

Aung Myoe. 2015. 'Myanmar's China Policy since 2011: Determinants and Directions'. *Journal of Current Southeast Asian Affairs* 34 (2): 21–54.

Chachavalpongpun, Pavin. 2005. *A Plastic Nation: The Curse of Thainess in Thai–Burmese Relations*. Lanham: University Press of America.

Chachavalpongpun, Pavin. 2014. 'The New Thailand–Myanmar Axis'. *The Diplomat*, 29 July.

CMB ASEAN Research Institute. 2015. 'Myanmar Economic Profile' Kuala Lumpur.

Edström, Bert. 2009. *Japan and the Myanmar Conundrum*. Stockholm: Institute for Security & Development Policy, October 2009.

Ganesan, N. 2006. 'Thai–Myanmar–ASEAN Relations: The Politics of Fun and Grace'. *Asian Affairs* 33 (3): 131–149.

Haacke, Jürgen. 2006. *Myanmar Foreign Policy: Domestic Influences and International Implications*. Abingdon: Routledge.

Haacke, Jürgen. 2009. 'Myanmar, the Responsibility to Protect, and the Need for Practical Assistance'. *Global Responsibility to Protect* 1 (2): 156–184.

Haacke, Jürgen. 2015. *Myanmar and the United States: Prospects for a Limited Security Partnership*. Sydney: United States Studies Centre at the University of Sydney.

Leifer, Michael. 1989. *ASEAN and the Security of South-East Asia*. London: Routledge.

Mahtani, Shibani. 2015. 'Myanmar Opens Japanese-Backed Economic Zone Amid Election Campaign'. *The Wall Street Journal*, 23 September. www.wsj.com/articles/myanmar-opens-japanese-backed-economic-zone-amid-election-campaign-1443006607.

Moe Thuzar. 2013. 'Myanmar and the 2014 ASEAN Chairmanship'. *ISEAS Perspective*, 18 March.

Popham, Peter. 2011. *The Lady and the Peacock: The Life of Aung San Suu Kyi of Burma*. London: Rider.

Roberts, Christopher B. 2010. *ASEAN's Myanmar Crisis: Challenges to the Pursuit of a Security Community.* Singapore: ISEAS.

Seekins, Donald M. 2007. *Burma and Japan Since 1940: From 'Co-Prosperity' to 'Quiet Dialogue'.* Copenhagen: NIAS.

Strefford, Patrick. 2006. 'Foreign Debt: Distorting Japan's ODA Diplomacy Towards Myanmar'. *Ritsumeikan Annual Review of International Studies* 19 (2): 157–168. www.ritsumei.ac.jp/acd/cg/ir/college/bulletin/vol.19-2/Strefford.pdf.

Taylor, Robert H. 2008. *The State in Myanmar.* London: C. Hurst and Publishing.

30

NEIGHBOURHOOD

Renaud Egreteau and Li Chenyang

Introduction: locating Myanmar in its neighbourhood

The political geography that post-independence Myanmar inherited from the British presented some formidable challenges. Sandwiched between two rising populous neighbours, China and India, the Indian Ocean and its potentially strategic maritime lanes, as well as a mainland Indochina rapidly drawn into Cold War power games, the country's first postcolonial leaders early on acknowledged that their approach to foreign and security policy had to reckon with Myanmar's peculiar geographic position. The Burmese polity indeed straddles several regions – South Asia, East Asia, Southeast Asia – but culturally, historically and economically belongs fully to none of them. Furthermore, the civil war that emerged in the late 1940s between the ethnic Bamar majority – who soon dominated the country's political elites – and a myriad of ethnic nationalities dwelling in Myanmar's border peripheries rapidly undermined its relations with its five direct neighbours. Ethnic and communist insurgents developed large-scale underground networks across the borders with China, Thailand, India, Laos and even Bangladesh (or East Pakistan before 1971) where they found sympathy, if not open political support, for their struggle against Myanmar's central authorities and other rival ethnic armed groups (Smith 1999; Lintner 1999).

Conflict, asymmetric threat perceptions, political instability and anti-state insurgency in the border areas have thus heavily factored in Myanmar's neighbourhood policy orientation since its independence and will continue to do so well into the 2010s, as this chapter highlights. The chapter first focuses on the two biggest neighbours Myanmar has had to deal with since independence – China and India. A fair amount of scholarship has since the early 1990s portrayed Myanmar as a potential nexus or cockpit of rivalry between Beijing and New Delhi, and in the long run the United States (Thant Myint-U 2012; Egreteau and Jagan 2013; Lintner 2015). While creating new opportunities for Myanmar in terms of development, economic growth, diplomatic support and even military assistance over the past two decades, the assertive ambitions of both rising giants in Myanmar have posed new strategic challenges for policymakers in Naypyitaw, where a deep tendency towards political xenophobia as well as anti-Chinese and anti-Indian nationalism still lingers well into the 2010s.

As this chapter continues, Thailand, the country's third largest neighbour, has also developed uneasy interactions with the Myanmar authorities, particularly over the past two decades.

The bilateral relationship has long been marred with age-old enmities, border disputes and military clashes, but also economic interdependence and a calculated diplomatic friendship within ASEAN. Bangladesh (erstwhile East Pakistan) has developed the most difficult relationship with Myanmar. Unresolved trans-border issues and the plight of the Rohingya communities in the northwestern districts of Myanmar's Rakhine State continue to undermine the bilateral relation with no resolution in sight, despite the settlement of a maritime boundary dispute in 2012. Lastly, Myanmar's trade and diplomatic relations with Laos, its fifth and tiniest neighbour located on the eastern banks of the Mekong River, can be viewed as far less significant, although Vientiane and Naypyitaw commonly support each other in international diplomatic fora.

China

The diplomatic relations between Myanmar and China are customarily referred to as *pauk phaw* (or kinsfolk) by officials (Maung Aung Myoe 2011; Steinberg and Fan 2012). Myanmar was among the first non-socialist states to establish diplomatic relations with Beijing in June 1950. Along with their Chinese counterparts, Myanmar's postcolonial leaders actively participated in the Non-Aligned Movement in the early 1950s and co-sponsored the Bandung Conference in 1955. This helped solve the boundary dispute between China and Myanmar through a bilateral agreement in 1960. However, Sino-Myanmar relations have regularly soured, in particular when anti-communist troops from the Kuomintang established their bases in Myanmar's northeastern Shan States in the 1950s or when anti-Chinese riots spread in Yangon in 1967.

In 1988, Myanmar's new junta dropped the autarkical policies professed by General Ne Win's regime, and attempted to open up and liberalize Myanmar's national economy. Following the coup d'état in Yangon and the subsequent crackdown on pro-democracy forces, Myanmar rapidly found itself isolated from most of the international community. Western countries led by the United States gradually imposed an array of sanctions on the country and its new regime. China offered a powerful policy alternative, and from 1989, Myanmar's new leadership embarked on what Chinese observers have coined as a 'Foreign Policy of Leaning to One Side'. For the two subsequent decades, China developed a unique economic and strategic partnership with its southwestern neighbour, which shares a more than 2,100 km-long border with Yunnan. It offered to this Chinese landlocked province an essential gateway to the south. A trade and infrastructure corridor was thus gradually shaped from Kunming down to Mandalay, along the historical 'Burma Road'. Chinese large-scale investments, as well as individual Yunnanese entrepreneurs, began to pour into Myanmar from the early 1990s and unchecked cross-border trades of all sorts – but especially of jade and timber – have developed dramatically ever since (Woods 2011; Egreteau 2012).

Myanmar's dependency over China has generated a noticeable resentment among its elites, and strong anti-Chinese sentiments expanded in Myanmar society during the 1990s and 2000s (Min Zin 2012; Farrelly and Olinga-Shannon 2015, 14–15). In March 2011, the advent of a new government led by President Thein Sein has, however, been perceived by many observers as an official attempt to gradually rebalance Myanmar's foreign relations and back away from China (Huang 2015, 204–05; Maung Aung Myoe 2015b, 26). Thein Sein visited Beijing in May 2011 and signed a joint statement establishing a comprehensive strategic cooperative partnership between the two neighbours (Li 2012). This partnership was meant to offer a reassurance that Myanmar would get China's full support for its ongoing economic and political transitions.

But soon after Thein Sein's trip, Sino-Myanmar relations began to encounter a series of setbacks. Responding to mounting popular Sinophobic views at home, Thein Sein ordered in

September 2011 the suspension of a US$3.6 billion Chinese hydropower project in Myanmar's northern Kachin State. Supported by a Chinese state-owned company – the China Power Investment Corporation – the Myitsone dam project was to be developed at the headwaters of the Irrawaddy (Ayeyarwaddy) River, Myanmar's highly symbolic waterway. Chinese officials have since kept on pushing for the construction of the dam to resume, in vain. Another Chinese-backed megaproject in Myanmar, the Letpadaung copper and gold mine (located northwest of Mandalay), has also drawn intense local resistance, as did the dual oil and gas pipeline built by the China National Petroleum Corporation between the Rakhine coastline and Kunming (Zhao Hong 2013).

Other issues have suddenly undermined the bilateral relations in the early 2010s. The resumption along Yunnan's borders of armed conflicts between the Myanmar armed forces (Tatmadaw) and various ethnic groups residing in Myanmar's northern borderlands, such as the Chinese-speaking Kokang and the Kachin Independence Organization (KIO), have much worried Beijing's officials (Yun Sun 2013, 2015). In April 2013, June 2014 and September 2015, President Thein Sein's subsequent diplomatic trips to China were openly purported to restore a comity lost between the two neighbours. If China's investments in Myanmar have exceptionally dropped since 2012, after a golden period of twenty years, Chinese state and private enterprises nonetheless continue to hold considerable sway over Myanmar's formal and informal economy. Between 1988 and 2015, China has officially invested some US$14.8 billion in Myanmar – or 27.3 per cent of the total of certified foreign direct investments received by the country in 27 years. As Myanmar remains vital to China's long-term economic goals for its southwestern provinces, there are reasons to believe that the Chinese leadership will more seriously address the fundamental distrust displayed by the Myanmar elites (Yun Sun 2012; Li and Char 2015). As an illustration, Aung San Suu Kyi was for the first time invited in June 2015 to pay an official visit to China by the Chinese Communist Party. The red carpet was rolled out for the then iconic opposition leader and Nobel laureate in Beijing, where she met President Xi Jinping (Haacke 2015). Her second visit to China in August 2016, this time as an elected leader, proved another opportunity to refine the damaged relationship.

Furthermore, the gradual lifting of international sanctions decided by Western governments in 2012 has rekindled Myanmar's relations to the outside world. The United States, long at odds with Myanmar's military leadership and an intransigent partisan of regime change in Myanmar, launched a policy review when President Barack Obama took office in 2009. Many experts have interpreted the multifaceted rapprochement between the Obama and Thein Sein administrations as a new thorn in China's ambitions in Southeast Asia (Maung Aung Myoe 2015b; Lintner 2015, 236). Hasty conclusions have indeed been popularly drawn on a new Sino-US 'great game' rising over Myanmar at the turn of the 2010s (Dai and Liu 2014). China's period of utmost dominance over its southern neighbour may have come to an end. But despite a perceptible economic slowdown in the mid-2010s, China remains a fast growing economy much in demand of underexploited resources available on its doorstep. Even more, since the NLD came into power, Naypyitaw has maintained high-level political contacts with Beijing. China was the first non-ASEAN country visited by Aung San Suu Kyi in August 2016. Yet, the economic partnership has not made any significant progress since 2016. The NLD government has not settled the Myitsone dam controversy in northern Kachin State and the Kyaukphhyu deep-water port project supported by Chinese state-owned enterprises has stalled. In the long run, geopolitical and economic factors will continue to determine Myanmar's policy towards China, a neighbour it cannot bluntly alienate.

India

Since both countries won their independence from the British in 1947 and 1948 respectively, India and Myanmar have developed a relationship that can range from cordial at best to uneasy at worst. Bitter colonial memories, distrust, wariness about a powerful neighbour on the Myanmar side, policy neglect and even condescendence on the Indian side have prevented the establishment of a relationship based on political affinities and common strategies throughout the second half of the twentieth century (Egreteau 2003). Nonetheless, the bilateral interactions have grown richer and more diversified with Myanmar's liberalization at the turn of the 2010s, and even more in 2014 with the advent of a regionally oriented government led by Prime Minister Narendra Modi in India (Egreteau 2011; Lee 2014; Bhatia 2015).

Since policy pundits in Delhi opted for a policy shift towards Myanmar in the early 1990s, India has sought to achieve three core objectives in Myanmar – policy objectives which twenty years later still stand at the heart of India's diplomacy vis-à-vis its eastern neighbour. First, encouraged by its own security establishment, India has long sought to pacify its northeastern borderlands. Echoing Myanmar's own internal turmoil, India's Northeast has been plagued with criminal insurgency and ethnic strife since the 1940s. Many ethnic separatist outfits fighting against India's central government – such as those formed by the Naga, Assamese or Meithei minorities – have routinely found roots, shelter and support on the Myanmar side of the 1,643 km-long border with India. From 1993 onwards, Indian security circles have sought new forms of cooperation with the Burmese security and intelligence forces (Egreteau 2003, 150–58; Nardi 2008). Still, India keeps in view the realities posed by a rugged and densely forested terrain as well as material limitations – and even reluctance to comply with all Indian demands – of the Burmese authorities themselves. As a matter of fact, during the 2010s, New Delhi has pursued its attempts to crush cross-border rebel networks on its own, without even seeking half-hearted support from Myanmar (Bhaumik 2015). However, efforts to boost defence cooperation have continued to be promoted at the highest level. In July 2015, the red carpet was rolled out by India for Myanmar's top military brass. Senior-General Min Aung Hlaing toured various Indian naval bases and was received by the highest authorities in New Delhi.

Second, in the late 1990s, Indian and Burmese policymaking circles started to consider each other as potential allies in their tentative containment policy towards China. Since 1988, Beijing's strategic and commercial influence in Myanmar has greatly worried India's traditionally Sinophobic elites. At the same time, Myanmar's multiple societies have proved increasingly uncomfortable with China's persistent shadow over the country. In this emerging context, India has thus sought to position itself as a logical geographic, strategic and democracy-oriented counterweight to China in Myanmar. Engaged in a massive diversification of its commercial, diplomatic and military partnerships since the advent of a reformist government in Naypyitaw in 2011, Myanmar has also been keen on finding a welcome source of diplomatic support and developmental assistance in India in order to start moving away from the Chinese orbit (Bhatia 2015, 168–69).

Third, while liberalizing and opening up its own domestic economy in 1991, India launched a 'look east policy', which aimed to take a foothold in the East and Southeast Asian booming economies. Delhi thus decided to cosy up to its Burmese neighbour in the hopes of securing new trade markets and energy supply routes in a long-isolated country rich in natural resources. After signing a border trade agreement in 1994, India began to plan strategic investments in Myanmar for the construction of roads (such as between Tamu and Kalewa in Sagaing region), ports (notably Sittwe), power plants and factories. Indian state-owned oil companies such as GAIL and ONGC-V also started to prospect and took position on Myanmar's hydrocarbon market. The bilateral trade rose from US$62 million in the 1988–89 fiscal year to US$345 million in 2001–01 and crossed the US$1 billion mark in 2007–08 (Egreteau 2011, 474).

However, after years of a tentative thrust into Myanmar, the Indian establishment became quite disillusioned, confessing the difficulties met as a result of building up more intimate ties with Myanmar's military-dominated elites. Underground networks run by Assamese, Meithei and Naga rebel groups still proliferate in Myanmar's remote Sagaing region with the enduring indulgence of easily-corrupted Burmese local authorities. Bilateral trade hardly reaches levels of commercial exchanges observed between India and faraway Poland or Kenya. Consequently, India's discourse on its role in Myanmar has evolved from the late 2000s. New Delhi has more enthusiastically defended projects of 'inter-connectivity' with Myanmar, as well as initiatives focused on 'capacity-building' and 'empowerment' of various Burmese communities, obviously insisting far less openly on security- or resources-driven objectives (Egreteau 2011; Lee 2014). India began offering training schemes to Burmese civil servants, journalists, teachers and, after 2011, even emerging the parliamentary workforce and Burmese legislators.[1] Training institutions in Myanmar, including those that focus on health care and higher education, were also supported by the Indian government in the cities of Yangon, Myingyan and Pakokku.

Recent high-profile inter-governmental exchanges have further attempted to boost the bilateral relationship. In 2011, with the advent of Thein Sein's reform-oriented administration, India grabbed the opportunity to influence the newly elected head of state. Thein Sein visited Delhi as early as October 2011, and welcomed Prime Minister Manmohan Singh in Naypyitaw in May 2012. In November 2012, Aung San Suu Kyi returned to India for the first time in 25 years. Mr Singh's successor, Narendra Modi, also travelled to Yangon in November 2014, lauding the potential benefits for Myanmar of India's revamped 'look east, act east' policy. However, India still appeared to lag behind in Myanmar (especially compared with China and Thailand), in terms of bilateral commercial exchanges and foreign direct investment. Bilateral trade, still heavily dominated by timber and agricultural products, has only reached US$2 billion in the 2014–15 fiscal year – thanks chiefly to bilateral banking arrangements made possible by the gradual lifting of international sanctions and the removal of administrative barriers and licence permits since 2011 by Naypyitaw.

Furthermore, ten years of promotion of a Thailand–Myanmar–India Trilateral Highway have still not proved successful, and efforts to complete the India-funded Kaladan Multi-modal fluvial port project in Sittwe have been rather slow since the early 2000s. Yet, many policy pundits in Delhi still want India to move deeper into Myanmar, especially from its northeastern region, despite the reluctance of India's own security establishment to open up a volatile and insurgency-ridden region bordering a potentially hostile China. Indian officials do not seem deterred and still aim to work for a broad, humble (yet quite welcomed locally) involvement in the democratization and development efforts of Myanmar in the 2010s, while at the same time including the country in India's own security-driven regional agenda for the twenty-first century. They reiterated this view when the newly elected NLD President Htin Kyaw and Aung San Suu Kyi's National Security Advisor Thaung Tun visited Delhi respectively in August 2016 and February 2017.

Bangladesh

Since Bangladesh was created from East Pakistan in 1971, Myanmar has developed an awkward relationship with its only Muslim neighbour. The two countries share only a 271 km-long land border, which includes 64 km of fluvial demarcation along the Naaf River (Ali Sheikh 1998, 471). Yet, over the past four decades, these swampy and porous borderlands have witnessed extensive waves of forced migration and political and communal unrest, as well as unbroken smuggling flows. Chief among the bilateral issues that Bangladeshi and Myanmar officials have discussed at the highest level since the 1970s is the plight of the Rohingya minority group – a Muslim community of about one million individuals segregated chiefly in the northwestern districts of Myanmar's Rakhine State and its capital, Sittwe.

Considered outsiders by Myanmar's authorities – but also the country's Buddhist-dominated society – the Rohingya have experienced decades of political discrimination, blunt segregation, forced displacement and cultural alienation, which culminated in 1978 and 1991 with two massive exoduses to Bangladesh (Ullah 2011). A remnant of the local Buddhist–Muslim fractures born of the Second World War, these repeated forced displacements have been fuelled by blatant racism observed among a handful of radical Buddhist Rakhine groups and a Myanmar state propaganda denouncing the underground activities of undesired foreign communities (Leider 2015). At the height of each humanitarian crisis, the UN High Commissioner for Refugees (UNHCR) has attempted to intervene. Two decades after the last exodus, the agency was still running two refugee camps in Bangladesh – Kutupalong and Nayapara – between the cities of Cox's Bazar and Teknaf. About 30,000 Rohingya were still registered as of June 2015.[2] Outside the camps dozens of thousands were said to be sheltered in unofficial settlements. Their numbers dramatically increased after a new exodus sparked by a crackdown launched by the Myanmar security forces in October 2016.

The spread of communal unrest inside Myanmar in the context of its post-2011 liberalization – and in particular the anti-Muslim riots that erupted in the Rakhine State in 2012 and spread to central and northern Myanmar in 2013 – has indeed further aggravated the alienation of the Rohingya and once more forced hundreds of families into exile (Human Rights Watch (HRW) 2013; International Crisis Group (ICG) 2014). These latest crises in 2012 and 2016 have had a spill-over effect on the bilateral relations between Myanmar and Bangladesh, which soured considerably. Dhaka continues to relentlessly deny Myanmar's enduring claims that the Rohingya are merely illegal Bangladeshi migrants who have recently entered the Rakhine State, while Naypyitaw accuses its Muslim neighbour of harbouring separatists, if not potential Islamist terrorist outfits.

Apart from the Rohingya conundrum which continues to considerably hinder the normalization of bilateral relations, other issues have been a major concern to both governments. The first is the delineation of the disputed maritime boundary between the two countries.[3] Since the early 2000s, the discovery of large gas and oil fields off the coastlines of Southeastern Bangladesh and the Rakhine State have prompted a necessary settlement, negotiations for which started in 2009 (Bissinger 2010). Both countries, eager to exploit untapped offshore resources, have pushed for a swift diplomatic agreement. An arbitration procedure under the United Nations Convention on the Law of the Seas (UNCLOS) has been accepted by both Naypyitaw and Dhaka and, notably, it helped resolved the dispute peacefully (Balaram 2012). The final judgment was given by the International Tribunal of the Law of the Sea in March 2012: it allowed Myanmar the larger parts of the disputed (c. 172,000 sq. km) while Bangladesh was granted about 110,000 sq. km around St Martin's Island.

Second, Bangladesh has long sought to establish a land connection with both Southeast Asia and China – a long-standing political ally of Dhaka and key commercial partner in position to balance the influence of Bangladesh's only other neighbour, India. However, the renovation of roads and the construction of direct transportation links between Bangladesh and Myanmar have never materialized. The volatility of the region, as well as the quasi-isolation of the Rakhine State from mainland Myanmar on the eastern side of the Yoma mountain range make it difficult for these links to form. Cross-border trade between Teknaf (in Bangladesh) and

Maungdaw (at the northwestern tip of the Rakhine State) was legalized only in 1994. Smuggling, however, has obviously remained the main channel for commerce in the region. In the 2013–14 fiscal year, the bilateral trade between the two countries lingered only at US$108 million.

A third related issue is border security. Land mines have long peppered the borderlands between Myanmar and Bangladesh. Skirmishes between Bangladeshi and Myanmar border patrols have also been reported on a regular basis, even after the Na-Sa-Ka (or Myanmar's Border Immigration Guard Force) was disbanded and replaced with a regular border police force in 2013. Pushed by local Rakhine elites who vehemently emphasize the multidimensional threats posed by Bangladesh and the local Muslim communities, Myanmar's national parliament voted in November 2014 in favour of strengthened border security measures. In November 2015, the chauvinistic and Buddhist-dominated Arakan National Party (ANP) grabbed a majority of seats in the Rakhine state assembly, causing renewed fears among local Muslim populations.

Truly, in the early days of Myanmar's transition, Dhaka and Naypyitaw tentatively tried to restore comity. The Bangladeshi government has proved intent on finding new economic opportunities in a country increasingly labelled as Asia's 'last frontier' for investments (Amin 2014). Sheikh Hasina, Bangladesh Premier since 2009, paid a landmark diplomatic visit to Myanmar in December 2011, promising assistance to solve the Rohingya conundrum and showing keen interest on importing electricity from Myanmar. However, Dhaka remains embroiled in deep political divides at home and has always been far more preoccupied with its relationship with India than with Myanmar. Besides, with the resurgence of communal violence in the Rakhine State and the scapegoating of the Rohingya communities throughout Myanmar since 2012, odds are that the bilateral relationship between Dhaka and Naypyitaw will continue to stall in coming years.

Thailand

Deep-rooted historical animosities have long lingered across the 2,096 km-long border between Thailand and Myanmar. Since the ransacking of the former capital of the Siamese kingdom, Ayutthaya, by Burmese troops in 1767, Myanmar has commonly been fictionalized as the Thais' archenemy (Chutintaranond and U-Sha 2001). This embittered history has been illustrated in the contemporary era with regular border disputes and a persistent mutual distrust between their respective elites (Chachavalpongpun 2005, 2010). Porous, mountainous borders as well as enduring inter-ethnic conflicts inside Myanmar have further given rise to a series of bilateral contentions since the 1950s, with particular acuity after Myanmar's 1988 uprising. The latter indeed prompted new waves of Burmese refugees and labour migrants flows into Thailand (Fink 2015). As of early 2017, Thailand was still providing tacit shelter to some 100,000 political refugees from Myanmar – mostly ethnic Karen (Kayin) and Karenni (Kayah) – in particular through nine UN-run camps based along its western borders.[4] Thailand has also welcomed hundreds of prominent Burmese political dissidents on its soil, especially in the border cities of Mae Sot, Mae Hong Son and Chiang Mai.

Diplomatic tensions have thus regularly undermined the bilateral relationship since the two countries recognized each other in August 1948. Ever since, Myanmar's ruling authorities have been suspicious of Thailand's cosy yet highly complex interactions with several of the rebel armed groups and ethnic insurgencies based in eastern Myanmar – all of which have fought against its central government – such as the Karen, Shan and Mon rebellions, the CIA-sponsored Kuomintang troops stationed in the Shan States in the 1950s and, until 1996, the Mong Tai Army (MTA) of Khun Sa, a notorious drug lord. In the polarized context of the Cold War,

Thailand's elites, anxious of the various menaces that Myanmar could pose, encouraged the development of a 'buffer policy' (Maung Aung Myoe 2015a, 122–23). The Thai military played an especially crucial role in the definition and then implementation of this type of policy, which combined logistic support to insurgents opposed to Myanmar's government with the development of informal cross-border trade exchanges bypassing the Burmese central authorities.

Despite unresolved political feuds, since the 1990s Thailand has stood among Myanmar's most important economic partners – the first in some sectors (such as energy, hydroelectricity and trade of basic commodities), and second only to China in many others. Thailand has become an economically vital partner for Myanmar since the turn of the twenty-first century. Various formal and informal investments from Thailand have fuelled Myanmar's national economy in many ways. The Thai opposition to the sanction policies imposed on Myanmar by Western governments between the mid-1990s and the early 2010s has also facilitated the thrust of Thai investors. Powerful Thai companies have been in position to develop deep interests inside Myanmar over the past two decades (Chachavalpongpun 2010). By late 2014, the total amount of Thai foreign direct investments in Myanmar reached some US$10 billion. Among the largest Thai investors stand the state-owned Petroleum Authority of Thailand (PTT, the country's sole gas supplier), Siam Cement Group, Toyo-Thai Corporation and Bangkok Dusit Medical. About a fifth of Thailand's total supplies of natural gas come from Myanmar, especially through Myanmar's two main offshore gas fields of Yadana and Yetagun in the Andaman Sea. Furthermore, the Thai economy – with few qualms – has made the most of the presence of an estimated two to three million Myanmar migrants on its soil since the 1990s (Fink 2015, 24).

In return, Myanmar has largely profited from the money these legal – and illegal – migrants have sent home in remittances (Pearson and Kusakabe 2012). Since Myanmar engaged in liberalization in the early 2010s, special economic zones have also sprung up on the Thai side of the border, notably in Tak province. Border trade has also dramatically expanded after Myanmar initiated several rounds of peace parleys with the ethnic armed groups in late 2011 that long used to act as 'buffers' with Thailand. Between the 2011–12 and 2014–15 fiscal years, border trade increased 18-fold to reach US$432 million. The total bilateral trade between the two neighbours amounted for US$8.15 billion in 2014–15. Several challenges remain though, as proved by the difficulties the Dawei deep-sea port project has experienced since the mid-2000s. This industrial zone project located in Myanmar's Tanintharyi region (in which Japan and Thailand have aimed to invest massively) has been stuck in a quagmire for a decade. A series of other bilateral contentious issues also remain unresolved, such as the relentless illegal fishing in Burmese territorial waters by Thai trawlers, the quasi-enslavement of Burmese labour migrants by Thailand-based networks of human traffickers, and the spread of diseases into Thailand such as HIV/AIDS. These issues are combined with the unmanageable flows of illegal drugs – heroin and methamphetamines chiefly – produced in the Burmese borderlands by local strongmen and drug barons.

Since the turn of the 2010s there has nonetheless been noteworthy improvement in the bilateral relationship. The general logic of geography, economic development and territorial proximity all seem to prevail. Since the late 1990s, each time a Democrat-led government had taken office in Bangkok, bilateral relations between Thailand and Myanmar have reached their lowest point, while the election of an administration led either by the controversial (but highly popular) tycoon Thaksin Shinawatra (2001–06) or his sister Yingluck Shinawatra (2011–14), has increased accommodation and appeasement between Bangkok and Naypyitaw. Since the late 2000s, however, policymakers in Naypyitaw have taken great care to not take sides in

Thailand's increasingly divided (and coloured) society (Chachavalpongpun 2010; Maung Aung Myoe 2015a). New forms of cooperation have even been thought of by both countries' elites, and a consensus appears to have emerged on the necessity to tone down criticism and reduce the opposition to the other government. From Myanmar's point of view, the long-term financial and commercial investments Thailand can provide to the country are vital, and securing a strong diplomatic and strategic ally within the ASEAN club is also of paramount importance. In June 2016, Aung San Suu Kyi focused her visit to Bangkok on the fate and rights of Burmese migrants. From a Thai perspective, the cooperation of the Burmese central government, whether led by the USDP or the NLD, is essential to the pacification and liberalization of the border regions.

Military relations have particularly improved since the late 2000s (Egreteau and Jagan 2013, 352–56). The Royal Thai Army has long been concerned with the regular incursions into and shelling of Thai territory by Tatmadaw troops hunting down rebels from the Karen National Union (KNU) or the Shan State Army–South (SSA–S). The last border clashes between Thai and Myanmar armed forces date back to 2001. Senior-General Min Aung Hlaing visited Thailand twice, in January 2012 and in July 2014. In September that latter year, the Thai premier and coup leader General Prayuth Chan-ocha paid a reciprocal trip to Naypyitaw; this was his first official trip abroad as junta chief. As personal relationships play a key role in the management of bilateral contention – as proved by the influence of Thaksin Shinawatra in the mid-2000s – they might augur smoother bilateral relations for the late 2010s. The relative pacification of Myanmar's eastern borders engaged in 2011 with new rounds of peace talks between Naypyitaw and various ethnic armed groups – some held on Thai territories – may have also helped smooth Thai–Myanmar interactions.

Laos

Laos is Myanmar's tiniest neighbour. Both countries share a 238 km-long border, naturally formed by the Mekong River. The official demarcation was finalized only in 1995 – 40 years after Myanmar and Laos established diplomatic relations in July 1955. A Myanmar–Lao Joint Commission for Bilateral Cooperation was created and has since convened somewhat regularly to discuss other bilateral issues. It met for the eleventh time in March 2015. Laos and Myanmar, especially since they both joined ASEAN in 1997, have regularly supported each other in regional and international arenas and are likely to continue being sympathetic to each other in the near future. Unlike its other direct neighbours, Naypyitaw does not perceive any immediate threats from Laos, although Myanmar's security forces have long been carefully watching whether any anti-state armed insurgency or militias have been using Laos as a retreat base. Myanmar military elites indeed appear to still share vivid memories of KMT troops spreading from Yunnan into the Shan States and French-controlled Lao territories in 1949 to continue their struggle against Mao's communist government. Regular dialogues between Naypyitaw and Vientiane on border security matters have been conducted since the 2000s and, unlike Thailand, Laos has proved receptive to Myanmar's security sensitivities in the matter over the years.

Since the advent of Thein Sein's administration in 2011, inter-governmental relations have obviously improved. Myanmar's president was in Vientiane in March 2012 to sign an agreement on what still remains the biggest joint economic project ever agreed by the two neighbours: the construction of a 700 metre-long bridge over the Mekong River, linking the district of Kenglup (Shan State) to Xieng Kok in Laos. The US$26 million project started in early 2013 and was completed in May 2015. This 'Friendship Bridge' is supposed to be part of the Greater Mekong

Subregion's northern economic corridor, which aims to link Vietnam's capital Hanoi with Myanmar's deep-sea port complex of Kyaukphyu on the Rakhine coastline. The Laotian president, Choummaly Sayasone, travelled to Myanmar in December 2013 to encourage the development of that corridor. However, informal trade remains the main channel for bilateral commerce, especially of illicit products such as narcotics produced in Myanmar's northeastern Shan State – and this continues despite the increasing pressure of China's anti-narcotics agencies on Myanmar and Laos (Su 2015). The first official trip in May 2016 of newly elected President Htin Kyaw and Aung San Suu Kyi, as Foreign Minister, was to Vientiane, at the invitation of the Laotian presidency.

Conclusion

Myanmar, 'hemmed in like a tender gourd among the cactus', according to its former Premier U Nu, developed a quite apprehensive neighbourhood policy as early as the 1950s. Sandwiched between India, China, Southeast Asia and the Indian Ocean, the country has long held the potential to become a point of convergence as well as a cockpit of strategic competitions between regional powers and neighbours. After a 'go-it-alone' diplomatic stance long-favoured by its military leaders since the 1960s, major events in regional politics have unavoidably had an influence on the country, especially since the end of the Cold War and the turn of the twenty-first century. The rise of India and China, as well as globalization, has already generated some noticeable effects. One example is the strong impact that the rapid development of the economies of Thailand, India and China has had on border areas in Myanmar. Myanmar's peripheries are now sites of unsuspected far-flung trans-border connections that make the country far more inter-connected with its immediate neighbourhood (and the rest of the world) than it has been since the British colonial era. Therefore, its own standing in Asia – and beyond – in the twenty-first century is highly likely to continue to be influenced by these basic geographic parameters. A carefully non-aligned, balanced, equidistant and probably reactive neighbourhood diplomacy may thus best suit Myanmar in the near future. The declarations of Aung San Suu Kyi, State Counsellor and Foreign Minister of the NLD-led government since March 2016, seem to have confirmed this perspective.

Notes

1 Chief among India's development programmes are various Foreign Institute Services schemes, the Indian Technical and Economic Cooperation Programme (ITEC) and the Colombo Plan's Technical Cooperation Scheme (TCS).
2 Updated figures available at http://reporting.unhcr.org/node/2539#_ga=1.47032804.2106796575.1487325365 [accessed on February 16, 2017].
3 A land boundary agreement was, however, signed in 1977.
4 Updated figures available at www.unhcr.or.th/en/about/thailand [accessed on February 16, 2017].

References

Ali Sheikh, Yunus. 1998. 'Bangladesh–Myanmar Relations: Making the Best of Proximity'. *BIISS Journal* 19 (4): 471–504.

Amin, Zahedul. 2014. 'Changing Dynamics in Myanmar Impacts Bangladesh Geopolitics'. *The Diplomat*, June 23.

Balaram, Ravi A. 2012. 'Case Study: The Myanmar and Bangladesh Maritime Boundary Dispute in the Bay of Bengal and its Implications for the South China Sea Claims'. *Journal of Current Southeast Asian Affairs* 31 (3): 85–104.

Bhatia, Rajiv. 2015. *India–Myanmar Relations: Changing Contours*. New Delhi: Routledge.

Bhaumik, Subir, 2015. 'Army's Transborder Raid in Myanmar: Interrogating the Claims'. *Economic and Political Weekly* 50 (25): 15–17.

Bissinger, Jared. 2010. 'The Maritime Boundary Dispute between Bangladesh and Myanmar: Motivations, Potential Solutions and Implications'. *Asia Policy* 10: 103–142.

Chachavalpongpun, Pavin. 2005. *A Plastic Nation: The Curse of Thainess in Thai–Burmese Relations*. Lanham: University Press of America.

Chachavalpongpun, Pavin. 2010. 'Thai–Myanmar Relations: Old Animosity in a New Bilateral Setting'. In *International Relations in Southeast Asia: Between Bilateralism and Multilateralism*, edited by N. Ganesan and Ramses Amer, 117–142. Singapore: ISEAS Publications.

Chutintaranond, Sunait and Kanokphan U-Sha, eds. 2001. *From Fact to Fiction: History of Thai–Myanmar Relations in Cultural Context*. Bangkok: IAS Monograph No. 54, Chulalongkorn University.

Dai, Yonghong and Hongchao Liu. 2014. *Rivalry and Cooperation: A New 'Great Game' in Myanmar*. Stockholm: Institute for Security and Development Policy Asia Paper.

Egreteau, Renaud. 2003. *Wooing the Generals: India's New Burma Policy*. New Delhi: CSH-Authorspress.

Egreteau, Renaud. 2011. 'A Passage to Burma? India, Development, and Democratization in Myanmar'. *Contemporary Politics* 17 (4): 467–486.

Egreteau, Renaud. 2012. 'The Burmese Jade Trail: Transnational Networks, China, and the (Relative) Impact of International Sanctions against Myanmar's Gems'. In *Myanmar's Transition: Openings, Obstacles, and Opportunities*, edited by Nick Cheesman, M. Skidmore and T. Wilson, 89–115. Singapore: ISEAS Publications.

Egreteau, Renaud and Larry Jagan. 2013. *Soldiers and Diplomacy in Burma: The Foreign Relations of the Burmese Praetorian State*. Singapore: NUS Press.

Farrelly, Nicholas and Stephanie Olinga-Shannon. 2015. *Interpreting Contemporary Chinese Life in Myanmar*. Singapore: ISEAS Trends No. 15.

Fink, Christina. 2015. 'Burmese Sanctuary-Seekers and Migrants in Thailand: Policies, Experiences and Prospects'. In *Trauma and Recovery in War's Border*, edited by Kathleen Allden and Nancy Murakami, 24–47. Lebanon, NH: Dartmouth College Press.

Haacke, Jürgen. 2015. 'Why Did Myanmar's Opposition Leader Just Visit China?' *The Diplomat*, June 15.

Huang, Chiung-Chui. 2015. 'Balance of Relationship: The Essence of Myanmar's China Policy'. *The Pacific Review* 28 (2): 189–210.

Human Rights Watch (HRW). 2013. *All You Can Do Is Pray*. Washington, DC: HRW.

International Crisis Group (ICG). 2014. *Myanmar: The Politics of Rakhine State*. Yangon/Brussels: Asia Briefing No. 261.

Lee, Lavina. 2014. 'Myanmar's Transition to Democracy: New Opportunities or Obstacles for India?' *Contemporary Southeast Asia* 36 (2): 290–316.

Leider, Jacques. 2015. 'Competing Identities and the Hybridized History of the Rohingyas'. In *Metamorphosis: Studies in Social and Political Change in Myanmar*, edited by Renaud Egreteau and François Robinne. Singapore: NUS Press.

Li, Chenyang. 2012. 'China–Myanmar Comprehensive Strategic Cooperation Partnership: A Regional Threat?' *Journal of Current Southeast Asian Affairs* 31(1): 53–72.

Li, Chenyang and James Char. 2015. *China–Myanmar Relations since Naypyidaw's Political Transition*. Singapore: RSIS Working Paper Series No. 288 (March 16).

Lintner, Bertil. 1999. *Burma in Revolt: Opium and Insurgency since 1948*. Chiang Mai: Silkworm Books.

Lintner, Bertil. 2015. *Great Game East: India, China, and the Struggle for Asia's Most Volatile Frontier*. [Revised Edition]. London: Yale University Press.

Maung Aung Myoe. 2011. *In the Name of Pauk-Phaw: Myanmar's China Policy since 1948*. Singapore: ISEAS Publications.

Maung Aung Myoe. 2015a. 'Legacy or Overhang? Historical Memory in Myanmar–Thai Relations'. In *Bilateral Legacies in East and Southeast Asia*, edited by N. Ganesan, 107–137. Singapore: ISEAS Publications.

Maung Aung Myoe. 2015b. 'Myanmar's China Policy Since 2011: Determinants and Directions'. *Journal of Current Southeast Asian Affairs* 34 (2): 21–54.

Min Zin. 2012. 'Burmese Attitude towards Chinese: Portrayal of the Chinese in Contemporary Cultural and Media Works'. *Journal of Current Southeast Asian Affairs* 31 (1): 115–131.

Nardi, Dominic J. 2008. 'Cross-Border Chaos: A Critique of India's Attempt to Secure Its Northeast Tribal Areas through Cooperation with Myanmar'. *SAIS Review* 28 (1): 161–171.

Pearson, Ruth and Kyoko Kusakabe. 2012. *Thailand's Hidden Workforce: Burmese Women Factory Workers.* London: Zed Books.

Smith, Martin. 1999. *Burma: Insurgency and the Politics of Ethnicity.* [2nd Edition]. London: Zed Books, 1999.

Steinberg, David I. and Hongwei Fan. 2012. *Modern China–Myanmar Relations: Dilemmas of Mutual Dependence.* Copenhagen: NIAS Press.

Su, Xiaobo. 2015. 'Non-traditional Security and China's Transnational Narcotics Control in Northern Laos and Myanmar'. *Political Geography* 48: 72–82.

Thant Myint-U. 2012. *Where China Meets India: Burma and the New Crossroads of Asia.* [Revised Edition]. New York: Farrar, Straus and Giroux.

Ullah, Akm Ahsan. 2011. 'Rohingya Refugees to Bangladesh: Historical Exclusions and Contemporary Marginalization'. *Journal of Immigrant & Refugee Studies* 9 (2): 139–161.

Woods, Kevin M. 2011. 'Conflict Timber along the China–Burma Border: Connecting the Global Timber Consumer with Violent Extraction Sites'. In *Chinese Circulations: Capital, Commodities and Networks in Southeast Asia*, edited by Eric Tagliacozzo, Chang Wen-chin and Wang Gungwu, 480–506. Durham, NC: Duke University Press.

Yun Sun. 2012. 'China's Strategic Misjudgement on Myanmar'. *Journal of Current Southeast Asian Affairs* 31 (1): 73–96.

Yun Sun. 2013. *China's Intervention in the Myanmar-Kachin Peace Talks.* Washington, DC: East-West Center, Asia-Pacific Bulletin No. 200 (February 20).

Yun Sun. 2015. *The Conflict in Northern Myanmar: Another Anti-China Conspiracy?* Washington, DC: East-West Center, Asia-Pacific Bulletin No. 302 (February 20).

Zhao Hong. 2013. *The China–Myanmar Energy Pipelines: Risks and Benefits.* Singapore: ISEAS Perspectives No. 30 (May 15).

31

INTERNATIONAL NON-GOVERNMENTAL ORGANISATIONS AND ADVOCACY

John Dale and Samantha Samuel-Nakka

Prior to the year 2000, most international non-governmental organisations (INGOs) and advocacy work in Myanmar either operated outside the country's borders or trod carefully under the suspicious surveillance of the military government's ministries. Today, however, this work is diversifying and expanding. There are complex organisations that intersect and openly work together within Myanmar to provide humanitarian services, traditional development projects, human rights education and democratic political reform. Nevertheless, the trajectory of Myanmar's humanitarian and democratic development remains uncertain.

This chapter highlights three organisational forces shaping civil society in Myanmar. Each of these organisational forces differently embeds this work in Myanmar's simultaneously changing state and economy: (1) bureaucratic structures of INGO coordination linking civil society to state (national and international) power; (2) transnational advocacy networks (TANs) of supporting civil society organisations linking local civil societies across diverse national cultures within and beyond Myanmar; and (3) an emerging social enterprise sector linking civil society to the disciplinary power of markets. These complex organisations shape the issues and impact of advocacy, and have competing visions and strategies for humanitarian and democratic development in Myanmar. The question for the future of advocacy during this critical transitional period in Myanmar is whether civil society can continue to find ways to deepen democracy as state bureaucratic and market forces are increasingly vying to shape the rapidly changing political, economic, legal, social and cultural institutional framework of development.

Before examining each of these forces, however, it is important to understand the division of labour and distinct political strategies that distinguished the projects of INGOs and TANs in Myanmar during the two decades prior to the transition from military to civilian governance. This helps to explain how the important work of pro-democracy activism fostered by TANs, which has contributed to Myanmar's democratic transition, has increasingly been tempered by state (Myanmar and international) bureaucratic organisational structures of governance.

State discipline: origins of bureaucratic advocacy

It might be tempting to attribute the burgeoning growth of INGOs and TANs in Myanmar to the country's democratic transition in the wake of the 2015 general elections that brought the National League for Democracy (NLD) to power. But such a view would miss what is more interesting about the complex and changing organisational topography of Myanmar civil society. Between 2001 and 2004, the INGO sector in Myanmar grew from 30 to 41 organisations, and doubled its budget from US$15 million to US$30 million. Many large INGOs, including World Vision, Population Services International and Médecins Sans Frontières – Holland, significantly expanded their programmes. Local non-governmental organisations (NGOs), many of which were unregistered and funded by international agencies, increased and expanded their humanitarian relief activities as well.

Driving the expansion of aid programmes in the early 2000s were both increased funding and changes in the operational environment for humanitarian agencies. Between the years of 2000 and 2005, humanitarian aid for Myanmar doubled from around US$75 million to US$150 million. Most aid agencies, like the United Nations Development Programme, the World Food Programme and the United Nations Population Fund, increased their activities during this period. At the same time, the military government in Myanmar increased permission to access and evaluate vulnerable populations for determining needs, delivering assistance and monitoring outcomes.

In short, between 2000 and 2005, the landscape for INGOs and advocacy in Myanmar was diversifying and expanding, much as it is today. What distinguishes today's period of expansion from the last one is the highly bureaucratic organisational structure within which INGOs now operate in Myanmar. Although many observers suggest that Cyclone Nargis, in 2008, created the opportunity for INGOs, local NGOs and other civil society organisations to forge new ties in a collective effort to provide emergency relief to victims in Myanmar, few have explained how these new ties became organised in the form of a highly bureaucratic structure. To explain this, we must understand the events that led to the contraction of INGO and advocacy work from mid-2005 to 2008. Moreover, these events unfolded within a less cooperative division of labour than existed between INGOs focused on humanitarian aid, technical assistance and traditional development, and those focused on human rights, democratic reform and community empowerment.

In August of 2005, The Global Fund, a financing institution designed to end epidemics such as malaria and HIV/AIDS, terminated a planned US$98 million health programme in Myanmar as a result of intense pressure from US-based lobby groups (notably the Institute for Asian Democracy). The political controversy over the termination of the programme undermined sensitive negotiation with the military government over the local operational conditions of foreign partnering organisations. Furthermore, the sudden termination of this programme in Myanmar made visible in a very public way the divide that existed between INGOs and advocacy networks that, on the one hand, had been working carefully to influence politico-military contacts within Myanmar to expand humanitarian operational space, and those that took a far less conciliatory approach towards the military government's abusive human rights practices and glacial movement towards democratic political reform. Generally, organisations taking the harder line worked in border areas of the country with only clandestine access to favourable pro-democracy contacts in central states and key cities, like Yangon and Mandalay. The former organisations worked inside the country, typically with locally registered organisations, and benefited from the relationship they had carefully cultivated with General Khin Nyunt, who served then as the military intelligence chief, and who actively facilitated broader humanitarian access for INGOs willing to work with him.

Over previous months, however, in late 2004, the well-cultivated influence of these humanitarian advocacy networks working inside Myanmar quickly began to weaken when Khin Nyunt was purged from power by an emerging military leadership that was uncompromising and more nationalistic in its views on permitting INGOs to expand their humanitarian work in Myanmar. This event severely limited the capacity of these INGOs and their partners within Myanmar. For example, even the International Committee of the Red Cross was forced to suspend most of its programmes operating in the country. The new seat of political government in Nyapyidaw was restructuring its power and laying plans for a referendum on the new constitution (which notably reserves 25 per cent of parliamentary seats for the military), new democratic elections and, as would only later become evident, a transition from a primarily military to a primarily civilian government.

In February 2006, the military government issued for the first time a set of formal 'Guidelines for UN Agencies, International Organisations and INGOs/NGOs'. This event suggested that the military had already been planning a systematic reassessment of its policy towards international assistance within the country. These guidelines established a new structure of committees at central, state/division and township levels to coordinate all aid activities in the areas. They also mandated the following: all agencies be registered with the Ministry of Home Affairs; all individual aid officials travelling outside Yangon and into conflict zones with ethnic minorities be accompanied by government escorts; national and international staff be vetted by the government; and all aid funds be channelled through the Myanmar Foreign Trade Bank. As many observers noted at the time, this language was not new, but prior to the publication of the guidelines, none of these stipulations and processes had been enforced. By 2006, the operational environment of humanitarian aid and advocacy was changing. The bureaucratic organisational structure of what today in Myanmar is called the INGO Forum conforms largely to the one proposed in these formal guidelines mandated by the military government.

But this landscape has also been rapidly changing in other ways since the general democratic elections in 2015. Constituting this emerging landscape is a complicated array of organisational structures with different visions and strategies, each of which intersects and complements, as well as constrains, the others.

The new state of social development for INGOs

Understanding the work of INGOs in Myanmar today begins with attention to the complex bureaucratic structures through which they are organised with the aim of addressing fundamental needs through the efficient, transparent and accountable delivery of humanitarian relief, technical services and community development assistance. These bureaucratic structures provide clear channels of responsibility among INGOs working in Myanmar, and link them to the work and oversight of key government ministries and international governmental organisations, as well as local NGOs, donors and embassies. These structures also have been rapidly incorporating new organisations and programmes that have only in recent years started operating in Myanmar, following the lifting of international (especially EU, UK and US) sanctions, and the subsequent influx of foreign direct investment, international development funding and humanitarian aid. Typically, these bureaucratic organisational structures coordinate the humanitarian and democratic action of civil society to facilitate its adaptation to Myanmar's political transition. Yet, they do not seek to foster in civil society an ongoing capacity to challenge the undemocratic rules or institutional arrangements of Myanmar's emerging capitalist markets nor inequitable social relations of economic production.

In 2008, Nargis devastated vast areas of Myanmar. The military government disallowed the cyclone or the subsequent flood of international assistance to halt the national referendum on the new constitution that was underway – claiming in the end that an incredible 92.48 per cent of voters in the 47 townships devastated by the cyclone participated in the election and approved the draft constitution by 98.12 per cent. Cyclone Nargis was both a catastrophe and a catalyst, undoubtedly transforming the organisational landscape of Myanmar's civil society. Yet, this transformation has occurred largely within the contours of the bureaucratic guidelines designed by the military prior to Nargis.

INGOs thwarted from entering the country nevertheless managed to engage from abroad local civil society organisations (CSOs) as important partners in humanitarian relief. Transnational partnerships with well-established local non-governmental organisations (LNGOs) provided a semblance of legal and political cover to the humanitarian work of domestic NGOs in Myanmar's then more ambiguous legal climate.

Legal reform under the new civilian government, since 2011, has brought greater clarity to the legal meaning (and thus permissibility) of operations and relations of INGOs, domestic NGOs and their partnerships. International and domestic NGOs now register their organisations under the new Association Registration Law Myanmar (No. 31/2014). The 2014 Association Registration Law envisions a decentralised registration system implemented by the Ministry of Home Affairs (MoHA), with six registration committees, including at the Union (national) level, region or state level, Naypyitaw Council level, self-administered region or state level, divisional level and township level. However, NGOs have expressed concern regarding pending legislation initiatives introduced by the Ministry of Labour, Immigration and Population – particularly drafts of the Law Concerning Foreigners and the Foreign Worker Law. If enacted, these draft laws have the potential to increase the burden on foreign workers and their employers, including those working in the civil society sector. They also could be selectively enforced against human rights activists.

An increasing number of local and international NGOs in Myanmar are bureaucratically organised to pursue a specific mandate to strengthen civil society. These actors serve as coordinating bodies to strengthen information sharing and coordinate humanitarian and development activities among INGOs working in Myanmar. For example, the Burnet Institute, an Australian NGO, formed in Yangon the Local Resource Centre (LRC) in 2008. LRC is a coordinating body that facilitates coordination for more than 1,800 civil society organisations working to promote humanitarian assistance, capacity building and information sharing. LRC has 809 local NGOs and 56 other networks working within their network (LNGO 2015 Annual Report Summary; and LNGO Directory 2017).

The Myanmar Information Management Unit (MIMU) is an independent mechanism for information management and serves as a resource for the development community in Myanmar. MIMU strengthens the coordination, collection, processing, analysis and dissemination of information. The MIMU Contact List is a searchable online directory of UN agencies, INGOs, LNGOs, diplomatic bodies and coordination teams working in Myanmar. It currently holds 2,690 individual contacts from 1,176 offices and 645 entities working in the humanitarian and development sectors across Myanmar.

MIMU established the INGO Forum in 2007 in an effort to support coordinated dialogue between the INGOs that are involved in humanitarian and development activities in Myanmar. The INGO Forum, as of March 2017, comprises 99 international civil society organisations. It serves as a platform for stakeholders to exchange information and share their expertise to strengthen analysis and decision-making in the humanitarian and development community.

LRC, MIMU and the INGO Forum provide different forms of information management services. The mutual governance of these bodies and the state ministries enables each to adapt to Myanmar's political transition that is taking place, but rarely does this relationship facilitate democratic or humanitarian challenges to the ways in which Myanmar's markets are being legally institutionalised.

Transnational advocacy networks

Overlapping, intersecting and sometimes conflicting with the bureaucratic structures reflected in these coordinating bodies are TANs linking civil society organisations that operate within and outside Myanmar. Worldwide, TANs have become increasingly influential in shaping international politics. In Myanmar, TANs have been operating since the 1990s to deepen democracy, human rights, humanitarianism and environmentalism, among other principled ideas. However, because the military government heavily repressed local political action in the pursuit of human rights or democratic change, or often understood this work to be a form of foreign political interference in Myanmar's national sovereignty, TANs typically operated clandestinely and without the support of the Myanmar government. Today, however, the work of TANs in Myanmar, like that of INGOs with which they often coordinate, is increasingly pulled into the orbit of bureaucratic structures for the delivery of technical assistance and relief.

This fact has not gone unnoticed by these TANs, and especially the local civil society organisations within them. In October of 2014, over 650 representatives from 257 organisations and networks in Myanmar gathered in Yangon for three days under the banner of the Myanmar People's Forum to discuss recent political developments and the transition process that started in 2011. Among the discussion points they proposed was a call for greater attention to deepening both political democracy through law reform and parliamentary accountability and economic democracy through meaningful local participation in economic development. Tellingly, they also addressed the role and involvement of INGOs in shaping the transition.

The Myanmar People's Forum called upon INGOs in particular to commit to the following principled action:

1 Continue aid and support progress and capacity building institutions, while operating in compliance with humanitarian and human rights principles, and to avoid activities that can lead to increased conflict;
2 Respect and acknowledge the capacity, equal entitlement and the important role of CSOs; and
3 Support processes that have emerged from consultations with local organisations and people as opposed to pre-arranged activities.

Myanmar Civil Society Organisations Forum 2014

Although Myanmar began a reform process in 2011 that aimed to transition to a more democratic and equitable society, there continue to be reports of human rights violations, suggesting an important obstacle to the process. The internationally reputable Assistance Association of Political Prisoners (AAPP) in Myanmar, which was formed as an unregistered NGO in the 1990s by former political prisoners sentenced from 7 to 21 years for their pro-democracy activism in Myanmar, produced on March 16, 2017 records of 86 political prisoners (including political activists, land rights activists and farmers) who were currently incarcerated in Myanmar's jails, and a further 206 political activists awaiting trial (AAPP 2017). In March 2017, the Rome-based Permanent People's Tribunal launched a session in London exploring allegations, based on witness testimony of Rohingya refugees and internally displaced Kachin, of state crimes (ranging from sexual violence to military air strikes and shelling of homes) against their ethnic communities in Myanmar. Representatives of the Myanmar government were invited to attend, but declined (Kantar 2017).

Myanmar has decades of experience in the pursuit of democracy, and its civil society has the potential to promote good governance and corporate accountability, encourage citizen participation and protect human rights. MIMU, the INGO Forum and the LRC all have networks of INGOs that are focusing on human rights and democracy issues. But there also are an increasing number of civil society organisations working through TANs towards these goals in Myanmar. The specific issues on which they focus are diverse, and the social relations through which they produce their transnational solidarity are varied.

In some cases, these TANs are created to deepen democratic change by linking local civil society to powerful networks of INGOs, diverse movement activists and states outside of Myanmar. For example, in February 2006, the Forum for Democracy in Burma (FDB), Asian Forum for Human Rights and Development (Forum-Asia) and Alternative ASEAN Network on Burma (ALTSEAN-Burma) organised a regional conference titled, 'Democratic Change by the People: Asia-Pacific Partnership on Burma'. Eighty participants representing 47 organisations from 16 countries attended the event held in Chiang Mai, Thailand. In addition to establishing partnership with Burma support groups across the Asia-Pacific region for developing and implementing a common strategy to mobilise a coordinated regional civil society movement for Burma, a key purpose of the event was to strengthen the support of civil societies to the Association of Southeast Asian Nations Inter-Parliamentary Myanmar Caucus (AIPMC) and national parliamentary caucuses on Burma (Myanmar), which had been working to discipline the human rights practices and stalled 'roadmap towards democracy' of Myanmar's military rulers. This conference established a new TAN – Burma Partnership, known prior to 2006 as the Asia-Pacific Peoples' Partnership on Burma (APPPB).

Burma Partnership is a network of organisations throughout the Asia-Pacific region that embraces a participatory approach in advocating for, and mobilising a movement for, democracy and human rights in Myanmar. Their network includes the multi-ethnic leadership of political and civil society organisations both inside Myanmar and in exile, as well as broad-based solidarity organisations in Myanmar, Indonesia, the Philippines, Korea, Hong Kong and Japan.

Another example of a coordinating body operating as a TAN to defend and advance human rights and democracy in Myanmar is the Network for Human Rights Documentation – Burma (ND Burma). ND Burma was formed in 2004 to provide a way for human rights organisations in Myanmar to collaborate on the human rights documentation process. They provide high-quality and high-volume data for ND Burma members and other advocacy groups, and continue to develop an accurate historical record that can be used for potential transitional justice mechanisms in Myanmar. ND Burma documented 67 cases of torture in 2016, a 150 per cent increase since the previous year.

This network of organisations includes the AAPP, Burma Issues, Chin Human Rights Organisation, Human Rights Foundation of Monland, Kachin Women's Association – Thailand, Lahu Women's Organisation, Palaung Women's Organisation and Ta'ang Students and Youth Organisation. It also includes four affiliate member organisations: All Arakan Students' and Youths' Congress; Pao Youth Organisation; Earthrights International; and Equality Myanmar (formerly the Human Rights Education Institute of Burma). The women's organisations and the student and youth organisations link this network to several other influential TANs, including the umbrella organisation Students and Youth Congress of Burma (identified above as a member of Burma Partnership's TAN, but which also represents 13 youth democratic and ethnic organisations), the United Nationalities Youth Forum (an umbrella of 13 member organisations of 11 ethnicities), and the Women's League of Burma (discussed below). The International Center for Transitional Justice also serves as a partner member of ND Burma.

Some TANs established in the wake of Cyclone Nargis also trace their origins to grassroots community leaders and organisations in Myanmar, even though their network's executive and agenda-setting power (Wong 2012) may be primarily dominated by international NGOs or foreign directors in national NGOs. For example, the Gender Equality Network (GEN), formerly the Women's Protection Technical Working Group, was formed in 2008 to work on gender equality and gender justice in Myanmar. This network comprises more than 100 national and international NGOs working for the fulfilment of women's rights in Myanmar. Since 2008, GEN and its member organisations have significantly strengthened the evidence base around key aspects of gender inequality and discrimination in Myanmar. This has included extensive research on gender-based violence, participation and representation in public life and social and cultural norms and practices. GEN, in turn, deploys these resources to target key actors at different levels of Myanmar society in an effort to address both structural causes of inequality – such as discriminatory laws and policies and the absence of implemented protective and gender-equal legislation – and the social and cultural norms and practices that contribute to gender inequality and discrimination in Myanmar.

Not all coordinating bodies operating as TANs began as the projects of INGOs tied to foreign states, or technical working groups within the post-Nargis state bureaucracy. Some began as grassroots community-based organisations that developed into TANs. A prominent example is the Women's League of Burma (WLB), which was established in 1999 with the objective of increasing women's participation in human rights and democracy work and engaging them as active drivers in the peace and reconciliation process. WLB is composed of 13 ethnically diverse community-based organisations led by women living and working in Myanmar and/or on the Myanmar–Thai border. WLB began its work with only local community resources in the 1990s, but soon started garnering transnational attention and clandestine support from other social movements outside of Myanmar. As Myanmar has transitioned from a military-ruled to a civilian parliamentary government, they have been able to use their experience and network of contacts developed during this time to transform themselves into a TAN.

Local NGOs and CBOs do not always find it in their interest to 'go transnational' (Bob 2005), or even to remain organised as a network once they have done so. In some cases, former consortia of NGOs are now transforming themselves into a single local NGO and working to strengthen local organisation and capacity building. These organisations focus on high-profile development projects including land conflict and religious tolerance. For example, the Food Security Working Group (FSWG) was established in 2002, and serves as a forum for networking, capacity building, information and knowledge sharing, as well as advocacy for organisations working on food security issues that cross-cut social, economic, ethnic and environmental issues. The FSWG membership consists of over 125 local and international NGOs and community-based organisations with links to other NGOs, universities, resource centres, government ministries and departments, as well as TANs, like the Greater Mekong Community Forestry Network.

Another example is Paung Ku, a civil society initiative established by a consortium of local and international NGOs that now operates as an independent local NGO to build the capacity of a range of civil society organisations through advocacy, training and small grants. It serves a critical role not only in linking international and local groups, facilitating working relationships between international NGOs and Myanmar's civil society, but also in directing support to local civil society groups throughout the country, with a particular focus on high-profile development projects and key issues relating to land, conflict, and development and religious tolerance.

TANs are not only strengthening the capacity of small farmers and civil society organisations through grants, information sharing and advocacy on local issues affecting community development but also by working to advance human rights norms and principles in ways that shape the business practices of foreign corporations operating in Myanmar. For example,

ALTSEAN-Burma – a network comprising human rights and social justice NGOs, political parties, think tanks, academics, journalists and student activists spanning the ASEAN member states – was first established in Thailand in 1996, and has been providing advocacy and training for democratic change, women's community leadership, and cross-cultural understanding and conflict resolution across ethnic nationalist boundaries of difference in Myanmar. Now, in addition to hosting CSO workshops throughout the country, they are supporting Myanmar's national efforts to conduct a baseline assessment of current implementation of business and human rights frameworks across the country, and then develop key recommendations for the development of the National Action Plan.

The newly registered Confederation of Trade Unions of Myanmar (CTUM), formerly the Federation of Trade Unions of Burma, provides a prominent example of how TANs are deepening economic democracy by shaping Myanmar's labour standards. Following the 1990s, when the military forced many pro-democracy labour leaders into exile, the unregistered FTUB was sustained in part through the international labour movement, the AFL-CIO and the Solidarity Center. In September 2012, after the government removed more than 2,000 people from a list of more than 6,000 pro-democracy supporters banned from entering the country, many of those living in exile returned – including the CTUM's current secretary general Maung Maung. Today the CTUM is working in ten states across Myanmar to deliver basic training about the international trade union movement and freely meet as union members to discuss labour rights and related issues like the country's new minimum wage law, one of the most progressive in Southeast Asia.

TANs are also working to ensure democratic space for civil society and communities in the activities of international financial institutions (IFI). For example, IFI Watch Myanmar facilitates dialogue among IFIs, the Myanmar government and local communities, ensuring ethnic nationalist and CSO representation from every state and region.

Myanmar's emerging social enterprise sector

Social enterprises represent a more recently emerging organisational structure that is significantly shaping the work of humanitarian and democratic development in Myanmar. Social enterprises are mainly distinguishable from NGOs because of their revenue model. Social entrepreneurs invest in social ventures and generate their own revenues to sustain themselves. A social enterprise is first and foremost a business, although like an NGO it constitutes part of the social sector. The main goal of an NGO is to create social value, without much regard for the business bottom-line, while the social enterprise aims, within a business model, to achieve sustainability in the financial and social (and often even the environmental) sense.

Reflecting the global trend in the rise of social enterprise, Myanmar is now home to many such ventures – most of which have emerged in the wake of the 2008 Cyclone Nargis disaster that occurred at the height of the global financial crisis. Proximity Designs, for example, winner of both the Skoll Foundation's and the Schwab Foundation's Award for Social Entrepreneurship, began in 2004 as a small social enterprise in Myanmar providing innovative irrigation foot-pumps to rural farmers in 600 villages. Today, Proximity Designs are accessible to 80 per cent of the rural population of Myanmar, a country in which 70 per cent of the population lives in rural areas. They have improved the incomes of roughly half a million farmers. They have diversified their design and product line of water pumps, and have developed drip irrigation systems, water storage tanks, and, more recently, solar lighting products.

They also have created innovative short-term financing solutions for rural smallholders in need of crop loans, and have begun spinning these off into Proximity Finance, which provides growers with ongoing access to credit. The creators of these social enterprises, particularly those in or from the US, UK or Western Europe, but increasingly in parts of Southeast Asia as well, say that they inhabit a social frontier, sometimes referred to as the 'emerging fourth sector', that for now straddles the sectors of business and civil society. It is becoming clear that, since 2014, Myanmar's emerging social enterprise sector is beginning to gain transnational access to a supportive institutional ecosystem that is largely operating outside the country (Dale and Kyle 2017).

Increasingly, international development institutions and impact investors embrace the notion that social enterprises can play an important role in promoting social inclusion in the formal economy and thereby reducing inequality. The collective consensus is that a thriving social enterprise sector might serve as a democratising force in Myanmar, helping to address what the British Council has described as an 'economic democracy deficit' (British Council 2015, 6–7).

Since 2011, major donors, bilateral agencies and development partners have increased support for capacity building and awareness raising activities for civil society organisations that are active inside Myanmar across a broad spectrum of sectors and geographic areas often delivering project-based support through third party INGOs, international development agencies and UN programmes (e.g., Open Society Institute, Partnership for Change, British Council, United States Agency for International Development and United Nations Development Programme). Increasingly, civil society capacity building is starting to integrate a focus on social entrepreneurship as a critical skill for financial sustainability. For example, Capacity Building Initiative (CBI) was established in 2000 by international NGOs in Yangon to meet their growing demand for skilled and trained staff. They are increasingly working with foreign experts to develop skills training seminars that support the changing organisational climate of development work in Myanmar, emphasising programme monitoring and evaluation, financial accountability and sustainability, as well as how to be creative and innovative in humanitarian work

But the socially transformative power of social enterprises does not lie in their ability to financially 'do-better' than traditional non-profit or donor-dependent 'do gooders'. Such a strategy could amount only to privatising the 'third sector', supplanting the work that activists and TANs had been doing, and possibly marginalising democratic political and economic development that focused on corporate accountability and capacity building for progressive democratic political engagement (Dale and Kyle 2015). Rather, the critical difference lies in the quality of social innovation that such a sector might bring to bear on the institutions that generate social inequality. The promise of social enterprises in Myanmar lies in their capacity to address social inequality in ways that deepen democracy. Yet, it remains unclear whether a vibrant social enterprise sector would pose any democratic challenge to the rules and institutional arrangements shaping Myanmar's emerging markets and economic transition (Dale and Kyle 2017). Combined with the state (national and international) discipline that bureaucratic structures are imposing on civil society, advocacy for deepening democracy and humanitarianism in Myanmar will require creating networks of actors that are capable of influencing these powerful organisational structures.

Conclusion

Although there is more work to do, INGOs have played a significant role in providing Myanmar with resources and technical assistance for community development, as well as in advocating for democracy and human rights in Myanmar's polity. More ambiguous in recent years is the democratic influence that NGOs have had on Myanmar's emerging economy and civil society.

This is an important concern as Myanmar seeks to institutionalise democratic reform and national reconciliation under new conditions of increased foreign direct investment, regional economic restructuring and disruptive technologies (Dale and Kyle 2015).

To the extent that INGOs are embedded in bureaucratic structures, they tend to adapt to, rather than challenge, the ways that Myanmar's markets and economic rights are being legally institutionalised and transformed to accommodate regional economic restructuring and new flows of global capital. Operating within these structures, they also have tended to marginalise local organisations, as the Myanmar People's Forum has brought to light, by prioritising without sufficient consultation individual agendas over local processes in ways that undermine the role and capacity of local organisations working to shape community relations and development.

To the extent that INGOs are embedded in TANs, INGOs have been more effective at deepening democratic and humanitarian norms and principles in Myanmar's economy, particularly with respect to labour laws, corporate and IFI accountability relating to human rights practices, and to some extent land use and migrant workers' rights. Also, within TANs, local CSOs have been better able to work with INGOs to enhance their role and capacity in deepening humanitarian and democratic development. However, as we have described, the strategy of 'going transnational' does not always enhance the agency of local organisations.

INGOs are also increasingly partnering with social enterprises in Myanmar that are embedded in transnational relations of their own. To the extent that social enterprises link civil society to markets – especially when seeking to solve social problems relating to community development while emphasising revenue-generating financial self-sustainability and measurable accountability – they have begun to challenge the means of support on which INGOs have traditionally relied. Many INGOs are starting to embrace, or atleast finding themselves forced to adhere to, these self-sustaining economic models and entrepreneurial values embodied in this organisational structure. Thus far, these structures have steered clear of projects that may be construed as politically challenging or even as enhancing local capacity for advancing democratic political reform.

Despite the fact that INGOs advocate for greater democracy and equality in Myanmar, each of the structures through which they pursue this goal, as we have described, introduces different ways of hierarchically organising social relations among the individual and collective bodies within them. How INGOs will manage the diverse roles they serve (often simultaneously) within these overlapping, intersecting and often competing organisational structures is a central question for the future of advocacy in Myanmar. Moreover, how INGOs address the sources of inequality that they themselves – organised within each of these structures – bring to the process is a central question for the future of democratic reform in Myanmar.

Bibliography

Alternative ASEAN Network in Burma. 2016. Web. Accessed April 7, 2016. www.altsean.org/Aboutus.htm.

Assistance Association of Political Prisoners (Burma). 2017. 'AAPP Monthly Chronology of February 2017 and Current Political Prisoners List'. March 16. Accessed March 21, 2017. http://aappb.org/2017/03/aapp-monthly-chronology-of-february-2017-and-current-political-prisoners-list/.

Bob, C. 2005. *The Marketing of Rebellion: Insurgents, Media, and International Action*. New York: Cambridge University Press.

British Council. 2015. *Think Global Trade Social: How Business with a Social Purpose Can Deliver more Sustainable Development*. London, UK: British Council.

Burma Partnership. 2016. Accessed March 7, 2016. www.burmapartnership.org/aboutus/.

Capacity Building Initiative. 2016. Accessed March 7, 2016. www.cbiinmyanmar.org/.
Dale, J. and Kyle, D. 2015. 'Smart Transitions? Foreign Investment, Disruptive Technology, and Democratic Reform in Myanmar'. *Social Research: An International Quarterly*, 'Special Issue: From Burma to Myanmar: Critical Transitions' 82 (2) (Summer): 291–326.
Dale, J. and Kyle, D. 2017. 'The Risky Business of Transformation: Social Enterprise in Myanmar's Emerging Democracy'. In *The Business of Transition: Law Reform, Development and Economics in Myanmar*, edited by Melissa Crouch. Cambride, UK: Cambridge University Press, pp. 81–121.
Food Security Working Group. 2016. Accessed March 21, 2017. www.myanmarfswg.org/en/member.
Gender Equality Network. 2016. Accessed March 7, 2016. www.genmyanmar.org/.
IFI Watch Myanmar. 2016. Accessed March 7, 2016. www.facebook.com/IFIWatchMyanmar/info/?tab=page_info.
INGO Forum. 2014. *INGO Forum Strategic Objectives July 2014–June 2016*. Yangon: INGO Forum.
International Center for Transitional Justice (ICTJ). Accessed April 21, 2016. www.ictj.org/about.
Kantar, S. 2017. 'People's Tribunal Emphasizes Solidarity across Ethnic, Religious Lines', *The Irrawaddy* (March 9). Accessed March 21, 2017. www.irrawaddy.com/news/burma/peoples-tribunal-emphasizes-solidarity-across-ethnic-religious-lines.html.
Local Resource Centre. 2015. Annual Report Summary. Accessed March 21, 2017. www.lrcmyanmar.org/en/resources/annual-report-2015-local-resourrce-centre.
Local Resource Centre. 2017. Local NGO Database. Accessed March 21, 2017. www.lrcmyanmar.org/en/cso-database.
www.lrcmyanmar.org/en/system/files/book/progressing_through_partnerships_eng.pdf.
Myanmar Civil Society Organisations Forum. 2014. 'Statement: Civil Societies' Review on Myanmar's Transition Process: Prospects for 2015 and Beyond'. Burma Partnership, October 17 Accessed March 7, 2016. www.burmapartnership.org/2014/10/civil-societies-review-on-myanmars-transition-process-prospects-for-2015-and-beyond/.
Myanmar Information Management Unit. 2017. Accessed March 21, 2017. www.themimu.info.
Network for Human Rights Documentation. 2016. Report on the Human Rights Situation in Burma, January–December, 2016. Accessed March 21, 2017. http://nd-burma.org/nd-burma-2016-report-finds-dramatic-increase-human-rights-violations/.
Proximity Designs. 2012a. 'Irrigation Products Game Changers: Smart designs that are having a major impact'. Accessed March 7, 2016. http://proximitydesigns.org/products-services/irrigation-products.
Proximity Designs. 2012b. 'Financial Services: Financial inclusion for rural entrepreneurs'. Accessed March 7, 2016. www.proximitydesigns.org/products-services/financial-services.
Solidarity Center. 2016. 'Myanmar Officially Recognizes Trade Union Confederation'. July 23, 2015. Accessed March 7, 2016. www.solidaritycenter.org/myanmar-officially-recognizes-trade-union-confederation/#sthash.sBkQdUOU.dpuf.
Women's League of Burma. 2016. Accessed February 22, 2016. http://womenofburma.org/.
Wong, W.E. 2012. *Internal Affairs: How the Structure of NGOs Transforms Human Rights*. Ithaca, NY: Cornell University Press.

32

INTERNATIONAL LAW AND INTER-GOVERNMENTAL ORGANISATIONS

Tyler Giannini and Matthew Bugher

For decades, Myanmar remained at the periphery of a globalising and increasingly interconnected international community. Myanmar's isolation not only muted the impact of lobbying by foreign governments and inter-governmental institutions but also dulled the power and influence of international law in the country. In Myanmar's recent steps towards a more democratic form of governance, one can recognise a growing sphere of influence for international law and the institutions through which it is enforced. Going forward, international law will play an important role in Myanmar's transition away from authoritarian rule by providing a normative framework for institutional and legal developments as well as the ground rules for international engagement with the country, including by other nations and inter-governmental organisations (IGOs).

This chapter begins by discussing the limited, but nonetheless important, influence of international law and IGOs on Myanmar's military-led governments during five decades of authoritarian rule. The chapter also considers recent developments that suggest the growing influence of international law in Myanmar's national public discourse and domestic affairs. International law touches on many issues, including economics, trade, the environment, social concerns, and topics in various other fields. In line with the authors' expertise, the chapter draws heavily from developments in international human rights law, international humanitarian law, and international criminal law. The authors believe that this focus informs broader conversations about international law and the rule of law relating to Myanmar.

This chapter concludes by examining two important functions that international law will play in Myanmar's continuing democratic transition. First, international law will provide an increasingly influential set of norms, principles, and standards that will guide the efforts of politicians, policy makers, civil servants, civil society, and others to reshape Myanmar society and governance structures. Second, international law will complement and reinforce the domestic legal regime in Myanmar, setting the ground rules for appropriate government action and helping establish a framework for how the domestic and international systems interact. Perhaps most importantly, international law establishes that Myanmar is primarily responsible for complying with international standards and fulfilling its legal obligations. However, international law and organisations have an important supporting role to play in this process, providing a backstop should Myanmar fail to comply with its obligations.

Myanmar's neglect of international law during decades of military rule was emblematic of the country's fraught relationship with the international community. Under prior military governments, Myanmar was loath to sign treaties or otherwise commit itself to respect for human rights, compliance with international standards, or rule-based engagement with the outside world. Nonetheless, notable treaty commitments and interactions with international bodies exerted significant influence in the country. Under Thein Sein's quasi-civilian administration that took power in 2011, Myanmar took small, but noteworthy, steps towards greater engagement with international law and international institutions. These steps were tentative and incomplete, however, with government officials sometimes paying lip service to international rights standards but failing to follow through on their commitments.

The National League for Democracy (NLD), which took the reins of government in early 2016, has not fundamentally changed Myanmar's relationship with international law during its first year in power. Rather, the government, along with the military institutions that control critical ministries, continues to show ambivalence and occasional hostility to IGOs and international actors—at least on matters relating to human rights. Despite the limits of change as of early 2017, hopes are high that respect for human rights and engagement with international law will improve significantly in the coming years.

The value of international law

Modern legal scholars have put forward a number of models that describe how international law influences the policies and actions of states. These range from noting the normative or standard-setting value of international law to focusing on the enforcement, or lack thereof, of international law. Each model tends to highlight a particular avenue of influence without diminishing the validity of other avenues. For example, Abram and Antonia Chayes put forward a 'managerial' model that focuses on the persuasive power of international discourse surrounding international legal regimes (Chayes & Chayes 1995) and Thomas Franck's 'fairness' model focuses on the legitimacy and moral weight of the standards themselves (Franck 1995). Ryan Goodman and Derek Jinks highlight the importance of 'acculturation' in communities of states that share a commitment to common sets of international standards (Goodman & Jinks 2004). Importantly, these models unanimously reject a pure 'enforcement model' of international law compliance that focuses exclusively on the coercive power of formal international enforcement mechanisms.

In rejecting an exclusive focus on state-to-state enforcement mechanisms, international legal scholar Harold Koh describes a process of 'norm-institutionalisation' that has particular relevance to modern day Myanmar. He argues that a broad spectrum of influences—touching upon several of the models put forward by other scholars—motivate governments to comply with international norms. These influences include coercion, self-interest, communitarian impulses, rule-legitimacy, and legal processes. Koh is careful to point out that it is not merely state-to-state relations that lead to the internalisation of new norms and highlights the role of NGOs and influential personalities in institutionalising human rights norms. Interestingly, Koh, writing in 1999, cites Aung San Suu Kyi as an example of a 'transnational norm entrepreneur', an individual who serves as a catalyst to mobilise support for human rights norms (Koh 1999).

International law and Myanmar's past

Myanmar's democratic leaders in the immediate post-independence era beginning in 1948 actively engaged with the international community. Although isolationism was advanced as an option in policy circles in Yangon, U Nu's civilian government ultimately pursued a proactive foreign policy focused on building 'international good will' through diplomatic dialogue and 'positive neutralism' (Egreteau & Jagan 2013, 86). Burma became a leading nation in the Non-Aligned Movement and thus punched above its weight in international circles. Perhaps symbolising optimism over Burma's role in the international community, U Thant, Burma's permanent representative to the UN, was appointed to be the UN Secretary-General in 1961, a position he would hold for the next ten years.

During the initial post-independence period, Burma accepted new obligations under international law and lent its support to the nascent development of the international human rights regime. In 1948, Burma was one of 48 countries to vote in favour of adoption of the Universal Declaration of Human Rights. Burma also signed the Genocide Convention in 1949 and ratified it in 1956. In addition, in 1955, Burma ratified two fundamental International Labour Organisation (ILO) conventions—the Forced Labour Convention and the Freedom of Association and Protection of the Right to Organise Convention.

Isolationism under military regimes

The 1962 coup by Ne Win marked the beginning of a dark period in Myanmar's engagement with the outside world. The introduction of a single-party system signalled a shift from an emerging law-based order to a command-based system of governance (Egreteau & Jagan 2013, 114). This shift had a profound impact on Burma's relationship with the international community and international law.

Between 1962 and the pro-democracy uprising in 1988, Burma did not ratify any significant multilateral international treaties. Thus, Burma was largely unengaged during this period when the international community was continuing to build the core framework of international human rights law, which included adopting the two foundational human rights treaties—the International Covenant on Civil and Political Rights (ICCPR) and the International Covenant on Economic, Social and Cultural Rights (ICESCR).

After the seismic upheavals of the 1988 uprising, the 1990 elections, and the subsequent repression of the pro-democracy movement, Myanmar's new military rulers sensed their vulnerability after years of isolation and temporarily embraced a partial opening to the outside world (Taylor 2009, 463).

This moment in Myanmar was accompanied by the ratification of a number of important treaties by the country's military rulers. The opening also corresponded with the end of the Cold War, a growing prominence of human rights internationally, and a developing fabric of international treaties, mechanisms, and institutions. While Myanmar already had obligations arising from customary international law, becoming a state party to a number of treaties was nonetheless an important step in establishing Myanmar's commitments and processes for enforcing its obligations. Notably, Myanmar became a party to the four Geneva Conventions, the foundational treaties of international humanitarian law, in 1992. Myanmar also acceded to the Convention on the Rights of the Child (CRC) in 1991 and the Convention on the Elimination of All Forms of Discrimination against Women (CEDAW) in 1997. In 1998, Myanmar acceded to the Vienna Convention on the Law of Treaties, a key international treaty concerning the application and interpretation of treaties between states.

Over the long term, this period of relative activity in joining several treaty regimes has had a significant and lasting impact on Myanmar's relationship with the international community and the activities of domestic actors. Although treaties often have limited direct enforcement value, they have normative power, meaning that actors can point out a government's obligations and the commitments made through a given treaty. This has been the case with Myanmar, where human rights and humanitarian organisations as well as numerous community-based organisations (CBOs) have for years framed programmes and advocacy efforts around standards based on Myanmar's treaty obligations dating to the 1990s.

This phase of treaty adoption during the 1990s, however, did not mitigate the preceding decades of neglect for rights nor did it lead to any significant improvement in Myanmar's human rights practices. When Myanmar's foreign relations moved again towards isolation—at least in regards to the West—in the late 1990s and 2000s, Myanmar remained a laggard in terms of both commitment and adherence to international law.

The limited treaty law applicable to Myanmar has particularly defined the options for formal international enforcement of violations of international law. In addition, during this period, Myanmar failed to incorporate international law obligations into its domestic legal framework, leaving international pressure and advocacy as the primary mechanisms for enforcing international law. Nevertheless, the international community, international institutions, and IGOs did make meaningful, law-based interventions during decades of military rule.

For example, between 1991 and 2015, the UN General Assembly passed annual resolutions regarding Myanmar. These resolutions condemned widespread and systematic human rights violations in Myanmar and called on the Myanmar government to embrace democratic processes, release political prisoners, and ratify human rights treaties, among other actions. Beginning in 1992, the Commission on Human Rights—subsequently reformed and renamed as the UN Human Rights Council—has also issued annual resolutions on Myanmar, covering similar topics. The resolutions from these bodies lean heavily on international law, often citing directly Myanmar's treaty obligations.

In 1992, the Commission on Human Rights established the position of the Special Rapporteur on the situation of human rights in Myanmar. This position has been renewed annually since, and the Special Rapporteur has regularly reported to the General Assembly, Commission on Human Rights, and Human Rights Council on pressing human rights issues in Myanmar. While successive Special Rapporteurs have been denied access to the country at times, they have played an extremely important role in highlighting human rights violations in the country, often holding the line on grave abuses when UN bodies and foreign governments prioritised diplomacy over human rights protections (Harvard Law School International Human Rights Clinic 2009).

International law played more than a merely symbolic role. Rather, international law had a tangible impact on Myanmar and its relationships with states and the international community. For example, Myanmar's violations of its international law obligations played a significant role in the imposition of economic and political sanctions by the United States and the European Union during the 1990s and 2000s. The UN and IGOs also focused attention on particular human rights issues, including the use of child soldiers and the monitoring of the political prisoner situation by organisations such as the International Committee for the Red Cross.

Perhaps most prominently, the ILO's engagement with Myanmar's military government demonstrated the power of treaty obligations to extract concessions from a recalcitrant, isolationist regime. In the 1980s and early 1990s, human rights organisations began to report about the prevalent use of forced labour, particularly by military personnel, in Myanmar. Pressure mounted on the ILO to act based on Myanmar's commitments under the ILO Forced Labour Convention, which it ratified in 1955. After a series of contentious exchanges with the Myanmar government, the ILO established a commission of inquiry to investigate the use of forced labour in the country. In 1998, the commission issued its report, citing the 'pervasive use of forced labour' in violation of the Convention (ILO 1998, 179). Using its power to take punitive measures—including by encouraging member states to impose economic sanctions—the ILO gained concessions from the Myanmar government, including the reform of laws that facilitated forced labour, the approval of regular ILO country visits, the posting of an ILO Liaison Officer in Yangon in 2002, and the establishment of a complaints mechanism to report instances of forced labour (Horsey 2011, 46–88). Although the Myanmar government often obstructed the ILO's interventions, scholars and human rights observers agree that tangible progress was made on combating forced labour under the SPDC government (Horsey 2011; MacLean 2012).

Tentative re-engagement under the Thein Sein administration and NLD government

Elections in 2010, held under Myanmar's new, military-drafted constitution, ushered in a period of reform and re-engagement with the West that picked up speed after Aung San Suu Kyi was released from house arrest and began political dialogue with Thein Sein's government. In his inaugural address, Thein Sein spoke openly about safeguarding 'fundamental rights of citizens and human rights' and 'work[ing] together with international organisations including the UN, INGOs, and NGOs'. Although the international community, perceiving the continuity of military leadership in the pre- and post-election regimes, largely dismissed the significance of Thein Sein's commitments at the time, they presaged a dramatic shift in how Myanmar would relate to the outside world (Steinberg 2015, 439).

In 2011, Myanmar underwent its first Universal Periodic Review (UPR), a process whereby the Human Rights Council reviews the human rights record of each country in the world. During the UPR process, numerous members of the Human Rights Council recommended that Myanmar become a party to key human rights treaties, including the ICCPR and ICESCR. Myanmar responded by indicating that it was 'considering to become party to the Human Rights instruments that it has not yet acceded to, depending on its resources and capacity to fully implement the obligations as a developing country'. In June 2013, the Myanmar National Human Rights Commission specifically recommended that Myanmar accede to the ICCPR, ICESCR, and the optional protocols to the two treaties.

Under the Thein Sein government, Myanmar became a party to a number of key human rights treaties relating to the rights of disabled persons and children and the use of various forms of weaponry. In July 2015, Myanmar finally signed the ICESCR, but at the time of writing it had not yet become a full party to the treaty. In September 2015, Myanmar also signed the Optional Protocol to the Convention on the Rights of the Child on the involvement of children in armed conflict. In its second UPR review in November 2015, Myanmar stated that it had been 'doing its utmost' to become a party to the ICESCR and was 'studying to become a signatory to the remaining international human rights treaties'. Since coming to power, the NLD has not taken formal action to advance Myanmar's treaty obligations, but has continued exploratory efforts regarding treaty adoption and incorporation.

These developments are significant and indicate a positive change in Myanmar's stance towards international law. However, Myanmar's adoption of key treaty obligations remains incomplete. Significantly, Myanmar has not signed or acceded to the ICCPR or the main human rights treaties relating to torture, racial discrimination, or enforced disappearance. Myanmar has not acceded to the ICESCR and has therefore not yet undertaken the full obligations of the treaty. Additionally, Myanmar has not become a party to optional protocols to the Geneva Conventions or key human rights treaties that provide a mechanism for individuals and groups to submit complaints to the committees monitoring compliance with human rights treaties to which Myanmar's is a party. Also, Myanmar has not become a party to the Rome Statute, severely hampering the jurisdiction of the International Criminal Court (ICC) over events occurring in Myanmar.

Just as importantly, Myanmar is at the very nascent stage of incorporating some international obligations into its domestic legal framework, further limiting the availability of domestic enforcement tools for individuals and communities. Thus, while Myanmar is increasingly making international commitments, which provide normative value and standards against which to evaluate government actions, formal mechanisms for holding state institutions and actors to account remain quite limited.

Thus, the shift to an international law-friendly country remains at best a work in progress. Indeed, at least in the arena of human rights, while the language of commitment changed, the pattern of resistance to international law and its mechanisms resembles the experience of the ILO in the previous decade. In 2012, for example, the Myanmar government formally invited the United Nations Office of the High Commissioner for Human Rights (OHCHR) to establish an office in Myanmar, a development that was warmly welcomed by OHCHR and the international community more broadly. A draft agreement concerning the office was exchanged between OHCHR and the Myanmar government, but the process soon unravelled. In late 2013, Myanmar's permanent representative at the UN rejected a General Assembly resolution calling for the process of opening the office to be expedited, stating that Myanmar 'reserves the right to choose the mandate of the office'. Although the opening of the office has remained a chief priority for the UN, foreign diplomats, and the human rights community, the process stalled in the two years leading up to the November 2015 elections. At the time of writing, the NLD government had not taken any formal, public steps to facilitate the establishment of the OHCHR office.

During Thein Sein's term in office, the relationship between the Myanmar government and two successive Special Rapporteurs was also contentious. Although both Rapporteurs at times experienced difficulties gaining visas or scheduling country visits, the government never broke off contact with either one for an extended period of time as the prior military government had done. However, the strong stance taken by the Special Rapporteurs on the Myanmar government's policies towards the Rohingya Muslim minority in Rakhine State led to frequent conflict with the Myanmar government. In 2014, Tomas Ojea Quintana invoked international criminal law, stating that discrimination and persecution against the Rohingya 'could amount to crimes against humanity', raising the ire of the government. Quintana's successor, Yanghee Lee, faced a severe backlash when she also attempted to highlight the situation of the Rohingya. In August 2015, Myanmar's Ministry of Foreign Affairs released a statement asserting that the government 'rejects country-specific mandates, including that of the Special Rapporteur'. After country visits during both the Thein Sein and NLD administrations, the Special Rapporteur expressed frustration about lack of access to areas in Kachin and Rakhine States and raised serious concerns that individuals with whom she spoke were vulnerable to retaliation by government authorities.

Following deadly attacks against Rakhine State border police outposts by Rohingya insurgents in October 2016, Myanmar security forces conducted systematic 'clearance' operations in the area. Human rights groups and UN bodies reported widespread human rights violations, including killings, torture, the destruction of homes and property, rape, and sexual violence. In particular, a February 2017 report by OHCHR, which depended on access to refugees in Bangladesh, presented highly credible evidence that these abuses had been committed on a massive scale. The NLD government initially denied that violations had occurred. Later, as evidence became overwhelming, the government avoided commenting directly on the veracity of specific allegations and instead cited the authority of several domestic investigation commissions with a mandate to investigate the situation. Human rights organisations and UN officials have cast doubt on the independence and credibility of those commissions. The lead government investigating body reported that it found no evidence of widespread human rights abuses, and instead cast doubt on the claims of victims and eyewitnesses. The complete failure of domestic investigations and accountability mechanisms to address these abuses led many to call for the establishment of a UN-mandated body to carry out an investigation. At the time of writing, the campaign for an independent international investigation was gaining momentum. The establishment of a UN commission of inquiry or similar body would be a major development in Myanmar's relationship with international law and international bodies.

During the Thein Sein era, the Myanmar government clearly recognised the importance of international law to its future, but the legacy of resistance to the international legal regime remained dominant, especially with regards to sensitive issues such as human rights. To date, the NLD government has not significantly departed from the positions and policies of its predecessor in regards to engagement with international law and institutions.

In the years to come, international law will undoubtedly play an important role in Myanmar's development and help shape Myanmar's relationship with the outside world. It remains to be seen how the process will proceed and whether the government will firmly embrace the rule of law and international law. The tentative first steps taken by the Thein Sein and NLD administrations provide a starting point for deeper and more meaningful engagement with the international community, but the actions of the NLD government will determine the tenor of that relationship and the speed with which international law becomes part of Myanmar's legal and policy framework.

International law and Myanmar's future

Despite its relatively disappointing track record to date, the NLD government is well-positioned to tip Myanmar from a country that resists international law to one that embraces it. The government could build on the limited progress made under the Thein Sein government, accelerate the country's pace of treaty ratification, and strengthen relationships with international institutions. It could also purposefully integrate international law into Myanmar's domestic landscape and institutions by actions such as promulgating policies, proposing legislation, and pursuing cases in the courts that advance international principles. However, regardless of the path charted—whether towards richer engagement with the international community or a retreat towards isolationism—international law will project normative power in Myanmar and play a vital role in shaping the government's relationship with domestic and international actors.

Domestic norm development and discourse

As described above, the limited scope of Myanmar's treaty obligations precludes the use of many international mechanisms and institutions to address international law violations in the country. However, the norm development function of international law is not directly dependent on formal enforcement mechanisms and relies heavily on the involvement of domestic actors, including political figures, civil society, journalists, and society at large. Indeed, the process of infusing international norms into Myanmar's domestic affairs has already picked up considerable speed and is unlikely to be halted.

During Thein Sein's presidency, the Myanmar government increasingly used the language of human rights and international law to justify its policies, programmes, and actions. The beginning of this shift was marked by Thein Sein's inaugural address. The speech expressed aspirations to military might and exalted the 'Three National Causes', the 'flourishing of Union Spirit', and the 'Five Principles of Peaceful Coexistence', reaffirming the values of past military governments. However, Thein Sein also explicitly referenced 'fundamental rights of citizens and human rights' and paid homage—albeit vaguely—to a number of other political rights and freedoms. Prior to the 2015 elections, Thein Sein touted his achievements in terms that explicitly referenced international human rights standards, going so far as to post a self-promoting video titled 'Opening the Freedom of Expression', on his Facebook page.

The change in government rhetoric was not a unilateral policy shift by Myanmar's political leaders, however. Rather, the government's change of tack was symptomatic of the infusion of international norms into Myanmar's public discourse. Political freedoms and human rights standards are increasingly becoming an important criteria by which domestic political actors, civil society, the media, and the public at large assess the actions of their government and their political opponents. This discussion is taking place openly inside the country to a much greater degree than pre-2010. Thus, while international law played a normative role both before and after 2010, it is now increasingly a point of reference in domestic debates concerning policy, legislative, and judicial matters rather than solely a measuring stick used by players outside the country.

To a certain degree, Myanmar's political opening, the influx of foreign money, people, and organisations, and the proliferation of internet access made the rise in awareness of international law an inevitability. However, civil society activists, educators, human rights defenders, and diplomats, among others, also proactively promoted international standards within Myanmar long before the recent changes. Activists and educators who ran rights awareness programmes under prior military governments deserve significant credit for their difficult, important, and impactful endeavours (Kinley & Wilson 2007). Since 2010, hundreds of human rights awareness campaigns, civic education courses, political affairs schools, and other programmes have sprung up in Myanmar. Additionally, exiled activists and organisations have returned home and brought with them their knowledge of international law and experiences of engaging with the international community. This genie cannot be easily put back in the bottle.

The conflict surrounding the National Education Law illustrates the way in which international norms—human rights standards, specifically—have increasingly infused public discourse inside Myanmar. Prior to passing the National Education Law in September 2014, the Myanmar government acknowledged the need for education reform in terms explicitly referencing international human rights law. At an education summit hosted by the UN General Assembly in New York in 2013, the government submitted a working paper which acknowledged the need for 'an overarching education law to ensure that rights to education are guaranteed under the law, in line with the Constitution of 2008 and international conventions Myanmar has committed to'.

While the government sought to bolster the National Education Law by referencing human rights norms, opponents attacked it on similar grounds, calling the law 'a little bit slack on human rights standards', and invoking rights language to criticise the law's failure to protect student unions and mother-tongue education for ethnic minorities, among other alleged shortcomings. After the law was passed, a student-led protest movement quickly formed, culminating in a brutal crackdown on protesters by police officers at the town of Letpadan, 70 miles north of Yangon.

In the aftermath of the crackdown, the government sought to justify the actions of the police officers, saying that they had employed international law enforcement standards as taught in European Union-sponsored training sessions. A report published in October 2014 by Fortify Rights and the Harvard Law School International Human Rights Clinic—and written, in part, by the authors of this chapter—accused the Myanmar government of violating the protesters' rights to freedom of assembly and expression and alleged that police used excessive force in violation of international law enforcement standards (Fortify Rights & Harvard Law School International Human Rights Clinic 2015).

Soon after the crackdown, authorities initiated charges against more than 70 protesters under the 2012 Peaceful Assembly and Peaceful Procession Law, a law that Thein Sein touted as demonstrating his commitment to respect the right to freedom of assembly. During the protest, its leaders refused to comply with the law's registration requirement, which they believed was undemocratic and violated international standards.

Upon coming to power, the NLD government immediately released scores of political prisoners, including the Letpadan protesters and others involved in public demonstrations. However, in violation of its international obligation to provide a full remedy, the government has not yet held anyone responsible for excessive use of force against, or arbitrary detention of, the protesters. In the first half of 2016, however, the NLD, citing human rights standards, used its parliamentary majority to amend the Peaceful Assembly and Peaceful Procession Law. Although the changes failed to bring the law into line with all relevant international standards, the changes succeeded in addressing some of the more repressive elements of the law.

That the NLD has acted to address these issues demonstrates the incremental yet incomplete progress to date. The invocation of international law by governmental and non-governmental stakeholders also highlights the normative and standard-setting power of international law in Myanmar. However, the shortcomings of reform efforts to date reveal possible limits to the NLD's current power or commitment to 'rule of law' and international law and show how enforcement mechanisms have so far had limited impact in Myanmar.

Overall, however, the prominence of international human rights standards in *domestic* public discourse about these events is remarkable when compared with the nature of such conversations under previous military regimes. Although the attempt to use human rights standards in defence of rights abusing policies and actions is unfortunate and harmful when it does occur, the fact that important national debates have been influenced by international law is a very positive development that should not be taken for granted. If the current trend continues, all key stakeholders, including the Myanmar government, civil society, and the international community should further extend the internalisation of international norms into public life in Myanmar.

International engagement

As described above, Myanmar's failure to sign, ratify, or accede to many key treaties limits opportunities to engage Myanmar through formal international processes and mechanisms. Nevertheless, international law provides important channels for engagement between domestic and international actors, in particular through monitoring and reporting activities.

Each of the core human rights treaties establishes a committee to monitor and promote compliance with the standards enshrined in the treaty. These committees undertake various functions to promote compliance with human rights standards, including through periodic reviews of the records of state parties in relation to their treaty obligations. These reviews usually involve consideration of national reports submitted by the state parties and independent submissions made by NGOs, CBOs, and others. As a party to CEDAW and CRC, Myanmar is subject to periodic reviews by the committees associated with those treaties. However, Myanmar is not subject to review by other treaty bodies, including the committees established by the ICCPR and ICESCR.

The UPR is a similar review process whereby the Human Rights Council examines the human rights record of each country in the world on a cycle that currently is four-and-a-half years long. Myanmar underwent its first UPR in 2011 and its second in 2015.

The record created during the UPR process and treaty committee reviews is extremely important. Diplomats, human rights organisations, CBOs, and journalists have frequently cited the 2011 and 2015 final reports of the UPR working group and Myanmar's response to the recommendations in those reports in order to highlight persistent human rights problems and remind the Myanmar government of its obligations and human rights commitments. Documents arising from the CEDAW and CRC review processes have received similar attention.

Equally important, however, is the collaborative process undertaken by human rights organisations and civil society in Myanmar during the UPR process and treaty committee reviews. In 2015, for example, activists from more than 100 organisations participated in the drafting of UPR submissions. Many received training in international law and report writing prior to drafting their submissions, further increasing their capacity. Moreover, the process of drafting and publishing submissions provides a centre-point to the advocacy efforts of these organisations and draws attention to pressing human rights concerns in the country.

Even on issues where there has yet to be significant domestic movement, the influence of international law and its normative power will continue in the coming years. Perhaps most prominently, the extremely contentious issue of possible enforcement of international criminal law against rights abusers in Myanmar has been, and will continue to be, centrally shaped by international law and standards (Harvard Law School International Human Rights Clinic 2009; 2014). Since Aung San Suu Kyi's rapprochement with Thein Sein's government in 2011, there has been little appetite among the international community for accountability-focused approaches to dealing with Myanmar's legacy of rights abuses. The recent well-documented allegations of grave abuses in Rakhine State may spur international action in the form of a UN-mandated investigation. However, even if the West's stance towards Myanmar shifted considerably, ICC referral or the establishment of an international tribunal would require UN Security Council action that could be blocked by a veto from China or Russia.

Despite these constraints, international criminal law serves as an important backstop to domestic justice processes and discourse as well as international diplomacy relating to Myanmar, shaping the strong and diverse opinions regarding accountability among political actors, civil society, and the public. On the one hand, a vocal contingent of human rights and women's activists, as well as many leaders from ethnic nationality communities, have strongly supported measures to hold those responsible for grave human rights abuses accountable in international fora. Many others, especially those involved in political processes in Yangon and Naypyitaw, have clearly articulated their belief that focusing on past abuses could undermine Myanmar's transition and democratic reforms.

Notwithstanding these debates, the threat of future accountability for violations of international criminal law has motivated elements in the Myanmar government to stay the course on reform efforts and has deterred retrogressive actions that could prompt a more aggressive international stance. Moreover, a distant threat of prosecution in ten or twenty years—a possibility strongly supported by events in other parts of the world—may incentivise lawful conduct by a new generation of military and political leaders in Myanmar. Regardless, international law will have a critical influence on discourse regarding the appropriate way forward for the country.

The gap in enforcement mechanisms

Despite international law's demonstrable effect on establishing norms and guiding Myanmar's engagement with the international community, there is a great need for stronger enforcement mechanisms. This gap spans both the domestic and the international arenas with regards to Myanmar. Domestic law inadequately incorporates international law, and there is widespread agreement on the need for greater judicial independence and improved rule of law within Myanmar. For example, domestic institutions such as the Myanmar National Human Rights Commission lack independence and have limited enforcement powers, and national courts have yet to address international law claims in any meaningful way, leaving domestic enforcement avenues very limited to date.

As described above, Myanmar's failure to adopt key treaties has significantly limited the available international processes and mechanisms for engaging Myanmar, in particular those that have traditional enforcement powers through courts. For example, most treaties now have optional protocols—treaties in their own right—that establish complaint mechanisms whereby state parties agree to allow the treaty's committee to hear complaints regarding violations of relevant treaty obligations that occurred in their territories. Myanmar has not acceded to such optional protocols, thus eliminating this avenue of enforcement for citizens. While Myanmar is a party to the Genocide Convention and thus subject to the jurisdiction of the International Court of Justice (ICJ) for disputes arising under the Convention, its citizenry cannot directly bring complaints to the ICJ, which relies primarily on states to bring claims against other states. Because Myanmar is not a party to the Rome Statute, the ICC may only exercise jurisdiction over Myanmar if the UN Security Council refers a case to the Court, which is extremely unlikely. In short, the number and strength of mechanisms open to individuals for redress and remedy of human rights violations remains extremely limited internationally as well as domestically.

Conclusion

Recent events suggest an expanding sphere of influence for international law in domestic conversations and policymaking in Myanmar. Formal interactions with international institutions and the infusion of international norms into public discourse within Myanmar are having a positive effect. Taking an optimistic view, the Myanmar government is likely to embrace an even greater role for international law in domestic affairs in the coming years, including by continuing to adopt key international treaties, by engaging in good faith with international bodies, and by promulgating policies and a legislative agenda in line with international standards. Equally important, Myanmar civil society will also likely continue to proactively incorporate international law into its programming and advocacy. Myanmar has a lot to gain by increasingly embracing international law rather than returning to the recalcitrant stance of prior military regimes.

References

Chayes, A. & Chayes, A.H. 1995. *The New Sovereignty: Compliance with International Regulatory Agreements.* Cambridge, Massachusetts: Harvard University Press.

Egreteau, R. & Jagan, L. 2013. *Soldiers and Diplomacy in Burma: Understanding the Foreign Relations of the Burmese Praetorian State.* Singapore: NUS Press.

Fortify Rights & Harvard Law School International Human Rights Clinic. 2015. Crackdown at Letpadan: Excessive Force and Violations of the Rights to Freedom of Peaceful Assembly and Expression. Cambridge, Massachusetts.

Franck, T. 1995. *Fairness in International Law and Institutions.* Oxford: Clarendon Press.

Goodman, R. & Jinks, D. 2004. 'How to Influence States: Socialization and International Human Rights Law'. *Duke Law Journal* 54 (3): 621–703.

Harvard Law School International Human Rights Clinic. 2009. Crimes in Burma. Cambridge, Massachusetts.

Harvard Law School International Human Rights Clinic. 2014. Legal Memorandum: War Crimes and Crimes Against Humanity in Eastern Myanmar. Cambridge, Massachusetts.

Horsey, R. 2011. *Ending Forced Labour in Myanmar: Engaging a Pariah Regime*. New York: Routledge.
International Labour Organization. 1998. Report of the Commission of Inquiry appointed under article 26 of the Constitution of the International Labour Organization to examine the observance by Myanmar of the Forced Labour Convention, 1930 (No. 29). Geneva: ILO.
Kinley, D. & Wilson, T. 2007. 'Engaging a Pariah: Human Rights Training in Burma/Myanmar'. *Human Rights Quarterly* 29 (2): 368–402.
Koh, H. 1999. 'How is International Human Rights Law Enforced?' *Indiana Law Journal* 74 (4): 1397–1417.
MacLean, K. 2012. 'Lawfare and Impunity in Burma since the 2000 Ban on Forced Labour'. *Asian Studies Review* 36 (2): 189–206.
Steinberg, D. 2015. 'Myanmar and the United States, Closing and Opening Doors: An Idiosyncratic Analysis'. *Social Research* 82 (2): 427–452.
Taylor, R.H. 2009. *The State in Myanmar*. London: Hurst.

33
INTERNATIONAL ASSISTANCE

Ian Holliday and Zaw Htet

International assistance to underdeveloped countries expanded considerably in the twentieth century, with key growth points occurring during World War I, World War II and the aftermath of the Cold War (Barnett 2011). By the end of the century, global engagement divided into two main categories, long-term development aid and short-term humanitarian assistance, with many agencies operating in specific spheres. Burma was underdeveloped at independence in 1948 and has remained so ever since. In 70 years as a sovereign state, however, the country has experienced an uneven pattern of global aid, while typically maintaining a neutralist foreign policy stance (Johnston 1963; Liang 1990). In the fragile democratic period from 1948 to 1962, marked by civil war and an 18-month authoritarian interlude in 1958–60, external engagement was increasingly important, though also questioned because of its impact on the neutralist stance. In those years, aid mostly took the form of official development assistance (ODA) deployed on a government-to-government basis, and grants and loans disbursed by international financial institutions (IFIs) such as the International Monetary Fund (IMF) and the World Bank. Following the 1962 military coup, a policy of extreme isolation curtailed most forms of aid. Gradual re-engagement with the wider world in the 1970s and 1980s was then halted when the 1988 democracy movement was crushed by a military junta. During the 1990s, global aid remained negligible. Since the mid-2000s, by contrast, there has been significant growth in foreign assistance, spurred by the humanitarian disaster of Cyclone Nargis in 2008, and by political reform in the 2010s. This chapter first surveys the historical context and then focuses on the current transitional period. It looks at multilateral engagement, mostly through the United Nations (UN) but also through the European Union (EU) and the Association of Southeast Asian Nations (ASEAN), at bilateral engagement led by Japan and featuring other major donors such as Britain and the United States (US), and at engagement undertaken by major international non-governmental organizations (INGOs).

Context: 1948–2011

In January 1948, when Burma gained independence from Britain, the war-ravaged country was in need of considerable assistance. In summer 1949, missions led by Deputy Prime Minister General Ne Win and Minister for Foreign Affairs E Maung visited London and Washington to request development aid (Liang 1990, 60). Although the new state took the unusual step of declining to join the British Commonwealth, the organization in 1950 allocated to Burma a loan of £6 million, with £3.75 million contributed by Britain (Government of the United Kingdom 1950). However, the loan was never drawn down, possibly because Burmese leaders were not only keen to distance their country from its former colonial master but also able to tap other sources of assistance (Adeleke 2003). Also important in the early years was the US, which as part of its engagement with non-communist Southeast Asia operated an economic assistance programme in 1948–53, and donated food aid in 1956–64. An economic and technical aid agreement worth $10 million when signed in 1950 ultimately expanded to $25 million (Foley 2009, 165). Political tensions generated problems, but no major change. After Japan resumed diplomatic relations in 1954, it paid Burma $200 million in war reparations and $50 million in technical assistance in 1955–65 (Nemoto 2007). Faced with weak economic growth in the late 1950s, the Burmese government sought increased help. Foreign aid constituted 46 per cent of capital expenditure in 1957–58, 74 per cent in 1958–59 and 82 per cent in 1959–60 (Taylor 2009, 266). During a January 1961 visit, Chinese Premier Zhou Enlai made available an interest-free loan, repayable over 10 years, of $84 million (Liang 1990, 81).

In common with other poor post-colonial nations, Burma also gained help from multilateral institutions such as the UN and IFIs. In the 1950s, the UN solidified its engagement by opening a United Nations Development Programme (UNDP) office inside the country. Additionally, Burma became a member of the International Bank for Reconstruction and Development (IBRD) in 1952, receiving three loans for transportation projects totalling $33 million between 1956 and 1961 (Liang 1990: 199). It joined the International Development Association (IDA) in 1962. (IBRD and IDA are two of the five members of the World Bank Group.)

Almost all forms of external engagement were curtailed, however, by a March 1962 military coup that destroyed Burmese democracy and set in place a Revolutionary Council (RC), headed by Ne Win. Deeply isolationist in orientation, the RC built on criticism of Western advisers in the democratic period to implement a policy of hostility to external engagement (Badgley 1962, 1963; Johnston 1963). No IBRD lending was requested between 1962 and 1973, for instance (Liang 1990, 199). The sole significant exception in the 1960s was an Economic and Technical Cooperation Treaty signed in 1963 with Japan, which provided for a $140 million extension of war reparations (Nemoto 2007, 99). By the mid-1960s, however, the RC's catastrophic economic impact was acknowledged even by Ne Win himself, and when the Burma Socialist Programme Party (BSPP) took over in the early 1970s foreign relations were reconstructed. The first BSPP Congress, held in June–July 1971, endorsed a proposal to seek foreign aid, opening the way in 1973 for Burma to resume borrowing from the World Bank and become a member of the Asian Development Bank (ADB). Wider re-engagement took place once a BSPP single-party state was instituted in 1974 (Steinberg 2006). The UN's Food and Agriculture Organization (FAO) established an office in Burma in 1978.

Leading the way as bilateral donor was Japan. 'According to statistics published by the Organization for Economic Cooperation and Development (OECD), between 1973 and 1988, Japan loaned or gave $1.87 billion to Burma, more than two-thirds of all bilateral aid disbursements to the country' (Seekins 1992, 250). Japanese aid was as high as $244 million in 1986, and $259 million in 1988, and was supplemented by funds channelled through multilateral institutions. Total ADB loans amounted to $530 million by 1987 (Bourne 2011). Also important was West Germany, which between 1969 and 1986 allocated to Burma $77 million in grants and $342 million in loans (Liang 1990, 173). From 1952 to 1986, Britain under the Colombo

Plan allocated $6.5 million for education and training, and $59 million for capital assistance (Liang 1990, 171). In 1979, China provided $64 million in development aid, and added a further $15 million in 1984 (Liang 1990, 95). The US resumed economic cooperation in 1980, and in the mid-1980s made available to Burma more than $10 million annually (Liang 1990, 167–8). However, problems in Burma's donor relations were also evident. Because of unpaid loans, the World Bank in 1987 stopped its assistance programme, worth $1 billion in cumulative IBRD and IDA credits (Liang 1990, 199).

Piecemeal re-engagement with Burma by the US and some of its principal allies was brought to a dramatic halt in 1988, when a mass uprising for democracy was crushed by military forces. Asian support was also called into question, with pressure from shareholders led by the US prompting not only the IMF and the World Bank but also the ADB to stop providing loans and technical assistance (Bourne 2011; Simpson and Park 2013). ODA fell from $435 million in 1988 to $175 million in 1989 (World Bank 2016). Furthermore, when the National League for Democracy (NLD) secured a landslide victory in the May 1990 general election, but was contemptuously excluded from power by an obdurate military elite, the country's pariah status was amply confirmed. Award of the 1991 Nobel Peace Prize to NLD leader Aung San Suu Kyi solidified the terms of global discourse on Myanmar, as the country was now known. The US and most of its main allies looked to sanctions to place pressure on the junta and secure a series of humanitarian gains that would pave the way for future development. Although most Asian states were prepared quietly to do business with the ruling generals, they did little to provide aid. As ever, the exception was Japan, which in 1989 restarted existing projects and in the 1990s endorsed more than $500 million in debt relief. Until 2001, however, even Tokyo suspended ODA (ICG 2002).

The result was that in the 1990s Myanmar became a true aid orphan. Unbending cross-party hostility in the US Congress ensured both that humanitarian aid was curtailed alongside ODA and that the UN and leading IFIs were prevented by the US from reaching out. In 1999, the World Bank initiated discussions about re-engagement, but broke them off when the US Treasury Department threatened to curtail all funding. Many allies and INGOs also fell in line with US policy, engaging only minimally with the most distressed sectors. In this context, the military government looked increasingly to China for assistance (Haacke 2006). A refugee crisis in Rakhine State in the mid-1990s triggered intervention by the UN High Commissioner for Refugees and a number of INGOs, but this was a special case. In 2002, the International Crisis Group (ICG) noted that from 1988 to 2000, 'only Japan provided significant humanitarian assistance, including half a dozen health care, education and food production projects, as well as a large and expanding grassroots assistance program' (ICG 2002, 6). In the second half of the 1990s, Myanmar received only about $50 million per year in ODA (World Bank 2016), and INGO engagement was minimal with no more than about 15 agencies registered with line ministries to work inside the country.

The late 1990s also turned out to be a period of reassessment. EU development assistance, focused mainly on healthcare and HIV/AIDS programmes, started up in a small way in 1996, though no aid strategy was articulated until 2007. Britain's Department for International Development (DfID) began to provide assistance for refugees in 1997, and the bilateral aid relationship was formalized in 2002 with the attachment of a DfID aid officer to the Yangon embassy. The United States Agency for International Development (USAID) returned in a small way by resuming targeted health programmes in 1998. Nevertheless, most of the global development and humanitarian aid business remained disengaged, raising deep questions for aid agencies. In its 2002 report, ICG noted that 'In June 2001, the heads of eight UN agencies operating in Myanmar, in an open letter to their head offices overseas, described the situation as being "on the brink of a humanitarian crisis" and called for "a dramatic overhaul of budget allocations to Myanmar"' (ICG 2002, 7).

In consequence, a gradual enhancement of global engagement took place. In 2005, the Global Fund to Fight AIDS, Tuberculosis and Malaria allocated funding of $98 million to Myanmar, though within six months the programme was closed down because of fresh restrictions on travel and procurement of medical supplies. In consequence, the Three Diseases Fund (3DF), focused on the same three medical conditions, was launched in 2006 with a pooled fund of $138 million contributed by a consortium of Western governments. Still conditions remained difficult. At the end of 2007 Charles Petrie, UN Resident Coordinator since 2003, was asked to leave Myanmar following comments made about the 2007 Saffron Revolution and the 'deteriorating humanitarian situation' inside the country.

The limited development of international assistance in the mid-2000s was thrown into sharp relief by the devastating damage wrought by Cyclone Nargis in Lower Myanmar in May 2008. A humanitarian catastrophe of the first order was exacerbated by the country's extreme isolation, making it impossible in the critical early days to mount a global relief effort. Not only the junta's paranoid security concerns but also the lack of technical links and networks ensured that it took weeks and months rather than hours and days for assistance to reach affected communities. In June 2008, the Myanmar government reported to an ASEAN roundtable that 84,537 had died as a result of Nargis, and 53,836 were missing (presumed dead). The official death toll of 138,000 is now widely used by governments, aid agencies and the news media, though it is quite possibly an under-estimate. At the same time, however, Nargis reshaped global engagement with Myanmar. Total ODA increased from $196 million in 2007 to $534 million in 2008, and stabilized at $355 million in 2009 and 2010 (World Bank 2016).

Perhaps more importantly, the international community started to build local capacity. In May 2008, an ASEAN Humanitarian Task Force was formed, with advisory board members from China, India, Bangladesh, the UN, the Red Cross and Red Crescent Movement, the World Bank, the ADB and major INGOs. To operationalize the initiative a Tripartite Core Group was created in Yangon, bringing together the Myanmar government, ASEAN and the UN, to serve as a channel for negotiating Nargis response efforts. Additional global–local partnerships were created. 'These examples of cross-sectoral cooperation, involving the government, international agencies, civil society and the private sector, offer the possibility of forging new partnerships for development beyond the immediate emergency phase, also outside the delta,' wrote the ICG (2008, 23).

Contemporary international engagement

In many respects, 2008 was the turning point in Myanmar's relations with the international aid business. Subsequent events bound up with the switch to quasi-civilian rule in the 2010s ensured that, in contrast to the 1980s, there was no reversal, but rather intensification. In particular, the suspension or removal of most Western sanctions within the first 2–3 years of the transition from direct military rule, and a public avowal by the new government of the importance of foreign assistance, meant that political constraints on international assistance soon disappeared. Nevertheless, it was in the immediate aftermath of Nargis that key step changes were made in aid disbursements, capacity, networks and projects. Today, the pattern of Myanmar's aid interactions looks increasingly like that of a normal developing state. In this section we first survey domestic developments and provide an overview of international engagement in the transitional period. We then present brief sectoral studies of poverty, healthcare, education, labour and human rights. We look finally at two special cases of global involvement in the peace process and Rakhine State.

The domestic setting for engagement with the international aid business itself changed in the 2000s as important local NGOs started to be established. Particularly significant were two organizations focused on support for communities affected by conflict and, more generally, the peace process: Metta Development Foundation, created in 1998; and Shalom (Nyein) Foundation, created in 2000. Subsequently, community-based organizations began to emerge. In 2007, Paung Ku was created by a consortium of local and international agencies, led by Save the Children, to strengthen civil society. In 2008, the Local Resource Centre was founded by national and international agencies, led by the Burnet Institute, to enhance coordination between civil society groups and international partners.

Having established a firm footing inside Myanmar in the late 2000s, the international community consolidated its aid presence in the early 2010s. The ADB re-established a small office at the end of 2012, for instance (Simpson and Park 2013, 1861). Large amounts of a total foreign debt of $11 billion were soon relieved, with Japan forgiving $3.7 billion, the Paris Club of major creditor countries $2.2 billion, and Norway $534 million. Substantial ODA commitments were also made, led by the World Bank with $2 billion for a multi-year development programme (including $200 million for healthcare), Japan with a $400 million aid and investment package, the US with $170 million over 2 years from 2012 (though $200 million was ultimately committed), the EU with annual development pledges of around $125 million, and Britain with similar pledges of around $95 million. Total ODA inflows continued to move up and soon registered a step change: $374 million in 2011, $504 million in 2012, $3.9 billion in 2013. This meant that per capita ODA, averaging little more than $1 for most of the 1990s and only around $3 for most of the 2000s, increased to $10 in 2012 and $74 in 2013, finally placing Myanmar above regional neighbours such as Cambodia ($54) and Laos ($62).

In January 2013, a Myanmar Development Cooperation Forum was convened in Naypyitaw, bringing together the government and a Development Partnership Group of international donors to establish ground rules. By December 2015, 25 UN agencies, funds, offices and associate entities, and 87 INGOs were operating inside the country (MIMU 2016). Additional external support was allocated to the 2014 Myanmar Population and Housing Census, the first such exercise in more than 30 years. Against an estimated cost of $60 million, roughly $45 million of both financial and technical assistance came from the United Nations Population Fund and bilateral donors.

Poverty remains endemic in Myanmar, a consequence of 50 years of economic mismanagement and isolation. In UNDP's *Human Development Report 2015*, Myanmar ranks 148 out of 188 jurisdictions, locating it in the low human development category populated mostly by sub-Saharan African nations. Using 2014 data, Myanmar is reported to have a life expectancy at birth of 65.9 years, and gross national income per capita of $4,608, at 2011 purchasing power parities (UNDP 2015). An earlier Integrated Household Living Conditions Assessment, conducted in 2009–10, indicated that 26 per cent of the population was living below the poverty line. An analysis undertaken by the World Bank (2014) put the proportion as high as 37.5 per cent. Global engagement with poverty, often concentrated in rural areas, has long been led by the FAO and the World Food Programme. In 2009, a multi-donor Livelihoods and Food Security Trust Fund (LIFT), with a budget of €136 million, was an important initiative. Once a Microfinance Business Law had been passed in 2011, LIFT began to offer loans of $60 to $600 to small-scale farmers. ODA devoted to agriculture nearly doubled from $172 million in 2011 to $315 million in 2015.

Health has long been a major concern, notably since 2002 when the World Health Organization ranked Myanmar 190 out of 191 countries (see Chapter 27). Following the abortive launch of the Global Fund in 2005, the 3DF operated from 2006 to 2012. It established a platform for creation of a Three Million Development Goal Fund, set up in 2012 with $330 million for 2012–16 contributed bilaterally by Australia, Denmark, the EU, Sweden, Switzerland, Britain and the US. The work of the 3DF was picked up by the Global Fund, which returned to Myanmar in 2013 with a budget of $451 million for 2013–16. In the transitional period external resources for health are significant, accounting for 9.4 per cent of total health expenditure in 2010, 7.1 per cent in 2011, 8.0 per cent in 2012 and 15.3 per cent in 2013. Another significant multi-donor fund is Gavi (the Vaccine Alliance), which has worked in Myanmar since its inception in 2000 and committed total funding of $156 million for 2000–20. Leading INGOs working in the health sector include Médecins Sans Frontières (MSF) Holland (since 1992), Malteser International (since 2001) and Medical Emergency Relief International (since 2005). ODA devoted to the sector increased from $30 million in 2010 to $173 million in 2011 and $595 million in 2014 (MAIMS, 2016).

Education is widely seen as a key development sector, with external engagement with basic provision led by the United Nations Children's Fund (UNICEF) (see Chapter 26). In 2015, UNICEF estimated that over one million children were out of school. It noted that '70 percent of primary school age children complete a full course of primary education at the correct age, and out of every 100 children entering primary school, only about 20 go on to finish lower secondary school' (UNICEF 2015).

Previously, in 2012, the first Comprehensive Education Sector Review in 20 years was launched, in part to generate a platform for engagement with international donors. A Joint Education Sector Working Group was formed to stimulate policy dialogue between the government and development partners. A considerable amount of funding is disbursed through the Multi Donor Education Fund (MDEF), supported by Australia, Denmark, the European Commission, Norway, UNICEF, the United Nations Educational, Scientific and Cultural Organization (UNESCO), and Britain. MDEF Phase I provided $86 million in 2012–15. Phase II, focused on primary education, contributed $65 million in 2012–16 and sought to build better coordination across ministries to support early childhood development. In 2013, World Vision (active in Myanmar since 1991), Save the Children (active since 1995) and the Burnet Institute (active since 2003) came together to establish the Myanmar Education Consortium with aid from the Australian Agency for International Development (AusAID), Britain's DfID and the Danish International Development Agency (DANIDA). It has provided financial support to some 30 civil society organizations. In general, higher education lacks assistance, though UNESCO has a capacity-building project funded by Open Society Foundations (OSF), the British Council has an English-language support programme, and AusAID and OSF have a project to help revitalize Mandalay University and the University of Yangon.

Labour has for many years been a controversial policy sector because of allegations of forced labour lodged by the International Labour Organization (ILO) and others during the junta period. In 1999, the ILO for the first time in its history adopted resolutions limiting assistance to a member state, and banning participation in ILO activities. ILO technical assistance to Myanmar ceased. In 2011, however, the ILO started to look beyond forced labour and child soldier issues to capacity building. At much the same time, domestic reform began to take place, with a Labour Organization Law passed in 2011. By early 2015, the number of registered labour organizations had increased to 1,500. However, Myanmar's legal framework is not fully in line with ILO Convention 87 on Freedom of Association and Protection of the Right to Organize, and may need to be amended. In 2012 and 2013 the ILO lifted sanctions, pledging to support the government to eliminate forced labour by 2015. In 2014, Myanmar and the US jointly launched an initiative to promote fundamental labour rights and practices. Additional support came from Japan, Denmark and the EU. In mid-2015, the Confederation of Trade Unions of Myanmar, previously known as the Federation of Trade Unions of Burma and based in Thailand as an underground organization, was recognized by the government. It soon delivered training and capacity building in ten regions and states.

Human rights remain contentious even during Myanmar's transitional period, chiefly because of conflict between the national army and a small number of ethnic armed groups, and also because of Buddhist–Muslim violence, notably in Rakhine State. Amnesty International first documented the detention of political prisoners in 1965, and since the 1990s has reported extensively on human rights abuse in Myanmar. In the 1990s and 2000s, the UN Commission on Human Rights, its successor the UN Human Rights Council and the UN General Assembly regularly passed critical resolutions. The position of special rapporteur on the situation of human rights in Myanmar was created in 1992, and the UN secretary-general appointed a special envoy in 1997. Since the 1990s, five rapporteurs and four envoys have served. In September 2011, at an early stage of the transition, the Myanmar National Human Rights Commission, comprising 15 retired government officials and academics, was formed to promote and protect rights embodied in the 2008 constitution. Full legal underpinnings were enacted in 2014, and the number of commissioners was reduced to 11. However, the commission's limited engagement with human rights issues and poor transparency ensure that it lacks credibility. Even under the NLD government, Yanghee Lee, rapporteur since 2014, routinely files highly critical reports. Organizations such as Amnesty, Human Rights Watch and the Asian Human Rights Commission continue to take a close interest, especially in violence against the Rohingya minority in Rakhine State.

The *peace process*, focused on the issue of nation-building that confronted Burma at independence in 1948 and remains deeply problematic to this day, is a special area of global engagement. In November 2012, the Myanmar Peace Centre (MPC) was established as a quasi-governmental agency with funding chiefly from the EU ($6.4 million), Nippon Foundation ($6.3 million) and Japan ($1.2 million). In November 2013, a Nationwide Ceasefire Coordination Team was created by a broader set of ethnic nationalities. International engagement with these domestic developments was led by the Myanmar Peace Support Initiative (MPSI), set up under Petrie. This was a short-term initiative designed to help implement projects supported mainly by the Peace Donor Support Group, established in 2012 by Norway, Australia, Britain, the EU, the UN and the World Bank to coordinate international support and provide aid worth $30 million in conflict-affected areas. MPSI was wound up in 2014, having spent $4 million on 13 education, health, water and sanitation, and capacity-building projects. In July 2016, MPC became the National Reconciliation and Peace Centre, chaired by State Counsellor Aung San Suu Kyi. In December 2016, a Joint Coordinating Body for Peace Process Funding, also led by Aung San Suu Kyi, was established to manage international assistance. Pledges of more than $100 million were made through the Joint Peace Fund, a multi-donor trust established in 2016.

Rakhine State presents special challenges for international assistance. In June 2012, sectarian tension erupted into widespread violence between Buddhist and Muslim communities, triggering a state of emergency and driving some 140,000 Rohingya Muslims into internally-displaced person (IDP) camps. In July 2012, Thein Sein informed Antonio Guterres, UN

High Commissioner for Refugees, that Myanmar would take responsibility only for its own citizens. He proposed that Rohingya Muslims, identified as illegal immigrants, be accommodated in UN-sponsored IDP camps or transferred to third countries. Guterres rejected the proposal. While aid agencies allocated $89 million to a Rakhine Response Plan for 2012–13, and high-level representatives joined exploratory missions, it quickly became clear that there was extensive grassroots resistance to international humanitarian engagement (UNHCR 2012). In February 2014, the activities of MSF Holland, built over a 20-year period into the biggest medical service in Rakhine, were suspended after MSF reported that it had treated Muslims for injuries sustained during sectarian violence the authorities said never took place. In March 2014, 33 UN and INGO offices and warehouses were ransacked by a Rakhine mob in Sittwe, and 300 staff were relocated. Not until several weeks later did the agencies resume operations, and not until December 2014 did a fresh memorandum of understanding enable MSF to restart its activities. In August 2016, the NLD government established an Advisory Commission on Rakhine State, chaired by former UN Secretary-General Kofi Annan, and asked it to report within one year. However, tension and conflict continued, Rohingya communities were clearly targeted for violence, and the national army was implicated in atrocities. Global pressure intensified on Aung San Suu Kyi to take a clear leadership role in responding to the crisis.

Conclusion

The formation of an NLD government in March 2016 further changed Myanmar's relationship with international donors. In one respect, it reinforced the trend of growing engagement registered since Nargis in 2008. In another respect, however, it marked a shift in the relationship. Soon after the November 2015 election, Aung San Suu Kyi met with major global agencies to inform them that in future the agenda for international assistance would be set by the government, not by the agencies. Her stance built on an awareness developed under Thein Sein, but not fully acted upon, that global engagement was marked by duplication, inefficiency and waste. In November 2016, she set up a Development Assistance Coordination Unit to identify and prioritize international development projects. It seems likely that much future assistance will be directed to agriculture, infrastructure development and urban planning. At the same time, global concern about human rights, especially in Rakhine State, continued to grow, creating tensions between Aung San Suu Kyi and international agencies.

Internal aid dynamics have also changed. Under sanctions in the 1990s and 2000s, Myanmar's development funding was channelled primarily through UN agencies. However, the enhanced international legitimacy of the NLD government, particularly with Western donors, means that aid is starting to flow directly to state agencies and the role of the UN is shifting towards technical assistance, as in most middle-income countries. At the same time, though, the Myanmar public sector is becoming over-burdened by the burst of development assistance directed to it. Furthermore, the role of the Ministry of Home Affairs, headed by a serving military officer, in overseeing all subnational bureaucracy complicates project implementation.

The days when Myanmar was an aid orphan are over, and a largely normal set of relations with international society has now been established. In the past 10 years patterns of international assistance have been transformed. At the same time, however, difficulties in managing global engagement through aid projects continue to face the NLD government.

References

Adeleke, A. 2003. 'The Strings of Neutralism: Burma and the Colombo Plan'. *Pacific Affairs* 76 (4): 593–610.

Badgley, J. 1962. 'Burma's Military Government: A Political Analysis'. *Asian Survey* 2 (1): 24–31.

Badgley, J. 1963. 'Burma: The Nexus of Socialism and Two Political Traditions'. *Asian Survey* 3 (2): 89–95.

Barnett, M. N. 2011. *Empire of Humanity: A History of Humanitarianism*. New York: Cornell University Press.

Bourne, S. 2011. *The ADB in Burma: Behind the Scenes*. Quezon City: NGO Forum on ADB.

Foley, M. 2009. *The Cold War and National Assertion in Southeast Asia: Britain, the United States and Burma, 1948–1962*. London: Routledge.

Government of the United Kingdom. 1950. 'Agreement between the Governments of the United Kingdom of Great Britain and Northern Ireland, Australia, India, Pakistan and Ceylon, and the Government of the Union of Burma Regarding a Loan to Burma'. June 28, 1950, Cmd 8007.

Haacke, J. 2006. *Myanmar's Foreign Policy: Domestic Influences and International Implications*. Abingdon: Routledge.

International Crisis Group [ICG]. 2002. *Myanmar: The Politics of Humanitarian Aid*. Bangkok & Brussels: ICG.

International Crisis Group [ICG]. 2008. *Burma/Myanmar after Nargis*. Bangkok & Brussels: ICG.

Johnston, W. C. 1963. *Burma's Foreign Policy: A Study in Neutralism*. Cambridge, MA: Harvard University Press.

Liang, C. S. 1990. *Burma's Foreign Relations: Neutralism in Theory and Practice*. New York: Praeger.

Mohinga Aid Information Management System [MAIMS]. 2016. Online Database. Accessed April 22, 2016. http://mohinga.info/en/.

Myanmar Information Management Unit [MIMU]. 2016. Online Database. Accessed April 22, 2016. www.themimu.info/.

Nemoto, K. 2007. 'Between Democracy and Economic Development: Japan's Policy towards Burma/Myanmar Then and Now'. In *Myanmar: State, Society and Ethnicity*, edited by N. Ganesan and K. Y. Hlaing. Singapore: Institute of Southeast Asian Studies: 96–108.

Seekins, D. M. 1992. 'Japan's Aid Relations with Military Regimes in Burma, 1962–1991'. *Asian Survey* 32 (3): 246–62.

Simpson, A. and S. Park. 2013. 'The Asian Development Bank as a Global Risk Regulator in Myanmar'. *Third World Quarterly* 34 (10): 1858–71.

Steinberg, D. I. 2006. 'Burma–Myanmar: The US–Burmese Relationship and Its Vicissitudes'. In *Short of the Goal: US Policy and Poorly Performing States*, edited by N. Birdsall, M. Vaishnav and R. L. Ayres. Washington, DC: Center for Global Development: 209–244.

Taylor, R. H. 2009. *The State in Myanmar*. London: Hurst & Company.

UNICEF Myanmar. 2015. Quality Basic Education Programme. Accessed April 22, 2016. www.unicef.org/myanmar/education_20838.html.

United Nations Development Programme [UNDP]. 2015. *Human Development Report: Work for Human Development*. New York: UNDP.

United Nations High Commissioner for Refugees [UNHCR]. 2012. Rakhine State Situation Update. July 19.

World Bank. 2014. *Myanmar: Ending Poverty and Boosting Shared Prosperity in a Time of Transition*. Washington, DC: World Bank Publications.

World Bank. 2016. World Development Indicators Online Database. Accessed April 22, 2016. http://data.worldbank.org/indicator/DT.ODA.ODAT.CD.

PART VII

Challenges

34
PEACE AND RECONCILIATION

Kim Jolliffe

Among the many challenges that were inherited by the NLD-led government in 2016, perhaps the most difficult is alleviating the country's seven-decade-old armed conflicts, which in recent years have seen their most intense period of violence since the 1980s. The conflicts emerged over constitutional disputes prior to independence and have persisted through more than five decades of rule by the Bamar military class, manifesting in sporadic armed conflict between countless Ethnic Armed Organisations (EAOs) and the Myanmar Armed Forces (Tatmadaw).

While the EAOs, along with successive non-violent ethnic political movements, have called for greater autonomy for their territories and a more equal stake in the national affairs of the country, the Bamar-dominated state has struggled persistently to bring all territories under centralised rule. In very few cases, EAOs have called for independence, but from the 1970s until today, the majority have been calling for a democratic federal system of government, while most others have focused primarily on achieving autonomy for their own areas. Throughout 49 years of outright military rule, the state sought to marginalise all forms of political opposition, while attempting to erode armed movements through containment offensives, and programmes to transform them into state-backed militia.

With the NLD coming to power in March 2016, there were high hopes for the administration to address long-standing grievances, and build sustainable peace. Since the NLD's inception, its interests and political positions have overlapped considerably with those of a core bloc of pro-democracy and pro-federal EAOs, including the Karen National Union (KNU), the Kachin Independence Organisation (KIO), the New Mon State Party (NMSP), the Chin National Front and the Karenni National Progressive Party (KNPP). The NLD and this bloc have long mirrored each others's calls for a federal, democratic constitution, and for it to be developed through broad-based national dialogue, including ethnic leaders, the NLD and other mostly Bamar pro-democrats, and the Tatmadaw.

Through the 1990s and 2000s, such calls were ignored by the military government, which instead pursued a near-unilateral constitutional drafting process, aimed at instituting a 'disciplined democracy'. However, in October 2015, the Tatmadaw and key government figures from the former regime committed for the first time on paper to a dialogue aimed explicitly at establishing 'a union based on the principles of democracy and federalism', as part of negotiations with EAOs. This commitment has provided an unprecedented opportunity for the NLD government to see through their long stated aim of achieving 'national reconciliation' through dialogue.

Nonetheless, recent years have actually seen a dramatic increase in levels of armed conflict overall, as long-standing ceasefires have broken with groups such as the KIO, Shan State Progress Party and the Myanmar National Democratic Alliance Army, and conflicts have broken out with two new groups, the Palaung State Liberation Front and the Arakan Army. Four of these EAOs have formed a formal alliance in northern Shan State, called the Northern Alliance – Burma (NA-B), and have become increasingly allied with the country's largest EAO, United Wa State Party (UWSP), whose relations with government have soured greatly. Conflicts have continued unabated since the NLD came to office, as the Tatmadaw carried out sustained air and ground offensives near the KIO's headquarters in Kachin State and the groups in northern Shan State has targeted key trade routes near the China border. Additionally, sectarian, predominantly intercommunal conflict in Rakhine State has escalated into an insurgency provoking a devastating Tatmadaw response, which the UN has described as a 'calculated policy of terror', to force populations to move (UNOHCHR 2017, 41).

Largely as a result of such violence, hope for a comprehensive peace settlement deteriorated significantly during the NLD's first year in government. The administration essentially continued the process established through the Nationwide Ceasefire Agreement (NCA), but has struggled to make the process fully inclusive, as the Tatmadaw and EAOs continued to deliberate over numerous terminological and procedural issues. In particular, the Tatmadaw has excluded Myanmar National Democratic Alliance Army (MNDAA), Palaung State Liberation Front (PSLF) and Arakan Army (AA), from the NCA. For example, in 2016, the military demanded these groups issue a signed statement denouncing the principle of armed struggle, prior to being allowed to sign the NCA. As these groups have refused to do so, they have been excluded, while their allies, including the KIO and UWSP, have refused to sign the NCA until inclusivity is achieved.

Underpinning the many intricate disputes that have marred proceedings is a systemic lack of trust among elements in EAOs and the Tatmadaw in the potential for a negotiated solution that suits their aims. While the Tatmadaw maintains an uncompromisingly forward posture in ceasefire and non-ceasefire areas and continues daily offensives on EAO positions, numerous EAOs continue to change the terms for signing the deal and generally express a lack of commitment to the current process. Meanwhile, the NLD has apparently committed to siding rhetorically with the Tatmadaw – in line with constitutional restraints that give it no direct influence over operational military matters – ensuring that state media and other official communications praise the 'valiant' actions of the Tatmadaw, while denouncing EAO aggression.

Therefore, there remain deep challenges to negotiating a solution in the near term. More broadly, as rural ethnic areas remain heavily militarised by the Tatmadaw, uncountable EAOs of various sizes, and an even larger number of state-backed militia, untangling the political and financial economies that have driven war will likely take decades, even if the state can strike a deal with a core group of EAOs.

This chapter provides a chronological overview of armed ethnic conflict in Myanmar, looking particularly at the 1988–2011 and 2011–2016 periods, and focusing largely on the approaches of former governments to handling ethnic armed conflicts. It then discusses the opportunities and challenges that the NLD-led government faces today in trying to bring a lasting peaceful settlement. The chapter concludes with a sober reflection on the reality that, despite good reason for hope, Myanmar likely has many more decades, at least, of ethnic armed conflict, and that the potential for meaningful change depends on the actions of the Bamar military elite.

Independence and military rule: 1948–1988

Within one year of the country's independence in 1948, Myanmar was in crisis, as a result of multiple socialist and communist insurgencies, including the Burma Communist Party (BCP) and the ethnonationalist armed movements of the KNU and various Mon, Rakhine, Mujahadin and Pa-O groups. At that time, the majority of Shan, Kachin, Chin and Karenni leaders were incorporated into the formal political structure as ministers and MPs in the governments and parliaments created for their regions or as local-level monarchs, called *Saophas*.[1]

In the 1950s, fighting between the government and the active armed movements, coupled with the arrival of Kuomintang insurgents retreating from China, led the country into deep instability. As ethnic units from the original Tatmadaw defected, the military became increasingly Bamar-dominated, and its expansion alongside Myanmar language teachers spurred grievances among Shan and Kachin leaders and communities. In the early 1960s, a 'Federal Movement' was launched by politicians in Shan State, which came to include ethnic politicians from other parts of the country, to call for greater powers to lie with the ethnic states. At the same time, Kachin and Shan armed movements were begun by students and peasants in the north of the country.

In 1962, on the second day of negotiations between the 'Federal Movement' and the central government, the military staged a coup d'état, arresting all of those involved. It then instated a highly centralised form of military government that removed the local governments and parliaments altogether. The Tatmadaw initiated its 'four-cuts' strategy which sought to cut support off from communities to insurgents, and manifested in decades of forced relocation campaigns and systematic violence against and oppression of ethnic communities in areas affected by armed conflict.

As Kachin and Shan armed movements rose in strength, the government became increasingly dependent on the mobilisation of state-backed militia, particularly in Shan State, where it allowed local armed actors including some former Kuomintang to remain armed and use government infrastructure for business in return for loyalty.

In the late 1960s and 1970s, the Bamar-led BCP made alliances with leaders from numerous ethnic groups, including Wa, Kokang, Kachin, Shan, Pa-O, Kayan and Karenni factions, among others. With the support of China it took control of large swaths of northeastern Shan State and northern parts of Kachin State and maintained patronage over groups across numerous other regions. In the same period, other ethnic armed movements, including today's KNU, KIO, NMSP and KNPP, became increasingly pro-federal and pro-democratic. In 1976, ten such groups formed an alliance called the National Democratic Front (NDF), which was later expanded to twelve groups. Numerous Shan, Naga and other groups maintained autonomy from both of these movements, but in continued resistance to the state.

The military junta era: 1988–2011

In 1988, mass demonstrations catalysed a second coup d'état, bringing to power a new military government. The State Law and Order Restoration Council, as the junta was called, then held elections in 1990 that were won by the newly established NLD in a landslide. However, as the SLORC refused to honour the result, large numbers of elected representatives joined the thousands of protestors who had fled in 1988, in exile and in territories held by the KNU. Before long, alliances were formed between Bamar pro-democracy networks and the NDF, unified in calls for the NLD to be allowed to form a government, and for the need for a new federal, democratic constitution.

Throughout its twenty-two-year reign, the SLORC (later renamed the State Peace and Development Council (SPDC)) placed great emphasis on achieving stability and 'consolidation of the union' through a new strategy for dealing with the EAOs. The strategy revolved around efforts to contain and slowly wear away at their territories, through a combination of military campaigns, strategic ceasefires and programmes to convert EAOs into state-backed militia. At the same time, the state explicitly disregarded EAO attempts to gain an equal stake in formal politics, marginalising them from processes of constitutional design and overriding their existing governance systems by exploiting ceasefires to expand the state's presence into new territories.

The beginnings of this strategy came in 1989, as the BCP collapsed after various ethnic factions at its headquarters area mutinied, and formed new EAOs, including the UWSP and the Myanmar National Democratic Alliance Army. Soon after, the SLORC's General Khin Nyunt reached out to these and other EAOs that had previously been supported by the BCP, and secured a run of ceasefires in quick succession. In the 1990s, the General then began reaching out to other EAOs, including some of those from the NDF, such as the KIO, KNPP and the Pa-O National Organisation (PNO). Although Khin Nyunt was ousted in 2004, these ceasefires continued and others were signed in following years. By 2011, the government recognised ceasefires with seventeen 'major' EAOs and with twenty-three 'minor' ones, with small groups and splinter factions. Through most of the 1990s, the Tatmadaw held dozens of ceasefires with most groups in Kachin State and northern Shan State, as well as the NMSP in the southeast (Kramer 2009b).

At first, each of these groups gained semi-official territories with borders that could not be crossed by the other side without prior coordination via EAO liaison offices. They were also awarded economic concessions such as mining and logging permissions (Kramer 2009b). Some of these groups, such as the PNO, the Karenni State Nationalities People's Liberation Front (KNPLF), National Democratic Army-Kachin (NDA-K), Kachin Defence Army (KDA) and the Democratic Karen Buddhist Army (DKBA), renounced their political aspirations, and effectively became armed proxies of the Tatmadaw, allowing government administration to be established in their areas. The most powerful ceasefire EAO, the UWSP, kept its own territory autonomous but allied with the Tatmadaw against a number of Shan EAOs, and was able to secure control of new areas with the government's permission.

Meanwhile, ceasefire EAOs that maintained their political opposition, such as the KIO, NMSP, Shan State Progress Party (SSPP), Palaung State Liberation Party (PSLP) and Shan State National Army (SSNA), came under increasing pressure on numerous fronts. Firstly, they saw their economic concessions reduced each year, as the Tatmadaw expanded its presence in areas surrounding their areas, cutting off trade and supply routes, and positioning its own bases inside their territories. In 2005, Tatmadaw forced two major ceasefire groups, the PSLP and the SSNA, to disband entirely. According to state media (*New Light of Myanmar* 2011), by 2011, fifteen EAOs had disbanded entirely and given up their arms to the state, though many of these were small splinter factions from other EAOs. Meanwhile, ceasefire areas and surrounding areas across the country became the sites of rampant resource extraction, agribusiness and hydropower development, leading to widespread land confiscation and environmental destruction (Buchanan, Kramer & Woods 2013).

These ceasefires allowed the Tatmadaw to focus its military counterinsurgency efforts on the KNPP, KNU and various Shan EAOs, which it generally offered less favourable ceasefire conditions or refused to speak with.[2] Intermittent campaigns utilising thousands of Tatmadaw infantrymen backed up by artillery were used to take positions throughout EAO territories and to link them up with heavily fortified roads. Peripheral areas remaining under EAO control were then designated as 'black zones', in which all remaining people were considered insurgents. In these areas, forced relocation campaigns – involving the issuing of orders to village heads, as well as the shelling and burning of villages – were undertaken to move entire populations to areas close to Tatmadaw facilities or to towns already under government control. According to annual surveys conducted by the relief organisation the Thai Burma Border Consortium (2011, 17), at least 3,700 villages were 'destroyed, relocated or abandoned' between 1996 and 2011. Meanwhile, the widespread placement of Tatmadaw battalions throughout civilian-populated areas led to rampant human rights abuses in these areas, including forced labour, extortion, torture, arbitrary detainment and sexual abuse (Karen Human Rights Group 2008; 2013).

These offensives expended huge resources and caused significant Tatmadaw casualties but did not achieve annihilation or dismantlement of the EAOs. However, by establishing networks of military facilities across EAO strongholds, the Tatmadaw gained access to resources and trade routes and secured a presence that became instrumental to expanding its administrative presence during ceasefires in later years.

Throughout this period, the military government resisted repeated calls from EAOs to engage in meaningful political discussion, through which they hoped to negotiate for decentralisation of government. Such requests were made by the KIO, NMSP and KNU among others during ceasefire talks, but the groups were told that the military government was just temporary and they would have to wait for a new constitution to be instated and a government to be formed.

To that end, the government held a National Convention between 1993 and 1996 and again between 2004 and 2007 in order to draft a new charter (Human Rights Watch 2008). The convention included ethnic representatives from twenty-eight ceasefire groups but they repeatedly complained of being given no meaningful space to influence proceedings (Seng 2003; Human Rights Watch 2008), and submitted detailed requests for the new constitution to ensure greater decentralisation of government (South 2008, 128–129; Human Rights Watch 2008). In 2005, the NMSP pulled out of the convention altogether in protest. In 2007, the KIO submitted a six-page, nineteen-point proposal to the National Convention with detailed requests for the formation of a federal government and armed forces with local defence force units under the control of each ethnic state. The military government rejected the proposal, and threatened to break its ceasefire with the KIO (Sakhong 2010).

The National Convention concluded in 2007 and a new constitution was promulgated in 2008 following a widely discredited referendum. The 2008 Constitution, which has been in use since 2011, provides for subnational governments for the fourteen states and regions, as long-requested by EAOs, but endows them with few autonomous legislative or executive powers.[3] Although President Thein Sein announced plans in 2013 to take steps towards greater decentralisation of government, very little was achieved during his term of office. The key provisions of a bill introduced to the Union legislatures in mid-2015 to allow greater powers to state/region governments were vetoed by the Tatmadaw, which is given such powers by the constitution (Htoo Thant, *The Myanmar Times*, 2 July 2015).

In 2009, the military government made demands for all ceasefire groups to come under the direct command of the Tatmadaw, by transforming into 326-man border guard forces (BGFs), each with a few dozen ordinary Tatmadaw officers and support personnel embedded in their ranks (Kramer 2009a). In 2009 and 2010, the KNPLF, NDA-K, a large faction of the DKBA, and numerous smaller groups formed a total of twenty-three BGFs. Fifteen other groups, including the PNO, KDA and a large faction of the SSPP, meanwhile, were able to form less formalised state-backed militia. Leaders from some of these groups then prepared to run in the 2010 elections with their own political parties, as independents or under the Tatmadaw-backed Union Solidarity and Development Party (USDP).

However, the large majority of EAOs rejected the BGF demands, leading to their ceasefires being annulled and their being blocked from forming official political parties. Tensions then escalated significantly with some of the larger EAOS, including the MNDAA, KIO, UWSP,

SSPP and NMSP. In 2009, the Tatmadaw conquered the oldest ceasefire territory, that of the MNDAA, forcing the majority faction into China, while a smaller group formed a BGF and joined the USDP (Jolliffe 2015, 23–26).

In late 2010, national elections that were widely criticised by the international community for fraud were held, bringing to power a new government under the 2008 Constitution, led by leaders from the former military government (International Crisis Group 2011). Trust between the Bamar military elite and the EAOs was at an extreme low, with all ceasefires null and void, and the chances of an inclusive political process to bring about governmental decentralisation more distant than ever. This was reflected in the outbreak of new conflict on election day, when a large faction of the DKBA, which had long acted as a Tatmadaw proxy, took up arms against the state, with a dramatic offensive on Myawaddy Town (Burma Centre of Ethnic Studies 2011).

In summary, during the 1990s and 2000s, the military government failed in both its military efforts and its political strategy to bring the country closer to stability. Militarily it was unable to defeat its opponents through counterinsurgency operations, and subordinated just a few significant groups to the role of state-backed militia. Politically, its marginalisation of EAOs from the constitutional design process meant that their areas remained outside of the constitutional order, defended by their armed wings, or hinged on the officially expired ceasefire arrangements.

The President Thein Sein era: 2011–2015

During President Thein Sein's 2011–2015 term of office, armed conflict in Myanmar escalated dramatically (see Figure 34.1). At the same time, however, unprecedented space for a negotiated settlement was created. This apparent paradox was due primarily to contradictory signals

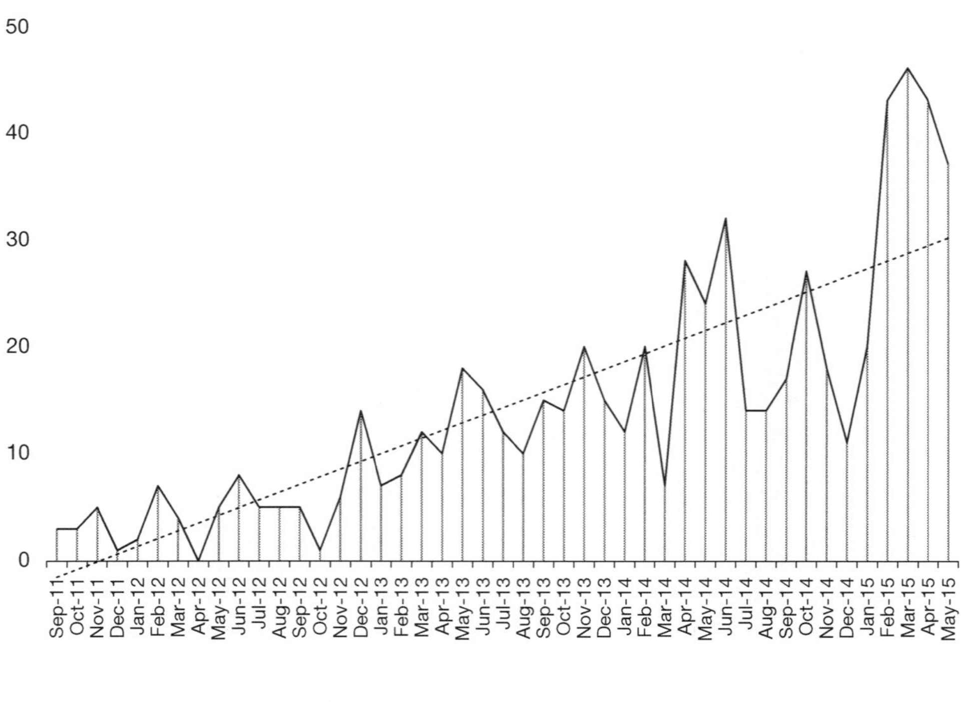

Figure 34.1 Armed clashes between the Tatmadaw and ethnic armed organisations, 2011–2015

Source: Stephen Gray, using Burma News International data.

and behaviours of the former regime figures remaining in power. On the one hand, President Thein Sein showed unprecedented eagerness to enter into negotiations with EAOs in the pursuit of peace. On the other, the Tatmadaw continued its existing strategy, most visibly by undertaking its most intensive counterinsurgency offensives in decades.

In the first few months of Thein Sein's presidency, Shan and Kachin States spiralled into intense conflicts that have continued into 2016. In early March that year, just weeks before the president's inauguration, the Tatmadaw broke its twenty-two-year ceasefire with the SSPP, unleashing an offensive involving around 2,000 troops across multiple townships (Keenan 2014). The same month, tensions were intensified between the government and the KIO, when the latter sent a letter to the Chinese government in opposition to the Myitsone mega hydropower dam, stating that the 'KIO would not be responsible for the civil war if the war broke out because of [the project]' (KIO 2011).

Following a number of violent incidents, including Tatmadaw shelling of KIO positions, and the maiming and killing of a KIO liaison officer, the ceasefire was irrevocably broken on 11 June 2011, when Tatmadaw troops from eleven light infantry battalions launched an attack on a KIO position near to a construction site of a different dam in KIO territory. The KIO had previously stated it would not disrupt this particularly project, but state media claims that it had (Burma Centre for Ethnic Studies 2013; *New Light of Myanmar* 2011). By the end of the year, an ally of both the KIO and SSPP, the Palaung State Liberation Front, which had splintered from the disbanded PSLP years before, re-entered the area with a new armed wing, the Ta'ang National Liberation Army. The TNLA rapidly rose in strength, primarily taking control of Ta'ang settlements left ungoverned or held by the KIO and SSPP and soon provoked regular Tatmadaw offensives against its new positions (Jolliffe 2015, 76). These EAOs were then joined in arms by a new EAO, the Arakan Army (AA), and a resurgent majority faction of the MNDAA. In 2015, both the AA and MNDAA went on to take positions in areas of their own ethnicity, Rakhine State and the Kokang region of Shan State respectively, leading to new conflicts.

Despite the the Tatmadaw's signing of a ceasefire with the SSPP in July 2011 and an agreement to reduce tensions with the KIO in February 2013, all of these conflicts have continued into 2016. Increasingly frequently since late 2012, Tatmadaw offensives have made use of aerial bombardments and strafing, as well as continued use of indiscriminate shelling. These conflicts have caused the protracted displacement of more than 100,000 civilians and more temporary periods of displacement for thousands of people each month. There have also been continuous allegations of human rights abuses, committed mostly by the Tatmadaw, but by EAOs too.

Contrastingly, the president made the pursuit of peace through negotiation a central aim of his term, managing to gain an unprecedented level of cooperation from the Tatmadaw in holding talks. A new wave of fourteen ceasefires was agreed in 2011 and 2012, seven of which were with groups that had never held meaningful ceasefires with the government before, including the state's oldest enemy, the KNU. In 2012, the EAOs then got commitments from the government to holding of political dialogue (*Mizzima* 2012). In 2013, amid calls from EAOs for the Tatmadaw to halt all offensives and begin the dialogue immediately, the government and Tatmadaw agreed to a compromise. Instead, the country's first ever multi-lateral talks would begin towards a nationwide ceasefire agreement that would, in turn, establish concrete terms for broad-based political talks.

However, on the ground, this shift in the military elite's rhetorical stance was undermined greatly by an apparent continuation of its old counterinsurgency strategy. While EAOs and communities in Kachin and Shan States experienced relentless offensives on territories that had been agreed in the 1980s and 1990s, new ceasefire areas experienced intensive expansion of the military and of the government's administration into EAO territories, particularly those of the

KNU and KNPP. This process of government expansion, achieved largely through the provision of development and social services to ceasefire regions, served to undermine the confidence of powerful factions of these groups, with certain leaders questioning the government's interest in genuine peace (Jolliffe 2015).

Meanwhile, although the Tatmadaw had quietly sidelined its BGF demands, it persisted in insisting that EAOs will need to agree to Disarmament Demobilisation and Reintegration (DDR). Commander-in Chief Min Aung Hlaing stated at least twice in 2015 that peace would ultimately depend on EAOs committing to DDR (*Mizzima* 2015). During negotiations between the UPWC and the EAOs during Thein Sein's term too, Tatmadaw representatives also demanded that the EAOs disarm prior to political dialogue, despite the government's formal statements seemingly accepting that this would not be forced (Larry Jagan, *Asia Times*, 8 October 2014).

Notwithstanding these difficulties, by autumn 2015, an NCA text was agreed by both delegations that would commit signees to the undertaking of a political dialogue aimed explicitly at establishing 'a union based on the principles of democracy and federalism' (The Nationwide Ceasefire Agreement 2015). While scepticism remained high among some EAO leaders, even its critics agreed that the text, 'encapsulates virtually every issue important to minority communities in war zones', despite a lack of binding commitments on most of these points (Zarni & Kapi 2015).

But ultimately due to trust being so low, the agreement was only signed by eight EAOs at a ceremony on 15 October 2015. Most non-signees refused explicitly due to a last minute government decision to block the PSLF, MNDAA and AA who they were allied with. More generally, however, most groups were reluctant to afford a political victory to the state without greater guarantees for a shift in Tatmadaw behaviour, for their territorial claims to be respected and for political dialogue to be meaningful. Furthermore, with an NLD election victory seemingly on the horizon, many EAO leaders were unsure what the incumbent government could achieve, and had more faith in the NLD's ambition for transformational political change. Nonetheless, the NCA signing signalled a breakthrough in that the commander-in-chief and numerous core members of the former regime signed a commitment to such dialogue for the first time.

Prospects for peace under the NLD-led government

In April 2016, with the NLD-led government newly in place, hopes were high for the much-awaited broad-based political dialogue. The holding of such talks had been the central aim not just of the NLD but of a large bloc of EAOs recently engaged in talks with government. The NLD's commitment to achieving peace through political dialogue was further confirmed in President Htin Kyaw's inaugural address, as he stated as his government's main policies: 'national reconciliation, internal peace, [and] pursuing a constitution toward a federal union'.

Following on from the NCA, the country's first Union Peace Conference was held in January 2016, and was attended by the former government, including President Thein Sein; the Tatmadaw, including the commander-in-chief, Min Aung Hlaing; the NLD, including Aung San Suu Kyi; EAOs that signed the NCA; and other politicians and influential persons. Given the limited mandate of the outgoing government, it was largely a symbolic affair, but a commitment was stated by all participants to continue talks and find ways to bring non-NCA signee EAOs in.

Confidence was also high that the NLD-led government would benefit from trust and support from some leaders of EAOs that aspire to create a democratic, federal system of government. Since the 1990s the KNU has always been forthright in its support for the NLD, regularly issuing statements in favour of the party and its political aims. Other NDF groups that held ceasefires, such as the NMSP, also often issued statements in Aung San Suu Kyi's favour. In a leaked US diplomatic cable from 2008, the KIO was said to view 'its relationship with the NLD as a friendship rather than an alliance, and emphasized it has goals beyond the NLD's, such as preserving their ethnic culture and language'. The KIO was said to be willing to work with any government that can ensure protection of Kachin ethnic rights (Wikileaks 2008). Meanwhile, the United Nationalities Alliance, made up of ethnic parties that competed in 1990 in alliance with the NLD, has maintained strong relations with pro-federal EAOs, and had held similar political demands, primarily for a federal constitution.

In 2014, Aung San Suu Kyi hosted, at her home, leaders from the United Nationalities Federal Council and a bloc of EAOs, including the KIO, NMSP, SSPP and KNPP among others. Later that year, the NLD had its first official meeting with the UNFC alongside other political parties in Thailand. The NLD delegation delivered a signed letter from Aung San Suu Kyi expressing support for the UNFC's political reform efforts (Mon News Agency 2014). Aung San Suu Kyi has also had numerous long meetings in recent years with KNU Vice President Zipporah Sein, who has been vocally sceptical of the peace process led by President Thein Sein. In a December 2015 statement, the KNU Vice President said, 'We accept and support the policies of NLD with regard to democratisation, constitutional amendments, rule of law, peace and national reconciliation. They are in line with the objectives of the EAOs' (Sein 2016).

Since then, however, hope for a comprehensive peace settlement has deteriorated significantly, as armed conflict has continued unabated, and the NLD has failed to demonstrate clear commitment to addressing the root causes of conflict through political reform. The NLD-led government has repeatedly commended the military, while blanketly denouncing the aggression of EAOs, despite the much greater intensity of Tatmadaw use of force. The government has also replaced many of the figures leading the peace process, meaning that crucial, particularly informal, lines of communication between the state and EAOs have been cut. At the same time, despite rhetorical commitment to federalism, the NLD has taken a highly centralised approach to governance and has yet to initiate any meaningful decentralisation reforms. While the NLD appears to be prioritising the building of trust with the Tatmadaw to gain more political elbow room, its recent rhetoric has greatly damaged the trust of EAOs in a negotiated solution.

Ultimately, successful dialogue will depend on the achievement of three-way consensus between the Tatmadaw, the NLD government and the EAOs, with relations between the three parties likely to remain fluid. According to the political dialogue framework agreed by the former government, the talks will conclude with the creation of a Union Accord to be submitted to Parliament, that will lay the 'basis for amending, repealing and adding provisions to the Constitution and laws'. This structure is premised on the hope that political talks can build trust and allow the former antagonists to find common cause and vision, leading to an accord that promises to reform the political order to reflect a basic consensus. Such an agreement would then depend on a carefully managed transition period that sees all parties take steps according to agreed milestones to transform the security environment and hand over governance responsibilities to new or reformed institutions.

In principle, such a transition could include armed actors from any or all sides disbanding, integrating, reforming or establishing new mandates and regulations. In the case of EAOs with deeply rooted administrative, governance and social service bodies, these structures too might be formally reconstituted or integrated into the state, or at least be given a formally agreed mandate. To galvanise the necessary momentum, a broad enough pact would need to be formed from across all parties of individuals that were committed not just to establishing the new order but also to defending it against actors from all sides that would aim to disrupt reforms for their own agendas. Essentially, the process would have to create a state structure that has the empirical capacity to maintain a monopoly over the legitimate use of force, by either incorporating or overriding the many power-holders that currently remain outside of it.

In practice, however, differences in vision and perspective seem so vast that it will be near impossible to negotiate a blueprint for reform that not only gets nominal support from enough parties but actually garners enough enthusiasm for them to agree to give up existing powers. As Tatmadaw negotiators confirmed at the conference in January 2016, they maintain that the current constitutional order does not require any drastic change and seem primarily concerned with determining what concessions they would have to give to persuade EAOs to undergo DDR.[4] The Tatmadaw, whose old slogan ran 'one voice, one blood, one nation', remains staunchly conservative and committed to a centralised and well-ordered system on its own terms, while individual commanders at all ranks benefit greatly from business interests in ethnic areas.

Meanwhile, EAO demands vary greatly, but are all highly ambitious. The pro-federal EAOs are seeking nothing less than an overhaul of the constitution to ensure their states' significant sovereign powers, and a security sector reform agreement that allows them to maintain arms as official but semi-autonomous units, as part of a 'Federal Union Army'. Other EAOs are more concerned with their own regions' autonomy and vary from the UWSP that wishes to constitute a Wa State, removed from Shan State, to the Restoration Council of Shan State, whose constitution maintains an emphasis on gaining self-determination for the Shan people. Meanwhile, Naga armed groups maintain that their region is still an independent nation under foreign occupation. Due to combinations of inertia, deep distrust of government and personal self-interests, individual leaders in these groups then vary greatly in the extent to which they are genuinely committed to reforms that would put them under the authority of future state institutions at all.

Despite the apparent asymmetrical nature of conflicts, EAOs remain extremely resilient and are not on the brink of being forced to cut their losses. In conflict, they often have the advantage of high morale among troops and the ability to quickly find sanctuary, due to knowledge of terrain, deep relations with communities and proximity to international borders. Furthermore, they can benefit greatly from maintaining ceasefires with the government for protracted periods, engaging in business to finance their movements, develop their areas and reap personal profits. They have become well embedded in the political economies of their areas, and are so numerous that the Tatmadaw will remain unable to remove them by force. Indeed, to this day, the Tatmadaw has yet to destroy a single EAO in its entirety. Therefore, they are unlikely to renege on their ultimate aims even if they appear unattainable.

A perhaps more likely, but in no way guaranteed, peace-building scenario is a multi-decade process of détente, whereby a gradual transition brings about a political and security environment that reflects and thus better manages the core interests of all parties. This would likely entail that the Bamar military elite makes incremental concessions to address core ethnic grievances and that institutions are slowly reformed to represent the diversity of politically active elites from different nationalities and societies. Only then would EAOs be likely to seriously consider disbandment or integration into the state system. In some cases, specific deals would be made for the integration of EAOs' governance or security structures into the state system. In other cases, EAOs would just lose their raison d'être as grievances decrease and the economy becomes better regulated, encouraging them to disband. Regrettably, this would likely mean that armed conflicts would continue to ebb and flow, and that coercion would continue to play a role in the processes of resistance and state consolidation. Even if the Myanmar state is able to eventually achieve the level of inclusivity and legitimacy necessary to end ethno-political resistance, it would then continue to face internal threats from a wide range of armed actors concerned primarily with profit.

Whether the political dialogue has the potential to form the kind of broad-based pact necessary to oversee a comprehensive peace transition, or if it will become a first step towards a much longer process of détente, central to its success will be the approach taken by the Bamar military elite. Without a serious commitment to significant decentralisation reforms and a shift away from current military methods, it will be nearly impossible for trust to be built. Without signs of a significant change in the attitude of those controlling the Tatmadaw, ethnic armed conflicts may well get worse before they get better.

Notes

1 Saophas only existed in Shan and Karenni (renamed Kayah in 1954) States. Kachin chiefs, called Duwa, and traditional leaders from Chin, Zomi and other nationalities did not have their positions formally inaugurated though many of them took positions as ministers and MPs.

2 For an overview of the military government's talks undertaken with the KNU, see Keenan (2012). On KNPP and RCSS, see Kramer (2009b, 11–13).

3 Under the charter, locally elected representatives are unable to elect or influence state/region ministers, and have no formal mandate to oversee the core functions of local everyday governance. They can pass laws in only a few limited areas, and these laws cannot contradict those of the Union (Nixon et al. 2013). The most influential government body at all levels, particularly below the states/regions at the district and township levels, is the General Administration Department, which falls under the entirely military-led Union Ministry of Home Affairs (Saw & Arnold 2014).

4 The final NCA text omitted references to DDR, however, and instead stated that 'security integration matters' would be discussed during the political dialogue phase (The Nationwide Ceasefire Agreement 2015). However, according to EAO negotiators, a handbook of materials on SSR compiled and shared at talks by the government in 2015 revolved primarily around DDR processes.

References

Buchanan, J., T. Kramer & K. Woods. 2013. *Developing Disparity—Regional Investment in Burma's Borderlands*. Amsterdam: The Transnational Insititute.

Burma Centre of Ethnic Studies. 2011. 'The Situation in Karen State After the Burmese Election'. In *Ending Armed Conflict in Burma: A Complicated Peace Process*, edited by L. H. Sakhong & P. Keenan, 287–294. Chiang Mai: Burma Centre for Ethnic Studies.

Burma Centre for Ethnic Studies. 2013. 'The Conflict in Kachin State: Time to Revise the Costs of War?' In *Ending Armed Conflict in Burma: A Complicated Peace Process*, edited by L. H. Sakhong & P. Keenan, 266–269. Chiang Mai: Burma Centre for Ethnic Studies.

Human Rights Watch. 2008. *Chronology of Burma's Constitutional Process*. www.hrw.org/sites/default/files/reports/burma0508chronology.pdf

International Crisis Group. 2011. *Myanmar's Post-Election Landscape*. Brussels.

Jolliffe, K. 2015. *Ethnic Armed Conflict and Territorial Administration in Myanmar*. Yangon: The Asia Foundation.

Karen Human Rights Group. 2008. *Village Agency: Rural Rights and Resistance in Militarized Karen State*. Karen Human Rights Group.

Karen Human Rights Group. 2013. KHRG Reports.

Keenan, P. 2012. *The Karen National Union Negotiations 1949–2012*. Chiang Mai: Burma Centre for Ethnic Studies.

Keenan, P. 2014. 'The Burmese Regime's Offensive Against the Shan State Progressive Party/Shan State Army'. In *Ending Ethnic Armed Conflict in Burma: A Complicated Peace Process*, edited by L. H. Sakhong & P. Keenan, 204–213. Chiang Mai: Burma Centre for Ethnic Studies.

KIO. 2011. Mali Nmai Confluence Dam Project. 16 March.

Kramer, T. 2009a. *Burma's Ceasefires at Risk: Consequences of the Kokang Crisis for Peace and Democracy*. Amsterdam: Transnational Insitute.

Kramer, T. 2009b. *Neither War nor Peace: The Future of the Cease-fire Agreements in Burma*. Amsterdam: The Transnational Institute.

Mizzima. 2012. 'Gov't, KIO Agree to Political Dialogue'. 1 November. Accessed 12 December 2015. http://reliefweb.int/report/myanmar/govt-kio-agree-political-dialogue.

Mizzima. 2015. 'Senior General Min Aung Hlaing Says Army Will Respect Election Result'. 20 July.
Mon News Agency. 2014. 'UNFC Congress Postpones Assembly to Meet with National Political Parties'. *Mon News*, September 1. Accessed 10 April 2016. http://monnews.org/2014/09/01/unfc-congress-postpones-assembly-meet-national-political-parties/.
New Light of Myanmar. 2011. 'Press Conference (1/2011) on Government's Efforts to Transform National Race Armed Groups in Accordance with State Constitution Held'. 13 August.
Nixon, H., C. Joelene, K. P. C. Saw, T. A. Lynn & M. Arnold. 2013. *State and Region Governments in Myanmar*. Yangon: The Asia Foundation.
Sakhong, L. H. 2010. 'The Kachin's Dilemma: Become a Border Guard Force or Return to Warfare'. In *Ending Ethnic Armed Conflict in Burma: A Complicated Peace Process*, edited by L. H. Sakhong & P. Keenan, 128–142. Chiang Mai: Burma Centre for Ethnic Studies.
Saw, K. P. C. & Arnold, M. 2014. *Administering the State in Myanmar: An Overview of the General Administration Department*. Yangon: The Asia Foundation.
Sein, Z. 2016. *A Brief NCA History: The NCA's Flaws and Failings*. Zipporah Sein.
Seng, N. 2003. 'Ceasefire Groups Prepare for National Convention'. *The Irrawaddy*, 22 October.
South, A. 2008. *Ethnic Politics in Burma: States in Conflict*. New York: Routledge.
Thai Burma Border Consortium. 2011. *Displacement and Poverty in South East Burma/Myanmar*. Thai Burma Border Consortium.
The Nationwide Ceasefire Agreement. 2015. The Nationwide Ceasefire Agreement Between the Government of the Republic of the Union of Myanmar and the Ethnic Armed Organizations. 15 October. Accessed 12 December 2015. www.mmpeacemonitor.org/images/2015/oct/nca%20contract%20eng.pdf.
United Nations Office of the High Commissioner on Human Rights (UNOHCHR). 2017. Report of OHCHR Mission to Bangladesh: Interviews with Rohingyas Fleeing from Myanmar Since 9 October 2016. Accessed 27 February 2017. www.ohchr.org/Documents/Countries/MM/FlashReport3Feb2017.pdf.
Wikileaks. 2008. Burma: Key Ethnic Cease-Fire Group Talks. 17 January. Accessed 10 April 2016. https://wikileaks.org/plusd/cables/08RANGOON38_a.html.
Zarni, M. & S. Kapi. 2015. 'Divisive Ceasefire Won't Bring Peace'. *DVB*, 9 August.

35

DEMOCRACY AND HUMAN RIGHTS

Morten B. Pedersen

The landslide victory of the National League for Democracy (NLD) in Myanmar's November 2015 elections and subsequent transfer of power to the country's first fairly elected government in more than half a century in April 2016 punctuated one of the most promising democratic breakthroughs anywhere in the world in recent decades. Myanmar, however, remains a limited democracy and establishing genuinely democratic institutions (procedural democracy) that protect human rights under the rule of law (substantive democracy) presents a difficult challenge. This chapter places recent political developments in a historical context, assesses the state of democracy and human rights in the country as the new NLD government approaches its one year anniversary, and considers the prospects for further democratisation. The analysis necessarily paints with broad strokes, but hopefully provides a useful framework for more detailed inquiry.[1]

Historical context

The first constitution of independent Myanmar (then Burma) established a parliamentary democracy. Development of the country's embryonic democratic institutions, however, was disrupted by the outbreak of civil war immediately upon independence in 1948, which prompted a rapid expansion of the military's role in government and eventual capture of power in 1962. Early hopes for freedom and equality thus gave way to the harsh realities of a national security state dominated by the military and oriented primarily towards national security goals.

Like their counterparts in South America around the same time, Myanmar's military leaders came to believe that only the military had the patriotism and discipline required to safeguard the Union against the grave internal and external threats facing it. Thus, they pushed aside the ineffectual parliamentary government and took full control of the country, at first temporarily under a military caretaker government (1958–1960) but then more permanently with the 1962 coup.

Over the following five decades, the military experimented with a succession of political and economic regimes as it sought to build a unified and legitimate state first under the Revolutionary Council (1962–1974) and later under the Burma Socialist Programme Party (1974–1988) and the State Law and Order Restoration Council/State Peace and Development Council (1988–2011). The core of the national security state, however, remained intact. The military maintained direct or indirect control of all three branches of government, as well as the civil service and key parts of the economy. It monopolised the media and established a host of mass organisations that populated the space normally filled by civil society. Through these institutions, the military was able to mobilise a large proportion of the population and the country's resources in support of its national security objectives, while pre-empting the emergence of alternative power structures. Any opposition to the centralising – and supposedly unifying – project of the national security state was harshly dealt with by the security forces, which at times seemed to view the entire population as potential enemies.

The past six years, since the end of direct military rule in 2011, have seen a rolling back of significant elements of the national security state, driven primarily by a reassessment of the country's national security needs. However, Myanmar's military leaders continue to insist that military guidance is required for at least another decade, depending on further consolidation of peace and maturation of democratic institutions. The institutional framework for this guided transition is laid out in the 2008 Constitution, which essentially establishes a dyarchic system with power shared between the elected government and the military.

Current situation

The initial phase of reform under former general President Thein Sein's Union Solidarity and Development Party (USDP) government (2011–2015) saw major progress in a short time across key dimensions of democracy and human rights. After 50 years of insular, security-oriented military rule, the military-as-an-institution stepped away from many areas of government, facilitating a broad shift towards more open and people-oriented governance. This was accompanied by a dramatic expansion of political freedoms, which prompted a virtual explosion in political debate and contestation, much of it driven by a flourishing private and social media. Significant efforts were made also to strengthen socioeconomic and cultural rights, for example, through legalisation of trade unions, increased investments in health and education and expansion of the use of ethnic languages in the media and schools. The national security state, however, still casts a deep shadow over the emerging political system and the country's new democratic institutions remain partial, shallow and low quality.

Partial democracy

The 2008 Constitution was drawn up under the tutelage of the military for the specific purpose of ensuring that the planned transfer of power to a civilian government would not threaten the military's national, corporate and personal interests, and reflects the authoritarian mind-set of its drafters, notably an insistence on centralised power to counter perceived centrifugal forces in society (Pedersen 2011). As such, it has helped create the confidence necessary within the military hierarchy to allow liberalisation, yet imposes fundamental limitations on democracy.

Although the charter formally establishes a multiparty democracy with regular elections and associated civil and political rights, key elements of a democratic system are lacking. Unelected active military officers wield significant executive and legislative influence; the military itself remains largely outside civilian control; and all democratic rights are subject to laws enacted for 'national security' and 'the prevalence of law and order'. Similarly, while the constitution nominally sets up a federal structure of government with a bicameral parliament and fourteen states/divisions of equal status – each with its own executive, legislature and judiciary – actual decentralisation of power is limited. Chief ministers of the states/divisions are appointed by and subject to the will of the president and local governance powers and budgets are extremely limited (Nixon et al. 2013). These shortcomings are compounded by the rules for amending the constitution, which effectively give the military veto power over any future changes.

Shallow democracy

While there is today broad, rhetorical commitment to the ideology of democracy – even within the military – and significant progress has been made also on putting in place key democratic institutions, the deeper political culture is proving highly resistant to change.

The USDP and NLD governments have both evinced deep-seated tensions between their formal commitment to openness and persistent authoritarian mind-sets, notably, in their relations with the media and civil society. While this was perhaps to be expected from an administration led by ex-generals, many have been shocked to witness very similar behaviour under the new leadership of Aung San Suu Kyi and a party which counts scores of ex-political prisoners among its MPs. However, as recent scholarship on Myanmar understandings of democracy and the rule of law has shown, the country's democratic elite may not be all that different from its military nemeses. In investigating different perceptions of democracy in Myanmar, Wells (2015), for example, found that many democracy activists share with the military an emphasis on strong leadership, unity and fulfilment of obligations (as opposed to democratic institutions, pluralism and rights); only they want to 'replace the [supposedly] self-interested dictators of the military era with the self-sacrificing and committed leadership of the opposition'. Similarly, Cheesman (2014) has observed that Aung San Suu Kyi in dealing with key human rights issues has tended to echo the military's understanding that 'the rule of law is achieved through obedience, rather than through substantive practices associated with democratic values'.

Surveys of popular attitudes reinforce these conclusions. Although Myanmar people generally express a strong preference for democracy in the abstract, they show little understanding of the principles and practices that underpin a democratic society, beyond associating it with freedom and a better life (Asia Foundation 2014; Welsh and Huang 2016). In fact, these surveys reveal very low public knowledge about the basic structure and functions of government, beyond the local level.

Low quality democracy

In addition to these legal and cultural limitations – and partly as a consequence of them – Myanmar's embryonic democracy has a long way to go on protecting basic human rights. Although the military's definition of national security threats has narrowed significantly, permitting much greater expression of diverse views – including open criticism of the government but still less so of the military – current law and practice continue to curtail individual freedom in favour of the state's interest in order and stability. This problem is particularly acute in areas of continuing armed conflict where the military essentially operates outside of the law and accusations of the use of excessive force and mistreatment of civilians remain commonplace.

If serious human rights violations were restricted to the hangovers of the national security state and its security agencies, one could perhaps be optimistic that this was a transitory phenomenon destined to diminish with the spread of democracy and peace. However, the problems go deeper than that. One major concern is socio-political and economic discrimination against Muslims in general and the Rohingya in particular, which has actually worsened since the start of reform due in part at least to the competition for votes among the major political parties in a context of widespread popular prejudices against this ethno-religious minority group. Although the NLD appears less openly anti-Muslim than, for example, the USDP and since coming to power has made at least some modest effort to restrain the burgeoning monk-led Buddhist nationalist movement and its incendiary message of 'the Muslim threat', the potential costs to any Myanmar government of upsetting majority Buddhist nationalist sensitivities are far greater than those of ignoring the rights of a small Muslim minority. In this area at least, it is far from assured that democracy in Myanmar will be compatible with international human rights.

Another very serious issue is land rights. Amidst the excitement about Myanmar's overall economic prospects and strong increases in foreign trade and investment since the start of reform, there is growing concern that growth is happening at the expense of ordinary people who are losing their land in the process. While there has been a reduction in the expropriation of land for public purposes, which was rife under the previous military regime, anecdotal evidence suggests that there has been an increase in 'land grabs' by private economic interests seeking to cash in on new economic opportunities. This is in part due to the inadequacies of new investment and land laws, which generally favour investors at the expense of local communities. However, the lack of appropriate legal safeguards is compounded by the weakness of the rule of law, which makes it very difficult for landowners to challenge major private companies that often collude with local administrative authorities to 'legally' displace them in the name of the public interest.

Future prospects

The peaceful transfer of power to the former main opposition party in 2016 is a major waypoint of democratisation, and also provides an opening for deeper reforms under a government that is at least formally committed to protecting international human rights. Yet, even a cursory analysis of the political, institutional and structural conditions for further democratisation reveals the daunting challenges facing the new government.

Political conditions

Comparative studies of the politics of democratic transitions direct our attention to the critical role of decisionmakers – and especially the importance of pacts between old and new elites that satisfy the vital interests of all sides. In Myanmar, this requires pro-democracy forces to find common ground not only with former powerholders in the military, but also ethnic nationalist leaders who have long pursued armed struggle against the Burman-dominated state for increased autonomy, ethnic rights and a fair share of the country's resources.

The military, so far, has played a largely constructive role in the political reform process, and both senior and lower level military officers today speak openly about democracy as the preferred system of government. This tentative buy-in appears to be rooted in four factors (Pedersen 2014a):

- *The institutional self-image and role perceptions of the military* Like the militaries in many developing countries, the Myanmar military considers politics to be part of its 'professional' duties. This reflects its role in the anti-colonial struggle, as well as the continuance since independence of serious internal security challenges to the Myanmar government, which has seen a gradual military role expansion to encompass political, social and economic functions (Myoe 2014). Contrary to conventional wisdom, however, the Tatmadaw has never seen itself as a ruling class. Rather, its self-image is that of 'guardian' of the state, which steps in at times of crisis to save the country. Thus, it was the declared policy of the post-1988 military regime from the beginning to hand back power to a democratically elected government, although one in which the military would continue to play a 'stabilising' role.

- *The failure of the previous military regime to develop the economy* As part of its self-prescribed national leadership role, the military historically has been committed to building a 'modern and developed nation'. Each military coup has been followed by efforts to restructure the economy in line with the ideology of the day – and each of these efforts has ultimately failed. This has been a source of internal military disquiet at least since the early 2000s (Pedersen 2014a), compounded by a growing realisation that Myanmar's continued under-development constitutes a potential existentialist threat to the country in an otherwise rapidly developing region (Crisis Group 2014). The current military leadership is keenly aware that, for Myanmar to re-integrate into the world economy, it needs a more legitimate government as well as better governance and peace in the borderlands.
- *The growing dependence on China* Myanmar's deepening political and economic isolation under the post-1988 military regime drove it into the arms of China, thus upsetting its long-standing non-alignment in international affairs and leaving it vulnerable to unwanted interference from its giant neighbour (Pedersen 2014b). The SLORC/SPDC tried to rebalance Myanmar's position by seeking closer relations with its Southeast Asian neighbours in ASEAN, as well as India and Russia. However, the military leadership recognises that the only effective counterbalance to China is the US and that re-establishing a strategic relationship with Washington requires political reform.
- *Internal concerns about the military's operational effectiveness* The role expansion associated with the national security state has been detrimental to the ability of the armed forces to undertake their primary security functions. The SLORC sought to overcome this problem by undertaking a dramatic expansion of the military. However, this created its own problems of management and discipline. Thus, Commander-in-Chief Min Aung Hlaing has repeatedly emphasised that he wants to develop an 'international standard, regular army', which can stand tall among its peers in the region. This should not be taken to mean that he envisions a total retreat of the military from politics – not yet – but he has taken a number of steps to enhance the army's motivation and fighting abilities (Selth 2015), and is keen to restore access to Western military training facilities and weapons systems (Callahan 2012).

Military support for further democratisation, however, cannot be taken for granted. While the military leadership appears to be quite satisfied with the way 'their' transition is unfolding, they harbour deep, historically rooted distrust of civilian politicians and what they derogatively refer to as 'party politics' (Pedersen 2004) and firmly believe that military supervision of the elected government is needed to safeguard national interests at least for a transitional period. This was relatively unproblematic during the initial phase of reform due to the dominance of retired generals in the Thein Sein administration who enjoyed the trust of their former colleagues in the military and, in turn, respected the military's 'red lines'. Yet, with the transition to an NLD-led administration (and parliament) this organic relationship between the government and the military has been disrupted and the coming years are bound to seriously test the durability of the existing political basis for reform including both its formal (constitutional) and informal elements. It would be particularly dangerous if the NLD were to openly challenge the reserve powers of the military, which are central to the implicit pact underlying the ongoing transition. This is something that the party has so far avoided but is under significant both internal and external pressure to attempt, and indeed must eventually achieve to build a fuller, deeper and higher quality democracy.

The key for the NLD to unlocking the national security state is to negotiate an end to the country's long-standing armed conflicts, which saw the establishment of that state in the first place. This, however, is a complex equation. The ethnic nationalist elite share with the pro-democracy elite a wish to end the dominance of the military in Myanmar politics. However, they are more concerned with self-determination and ethnic rights than democracy per se, and some of the demands implied in their call for 'genuine federalism' do not align easily with the values of either the NLD or the military.

The prospects for successful cooperation between the NLD and ethnic nationalists seemed greatly improved by the emergence in the lead up to the 2015 elections of a large number of ethnic political parties that pursue ethno-nationalist agendas within a democratic political framework and thus in support of the democratisation process. The NLD's landslide election victory, however, had the paradoxical result of marginalising these parties, and the new government has done little to rebuild a pan-ethnic movement for democracy within the parliamentary system. This places a further premium on reaching a successful peace settlement with the older, more established ethnic *armed* groups, which have been fighting the central government for decades and so far are refusing to give up their arms. Without it, militant ethnic nationalists are likely to continue to pursue their goals through military means.

Further complicating matters, the ethnic armed groups are highly diverse. Some, such as the Karen National Union and the New Mon State Party, have a clear political agenda (a 'genuine federal and democratic state') and enjoy broad support among local populations. They have long been providing for the security and social needs of local communities in areas under their control, and since the advent of ceasefires, have generally been acting as 'political parties in waiting'. At the other end of the spectrum, however, are groups such as the United Wa State Army and several other smaller groups in Northern Shan State whose interests lie more in self-enrichment than in providing for local needs. These latter groups have prospered in the absence of any form of state control or rule of law, typically through a mix of shady business and outright criminal activities; they generally have an exploitative, almost feudal, relationship with local communities and have no interest in the democratisation of local politics. In these areas, even a successful peace settlement may do little to advance local democracy and human rights. In fact, any government in Naypyitaw committed to bringing substantive democracy to the Wa region may ultimately have to rely on the threat of military force.

Although all the major groups in Myanmar's highly contested politics appear to recognise that it is not only in the country's but also their own best interest to end decades of bitter conflict and move forward together, the very duration and intensity of those past conflicts and their legacy of deep distrust makes that a very difficult goal to achieve.

Institutional conditions

While committed leaders may be able to establish basic democratic institutions, the failure of many recent democratic transitions to significantly improve human rights demonstrates the importance of the broader institutional context. This dimension has tended to be overshadowed in Myanmar politics and scholarship alike by the long-standing focus on overcoming military resistance to reform, but institutional deficiencies present an equally fundamental obstacle to improving governance and human rights outcomes.

Five decades of top-down military rule, low prioritisation of education and international isolation have dramatically reduced the capacity of Myanmar's once proud civil service to devise and implement good policy (Pedersen 2008). Although there are of course many individual exceptions – and indeed some exceptional individuals – the majority of civil servants lack appropriate education, training and experience, and are often fearful of taking initiative. There are also major problems with corruption, which is pervasive at all levels of the state, reflecting widespread disillusionment with public service jobs and low wages. The weakness of the judicial system is a particular concern since citizens are mostly denied the possibility of seeking protection from and redress of violations of their entitlements.

The NLD government has taken steps to strengthen leadership, streamline procedures and cajole civil servants to recommit to public service. However, the pool of new talent is limited and changing the underlying institutional culture and behaviour patterns is a long-term challenge. Thus, the new government – like previous ones – is likely for the foreseeable future to struggle to ensure that new policies are properly implemented and results are felt on the ground. This will be particularly challenging within policy areas where it shares power with the military, requiring an extra layer of negotiations, as well as in conflict-affected areas where all central government authorities suffer from a serious lack of legitimacy, if indeed they have access at all.

Meanwhile, it must be recognised that the political parties and civil society organisations driving the new reform agenda have internal limitations too. Most if not all political parties, including the NLD, have a strongly hierarchical structure with decision-making centralised at the top level and communicated downwards. There is little role for local party chapters – except in helping identify local candidates for elections – and links with local constituencies, as well as civil society organisations, are weak (Kempel et al. 2015). The parties' ability to aggregate and articulate citizens' interests before the state is therefore very limited. They are also generally weak in engaging and involving citizens – or even their own members – in democratic participation.

Myanmar's civil society organisations, similarly, are dominated by members of the narrow, but growing, intellectual/educated middle class. This is especially the case for the more political-oriented organisations, including the media. They represent a counter-elite – and perhaps politicians-in-waiting – rather than a genuine grassroots response (although this of course does not preclude them from genuinely working to promote the interests of local communities). The Sangha and the churches are more genuinely mass-based organisations, but the former has played a distinctly ambiguous role in the reform process due to its role in the rise of extremist Buddhist nationalism and the latter lack national political influence. Most religious leaders are active mainly in humanitarian work.

Structural conditions

Underlying the institutional deficiencies of the Myanmar state and society are a number of deeper structural factors even less amenable to negotiation and reform, including the country's lack of historical experience with democracy, deep ethnic divisions, economic underdevelopment and its location in a region where democracy has yet to gain a strong foothold.

Empirically, countries that have prior – and especially recent – experience with democracy tend to democratise faster and more thoroughly. This is likely because elements of democratic culture and behaviour have survived alongside later authoritarian structures. Myanmar has no such head start. Its prior experience with democracy in the 1950s was not only short and limited in depth but also a long time ago. Anyone who was politically aware and active in the period of parliamentary democracy is at least 70 years old today. With the partial exception of exiles who have spent significant parts of their lives abroad, any knowledge of democracy is therefore theoretical and contrasts sharply with a lifetime of practical experience of highly authoritarian, militarised structures. This invariably means that it will take time for practice to catch up with the form of Myanmar's new democratic institutions.

The challenges arising from the absence of democratic roots are compounded by the difficulty of instituting a system of majority rule in a country which has several major ethnic minority groups with long-standing aspirations for self-determination and self-expression. While comparative scholars disagree whether ethnic diversity is inherently detrimental to the success of democratic government, Myanmar faces a steep challenge in overcoming the deep-rooted divisions of the past.

The incessant wars since independence have caused a hardening of ethnic identities, which today permeate all areas of politics. Most political parties have ethnic designations and civil society groups, too, mostly form along ethnic lines. This is problematic because – even more so than other socio-political cleavages – ethno-religious identity tends to divide groups deeply, making moderation and compromise difficult. Even if different ethnic elites could find a way to work together, the brutality of the military's decades-long counter-insurgency operations – which have relied primarily on violence rather than winning hearts and minds – has left deep scars of enmity and distrust of state institutions among minority communities. Many people in Myanmar's borderlands simply do not feel part of the Union of Myanmar. This greatly complicates efforts to strengthen state institutions and deliver any substantive benefits of democratic government to these communities.

The recent communal conflict between Buddhist and Muslim communities has added a further and potentially even harsher dimension to this problem since it overlaps with a deep-rooted xenophobic element of Burman culture. Thus, while most Burman do see, for example, the Shan, Karen and Rakhine as legitimate members of the Myanmar polity, many consider the majority of Muslims to be foreigners and a potential threat to both race and religion. Similar attitudes apply, although with less vehemence, to other citizens of Chinese or South Asian origin, although the main concern here is less race and religion than it is economic exploitation.

Economically, too, Myanmar would appear a poor candidate for democracy. Despite significant economic growth in recent years, it remains one of the poorest countries in Asia. This may not be an obstacle to democratisation per se, but it does make it much harder for democracy to thrive, mostly due to its negative implications for political participation. Faced with grinding poverty, people naturally withdraw into the household to address pressing needs. They have neither the time nor resources to take an active interest in public affairs. This is confirmed by recent national surveys, which show that traditional, 'survival' values are far more prevalent in Myanmar than the modern, 'self-expression' values normally associated with democratic progress (Asia Foundation 2014; Welsh and Huang 2016). Although recent growth in communications, media and civil society activity is very positive, it is still primarily an urban, middle class phenomenon. The large majority of Myanmar people remain isolated from the country's new democratic politics; they participate at most through their vote on elections day and have limited understanding of the basis and function even of that process. Even if fully implemented, a system of one citizen–one vote would leave large segments of the population effectively unable to make meaningful demands on the government because they lack the political resources to do so. The dangers in this are all too evident in the failure of elites on all sides to protect the interests of some of the most vulnerable groups in the country.

The country's low economic development level also makes it harder to maintain moderate politics. Poverty is generally associated with higher levels of conflict over the distribution of scarce resources. Moreover, it increases the risk that demagogues can successfully mobilise people against outgroups such as ethnic or religious minorities. These phenomena are currently playing out with particular force in Rakhine State where democratisation has been accompanied by an escalation in long-standing communal conflict between Buddhist and Muslim communities. However, it could easily become a broader problem if the NLD government's economic reform programme fails to bring sufficient benefits quickly and equally.

Finally, it is important to consider the political systems of Myanmar's regional neighbours. While much attention has been paid recently to the democratising impact of increased cooperation with Western countries and international organisations, the more diffuse effects of regional contagion are likely to matter more in the long run, after the initial excitement evaporates. Myanmar's neighbours are not only *not* committed to exporting political freedom, rule of law and human rights; the majority are in fact models of something far less appealing. As such, they provide rich examples of alternative paths to modernity should key Myanmar elites come to view democracy as threatening.

None of this is to suggest that Myanmar's limited democracy is doomed. However, it is crucial to recognise that rather than simply undergoing a transition from military to democratic rule, the country is in fact in the midst of several simultaneous transformations, which include also shifts from war to peace, state capitalism to a liberal market economy, and towards much greater integration into the global community and economy. In some respects, this complexity may be an advantage as different groups can 'win' in different areas, thus moderating the intensity of competition over any given value. However, it also multiplies the potential flash points and places enormous demands on a government which has little capacity to fulfil them.

Conclusion and reflection

Unlike recent transitions in the Middle East and North Africa, the reform process in Myanmar was initiated by the previous military government from a position of strength and remains carefully managed. Indeed, the military leadership does not claim that the new system is democratic, but rather that they are effecting a gradual transition to democracy, the scope and speed of which will depend on broader social conditions.

The constitutional limits currently placed on Myanmar's embryonic democratic institutions are not necessarily detrimental to the country's long-term political development, as they ensure that reforms remain in line with the realities of power in the country and thus may help maintain stability in a period of great flux and uncertainty. However, they do hamper efforts to deal with deep-rooted governance problems and issues of injustice, and risk becoming an entrenched feature of the new political system.

As in other emerging democracies, the fundamental challenge in Myanmar is to move from procedural to a more substantive democracy (even as the former remains a work in progress). This is, to borrow from Carothers (2006), essentially an issue of 'representation' – i.e. of establishing a government that is not merely elected by the people but actually serves the people. Representation, in turn, requires an interconnected set of institutions and socio-political conditions, including a citizenry capable of expressing its interests, a state capable of meaningfully responding to citizens' needs, and organisations capable of effectively connecting citizens and the state. To develop those will take time, effort and probably quite a bit of luck.

Note

1 Although the overall argument presented in the present chapter is novel, the supporting analysis draws on a number of other publications and unpublished policy papers by the author on the same topic, in particular Pedersen (2004, 2008, 2011 and 2014a).

References

Asia Foundation. 2014. *Myanmar 2014: Civic Knowledge and Values in a Changing Society*. San Franciso: The Asia Foundation.

Callahan, Mary. 2012. 'The Generals Loosen Their Grip'. *Journal of Democracy* 23 (4): 120–130.

Carothers, Thomas. 2006. *Confronting the Weakest Link: Aiding Political Parties in New Democracies*. Washington, DC: Carnegie Endowment for International Peace.

Cheesman, Nick. 2014. 'What Does the Rule of Law Have to Do with Democratization in Myanmar?' *Southeast Asia Research* 22 (2): 213–232.

Crisis Group. 2014. *Myanmar's Military: Back to the Barracks?* Asia Briefing No. 143. Yangon/Brussels, 22 April. Available at https://www.crisisgroup.org/asia/south-east-asia/myanmar/myanmar-s-military-back-barracks (accessed 30 September 2017).

Kempel, Susanne, Chan Myawe Aung Sun, and Aung Tun. 2015. *Myanmar Political Parties at a Time of Transition: Political party dynamics at the national and local level*. Report prepared for Pyoe Pin Programme.

Myoe, Maung Aung. 2014. 'The Soldier and the State: The Tatmadaw and Political Liberalization in Myanmar since 2011'. *Southeast Asia Research* 22 (2): 1–16.

Nixon, Hamish, et al. 2013. *State and Region Governments in Myanmar*. San Francisco: The Asia Foundation.

Pedersen, Morten B. 2004. 'The World According to Burma's Military Rulers'. In *The Illusion of Progress: The Political Economy of Reform in Burma/Myanmar*, edited by David Mathieson and Ron J. May. Adelaide: Crawford House.

Pedersen, Morten B. 2008. *Promoting Human Rights in Burma: A Critique of Western Sanctions Policy*. Denver: Rowman & Littlefield.

Pedersen, Morten B. 2011. 'The Politics of Transition in Burma: Opportunities for Change and Options for Democrats'. *Critical Asian Studies* 43 (1): 49–68.

Pedersen, Morten B. 2014a. 'Myanmar's Democratic Opening: The Process and Prospects of Reform'. In *Debating Democratization in Myanmar*, edited by Nick Cheesman et al., 19–42. Singapore: ISEAS.

Pedersen, Morten B. 2014b. 'Myanmar Foreign Policy in a Time of Transition'. In *Myanmar's Growing Regional Role*, edited by Abraham Denmark and Meredith Miller. Washington, DC: National Bureau of Asian Research.

Selth, Andrew. 2015. *Strong, Fully Efficient and Modern: Myanmar's New Look Armed Forces*. Regional Outlook Paper No. 49. Brisbane: Griffith Asia Institute.

Wells, Tamas. 2015. 'Behind Myanmar's Elections: Contrasting Narratives of Democratization'. Paper presented at the Myanmar Update Conference, Australian National University, June 6–7.

Welsh, Bridget and Kai-Ping Huang. 2016. *Myanmar's Political Aspirations & Perceptions 2015 Asian Barometer Survey Report*. Selangor, Malaysia: Strategic Information and Research Development Centre. Available at www.asianbarometer.org/publications//db7ebcc178a8b76d98d083e920.

36
GENDER

Ma Khin Mar Mar Kyi

Myanmar is at last entering a period of democratisation. Daw Aung San Suu Kyi not only won a landslide victory in the elections of 8 November 2015, but within the first week of the new parliament, she successfully managed to choose a well-educated, loyal comrade-in-arms to be President of Myanmar. She outsmarted the military by creating a designation of her role as 'state counsellor', to circumvent the much anticipated military restriction in the very Constitution that bars her from the presidency, no doubt causing irritation for the military. This role gives her greater authority to guide both the government and the parliament and cements her influence over the executive and legislative branches. Notwithstanding, it is the first time in the history of Myanmar that a Burmese female politician has managed to lead the country. Males still overwhelmingly dominate parliament, especially compared with other ASEAN member states. This chapter will discuss how women continue to face structural gender-based discrimination and decline of their positions in society as a result of the prolonged period of military rule and its associated militarisation of culture with political ideologies.

Women and political representation

Myanmar was ruled by military and para-military regimes from the time it gained independence from the British in 1948, except for a brief period of democracy in the 1950s. More than half a century of military rule has impacted on every aspect of society, particularly gender power relations, due to the introduction of extreme patriarchal ideologies and policies of the military. Myanmar is a country with a diverse, multi-ethnic population of over 51 million people. According to the 2014 census, the first census in 30 years, the female population outnumbers males: 26.59 million to 24.82 million out of a total population of 51,419,420 (UNFPA 2015).

There was not a single woman in the State Law and Order Restoration Council (SLORC) (1988–1997) or its 39-member cabinet, or in all 19 State Peace and Development Councils (1997–2010). The 2006 National Convention included only 67 women among its 1,013 representatives and only 20 women were among the 659 members 'elected' to parliament in 2010 (Khin Mar Mar Kyi 2014). The Union Solidarity and Development Party (USDP) (2010–2015) had only 2 per cent female representatives in the 2010 election. In the 2012 by-elections, the National League for Democracy won seats for 12 females, including party leader Daw Aung San Suu Kyi, out of 43 elected parliamentarians, yet female representation made up just 4.6 per cent of nation-wide female representatives. Myanmar recorded the lowest level of female representatives in the Asia region (Khin Mar Mar Kyi 2014; see also Aung & Solomon 2015).

In order to achieve her position as Myanmar's first female political leader, Daw Aung San Suu Kyi took nearly 26 years, two landslide victories (1990, 2015), 15 years of house arrest, and many turbulent years in both her personal and political life. She had to win 83 per cent of the seats (in order to outvote the combined bloc of ex-military USDP and military, which automatically makes up 25 per cent of the seats in parliament). The military still managed to bar her appointment to her rightful position of president via the 2008 Constitution that they carefully instituted.

Although her achievement is remarkable, the National League for Democracy (NLD) set up a new cabinet on 1 April 2016 with 18 members, and there is no woman in the cabinet apart from Daw Aung San Suu Kyi herself. To put it differently, the current parliament has overall doubled the number of female parliamentarians, but women still represent less than 10 per cent of parliamentarians, and Myanmar remains at the bottom of the gender equality index in Asia. The NLD party itself decreased by half the number of women candidates in the 2015 election compared with the 2012 by-elections. The democratic government is still male dominated; nine out of ten newly elected MPs (87 per cent) are male.

It is also ironic, as the 2016 current democratic parliament has many (compared with previous parliaments) able, confident, politically, socially and economically successful and proven self-educated women leaders. They have succeeded in their fight to reach their positions as parliamentarians at the highest decision-making level of the country, and likely by their own efforts without much support from their families and against social norms, as well as counter to religion and the prevailing political culture in Myanmar. Some have faced imprisonment with the sheer courage of commitment, yet now face the glass-ceiling of gender relations in Myanmar. The exclusion of such able women leaders, who are already present in the parliament, from the cabinet indicates the glass-ceiling of gender in the parliament in Myanmar, even under a democratic female leader who herself has to continue to struggle to take her rightful place as elected leader of the country.

When asked the reason for the lack of support for female political representation, the NLD spokesperson said there is a popular tendency to think that the inequality of women is due to their culture and religion (Macgregor 2015). Myanmar needs to mandate the adoption of affirmative action to ensure women's equal participation at all levels via a quota system, reservation or mandatory policies, which may open up political space for women. Historically, there is evidence of female leadership in the history of Myanmar, with women acting as judges, village heads, official ministers, government officials, influential queens and mayors (BSPP 1975; Tin 1935; Khaing 1984; U Hla 1966), though they may not have been equal in numbers to males in these roles.

Buddhism and gender

Myanmar has been a Buddhist country since the eleventh century (Khin Mar Mar Kyi 2013). Buddhism will continue to influence Burmese gender relations, as it stresses different values, responsibilities and norms between the sexes, though it offers contradictory gendered roles and meanings (see Horner 1961(1930); Thitsa 1980; Gross 1993).

Indeed, the role of women in Buddhism was also changed because of the loss of Burmese Bhikkhuni, or female monks, since the end of Bagan in the 13th century. There is evidence of female monks' equal title, honour and participation in religious ceremonies as 'the same honor as monks' at the time (Tin 1935, 413; Sein 1986, 233). Attempts to revive the female

Bhikkhuni monastic order is by law a criminal offence in 2015 under section 295 (a) for 'abusing religion' (Radio Free Asia 7 August 2005; *The Irrawaddy* 31 December 2005). The disappearance of female Bhikkhuni in Myanmar may have influenced gender relations.

The Burmese believe that the fundamental difference between men and women is *hpon* (glory, power and charisma). Although the origin and the meaning of *hpon* are obscured, Burmese believe that *hpon* is the fundamental difference between men and women. Men are considered to be born with *hpon* on their right shoulder, and women are considered spiritually lower because they are born without *hpon* (glory, power and charisma) (Khin Mar Mar Kyi 2004). As men alone have *hpon*, men alone can become *hpon-ji* (big *hpon* or male monks), thus securing one of the highest social orders, access to monastic institutions.

Women who cannot be monks are treated as having a lower spiritual status. They are called *Thilashin*, 'keepers of the precepts', only. They are viewed as women 'whose sons are dead, who are widowed, bankrupt, in debt, and broken-hearted' and they have to struggle against 'hardship and discrimination in society, within the nunnery . . . in the hierarchy of the monastic institution itself' (Kawanami 1990, 163–164). At best, they can only be the best supporter of the Sangha by their deeds in this life and earn merit to be reborn as a man in the next life (Khin Mar Mar Kyi 2004). With up to 90 per cent of the population being Buddhist, these Buddhist practices and beliefs reinforce women's inferior status.

Gender and sexuality

Traditional Burmese culture provided women with a high degree of gender equality, particularly 'sexual egalitarianism in social and economic affairs that may be unique in the Southeast Asian region' (Muller 1994). Myanmar was annexed by the British in three wars in 1824–1826, 1852–1853 and 1885. Most British colonial administrators and missionaries had recorded the remarkable position of women in Myanmar. For example, a colonial administrator, V.C. Scott O'Connor, notes that '*every writer* on Burma recorded the remarkable status attained by Burmese women in the public sphere, decision-making and control over finance . . . in advance of more reputedly civilized countries in the status it accords to its women' (O'Connor 1983, 42; italics mine) who are 'much more independent than any European even in the most advanced nations' (Scott 1882/1989, 52), and 'more surprising [this is the case] *in marriage and divorce*' (Brown 1926; italics mine).

Nonetheless, these colonial men's gazes were fixed only on the remarkable position of Burmese women, and were twisted, by the British Victorian mode of masculinity at the time, to see this as an indicator of 'barbaric' and 'uncivilised' social customs that favoured women (Brown 1926; Hall 1945; Kelly 1905). Some even linked the positions of Burmese women with the apparent failure of the nation and men, and even appealed to Burmese men that 'the world is a man's world, [Burmese men] must learn to be a man . . . for the future of the nation' (Fielding 1906, 266–267).

The impact of such gender discrimination was clearest in their views of Burmese women's sexuality. Traditionally, Burmese marriage is civil, and according to Burmese traditional customs a marriage was legalised if a couple were: (i) given in marriage by their parents, (ii) by the intervention of a go-between and (iii) by mutual consent, or (iv) by living and eating together. Other public acceptance of marriage occurred if a woman allowed a man to hang his clothing on a *paso* – a beam inside a woman's house – that would result in their recognition as a married couple, *paso-tan–tin–akyin–lin–maya* (Khin Mar Mar Kyi 2013).

Intermarriage between Burmese women and foreigners rapidly increased in the colonial era. However, because of the different cultural attitudes towards marriage, the traditional rights of women in marriage were no longer recognised. Although Buddhist Law in section 6 of the Burma Courts Act of 1872 dealt with succession, inheritance or marriage, for the Burmese, there was no provision regarding mixed marriages (Gutter 2001). Because of Burmese cultural resistance to gender equality, the Special Marriage Act of 1872 was amended in 1923, followed by the 1939 Act, the predecessor of The Buddhist Women's Special Marriage and Succession Act, or The Buddhist Women's Special Marriage and Succession Act of 1954, which was amended.[1] It means that, under section 21, if a Buddhist woman lived with a non-Buddhist man even without registration or religious authority, they were recognised as a husband and wife in line with Burmese culture (Gutter 2001).[2] This is the only Special Marriage Act in Asia that aims to protect the rights of Buddhist women (Kyaw 1988; Khin Mar Mar Kyi 2004). In other words, Myanmar already had progressive laws and only needed to add other laws with consultation with women to protect them.

Furthermore, the Married Property Act (1828), Matrimonial Causes Act (1857) and Married Women's Property Act (1893) also ensured a divorced Burmese Buddhist wife could keep the property that she had earned. Indeed, the first Married Women's Property Act laws for the protection of Burmese women were more advanced than those introduced in England in 1870. Thus, some argued that, long before it was the case in England, Burmese women could own property both before and after marriage (Sein 1972, 291).

Nonetheless, nationalism has further disadvantaged women more than their male counterparts. Burmese nationalists re-invented traditional culture with reference to Western concepts of a modern nation state, and stressed the legitimacy of masculine dominance to suit their needs (Khin Mar Mar Kyi 2013; see also Chatterjee 1989; McClintock 1995). They even managed to promote the view that women who had sexual relationships with men of other racial, religious and national backgrounds were 'traitors' to the nation, sovereignty, race and religion with ethno-centric Burmese identity, with the motto of 'to be Burmese is to be a Buddhist'(Ma Ma Lay 1955, 1973; Khin Mar Mar Kyi 2004). Women who married Muslims were particularly denounced, to such an extent that mixed marriages were the main reason for the third Burmese Indo racial riots in 1938, and the foundation of the Do Bamar 'Our Burma' or 'We Burmese' organisation (see Yi 1988). The Burmese military regime's inherited gender ideologies were once again revived as they faced an opposition led by a woman who was married to a man from a former coloniser.

Gender and the Constitution

The endorsement of Myanmar's Constitution via a referendum in 2008 aimed to legalise structural discrimination against women. Sections 347 and 348 of the 2008 Constitution guarantee legal equality of all citizens, regardless of gender, and prohibit discrimination based on sex. Section 249 ensures equal opportunities in public employment and occupation, and section 350 provides for equal pay for equal work. However, the Constitution also, ironically, requires that the president have a military 'vision' or 'outlook' (Constitution 2008). It is therefore very difficult for a woman to become president, as the military is considered to be a male profession and a male dominated area. Women hold a little over 1 per cent of the lower positions in the current military, out of half a million members.

This is despite the fact that Myanmar is party to the Convention on the Elimination of all forms of Discrimination against Women (CEDAW), which commits signatories to eliminate discrimination against women. Unsurprisingly, the 2008 Constitution was an attempt to exclude a particular woman from the presidency, Daw Aung San Suu Kyi, and to ensure exclusive masculine dominance in politics and the legal institutionalisation of structural discrimination towards women.

More disturbingly, section 352 of the Constitution specifically refers to 'positions that are suitable for men only' (Constitution 2008). This explicitly illustrates the structural nature of gender discrimination in politics and the Constitution. While the Constitution discriminates against women, it provides a guarantee for the permanent role of the military in the country's decision-making processes, accounting for 25 per cent of the seats in both houses of the parliament. This does not bode well for Myanmar, as research has found that countries where women hold more than 33 per cent of the seats in parliament have higher scores in human development indices than nations with a lower female representation (Bari 2000).

Women's rights in the reform era

Even in the reform era (2012–2015) the military regime has managed to further diminish the customary rights of women in marriage. The outbreak of racial, communal and sectarian conflicts in many parts of Burma were ostensibly inflamed by the rape case of Ma Thida Htwe – a 26-year-old Rakhine woman who was gang raped and killed by three young Muslim men in Rakhine state on 26 May 2012. The brutal rape was quickly politicised, and led to the foundation of the Organisation for the Protection of Race, Religion and Belief, better known by its Burmese acronym Ma Ba Tha. However, the actual gender violence that women in general face in Rakhine state was moved out of the political gaze, even though the motto of Ma Ba Tha was a 'Buddhist woman raped in every town' (Radio Free Asia 16 January 2014; Mann 2014).

In 2013, within six months, U Wirathu, the leader of Ma Ba Tha, submitted to parliament a set of four interconnected 'Laws for the Protection of Race & Religion' or Myanmar Women's Special Marriage Law. Myanmar's two most powerful exclusive male institutions – the military regime and religious institutions – have supported these laws. Many people respect monks, and believing that these laws will provide much needed security for them, supported the laws (Khin Mar Mar Kyi 2014).

Ma Ba Tha used threat and intimidation to warn Burmese not to oppose these laws. Many women activists, including the UN Special Rapporteur on Myanmar, Ms Yanghee Lee, were verbally attacked by the head of Ma Ba Tha, U Wirathu, a teaching abbot of thousands of monk-students, at a public assembly in Rangoon. In front of the crowd and with the support of the monks, he then verbally abused the female UN Special Rapporteur, with gender-specific discriminative, vulgar and profane words denouncing her anatomy, morality, dignity and promiscuity to humiliate and shame her (Mann & Michaels 2013).

Even more worrying, U Wirathu threatened to use physical violence, stating 'let us find ways and means to teach the beastly woman a lesson . . . by beating with my slipper' (Mann & Michaels 2013). The use of sexually coarse and vulgar language was aimed to humiliate a prominent woman publicly, and suggests how ordinary Burmese women are to be silenced by the normalisation of masculine violence in Myanmar. Almost entirely without any participation by women in the decision, the entire package of 'Race and Religion Protection Laws', or Myanmar Women's Special Marriage Law, was passed. These laws included the Population Control Bill No. 28/2015 (May 2015), Religious Conversion Bill No. 48/2015 (28 August 2015),[3] Buddhist Women Special Marriage Law No. 50/2015 (31 August 2015)[4] and Law on the Practice of Monogamy No. 54/2015 (August 2015).[5]

Human rights and the anti-interfaith marriage laws

Unsurprisingly, another indicator of male dominance is also reflected in the approval of the new anti-interfaith marriage laws of 2015.These anti-interfaith marriage laws contravene the Universal

Declaration of Human Rights. Article 16 states that 'Men and women of full age, without any limitation due to race, nationality or religion, have the right to marry.' The new bill, which effectively denies women the right of choosing a husband of a different religion without official permission, is not only a violation of basic human rights but also contrasts and reduces her customary and traditional rights (Khin Mar Mar Kyi 2013).

These laws will impact severely on women in Myanmar. Take, for example, the new Population Control Healthcare Bill, which criminalises women by mandating a three-year gap between births. This law legally removes Burmese women's autonomy over their body and reproductive rights. Myanmar does not have an adequate domestic violence law, while under the current penal code spousal rape is criminalised only if the wife is under 14 years of age. Pregnancies may not be by the choice of women, yet they are responsible for their reproductive health.

Culturally Burmese believe that reproductive health issues are women's sole responsibility, thus their husbands may not be liable on such issues. Abortion is strictly illegal – unless the woman's life is in danger. Even if they survive, they will experience the social stigma attached to abortion. It may lead women in desperate situations to risk their health, as they may seek unlawful and unsafe abortions. Now women are confronted with impossible choices: to risk their life or to face imprisonment. There are no refuge centres, helplines or counselling available regarding women's health care and welfare issues such as sexual health or domestic violence. Unsurprisingly, the underlying theme of the Ma Ba Tha's rhetoric is similar to that of the military regime and is based on men's interests alone.

Gender and development

Evidence has indicated that economic development and the empowerment of women are closely related (UNDP 2015). Yet despite some progress, Burmese women continue to face a number of challenges, including deteriorating conditions of employment, income and job security. Empowering women is crucial to economic development. Amartya Sen, Nobel laureate, Harvard economist and a founder of UNDP's Human Development Index, has long argued that women's agency and freedom are two crucial ingredients for economic development (Sen 1990). Evidence has indicated that the majority of the world's poor are women (Global Citizen 2012). UNIFEM has argued that a major factor underlying the feminisation of poverty is the lack of power of women (Khin Mar Mar Kyi 2014, 309) and women are central actors making the case for sustainable development (Sen 1999; UNDP 2012).

Women experience a higher incidence and a more extreme and structural experience of poverty, and more barriers to escape out of poverty, than men. Female-headed households are often the 'poorest of the poor', as they are mostly engaged in agriculture, industry and the informal sector. The equal participation of women is one of the key ingredients for the development of a nation (Sen 1999). It is crucial to remove social, political and cultural constraints and barriers that handicap women. Women's alternative skills, experiences, values and solutions would be crucial to solving extraordinary challenges that the current democratic government is facing.

Decades of militarisation and the military's promotion of patriarchal values have resulted in limited opportunities and independence for women in employment. Indeed, the gender gap is particularly apparent in the labour market. In general, female workers predominate in low paid jobs, especially in textile, shoe and hat factories, where more than 90 per cent of 300,000 workers are women and the majority are under 25 (Oxfam 2016), and they are often recruited at between 13 and 15 years of age (Htun 2012, 13). The labour process has heavily gendered assumptions: women can be paid lower wages (wages for a man are 2,500 kyats and for a woman 2,000 kyat for the same job), are seen as easier to control, desperate to work, and likely to be obedient and able to be pressured to work harder to meet the quota of the daily production line. Also, there is almost always a male manager who controls, instructs and disciplines female employees in these factories. Structural inequality, which includes ideologically charged and gender-specific values and responsibilities, leads women to accept these arrangements.

Since reform, there has been an increase in protests at factories in industrial areas. For example, from May to June in 2012, a total of 56,551 workers across 90 textile, shoe and hat factories staged protests against their working conditions (Lwin 2014).

They have long working days (7am to 7pm are normal working hours), are without sanitary drinking water and face other inhumane conditions. Analysis of their wages paints a disturbing picture of how these women's labour and human rights are exploited. For example, many workers receive basic pay of as little as 350 kyats (30 cent per day or almost 30 kyat per hour), and make a little over 10,000 kyats per month (US$8), which covers 50 per cent of their rent for a place in a shared room. In order to survive, they must work obediently and diligently to complete an almost impossible daily quota to get an extra 'dutiful bonus' of 22,000 kyats, without 'absence' bonus of 4,000 kyats, so called 'pocket money and travel allowance' of 2,700 kyats and the cost of living allowance of 5,000 kyat (US$1=1,200 kyat, 2016). Only then, a worker would earn as little as around 50,000 kyats per month, after having 465 kyats deducted for the social security scheme (Lwin 2014).

For mere survival, they have to work overtime, and yet 'half of them are in debt and constantly borrowing money for basic needs such as food, medicine and transportation' while they are working 11 hours a day 6 days a week' (Oxfam 2016). Although these women are working on Western high street fashion labels such as Gap, Primark, H&M and Tesco, and working in profitable industries, their basic rights are simply ignored.

Similarly Action Labour Rights released a report entitled 'Under Pressure' in March 2016 after collecting data from 1,200 employees in 39 factories in April–June 2015. Of these employees, 30 per cent were forced to work overtime of 16 hours a week, and 62 per cent reported that they were not allowed to refuse to work overtime. As many as two-thirds of workers (63 per cent) said that they did not have enough money to survive; 30 per cent of workers said they were provided pay slips in English or Korean only (Action Labour Rights 2016).

Health, occupational safety and proper fire exits are almost non-existent, and one in three workers has been injured at work (Oxfam 2016). The gender relations in the informal labour sector suggest how gender-specific conservative patriarchal norms and policies harm women, who form the majority of the population in Myanmar. These problems are reinforced by a lack of awareness, and inequality, which is so culturally ingrained that many think it is normal.

Growing protests over land rights issues involving women in recent years suggest the extent of land rights issues face by women, particularly involving development projects. As 70 per cent of the population live and work in the agricultural sector, it is a critical area for the socio-economic development of the country. Although the National Land Use Policy Paragraph 10(b) of the National Land Law seems to 'provide equal rights in all sectors for women for land use and secure land tenure', men and women have different access to land and land-related decision-making processes (Thein 2015).

A Transnational Institute (2015) report also suggests that land rights and agriculture are gendered. While there is a zero illiteracy rate among farmers who are male heads of house, this compares with 8 per cent for female household heads (Kyaw & Routray 2006). Female farmers earn 20 per cent less than men for the same job (Oxfam 2014, 12). Women also outnumber men as landless farmers; 20 per cent of female workers had no land compared with 6 per cent of male farmers. Even if they own land, women own smaller farms compared with men, with an average of 4.4 acres for men and 2.2 acres for women (Kyaw & Routray 2006). This has forced women to migrate, both internally and overseas, including to Thailand, to work in labour intensive jobs, as they lack alternative economic opportunities in Burma compared with men (Khin Mar Mar Kyi 2013).

The Draft National Land Use Policy, Paragraph 78, also refers to women's inheritance rights and yet, in most cases, wives' names or signatures do not appear on land title documentation at the registry (Transnational Institute 2015). Protecting and securing women's access to land can reduce the vulnerability of women in many ways. As Rasghida Manjoo, the Special Rapporteur on Violence Against Women, emphasises: 'The empowerment and equal right of women in agricultural and land rights, is the single most critical contributor to violations of the economic, social and cultural rights of women among the agrarian economies of most developing countries' (Manjoo 2011). The security of women's land and property rights can increase agricultural productivity. The Convention on the Elimination of Discrimination Against Women (CEDAW) highlights 'the significant roles which rural women play in the economic survival of their families' (FAO 2011), which in turn 'determines the ability of family members, especially children, to prosper' (Oxfam 2014, 17). Thus, women's lack of access to land will affect the welfare of the family as well as the future of their children, and can lead to negative consequence for their independence, survival, safety, security and rights. This is why gender issues related to land and agricultural policies need to be addressed in gender sensitisation programmes. It is not a coincidence that, as the United Nations Human Development index reflects, Myanmar was ranked 149th out of 186 countries in 2013 and was one of the lowest ranked ASEAN nations on the index (UNDP 2013).

Women in education

Although evidence indicates that education plays a crucial role, and is one of the main forms of capital for human development, government funding for education in Myanmar is minimal, tied only with the health sector. The government of Myanmar spent the lowest proportion of GDP in the region on education, with as little as 1.4 per cent of GDP in 2011/2012 and 2012/2013 (JICA 2013). Education is a female dominated profession. Women outnumber men in all ranks of students from the undergraduate to the postgraduate level, as well as among staff, as tutors, demonstrators, lecturers, assistant lecturers, professors and assistant professors (see Table 36.1).

Table 36.1 Gender breakdown of higher education students, by level, 2012

	Male	*Female*	*% of total student population*	*Total*
Undergraduates	201,762	296,725	59	498,487
MA/MSC qualifying	156	915	87	1,071
Postgraduate diploma	473	1,309	73	1,782
Master's degree	1,315	5,473	80	6,788
Masters of research	69	407	85	476
PhD	429	1,858	81	2,287
Total	204,204	306,687	60	510,891

Source: Ministry of Education, Department of Education Planning and Training 2012.

The glass-ceiling of gender is extremely apparent in decision-making positions, which are given to women's male counterparts. Table 36.2 shows that there were 178 male professors out of 783 professors in Myanmar, and yet there were no female rectors in Myanmar until 2015. In 2015, after increased criticism from Burmese feminists and activists, four rectors were appointed in the education sector, meaning only 0.51 per cent of rectors are female in the female dominated area of education. In other words, there is clear evidence of how structural inequality and discrimination exist in Myanmar, and how women still encounter glass-ceilings, even if they excel in their chosen professions.

Gender-based violence

Cultural norms, gender inequality and discrimination can lead to gender-based violence, and structural violence of poverty. In Rangoon, rape is the second largest crime following murders. Since the reforms of 2012, there have been increasing numbers of reports of gender-based violence, including rape cases, particularly involving under-age girls (see Table 36.3). In 2015, rape was the second most recorded crime, with more than 682 cases in Myanmar, while there were 1,264 murder cases, according to the police department in Myanmar (Eleven News 17 January 2015). More disturbingly, rape cases involving under-age girls are common. According to the police department of Yangon Region, 73 rape cases were reported in the first half of 2015 and 44 of them (over 60 per cent) involved a child (Htwe 2015).

Gender-based violence is a result of not just isolated individual pathology but also widespread collective pathologies. Women also suffer because of inadequate reproductive health care and education. Lack of accessibility, the affordability of contraceptive pills and high maternal mortality rates also need to be addressed, together with sex education. Otherwise incidence of sexually transmitted diseases like HIV/AIDS will continue to rise.

Not having specific laws to address the issue of gender-based violence, and the rejection of the existence of gender-based violence in society, including by those in power, further makes these crimes invisible. Executive government as well as prominent women have repeatedly

Table 36.2 Gender breakdown of higher education teachers, 2012

No.	*Designation*	*No. of male teachers*	*No. of female teachers*	*Total*
1	Professor	178	605	783
2	Associate Professor	153	614	767
3	Lecturer	513	3,134	3,647
4	Assistant Lecturer	531	2,580	3,111
5	Tutor/Demonstrator	534	2,188	2,722
	Total	1,909	9,121	11,030

Source: Department of Higher Education (Lower Myanmar), MOE, 31 May 2012.

Table 36.3 Rape cases

Year	*Murders*	*Rapes*
2014	1,333	741
2013	1,305	734
2012	1,323	654

denied that fact, arguing that women suffer no discrimination in Myanmar and legally enjoy equal rights with men in political, economic, administrative and social areas (DVB 2014).

The pervasive level of sexual violence led to the UN security council passing a resolution that 'women and girls are particularly targeted by the use of sexual violence, including as a tactic of war to humiliate, dominate, instill fear in, disperse and/or forcibly relocate civilian members of a community or ethnic group' in 2008 (United Nations Human Rights Office of the High Commissioner n.d.).

On 20 January 2014, two young female Kachin volunteer teachers were repeatedly gang raped and killed in Shan state, and many accused the Burmese army of the rape, as they were stationed at the village that night. Instead of carrying out an effective investigation, the military issued a warning, saying that 'Tatmadaw will not tolerance such accusations' (Mon 2015). Such attitudes and unwillingness, even defensive attitudes and threats of authority, will undoubtedly hinder the ability to seek justice for women.

Conclusion

Burmese women have experienced structural violence and discrimination, because of prolonged military rule unlike anywhere else in Asia. Women's skills can be an alternative source of solutions for the new government. The government needs to mandate the adoption of affirmative action initiatives to ensure women's equal participation at all levels, with quota systems, reservation or mandatory policies to open up political space for women. It can help to create strategic opportunities for them to contribute based on equality and social justice. It will help to build democracy, a fundamental ingredient of which is based on the equal access and equal participation of both women and men.

Notes

1 In 1927 the High Court at Rangoon changed the term 'Buddhist Law' to 'Burmese Buddhist Law' and in 1956 to 'Customary Law of the Burmese Buddhists'. In 1969 this law was changed to read 'Burmese Customary Law'.
2 'The Burma Code', Vol. I, Officially Published under the Authority of the Government of the Union of Myanmar, 1955, p. 9 (Article 13, section 3), followed by Act No. 24 of 1939 and Act No. 32 of 1954.
3 The Religious Conversion Bill stipulates that anyone who wants to convert to a different faith needs written permission from local 'Registration Boards' (government officials and community members) for conversion.
4 The Buddhist Women's Special Marriage Bill criminalises the civil marriage of Buddhist women if they marry non-Buddhist men without written permission from her parents and the local authorities; those not complying face ten years imprisonment.
5 The Monogamy Bill introduces new provisions that could constitute arbitrary interference with one's privacy and family.

References

Action Labour Rights. 2016. 'Under Pressure'. Action Labour Rights Publications, 25 March. Accessed 5 April 2016. www.burmalibrary.org/docs22/Under%20Pressure.pdf.

Aung, S.Y. and Solomon, F. 2015. 'Political Parties Pilot Gender Quotas'. *The Irrawaddy*, 4 February.

Bari, F. 2000. *Women in Pakistan: Country Briefing Paper*. Islamabad: Asian Development Bank: Office of Environment and Social Development.

Brown, R.G. 1926. *Burma as I Saw it: 1889–1917*. London: Methuen.

Burmese Socialist Programme Party (BSPP). 1975. *Myanma Amyothami Lawka* (trans. *The World of Burmese Women*). Rangoon: Sapei Beinman.

Chatterjee, P. 1989. 'Colonialism, Nationalism and Colonized Women: The Contest in India'. *American Ethnologist* 16 (4): 622–633.

Democratic Voice of Burma (DVB). 2014. 'Sexual Harassment in Burma (English)'. Debates, 18 November. Accessed 26 March 2016. www.youtube.com/watch?v=VnXCKdKg-Oo.

FAO (United Nations Food and Agriculture Organisation). 2011. The State of Food and Agriculture: 2010–2011.

Fielding, H. 1906. *A People at School*. London: MacMillan & Co.

Global Citizen. 2012. 'Introduction to the Challenges of Achieving Gender Equality'. Global Poverty Project, 10 October. Accessed 26 March 2016. www.globalcitizen.org/en/content/introduction-to-the-challenges-of-achieving-gender.

Gross, R. 1993. *Buddhism After Patriarchy: A Feminist History, and Reconstruction of Buddhism*. Albany: State University of New York Press.

Gutter, P. 2001. '"Law and Religion in Burma", Burma Lawyer Council: Legal Issues on Burma Journal'. 8 August, Accessed 10 November 2015. www.ibiblio.org/obl/docs/LIOB08-pgutter.law%20and religion.htm.

Hall, D.G.E. 1945. *Europe and Burma: A Study of European Relations with Burma to the Annexation of Thibaw's Kingdom, 1886*. Oxford: Oxford University Press.

Horner, I.B. 1961(1930). *Women Under Primitive Buddhism: Laywomen and Alas Women*. Colombo: The Wheel Publication, 30 (xxiv).

Htun, S.Y. 2012. 'The Labour Community Desires the Development of Labour Associations'. *People's Age Journal* 98: 13.

Htwe, Z.Z. 2015. 'More Than Half of Rape Cases Involve Children'. *The Myanmar Times*, 20 August.

JICA (Japan International Cooperation Agency). 2013. 'Data Collection Survey on Education Sector in Myanmar'. Japan International Cooperation Agency. Accessed 31 December 2015. http://open_jicareport.jica.go.jp/pdf/12113635.pdf.

Kawanami, H. 1990. 'The Religious Standing of Burmese Buddhist Nuns (*Thilashin*): the Ten Precepts and Religious Respect Words'. *The Journal of the International Association of Buddhist Studies* 13 (1): 17–39.

Kelly, Tabbot, 1905. *Burma, Painted and Described*. London: Adam and Charles Black.

Khaing, D.M.M. 1984. *The World of Burmese Women*. London: Zed Books.

Khin Mar Mar Kyi. 2004. 'Race, Gender and Sexuality in the Reconstruction of Politics in 20th Century Burma/Myanmar'. In *The Illusion of Progress: The Political Economy of Reform in Burma/Myanmar*, edited by D. Matheson and R. May. Adelaide: Crawford House Publication.

Khin Mar Mar Kyi. 2013. *'Dreams of Dutiful Daughters'. The Digital Humanities Hub: Research School of Humanities*. Canberra: Australian National University.

Khin Mar Mar Kyi. 2014. 'Engendering Development in Myanmar: Women's Struggle for San, Si, Sa'. In *Debating Democratization in Myanmar*, edited by N. Cheeseman, N. Farrelly and T. Wilson, 305–331. Singapore: Institute of Southeast Asian Studies.

Kyaw, A. 1988. 'Status of Women in Family Law in Burma and Indonesia'. *Crossroads* 4 (1): 100–120.

Kyaw, D. and Routray, J.K. 2006. 'Gender and Rural Poverty in Myanmar: A Micro Level Study in the Dry Zone'. *Journal of Agriculture and Rural Development* 107 (2): 103–114.

Lwin, K.S. 2014. 'Understanding Recent Labour Protests in Myanmar'. In *Debating Democratization in Myanmar*, edited by N. Cheeseman, N. Farrelly and T. Wilson, 137–159. Singapore: Institute of Southeast Asian Studies.

Ma Ma Lay 1955. *Not Out of Hate*. Rangoon.

Ma Ma Lay 1973. *Blood*. Rangoon.

McClintock, A. 1995. *Imperial Leather: Race, Gender and Sexuality in the Colonial Contest*. New York: Routledge.

Macgregor, F. 2015. 'No Confidence, or No Opportunity?' *The Myanmar Times*, 20 November.

Manjoo, R. 2011. 'Special Rapporteur on Violence against Women'. UN Commission on the Status of Women: 56th Session, 28 February, New York.

Mann, Z. 2014. 'Monk Conference Backs Bills to Restrict Interfaith Marriage, Rohingya Voting'. *The Irrawaddy*, 1 January.

Mann, Z. & S. Michaels. 2013. 'Petition to Restrict Interfaith Marriage Garners 2.5 Million Signatures in Burma'. *The Irrawaddy*, 16 January.

Ministry of Education. 2012. 'Education Development in Myanmar and Education System in Myanmar: Self Evaluation and Future Plans'. Ministry of Education. Accessed 31 December 2015. www.myanmar education.edu.mm/dhel/educationsysteminmyanmar/educationstructure.

Mon, Y. 2015. 'Police Name Local Suspects in Kachin Teachers' Murder'. *The Myanmar Times*, 1 July.

Muller, H. 1994. 'Women in Urban Burma: Social Issues and Political Constraints'. *Women Studies International Forum* 17 (6): 609–620.

O'Connor, R. 1983. *A Theory of Indigenous Southeast Asian Urbanism*. Singapore: Institute of Southeast Asian Studies.

Oxfam. 2014. 'Delivering Prosperity in Myanmar's Dry Zone'. Oxfam Briefing Paper, 28 August. Accessed 20 January 2016. www.oxfam.org/sites/www.oxfam.org/files/file_attachments/bp-myanmar-dryzone-smallscale-farmers-280814-en.pdf.

Oxfam. 2016. 'From Sweatshops to Switzerland, the Women in Myanmar Behind the Billionaires.' Oxfam Publication, 4 March. Accessed 29 March 2016. https://oxfamblogs.org/fp2p/from-sweatshops-to-switzerland-the-women-in-myanmar-behind-the-billionaires-fortunes.

Scott, G. 1882/1989. *The Burman: His Life and Notions*. Scotland: Kiscadale Publications.

Sein, D.M. 1972. *Towards Independence in Burma: The Role of Women*. Oxford: Oxford University Press.

Sein, D.K.K. 1986. *Pagan Yinkyehmuouqchuqye, Tayasiyinye Luhmuye* (trans. *Bagan Literature and Culture*). Rangoon: Sarpebainmun.

Sen, A. 1990. 'Development as Capability Expansion'. In *Human Development and the International Development Strategy for the 1990s*, edited by K. Griffin and J. Knight, 41–58. London: Macmillan.

Sen, A. 1999. *Women's Agency and Social Change*. Oxford; New York: Oxford University Press.

Thein, U.S. 2015. 'Recognition and Protection of Customary Tenure'. Paper presented at Workshop on Opportunities for Development-Oriented Drug Control in Myanmar, NayPyiTaw, at the Central Committee for Drug Abuse Control (CCDAC) and the Transnational Institute (TNI) Conference, 21–22 January.

Thitsa, K. 1980. *Providence and Prostitution: Women in Buddhist Thailand*. London: Change International Reports.

Tin, U.P.M. 1935. 'Women in the Inscriptions of Pagan'. *Journal of the Burma Research Society* 25: 149–159.

Transnational Institute. 2015. 'Linking Women and Land in Myanmar'. Transnational Institute, February. Accessed 31 March 2016. www.tni.org/files/download/tni-nlup-gender_0.pdf.

U Hla, L. 1966. *Thusamya ka Pyawkheteh Theipun Maung Wa Akyaung* (trans. *The Story of Theipan Maung Wa*). Rangoon: Kyipwaye.

UNDP (The United Nations Development Programme). 2012. 'Empowering Women is Key to Building a Future We Want, Nobel Laureate Says'. 27 September. Accessed 12 December 2015. www.undp.org/content/undp/en/home/presscenter/articles/2012/09/27/empowering-women-is-key-to-building-a-future-we-want-nobel-laureate-says.html.

UNDP. 2013. *Human Development Report 2013. The Rise of The South: Human Progress in a Diverse World*. New York: UNDP.

UNDP. 2015. 'Social Inclusion of Women: From Beijing to Post-2015'. UNDP conference, Buenos Aires, 6–8 May.

UNFPA (The United Nations Population Fund). 2015. 'The 2014 Myanmar Population and Housing Census'. The Republic of the Union of Myanmar Report, UNFPA and Department of Population Ministry of Immigration and Population, May, NayPyiTaw.

United Nations Human Rights Office of the High Commissioner. n.d. 'Rape: Weapon of War'. www.ohchr.org/EN/NewsEvents/Pages/RapeWeaponWar.aspx.

Yi, D.K. 1988. *The Dobama Movement in Burma (1930–1938)*. Ithaca: Southeast Asia Program, Cornell University.

37

NATION-BUILDING

Matthew J. Walton

Josef Silverstein (1980), a scholar of politics in Burma, remarked at the end of his 1980 book *Burmese Politics: The Dilemma of National Unity*, that 'claiming unity without demonstrating it to the satisfaction of all is no answer, and the continuation of armed struggle seems to bear that out' (249). Silverstein's book remains one of the few volumes to focus solely on the overarching question of national unity in Myanmar, although the concept, along with the corollary issue of nation-building, is certainly at the heart of many studies of politics and identity in the country, especially those that deal with the development of national identity among the non-Burman ethnic groups. Silverstein was correct in his analysis then and the point remains salient today: political leaders in Myanmar have made a habit of declaring (even insisting on) the unity of the Burmese/Myanmar nation, yet the persistence of conflict and the militant assertion of sub-national identities would suggest that there is no coherent, unifying Myanmar national identity.

I follow that line of argument in this chapter, arguing that there is no Myanmar 'nation', despite Burman Buddhist leaders' multiple attempts in the modern era to create one. These attempts have mostly been through the use of force, particularly since independence in 1948. As a result, non-Burman ethnic groups and other non-dominant groups have solidified their own identities, often in opposition to a brutally repressive state and military. Yet along the way, there have been times when the boundaries of inclusion and exclusion have shifted, both among Burmans seeking to create a 'Myanmar' identity and among various ethnic groups that have attempted to do the same within their own communities. Laying the foundations of an inclusive, egalitarian national community in Myanmar is now possible in new ways since the transition, although it is certainly not assured and faces formidable obstacles. The political freedoms that have emerged since 2011 and the power shift to a National League for Democracy (NLD)-led government in 2016 have created some measure of space for a critical and honest discussion of national identity and of the terms of inclusion in the polity. However, most of the key dynamics considered here that have inhibited the creation of that inclusive national community have persisted under the NLD government, making the prospects for nation-building bleak.

The chapter begins with a brief consideration of the linguistic aspects of discussing identity in Myanmar. I then consider the ways in which the content of the national community (and its constructed Others) shifted during the first half of the twentieth century, culminating in the solidification of an ethno-religious core of the nation, as a result of the military's pacification efforts throughout the 1950s. I then consider various nation-building efforts among several of the non-Burman ethnic groups and the Rohingya ethno-religious minority. Finally, I look at education as a tool that has contributed to exclusionary conceptions of national and sub-national identity, but could also be reconfigured to be the vehicle through which a new understanding of Myanmar national identity could be discussed, critiqued, and inculcated.

The language of national identity

One of the challenges in navigating discourses of nation-building and national identity in Myanmar is linguistic. That is, the language that people use to describe themselves, their various identities, and the boundaries of national inclusion does not always neatly map on to English language terms commonly associated with citizenship and belonging in a modern nation-state. For example, the word *lu myo* literally means 'type of person'. It is usually translated as either 'race' or 'ethnicity', already demonstrating the lack of direct correspondence between the Burmese and English terms that mean very different things. In practice, asking someone what *lu myo* they are could elicit a range of possible answers, including ethnicity, religion, race, or nationality.

Another term denoting ethnic group is *tain yin tha*, which is frequently deployed in different ways depending on the identity and intentions of the speaker. A non-Burman would almost invariably include herself in the category of *tain yin tha*. However, many Burmans unconsciously use the term *tain yin tha* to signify minority (that is, *non*-Burman) ethnic groups, although if they are seeking to reinforce the claim that all ethnic groups are brothers and sisters in the same Myanmar identity, they may insist that Burmans are also included in *tain yin tha*. Nick Cheesman (2017) has demonstrated how *tain yin tha* has, in recent decades, become the unavoidable conceptual lens through which claims to citizenship must be made in Myanmar. Just these examples and their varying usage suggest that there is an indigenous categorisation system (or systems, since members of different ethnic groups might also understand the terms differently) that does not neatly map on to the race/ethnicity distinction and that, furthermore, that system is itself continually being contested and reformulated. In a country with the diversity of Myanmar, none of these axes of identity have ever completely defined the national identity, although a Burman Buddhist core has been dominant and ascendant nationally at least since independence.

Additionally, while it appears to be scholarly convention today to use Burman, Bama, or Bamar to refer to the majority ethnic group in English, many non-Burmans continue to use the term 'Burmese' to mean 'Burman'. It is also worth mentioning that in popular usage, although the word 'Myanmar' is officially intended to refer to all citizens of the country, in practice many people elide its usage to mean, at different times, the majority ethnic group or all citizens of the country (and occasionally, all officially-recognised ethnic groups). I would classify this as an indicator of majority privilege for Burmans (Walton 2013). That is, Burmans are always unproblematically 'Myanmar'; and while non-Burman groups can (under the right circumstances) be included in the national identity, their membership in the category is always provisional and contingent on factors such as how much they have assimilated to a Myanmar cultural identity and what type and degree of opposition they might manifest towards the state.

Shifting boundaries of inclusion in the 'nationalist' and 'independence' eras

The common narrative in studies of nationalism in colonial Burma has depicted a nationalist movement in two stages, initially led by monks and Buddhist actors from the beginning of the twentieth century, then shifting to become a secularly led and oriented movement by the 1920s and 1930s, brought on in part because of the allegedly destructive factionalism of monk-led politics. Alicia Turner's (2014) groundbreaking study of the period 1890–1920 has fundamentally challenged this narrative, demonstrating that the primary referent of activism during that time was strengthening and protecting the *sasana* (Buddhist religion and religious community), not a still-emerging and coalescing Burmese national identity. Turner relates how, in response to fears of the deterioration of the *sasana*, Buddhists began to take upon themselves the tasks of *sasana*-preservation by forming hundreds of lay Buddhist associations, studying the scriptures, practising meditation, promoting Buddhist education, and conducting public morality campaigns against drinking and gambling.

Turner's explanation of the origins of this misreading of a critical period of Burmese history is important in understanding the role of historical memory in nation-building and national narratives. She argues that a 1920 pamphlet entitled *The History of Myanma Buddhist Associations* was written by the 'winners' of the 1919 debate within the YMBA (Young Men's Buddhist Association) over whether the organisation would take up political issues. This faction's version of history became the dominant one that was reproduced and reinforced by scholars and political leaders, and through standardised educational texts, obscured the diversity of interests and objectives among Buddhist groups during that time period (Turner 2009, 47ff). Visions of the membership and boundaries of inclusion of any group will have dominant articulations as well as contesting alternative depictions; the nation is probably the most politically-consequential of these groups and as such, control of the national narrative is particularly important to political authorities.

While the opening decades of the twentieth century may not have included self-conscious 'nationalist' activism, they are still of critical importance to a study of nation-building in Myanmar. This period strongly reinforced the boundaries of a Buddhist community of religious identity and practice that would, in the 1920s and 1930s, be intertwined with an emerging (albeit still shifting and contentious) political national identity. This occurred to such a degree that the two would quickly be seen as essentially and inextricably interconnected, both in the view of dominant political discourses and in almost all scholarly analysis of Burmese national identity. The commonly-cited phrase 'To be a Burman is to be Buddhist' probably had more general cultural implications in its pre-colonial and colonial usage, but following the activism of groups like the *Dobama Asiayone* in the 1930s, gradually came to refer to a more bounded religio-political community.

The India-educated and politically active Burmese monk U Ottama was one of the first to explicitly weave together notions of religious and political identity in the 1920s. He argued that British rule had actually inhibited Buddhist moral practice in Burma; Burmese Buddhists needed self-rule to regain access to the spiritual liberation of enlightenment (Smith 1965). But while he and other activists of the period were united in their opposition to the British, their sense of who ought to constitute the national community of Burma (or what 'self-rule' would actually imply in practice) was less well-defined and certainly more porous and open than the Burman Buddhist-dominated national identity that would eventually solidify. Although U Ottama did use religious symbolism and arguments in his appeals, he also 'spoke in Hindustani frequently and urged the unity of the Muslims, Hindus, and Buddhists' (Smith 1965, 97–98). It is difficult to know how typical his more inclusive perspective was, but it does reflect the varied and constantly shifting configurations of national and religious identity and belies a simplistic, unitary label of 'Buddhist nationalism' for the period. This ambiguity would continue in the rhetoric and activism of the most prominent and influential nationalist group, the *Dobama Asiayone*, formed in the early 1930s.

Kei Nemoto's important research on this organisation highlights a number of points relevant to a discussion of nation-building in Myanmar. Chief among those is the way in which language, labels, and meaning regularly shift over time. The word *dobama* in *Dobama Asiayone* (*asiayone* simply means group or organisation) is variously translated as 'We, the Burmese', 'We Burmans', 'Our Burma', or 'Our [kind of] Burmese'. Nemoto points out that *Bama* was explicitly chosen over *Myanma*, as at the time, the latter connoted solely the majority Burman ethnic group. In fact, the term *Bama* also held similarly circumscribed ethnic connotations, but the *Dobama* 'decided to redefine it to denote all indigenous people living in British-dominated Burma' (Nemoto 2000, 3). This is exactly the opposite of the meaning that these terms hold today, at least in official usage, since the government changed the name of the country to 'Myanmar' in 1989 with a stated intention of lessening the rhetorical association of the name of the country with the name of the majority ethnic group.

The *Dobama*'s usage of its namesake category, alongside what Nemoto claims was a more frequent usage of its opposite, *thudobama* ('their Burma', or 'those Burmese'), reflects the changing (and sometimes contradictory) referents of these important identity terms in a period when the boundaries of the national community were still being asserted and contested. The initial impetus of the *Dobama*'s activism was the May 1930 dock riots that took place primarily between Indians and Burmans, but Burmese scholar Khin Yi argues that the group's 1930 manifesto analysed the riots primarily through an economic lens and urged Burmans 'not to hate the Indians but to love one another more' (quoted in Khin Yi 1988, 5). *Thudobama* was also not necessarily an ethnic, racial, *or* national category. The term was initially directed at those who either supported colonial rule or were not working to oppose it. Throughout the late 1930s and 1940s, *thudobama* acquired more of an ideological character as leftists used it to criticise each other, but the term's meaning shifted again at the end of the Japanese occupation in 1944 when the Japanese fascists and their collaborators became *thudobama*, with the former *thudobama* of Burmans and non-Burman ethnic groups that had supported the British moving (temporarily, at least) into the *dobama* category (Nemoto 2000, 9).

Examining the shifting meanings associated with the terms *dobama* and *thudobama* reminds us how, even throughout this formative period of nationalist activism, the primary referents of national inclusion remained flexible. There was disagreement over who ought to be considered *dobama* and *thudobama* and for what reasons. There were also competing political structures that recognised different principles of political inclusion and representation. Not only this, influential political leaders and groups changed their views on who ought to be included in the national community according to the political situation, sometimes for reasons of expediency. We often view the 1930s as a period in which Burmese national identity coalesced, forming around a Burman and Buddhist core. While this was one strand of the nationalist discourse of the time, it probably did not achieve ascendancy until the ethnic conflicts of the 1950s further alienated most non-Burman ethnic groups and military rule solidified national identity as both ethnically Burman and religiously Buddhist. Nemoto is right to rescue the *dobama* discourse as an 'effort to reconceptualise the Burmese nation in significantly progressive ways' (2000, 3). But the uncomfortable fact remains that, even within this sometimes progressive effort, the articulation of a national identity required an Other that was probably more central to the process of differentiation than the core group itself. That was certainly the case in the 1950s and 1960s, as religious, ethnic, and ideological conflicts tore a newly independent Burma asunder, opening up space for military rule and the building and policing of a national community through increasingly repressive policies and force of arms.

Mary Callahan (2003a) has written the narrative of how the modern military-led state emerged in Burma, through internally-directed conflict. Upon independence in 1948, the newly formed Burmese government was forced to contend with various religious, political, and ethnic rebellions that expanded in scope, intensity, and efficacy throughout the early 1950s. Faced with civil conflict across the country, the Burmese military began a campaign of pacification that, by the late 1950s, brought much of the territory under its control, although sporadic civil conflict has continued to the present. The crucial part of Callahan's analysis with respect to nation-building is that, in conducting its operations, the military and its leaders gradually came to see their own fellow citizens as potential enemies and themselves as the only institution capable of holding the country together, by force if necessary. This was the period in which persistent ethnic conflict reinforced the military's growing distrust of non-Burmans and, concurrently, non-Burmans' belief that Burman chauvinism and military repression were part of the fundamental character of the Burmese state. Although the Burmese security forces would occasionally turn their brutality on Burman Buddhist citizens, this was usually in response to direct opposition, whereas ethnic populations faced atrocities whether they were part of an armed resistance or not (Walton 2013). Direct military rule beginning in 1962 was characterised by this distrust of ethnic populations and further solidified the Burman Buddhist core of the Myanmar nation.

Nation-building among non-Burmans

The counterparts to Myanmar government and military attempts at nation-building are the efforts by various non-Burman ethnic groups to build and strengthen what they consider to be their own national identities. Unsurprisingly, the military perceives these efforts as inherently divisive, hostile, and, if unchecked, likely to lead to the political disintegration of the country. Decades of military government propaganda, combined with limited access to information, have ensured that this view has also been prevalent among the general Burman population, at least until recently. But, while increasing numbers of Burmans appear to be sympathetic to non-Burman calls for increased political autonomy and representation, many still see the cultivation of separate ethnic-national identities as an impediment to national reconciliation and the contemporary nation-building project. Additionally, the internal processes within many of these groups have at times been as exclusionary and hegemonic as Burman-led attempts at nation-building, repressing critical or minority perspectives and, for strategic reasons, attempting to present a unitary, unified image that belies the diversity of identities and experiences *within* Myanmar's many non-dominant ethnic groups.

Nick Cheesman has described the challenge faced by Karen leaders who must attempt to fashion a common narrative of identity among people as diverse as 'a S'gaw Karen highland animist swidden farmer who speaks only her own language and a Western Pwo Karen delta Christian civil servant whose first language is Burmese' (2002, 200). Ashley South (2007) has called this the 'problem' of Karen diversity, and has highlighted a Christian-dominated paradigm of 'Karen-ness' that has been reinforced not only by Karen National Union (KNU) elites in Myanmar and Thailand but also by other diaspora groups. The projection of this unitary Karen identity generated feelings of exclusion among Buddhist Karen that, among other factors, contributed to a major split in 1994 in which the newly formed DKBA (Democratic Karen Buddhist Army, later renamed the Democratic Karen Benevolent Army) allied with government forces and facilitated the fall of the KNU headquarters at Manerplaw in 1995, a decisive moment in Myanmar's long-running civil conflict.

Jessica Harriden, in her study of the development of Karen identity, notes the ways in which Karen nationalist leaders (and probably leaders of other ethnic identity groups as well) have been influenced by the ascriptive conceptual models that were prominent in early twentieth-century studies of ethnic groups in Burma and that posited ethnic identity as given. Those studies 'simultaneously encouraged notions of Karen distinctiveness vis-à-vis other ethnic groups and emphasised the unity of all Karen cultures by adopting a pan-Karen perspective' (Harriden 2002, 88). They were also the intellectual precursors of statements like this from the KNU in 1947: 'A KAREN IS A KAREN; one in blood brotherhood; one in sentiment; one in diversity and one mass of a Karen nationhood [sic]' (*ibid.*, 109). Statements like this, however, belied persistent disagreement over such fundamental questions as who could be considered Karen, what an autonomous Karen State might look like, what territory it might claim, etc. (Thawnghmung 2008, 6–10).

Ananda Rajah (2002) has argued that, despite the different sub-identities among the Karen, a relatively consistent genealogy of contemporary Karen ethno-national and nationalist identity can be traced back to the writings of Christian missionaries in the nineteenth century. These writings laid the groundwork for the Karen to see themselves as a 'nation of intent' which continued through the creation of the KNU in 1949, and is replicated today through the social, political, and educational structures that exist in Karen-controlled areas of Myanmar as well as some of the Karen-dominated refugee camps on the Thai–Myanmar border. The conjectures of early missionaries encouraged Karen elites to conceptualise—and more critically, *organise*—their community trans-locally (2010, 533). These self-depictions were oriented towards establishing Karen 'indigeneity' and increasingly articulated in light of Burman oppression. Although Rajah acknowledged the ways in which the fall of Manerplaw splintered Karen national imaginings (by removing the existence of a tangible Karen-controlled homeland), he argued that Karen-ness had effectively transcended the locales to which it might have formerly been attached and will continue to anchor expressions of Karen ethno-nationalism and nationalism (2010, 533).

Christianity has played a similar role in developing a distinct sense of nation-hood among the Chin. Lian Sakhong, in his study of the development of Chin identity, notes the way in which theological similarities between Christianity and traditional Chin religion allowed for a sense of continuity between the past and the present. Specifically, a shift from a *Khua-hrum* (guardian gods)-centric belief system to a *Khua-zing* (Supreme God)-centric belief system facilitated the recognition of common religious practice and thought that, 'offered the Chin a national identity, which they never had a chance to create under their traditional religious worship' (Sakhong 2003, 243). This was also the basis for asserting a political identity, particularly against the dominant Burman Buddhist majority, but also as distinct from other Christian groups in Myanmar.

Ashley South (2003) has argued that in one key respect, Mon national sentiment has differed from that of the other non-Burman groups: Mons have looked back to a classical era of dominant and influential Mon civilisation as a way of preserving their cultural identity and as the basis for asserting the legitimacy of an independent or autonomous Monland. But he has also noted the ways in which the repressive actions of the Burmese government and military, which have forced refugees to become more dependent on ethnic armed groups such as the New Mon State Party (NMSP), are 'likely to have reinforced their public identification with Mon ethnicity' (2003, 194).

It is possibly easier for Mons to orient their national identity in this way as Burman historical narratives tend to position Mon culture as the predecessor to the Burman political empire. Historians and political leaders of two of the other majority Buddhist ethnic minorities with substantial written civilisational histories, the Shan and the Rakhine, have also written works that establish thriving and independent cultural histories of their national identity groups. Despite a common religious belief, Shan narratives focus on the relative independence of Shan principalities, under both Burman kings and colonial rule and cultural connections to Tai communities in neighbouring Thailand (see Sai Aung Tun 2008). Rakhine expressions of national identity, on the other hand, regularly highlight what is portrayed as a beleaguered nationality, subjected to Burmanisation since the kingdom of Arakan was conquered in 1785 (examined from a historical perspective in Leider 2008) and assaulted by Muslim incursions that are personified most recently in the present Rohingya 'threat' (as described in Aye Chan 2005).

Mandy Sadan's authoritative study of the emergence and development of a Kachin ethno-national identity provides several important lessons for understanding nation-building in Myanmar. She challenges overly simplistic accounts that posit Kachin alliances with the British during the colonial period as foundational to a national identity oriented against the Burman-led state, revealing a wide range of Kachin attitudes (including strong antagonism) towards the British (Sadan 2013, Chapter 4). She also contests the central role of Burman repression as fostering the distinct ethno-nationalist perspective of the currently-dominant Kachin Independence Organisation (KIO), demonstrating lively and contentious debates within the community over leadership, the constituent components of Kachin identity, and the relationship of Kachin elites with the central authorities. Most importantly, she demonstrates the contingency of the emergence of the KIO and Kachin ethno-national identity in their current forms by considering the historical dynamics that allowed certain groups to be able to 'claim authority over ideologies of political and social identity' (2013, 37). This approach could be fruitfully adopted not only with regard to the study of national identity formation among non-Burman groups, but to various iterations of Myanmar national identity as well.

The case of the Rohingya complicates Myanmar's already muddled identity categories even further. Advocates for this Muslim minority that is actually a majority in some townships along the Myanmar–Bangladesh border assert that the group has been a part of the Myanmar national community for many generations. The opposing stance of the former government and, indeed, seemingly much of the population of the country is that they are primarily made up of illegal immigrant 'Bengalis' who entered during the colonial period and over porous borders since that time. While there is undisputable evidence of the presence of Muslim communities in what is now Rakhine state for centuries, Rohingya advocates are at pains to demonstrate that they are the direct descendants of those communities and there is strong evidence to suggest that, whatever the historical lineage, the label 'Rohingya' only came into regular and consistent use for members of the community in the post-WWII period (Leider 2013). But, as Nick Cheesman (2017) makes clear, the language of the 1982 Citizenship Law as well as the dominant conceptual norm of *tain yin tha* require the Rohingya to articulate their belonging in this way, and to insist that they are an 'indigenous' ethnic group rather than a nationality, even one that has been resident within Myanmar for many years. And, it should be noted, the constructed nature of Rohingya identity as such in the middle of the twentieth century is no more problematic or artificial than the former military regime's construction (or possibly re-consolidation) of 'Myanmar' identity in 1989, or any of the ethno-national identities considered in this chapter.

While it seems clear that most of the non-Burman ethnic identities have been fostered in response to Burman dominance, it remains the case that there has been a range of attitudes adopted by non-Burmans towards Burmans; this has significant implications for the project of nation-building for Myanmar as a whole. Martin Smith provides a useful example in the case of the dispute between the Karen National United Party (KNUP) and the Karen Revolutionary Council (KRC) in the late 1950s and early 1960s (Smith 1999, 213–218). Although there were multiple dimensions to this intra-Karen conflict, one fundamental disagreement stemmed from perceptions of who the 'enemy' was. Hunter Tha Hmwe, the leader of the KRC, saw 'Burmans' as the enemy, whereas the KNUP perspective, influenced no doubt by the geographical positioning of many of its leaders in the ethnically mixed Delta region, saw 'Burman chauvinism' to be the primary impediment. One of these framings could potentially make space for an ethnically integrated Myanmar while one simply reinforced and naturalised inter-group antagonism. While acknowledging that viewing 'Burmans' as the enemy is a reasonable conclusion to reach from the perspective of ethnic groups that have been brutally repressed for decades, the prospects for inclusive nation-building are significantly dampened if this becomes the dominant view. One area that is critical for shaping views of an ethnic 'Other' is education.

Nation-building through education

Education is central to the creation and maintenance of identities, and changes to the educational system and curricular materials will be an essential part of a revised nation-building project in Myanmar. It should not be surprising that, just as official Myanmar state curricula present a particular (Burman Buddhist-dominant) narrative of the Myanmar nation, materials developed by non-Burman ethnic groups have offered contrasting pictures, often rooted in antagonism to the Burman-led military state. In recent years there have been attempts to bridge this gap, looking forward to the integration of the state education system with ethnic-administered systems. The Myanmar government is also gradually easing restrictions on native language education, a process that—along with significant curricular revision—will have to occur more rapidly if various minority groups are to feel that they have a voice and a place within the national narrative.

The dominant Burman Buddhist identity has been reinforced through government textbooks that privilege a particular historical narrative of the founding of the Burmese polity and depict non-Burmans either as minor players or as attempting to split the national community. Since the early 1990s, the government has extensively re-written textbooks in order to emphasise a common 'Myanmar' identity, although still with content that generally reflects Burman Buddhist history and cultural norms and practices (Metro 2011). Ostensibly included in this 'Myanmar' national identity, non-Burmans and non-Buddhists often appear in roles that oversimplify their historical political positions. For example, depictions of non-Burmans as being opposed to the British during the colonial period ignore not only the fact that many supported the British but also that their participation in modern Burma's founding was contingent and motivated by factors other than a presumed national Burmese unity (Walton 2008). When non-Burman figures are included as prominent or consequential actors, they are often de-ethnicised and appropriated as 'Myanmar' heroes. One classic example is the ethnic Arakanese (Rakhine) monk U Ottama (mentioned earlier in this chapter), who is championed in Burmese history books for his anti-colonial agitation but rarely recognised for his work on behalf of Arakanese cultural recognition. And non-Burmans who struggled *against* Burman kings or the Burmese military in the past century find no place in the government histories, being relegated to the textbooks written and used by non-Burman groups (Salem-Gervais and Metro 2012).

As described in the previous section, non-Burman national sentiment has varied in the degree to which it is oriented primarily in opposition to a dominant Burman national identity. The educational regimes and curricula developed by non-Burman groups in the areas they control inside of Myanmar and in refugee and exile communities on the Thai–Myanmar border have played an important role in shaping non-Burman attitudes towards Burmans, their sense of their own ethnic and national identities, and the degree to which they feel a part of a national community in Myanmar. In a (2014) study of non-state education provision among the Karen and Mon, Marie Lall and Ashley South conclude that the predominantly 'separatist' approach adopted by the Karen will disadvantage students who are unprepared to learn in the Myanmar language and unable to integrate with the national education system. By contrast, the Mon ethnic education model follows a government curriculum but augments this with classes in Mon language, history, and culture, preparing students to move on to tertiary education. While recognising that educational possibilities are shaped by various exogenous factors (including, in this case, the persistence of active conflict in Karen areas, contrasted with a ceasefire in Mon areas since 1995), the authors recommend the further development of the Mon model (with appropriate adaptation for areas with varying degrees of ethno-linguistic diversity). This will minimise the linguistic and social disadvantages that non-Burman students experience and lay the groundwork for an integrated national education system. (Also see Lall's chapter on Education in this volume.)

For an integrated national education system to be effective in creating an inclusive and equitable national community, it will require the development of an equally inclusive curriculum that allows students to critically assess national myths and narratives (of all groups in the country). One notable model is the *Histories of Burma* textbook, written by Rosalie Metro (2013) and published by the Myanmar education NGO Mote Oo.[1] After her dissertation research into education in Myanmar and on the Thai–Myanmar border revealed that a primary source textbook would be more effective in fostering inter-ethnic reconciliation than a history textbook written from a single perspective, Metro worked with Burmese colleagues to create a textbook that includes documents that span Myanmar's contemporary history (Metro 2011). Foundational documents such as the 1947 Panglong Agreement sit alongside similar manifestos from ethnic and political resistance movements and speeches from key figures in Myanmar's politics. Students are encouraged to interrogate the perspectives and assumptions contained within these documents, in the process revealing multiple and contested strands of 'Burmese' history, along with possibilities for imagining a different set of terms on which a national union could be constructed.

The construction of a national identity relies not only on curricular materials that promote particular narratives of the nation but also on a common language. Other scholars have documented the many restrictions on both education and publishing in languages other than Burmese (Callahan 2003b; Houtman 1999). Those restrictions have gradually eased since 2011, with the Mon State Parliament passing a bill in April 2014 to allow certain classes at government schools to be taught in Mon language. Local governments across the country that would like to begin gradually implementing similar programmes face obstacles of central administrative resistance and a lack of resources and technical expertise, even under an NLD-led government. While this is a critical aspect of inclusive nation-building, additional progress is likely to be piecemeal and to be disproportionately implemented across the country.

Conclusion

While all national identities are constructed and contested, multiple nation-building projects in Myanmar since the beginning of the twentieth century reveal the fundamentally fragmented nature of belonging in the country. Identities at the national and sub-national levels have more often than not been forcibly imposed, often coupled with disciplining discourses of 'unity' that repress dissenting voices (Walton 2015). To say that there is not currently a Myanmar 'nation' is not to say that one cannot emerge. However, it will have to take seriously the multiple perspectives of the country's diverse ethnic and religious groups, be built on principles of inclusion rather than exclusion, and most importantly, recognise that the nation-building efforts of the country's Burman, Buddhist elites (both military and civilian) have usually been experienced by the country's minorities as hegemonic impositions more likely to divide than to unite.

Note

1 The *Sourcebook*, *Student's Book*, and *Teacher's Book* can be downloaded from Metro's website at https://sites.google.com/site/rosaliemetro/home/curriculum-design (Accessed 15 August 2015). Information about Mote Oo's other curriculum materials can be found at www.moteoo.org/curriculum/ (Accessed 15 August 2015).

References

Aye Chan. 2005. 'The Development of a Muslim Enclave in Arakan (Rakhine) State of Burma (Myanmar)'. *SOAS Bulletin of Burma Research* 3 (2): 396–420.

Callahan, Mary. 2003a. *Making Enemies: War and State Building in Burma*. Ithaca: Cornell University Press.

Callahan, Mary. 2003b. 'Language Policy in Modern Burma'. In *Fighting Words: Language Policy and Ethnic Relations in Asia*, edited by Michael E. Brown and Sumit Ganguly, 143–175. Cambridge, MA: MIT Press.

Cheesman, Nick. 2002. 'Seeing "Karen" in the Union of Myanmar'. *Asian Ethnicity* 3 (2): 199–220.

Cheesman, Nick. 2017. 'How in Myanmar "National Races" Came to Surpass Citizenship and Exclude Rohingya'. *Journal of Contemporary Asia* 43(3): 461–483.

Harriden, Jessica. 2002. 'Making a Name for Themselves: Karen Identity and the Politicization of Ethnicity in Burma'. *Journal of Burma Studies* 7: 84–144.

Houtman, Gustaaf. 1999. *Mental Culture in Burmese Crisis Politics: Aung San Suu Kyi and the National League for Democracy*. Tokyo: Institute for the Study of Languages and Cultures of Asia and Africa, Tokyo University of Foreign Studies.

Khin Yi. 1988. *The Dobama Movement in Burma (1930–1938)*. Ithaca, NY: Southeast Asia Program, Cornell University.

Lall, Marie and Ashley South. 2014. 'Comparing Models of Non-state Ethnic Education in Myanmar: The Mon and Karen National Education Regimes'. *Journal of Contemporary Asia* 44 (2): 298–321.

Leider, Jacques P. 2008. 'Forging Buddhist Credentials as a Tool of Legitimacy and Ethnic Identity: A Study of Arakan's Subjection in Nineteenth-Century Burma'. *Journal of the Economic and Social History of the Orient* 51: 409–459.

Leider, Jacques P. 2013. 'Rohingya: The Name, the Movement, the Quest for Identity'. In *Nation Building in Myanmar*. Yangon: Myanmar EGRESS/Myanmar Peace Center.

Metro, Rosalie. 2011. 'History Curricula and the Reconciliation of Ethnic Conflict: A Collaborative Project with Burmese Migrants and Refugees in Thailand'. PhD diss., Cornell University.

Metro, Rosalie. 2013. *Histories of Burma*. Yangon: Mote Oo.

Nemoto, Kei. 2000. 'The Concepts of Dobama (Our Burma) and *Thudo-Bama* (Their Burma) in Burmese Nationalism, 1930–1948'. *Journal of Burma Studies* 5: 1–16.

Rajah, Ananda. 2002. 'A "Nation of Intent" in Burma: Karen Ethno-Nationalism, Nationalism and Narrations of Nation'. *The Pacific Review* 15 (4): 517–537.

Sadan, Mandy. 2013. *Being and Becoming Kachin: Histories Beyond the State in the Borderworlds of Burma*. Oxford: Oxford University Press.

Sai Aung Tun. 2008. *History of the Shan State: From its Origin to 1962*. Chiang Mai: Silkworm Books.

Sakhong, Lian H. 2003. *In Search of Chin Identity: A Study in Religion, Politics and Ethnic Identity in Burma*. Richmond: NIAS Press.

Salem-Gervais, Nicholas and Rosalie Metro. 2012. 'A Textbook Case of Nation-Building: The Evolution of History Curricula in Myanmar'. *Journal of Burma Studies* 16 (1): 27–78.

Silverstein, Josef. 1980. *Burmese Politics: The Dilemma of National Unity*. New Brunswick, NJ: Rutgers University Press.

Smith, Donald Eugene. 1965. *Religion and Politics in Burma*. Princeton, NJ: Princeton University Press.

Smith, Martin. 1999. *Burma: Insurgency and the Politics of Ethnicity*. London: Zed Books.

South, Ashley. 2003. *Mon Nationalism and Civil War in Burma: The Golden Sheldrake*. Richmond: Routledge Curzon.

South, Ashley. 2007. 'Karen Nationalist Communities: The "Problem" of Diversity'. *Contemporary Southeast Asia* 29 (1): 55–76.

Thawnghmung, Ardeth Maung. 2008. 'The Karen Revolution in Burma: Diverse Voices, Uncertain Ends'. In *East–West Center Policy Studies Series*. Vol. 45. Singapore; Washington, DC: Institute of Southeast Asian Studies; East–West Center.

Turner, Alicia Marie. 2009. 'Buddhism, Colonialism and the Boundaries of Religion: Theravada Buddhism in Burma, 1885–1920'. PhD diss., University of Chicago, Divinity School.
Turner, Alicia Marie. 2014. *Saving Buddhism: The Impermanence of Religion in Colonial Burma*. Honolulu: University of Hawai'i Press.
Walton, Matthew J. 2008. 'Ethnicity, Conflict, and History in Burma: The Myths of Panglong'. *Asian Survey* 48 (6): 889–910.
Walton, Matthew J. 2013. 'The Wages of Burman-ness: Ethnicity and Burman Privilege in Contemporary Myanmar'. *Journal of Contemporary Asia* 43 (1): 1–27.
Walton, Matthew J. 2015. 'The Disciplining Discourse of Unity in Burmese Politics'. *Journal of Burma Studies* 19 (1): 1–26.

38

CLASS AND INEQUALITY

Elliott Prasse-Freeman and Phyo Win Latt

As Myanmar continues its transition from a military state to a quasi-democratic one, its economic growth rates have risen concomitantly (World Bank Group 2014, 7). Given the penury to which the country descended over the military period, Myanmar's masses would appear poised to reap benefits from this growth, as the rising tide lifts all boats (Farrelly 2016). However, closer examination of the structure of the political economy (see Chapter 18; Nyo Tun 2016) dampens enthusiasm: average Myanmar people face four interlacing challenges – a highly resource-extractive growth model; agrarian displacement; few good jobs to reabsorb displaced labourers; and inadequate or eroding safety nets – that may leave them materially worse off.

First, Myanmar's growth model remains dependent on natural resource extraction (Bissinger 2012; World Bank Group 2014, 16), a phenomenon which in comparative cases has led to marked increases in inequality (Gylfason & Zoega 2002). Such extractive sectors, which in Myanmar include the illicit drugs trade (Winn 2015), have few economic linkages – meaning they create few jobs relative to the rents they generate. Current market liberalisation is merely facilitating an intensification of such resource exploitation, as foreign investment skews massively towards the extractive sector (World Bank Group 2014, 16). Myanmar's exceedingly thin political-economic elite (only 7.5 per cent of the population is middle class or affluent – see Shein Thu Aung 2013) has benefited by illicitly capturing resource rents, policing entrance to this rarefied stratum by requiring personalised connections to a military-elite clique (Larkin 2015); by entrenching themselves as the only viable businesses (Ford et al. 2016) they potentially crowd out non-aligned prospective entrants.

Second, legal 'reforms' have made land an alienable asset, providing an alluring investment opportunity for agribusinesses, industrial zone managers, narcotics money launderers (Meehan 2011) and land speculators. These reforms together with the aforementioned land-intensive resource extraction put immense pressure on the livelihood base of Myanmar's poor: land is being stripped from both peasants and urbanites through means both 'legal' (evictions and debt dispossession) and extra-legal (violent land grabs).

Third, infrastructure and logistics deficits – not to mention a global political-economic structure that provides barriers to economic 'structural transformation' for such a late 'late developer' (Waldner 1999) – mean that displaced masses are not reabsorbed into any bourgeoning high-productivity economic sector such as manufacturing.

Finally, meagre public services do not provide the marginalised with opportunities to break the cycle of underemployment: education and health in particular are sectors in which the wealthy consume high-quality private services (often outside Myanmar), while the poor survive on underfunded and under-qualified public options. Further, resource rent management processes remain inscrutable (World Bank Group 2014, 42) and hence revenues may be siphoned off rather than being allocated to those starved public good sectors. Added to this, traditional networks of care and support may be eroding: increasingly necessary migration (ILO 2015) disrupts village life and *horizontal* community bonds therein (Boutry 2013), while an ascendant bourgeois ethos celebrating individual accomplishment combined with elite reorientation to a now-accessible global consumptive marketplace means that *vertical* patronage bonds may degrade.

Myanmar is hence rapidly becoming a visibly unequal place, as a military-business elite asserts itself, flaunting luxuriant lifestyles (Mahtani 2014) that flourish in the interstices of the country's largely destitute environment. This is a moment of explicit class consolidation – complete with the ideological succour provided by self-help gurus justifying accumulation as available to all with 'positive' attitudes. How will the excluded respond: will the pullulating protests roiling in Myanmar today mobilise broader movements? Or will the poor feel placated by the country's ubiquitous 'development' discourse, believing broad benefits (either material or only symbolic) will trickle down to them (Prasse-Freeman 2014)?

This chapter will proceed by sketching Myanmar's political economy over the past two centuries, focusing on facets that prevented both grossly unequal conditions from developing and class-consciousness from forming. It will then turn to the current political economy, further elaborating the four challenges sketched above. The chapter will then conclude with a discussion of perceptions of class and inequality in the country.

Historical equality in shared exploitation

As elaborated by scholars of dynastic Myanmar and Southeast Asia (Scott 2009, Aung-Thwin 1990, and Lieberman 1984, *inter alia*), Myanmar's pre-colonial political economy revolved around the control of rice paddy production. Authorities built decentralised systems of taxation and regulation through which they garnered tribute from regional leaders, who in turn extracted resources from those further away institutionally and physically. Critical for our purposes, within this political economy key institutions helped peasants manage exploitation. Aung-Thwin (1984) outlines the way subjects sought out bonded relationships to patrons or institutions that secured their lives and livelihoods, while Scott (1972) describes how the political-economic 'terms of trade' were relatively decent for a peasant producer who could nonetheless rely on kin and village to mitigate shocks. In later work, Scott (2009) posits that if elites violated the terms of these bonds, the hills and swamps surrounding Myanmar's lowlands provided areas to which subjects could flee (cf. Lieberman 2010, 339–342).

While more research is necessary to assess whether this compelled any concessions by rulers, at the very least the evidence suggests that conditions eroded for peasants during the colonial period. The British colonial project (1824–1947) generally undermined village risk management mechanisms (by enclosing common resources and inducting peasants into the perilous cash economy – see Scott 1972, 25–26), and in particular radically transformed the Delta areas of the Ayeyawaddy river into an enormous rice producer by inducing peasants to clear swamps and plant paddy. While this turned Myanmar into 'the rice bowl of Asia', historian Ian Brown describes the ultimately disastrous effects of this colonial rice-export economy: by continually rejecting legal and policy protection schemes for farmers (such as conditional debt forgiveness laws or crop diversification policies), the colonial administration made peasants vulnerable to cycles of dispossession. The British themselves noted the way they were undermining the long-term health of the Burmese political economy, and yet chose to only deepen their extraction practices (Brown 2013, 37–44). Moreover, this myopic focus on rice retarded the development of any non-rice sectors (including more human capital-intensive ones); further, by importing Indian clerks to run the administration, and by promoting Indian (and Chinese) capital to lubricate the economy, the colonial period systematically excluded Burmese from the state and the few advanced sectors of the economy. Hence, external shocks such as the Great Depression and World War II decimated the brittle economy, and Burma staggered into independence with little capital (Indians had fled or been expelled), rice fields destroyed, infrastructure cut, without domestic manufacturing, with few experienced administrators and facing a country-wide insurgency exacerbating those challenges. Against conventional wisdom about Burma's bright post-independence future, the country was hardly poised to be a successful economy *before* the mismanagement of the military period.

The military era further exacerbated Myanmar's decline. In the context of economic and administrative ruin, and numerous insurgencies mobilised along ideological and ethnic lines, Burma's military emerged as an ambitious and capable actor (Callahan 2003), ultimately able to build a hybrid rentier state (Prasse-Freeman 2012): while fighting off those many insurgencies, the military-state apparatus extracted the country's natural resources and cut a set of 'bargains' with the populace. Rural dwellers got land, but were compelled to give up much of their rice yield to the state; urbanites got cheap rice, but there was no competent industrialisation and no growth. Both groups were denied political freedoms. The military was able to violate those bargains at whim – as in the Delta area where thousands of farmers were dispossessed of their land after not delivering their rice yield quotas (GRET 2015). Yet, such expedient violations bring into question claims such as Brown's that the military governments of this era 'stressed equity rather than increased productivity' (Brown 2013, 185); when read through the lens of the military's interests, low inequality was less a policy goal – less a choice for which 'productivity' was sacrificed – than a secondary effect derived from the military's prosecution of its organisational objectives. As Brown himself notes, the military never addressed landlessness (in fact, scholars at GRET show that the military *created* it), and by 2000 'nearly ten million people [were] largely dependent on laboring wages alone' (Brown 2013, 185). Unlike other so-called late-developers in the greater region (such as Taiwan and South Korea – see Waldner 1999), the rents extracted by the military were not reinvested into the building of an advanced manufacturing sector (hence structurally transforming the economy), but were rather directed at maintaining a system of political domination through an ever-growing apparatus of organised violence. As we will elaborate on below, the military's self-interests subverted any rhetorical pretence for equality and socialism; people were equal in their poverty (Khin Maung Kyi et al. 2000, 130–131).

As the military continued throughout the 1990s and 2000s to consolidate its position within the state, it relinquished some direct control of the economy, pivoting towards market experimentation by encouraging an improvisational quasi-entrepreneurial form of wealth extraction, one that resulted in two significant transfers of productive resources. The first saw the dispossession of average Burmese people: various state agencies were encouraged to embrace the market economy by setting up their own 'development' projects, meaning that ill-equipped ministries grabbed land from farmers and attempted to establish industrial projects (sugar production, etc.), with predictably disastrous results (see Woods 2014); as the military continued to win wars against ethnic and other various non-state armed groups, it collaborated with those vanquished elites for shared resource exploitation (Woods 2011), resulting in marginalisation of ethnic masses (Brenner 2015).

If the first transfer was from individual people to the state, the second was from the state – and hence ostensibly *all* Myanmar people – into the hands of private actors. Here the military set up its own economic corporations devoted to capital accumulation mostly through the extraction of natural resources; moreover, various generals cultivated relationships with business leaders (called 'national entrepreneurs'), empowering them to carry out the exploitation of key domains of the economy. These tycoons would receive effective monopolies in natural resource extraction (timber, gems) or import licence monopolies for certain key products (automobiles, cement, etc.), allowing them to keep prices otherwise artificially high, reaping enormous windfalls for themselves and their patrons (Larkin 2015; Ford et al. 2016).

The transition from austere faux-socialism to authoritarian capitalism created new conceptions of opportunity and value, particularly pertaining to land, with significant consequences for inequality today. But before taking up those themes, we will now linger briefly on the historical period to discuss how the phenomena just outlined shaped popular conceptions of class and inequality.

Arrested class-consciousness

Throughout this history Burmese people often identified 'foreign' (British, Indian, Chinese, etc.) forces, and then the military itself, as the precipitators of economic devastation. Indeed, the internal stratification of wealth and opportunities amongst Burmese that occurred from colonial occupation through the BSPP period to today has not been interpreted as a schism between those Burmese who controlled the means of production or who set the terms of market integration and those who did not. Rather, ascription of the cause of the material inequality was displaced on to interests *external* to that dialectic: on to either transnational forces (such as Indians, Chinese or Westerners), or on to the military as responsible for the immiseration of the people.

As Taylor (1981, 45) argues, because of the ways the colonial state facilitated access for Indian capitalists, and because of the wealth acquisition the Chinese enjoyed during colonial rule, what might have developed into class critiques became obscured under the perceived ethnic difference embodied by those two groups and the Western colonisers behind them. The rise of ethno-racial consciousness was exacerbated by a series of Indo-Burman riots and a number of Sino-Burman scuffles (Lintner 1990, 20). The trope of the illegitimate foreign usurper winnowed its ways into popular media of this period – for instance, a popular song in the 1930s about Chettiars went thus: 'They take the gold, they take the silver, they take the land, and then, they take the women; we are afraid that [our] race will disappear.' More important, however, was the conflation of economic exploitation and foreignness into a single concept. Nemoto (2000) shows that even as the powerful nationalist movement *Dobama Asiayoun* defined themselves ('We Burmese') as poor and honest (rather than as a particular 'race' *per se*), they fashioned their 'We Burmese'-ness against a 'Those Burmese' who were internal enemies because of their alignment with external interests.

Further, the Communist Party of Burma (CPB), which emerged after independence to contest the constitutional regime and then the military that succeeded it, retained the external focus. It preferred to portray Myanmar's governments as semi-feudal neocolonialisms rather than focusing on intra-social conflict over the control of resources (Yin Htun 2015). Moreover, by taking to the hills and becoming involved in the narcotics trade, Lintner argues that by the mid-1980s 'Communist ideology became a hollow concept' (Lintner 1990, 41).

Finally, the one institution that did discuss class – the BSPP regime – alienated nearly the entire country, giving class discussion itself a bad name. Even as the military-state extracted surplus from farmers through the fixing of rice procurement prices, even as it amassed wealth from natural resource sales, the party simultaneously called for a classless society, adopting a rhetoric of dialectical historical materialism infused with some Buddhist values (Union of Burma 1964). This rhetoric often made assertions that were incongruent with people's daily realities. For instance, the BSPP permitted many literary works depicting the miserable lives of working class people (by Bhamo Tin Aung (2011), Maung Htin, Naing Win Swe, etc.) so as to justify the revolution. However, these novels often (intentionally or inadvertently) called attention to the hollowness of the BSPP's claims. For instance, while a recurring theme in these works was how poor people were preyed on by the black market (Kyaw Yin Hlaing 2001), poor (and the well-off!) depended on the black market for consumer essentials. Indeed, when Ne Win demonetised the currency in 1988 to eliminate the black markets, people suffered from losing their savings, but those challenges were significantly exacerbated by the sudden absence of black market-provided goods (Brown 2013, 166, 200). In sum, as the BSPP destroyed the economy, 'socialism' became a condemned word – signifying a toxic mix of cynicism and incompetence.

The BSPP legacy is reflected in discourse today. Class conflict itself is condemned as an atavistic and regressive legacy of the Ne Win years. For instance, the populist journal *Thuriya Naywun* recently ran a scathing two-part article entitled 'Leftist doctrine and class warfare, have we arrived [again] to Ne Win's time?' (Bobo Kyaw Nyein 2015). Moreover, while there are terms about the poor that can be expressed in explicit 'class' terms – such as 'the oppressed class' and 'lower class', the proletariat ('people without things') – they do not appear often. In dozens of ethnographic interviews and observations of contemporary discourse, we heard instead of 'the poor' or the 'lower people'. When class *is* explicitly used, it is not only (or very often) applied in the context of *classes* opposed to each other because of clear delineations between them (as in Marxist conceptualisations), but rather it is used as a mode of *general* social differentiation. For instance, one hears about the 'educated class' or the 'people who live in cities class' or even 'the taxi riding class'. A point here, following Campbell (n.d.; see also Soe Lin Aung 2014), is that molar institutions such as the BSPP and CPB have obscured and even arrested articulations of emancipatory political orientations from below.

Instead of class: the promise of development for all

Indeed, in the context of the false promises of the BSPP's 'socialism' and the legacy of animus toward 'foreigners' as the vectors of exploitation, in fieldwork we have observed that often the promise of 'development' eclipses or preempts the idea of class conflict. In this, the country is split into two parts: development promises to transform the current state of the nation (fractious and economically backward) into its future incarnation (the 'developed' nation).

This development rhetoric has long been ubiquitous in Burmese-language discourse and symbolic life. Since independence Myanmar people have been treated to a continual effluent of propaganda heralding development successes and promising others: models of suspension bridges and photographs of dams dominate the National Museum in Yangon's one hall devoted to contemporary government initiatives; state school facades have 'with education, modern development' plastered on them; for years a billboard declaring the hopeful assurance 'To a more modern and developed nation' has greeted visitors entering Yangon from Mingaladon Airport. It is not surprising that the military's party, the United State Development Party (USDP), made its slogan for the 2015 elections: '[We] will continue to work to bring about the development of the country's social prosperity'. In September of 2015, President Thein Sein released a video entitled 'Moving Forward' touting his accomplishments (President's Office 2015). Although the video features in its subtitles a range of policy victories, the *images* are preoccupied to a comical degree with representations of ports, construction sites and bustling business districts (often shown in time-lapse to suggest their imminent becoming). Even when written subtitles tout the solutions to the country's ethnic conflict, the video presents the same images of 'development' and 'modernity'. This is particularly striking given that ethnic nationalities often see 'development' as giving rhetorical cover for state occupation of indigenous land and resources (KHRG 2007; TNI 2013).

Indeed, the invocation of development often obscures current challenges; it has been presented as the *deus ex machina* for problems as varied as ethnic conflict, democratisation and poverty. For instance, when Speaker of Parliament Shwe Mann addressed an audience of Rakhine nationalists in 2013, he presented development as the panacea for all of these problems: 'Our country was left behind for many years because we didn't trust each other and lacked cooperation. Let's build trust, cooperate and work together for the development of the state' (Saga Wa 2013).

The National League for Democracy (NLD), now the country's ruling party, has done little better. For instance, note the sad and cynical rhetoric that NLD leader Aung San Suu Kyi used while defending the Letpadaung copper mine project's continuation. This mine, built on land expropriated from villagers and given to a Chinese company, had been picketed by displaced villagers before a brutal police crackdown on Buddhist monks raised their cause to the national stage. Aung San Suu Kyi chaired a commission to investigate the issue and ultimately argued that the villagers would have to accept the compensation offered. Her justification is critical: saying *she had to do what was good for the country*, she sacrificed the desires of the villagers because, she said, foreign capital would be frightened by capitulation to protesters' demands (*The Voice Weekly* 2013). By attempting to silence the farmers by invoking the country's future benefits, she implied that all those stolen from today will somehow benefit from their dispossession in the long run. They must sacrifice and then they must wait.

Finally, take an experience by one of the authors: in a courthouse in Mandalay in April 2015 an altercation occurred between police and defendant Thein Aung Myint as the latter was being escorted into court to be tried for leading a protest; the police chief later told the defendant's comrades, by way of assuaging their anger: 'We are not against [Thein Aung Myint]. After all, we are both on the same side. We both want development for the country.' In those examples, currently irreconcilable issues of, respectively, ethnic conflict, land grabs and draconian sanctioning of democratic citizen participation are deferred. Such discourse elides the causes of current problems through a promise of messianic transformation, actually neglecting and even undermining the future it gestures towards.

Inequality today: dispossession, joblessness, no opportunity

With the Letpadaung land grab just discussed in mind, we turn now to the current political economy, asking: in the shadow of development rhetoric, what are the prospects for 'development' to be delivered to all?

Poor. A number of factors are conspiring to significantly increase wealth stratification. Natural resource extraction has been covered sufficiently above, and so we will here focus on the latter three: forces of dispossession; arrested 'structural transformation'; and few opportunities for average people to acquire the human capital necessary to participate in a growing economy.

Dispossession

A significant percentage of rural dwellers (who still comprise 70 per cent of Myanmar's population) generally avoided destitution during the historical periods covered above because they retained de facto ownership of land on which they could implement productive activities (usually food cultivation). Indeed, land is still the most important single variable predicting economic security for a median Burmese person, and the landless are much poorer than those with land (Rammohan & Pritchard 2014). However, political, legal, economic and regulatory changes have precipitated significant dispossession – and have left many others vulnerable. First, displacement has long been a counter-insurgency strategy pursued by the Burmese military against local populations during its wars (Woods 2011; Ferguson 2014). Second, violent land grabs – often for agribusiness projects – remain a scourge (Global Witness 2015), and there has been no systematic policy or law promulgated to redress their concerns (more on this below). What's worse, these extra-legal grabs have been supplemented by increasing displacement of 'squatters' (ILO 2015, 48) and those who have forfeited land because of inabilities to repay debt (Woods 2015; Salaing Thant Sin 2014). These more insidious, 'natural' forms of dispossession – in which people are removed from land to which they lack legal 'rights' – have emerged as a function of the broader political-economic context: the normalisation of external diplomatic relations has made possible agribusiness development (Scurrah et al. 2015), the proliferation of industrial zones (including SEZs) (see Nishimura 2017), and massive resource extraction projects – the last especially in the uplands (TNI 2013). Millions of acres of land have been transferred to companies to carry out these land-intensive endeavours, and the government promises to convert 10 million acres by 2030 (Andersen 2016, 11).

As sociologist Henry Bernstein (1981) pointed out long ago, under normal conditions peasants face significant challenges to make ends meet year-to-year – a phenomenon he calls the 'simple reproduction squeeze'. This intrinsic vulnerability becomes potentially disastrous when vested and powerful actors desire the same land, and when legal reforms (in this case Myanmar's 2012 Farmland Law and 2012 Vacant, Fallow, and Virgin Law) make land suddenly officially alienable and transferable. The insertion of land into markets creates what can be called the quotidian land grab, in which commons 'are being fenced off by some local authorities to generate revenue for themselves and the common rights are no longer available to the village folk', as government economist U Myint (2011) has put it. Without the commons, farmers often cannot survive.

Land's commodification is generating a secondary and compounding pressure: investment in land. Patrick Meehan perceives land purchases as a way of laundering drug cash, arguing that:

> for an inflated price drug lords have been able to purchase property, allowing the state to exact a fee (the inflated cost paid over the actual value of the asset) in return for which drug revenue is converted into legitimate real estate.
>
> *Meehan 2011, 391*

Elizabeth Rhoads (forthcoming) has explored a transfer of land resources in early 2010 so vast that it is colloquially referred to as 'the fire sale' (see *The New York Times* 2010). As vast swaths of public land have been effectively given away to well-connected individuals, Rhoads has marked a concomitant transformation in the way land is valued: whereas in the previous era urban land owners rented out land to tenants to generate a small but stable income stream, now land is meant to provide real and fairly immediate returns. Investment in land has hence gone from a risk management (see MDRI/Mastercard 2014, 59, 68, 73) to a capital accumulation strategy. Urban poor are directly affected by this land investment (Myat Nyein Aye 2016) as affordable housing proves elusive (AFP 2013); the World Bank notes that urban poverty in Yangon is 'surprisingly high' (2014, 23) while Boutry (n.d.) outlines the vulnerability created in part by the housing crisis.

Whither structural transformation?

The processes described above seem at first glance homologous to historical enclosure movements – for instance, the privatisation of the English commons described famously by Karl Polanyi (2001). But in that era there were jobs in factories and mines (as miserable as they were) awaiting the people recently made 'free' of their land and security (Marx 1977, 875). While the World Bank today uses language (if not connotation) similar to Marx when describing the liberated poor ('The prospects for poverty reduction are greater when *newly released farm labor* can find its way to good, formal sector jobs' (World Bank Group 2014, 28, emphasis added)), there are marked differences in the *opportunities* for those labourers to find good work. As the World Bank itself notes, 'there is likely to be some substitution of capital for labor [in the agricultural sector]' (ibid., 45) but 'the pace of structural transformation has been limited . . . the reallocation of labor appears to have stalled' (ibid., 13). In other words, as bodies are made superfluous (by technology or land grabs alike) they are not reabsorbed in other production processes elsewhere.

Here it is worth examining comparable contexts to see how similar phenomena – dispossession of farmers for agribusiness or extraction projects – have affected the displaced. In Indonesia, anthropologist Tania Li has found that agribusinesses do not provide stable and beneficial employment. 'In Southeast Asia, plantations have routinely been bad news for the "locals": their land is needed, but their labor is not' (Li 2011, 286), and elsewhere she challenges the entire structural transformation model, questioning whether in a globalised market it is reasonable to assume that labourers can be absorbed by *domestic* economies (Li 2009). Returning to Myanmar's economy, the ILO's recent comprehensive migration report shows a strikingly high degree of rural-to-rural migration, suggesting that displaced or underemployed individuals are not being drawn by jobs generated by urban growth (ILO 2015, 3). The World Bank's migration report finds that urban jobs are so poor that 'earning differentials [between rural and urban] are not significant' (World Bank Group 2016, 10); rural people who do leave for cities mostly do so because rural economies no longer provide work (ibid., 61). Further, out-migration to Thailand continues apace (Rhoden & Unger 2015), despite precarious conditions there (Arnold & Pickles 2011). Finally, where employment opportunities emerge as a result of industrialisation, these benefits have been mitigated by rampant labour abuses and a suppression of wages (Labor Rights Clinic et al. 2013).

Few avenues of social mobility

Finally, not only does the allocative mechanism of economic growth not accrue to the poorest, it also does not appear that *distributive* interventions will be implemented to serve the poor's needs. Even if, as David Dapice et al. (2011) show, increased investment in the agrarian sector could assist the rural poor, there are a number of factors that militate against those benefits being delivered. Adequate sectoral support to farmers – in the form of sufficient provision of credit and inputs, or debt relief – has simply never been delivered, and has not improved during this era of putative reform. This derives from the state's inability to effectively tax its citizens (Wood 2014), especially the wealthy (Lawi Weng & Thet Swe Aye 2013); hence there is little revenue for supporting the agrarian sector, let alone assisting those made vulnerable by dislocations wrought by economic changes. Indeed, the state's social protection programme, which aspires to deliver a universal pension, has thus far gone unfunded (Htoo Thant 2015); the state devotes a stunningly meagre 0.01 per cent of GDP to social safety net programmes, far below other comparably poor countries (World Bank Group 2014, 44). Moreover, investment in education and public health remains below international standards, and what recent investments there have been in health have been mostly in low-impact capital expenditures (ibid., 38). Finally, even if equity-directed policies were designed and funded, there is a question of state capacity and will to deliver them.

Conclusion: class consolidation, nascent class-consciousness?

Another reason to speculate that lives for Myanmar's poor will become more precarious derives from the potential for elites who had previously seen themselves as patrons (to local communities, to the poor) to reorient away from that role towards an exclusivist global or Asian-regional consumption culture. Returning to Scott, who insists that patron–client ties are not atavistic vestiges of 'pre-modern' political economies but 'serve as a formula for bringing together individuals who are not kinsmen and as building-blocks for elaborate chains of vertical integration' (1972, 8), we are suggesting that currently there are fewer reasons to create these integrative chains. And while performing wealth and power – especially through public donations to religious associations and especially during natural disasters – retains its social importance, such demonstrations are sporadic and arbitrary: the social function of responsibility for the less well-off runs the risk of inexorably eroding.

This is because the transition facilities a consolidation of a new authoritarian-capitalist oligarch-military class, complete with a new consciousness circulating amongst its members. Tycoons (often called 'cronies') who once kept low profiles now audaciously assert their centrality to the economy; while this centrality may be true (Ford et al. 2016), the blatant proclamation of it, often combined with a rejection of the term 'crony' and an explicit assertion of the tycoons' principled entrepreneurialism (Ye Naing Oo 2016), suggests a robust ideological project. This consciousness is developed through self-help memes circulated on social media which focus on hard work and 'smart' investment, and through the stunning rise of self-help figures such as Lin Thaiq Nyunt, a business achievement guru peddling easy answers about the efficacy of positive thinking and the non-existence of any structural barriers to success. 'In the world we cannot talk about separation between classes. There is only a difference in effort and striving,' is his tagline; his slogan is 'See you at the top' (in English). Lin Thaiq Nyunt is not so much causative of this consciousness, but an index of it, and provides another site (in addition to yacht clubs, night clubs, shopping malls) that beckons others to participate in the 'principled entrepreneurial' mission.

On the other end of this increasingly stark divide, non-elites struggle to navigate the co-existence of, on one hand, visible wealth accumulation, 'development' rhetoric and apparent explosions in opportunity, and, on the other, the erosion of social bonds linking high and low status groups in the context of increasingly difficult structural economic conditions (Boutry 2013). While radical farmer, labour and livelihood movements have rejected the discourse of inclusive amelioration by grounding their militant actions in their material conditions – providing powerful exemplars for broader consumption by national publics (Prasse-Freeman 2016a) – these publics often appear ambivalent: there is condemnation of the 'crony economy', the 'failed law' and the durability of effective military elite control, but there is also a durable displacement of responsibility on to 'foreigners' (Muslims and Chinese) and an uncertain perspective on those very 'crony' businesspeople who have devoured the country.

To wit, over the past year we have looked at hundreds of political cartoons featured in major newspapers and journals and have observed a preponderance of ethnic scapegoating: Chinese in caricatured dress, Muslims who mispronounce 'proper' Burmese both flout the law and exploit the country. Yet while they are often identified as exploiters, the corrupt *Burmese* politician (marked by the *konbaung* headpiece) is often the intermediary who is actually making the exploitation possible. The Chinese or Muslim is portrayed almost as an unreflective force of nature – often talked about rather than being featured – while the space of the cartoon is instead occupied by the object of the public's derision: the betrayer of the nation who is selling it off. It is in this ambiguity that we trace the seeds of a class politics that identifies the economic exploitation being forged by 'Burmese' over other 'Burmese' people.

And yet, the inability to assert this claim may also be emblematic of a structural devalorisation of Myanmar's non-elites: while those working the land were historically necessary to create the polity's wealth, the evolution of the global economy (which has substituted capital for labour as technology has advanced), and the general transformation of land into a commodity (on which capital-intensive endeavours can be pursued), has meant that wealth is increasingly generated through means *not* involving labourers. These masses may feel they lack the bargaining strength to beat this new class, and must find ways to join them.

Of course, structural impediments can be circumvented or even dismantled with concentrated political action. It is here that the NLD's installation into government in the 2015 elections has brought some initial hope. The NLD came to power under a mantle of change, and its leaders have occasionally said the right things about poverty and pro-poor policies. For instance, the party pledged a resolution of *all* land grabs by the end of 2016 (Htet Naing Zaw 2016), and its economic platform, announced in July 2016, promised *inter alia* a suspension of mining until proper regulations were instituted, credit and support for farmers, and a commitment to tackling poverty and inequality (Aye Thidar Kyaw & Hammond 2016).

Yet, some of the party's other discourse has been troubling. Rather than taking a principled stand against cronyism, Aung San Suu Kyi caused a stir when she seemed to argue for its necessity and merely implored cronies to behave a bit better (Inkyin Naing 2016). Further, despite the party's grand proclamations to redress land grabs, Jenny Franco (2016) points out that NLD statements assert only tepid support for farmers' land tenure security. Franco writes that language in its election manifesto

> does not sound like a very strong commitment to remedying a grave injustice, and no mention is made of the extensive guidance to be found in international human rights and humanitarian law... [or] even the NLUP [National Land Use Policy].

Even more importantly, Franco points out that proceeding with land titling without addressing land grabs and general farmer vulnerability is a great example of how liberalisation can harm the least well-off: 'Securing legal land rights can even open the door to losing their land, for example in cases of economic distress or indebtedness.'

In the context of such conflicting rhetoric, it becomes imperative to assess instead the party's *actions*. Returning to Letpadaung may prove instructive: when this chapter was written the case was still far from being resolved; on 22 February 2017 protesters barricaded roads to block mining company activities (Zarni Mann 2017). One of the authors visited four villages there in June 2016 and was told about the project's degradation of the environment, the inadequate compensation given for seized lands, and *additional* land grabs – facts corroborated in an early 2017 Amnesty International report (Amnesty International 2017).

The persistence of the conflict in Letpadaung is emblematic of the general pattern of continuing and deepening displacement: the deadline for resolving all land grab cases has passed without any meaningful NLD action; instead, every week more dispossessed farmers are arrested for protests (Htay Hla Aung 2017). All of this is occurring beneath the discursive cover of democracy and liberalisation, producing a situation in which long-standing political activists feel ambivalent about critiquing the new government (Prasse-Freeman 2016b). Ultimately, they want to know if the NLD will meaningfully contest the entrenching military-elite class, or if, more alarmingly, its members would prefer to join it. How the NLD answers that question, and how activists and other political actors in turn respond to that answer, may significantly impact the future trajectories for the poor in Myanmar today.

References

AFP. 2013. 'Soaring land prices push Myanmar's poor into streets'. AFP, 11 September.

Amnesty International. 2017. *Mountain of Trouble: Human Rights Abuses Continue at Myanmar's Letpadaung Mine*. London: Amnesty International.

Andersen, Kirsten Ewers. 2016. 'Study of Upland Customary Communal Tenure in Chin and Shan States'. Land Core Group.

Arnold, Dennis and John Pickles. 2011. 'Global Work, Surplus Labor, and the Precarious Economies of the Border'. *Antipode* 43 (5): 1598–1624.

Aung-Thwin, Michael. 1984. 'Hierarchy and Order in Pre-Colonial Burma'. *Journal of Southeast Asian Studies* 15 (2): 224–232.

Aung-Thwin, Michael. 1990. *Irrigation in the Heartland of Burma*. Northern Illinois University Occasional Paper No. 15.

Aye Thidar Kyaw and Clare Hammond. 2016. 'Government reveals 12-point economic policy', *The Myanmar Times*, 29 July.

Bernstein, Henry. 1981. 'Concepts for the Analysis of Contemporary Peasantries'. In *The Political Economy of Rural Development: Peasants, International Capital, and the State*, edited by Rosemary Galli, 3–24. Albany: SUNY Press.

Bissinger, Jared. 2012. 'Foreign Investment in Myanmar: A Resource Boom but a Development Bust?' *Contemporary Southeast Asia* 34 (1): 23–52.

Bobo Kyaw Nyein. 2015. 'Leftist Doctrine and Class Warfare, Have We Arrived [again] to Ne Win's Time?' *Thuriya Naywun* 1 (50) [Burmese].

Boutry, Maxime. n.d. 'Urban Poverty in Yangon Greater City'. Report for World Food Program Yangon.

Boutry, Maxime. 2013. 'From British to Humanitarian Colonization: the "Early Recovery" Response in Myanmar after Nargis'. *South East Asia Research* 21 (3): 381–401.

Brenner, David. 2015. 'Ashes of Co-optation: From Armed Group Fragmentation to the Rebuilding of Popular Insurgency in Myanmar'. *Conflict, Security & Development* 15 (4) 337–358.

Brown, Ian. 2013. *Burma's Economy in the Twentieth Century*. New York: Cambridge University Press.

Callahan, Mary Patricia. 2003. *Making Enemies: War and State Building in Burma*. Ithaca: Cornell University Press.

Campbell, Stephen. n.d. 'Rethinking Myanmar's Left Intellectual History: The Subaltern Politics of Banmaw Tin Aung and Thakin Po Hla Gyi'.

Dapice, David O., Thomas J. Valley, Ben Wilkinson, Malcolm McPherson, and J. Michael 2011. 'Myanmar Agriculture in 2011: Old Problems and New Challenges'. Research paper prepared for Proximity Designs, Myanmar. Cambridge: Ash Center for Democratic Governance and Innovation, Harvard Kennedy School.

Farrelly, Nicholas. 2016. 'Misplaced Affection for Myanmar's old Days'. *New Mandala*, 9 March.

Ferguson, Jane. 2014. 'The Scramble for the Waste Lands'. *Singapore Journal of Tropical Geography* 35: 295–311.

Ford, Michele, Michael Gillan and Htwe Htwe Thein. 2016. 'From Cronyism to Oligarchy? Privatisation and Business Elites in Myanmar'. *Journal of Contemporary Asia* 46: 1.

Franco, Jenny. 2016. 'The Right to Land at Crossroads in Myanmar', *Transnational Institute*, 5 July.

Global Witness. 2015. *Guns, Cronies and Crops*. London: Global Witness.

GRET. 2015. 'Land Tenure in Rural Lowland Myanmar', Draft Report, September.

Gylfason, Thorvaldur and Gylfi Zoega. 2002. 'Inequality and Economic Growth: Do Natural Resources Matter?' April. CESifo Working Paper Series No. 712.

Htay Hla Aung. 2017. '350 protesting farmers face court', *Eleven*, 23 February.

Htet Naing Zaw. 2016. 'Govt committee to settle all land grab cases in six months', *The Irrawaddy*, 1 July.

Htoo Thant. 2015. 'Budget concerns cripple pension expansion'. *The Myanmar Times*, 16 January.

Inkyin Naing. 2016. 'Daw Su gives warning to cronies to not act with intentions like before' *Voice of America* [Burmese], 23 October.

International Labour Organization (ILO). 2015. 'Internal Labour Migration in Myanmar: Building an Evidence-Base on Patterns in Migration, Human Trafficking and Forced Labour'. Yangon: ILO.

Karen Human Rights Group 2007. 'Development by decree: the politics of poverty and control in Karen State'. 24 April. Chiang Mai.

Khin Maung Kyi, Ronald Findlay, Sundrum Mya Maung R.M. and Myo Nyunt, Zaw Oo. 2000. *A Vision and a Strategy: Economic Development of Burma*. Stockholm: Olof Palme International Center.

Kyaw Yin Hlaing. 2001. The Politics of State–Business Relations in Post-Colonial Burma. Cornell.

Labor Rights Clinic, Cooperation Programme of Independent Laborers, Construction-based Labour Union, Workers Support Group. 2013. 'Modern Slavery: A Study of Labour Conditions in Yangon's Industrial Zones (2012–2013)'. PhD dissertation. Ithaca: Cornell University.

Larkin, Stuart. 2015. 'Myanmar's Tycoons: Vested Interests Resisting Reform or Agents of Change?' *ISEAS Perspective* 39: 1–14.

Li, Tania. 2009. 'Exit from Agriculture: A Step Forward or a Step Backward for the Rural Poor?' *Journal of Peasant Studies* 36 (3): 629–636.

Li, Tania. 2011. 'Centring Labour in the Land Grab Debate'. *Journal of Peasant Studies* 38 (2): 281–298

Lieberman, Victor. 1984. *Burmese Administrative Cycles: Anarchy and Conquest, c. 1580–1760*. Princeton: University Press.

Lieberman, Victor. 2010. 'A Zone of Refuge in Southeast Asia? Reconceptualizing Interior Spaces'. *Journal of Global History* 5 (2): 333–346.

Lintner, Bertil. 1990. *The Rise and Fall of the Communist Party of Burma (CPB)*. No. 6. SEAP Publications, 20. Ithaca: Cornell University.

Mahtani, Shibani. 2014. 'Meet the New Rich . . . in Myanmar'. *Wall Street Journal*, 4 September.

Marx, Karl. 1977. *Capital: Volume 1*, trans. Ben Fowkes. New York: Vintage.

MDRI/Mastercard. 2014. 'Cash in Context: Uncovering Financial Services in Myanmar'.

Meehan, Patrick. 2011. 'Drugs, Insurgency and State-Building in Burma: Why the Drugs Trade is Central to Burma's Changing Political Order'. *Journal of Southeast Asian Studies* 42 (3): 376–404.

Myat Nyein Aye. 2016. 'Speculation squeezes potential gains from Dala property'. *The Myanmar Times*, 3 March.

Nemoto, Kei. 2000. 'The Concepts of Dobama (Our Burma) and Thudo-Bama (Their Burma) in Burmese Nationalism, 1930–1948'. *Journal of Burma Studies* 5: 1–16.

The New York Times. 2010. 'Myanmar's ruling junta is selling state's assets'. 7 March.

Nishimura, Lauren. 2017. 'Facing the Concentrated Burden of Development: Local Responses to Myanmar's Special Economic Zones'. In *The Business of Transition: Law Reform, Economics and Development in Myanmar*, edited by Melissa Crouch. Cambridge: Cambridge University Press.

Nyo Tun. 2016. 'Betrayed by statistics: GDP "'growth" leaves Burmese no richer'. *Democratic Voice of Burma*, 1 February.

Polanyi, Karl. 2001. *The Great Transformation*. Boston: Beacon.

Prasse-Freeman, Elliott. 2012. 'Power, Civil Society, and an Inchoate Politics of the Daily in Burma/Myanmar'. *Journal of Asian Studies* 71 (2): 371–397.

Prasse-Freeman, Elliott. 2014. 'Aung San Suu Kyi and her Discontents'. Kyoto Review.

Prasse-Freeman, Elliott. 2016a. 'Grassroots Protest Movements and Mutating Conceptions of "the Political" in an Evolving Burma'. In *Metamorphosis: Studies in Social and Political Change in Myanmar*, edited by Renaud Egreteau and Francois Robinne. Singapore: NUS Press.

Prasse-Freeman, Elliott. 2016b. 'The New Burma is Starting to Look Too Much Like the Old Burma', *Foreign Policy*, 28 June.

Rammohan, Anu and Bill Pritchard. 2014. 'The Role of Landholding as a Determinant of Food and Nutrition Insecurity in Rural Myanmar'. *World Development* 64: 597–608.

Republic of the Union of Myanmar President's Office. 2015. 'Shwe-tho Myanmar (Moving Forward)'. [Burmese] 11 September. www.facebook.com/myanmarpresidentoffice.gov.mm/videos/899593970088340/.

Rhoads, Elizabeth. Forthcoming. 'The Yangon Fire Sale and Evolutions in Land Value in Myanmar'.

Rhoden, T.F. and Danny Unger. 2015. 'No Burmese Returning: Economics Across Myanmar–Thailand Border'. *The International Journal of East Asian Studies*, 19 (2) 51–70.

Saga Wa. 2013. 'The Rakhine people are protecting the union's culture, customs, and traditions in addition to its autonomy and the ownership of the land'. [Burmese.] Myawady, 30 September.

Salaing Thant Sin. 2014. 'In the Labyrinth of Debt, the Downtrodden Farmers'. [Burmese]. *Irrawaddy Weekly Journal* 1 (46).

Scott, James C. 1972. 'The Erosion of Patron–Client Bonds and Social Change in Rural Southeast Asia'. *Journal of Asian Studies* 32 (1): 5–37.

Scott, James C. 2009. *The Art of Not Being Governed.* New Haven: Yale University Press.

Scurrah, Natalia, Kevin Woods and Philip Hirsch. 2015. 'The Political Economy of Land Governance in Myanmar'. Mekong Region Land Governance.

Shein Thu Aung. 2013. 'Middle class in Myanmar to double by 2020'. *Myanmar Business Today,* 30 December.

Soe Lin Aung. 2014. 'Syncretism and Historicity: Towards a Translational Reading of Burmese Marxism'. Paper presented at 2014 Cornell Burma Conference.

Tin Aung (Bhamo). 2011. *Colonial Era Myanmar History.* Yangon: KantKaw WutYeh Publishing [Burmese].

Transnational Institute (TNI). 2013. 'Developing Disparity Regional Investment in Burma's Borderlands'. Amsterdam, February.

U Myint. 2011. 'Reducing Poverty in Myanmar: the Way Forward'. Paper presented to the 'Forum on Poverty' sponsored by the Burmese government in Naypyitaw on 20–21 May 2011.

Union of Burma. 1964. *The System of the Correlation of Men and His Environment.* Union of Burma Rangoon.

Taylor, Robert H. 1981. 'Party, Class and Power in British Burma'. *The Journal of Commonwealth & Comparative Politics*, 19 (1): 44–62.

The Voice Weekly. 2013. 'The person behind the Letpadaung Mountain'. 16 March. www.facebook.com/thevoiceweekly/posts/551253048228292 [Burmese language].

Waldner, David. 1999. *State Building and Late Development.* Ithaca: Cornell University Press.

Weng, Lawi and Thet Swe Aye. 2013. 'Amid mass tax evasion, Burmese public demands reform'. *The Irrawaddy*, April 10.

Winn, Patrick. 2015. 'Myanmar's state-backed militias are flooding Asia with meth'. *Global Post,* 12 November.

Wood, Josh. 2014. 'Fiscal cloud taxes Myanmar optimism'. *Asia Times*, 8 January.

Woods, Kevin. 2011. 'Ceasefire Capitalism: Military–Private Partnerships, Resource Concessions and Military–State Building in the Burma–China Borderlands'. *Journal of Peasant Studies* 38 (4): 747–770.

Woods, Kevin. 2014. 'Political anatomy of land grabs'. *The Myanmar Times*, 3 March.

Woods, Kevin. 2015. 'CP Maize Contract Farming in Shane State, Myanmar'. BICAS Working Paper 14, May. https://www.iss.nl/fileadmin/ASSETS/iss/Research_and_projects/Research_networks/BICAS/BICAS_WP_14-Woods.pdf.

World Bank Group. 2014. 'Ending Poverty and Boosting Shared Prosperity in a Time of Transition'. Nov, Report No. 93050-MM.

World Bank Group. 2016. 'A Country on the Move: Domestic Migration in Two Regions of Myanmar'. Qualitative Social and Economic Monitoring project, January.

Ye Naing Oo. 2016. 'Interview with Khin Shwe (Zaygabar)'. *The Voice,* 29 March.

Yin Htun (Suseethee). 2015. *Thakin Than Thun's Speeches.* Yangon: Yin Myo Literature [Burmese].

Zarni Mann. 2017. 'Local protesters block road to Letpadaung Copper Mine', *The Irrawaddy*, 22 February.

39

ENVIRONMENT AND NATURAL RESOURCES

Adam Simpson

One of the key challenges facing Myanmar is to exploit its natural resources in a way that results in equitable development, while protecting the country's core ecosystems and promoting respect for its environment. 'The environment' is a social and political construct, the meaning of which is contested by competing interests within society. In Myanmar, as in many other parts of Southeast Asia, 'the environment' is often conflated with 'natural resources': a resource to be exploited with the benefits extracted by the privileged few while the resultant pollution, deforestation and other negative environmental externalities afflict the less powerful (Simpson 2018b). The environment in Myanmar is therefore inextricably linked to its turbulent and authoritarian political history and the associated issues of justice, inequality and social activism. As Hirsch (2017) notes in relation to Southeast Asia more broadly, 'the environment is firmly embedded in the wider social, economic and political dynamics of the region as a whole and of its constituent countries'.

Myanmar's ethnic, cultural and religious diversity results in many attitudes and approaches to the environment and natural resources. Although Buddhism is the country's dominant religion there are also sizeable populations of Christian, Muslim and other religious minorities. For many ethnic groups in the mountainous border regions these religions overlie, and merge with, longstanding animist belief systems, resulting in complex syncretic perspectives towards human–nature interaction. Respecting these belief systems while applying scientific rigour and analysis to ecosystem impacts would significantly improve Myanmar's evolving environmental governance system, while an increased role for ethnically diverse local communities in the management of natural resources would promote the process of national reconciliation as well as providing ecological benefits.

Like its ethnicity and culture, Myanmar's geography and ecology are extremely diverse, and include mountainous borderlands that extend the length of the country, the flat lands of the central dry-zone and relatively pristine beaches on the southern tropical coasts and islands. Historically, however, the governance of these ecosystems has been woefully inadequate with mismanagement and endemic corruption combining to exacerbate environmental destruction. In some respects, the lack of economic development in the country throughout five decades of authoritarian rule resulted in a less disastrous environmental impact on the local environment than in its neighbour, Thailand, which developed large and highly polluting heavy industries over the same period. Fragile coastal areas have not been degraded to the same extent as in Thailand because mass tourism and heavy industries remain in their infancy. In other respects, however, corruption and the lack of coherent environmental governance and policy making resulted in widespread and ad hoc mining, logging and energy projects that were undertaken without regard for the adverse environmental consequences, a situation compounded by civil conflict between the central government and ethnic minorities in the mountainous and resource-rich border regions. While Thailand's forests have recovered somewhat since 1990, Myanmar has spent much of the intervening period deforesting the country at a furious pace.

Despite a surge in environmentally destructive 'development' activities associated with Myanmar's transition, the Thein Sein-led USDP government's approach to governance of natural resources and the environment gradually started to shift in tandem with other political reforms, resulting in new policy tools that were more accessible to civil society. Most notable amongst these was Myanmar's embrace of the Extractive Industries Transparency Initiative (EITI), which represents a global movement towards transparency and civil society engagement in natural resource governance. While the global movement has taken decades to evolve, Myanmar undertook a fast-track transition from residual direct military rule in early 2011 to a nominally civil society-centred governance process in some extractive industries within a few years. The impediments and difficulties in this transition epitomise some of the broader governance limitations within the country and illustrate the formidable challenges in environmental governance facing the NLD government.

The rest of this chapter explores the dynamics of environmental and natural resource governance in Myanmar and proceeds in four main sections. The first section provides a brief overview of how corruption in Myanmar has impacted on its environment and natural resources. The second section examines the historical challenges to environmental governance and security during the period of military rule. The third section explores the emerging state-led forms of environmental governance under the Thein Sein government and the fourth section examines the prospects for effective environmental governance under the NLD government.

Corruption and the environment in Myanmar

Agriculture and natural resources are the most significant components of Myanmar's economy: they dominate exports and provide the vast majority of its foreign exchange, whether official or unofficial. Corruption at various levels, mismanagement and civil conflict have allowed much of the activity to occur in the black economy, resulting in ineffective environmental governance and accompanying widespread environmental degradation (Simpson 2018a). These issues are interrelated and partly result from the central role the military has historically played in the country's political economy (see Chapter 18). The role of the military in politics and the economy will be a long-term issue for society to address but the effect of corruption itself has had a highly debilitating effect on environmental protection, equitable development and sustainability.

Corruption occurs when people in public office breach the 'impartiality principle', whereby everyone should be treated more or less equally by the state (Kurer 2005); it usually occurs as a result of some sort of private payment. In natural resources, it often entails public officers receiving private financial benefit to treat a company or individual favourably by unfairly awarding a licence, a mining or forestry lease or a state production quota. The financial benefit is usually a 'kickback': a direct cash payment or a profit-sharing interest in the business.

Corruption is more likely to occur in societies such as Myanmar with highly unequal power and resource distributions, which reinforce in-group trust within privileged circles but reduce it between these circles and less favoured citizens, resulting in an 'inequality–mistrust–corruption' trap (Le Billon 2014). Likewise, when the public perceives that the government is making genuine efforts to reduce corruption they are more likely to fight corruption themselves (Peiffer and Alvarez 2015). Perceptions are therefore clearly important in increasing or reducing corruption.

Corruption relating to natural resources differs amongst types of natural resources, and the society within which they are exploited. Dependency on natural resource exports can increase corruption, but in some cases it can actually decrease it. According to Petermann et al. (2007) non-fuel mineral exports tend to increase corruption only in developing countries, and particularly in those that export high value mineral commodities such as diamonds and gold. Myanmar is particularly vulnerable here due to its enormous jade industry.

In the forestry sector, corruption and resource dependency results in increased deforestation (Barbier et al. 2005). Attempts by international organisations to promote forestry governance norms in developing countries in Southeast Asia have depended to a large extent on their endorsement and adoption by local politicians and vested interests; widespread corruption, particularly in the palm oil business, has perpetuated unsustainable deforestation for land conversion that has resulted in the visible governance failure of the annual regional haze (Hameiri and Jones 2015; McCarthy 2014; Varkkey 2016). Myanmar has lost close to 20 per cent of its forest cover since 1990 and most military-backed governments showed little interest in halting the decline.

Post-conflict countries, which are often poor to begin with, are particularly susceptible to corruption in their natural resource sector due to disrupted and resource-poor bureaucracies governing highly profitable industries, which can undermine transitions to peace (Le Billon 2014). Myanmar has been afflicted by civil conflict since independence and while some regions of conflict have improved, intractable conflicts continue in other parts of the country.

For all these reasons, natural resource governance in Myanmar has been limited, opaque and corrupt. Some industries are better governed than others – natural gas is increasingly transparent and open to investment by international corporations, while much of the jade industry remains hidden. Nevertheless, remnants of deep military–state involvement in the drug trade (Meehan 2011), forestry (McCarthy 2014), rubber (Woods 2011) and particularly jade (Global Witness 2015) have ensured that well-connected vested interests continue to oppose governance reforms aimed at reducing corruption. Like many other sectors of the economy, the jade industry in Myanmar is run by an oligopoly of military-owned corporations and associated cronies (Ford et al. 2016; Jones 2014). This dominance creates impediments to removing corruption within the natural resources sector, which is particularly problematic given Myanmar's structural position as a producer and exporter of raw commodities.

Corruption within Myanmar is clearly endemic. In Transparency International's Corruptions Perception Index 2016 Myanmar was perceived as one of the most corrupt countries in the world, ranked 136 out of 176 countries, although this was a significant improvement compared with during direct military rule (Transparency International 2017). This corruption is particularly embedded within the natural resources sector. In the inaugural Resource Governance Index in 2013 Myanmar ranked last out of 58 resource-rich countries in terms of the quality of governance in the extractive sector with a score of 4 out of 100 (Natural Resource Governance Institute 2013). Although a broad range of governance reforms will be required to overcome ingrained corrupt practices, a first step towards improving governance would be to increase transparency within the natural resource sector. The rest of the chapter therefore outlines the impacts of various epochs on Myanmar's environment and the recent development of more effective environmental governance tools, including greater transparency in the natural resources sector.

The environment and natural resources under military rule

During military rule there was no serious attempt to develop comprehensive environmental laws and policies with state-led environmental governance limited to a patchwork of isolated and limited ad hoc laws that, due to a lack of both government commitment and bureaucratic capacity, were inconsistently enforced. While there existed forestry laws, including those that recognised community forests, and a Land Acquisition Act, which was meant to regulate compensation for farmers, there were no laws that adequately regulated pollution or protected biodiversity and no law existed that took a holistic approach to the management or protection of the environment overall. A National Environmental Policy had existed since 1940 but it was largely ignored by military governments and had not been updated since 1994. While most countries by 2011 had well-entrenched laws ensuring that public participation, environmental impact assessment (EIA) and social impact assessment were key components of major development activities, these types of legislated requirements were still absent from Myanmar.

Natural resources were extracted without environmental constraint by military-owned companies or associated cronies in government-controlled areas while ethnic armed groups survived on the revenues from unregulated extractive industries in the regions they controlled. As a report on the extractives industry undertaken during the Thein Sein era noted, during military rule, 'many grievances with the extractive industries sector were resolved by fiat or use of force, rather than through policy-making, mediation or dialogue' (Adam Smith International 2015: 9). All levels of government and bureaucracy had extremely limited capacity and resources: government data, such as it was, existed on paper rather than computers. Due to conflict and corruption there was a significant black economy that meant many environmental and natural resource indicators were not accurately captured in official statistics.

Myanmar's economy and society was dominated by agriculture (see Chapter 19), but the historical lack of an overarching land use policy, together with the existence of a range of outdated, ad hoc and incoherent rules and regulations related to land management, resulted in the abuse of land use rights and widespread land degradation (Tin Htut Oo 2012). Government regulation, when it occurred, was often misguided, with a top-down counterproductive focus. Agricultural production was largely controlled through directives specifying the commodities that individual farmers were to produce. These directives were based on whims of the generals rather than effective environmental governance, and the results were often inappropriate for a particular climate or region, resulting in poor yields and environmental degradation.

Likewise, large-scale, artisanal and small-scale mining together had an enormous environmental impact due to the lack of environmental regulations, resulting in deforestation and the pollution of rivers from mine tailings. Mines throughout Myanmar produce zinc, lead, silver, tin, gold, iron, coal and gemstones, particularly jade. The largest copper mine in the country, the Letpadaung (Monywa) Copper Mine in Sagaing Region, was a site of regular community opposition due to land grabs and environmental destruction. These unregulated exploitative activities had dire impacts for the environmental security of many communities in Myanmar, particularly ethnic minorities. In the early decades of military rule, during the period of 'the Burmese road to socialism', state authoritarianism and incompetence depleted ecosystems while running down the economy. Although much environmental degradation occurred, the civil conflict and lack of economic dynamism limited the level of destruction compared with neighbouring Thailand. According to the World Bank, by 1990 forests still covered 60 per cent of Myanmar while in Thailand the coverage was less than half this level (World Bank 2016a).

Following the protests of 1988, the subsequent military regime created a quasi-market economy by opening the door to joint ventures between state or military-backed domestic enterprises and foreign companies that were interested in exploiting Myanmar's natural resources through the Union of Myanmar Foreign Investment Law. The shift towards a market economy in agriculture brought in international investors and a rapid expansion of large-scale commercial agriculture with export-oriented plantations established on land designated as 'wasteland', resulting in increased use of chemical fertilisers and the removal of small-scale farmers from their customary land. This practice resulted in widespread land appropriation and conflict across the country.

With the shift towards a market economy there were also some tentative steps to re-engage with international organisations (see Chapter 32), resulting in some state-led environmental governance initiatives. In 1990 the National Commission for Environmental Affairs (NCEA) was formed to regulate the use of natural resources and set environmental standards but it was severely limited by its own resources. Ten years after its formation its budget was still only approximately US$6,000 and although this had doubled by 2004/5 it was still barely enough to meet the administrative costs. By 2006 it had collaborated with UNEP and the ADB to prepare a National Environmental Performance Assessment Report, which provided useful baseline data on Myanmar's environment (BEWG 2011: 18; NCEA and UNEP 2006: 72). In the absence of a clear, effective and unified legislative framework, however, the report languished on office desks while the rapacious exploitation of the country's natural environment continued unabated.

The limited contact with outside organisations and the lack of official IFI aid during this period (Simpson 2014; Simpson and Park 2013) meant that the government was somewhat insulated from global governance developments associated with climate change. Nevertheless, the government's attempts to normalise its international relations in the early 1990s led it to sign the UN Framework Convention on Climate Change (UNFCCC) in 1992. With UNFCCC funding through the UN Global Environment Facility (GEF), Win Myo Thu, an activist, and his NGO, ECODEV, began a project of national communication while the country was still under military rule, including organising the country's first national climate change conference. Win Myo Thu was a key environmental advocate during this period, being the climate change adviser to the NCEA and a national consultant for the National Biodiversity Strategy and Action Plan on conservation (NBSAP) (Simpson 2015: 156–7).

Despite the potentially devastating impacts of climate change, however, the government demonstrated little commitment in mitigation or adaptation. Myanmar was one of the three countries globally most affected by climate disasters 1993–2012 (Kreft 2013 and Eckstein). Most of this ranking was due to the catastrophic impact of Cyclone Nargis in May 2008, which killed more than 140,000 people, destroyed 800,000 houses and left millions of Ayeyarwady (Irrawaddy) Delta residents, mostly ethnic Kayin (Karen), homeless and facing disease and malnutrition. The cyclone path along the Delta meant that it caused maximum destruction but it was clear that the widespread destruction of forests and mangrove ecosystems exacerbated the impacts of the cyclone. Mangroves provide a natural barrier against storm surges. The growth of military-run shrimp and fish farms along the coast had weakened these natural barriers while deforestation had intensified river flooding.

One of the key aspects of climate change policy is energy policy, but as with the other forms of environmental governance, energy policies during this period contributed little towards national development or sustainability. Electricity access and usage throughout the country was extremely low with the electrification rate estimated at 26 per cent in 2011 by the Asian Development Bank (ADB) (Asian Development Bank 2012b: 23). This ADB figure included an average of 16 per cent across rural areas while Yangon, the commercial capital, recorded the highest rate of 67 per cent. Even these electrification rates provide an overly optimistic picture because rationing and unscheduled blackouts were ubiquitous, even in Yangon. Outside of the major centres electrification was limited and, in some ethnic minority regions, virtually non-existent. Total installed capacity of the grid in 2011 was 3,361 megawatts (MW), with the energy sources being hydropower (75 per cent), gas (21 per cent) and coal (4 per cent). Due to poor maintenance of the gas and coal power plants and a lack of water during the dry season, however, the peak load during the driest months was only 1,533MW. As with many other developing countries simple biomass technologies such as fuelwood, charcoal, agricultural residue and animal waste have historically provided the dominant fuel source, supplying almost 70 per cent of the country's primary energy (Asian Development Bank 2012b: 3).

These extreme energy shortages existed in the context of the development, throughout the 1990s and 2000s, of the country's energy sector for exports in return for foreign exchange, initially to Thailand but increasingly to China too (Haacke 2010; Simpson 2007). Natural gas was the most successful of Myanmar's forays into this area with several projects being instigated and developed during military rule, although some were completed during the Thein Sein government: the Yadana and Yetagun Natural Gas Pipelines exported gas from Myanmar to Thailand from the turn of the century and earned approximately US$3 billion gross and US$1.5 billion net by 2010–11 (Turnell 2012: 146), constituting about 45 per cent of the country's total exports; the Zawtika Gas Pipeline sent gas in the same direction from 2014; and the Shwe Gas Pipeline exported gas from Rakhine State to Yunnan Province in China from 2013. Less successful was the hydropower dam building programme: the China Power Investment Corporation and its partners started building the US$3.6 billion Myitsone Dam on the Ayeyarwady (Irrawaddy) River in Kachin State, which was expected to provide up to 6,000MW of electricity, primarily for export to China, while a cascade of dams was planned for the Thanlwin (Salween) River in Shan, Kayah (Karenni) and Kayin (Karen) States to export electricity to both Thailand and China (Simpson 2013).

All these major development projects were undertaken in the absence of any significant or rigorous state-led environmental governance and without any significant local consultation or participation. EIAs were either not undertaken at all or lacked any formal processes for public or civil society input or response. Nevertheless, while the gas pipelines all reached completion, progress on the dams was often slow due to civil conflict and opposition from local communities, however limited the formal modes of participation (Kirchherr et al. 2016). The projects tended to cause a variety of environmental problems, mainly in the ethnic minority areas of Myanmar's mountainous border regions. Hydropower and natural gas are less harmful in relation to climate change and local pollution than coal, but large-scale hydropower projects have dire ramifications for fisheries, downstream water security and displaced local communities. The exploitation of natural gas rather than coal or oil also had less to do with conscious government policy and more to do with the geological serendipity of plentiful reserves. For the many destitute and energy-poor communities of Myanmar, the exporting of most of these energy resources to fund ongoing authoritarian rule provided little hope for improved energy and environmental security: the two ethnic minority areas that hosted the gas pipelines, Tanintharyi (Tenasserim) Region and Rakhine (Arakan) State, had the two lowest per capita levels of electricity usage in the country (Simpson 2017a: 84).

During military rule there was little opportunity for local dissent, and domestic environmental activists, particularly those based in ethnic minority areas, who questioned the necessity or rationale behind these projects were harassed by the military and its intelligence service, including with arrests and torture (Doyle and Simpson 2006). As a result of this repression, and particularly the crackdown of 1988, many activists removed themselves from Myanmar-proper to the 'liberated' border regions controlled by ethnic minorities or neighbouring countries such as Thailand. In the absence of effective state-led environmental governance this 'activist diaspora', which included numerous ethnically based environmental NGOs, provided the most fertile and important 'activist environmental governance' of energy projects in Myanmar during this period (Simpson 2013; 2017a). These activists undertook dangerous covert research in Myanmar-proper and the liberated areas to produce environmental reports and assessments, with a strong justice focus on security and human rights, which were then used to pressure corporations and Western governments to divest from these destructive projects. They did not lobby Myanmar's government itself, as it had generally ignored such petitions, but from 2011 the new Thein Sein government offered new opportunities for civil society engagement, along with the development of a more comprehensive environmental governance regime.

Environmental governance under Thein Sein and the USDP

The broader governance improvements instigated by the Thein Sein government from 2011 were accompanied by the establishment of more cohesive environmental policies and, gradually, by improved processes of consultation with the public, international agencies and civil society. The most significant message to both the public and the international community that the government's approach to the environment and natural resources would be different was Thein Sein's announcement, on 30 September 2011, that in response to community environmental concerns over the project the Myitsone Dam would be suspended for the remainder of his five-year term. This was a stunning diplomatic rebuke against China, which supported the project, but was also the first significant decision the government had nominally made on the basis of community opposition. This was an unprecedented acknowledgement by the government that it would no longer *automatically* force through large-scale environmentally destructive development projects that were strongly opposed by the community. This decision gave more confidence to local activists that they could challenge existing developments, and in January 2012 the Dawei Development Association, a newly formed NGO promoting 'green development', held a protest on the beach near the proposed site of the Dawei Development Project: later that month the government announced the cancellation of the Dawei 4,000MW coal-fired power station. This announcement further reinforced the view that local communities and domestic environmental groups would now be able to influence some development decisions, particularly those related to the export of energy.

The new relative openness to public consultation was accompanied by the development of a more comprehensive suite of environmental conservation laws and policies to regulate development activities. In 2012 the Ministry of Environmental Conservation and Forestry (MOECAF) was formed, giving environmental conservation a ministerial prominence it had never previously enjoyed. An Environmental Law, which had been drafted and redrafted over 15 years, was passed in March 2012 (Government of Myanmar 2012). This law was entirely dependent on the various rules and procedures that were required to implement it so, despite this law passing in 2012, it had little overt impact on development decisions throughout the Thein Sein era because these rules and procedures took several years to be finalised. Due to the governments's lack of experience and expertise in this area the ADB assisted with the drafting of the EIA Procedures, Rules and National Environmental Quality Standards through a Technical Assistance Grant under the Greater Mekong Subregion Core Environment Programme (Asian Development Bank 2014). While the ADB's participation and environmental safeguards are not always adequate, Myanmar's historical lack of safeguards made the ADB's look relatively comprehensive (Simpson and Park 2013). Although there was limited consultation with civil society prior to passing the law in 2012, the development of the rules and procedures was undertaken via workshops with public and private stakeholders throughout 2012–15 in a consultation process that, until the political reforms, was entirely foreign to Myanmar. Both the EIA Procedures and National Environmental Quality (Emission) Guidelines were finally launched in January 2016 in the last days of the Thein Sein government (Asian Development Bank 2016).

The evolution of engagement practices throughout the Thein Sein government was also evident in the development of land use policy. In 2012 the parliament passed, with no consultation, the Farmland Law and Vacant, Fallow and Virgin Lands Management (VFV) Law, which were criticised by groups such as the Food Security Working Group's Land Core Group as providing 'weak protection of the rights of smallholder farmers in upland areas [and] remain[ing] designed primarily to foster promotion of large-scale agricultural investment' (Oberndorf 2012: iii). They argued that the laws were likely to perpetuate widespread land appropriation and conflict across the country.

By 2014 the government had become much more open to civil society engagement and the process of consultation per se. A draft National Land Use Policy (NLUP) was released for feedback in October 2014. According to Oberndorf (2014) the draft NLUP emphasised strengthening the land tenure security of smallholder farmers, ethnic communities, women and other vulnerable groups and also included important provisions on: ensuring the use of effective environmental and social safeguard mechanisms; improving public participation in decision-making processes related to land use planning; improving public access to accurate information related to land use management; and developing independent dispute resolution mechanisms. The Transnational Institute was more critical of the draft NLUP, arguing that it fell far short of international standards, but saw it as an important improvement on the previous approach to land use policy. Its response to the draft NLUP (Franco et al. 2015) emphasised that the Myanmar government was a signatory of the FAO's *Voluntary Guidelines on the Responsible Governance of Tenure of Land, Fisheries and Forests in the Context of National Food Security* (Food and Agriculture Organization 2012). These guidelines provide the highest international standard on tenure of land, fisheries and forests and the government's draft NLUP could therefore be judged against these standards.

The government released the sixth draft of the NLUP in May 2015 and the final version was released in the last days of the outgoing parliament in January 2016. As with the Environmental Conservation Law the full impact of the NLUP will be determined by the composition and actions of the various councils and committees mandated within the policy in addition to the laws, rules and regulations that underpin it, but it was clear that the policy provided a new best practice approach to land use policy: it consistently referred to a need for participatory, transparent and accountable processes and sought the recognition of customary land tenure and dispute resolution (Aguirre 2016). The crucial element of the policy development process, however, was the extensive consultation with, and participation of, civil society in the development of the policy, which stood in stark contrast to the opaque development and delivery of the lands laws of 2012.

In relation to the formal climate change negotiations, the Myanmar government submitted its Intended Nationally Determined Contribution (INDC) to the UNFCCC in September 2015 as its commitment to the Paris Agreement (Ministry of Environmental Conservation and Forestry 2015). The government committed to reduce the country's per capita emissions of 2 tonnes of carbon dioxide equivalent (tCO2eq) in 2010 by 6 per cent by 2030. The current emissions level ranks Myanmar around 46th-lowest out of 198 countries (Australian-German Climate and Energy College 2015). Given the existing low level of per capita emissions – compared with, for example, Australia at 25.3 tCO2eq – the commitment appears quite significant, if it is achieved.

While these improvements in environmental governance occurred throughout the Thein Sein government there continued to be significant environmental destruction, particularly that linked to military or crony-operated companies, which may also call into question the INDC commitments. According to the Global Forest Resources Assessment 2015, Myanmar had the third largest area of annual deforestation – after Brazil and Indonesia – between 2010 and 2015, losing 546,000 hectares, or 1.7 per cent of the country, of forest per annum (Food and Agriculture Organization 2015: 15). By 2015 the forested area had decreased to approximately 44.5 per cent (World Bank 2016a). Despite an export ban on timber from 1 April 2014 discrepancies in figures between the Myanmar government and its trading partners indicated that the corrupt and illegal export of logs continued. According to the government, after the ban came into effect Myanmar received US$44 million from timber exports in the 2014–15 fiscal year compared with US$900 million the year before. These figures were not borne out by figures from its six major trading partners, which indicated Myanmar's log exports were only slightly down to US$1.3 billion from US$1.5 billion the year before with timber trade with China increasing from US$622 million to US$677 million in the same period (NCRA 2015b). This result was consistent with research demonstrating that military-connected companies in the border regions often receive agricultural concessions as a cover for logging operations that appear to be the primary objective (Woods 2015).

In the mining sector, the environmental destruction and poor working conditions, particularly in jade mines, were highlighted with a major landslide in Hpakant, Kachin State, in November 2015, that killed at least 116 people. Conflict and community protests over mines were widespread throughout the country during the government's term and particularly around the Letpadaung (Monywa) Copper Mine in Sagaing Region, where protests over land grabs and environmental degradation were common. Despite the government re-negotiating the contract to provide more favourable terms for the government and local communities at the expense of China's Wanbao Mining Ltd in 2013, activists maintained that local communities had still not been consulted. Protesters were regularly arrested and jailed at the site and in December 2014 an activist was shot and killed, provoking greater unrest. The government had passed legislation that permitted public protest for the first time in Myanmar but it required the assent of the local authorities, which was not always forthcoming. Conflict at the Letpadaung Mine, and particularly the death of the protester, were issues that were taken up by activists within the EITI, a process which became emblematic of the reforms under the Thein Sein government, but also of the limitations that remained in environmental and natural resource governance in a country still dominated by the military.

The Extractive Industries Transparency Initiative

The EITI is a 'global Standard to promote open and accountable management of natural resources' (EITI International Secretariat 2017). Once a country joins the initiative it becomes mandatory for all extractive industry operators operating within that country to cooperate in the requirements of the EITI. Annual EITI reports for the country that disclose information on tax payments, licences, contracts and production from natural resource extraction are compiled by an Independent Administrator, allowing civil society and community groups to track the revenue from natural resources from production to the government accounts. President Thein Sein announced Myanmar's intention to join the EITI in December 2012 and it submitted its first report in January 2016. If the first and second EITI reports (due 2018) are validated by the EITI Board, Myanmar is likely to be assessed as having made Meaningful Progress towards implementing the EITI 2016 Standard (Simpson 2017b). In addition to reconciling company payments with government revenues, the key component of the EITI process is the Multi-Stakeholder Group (MSG), which manages the EITI in each country, with equal votes between civil society, industry and government. Civil society therefore played a key decision-making role throughout Myanmar's EITI accession process, creating a corporatist body that was hitherto entirely foreign to governance in Myanmar.

In support of Myanmar joining the EITI AusAID sponsored a delegation of civil society activists and government officials to visit Australia in May 2013 for the Global EITI Conference. This was the first time that government ministers and senior civil servants had spent time in such close quarters with activists and it was a watershed moment in breaking down the barriers between government and civil society (Simpson 2017b). The EITI will not be a panacea for natural resource governance in Myanmar, despite high expectations throughout the country, but it will play an important role in both legitimating civil society participation in governance processes and providing some much-needed transparency in the extractive industries, particularly gemstones and jade, which currently constitute an enormous black market in Myanmar.

Officially all gemstones and jade produced in Myanmar must be sold at the government's annual Myanmar Gems Emporium, and the Thein Sein government insisted that this was the figure to be used in the EITI. In the 2015 Emporium, gemstone sales were US$1.26 billion, down from a record US$3.4 billion in 2014, with jade accounting for about 90 per cent of the total sales (Reuters 2015). According to Myanmar's Central Statistical Organisation jade *exports* were approximately US$1 billion, or 10 per cent of the total, in the financial year April 2013–March 2014, with around the same amount in 2014–15 (Central Statistical Organisation 2016; Moore Stephens 2015, 15). However, according to Chinese customs data provided to the UN's Comtrade database, China imported US$12.3 billion of gemstones in 2014, with most of the trade being jade (NCRA 2015a). While it appears that almost all of Myanmar's jade is ultimately exported to China, the discrepancy between these figures indicates that there was far more jade being mined and exported than the government acknowledged. The Chinese figures also only include official exports; there are likely to be significant flows of gemstones in the black economy not being accounted for in these figures.

Furthermore, a report by Global Witness (2015) employed two separate estimates of the jade sector – the secondary one based on the aforementioned Chinese data – with both methods concluding that the value of the amount of jade mined in 2014 was worth over US$30 billion, which was almost half Myanmar's total estimated 2014 GDP of US$64 billion (World Bank 2016b). Both estimates were based on official production data that took no account of the jade production kept entirely off the books, which is, again, likely to be significant. More recent Chinese UN Comtrade data suggest gemstone imports from Myanmar have almost disappeared. In 2015 imports fell to US$2.3 billion and in 2016 they collapsed even further to US$179 million, possibly due to the corruption crackdown in China (Simpson 2017b). Despite, these changes, the overall uncertainty and unreliability of most gemstone data suggests that the figures used in the first EITI Report for gemstones was a small fraction of what the industry actually produced and highlighted a severe limitation of the EITI process that the new NLD government inherited.

The road ahead: prospects for environmental governance under the NLD

One of the first decisions of the new NLD government was to halve the number of government ministries, with MOECAF rebranded as the Ministry of Natural Resources and the Environmental Conservation (MONREC). The most significant change to the ministry was the addition of mining to the forestry and environmental conservation portfolios. The new minister, U Ohn Win, had a strong background in forestry and was one of the few ministers appointed from outside the NLD. While the minister was conservation-oriented he may not have the political experience and authority to constrain and adequately confront the sprawling and largely unregulated mining sector. The environmental challenges facing the government are severe, particularly the need to find a balance between exploiting natural resources for sustainable and equitable development and repairing some of the past environmental damage caused by unfettered deforestation, mining and previous destructive development projects. Adequate support for the EITI process will be crucial to improving governance of the mining sector: after allowing the process to stagnate during their first year in office (Simpson 2017b), the NLD government finally appointed a new EITI Leading Committee in December 2016 and in April 2017 they were granted 12 month extensions by the EITI International Board, resulting in the second EITI Report being due 31 March 2018 and validation commencing 1 July 2018 (EITI International Secretariat 2017). Reorganisation of Myanmar's state-owned enterprises, particularly in the natural resources sector, will be a key indicator of the government's commitment to broader governance reforms (Heller and Delesgues 2016).

One of the minister's first announcements, to the upper house of parliament in June 2016, was that logging would be suspended nationwide by the end of that fiscal year in April 2017. Building on the export ban in April 2014 the policy, if fully implemented, will stem the haemorrhaging of Myanmar's forest cover that had occurred over the previous decades. The prospects for the success of this policy are substantially greater under the new government than if such a policy had been proposed under the Thein Sein government. The new government has few of the links to the military and their associated businesses that have stymied conservation attempts in the past (Woods 2015). While deforestation is still likely to continue in pockets due to illegal logging for agriculture or mining, the country-wide unregulated destruction of forests is likely to come to a halt with some reforestation of recently forested areas and afforestation of long-denuded areas likely.

This forestry policy will have numerous beneficial flow-on effects including reduced flooding, of the sort that devastated large swaths of the country in mid-2015, reduced erosion of arable land and soils and more amenable microclimates. As with most countries, climate change will be the most significant environmental issue for Myanmar's future because it is likely to exacerbate most existing environmental problems and also create new ones: storms and cyclones such as Nargis are likely to become more frequent and more intense, together with a more unpredictable monsoon, higher sea-levels and longer and more severe droughts. The ADB lists climate change and pollution as two of the key risks facing Myanmar, highlighting the importance of environmental issues to Myanmar's long-term development (Asian Development Bank 2012a: 32–33). Crucial strategies to deal with these global environmental changes include increasing the amount of forested areas in fragile watersheds and repairing mangrove ecosystems that provide natural buffer zones. In addition, energy policies that minimise carbon emissions while protecting local ecosystems and cultural practices will promote sustainable local practices while assisting global efforts to reduce climate change. These policies can be drawn from a critical approach to energy security (Simpson 2017a: 191–6), which would prohibit the use of mega-dams across large free flowing rivers such as the Ayeyarwady and Thanlwin.

The battle for competing land uses in Myanmar is most evident in Dawei in Tanintharyi (Tenassarim) Region where a Special Economic Zone (SEZ) including a petrochemical industry and deep-sea port is competing with local attempts to develop ecotourism. This area of essentially unspoiled beaches has enormous ecotourism potential, an industry which could provide much-needed foreign exchange without destroying the country's ecosystems (Nuwer 2016). The location of the SEZ has attracted other interest including a Chinese energy company, which received approval from the outgoing Myanmar Investment Commission in March 2016 for Myanmar's first large-scale oil refinery. These industries are clearly incompatible – ecotourists do not want to swim near oil refinery outlets – and while some form of industrial development within Myanmar is necessary, the poor health outcomes associated with Thailand's polluted eastern seaboard should be instructive.

Effective state-led environmental governance is desperately needed in Myanmar, both to address the historical environmental degradation that occurred during the mismanagement of military rule and the environmental strains being unleashed by the current political and economic reform process. While the policy architecture to improve environmental outcomes is still embryonic there are clear signs that a process of comprehensive and integrated environmental governance is emerging. A revised National Environmental Policy, which was funded by the UNDP and underwent several drafts and national consultation rounds, is expected to be released in 2017, as is the Myanmar Climate Change Strategy and Action Plan, but, as with all recent legislation and policies in Myanmar, it will be the implementation of the policy that provides the challenge. Civil society will play a crucial role in the development and effectiveness of this environmental governance architecture but it will also require immense leadership and commitment from the NLD government to reverse decades of neglect.

References

Adam Smith International. 2015. *Institutional and Regulatory Assessment of the Extractive Industries in Myanmar.* London: Adam Smith International and MDRI-CESD.

Aguirre, D. 2016. 'A sound basis for land reform'. *Frontier Myanmar*, 19 February. Accessed 10 June 2016. http://frontiermyanmar.net/en/sound-basis-land-reform.

Asian Development Bank. 2012a. *Myanmar in Transition: Opportunities and Challenges.* Manila: Asian Development Bank.

Asian Development Bank. 2012b. *Myanmar: Energy Sector Initial Assessment.* Manila: Asian Development Bank.

Asian Development Bank. 2014. 'Greater Mekong Subregion: Core Environment Program'. Manila: Asian Development Bank. Accessed 15 May 2016. www.gms-eoc.org/.

Asian Development Bank. 2016. Launch Ceremony: EIA Procedures and Environmental Quality Guidelines. 'Asian Development Bank, Greater Mekong Subregion, Core Environment Program. Bangkok'. Accessed 10 October 2016. www.gms-eoc.org/events/launch-ceremony-eia-procedure-and-environmental-quality-guidelines.

Australian–German Climate and Energy College. 2015. *INDC Factsheets.* (Australian–German Climate and Energy College, Melbourne). www.climate-energy-college.net/indc-factsheets. Accessed 10 June 2016.

Barbier, E. B., R. Damania and D. Léonard. 2005. 'Corruption, trade and resource conversion'. *Journal of Environmental Economics and Management* 50 (2): 276–99.

BEWG. 2011. *Burma's Environment: People, Problems, Policies.* Chiang Mai, Thailand: The Burma Environmental Working Group (BEWG).

Central Statistical Organization. 2016. *Central Statistical Organization.* Naypyitaw: Ministry of National Planning and Economic Development. Accessed 1 December 2016. www.csostat.gov.mm/.

Doyle, T. and A. Simpson. 2006. 'Traversing more than speed bumps: Green politics under authoritarian regimes in Burma and Iran'. *Environmental Politics* 15 (5): 750–67.

EITI International Secretariat. 2017. *Extractive Industries Transparency Initiative.* Oslo: Extractive Industries Transparency Initiative (EITI). Accessed 1 June 2017. http://eiti.org/.

Food and Agriculture Organisation. 2012. *The Voluntary Guidelines on the Responsible Governance of Tenure of Land, Fisheries and Forests in the Context of National Food Security.* Rome: Food and Agriculture Organisation (FAO) of the United Nations.

Food and Agriculture Organisation. 2015. *Global Forest Resources Assessment 2015.* Rome: Food and Agriculture Organisation of the United Nations. Accessed 15 September 2015. www.fao.org/3/a-i4793e.pdf.

Ford, M., M. Gillan and H. H. Thein. 2016. 'From cronyism to oligarchy? Privatisation and business elites in Myanmar'. *Journal of Contemporary Asia* 46 (1): 18–41.

Franco, J., P. Vervest, T. Kramer, A. A. Fradejas and H. Twomey. 2015. *The Challenge of Democratic and Inclusive Land Policymaking in Myanmar: A Response to the Draft National Land Use Policy.* Amsterdam: Transnational Institute.

Global Witness. 2015. Jade: Myanmar's 'Big State Secret'. Global Witness. Accessed 23 October 2015. www.globalwitness.org/reports/myanmarjade/.

Government of Myanmar. 2012. The Environment Conservation Law. Naypyitaw, 30 March.

Haacke, J. 2010. 'China's role in the pursuit of security by Myanmar's State Peace and Development Council: Boon and bane?' *The Pacific Review* 23 (1): 113–37.

Hameiri, S. and L. Jones. 2015. *Governing Borderless Threats: Non-Traditional Security and the Politics of State Transformation*. Cambridge: Cambridge University Press.

Heller, P. R. P. and L. Delesgues. 2016. *Gilded Gatekeepers: Myanmar's State-Owned Oil, Gas and Mining Enterprises*. New York: Natural Resource Governance Institute (NRGI), January. Accessed 18 February 2016. www.resourcegovernance.org/sites/default/files/nrgi_Myanmar-State-Owned-Enterprises_Full-Report.pdf.

Hirsch, P. 2017. 'Introduction: The environment in Southeast Asia's past, present and future'. In *Routledge Handbook of the Environment in Southeast Asia*, edited by P. Hirsch. London and New York: Routledge.

Jones, L. 2014. 'The political economy of Myanmar's transition'. *Journal of Contemporary Asia* 44 (1): 144–70.

Kirchherr, J., K. J. Charles and M. J. Walton. 2016. 'The interplay of activists and dam developers: The case of Myanmar's mega-dams'. *International Journal of Water Resources Development* 33 (1): 111–31. doi: 10.1080/07900627.2016.1179176.

Kurer, O. 2005. 'Corruption: An alternative approach to its definition and measurement'. *Political Studies* 53 (1): 222–39.

Le Billon, P. 2014. 'Natural resources and corruption in post-war transitions: Matters of trust'. *Third World Quarterly* 35 (5): 770–86.

McCarthy, S. (2014). 'Norm diffusion and the limits to forestry governance reform in Southeast Asia's new democracies'. *The Pacific Review* 27(5): 755–78.

Meehan, P. 2011. 'Drugs, insurgency and state-building in Burma: Why the drugs trade is central to Burma's changing political order'. *Journal of Southeast Asian Studies* 42 (3): 376–404.

Ministry of Environmental Conservation and Forestry. August 2015. *Myanmar's Intended Nationally Determined Contribution – INDC*. Yangon: Ministry of Environmental Conservation and Forestry (MOECAF), The Republic of the Union of Myanmar.

Moore Stephens. November 2015. *Myanmar Extractive Industries Transparency Initiative: Scoping Study for the First EITI Report – For the Period April 2013–March 2014*. London: Moore Stephens.

Natural Resource Governance Institute. 2013. *The 2013 Resource Governance Index: A Measure of Transparency and Accountability in the Oil, Gas and Mining Sector*. New York: Natural Resource Governance Institute (formerly Revenue Watch Institute). Accessed 16 June 2016. www.resourcegovernance.org/sites/default/files/rgi_2013_Eng.pdf.

NCEA and UNEP. December 2006. *Myanmar: National Environmental Performance Assessment (EPA) Report*. Yangon: National Commission for Environmental Affairs (NCEA), Myanmar and Project Secretariat UNEP Regional Resource Center for Asia and the Pacific.

NCRA. June, 2015a. *A $12bn Jade and Gem Industry Rides to the Kyat's Rescue*. Yangon: New Crossroads Asia. Accessed 10 November 2015. www.newcrossroadsasia.com/.

NCRA. September, 2015b. *Myanmar Business Update*. Yangon: New Crossroads Asia.

Nuwer, R. 2016. 'The race to save Myanmar's remarkable biodiversity'. *Scientific American* 314 (5): 44–9.

Oberndorf, R. B. November 2012. *Legal Review of Recently Enacted Farmland Law and Vacant, Fallow and Virgin Lands Management Law*. Yangon: Food Security Working Group's Land Core Group. Accessed 1 June 2016. www.forest-trends.org/documents/files/doc_3274.pdf.

Oberndorf, R. B. 2014. *Burma Draft National Land Use Policy Open For Public Consultations*. USAID Accessed 4 October 2017. https://usaidlandtenure.net/2014/11/burma-draft-national-land-use-policy-open-for-public-consultations/.

Peiffer, C. and L. Alvarez. 2015. 'Who will be the "principled-principals"? Perceptions of corruption and willingness to engage in anticorruption activism'. *Governance* 29 (3): 351–69.

Petermann, A., J. I. Guzmán and J. E. Tilton. 2007. 'Mining and corruption'. *Resources Policy* 32 (3): 91–103.

Reuters. 2015. 'Myanmar gems sales slump as conflict stems jade supply'. Reuters, 9 July. Accessed 10 November 2015. www.reuters.com/article/2015/07/09/myanmar-jade-idUSL3N0ZP2DH20150709.

Simpson, A. 2007. 'The environment–energy security nexus: Critical analysis of an energy "love triangle" in Southeast Asia'. *Third World Quarterly* 28 (3): 539–54.

Simpson, A. 2013. 'Challenging hydropower development in Myanmar (Burma): Cross-border activism under a regime in transition'. *The Pacific Review* 26 (2): 129–52.
Simpson, A. 2014. 'Market building and risk under a regime in transition: The Asian Development Bank in Myanmar (Burma)'. In *The Politics of Marketising Asia*, edited by T. Carroll and D. S. L. Jarvis. Basingstoke and New York: Palgrave Macmillan.
Simpson, A. 2015. 'Starting from year zero: Environmental governance in Myanmar'. In *Environmental Challenges and Governance: Diverse Perspectives from Asia*, edited by S. Mukherjee and D. Chakraborty. London and New York: Routledge.
Simpson, A. 2017a. *Energy, Governance and Security in Thailand and Myanmar (Burma): A Critical Approach to Environmental Politics in the South*. Updated Edition. Copenhagen: NIAS Press.
Simpson, A. 2017b. 'The Extractive Industries Transparency Initiative: New openings for civil society in Myanmar'. In *The Business of Transition: Law Reform, Development and Economics in Myanmar*, edited by M. Crouch. Melbourne: Cambridge University Press.
Simpson, A. 2018a. 'Corruption, investment and natural resources'. In *International Natural Resources Law, Investment and Sustainability*, edited by S. Alam, J. Bhuiyan and J. Razzaque. London and New York: Routledge.
Simpson, A. 2018b. 'The environment in Southeast Asia: Injustice, conflict and activism'. *Contemporary Southeast Asia*, edited by M. Beeson and A. Ba. Third edition. New York: Palgrave Macmillan.
Simpson, A. and S. Park. 2013. 'The Asian Development Bank as a global risk regulator in Myanmar'. *Third World Quarterly* 34 (10): 1858–71.
Tin Htut Oo. 2012. 'Devising a new agricultural strategy to enhance Myanmar's rural economy'. In *Myanmar's Transition: Openings, Obstacles and Opportunities*, edited by N. Cheesman, M. Skidmore and T. Wilson. Singapore: ISEAS, 156–81.
Transparency International. 2017. 'Corruption Perceptions Index 2016'. Transparency International, Berlin. Accessed 29 January 2017. www.transparency.org/news/feature/corruption_perceptions_index_2016.
Turnell, S. 2012. 'Reform and its limits in Myanmar's fiscal state'. In *Myanmar's Transition: Openings, Obstacles and Opportunities*, edited by N. Cheesman, M. Skidmore and T. Wilson. Singapore: ISEAS, 137–55.
Varkkey, H. 2016. *The Haze Problem in Southeast Asia: Palm Oil and Patronage*. London and New York: Routledge.
Woods, K. 2011. 'Ceasefire capitalism: Military–private partnerships, resource concessions and military–state building in the Burma–China borderlands'. *The Journal of Peasant Studies* 38 (4): 747–70.
Woods, K. March, 2015. 'Commercial Agriculture Expansion in Myanmar: Links to Deforestation, Conversion Timber, and Land Conflicts. Forest Trends and UK Aid, DfID'. Accessed 10 March 2016. http://forest-trends.org/releases/uploads/Conversion_Timber_in_Myanmar.pdf.
World Bank. 2016a. *Forest Area*. Washington, DC: World Bank. Accessed 11 June 2016. http://data.worldbank.org/indicator/AG.LND.FRST.ZS.
World Bank. 2016b. *Myanmar*. Washington, DC: World Bank. Accessed 15 June 2016. www.worldbank.org/en/country/myanmar.

Conclusion

40
MYANMAR FUTURES

Adam Simpson, Ian Holliday and Nicholas Farrelly

Myanmar is in the midst of a momentous political and economic transition, the outcome of which will have ramifications not only for the country itself but also for the rest of Southeast Asia and much of continental Asia. This volume has provided an in-depth survey and analysis of the many cultural, political and economic shifts currently underway and the key challenges that the country faces. It is now therefore worth considering what a successful transition in Myanmar might look like.

There can be little doubt that for most people in Myanmar, and for the country's many supporters elsewhere in the world, a successful transition will result in a prosperous and peaceful democracy: many of its people took to the streets demanding democracy in 1988 and electoral support for the National League for Democracy (NLD) was overwhelming in both 1990 and 2015 (Ardeth Thawnghmung 2016). However, as with all political concepts, the form and function of democratic rule is heavily contested. In Myanmar, the military's roadmap to 'discipline-flourishing democracy', put into practice with the 2008 constitution, reserves a quarter of legislative seats for serving military personnel, mandates direct military appointments to the executive and allocates the *Tatmadaw* a key role in many aspects of national governance. Such enduring military dominance does not satisfy most definitions of democracy. Nevertheless, with the gradual loosening of constraints on political debate and the NLD government coming to power in 2016, Myanmar is becoming more democratic than at any point in the past half century. Whether the transition can continue in this democratic direction is still unclear.

A fundamental component of any transition to a democratic society is adherence to international norms relating to democracy and a broad portfolio of human rights in the political, civil, economic, social and cultural realms. The political reform process underway in Myanmar therefore has major implications for the country's economic and cultural future. Genuine respect for democratic norms and human rights should lead to a more equitable and ecologically sustainable model of economic development. It should also support the recognition and respect of social and cultural diversity, whether based on ethnicity, sexual orientation, ability or gender. Democracy, human rights, sustainability and equitable economic development are often treated as separate issues, but this is usually the result of applying unduly narrow definitions. More comprehensive visions of sustainable and just states provide useful insights on the interdependence of these issues (Eckersley 2004). In 2015, Myanmar finally signed the International Covenant on Economic, Social and Cultural Rights (ICESCR), which sets out a range of state obligations in these areas.

A democratic, just and sustainable future for Myanmar therefore relies on the notion of inclusion. An inclusive polity, economy and society do not discriminate on the basis of religion, ethnicity, gender or sexual orientation. With ongoing civil conflict in Myanmar's north, east and west, and the religious tensions between Buddhists and Muslims in much of the country, this may seem like a utopian vision, but it remains a precursor for any truly liberal or social democratic state.

Political and economic inclusion is generated by adherence to human rights norms but it is also necessary for any successful strategy of sustainable development. Inequality in Myanmar is significant and there is a growing global recognition, even in institutions such as the IMF, that inequality and neoliberal economic models can stifle the full potential of economic development (Dabla-Norris et al. 2015; Ostry et al. 2016; Wilkinson and Pickett 2009). Myanmar's natural resources and agricultural development provide avenues for addressing poverty throughout the country but only if such development is achieved through ecologically sustainable strategies that respect the rights of ethnic minority and local communities in decision-making. Policies that promote free, high-quality education for all, particularly in ethnic languages, not only improve understanding and tolerance of difference but also provide the human capital for future economic development (Jolliffe and Mears 2016; Lall and South 2013).

Political inclusion is possibly the most significant issue facing Myanmar, with questions of ethnicity a key contributor to historical and contemporary conflicts. Ethnicity feeds directly into Myanmar's unresolved citizenship crisis (Holliday 2014). As Walton (2013) has shown, many in the ethnic Bamar (Burman) community are oblivious of the systematic marginalisation of other ethnic cultures, languages and religions. This unacknowledged privilege is not, however, unique to the Bamar community, as some 'accepted' national ethnic minorities also receive unacknowledged privilege and reinforce the marginalisation of other minority communities.

The key document in this area is the 1982 Citizenship Law, which set out the country's 135 officially designated ethnic groups, the 'national races'. The law was passed during military rule under Ne Win, which was opposed by the NLD and many ethnic groups for its authoritarian and chauvinist practices. While arguing that laws made under Ne Win were unjust and illegitimate, in the new political climate many ethnic minority activists have been happy to cite and promote this law to justify the exclusion of other minorities, notably the Muslim Rohingya in Rakhine State, although this is part of a broader scapegoating of Muslims throughout Myanmar (Cheesman 2017; van Klinken and Su Mon Thazin Aung 2017). There is no easy political solution to the issue of inclusion in Myanmar but a useful first step could be the technical separation of ethnicity from eligibility for citizenship (see Farrelly 2016).

An intermediate point for the transition currently underway in Myanmar might, therefore, see the law redrafted to remove ethnicity as a primary determinant of citizenship. There are of course significant political impediments to implementing such a change but, just as the concept of federalism is, for the first time, being openly debated in Myanmar, the emergence of a new definition of citizenship, founded on liberal values rather than arbitrary and often ethnologically dubious categorisations, should not be entirely ruled out. Such a shift would take courage on the part of Myanmar's democrats to make the necessary adjustments in what is currently a rigid set of social expectations about ethnic belonging.

In government, the NLD has made efforts to promote what they consider neutral language on sensitive ethnic issues, particularly the Rohingya. Their terminological revisions have caused consternation among 'nationalist' Buddhists, and have also been opposed by some Rohingya themselves. There were reports that Muslims in Rakhine State townships refused to accept new government-issued national verification cards, or 'green cards', as part of a citizenship verification pilot programme because their race and religion were omitted (*The Myanmar Times*, 16 June 2016).

These Muslims wanted their ethnicity listed on the card both to emphasise their identity and because they thought its absence could reduce their chances of eventually gaining citizenship. There is, in such cases, a lack of trust between ethnic minorities and the government due to deep-seated historical animosities. While the NLD government generates much more goodwill than its predecessors, there are obvious challenges when it comes to contentious ethnic and religious fault lines. The removal of ethnicity and religion from government identification cards is, however, a worthwhile ambition for a pluralist democracy. The official diminution of ethnic classification may be possible if supposedly discrete groups accept that they are all, fundamentally, the same.

An attempt to reduce communal tensions came with the government announcement in mid-2016 that it would use the religiously determined, but ethnically neutral, terminology of 'Buddhist community in Rakhine State' and 'Muslim community in Rakhine State' in state-owned publications (*The Irrawaddy*, 21 June 2016). The previous USDP government commonly referred to the Rohingya as 'Bengalis', a pejorative and ethnologically suspect term. Under the NLD government these tentative steps towards more ethnically neutral governance were shaped by the need to balance the competing demands of local nationalists and external critics. In championing such difficult changes, the NLD were encouraged by their landslide triumph at the 2015 election in the face of large-scale 'nationalist' Buddhist protests, including exhortations by prominent monks not to vote for the leading democratic politicians. Even with that popular mandate, the NLD's efforts have foundered amongst the Buddhist majority of Rakhine State who continued to insist on identifying their Muslim neighbours as 'Bengali'.

The NLD attempted to placate international criticism on the treatment of the Rohingya by the appointment of an international advisory commission in August 2016, led by former UN Secretary General Kofi Annan (Reuters, 24 August 2016), and by October the situation in northern Rakhine State was relatively stable, despite the ongoing incarceration of over 100,000 Rohingya in internally displaced peoples (IDP) camps. On 9 October 2016, however, coordinated armed attacks on three border posts near Maungdaw township in northern Rakhine State killed nine Myanmar police officers and eight assailants (*The Myanmar Times*, 10 October 2016). As a result, the region again became heavily militarised with widespread allegations of *Tatmadaw* abuse of the Muslim community and an exodus of 70,000 Rohingya to Bangladesh (OHCHR 2016; 2017).

On 24 August 2017 the commission delivered their final report, which included comprehensive and productive recommendations on pathways to peace in Rakhine State. The NLD government quickly committed to implement the recommendations 'to the fullest extent, and within the shortest timeframe possible'. In the early hours of the next morning, militants attacked 30 police posts and an army barracks in northern Rakhine State, resulting in a brutal military operation which the UN High Commissioner for Human Rights labelled 'a textbook example of ethnic cleansing'. At the time of writing over 400,000 Rohingya had fled across the border to Bangladesh in the three weeks following the attacks. The outlook for the Rohingya and peace in Rakhine State is now even more bleak (Simpson 2017a).

Broader concerns by ethnic minorities over the NLD as primarily a Bamar party were reinforced around the one year anniversary of the NLD government over a bridge-naming dispute in Chaungzon, Mon State. The government insisted on naming the bridge after the Bamar General Aung San, Aung San Suu Kyi's father, while the Mon ethnic community were in favour of a more locally sensitive name. By-elections for parliament were held on 1 April 2017 to replace government appointees, including for the seat surrounding the bridge, and to fill several seats left vacant due to civil conflict in Shan State during the 2015 elections. The dispute resulted in a 17 per cent collapse in the NLD vote in Chaungzon and they lost the seat.

Similarly, in Shan State the Shan Nationalities League for Democracy (SNLD) won all six previously empty seats with a negligible NLD vote registered in several electorates. The tactical voting in ethnic areas that delivered the NLD its landslide in 2015 is unlikely to be repeated (Simpson 2017b).

Ethnic concerns fed into broader dissatisfaction with the performance of the NLD and Aung San Suu Kyi in their first year in office. Little progress was made on the peace process, despite Aung San Suu Kyi expending considerable political capital in this area. Furthermore, there were relatively few detailed plans for development with Aung San Suu Kyi continuing to promote a 'socially conservative ideology of radical self-sufficiency and *laissez-faire* relations between the state and society' (Mary Callahan, *Nikkei Asian Review*, 29 March 2017), arguing citizens should muster 'courage' and 'self-confidence' rather than rely on government action or support; an exhortation unlikely to be received with equanimity in ethnic areas facing off against the state's military. The NLD was undoubtedly left a shambolic economic legacy by the previous USDP government and the military operates independently, but the government came to power with unprecedented goodwill and it is striking how this has metamorphosed into an aloof sense of entitlement within the NLD.

One sector with which the NLD needs to engage further is civil society. Since the opening of political space in Myanmar it has been apparent that civil society is not always civil, with chauvinist 'nationalist' movements becoming more prominent. Nonetheless, civil society is an essential component of any thriving democratic system and it has a pivotal role to play in engaging community and government stakeholders. Civil society provides an outlet for pursuing cultural goals, as well as political ones, and provides mechanisms for minorities or groups unable, or unwilling, to enter the formal political process. There are concerns that the NLD government does not consider civil society an active partner in the transition, since it lacks the electoral legitimacy of the NLD. It would be a missed opportunity, and do little for democratic development, if local activists were merely expected to follow the lead set by elected politicians (Simpson and Smits 2018).

After decades of military rule, a free media in Myanmar will also be crucial for the development of a vibrant, inclusive and democratic society but here again the NLD's record is mixed. The rapid expansion of newspapers and news outlets in the country under the USDP government was welcome and there have been some moves by the NLD to continue relaxing restrictions on the media. For politicians and government officials, however, there is still a need to embrace the scrutiny offered by journalists, even when it proves uncomfortable. The media, including its rambunctious online elements, should be considered an essential component of democracy rather than an impediment to smooth national development. Unfortunately, journalists and political activists continued to be arrested and jailed under residual legislation, such as section 66(d) of the 2013 Telecommunications Act, during the NLD's first year in office (Simpson 2017b). The ongoing difficulties and restrictions in reporting on civil conflicts, particularly in Rakhine State, demonstrate that there remain clear limits on press freedom in the country (Brooten and Verbruggen 2017).

Free and fair elections are a key component of successful democracies and the 2015 election was, given Myanmar's recent history, undoubtedly a success by almost any measure. However, Myanmar's first-past-the-post electoral system, while delivering the NLD a useful majority, is actually not the best system for pursuing inclusive democracy. A system of proportional representation, with preferential voting, would result in more representative and inclusive legislatures (Dryzek and Dunleavy 2009). If Myanmar's parliaments are seen as accurately reflecting the will of all communities, ethnic groups are more likely to pursue their interests through democratic means rather than armed struggle.

A related factor in the potential success of Myanmar's transition is the continuing centrality of Myanmar's military in the country's political and economic life. While the NLD government gains most of the media attention for its activities, it still only governs with the acquiescence of the *Tatmadaw*. The military may have receded from the frontline of government but it remains a powerful force that, under its own 2008 constitution, is an autonomous institution, free from civilian control or oversight. The military clearly runs its own operations in the restive ethnic regions. The assassination in January 2017 of Ko Ni, a key legal adviser to the NLD, at Yangon International Airport reinforced the views of some that military subterfuge was consciously undermining the government. That he was the NLD expert on understanding and challenging the military-authored constitution, as well as being one of the few prominent Muslims in political life, cast further doubt on hopes that Myanmar had entered a new more liberal and democratic era.

While the constitution ensures that the military plays a dominant role in Myanmar's politics, its role in Myanmar's economy is much less formalised, but no less significant (Ford et al. 2016; Jones 2014). To consolidate democratic rule the NLD must also democratise economic development; if the poor see continuing inequality and little material gain from democratic rule they may be inclined to accept more authoritarian options in future if they come attached with promises of economic relief. During the first year in office Aung San Suu Kyi focused almost exclusively on the peace process at the expense of economic development; in reality, the two goals are interdependent.

Finally, the transition inside Myanmar will inevitably be shaped by events in the wider world as the country continues to embrace international society. External actors are increasingly present in Myanmar as major foreign powers, corporations and INGOs look for opportunities in what is an emerging site for regional competition. Aung San Suu Kyi rightly insists that the Myanmar government, not international actors, will decide on the country's policies both big and small. Nevertheless, no country is immune to the pressures of globalisation, and Myanmar will certainly need to account for many transborder considerations.

To build a modern democratic state, political leaders in Myanmar will need to effectively manage a daunting set of interrelated challenges. As well as establishing robust foundations for democracy inside the country, they will be forced to balance external influences seeking leverage at a time of national vulnerability. It helps that the elected NLD government claimed a strong popular mandate to improve the economy and increase political participation but inadequate state resourcing is likely to remain a persistent constraint. As Myanmar continues its transition towards a more inclusive government and society it remains far too early to claim that the nascent process has been a success.

References

Ardeth Thawnghmung (2016). 'The Myanmar Elections 2015: Why the National League for Democracy won a landslide victory'. *Critical Asian Studies*, 48(1): 132–42.

Brooten, L. and Y. Verbruggen (2017). 'Producing the news: Reporting on Myanmar's Rohingya crisis'. *Journal of Contemporary Asia*, 47(3): 440–60. doi: 10.1080/00472336.2017.1303078.

Cheesman, N. (2017). 'How in Myanmar "National Races" came to surpass citizenship and exclude Rohingya'. *Journal of Contemporary Asia*, 47(3): 461–83. doi: 10.1080/00472336.2017.1297476.

Dabla-Norris, E., K. Kochhar, N. Suphaphiphat, F. Ricka and E. Tsounta (2015, June). *Causes and Consequences of Income Inequality: A Global Perspective*. (International Monetary Fund, Washington, DC).

Dryzek, J. and P. Dunleavy (2009). *Theories of the Democratic State*. (Basingstoke: Palgrave Macmillan).

Eckersley, R. (2004). *The Green State: Rethinking Democracy and Sovereignty*. (Cambridge, Massachusetts and London: The MIT Press).

Farrelly, N. (2016, May). 'Should ethnicity be reconsidered?' *The Myanmar Times*.

Ford, M., M. Gillan and H. H. Thein (2016). 'From cronyism to oligarchy? Privatisation and business elites in Myanmar'. *Journal of Contemporary Asia*, 46(1): 18–41.

Holliday, I. (2014). 'Addressing Myanmar's citizenship crisis'. *Journal of Contemporary Asia*, 44(3): 404–21.

Jolliffe, K. and E. S. Mears (2016, October). *Strength in Diversity: Towards Universal Education in Myanmar's Ethnic Areas*. (Yangon: Asia Foundation). http://asiafoundation.org/wp-content/uploads/2016/10/Strength-in-Diversity-Toward-Universal-Education-Myanmar-Ethnic-Area.pdf. Accessed: 10 April 2017.

Jones, L. (2014). 'The political economy of Myanmar's transition'. *Journal of Contemporary Asia*, 44(1): 144–70.

Lall, M. and A. South (2013). 'Comparing models of non-state ethnic education in Myanmar: The Mon and Karen national education regimes'. *Journal of Contemporary Asia*, 44(2): 298–21.

OHCHR (2016, October). *UN Experts Urge Myanmar to Address Serious Violations of Human Rights in Northern Rakhine State*. (Office of the High Commissioner on Human Rights, United Nations, Geneva). www.ohchr.org/EN/NewsEvents/Pages/DisplayNews.aspx?NewsID=20742&LangID=E. Accessed: 25 March 2017.

OHCHR (2017, February). *Interviews with Rohingyas Fleeing from Myanmar Since 9 October 2016*. (Office of the High Commissioner on Human Rights, United Nations, Geneva).

Ostry, J. D., P. Loungani and D. Furceri (2016, June). 'Neoliberalism: Oversold?' *Finance and Development*, 53(2): 38–41.

Simpson, A. (2017a). 'Dark clouds over Rakhine State'. East Asia Forum. 19 September. www.eastasiaforum.org/2017/09/19/dark-clouds-over-rakhine-state/. Accessed: 21 September 2017.

Simpson, A. (2017b). *Energy, Governance and Security in Thailand and Myanmar (Burma): A Critical Approach to Environmental Politics in the South*. Updated edition. (Copenhagen: NIAS Press).

Simpson, Adam and Mattijs Smits. (2018). 'Transitions to energy and climate security in Southeast Asia? Civil society encounters with illiberalism in Thailand and Myanmar'. *Society and Natural Resources* doi: 10.1080/08941920.2017.1413720.

van Klinken, G. and Su Mon Thazin Aung (2017). 'The contentious politics of anti-Muslim scapegoating in Myanmar'. *Journal of Contemporary Asia*, 47(3): 353–75. doi: 10.1080/00472336.2017.1293133.

Walton, M. J. (2013). 'The "wages of Burmanness": Ethnicity and Burman privilege in contemporary Myanmar'. *Journal of Contemporary Asia*, 43(1): 1–27.

Wilkinson, R. G. and K. Pickett (2009). *The Spirit Level: Why More Equal Societies Almost Always Do Better*. (London: Allen Lane).

INDEX

FSC
www.fsc.org
MIX
Papier | Fördert gute Waldnutzung
FSC® C083411

Kolibri 360 GmbH
Ferdinand-Jühlke-Straße 7
99095 Erfurt, Deutschland
produktsicherheit@kolibri360.de